# THE COLLECTED WORKS OF JOHN REED

# THE COLLECTED
# WORKS OF
# JOHN REED

INTRODUCTION BY
ROBERT A. ROSENSTONE

THE MODERN LIBRARY
NEW YORK

1995 Modern Library Edition

Introduction copyright © 1995 by Robert A. Rosenstone

Jacket portrait courtesy Culver Pictures

Printed on recycled, acid-free paper

Library of Congress Cataloging-in-Publication Data

Reed, John, 1887–1920.
   [Works. 1995]
   The collected works of John Reed.
      p.  cm.
   Contents: Insurgent Mexico—The war in Eastern Europe—Ten
days that shook the world.
   ISBN 0-679-60144-9
   1. War in the press.   I. Title.
PN4784.W37R44   1995
070'.92—dc20     94-32160

Manufactured in the United States of America

2  4  6  8  9  7  5  3  1

# Contents

# Wars and Revolution:
# The Reporting of John Reed
# by Robert A. Rosenstone

To his contemporaries, John Reed always seemed larger than life. He was a venturesome man who lived out the fantasies of others, a culture hero, a celebrity in an era when the medium of mass communication was the printed page. During his short, hectic life, he played many roles—adventurer, playboy, Bohemian, lover, radical, antiwar activist, revolutionary agitator. But three-quarters of a century after his death in 1920 at the age of thirty-three (in a Moscow hospital during the fourth grim winter of the Russian Revolution), he is best remembered by the profession he chose during his teens: writer. Not, it is true, as the poet and novelist the young Jack Reed had dreamed of becoming, but as a kind of writer particularly well suited to the world-shaking events of the era in which he lived. Reed was a journalist. To be more precise, a foreign correspondent in a time when that job required bravado, fearlessness, and literary talent in equal measure.

In his case, the talent was enormous enough to raise reporting to the level of an art. That is one major reason why his three books remain alive and compelling today. Another lies in the enduring interest of the subjects which attracted him: the political hopes and military campaigns of Pancho Villa and his horseback soldiers in Mexico during the first of the century's great revolutions; the Balkans and Russia in the First World War, where internecine war flourished on both sides of the lines; the ten great Bolshevik days of October 1917, which Reed's words would both define and transform into a model for how Socialism could come to power.

He did not just stumble upon such stories or arrive in the right place at the right time because an editor sent him on assignment. He was a witness to, and occasional participant in, some of the momentous events of the second decade of the century because his desires, ambitions, needs, beliefs, and talents drew him there. Never a detached journalist, rarely aloof or analytical, Reed wrote best when he was fully engaged in and committed to the outcome of great events that were colorful, dramatic, and full of possibilities for social change and renovation.

The heritage of this man who sought out upheaval and revolution was divided. Born in Portland, Oregon, in 1887, Reed was a sickly, delicate child, raised by an ambitious mother from one of the city's wealthiest families, and a self-made father whose contempt for the cultural narrowness of his business peers led him into political crusades as a Progressive. A combination of familial and personal ambition took Jack to Harvard, where he never fit in with the New England social elite, but instead made a reputation as a writer for both the literary *Monthly* and the comic *Lampoon*. His post-graduation trip to Europe in 1910 was emblematic. Classmates went in style on luxury liners and traveled in first-class compartments around the continent. Jack worked across the Atlantic on a cattle boat, then hiked and hitched rides across England, France, and Spain.

In 1911 he settled in Manhattan, the publishing center of the nation. From the first, his professional work straddled two worlds. He wrote humorous and romantic short stories and pieces of commercial reportage for mass-circulation magazines; poetry and serious, hard-edged stories about city life for small journals like *Poetry* and *The Masses*. Contacts with the latter drew him into Greenwich Village, the center of a growing subculture of artists and intellectuals that vibrated with theories about how to revolutionize art, sex, life, and politics. By 1913 Jack was one of the stars of this Bohemia, called by some the Golden Boy of the Village.

Success came quickly for Jack—but almost as quickly he learned that for him success would never be enough. Like his peers in the Village, Reed felt the world to be on the edge of great social transformations that would make modern societies more egalitarian, just, and creative. But he was no theorist. Much of his desire for radical change came from a strong identification with outsiders—with the weak, the exploited, the unemployed, with foreigners and ethnic minorities. Such identification led directly to his first arrest. While covering a strike against the silk mills in Paterson, New Jersey, in the spring of 1913, he disobeyed a cop and spent four days in jail with the immigrant Italian, Polish, and Jewish members of the Industrial Workers of the World.

Six months later, he was off to Mexico to cover a revolution just beginning to touch American consciousness. While other reporters sat in the bars of El Paso, gathering stories from the conflict's refugees, Reed, writing for *Metropolitan Magazine*, slipped across the border and rode on trains and wagons until he caught up with Pancho Villa's army in Chihuahua. Getting to know the Mexican leader and sharing his dreams for a better world, Reed spent several weeks riding with a horseback troop, then joined foot soldiers during the important battle of Torreón. So vivid were his reports from the front in *Metropolitan Magazine* that Walter Lippman wrote, "I say that with Jack Reed reporting begins . . . incidentally, the stories are literature."

He returned from Mexico a celebrity, much sought at the dinner tables, salons, and publishing houses of Manhattan. The *Metropolitan* raised his salary to $500 a week (making him one of the highest paid reporters in the country) and in the fall of 1914 sent him off to cover the Western front of the war that had erupted in August. His months there were a personal and professional disaster. For him the war had no meaning. The armies of the continent were cold, impersonal machines that, in the name of blind patriotism, were slaughtering the culture of hope, art, and creativity that Reed and his friends believed in.

A trip to the Eastern Front in 1915 was more productive. The bloody conflict in the Balkans might be fueled by ancient ethnic conflicts and hatreds, but at least it was human in its waste and inefficiency, full of undercurrents that hinted at coming social change. This was most obvious in Russia, where Reed was spied upon, arrested more than once, and finally expelled from the country. It didn't matter. The vastness of the landscape, the passion of the people, the heated dialogues in Moscow's all-night salons, and the political maneuverings of radical parties all convinced him that here was a land where great social change was imminent.

As the United States moved toward entering the conflict, Reed's antiwar sympathies put him at increasingly sharp odds with much of American society. After the declaration of war against Germany in April 1917, government and vigilantes engaged in severe repression of dissent. Along with other editors of *The Masses*, Reed stood trial twice for sedition. Although the juries refused to bring in convictions, one by one the magazines and newspapers that had once welcomed anything he wrote began to refuse his articles. Eventually he could find no outlets for his work.

Superb intuition saved him. Sensing that the revolution of February 1917 in Russia was only the beginning of a larger story, he went to Petrograd in September and plunged into the feverish atmosphere of political and military maneuvering and intrigue. For weeks he lived at a peak, going from the homes of the old nobility to political meetings at steel factories, from the Winter Palace of Prime Minister Kerensky to Smolny Institute, headquarters of the Petrograd Soviet, interviewing industrialists and workers, right-wing politicians and revolutionary leaders. When the Bolsheviks seized power, he was so hopeful that the revolution might end the war that he spent a few weeks in the ministry of propaganda, writing leaflets meant to convince German soldiers to lay down their arms.

He came home to a hostile America, where his papers were seized and held by the government for more than a year. But so well had he absorbed the atmosphere of Petrograd that when the documents were returned, he was swiftly able to distill the vibrancy, confusion, and hope of the period into *Ten Days That Shook the World*, a work that would become a kind of Bible for revolutionaries in the next half century. The same ten days would help shape the remainder of Reed's short life, move him toward organizing a Communist Party in the United States, then take him back to Russia as a delegate to the Second Congress of the

Communist International. Like millions of Russians, he would die of typhus that could not be treated because of a blockade on food and medical supplies imposed on the fledgling Soviet Union by the victorious Allies.

Today his three major books can be read as a measure of the hopes, dreams, and potentialities of America in the early twentieth century—not just for Reed or the Bohemian subculture of the time, but also for the United States as its political and cultural isolation came to an end and the nation stepped onto a world stage. All three books function on a personal, a historical, and an artistic level. *Insurgent Mexico* is a story of initiation, the tale of a young man both testing his personal courage and learning to write as he comes into contact with the weight of the past as embodied in a traditional society. *The War in Eastern Europe* records the intractable ethnic conflicts of people who continually struggle with the legacy of history; simultaneously it is a work in which one can see a writer honing his skills, learning how to move beyond his own adventures to create on the page a reality that is at once literal and symbolic. *Ten Days That Shook the World* is a masterpiece of compression and insight, a mixture of drama, analysis, and canny guesswork about a revolution still in progress. Lenin endorsed it as "truthful" and recommended it to the workers of the world, but one does not have to be a revolutionary to find in this book John Reed's most deeply American impulse— the notion that through human energies it is possible to overcome the burden of history and mold both our personal destinies and the shape of the society in which we live.

# Insurgent
# Mexico

To
Professor Charles Townsend Copeland
of Harvard University

Dear Copey:
I remember you thought it strange that my first trip abroad didn't make me want to write about what I saw there. But since then I have visited a country which stimulated me to express it in words. And as I wrote these impressions of Mexico I couldn't help but think that I never would have seen what I did see had it not been for your teaching me.

I can only add my word to what so many who are writing already have told you: That to listen to you is to learn how to see the hidden beauty of the visible world; that to be your friend is to try to be intellectually honest.

So I dedicate this book to you with the understanding that you shall take as your own the parts that please you, and forgive me the rest.

As ever,
Jack

New York,
July 3, 1914

# Contents

# On the Border

---

$M$ERCADO's Federal army, after its dramatic and terrible retreat four hundred miles across the desert when Chihuahua was abandoned, lay three months at Ojinaga on the Rio Grande.

At Presidio, on the American side of the river, one could climb to the flat mud roof of the Post Office and look across the mile or so of low scrub growing in the sand to the shallow, yellow stream; and beyond to the low *mesa*, where the town was, sticking sharply up out of a scorched desert, ringed round with bare, savage mountains.

One could see the square, gray adobe houses of Ojinaga, with here and there the Oriental cupola of an old Spanish church. It was a desolate land, without trees. You expected minarets. By day, Federal soldiers in shabby white uniforms swarmed about the place desultorily digging trenches, for Villa and his victorious Constitutionalists were rumored to be on the way. You got sudden glints, where the sun flashed on field guns; strange, thick clouds of smoke rose straight in the still air.

Toward evening, when the sun went down with the flare of a blast furnace, patrols of cavalry rode sharply across the skyline to the night outposts. And after dark, mysterious fires burned in the town.

There were thirty-five hundred men in Ojinaga. This was all that remained of Mercado's army of ten thousand and the five thousand which Pascual Orozco had marched north from Mexico City to reinforce him. Of this thirty-five hundred, forty-five were majors, twenty-one colonels, and eleven generals.

I wanted to interview General Mercado; but one of the newspapers had printed something displeasing to General Salazar, and he had forbidden the reporters the town. I sent a polite request to General Mercado. The note was intercepted by General Orozco, who sent back the following reply:

> ESTEEMED AND HONORED SIR: If you set food inside of Ojinaga, I will stand you sideways against a wall, and with my own hand take great pleasure in shooting furrows in your back.

But after all I waded the river one day and went up into the town. Luckily, I did not meet General Orozco. No one seemed to object to my entrance. All the sentries I saw were taking a siesta on the shady side of adobe walls. But almost immediately I encountered a courteous officer named Hernandez, to whom I explained that I wished to see General Mercado.

Without inquiring as to my identity, he scowled, folded his arms, and burst out:

"I am General Orozco's chief of staff, and I will not take you to see General Mercado!"

I said nothing. In a few minutes he explained:

"General Orozco hates General Mercado! He does not deign to go to General Mercado's cuartel, and General Mercado does not *dare* to come to General Orozco's cuartel! He is a coward. He ran away from Tierra Blanca, and then he ran away from Chihuahua!"

"What other Generals don't you like?" I asked.

He caught himself and slanted an angry look at me, and then grinned:

"*Quien sabe . . . ?*"

I saw General Mercado, a fat, pathetic, worried, undecided little man, who blubbered and blustered a long tale about how the United States army had come across the river and helped Villa to win the battle of Tierra Blanca.

The white, dusty streets of the town, piled high with filth and fodder, the ancient windowless church with its three enormous Spanish bells hanging on a rack outside and a cloud of blue incense crawling out of the black doorway, where the women camp followers of the army prayed for victory day and night, lay in hot, breathless sun. Five times had Ojinaga been lost and taken. Hardly a house that had a roof, and all the walls gaped with cannon shot. In these bare, gutted rooms lived the soldiers, their women, their horses, their chickens and pigs, raided from the surrounding country. Guns were stacked in the corners, saddles piled in the dust. The soldiers were in rags; scarcely one possessed a complete uniform. They squatted around little fires in their doorways, boiling cornhusks and dried meat. They were almost starving.

Along the main street passed an unbroken procession of sick, exhausted, starving people, driven from the interior by fear of the approaching rebels, a journey of eight days over the most terrible desert in the world. They were stopped by a hundred soldiers along the street, and robbed of every possession that took the Federals' fancy. Then they passed on to the river, and on the American side they had to run the gantlet of the United States customs and immigration officials and the Army Border Patrol, who searched them for arms.

Hundreds of refugees poured across the river, some on horseback driving cattle before them, some in wagons, and others on foot. The inspectors were not very gentle.

"Come down off that wagon!" one would shout to a Mexican woman with a bundle in her arm.

"But, señor, for what reason? . . ." she would begin.

"Come down there or I'll pull you down!" he would yell.

They made an unnecessarily careful and brutal search of the men and of the women, too.

As I stood there, a woman waded across the ford, her skirts lifted unconcernedly to her thighs. She wore a voluminous shawl, which was humped up in front as if she were carrying something in it.

"Hi, there!" shouted a customs man. "What have you got under your shawl?"

She slowly opened the front of her dress, and answered placidly:

"I don't know, señor. It may be a girl, or it may be a boy."

. . .

THESE were metropolitan days for Presid̤ː, a straggling and indescribably desolate village of about fifteen adobe houses, scattered without much plan in the deep sand and cotton-wood scrub along the river bottom. Old Kleinmann, the German storekeeper, made a fortune a day outfitting refugees and supplying the Federal army across the river with provisions. He had three beautiful adolescent daughters whom he kept locked up in the attic of the store, because a flock of amorous Mexicans and ardent cowpunchers prowled around like dogs, drawn from many miles away by the fame of these damsels. Half the time he spent working furiously in the store, stripped to the waist; and the remainder, rushing around with a large gun strapped to his waist, warning off the suitors.

At all times of the day and night, throngs of unarmed Federal soldiers from across the river swarmed in the store and the pool hall. Among them circulated dark, ominous persons with an important air, secret agents of the Rebels and the Federals. Around in the brush camped hundreds of destitute refugees, and you could not walk around a corner at night without stumbling over a plot or a counterplot. There were Texas rangers, and United States troopers, and agents of American corporations trying to get secret instructions to their employees in the interior.

One MacKenzie stamped about the Post Office in a high dudgeon. It appeared that he had important letters for the American Smelting and Refining Company mines in Santa Eulalia.

"Old Mercado insists on opening and reading all letters that pass through his lines," he shouted indignantly.

"But," I said, "he will let them pass, won't he?"

"Certainly," he answered. "But do you think the American Smelting and Refining Company will submit to having its letters opened and read by a damned greaser? It's an outrage when an American corporation can't send a private letter to its employees! If this don't bring Intervention," he finished, darkly, "I don't know what will!"

There were all sorts of drummers for arms and ammunition companies, smugglers and *contrabandistas*; also a small, bantam man, the salesman for a portrait company, which made crayon enlargements from photographs at $5 apiece. He was scurrying around among the Mexicans, getting thousands of orders for pictures which were to be paid for upon delivery, and which, of course, could never be delivered. It was his first experience among Mexicans, and he was highly gratified by the hundreds of orders he had received. You see, a Mexican would just as soon order a portrait, or a piano, or an automobile as not, so long as he does not have to pay for it. It gives him a sense of wealth.

The little agent for crayon enlargements made one comment on the Mexican revolution. He said that General Huerta must be a fine man, because he understood he was distantly connected, on his mother's side, with the distinguished Carey family of Virginia!

The American bank of the river was patrolled twice a day by details of cavalry, conscientiously paralleled on the Mexican side by companies of horsemen. Both parties watched each other narrowly across the Border. Every once in a while a Mexican, unable to restrain his nervousness, took a pot shot at the Americans, and a small battle ensued as both parties scattered into the brush. A little way above Presidio were stationed two troops of the Negro Ninth Cavalry. One colored trooper, watering his horse on the bank of the river, was accosted by an English-speaking Mexican squatting on the opposite shore:

"Hey, coon!" he shouted, derisively, "when are you damned gringos going to cross that line?"

"Chile!" responded the Negro. "We ain't agoin' to cross that line at all. We're just goin' to pick up that line an' carry it right down to the Big Ditch!"

Sometimes a rich refugee, with a good deal of gold sewed in his saddle blankets, would get across the river without the Federals discovering it. There were six big, high-power automobiles in Presidio waiting for just such a victim. They would soak him one hundred dollars gold to make a trip to the railroad; and on the way, somewhere in the desolate wastes south of Marfa, he was almost sure to be held up by masked men and everything taken away from him. Upon these occasions the High Sheriff of Presidio County would bluster into town on a small pinto horse—a figure true to the best tradition of "The Girl of the Golden West." He had read all Owen Wister's novels, and knew what a Western sheriff ought to look like: two revolvers on the hip, one slung under his arm, a large knife in his left boot, and an enormous shotgun over his saddle. His conversation was larded with the most fearful oaths, and he never caught any criminal. He spent all of his time enforcing the Presidio County law against carrying firearms and playing poker; and at night, after the day's work was done, you could always find him sitting in at a quiet game in the back of Kleinmann's store.

War and rumors of war kept Presidio at a fever heat. We all knew that sooner or later the Constitutionalist army would come overland from Chihuahua and attack Ojinaga. In fact, the major in command of the Border Patrol had already been approached by the Federal generals in a body to make arrangements for the retreat of the Federal army from Ojinaga under such circumstances. They said that when the rebels attacked they would want to resist for a respectable length of time—say two hours—and that then they would like permission to come across the river.

We knew that some twenty-five miles southward, at La Mula Pass, five hundred rebel volunteers guarded the only road from Ojinaga through the mountains. One day a courier sneaked through the Federal lines and across the river with important news. He said that the military band of the Federal army had been marching around the country practicing their music, and had been captured by the Constitutionalists, who stood them up in the market place with rifles pointed at their heads, and made them play twelve hours at a stretch. "Thus," continued the message, "the hardships of life in the desert have been somewhat alleviated." We could never discover just how it was that the band happened to be practicing all alone twenty-two miles from Ojinaga in the desert.

FOR a month longer the Federals remained at Ojinaga, and Presidio throve. Then Villa, at the head of his army, appeared over a rise of the desert. The Federals resisted a respectable length of time—just two hours, or, to be exact, until Villa himself at the head of a battery galloped right up to the muzzles of the guns— and then poured across the river in wild rout, were herded in a vast corral by the American soldiers, and afterward imprisoned in a barbed-wire stockade at Fort Bliss, Texas.

But by that time I was already far down in Mexico, riding across the desert with a hundred ragged Constitutionalist troopers on my way to the front.

# PART I

## DESERT WAR

# 1

## Urbina's Country

A PEDDLER from Parral came into town with a mule-load of *macuche*—you smoke *macuche* when you can't get tobacco—and we strolled down with the rest of the population to get the news. This was in Magistral, a Durango mountain village three days' ride from the railroad. Somebody bought a little *macuche*, the rest of us borrowed from him, and we sent a boy for some corn shucks. Everybody lit up, squatting around the peddler three deep; for it was weeks since the town had heard of the Revolution. He was full of the most alarming rumors: that the Federals had broken out of Torreon and were headed this way, burning ranches and murdering *pacificos*; that the United States troops had crossed the Rio Grande; that Huerta had resigned; that Huerta was coming north to take charge of the Federal troops in person; that Pascual Orozco had been shot at Ojinaga; that Pascual Orozco was coming south with ten thousand *colorados*. He retailed these reports with a wealth of dramatic gesture, stamping around until his heavy brown-and-gold sombrero wabbled on his head, tossing his faded blue blanket over his shoulder, firing imaginary rifles and drawing imaginary swords, while his audience murmured: *"Ma!"* and *"Adio!"* But the most interesting rumor was that General Urbina would leave for the front in two days.

A hostile Arab named Antonio Swayfeta happened to be driving to Parral in a two-wheeled gig the next morning, and allowed me to go with him as far as Las Nieves, where the General lives. By afternoon we had climbed out of the mountains to the great upland plain of northern Durango, and were jogging down the mile-long waves of yellow prairie, stretching away so far that the grazing cattle dwindled into dots and finally disappeared at the base of the wrinkled purple mountains that seemed close enough to hit with a thrown stone. The Arab's hostility had thawed, and he poured out his life's story, not one word of which I could understand. But the drift of it, I gathered, was largely commercial. He had once been to El Paso and regarded it as the world's most beautiful city. But business was better in Mexico. They say that there are few Jews in Mexico because they cannot stand the competition of the Arabs.

WE passed only one human being all that day—a ragged old man astride a burro, wrapped in a red-and-black checked serape, though without trousers, and hugging the broken stock of a rifle. Spitting, he volunteered that he was a soldier; that after three years of deliberation he had finally decided to join the Revolution and fight for Libertad. But at his first battle a cannon had been fired, the first he had ever heard; he had immediately started for his home in El Oro, where he intended to descend into a gold mine and stay there until the war was over. . . .

We fell silent, Antonio and I. Occasionally he addressed the mule in faultless Castilian. Once he informed me that that mule was "all heart" *(pura corazon)*. The sun hung for a moment on the crest of the red porphyry mountains, and dropped behind them; the turquoise cup of sky held an orange powder of clouds. Then all the rolling leagues of desert glowed and came near in the soft light. Ahead suddenly reared the solid fortress of a big rancho, such as one comes on once a day in that vast land—a mighty square of blank walls, with loop-holed towers at the corners, and an iron-studded gate. It stood grim and forbidding upon a little bare hill, like any castle, its adobe corrals around it; and below, in what had been a dry arroyo, all day the sunken river came to the surface in a pool, and disappeared again in the sand. Thin lines of smoke from within rose straight into the high last sunshine. From the river to the gate moved the tiny black figures of women with water-jars on their heads: and two wild horsemen galloped some cattle toward the corrals. Now the western mountains were blue velvet, and the pale sky a blood-stained canopy of watered silk.

But by the time we reached the great gate of the rancho, above was only a shower of stars.

Antonio called for Don Jesus. It is always safe to call for Don Jesus at a rancho, for that is invariably the *administrador's* name. He finally appeared, a magnificently tall man in tight trousers, purple silk undershirt, and a gray sombrero heavily loaded with silver braid, and invited us in. The inside of the wall consisted of houses, running all the way around. Along the walls and over the doors hung festoons of jerked meat, and strings of peppers, and drying clothes. Three young girls crossed the square in single file, balancing *ollas* of water on their heads, shouting to each other in the raucous voices of Mexican women. At one house a woman crouched, nursing her baby; next door another kneeled to the interminable labor of grinding corn meal in a stone trough. The menfolk squatted before little corn-husk fires, bundled in their faded serapes, smoking their *hojas* as they watched the women work. As we unharnessed they rose and gathered around, with soft-voiced *"Buenos noches,"* curious and friendly. Where did we come from? Where going? What did we have of news? Had the Maderistas taken Ojinaga yet? Was it true that Orozco was coming to kill the *pacificos*? Did we know Panfilo Silveyra? He was a *sergento*, one of Urbina's men. He came from that house, was the cousin of this man. Ah, there was too much war!

Antonio departed to bargain for corn for the mule. "A *tanito*—just a little corn," he whined. "Surely Don Jesus wouldn't charge him anything. . . . Just so much corn as a mule could eat . . . !" At one of the houses I negotiated for dinner. The woman spread out both her hands. "We are all so poor now," she said. "A little water, some beans—*tortillas*. . . . It is all we eat in this house. . . ." Milk? No. Eggs? No. Meat? No. Coffee? *Valgame Dios*, no! I ventured that with this money they might be purchased at one of the other houses. *"Quien sabe?"* replied she dreamily. At this moment arrived the husband and upbraided her for her lack of hospitality. "My house is at your orders," he said magnificently, and begged a cigarette. Then he squatted down while she brought forward the two family chairs and bade us seat ourselves. The room was of good proportions, with a dirt floor and a ceiling of heavy beams, the adobe showing through. Walls and ceiling were whitewashed, and, to the naked eye, spotlessly clean. In one corner was a big iron bed, and in the other a Singer sewing machine, as in every other house I saw in Mexico. There was also a spindle-legged table, upon which stood a picture postcard of Our Lady of Guadelupe, with a candle burning before it. Above this, on the wall, hung an indecent illustration clipped from the pages of *Le Rire*, in a silver-gilt frame—evidently an object of the highest veneration.

Arrived now various uncles, cousins, and *compadres*, wondering casually if we dragged any cigarros. At her husband's command, the woman brought a live coal in her fingers. We smoked. It grew late. There developed a lively argument as to who would go and buy provisions for our dinner. Finally they compromised on the woman; and soon Antonio and I sat in the kitchen, while she crouched upon the altar-like adobe platform in the corner, cooking over the open fire. The smoke enveloped up, pouring out the door. Occasionally a pig or a few hens would wander in from the outside, or a sheep would make a dash for the *tortilla* meal, until the angry voice of the master of the house reminded the woman that she was not doing five or six things at once. And she would rise wearily and belabor the animal with a flaming brand.

All through our supper—jerked meat fiery with *chile*, fried eggs, *tortillas*, *frijoles*, and bitter black coffee—the entire male population of the rancho bore us company, in the room and out. It seemed that some were especially prejudiced against the Church. "Priests without shame," cried one, "who come when we are so poor and take away a tenth of what we have!"

"And us paying a quarter to the Government for this cursed war!" . . .

"Shut your mouth!" shrilled the woman. "It is for God! God must eat, the same as we. . . ."

Her husband smiled a superior smile. He had once been to Jimenez and was considered a man of the world.

"God does not eat," he remarked with finality. "The *curas* grow fat on us."

"Why do you give it?" I asked.

"It is the law," said several at once.

And not one would believe that that law was repealed in Mexico in the year 1857!

I asked them about General Urbina. "A good man, all heart." And another: "He is very brave. The bullets bound off him like rain from a sombrero. . . ." "He is the cousin of my woman's first husband's sister." "He is *bueno para los negocios del campo*" (that is to say, he is a highly successful bandit and highwayman). And finally one said proudly: "A few years ago he was just a peon like us; and now he is a General and a rich man."

But I shall not soon forget the hunger-pinched body and bare feet of an old man with the face of a saint, who said slowly: "The Revolución is good. When it is done we shall starve never, never, never, if God is served. But it is long, and we have no food to eat, or clothes to wear. For the master has gone away from the hacienda, and we have no tools or animals to do our work with, and the soldiers take all our corn and drive away the cattle. . . ."

"Why don't the *pacíficos* fight?"

He shrugged his shoulders. "Now they do not need us. They have no rifles for us, or horses. They are winning. And who shall feed them if we do not plant corn? No, señor. But if the Revolución loses, then there will be no more *pacíficos*. Then we will rise, with our knives and our horsewhips. . . . The Revolución will not lose. . . ."

As Antonio and I rolled up in our blankets on the floor of the granary, they were singing. One of the young bucks had procured a guitar somewhere, and two voices, clinging to each other in that peculiar strident Mexican "barber-shop" harmony, were whining loudly something about a *trista historia d'amor*.

THE rancho was one of many belonging to the Hacienda of El Canotillo, and all next day we drove through its wide lands, which covered more than two million acres, I was told. The *hacendado*, a wealthy Spaniard, had fled the country two years before.

"Who is owner now?"

"General Urbina," said Antonio. And it was so, as I soon saw. The great haciendas of northern Durango, an area greater than the State of New Jersey, had been confiscated for the Constitutionalist government by the General, who ruled them with his own agents, and, it was said, divided fifty-fifty with the Revolution.

We drove steadily all day, only stopping long enough to eat a few *tortillas*. And along about sundown we saw the brown mud wall that hemmed El Canotillo round, with its city of little houses, and the ancient pink tower of its church among the alamo trees—miles away at the foot of the mountains. The village of Las Nieves, a straggling collection of adobes the exact color of the earth of which they are built, lay before us, like some strange growth of the desert. A flashing river, without a trace of green along its banks to contrast it with the scorched plain, made a semicircle around the town. And as we splashed across the ford, between the women kneeling there at their washing, the sun suddenly went behind the western mountains. Immediately a deluge of yellow light, thick as water, drowned the earth, and a golden mist rose from the ground, in which the cattle floated legless.

I knew that the price for such a journey as Antonio had carried me was at least ten pesos, and he was an Arab to boot. But when I offered him money, he threw his arms around me and burst into tears. . . . God bless you, excellent Arab! You are right; business is better in Mexico.

# The Lion of Durango at Home

At General Urbina's door sat an old peon with four cartridge belts around him, engaged in the genial occupation of filling corrugated iron bombs with gunpowder. He jerked his thumb toward the patio. The General's house, corrals and storerooms ran around all four sides of a space as big as a city block, swarming with pigs, chickens and half-naked children. Two goats and three magnificent peacocks gazed pensively down from the roof. In and out of the sitting room, whence came the phonographic strains of the "Dollar Princess," stalked a train of hens. An old woman came from the kitchen and dumped a bucket of garbage on the ground; all the pigs made a squealing rush for it. In a corner of the house wall sat the General's baby daughter, chewing on a cartridge. A group of men stood or sprawled on the ground around a well in the center of the patio. The General himself sat in their midst, in a broken wicker armchair, feeding *tortillas* to a tame deer and a lame black sheep. Before him kneeled a peon, pouring from a canvas sack some hundreds of Mauser cartridges.

To my explanations the General returned no answer. He gave me a limp hand, immediately withdrawing it, but did not rise. A broad, medium-sized man of dark mahogany complexion, with a sparse black beard up to his cheekbones, that didn't hide the wide, thin, expressionless mouth, the gaping nostrils, the shiny, small, humorous, animal eyes. For a good five minutes he never took them from mine. I produced my papers.

"I don't know how to read," said the General suddenly, motioning to his secretary. "So you want to go with me to battle?" he shot at me in the coarsest Spanish. "Many bullets!" I said

23

nothing. *"Muy bien!* But I don't know when I shall go. Maybe in five days. Now eat!"

"Thanks, my General, I've already eaten."

"Go and eat," he repeated calmly. *"Andale!"*

A dirty little man they all called Doctor escorted me to the dining room. He had once been an apothecary in Parral, but was now a major. We were to sleep together that night, he said. But before we reached the dining room there was a shout of "Doctor!" A wounded man had arrived, a peasant with his sombrero in his hand, and a blood-clotted handkerchief around his head. The little doctor became all efficiency. He dispatched a boy for the family scissors, another for a bucket of water from the well. He sharpened with his knife a stick he picked up from the ground. Seating the man on a box, he took off the bandage, revealing a cut about two inches long, caked with dirt and dried blood. First he cut off the hair around the wound, jabbing the points of the scissors carelessly into it. The man drew in his breath sharply, but did not move. Then the doctor slowly *cut the clotted blood away from the top*, whistling cheerfully to himself. "Yes," he remarked, "it is an interesting life, the doctor's." He peered closely at the vomiting blood; the peasant sat like a sick stone. "And it is a life full of nobility," continued the doctor. "Alleviating the sufferings of others." Here he picked up the sharpened stick, thrust it deep in, *and slowly worked it the entire length of the cut!*

"Pah! The animal has fainted!" said the doctor. "Here, hold him up while I wash it!" With that he lifted the bucket and poured its contents over the head of the patient, the water and blood dribbling down over his clothes. "These ignorant peons," said the doctor, binding up the wound in its original bandage, "have no courage. It is the intelligence that makes the soul, eh?" . . .

When the peasant came to, I asked: "Are you a soldier?" The man smiled a sweet, deprecating smile.

"No, señor, I am only a *pacifico*," he said. "I live in the Canotillo, where my house is at your orders. . . ."

Some time later—a good deal—we all sat down to supper. There was Lieutenant-Colonel Pablo Seañes, a frank, engaging youth of twenty-six, with five bullets in him to pay for the three years' fighting. His conversation was sprinkled with soldierly curses, and his pronunciation was a little indistinct, the result of a bullet on the jawbone and a tongue almost cut in two by a sword. He was a demon in the field, they said, and a killer (*muy matador*) after it. At the first taking of Torreon, Pablo and two other officers, Major Fierro and Captain Borunda, had executed alone eighty unarmed prisoners, each man shooting them down with his revolver until his hand got tired pulling the trigger.

"*Oiga!*" Pablo said. "Where is the best institute for the study of hypnotism in the United States? . . . As soon as this cursed war is over I am going to study to become a hypnotist. . . ." With that he turned and began to make passes at Lieutenant Borrega, who was called derisively "The Lion of the Sierras," because of his prodigious boasting. The latter jerked out his revolver: "I want no business with the devil!" he screamed, amid the uproarious laughter of the others.

Then there was Captain Fernando, a grizzled giant of a man in tight trousers, who had fought twenty-one battles. He took the keenest delight in my fragmentary Spanish, and every word I spoke sent him into bellows of laughter that shook down the adobe from the ceiling. He had never been out of Durango, and declared that there was a great sea between the United States and Mexico, and that he believed all the rest of the earth to be water. Next to him sat Longinos Güereca, with a row of decayed teeth across his round, gentle face every time he smiled, and a record for simple bravery that was famous throughout the army. He was twenty-one, and already First Captain. He told me that last night his own men had tried to kill him. . . . Then came Patricio, the best rider of wild horses in the State, and Fidencio next to him, a pure-blooded Indian seven feet tall, who always fought standing up. And last Raphael Zalarzo, a tiny hunchback that Urbina carried in his train to amuse him, like any medieval Italian duke.

When we had burned our throats with the last *enchilada*, and scooped up our last *frijole* with a *tortilla*—forks and spoons being unknown—the gentlemen each took a mouthful of water, gargled it, and spat it on the floor. As I came out into the patio, I saw the figure of the General emerge from his bedroom door, staggering slightly. In his hand he carried a revolver. He stood for a moment in the light of another door, then suddenly went in, banging it behind him.

I was already in bed when the doctor came into the room. In the other bed reposed the Lion of the Sierras and his momentary mistress, now loudly snoring.

"Yes," said the Doctor, "there has been some little trouble. The General has not been able to walk for two months from rheumatism. . . . And sometimes he is in great pain, and comforts himself with *aguardiente*. . . . Tonight he tried to shoot his mother. He always tries to shoot his mother . . . because he loves her very much." The Doctor peeped at himself in the mirror, and twisted his mustache. "This Revolución. Do not mistake. It is a fight of the poor against the rich. I was very poor before the Revolución and now I am very rich." He pondered a moment, and then began removing his clothes. Through his filthy undershirt the Doctor honored me with his one English sentence: "I have mooch lices," he said, with a proud smile. . . .

I went out at dawn and walked around Las Nieves. The town belongs to General Urbina, people, houses, animals and immortal souls. At Las Nieves he and he alone wields the high justice and the low. The town's only store is in his house, and I bought some cigarettes from the Lion of the Sierras, who was detailed store-clerk for the day. In the patio the General was talking with his mistress, a beautiful, aristocratic-looking woman, with a voice like a handsaw. When he noticed me he came up and shook hands, saying that he'd like to have me take some pictures of him. I said that that was my purpose in life, and asked him if he thought he would leave soon for the front. "In about ten days, I think," he answered. I began to get uncomfortable.

"I appreciate your hospitality, my General," I told him, "but my work demands that I be where I can see the actual advance upon Torreon. If it is convenient, I should like to go back to Chihuahua and join General Villa, who will soon go south." Urbina's expression didn't change, but he shot at me: "What is it that you don't like here? You are in your own house! Do you want cigarettes? Do you want *aguardiente*, or *sotol*, or cognac? Do you want a woman to warm your bed at night? Everything you want I can give you! Do you want a pistol? A horse? Do you want money?" He jerked a handful of silver dollars from his pocket and threw them jingling on the ground at my feet.

I said: "Nowhere in Mexico am I so happy and contented as in this house." And I was prepared to go further.

For the next hour I took photographs of General Urbina: General Urbina on foot, with and without sword; General Urbina on three different horses; General Urbina with and without his family; General Urbina's three children, on horseback and off; General Urbina's mother, and his mistress; the entire family, armed with swords and revolvers, including the phonograph, produced for the purpose, one of the children holding a placard upon which was inked: "General Tomas Urbina R."

# 3

## The General Goes to War

W E had finished breakfast and I was resigning myself to the ten days in Las Nieves, when the General suddenly changed his mind. He came out of his room, roaring orders. In five minutes the house was all bustle and confusion—officers rushing to pack their serapes, *mozos* and troopers saddling horses, peons with armfuls of rifles rushing to and fro. Patricio harnessed five mules to the great coach—an exact copy of the Deadwood Stage. A courier rode out on the run to summon the Tropa, which was quartered at the Canotillo. Rafaelito loaded the General's baggage into the coach; it consisted of a typewriter, four swords, one of them bearing the emblem of the Knights of Pythias, three uniforms, the General's branding-iron, and a twelve-gallon demijohn of *sotol*.

And there came the Tropa, a ragged smoke of brown dust miles along the road. Ahead flew a little, squat, black figure, with the Mexican flag streaming over him; he wore a floppy sombrero loaded with five pounds of tarnished gold braid—once probably the pride of some imperial *hacendado*. Following him closely were Manuel Paredes, with riding boots up to his hips, fastened with silver buckles the size of dollars, beating his mount with the flat of a saber; Isidro Amaya, making his horse buck by flapping a hat in his eyes; José Valiente, ringing his immense silver spurs inlaid with turquoises; Jesus Mancilla, his flashing brass chain around his neck; Julian Reyes, with colored pictures of Christ and the Virgin fastened to the front of his sombrero; a struggling tangle of six behind, with Antonio Guzman trying to lasso them, the coils of his horsehair rope soaring out of the dust. They came on the dead run, all Indian shouts and cracking revolvers, until they were only a hundred feet away, then jerked their little cow ponies cruelly to a staggering halt with bleeding mouths, a whirling confusion of men, horses and dust.

This was the Tropa when I first saw them. About a hundred, they were, in all stages of picturesque raggedness; some wore overalls, others the *charro* jackets of peons, while one or two sported tight *vaquero* trousers. A few had shoes, most of them only cowhide sandals, and the rest were barefooted. Sabas Gutierrez was garbed in an ancient frockcoat, split up the back for riding. Rifles slung at their saddles, four or five cartridge belts crossed over their chests, high, flapping sombreros, immense spurs chiming as they rode, bright-colored serapes strapped on behind—this was their uniform.

The General was with his mother. Outside the door crouched his mistress, weeping, her three children around her. For almost an hour we waited, then Urbina suddenly burst out of the door. With scarcely a look at his family, he leaped on his great, gray charger, and spurred furiously into the street. Juan Sanchez blew a blast on his cracked bugle, and the Tropa, with the General at its head, took the Canotillo road.

In the meanwhile Patricio and I loaded three cases of dynamite and a case of bombs into the boot of the coach. I got up beside Patricio, the peons let go of the mules' heads, and the long whip curled around their bellies. Galloping, we whirled out of the village, and took the steep bank of the river at twenty miles an hour. Away on the other side, the Tropa trotted along a more direct road. The Canotillo we passed without stopping.

"*Arré mulas! Putas! Hijas de la Ho——!*" yelled Patricio, the whip hissing. The *Camino Real* was a mere track on uneven ground; every time we took a little arroyo the dynamite came down with a sickening crash. Suddenly a rope broke, and one case bounced off the coach and fell upon rocks. It was a cool morning, however, and we strapped it on again safely. . . .

Almost every hundred yards along the road were little heaps of stones, surmounted by wooden crosses—each one the memorial of a murder. And occasionally a tall, white-washed cross uprose in the middle of a side road, to protect some little desert rancho from the visits of the devil. Black shiny chaparral, the height of a mule's back, scraped the side of the coach; Spanish bayonet and the great barrel-cactus watched us like sentinels from the skyline of the desert. And always the mighty Mexican vultures circled over us, as if they knew we were going to war.

Late in the afternoon the stone wall which bounds the million acres of the Hacienda of Torreon de Cañas swung into sight on our left, marching across deserts and mountains like the Great Wall of China, for more than thirty miles; and, soon afterward, the hacienda itself. The Tropa had dismounted around the Big House. They said that General Urbina had suddenly been taken violently sick, and would probably be unable to leave his bed for a week.

The Casa Grande, a magnificent porticoed palace but one story high, covered the entire top of a desert rise. From its doorway one could see fifteen miles of yellow, rolling plain, and, beyond, the interminable ranges of bare mountains piled upon each other. Back of it lay the great corrals and stables, where the Tropa's evening fires already sent up myriad columns of yellow smoke. Below, in the hollow, more than a hundred peons' houses made a vast open square, where children and animals romped together, and the women kneeled at their eternal grinding of corn. Out on the desert a troop of *vaqueros* rode slowly home; and from the river, a mile away, the endless chain of black-shawled women carried water on their heads. . . . It is impossible to imagine how close to nature the peons live on these great haciendas. Their very houses are built of the earth upon which they stand, baked by the sun. Their food is the corn they grow; their drink the water from the dwindled river, carried painfully upon their heads; the clothes they wear are spun from the wool, and their sandals cut from the hide of a newly slaughtered steer. The animals are their constant companions, familiars of their houses. Light and darkness are their day and night. When a man and a woman fall in love they fly to each other without the formalities of a courtship—and when they are tired of each other they simply part. Marriage is very costly (six pesos to the priest), and is considered a very swagger extra; but it is no more binding than the most casual attachment. And of course jealousy is a stabbing matter.

We dined in one of the lofty, barren *salas* of the Casa Grande; a room with a ceiling eighteen feet high, and walls of noble proportions, covered with cheap American wallpaper. A gigantic mahogany sideboard occupied one side of the place, but we had no knives and forks. There was a tiny fireplace, in which a fire was never lighted, yet the chill of death abode there day and night. The room next door was hung with heavy, spotted brocade, though there was no rug on the concrete floor. No pipes and no plumbing in all the house—you went to the well or the river for water. And candles the only light! Of course the *dueño* had long fled the country; but the hacienda in its prime must have been as splendid and as uncomfortable as a medieval castle.

The *cura* or priest of the hacienda church presided at dinner. To him were brought the choicest viands, which he sometimes passed to his favorites after helping himself. We drank *sotol* and *aguamiel*, while the *cura* made away with a whole bottle of looted anisette. Exhilarated by this, His Reverence descanted upon the virtues of the confessional, especially where young girls were concerned. He also made us understand that he possessed certain feudal rights over new brides. "The girls, here," he said, "are very passionate. . . ."

I noticed that the rest didn't laugh much at this, though they were outwardly respectful. After we were out of the room, José Valiente hissed, shaking so that he could hardly speak: "I know the dirty———! And my sister. . . . ! The Revolución will have something to say about these *curas!*" Two high Constitutionalist officers afterward hinted at a little known program to drive the priests out of Mexico; and Villa's hostility to the *curas* is well known.

Patricio was harnessing the coach when I came out in the morning, and the Tropa were saddling up. The doctor, who was remaining with the General, strolled up to my friend, Trooper Juan Vallejo.

"That's a pretty horse you've got there," he said, "and a nice rifle. Lend them to me."

"But I haven't any other————" began Juan.

"I am your superior officer," returned the doctor. And that was the last we ever saw of doctor, horse and rifle.

I said farewell to the General, who was lying in torture in bed, sending bulletins to his mother by telephone every fifteen minutes. "May you journey happily," he said. "Write the truth. I commend you to Pablito."

# 4

## La Tropa on the March

$A$ND so I got inside the coach, with Rafaelito, Pablo Seañes, and his mistress. She was a strange creature. Young, slender, and beautiful, she was poison and a stone to everybody but Pablo. I never saw her smile and never heard her say a gentle word. Sometimes she treated us with dull ferocity; sometimes with bestial indifference. But Pablo she cradled like a baby. When he lay across the seat with his head in her lap, she would hug it fiercely to her breast, making noises like a tigress with her young.

Patricio handed down his guitar from the box, where he kept it, and to Rafael's accompaniment the Lieutenant-Colonel sang love ballads in a cracked voice. Every Mexican knows hundreds of these. They are not written down, but often composed extemporaneously, and handed along by word of mouth. Some of them are very beautiful, some grotesque, and others as satirical as any French popular song. He sang:

> *Exiled I wandered through the world—*
> *Exiled by the government.*
> *I came back at the end of the year,*
> *Drawn by the fondness of love.*
> *I went away with the purpose*
> *Of staying away forever.*
> *And the love of a woman was the only thing*
> *That made me come back.*

And then *"Los Hijos de la Noche"*:

> *I am of the children of the night*
> *Who wander aimlessly in the darkness.*

*The beautiful moon with its golden rays*
*Is the companion of my sorrows.*

*I am going to lose myself from thee,*
*Exhausted with weeping;*
*I am going sailing, sailing,*
*By the shores of the sea.*

*You will see at the time of our parting*
*I will not allow you to love another.*
*For if so it should be, I would ruin your face,*
*And many blows we would give one another.*

*So I am going to become an American.*
*Go with God, Antonia.*
*Say farewell to my friends.*
*O may the Americans allow me to pass*
*And open a saloon*
*On the other side of the River!*

The Hacienda of El Centro turned out to give us lunch. And there Fidencio offered me his horse to ride for the afternoon.

The Tropa had already ridden on ahead, and I could see them, strung out for half a mile in the black mesquite brush, the tiny red-white-and-green flag bobbing at their head. The mountains had withdrawn somewhere beyond the horizon, and we rode in the midst of a great bowl of desert, rolling up at the edges to meet the furnace-blue of the Mexican sky. Now that I was out of the coach, a great silence, and a peace beyond anything I ever felt, wrapped me around. It is almost impossible to get objective about the desert; you sink into it—become a part of it. Galloping along, I soon caught up with the Tropa.

"Aye, Meester!" they shouted. "Here comes Meester on a horse! *Que tal*, Meester? How goes it? Are you going to fight with us?"

But Captain Fernando at the head of the column turned and roared: "Come here, Meester!" The big man was grinning with delight. "You shall ride with me," he shouted, clapping me on the back. "Drink, now," and he produced a bottle of *sotol* about half full. "Drink it all. Show you're a man." "It's too much," I laughed. "Drink it," yelled the chorus as the Tropa crowded up to see. I drank it. A howl of laughter and applause went up. Fernando leaned over and gripped my hand. "Good for you, *compañero!*" he bellowed, rolling with mirth. The men crowded around, amused and interested. Was I going to fight with them? Where did I come from? What was I doing? Most of them had never heard of reporters, and one hazarded the opinion darkly that I was a gringo and a Porfirista, and ought to be shot.

The rest, however, were entirely opposed to this view. No Porfirista would possibly drink that much *sotol* at a gulp. Isidro Amayo declared that he had been in a brigade in the first Revolution which was accompanied by a reporter, and that he was called *Corresponsal de Guerra*. Did I like Mexico? I said: "I am very fond of Mexico. I like Mexicans too. And I like *sotol, aguardiente mescal, tequila, pulque,* and other Mexican customs!" They shouted with laughter.

Captain Fernando leaned over and patted my arm. "Now you are with the men (*los hombres*). When we win the Revolución it will be a government by the men—not by the rich. We are riding over the lands of the men. They used to belong to the rich, but now they belong to me and to the *compañeros.*"

"And you will be the army?" I asked.

"When the Revolución is won," was the astonishing reply, "there will be no more army. The men are sick of armies. It is by armies that Don Porfirio robbed us."

"But if the United States should invade Mexico?"

A perfect storm broke everywhere. "We are more *valiente* than the Americanos—The cursed gringos would get no further south than Juarez—Let's see them try it—We'd drive them back over the Border on the run, and burn their capital the next day . . . !"

"No," said Fernando, "you have more money and more soldiers. But the men would protect us. We need no army. The men would be fighting for their houses and their women."

"What are you fighting for?" I asked. Juan Sanchez, the color-bearer, looked at me curiously. "Why, it is good, fighting. You don't have to work in the mines . . . !"

Manuel Paredes said: "We are fighting to restore Francisco I. Madero to the Presidency." This extraordinary statement is printed in the program of the Revolution. And everywhere the Constitutionalist soldiers are known as "Maderistas." "I knew him," continued Manuel, slowly. "He was always laughing, always."

"Yes," said another, "whenever there was any trouble with a man, and all the rest wanted to fight him or put him in prison, Pancho Madero said: 'Just let me talk to him a few minutes. I can bring him around.'"

"He loved *bailes*," an Indian said. "Many a time I've seen him dance all night, and all the next day, and the next night. He used to come to the great Haciendas and make speeches. When he began the peons hated him; when he ended they were crying. . . ."

Here a man broke out into a droning, irregular tune, such as always accompanies the popular ballads that spring up in thousands on every occasion:

> *In Nineteen hundred and ten*
> *Madero was imprisoned*
> *In the National Palace*
> *The eighteenth of February.*
>
> *Four days he was imprisoned*
> *In the Hall of the Intendancy*
> *Because he did not wish*
> *To renounce the Presidency.*
>
> *Then Blanquet and Felix Diaz*
> *Martyred him there*
> *They were the hangmen*
> *Feeding on his hate.*
>
> *They crushed. . . .*
> *Until he fainted*
> *With play of cruelty*
> *To make him resign.*
>
> *Then with hot irons*
> *They burned him without mercy*

*And only unconsciousness*
*Calmed the awful flames.*

*But it was all in vain*
*Because his mighty courage*
*Preferred rather to die*
*His was a great heart!*

*This was the end of the life*
*Of him who was the redeemer*
*Of the Indian Republic*
*And of all the poor.*

*They took him out of the Palace*
*And tell us he was killed in an assault*
*What a cynicism!*
*What a shameless lie!*

*O Street of Lecumberri*
*Your cheerfulness has ended forever*
*For through you passed Madero*
*To the Penitentiary.*

*That twenty-second of February*
*Will always be remembered in the Indian Republic.*
*God has pardoned him*
*And the Virgin of Guadelupe.*

*Good-bye Beautiful Mexico*
*Where our leader died*
*Good-bye to the palace*
*Whence he issued a living corpse.*

*Señores, there is nothing eternal*
*Nor anything sincere in life*
*See what happened to Don Francisco I. Madero!*

By the time he was halfway through, the entire Tropa was humming the tune, and when he finished there was a moment of jingling silence.

"We are fighting," said Isidro Amayo, "for Libertad."

"What do you mean by Libertad?"

"Libertad is when I can *do what I want!*"

"But suppose it hurts somebody else?"

He shot back at me Benito Juarez' great sentence:

"Peace is the respect for the rights of others!"

I wasn't prepared for that. It startled me, this barefooted *mestizo's* conception of Liberty. I submit that it is the only correct definition of Liberty—*to do what I want to!* Americans quote it to me triumphantly as an instance of Mexican irresponsibility. But I think it is a better definition than ours—Liberty is the right to do what the Courts want. Every Mexican schoolboy knows the definition of peace and seems to understand pretty well what it means, too. But, they say, Mexicans don't want peace. That is a lie, and a foolish one. Let Americans take the trouble to go through the Maderista army, asking whether they want peace or not! The people are sick of war.

But, just to be square, I'll have to report Juan Sanchez' remark: "Is there war in the United States now?" he asked.

"No," I said untruthfully.

"No war at all?" He meditated for a moment. "How do you pass the time, then . . . ?"

Just about then somebody saw a coyote sneaking through the brush, and the entire Tropa gave chase with a whoop. They scattered rollicking over the desert, the late sun flashing from cartridge belts and spurs, the ends of their bright serapes flying out behind. Beyond them, the scorched world sloped gently up, and a range of far lilac mountains jumped in the heat waves like a bucking horse. By here, if tradition is right, passed the steel-armored Spaniards in their search for gold, a blaze of crimson and silver that has left the desert cold and dull ever since. And, topping a rise, we came upon the first sight of the Hacienda of La Mimbrera, a walled enclosure of houses strong enough to stand a siege, stretching steeply down a hill, with the magnificent Casa Grande at the top.

In front of this house, which had been sacked and burned by Orozco's General, Che Che Campa, two years before, the coach was drawn up. A huge fire had been kindled, and ten *compañeros* were slaughtering sheep. Into the red glare of the firelight they staggered, with the struggling, squealing sheep in their arms, its blood fountaining upon the ground, shining in the fierce light like something phosphorescent.

The officers and I dined in the house of the *administrador* Don Jesus, the most beautiful specimen of manhood I have ever seen. He was much over six feet tall, slender, white-skinned—a pure Spanish type of the highest breed. At one end of his dining room, I remember, hung a placard embroidered in red, white and green: "Viva Mexico!" and at the other, a second, which read: "Viva Jesus!"

It was after dinner, as I stood at the fire, wondering where I was to sleep, that Captain Fernando touched me on the arm.

"Will you sleep with the *compañeros?*"

We walked across the great open square, in the furious light of the desert stars, to a stone storehouse set apart. Inside, a few candles stuck against the wall illumined the rifles stacked in the corners, the saddles on the floor, and the blanket-rolled *compañeros* with their heads on them. One or two were awake, talking and smoking. In a corner, three sat muffled in their serapes, playing cards. Five or six had voices and a guitar. They were singing "Pascual Orozco," beginning:

> They say that Pascual Orozco has turned his coat
> Because Don Terrazzas seduced him;
> They gave him many millions and they bought him
> And sent him to overthrow the government.
>
> Orozco believed it
> And to the war he went;
> But the Maderista cannon
> Was his calamity.
>
> If to thy window shall come Porfirio Diaz,
> Give him for charity some cold tortillas;
> If to thy window shall come General Huerta,
> Spit in his face and slam the door.
>
> If to thy window shall come Inez Salazar,
> Lock your trunk so that he can't steal;

*If to thy window shall come Maclovio Herrera,*
*Give him dinner and put the cloth on the table.*

They didn't distinguish me at first, but soon one of the card-players said: "Here comes Meester!" At that the others roused, and woke the rest. "That's right—it's good to sleep with the *hombres*—take this place, *amigo*—here's my saddle—here there is no crookedness—here a man goes straight. . . ."

"May you pass a happy night, *compañero*," they said. "Till morning, then."

Pretty soon somebody shut the door. The room became full of smoke and fetid with human breath. What little silence was left from the chorus of snoring was entirely obliterated by the singing, which kept up, I guess, until dawn. The *compañeros* had fleas. . . .

But I rolled up in my blankets and lay down upon the concrete floor very happily. And I slept better than I had before in Mexico.

AT dawn we were in the saddle, larking up a steep roll of barren desert to get warm. It was bitter cold. The Tropa were wrapped in serapes up to their eyes, so that they looked like colored toad-stools under their great sombreros. The level rays of the sun, burning as they fell upon my face, caught them unaware, glorify-ing the serapes to more brilliant colors than they possessed. Isidro Amayo's was of deep blue and yellow spirals; Juan Sanchez had one brick red, Captain Fernando's was green and cerise; against them flashed a purple and black zigzag pattern. . . .

We looked back to see the coach pulled to a stop, and Patricio waving to us. Two of the mules had given out, raw from the traces, and tottering with the fatigue of the last two days. The Tropa scattered to look for mules. Soon they came back, driving two great beautiful animals that had never seen harness. No sooner had they smelled the coach than they made a desperate break for freedom. And now the Tropa instantly went back to their native profession—they became *vaqueros*. It was a pretty sight, the rope coils swinging in the air, the sudden snake-like shoot of the loops, the little horses bracing themselves against the shock of the running mule. Those mules were demons. Time after time they broke the *riatas;* twice they overturned horse and rider. Pablo came to the rescue. He got on Sabas's horse, drove in the spurs, and went after one mule. In three minutes he had roped him by the leg, thrown him, and tied him. Then he took the second with equal dispatch. It was not for nothing that Pablo was Lieutenant-Colonel at twenty-six. Not only could he fight better than his men, but he could ride better, rope better, shoot better, chop wood better, and dance better.

The mules' legs were tied, and they were dragged with ropes to the coach, where the harness was slipped on them in spite of their frantic struggles. When all was ready, Patricio got on the box, seized the whip, and told us to cut away. The wild animals scrambled to their feet, bucking and squealing. Above the uproar came the crack of the heavy whip, and Patricio's bellow: *"Andale! hijos de la Gran' Ch——!"* and they jerked forward, running, the big coach taking the arroyos like an express train. Soon it vanished behind its own pall of dust, and appeared hours afterward, crawling up the side of a great hill, miles away. . . .

Panchito was eleven years old, already a trooper with a rifle too heavy for him, and a horse that they had to lift him on. His *compadre* was Victoriano, a veteran of fourteen. Seven others of the Tropa were under seventeen. And there was a sullen, Indian-faced woman, riding sidesaddle, who wore two cartridge belts. She rode with the *hombres*—slept with them in the cuartels.

"Why are you fighting?" I asked her.

She jerked her head toward the fierce figure of Julian Reyes.

"Because he is," she answered. "He who stands under a good tree is sheltered by a good shade."

"A good rooster will crow in any chicken coop," capped Isidro.

"A parrot is green all over," chimed in someone else.

"Faces we see, but hearts we do not comprehend," said José, sentimentally.

AT noon we roped a steer, and cut his throat. And because there was no time to build a fire, we ripped the meat from the carcase and ate it raw.

"*Oiga*, Meester," shouted José. "Do the United States soldiers eat raw meat?"

I said I didn't think they did.

"It is good for the *hombres*. In the campaign we have no time for anything but *carne crudo*. It makes us brave."

By late afternoon we had caught up with the coach, and galloped with it down through the dry arroyo and up through the other side, past the great *ribota* court that flanks the Hacienda of La Zarca. Unlike La Mimbrera, the Casa Grande here stands on a level place, with the peons' houses in long rows at its flanks, and a flat desert barren of chaparral for twenty miles in front. Che Che Campa also paid a visit to La Zarca. The big house is a black and gaping ruin.

# 5

---

# White Nights at Zarca

Of course, I took up quarters at the cuartel. And right here I want to mention one fact. Americans had insisted that the Mexican was fundamentally dishonest—that I might expect to have my outfit stolen the first day out. Now for two weeks I lived with as rough a band of ex-outlaws as there was in the army. They were without discipline and without education. They were, many of them, gringo-haters. They had not been paid a cent for six weeks, and some were so desperately poor that they couldn't boast sandals or serapes. I was a stranger with a good outfit, unarmed. I had a hundred and fifty pesos, which I put conspicuously at the head of my bed when I slept. And I never lost a thing. But more than that, I was not permitted to pay for my food; and in a company where money was scarce and tobacco almost unknown, I was kept supplied with all I could smoke by the *compañeros*. Every suggestion from me that I should pay for it was an insult.

The only thing possible was to hire music for a *baile*. Long after Juan Sanchez and I rolled up in our blankets that night, we could hear the rhythm of the music, and the shouts of the dancers. It must have been midnight when somebody threw open the door and yelled: "Meester! *Oiga*, Meester! Are you asleep? Come to the *baile! Arriba! Andale!*"

"Too sleepy!" I said. After some further argument the messenger departed, but in ten minutes back he came. "El Capitan Fernando orders you to come at once! *Vamonos!*" Now the others woke up. "Come to the *baile*, Meester!" they shouted. Juan Sanchez sat up and began pulling on his shoes. "Now we're off!" said he. "The Meester is going to dance! Captain's orders! Come on, Meester!"

"I'll go if all the Tropa does," I said. They raised a yell at that, and the night was full of chuckling men pulling on their clothes.

Twenty of us reached the house in a body. The mob of peons blocking door and window opened to let us pass. "The Meester!" they cried. "The Meester's going to dance!"

Capitan Fernando threw his arms about me, roaring: "Here he comes, the *compañero*! Dance now! Go to it! They're going to dance the *jota*!"

"But I don't know how to dance the *jota*!"

Patricio, flushed and panting, seized me by the arm. "Come on, it's easy! I'll introduce you to the best girl in the Zarca!"

There was nothing to do. The window was jammed with faces, and a hundred tried to crowd in at the door. It was an ordinary room in a peon's house, whitewashed, with a humpy dirt floor. In the light of two candles sat the musicians. The music struck up *"Puentes a Chihuahua."* A grinning silence fell. I gathered the young lady under my arm, and started the preliminary march around the room customary before the dance begins. We waltzed painfully for a moment or two, and suddenly they all began to yell: *"Ora! Ora!* Now!"

"What do you do now?"

*"Vuelta! Vuelta!* Loose her!" a perfect yell.

"But I don't know how!"

"The fool doesn't know how to dance," cried one.

Another began the mocking song:

> *The gringos all are fools,*
> *They've never been in Sonora,*
> *And when they want to say: "Diez Reales,"*
> *They call it 'Dollar an' a quarta'....*

But Patricio bounded into the middle of the floor, and Sabas after him; each seized a *muchacha* from the line of women sitting along one end of the room. And as I led my partner back to her seat, they *"vuelta'd."* First a few waltz steps, then the man whirled away from the girl, snapping his fingers, throwing one arm up to cover his face, while the girl put one hand on her hip and danced after him. They approached each other, receded, danced around each other. The girls were dumpy and dull, Indian-faced and awkward, bowed at the shoulder from much grinding of corn and washing of clothes. Some of the men had on heavy boots, some none; many wore pistols and cartridge belts, and a few carried rifles slung from their shoulders.

The dance was always preceded by a grand march-around; then, after the couple had danced twice the circuit of the room, they walked again. There were two-steps, waltz and mazurka beside the *jota*. Each girl kept her eyes on the ground, never spoke, and stumbled heavily after you. Add to this a dirt floor full of arroyos, and you have a form of torture unequaled anywhere in the world. It seemed to me I danced for hours, spurred on by the chorus: "Dance, Meester! *No floje!* Keep it up! Don't quit!"

Later there was another *jota*, and here's where I almost got into trouble. I danced this one successfully—with another girl. And afterward, when I asked my original partner to two-step, she was furiously angry.

"You shamed me before them all," she said. "*You*—you said you didn't know how to dance the *jota!*" As we marched around the room, she appealed to her friends: "Domingo! Juan! Come out and take me away from this gringo! He won't dare to do anything!"

Half a dozen of them started onto the floor, and the rest looked on. It was a ticklish moment. But all at once the good Fernando glided in front, a revolver in his hand.

"The Americano is my friend!" said he. "Get back there and mind your business! . . ."

THE horses were tired, so we rested a day in La Zarca. Behind the Casa Grande lay a ruined garden, full of gray alamo trees, figs, vines, and great barrel-cactuses. It was walled around by high adobe walls on three sides, over one of which the ancient white tower of the church floated in the blue sky. The fourth side opened upon a reservoir of yellow water, and beyond it stretched the western desert, miles upon miles of tawny desolation. Trooper Marin and I lay under a fig tree, watching the vultures sail over us on quiet wing. Suddenly the silence was broken by loud, swift music.

Pablo had found a pianola in the church, where it had escaped Che Che Campa's notice the previous year; with it was one roll, the "Merry Widow Waltz." Nothing would do but that we carry the instrument out into the ruined patio. We took turns playing the thing all day long; Rafaelito volunteering the information that the "Merry Widow" was Mexico's most popular piece. A Mexican, he said, had composed it.

The finding of the pianola suggested that we give another *baile* that night, in the portico of the Casa Grande itself. Candles were stuck upon the pillars, the faint light flickering upon broken walls, burned and blackened doorways, the riot of wild vines that had twisted unchecked around the roof beams. The entire patio was crowded with blanketed men, making holiday, even yet a little uncomfortable in the great house which they had never been allowed to enter. As soon as the orchestra had finished a dance, the pianola immediately took up the task. Dance followed dance, without any rest. A barrel of *sotol* further complicated things. As the evening wore on the assembly got more and more exhilarated. Sabas, who was Pablo's orderly, led off with Pablo's mistress. I followed. Immediately afterward Pablo hit her on the head with the butt end of his revolver, and said he'd shoot her if she danced with anyone else, and her partner too. After sitting some moments meditating, Sabas rose, pulled his revolver, and informed the harpist that he had played a wrong note. Then he shot at him. Other *compañeros* disarmed Sabas, who immediately went to sleep in the middle of the dance floor.

The interest in Meester's dancing soon shifted to other phenomena. I sat down beside Julian Reyes, he with the Christ and Virgin on the front of his sombrero. He was far gone in *sotol*—his eyes burned like a fanatic's.

He turned on me suddenly:

"Are you going to fight with us?"

"No," I said. "I am a correspondent. I am forbidden to fight."

"It is a lie," he cried. "You don't fight because you are afraid to fight. In the face of God, our Cause is Just."

"Yes, I know that. But my orders are not to fight."

"What do I care for orders?" he shrieked. "We want no correspondents. We want no words printed in a book. We want rifles and killing, and if we die we shall be caught up among the saints! Coward! Huertista! . . ."

"That's enough!" cried someone, and I looked up to see Longinos Güereca standing over me. "Julian Reyes, you know nothing. This *compañero* comes thousands of miles by the sea and the land to tell his countrymen the truth of the fight for Liberty. He goes into battle without arms, he's braver than you are, because you have a rifle. Get out now, and don't bother him any more!"

He sat down where Julian had been, smiled his homely, gentle smile, and took both my hands in his.

"We shall be *compadres*, eh?" said Longinos Güereca. "We shall sleep in the same blankets, and always be together. And when we get to the Cadena I shall take you to my home, and my father shall make you my brother. . . . I will show you the lost gold mines of the Spaniards, the richest mines in the world. . . . We'll work them together, eh? . . . We'll be rich, eh? . . ."

And from that time on until the end, Longinos Güereca and I were always together.

But the *baile* grew wilder and wilder. Orchestra and pianola alternated without a break. Everybody was drunk now. Pablo was boasting horribly of killing defenseless prisoners. Occasionally, some insult would be passed, and there would be a snapping of rifle levers all over the place. Then perhaps the poor exhausted women would begin to go home; and what an ominous shout would go up: "*No vaya!* Don't go! Stop! Come back here and dance! Come back here!" And the dejected procession would halt and straggle back. At four o'clock, when somebody started the report that a gringo Huertista spy was among us, I decided to go to bed. But the *baile* kept up until seven. . . .

# "Quien Vive?"

Aт dawn I woke to the sound of shooting, and a cracked bugle blowing wildly. Juan Sanchez stood in front of the cuartel, sounding reveille; he didn't know which call reveille was, so he played them all.

Patricio had roped a steer for breakfast. The animal started on a plunging, bellowing run for the desert, Patricio's horse galloping alongside. The rest of the Tropa, only their eyes showing over their serapes, kneeled with their rifles to their shoulders. Crash! In that still air, the enormous sound of guns labored heavily up. The running steer jerked sideways—his screaming reached us faintly. Crash! He fell headlong. His feet kicked in the air. Patricio's pony jerked roughly up, and his serape flapped like a banner. Just then the enormous sun rose bodily out of the east, pouring clear light over the barren plain like a sea. . . .

Pablo emerged from the Casa Grande, leaning on his wife's shoulder. "I am going to be very ill," he groaned, suiting the action to the word. "Juan Reed will ride my horse."

He got into the coach, took the guitar, and sang:

> *I remained at the foot of a green maguey*
> *My ungrateful love went away with another.*
> *I awoke to the song of the lark:*
> *Oh, what a hangover I have, and the barkeeps won't trust me!*
>
> *O God, take away this sickness,*
> *I feel as if I were surely going to die—*
> *The Virgin of pulque and whiskey must save me:*
> *O what a hangover, and nothing to drink! . . .*

It is some sixty-five miles from La Zarca to the Hacienda of La Cadena, where the Tropa was to be stationed. We rode it in one day, without water and without food. The coach soon left us far behind. Pretty soon, the barrenness of the land gave way to spiny, hostile vegetation—the cactus and the mesquite. We strung out along a deep rut between the gigantic chaparral, choked with the mighty cloud of alkali dust, scratched and torn by the thorny brush. Sometimes emerging in an open space, we could see the straight road climbing the summits of the rolling desert, until the eye couldn't follow it; but we knew it must be there, still farther and farther again. Not a breath of wind stirred. The vertical sun beat down with a fury that made one reel. And most of the troop, who had been drunk the night before, began to suffer terribly. Their lips glazed, cracked, turned dark blue. I didn't hear a single word of complaint; but there was nothing of the light-hearted joking and rollicking of other days. José Valiente taught me how to chew mesquite twigs, but that didn't help much.

When we had been riding for hours, Fidencio pointed ahead, saying huskily: "Here comes a *christiano!*" When you realize that word *christiano*, which now means simply Man, is descended among the Indians from immeasurable antiquity—and when the man that says it looks exactly as Guatemozin might have looked, it gives you curious sensations. The *christiano* in question was a very aged Indian driving a burro. No, he said, he didn't carry any water. But Sabas leaped from his horse and tumbled the old man's pack on the ground.

"Ah!" he cried; "fine! *Tres piedras!*" and held up a root of the *sotol* plant, which looks like a varnished century plant, and oozes with intoxicating juices. We divided it as you divide an artichoke. Pretty soon everybody felt better. . . .

It was at the end of the afternoon that we rounded a shoulder of the desert and saw ahead the gigantic ashen alamo trees that surrounded the spring of the Hacienda of Santo Domingo. A pillar of brown dust, like the smoke of a burning city, rose from the corral, where *vaqueros* were roping horses. Desolate and alone stood the Casa Grande, burned by Che Che Campa a year ago. And by the spring, at the foot of the alamo trees, a dozen wandering peddlers squatted around their fire, their burros munching corn. From the fountain to the adobe houses and back moved an endless chain of women water-carriers—the symbol of northern Mexico.

"Water!" we shouted, joyously, galloping down the hill. The coach horses were already at the spring with Patricio. Leaping from their saddles, the Tropa threw themselves on their bellies. Men and horses indiscriminately thrust in their heads, and drank and drank. . . . It was the most glorious sensation I have ever felt.

"Who has a cigarro?" cried somebody. For a few blessed minutes we lay on our backs smoking. The sound of music—gay music—made me sit up. And there, across my vision, moved the strangest procession in the world. First came a ragged peon carrying the flowering branch of some tree. Behind him, another bore upon his head a little box that looked like a coffin, painted in broad strips of blue, pink and silver. There followed four men, carrying a sort of canopy made of gay-colored bunting. A woman walked beneath it, though the canopy hid her down to the waist; but on top lay the body of a little girl, with bare feet and little brown hands crossed on her breast. There was a wreath of paper flowers in her hair, and her whole body was heaped with them. A harpist brought up the rear, playing a popular waltz called *"Recuerdos de Durango."* The funeral procession moved slowly and gaily along, passing the *ribota* court, where the players never ceased their handball game, to the little Campo Santo. "Bah!" spat Julian Reyes furiously. "That is a blasphemy to the dead!"

In the late sunshine the desert was a glowing thing. We rode in a silent, enchanted land, that seemed some kingdom under the sea. All around were great cactuses colored red, blue, purple, yellow, as coral is on the ocean bed. Behind us, to the west, the coach rolled along in a glory of dust like Elijah's chariot. . . . Eastward, under a sky already darkening to stars, were the rumpled mountains behind which lay La Cadena, the advance post of the Maderista army. It was a land to love—this Mexico—a land to fight for. The ballad-singers suddenly began the interminable song of "The Bull-Fight," in which the Federal chiefs are the bulls, and the Maderista generals the *torreros;* and as I looked at the gay, lovable, humble *hombres* who had given so much of their lives and of their comfort to the brave fight, I couldn't help but think of the little speech Villa made to the foreigners who left Chihuahua in the first refugee train:

"This is the latest news for you to take to your people. There shall be no more palaces in Mexico. The *tortillas* of the poor are better than the bread of the rich. Come! . . ."

It was late night—past eleven—when the coach broke down on a stretch of rocky road between high mountains. I stopped to get my blankets; and when I started on again, the *compañeros* had long vanished down the winding road. Somewhere near, I knew, was La Cadena. At any minute now a sentinel might start up out of the chaparral. For about a mile I descended a steep road that was often the dried bed of a river, winding down between high mountains. It was a black night, without stars, and bitter cold. Finally, the mountains opened into a vast plain, and across that I could faintly see the tremendous range of the Cadena, and the pass that the Tropa was to guard. Barely three leagues beyond that pass lay Mapimi, held by twelve hundred Federals. But the hacienda was still hidden by a roll of the desert.

I was quite upon it, without being challenged, before I saw it, an indistinct white square of buildings on the other side of a deep arroyo. And still no sentinel. "That's funny," I said to myself. "They don't keep very good watch here." I plunged down into the arroyo, and climbed up the other side. In one of the great rooms of the Casa Grande were lights and music. Peering through, I saw the indefatigable Sabas whirling in the mazes of the *jota,* and Isidro Amayo, and José Valiente. A *baile!* Just then a man with a gun lounged out of the lighted doorway.

"*Quien vive?*" he shouted, lazily.

"Madero!" I shouted.

"May he live!" returned the sentinel, and went back to the *baile.* . . .

# An Outpost of the Revolution

T HERE were a hundred and fifty of us stationed at La Cadena, the advance guard of all the Maderista army to the west. Our business was to guard a pass, the Puerta de la Cadena; but the troops were quartered at the hacienda, ten miles away. It stood upon a little plateau, a deep arroyo on one side, at the bottom of which a sunken river came to the surface for perhaps a hundred yards, and vanished again. As far as the eye could reach up and down the broad valley was the fiercest kind of desert—dried creek beds, and a thicket of chaparral, cactus and sword plant.

Directly east lay the Puerta, breaking the tremendous mountain range that blotted out half the sky and extended north and south beyond vision, wrinkled like a giant's bedclothes. The desert tilted up to meet the gap, and beyond was nothing but the fierce blue of stainless Mexican sky. From the Puerta you could see fifty miles across the vast arid plain that the Spaniards named *Llano de los Gigantes*, where the little mountains lie tumbled about; and four leagues away the low gray houses of Mapimi. There lay the enemy; twelve hundred *colorados*, or Federal irregulars, under the infamous Colonel Argumedo. The *colorados* are the bandits that made Orozco's revolution. They were so called because their flag was red, and because their hands were red with slaughter, too. They swept through northern Mexico, burning, pillaging and robbing the poor. In Chihuahua, they cut the soles from the feet of one poor devil, and drove him a mile across the desert before he died. And I have seen a city of four thousand souls reduced to *five* after a visit by the *colorados*. When Villa took

Torreon, there was no mercy for the *colorados;* they are always shot.

The first day we reached La Cadena, twelve of them rode up to reconnoiter. Twenty-five of the Tropa were on guard at the Puerta. They captured one *colorado.* They made him get off his horse, and took away his rifle, clothes and shoes. Then they made him run naked through a hundred yards of chaparral and cactus, shooting at him. Juan Sanchez finally dropped him, screaming, and thereby won the rifle, which he brought back as a present to me. The *colorado* they left to the great Mexican buzzards, which flap lazily above the desert all day long.

When all this happened, my *compadre,* Captain Longinos Güereca, and Trooper Juan Vallejo, and I, had borrowed the Colonel's coach for a trip to the dusty little rancho of Bruquilla—Longinos' home. It lay four desert leagues to the north, where a spring burst miraculously out of a little white hill. Old Güereca was a white-haired peon in sandals. He had been born a slave on one of the great haciendas; but years of toil, too appalling to realize, had made him that rare being in Mexico, the independent owner of a small property. He had ten children—soft, dark-skinned girls, and sons that looked like New England farmhands—and a daughter in the grave.

The Güerecas were proud, ambitious, warm-hearted folk. Longinos said: "This is my dearly loved friend, Juan Reed, and my brother." And the old man and his wife put both their arms around me and patted me on the back, in the affectionate way Mexicans embrace.

"My family owes nothing to the Revolución," said 'Gino, proudly. "Others have taken money and horses and wagons. The *jefes* of the army have become rich from the property of the great haciendas. The Güerecas have given all to the Maderistas, and have taken nothing but my rank. . . ."

The old man, however, was a little bitter. Holding up a horsehair rope, he said: "Three years ago I had four *riatas* like this. Now I have only one. One the *colorados* took, and the other Urbina's people took, and the last one José Bravo. . . . What difference does it make which side robs you?" But he didn't mean it all. He was immensely proud of his youngest son, the bravest officer in all the army.

We sat in the long adobe room, eating the most exquisite cheese, and *tortillas* with fresh goat butter—the deaf old mother apologizing in a loud voice for the poverty of the food, and her warlike son reciting his personal Iliad of the nine-days' fight around Torreon.

"We got so close," he was saying, "that the hot air and burning powder stung us in the face. We got too close to shoot, so we clubbed our rifles——" Just then all the dogs began to bark at once. We leaped from our seats. One didn't know what to expect in the Cadena those days. It was a small boy on horseback, shouting that the *colorados* were entering the Puerta—and off he galloped.

Longinos roared to put the mules in the coach. The entire family fell to work with a fury, and in five minutes Longinos dropped on one knee and kissed his father's hand, and we were tearing down the road. "Don't be killed! Don't be killed! Don't be killed!" we could hear the Señora wailing.

We passed a wagon loaded with cornstalks, with a whole family of women and children, two tin trunks, and an iron bed, perched on top. The man of the family rode a burro. Yes, the *colorados* were coming—thousands of them pouring through the Puerta. The last time the *colorados* had come they had killed his daughter. For three years there had been war in this valley, and he had not complained. Because it was for the Patria. Now they would go to the United States where——But Juan lashed the mules cruelly, and we heard no more. Farther along was an old man without shoes, placidly driving some goats. Had he heard about the *colorados*? Well, there *had* been some gossip about *colorados*. Were they coming through the Puerta, and how many?

*"Pues, quien sabe, señor!"*

At last, yelling at the staggering mules, we came into camp just in time to see the victorious Tropa straggle in across the desert, firing off many more rounds of ammunition than they had used in the fight. They moved low along the ground, scarcely higher on their broncos than the drab mesquite through which they flashed, all big sombreros and flapping gay serapes, the last sunshine on their lifted rifles.

That very night came a courier from General Urbina, saying that he was ill and wanted Pablo Seañes to come back. So off went the great coach, and Pablo's mistress, and Raphaelito, the hunchback, and Fidencio, and Patricio. Pablo said to me: "Juanito, if you want to come back with us, you shall sit beside me in the coach." Patricio and Raphaelito begged me to come. But I had got so far to the front now that I didn't want to turn back. Then the next day my friends and *compañeros* of the Tropa, whom I had learned to know so well in our march across the desert, received orders to move to Jarralitos. Only Juan Vallejo and Longinos Güereca stayed behind.

The Cadena's new garrison were a different kind of men. God knows where they came from, but it was a place where the troopers had literally starved. They were the most wretchedly poor peons that I have ever seen—about half of them didn't have serapes. Some fifty were known to be *nuevos* who had never smelled powder, about the same number were under a dreadfully incompetent old party named Major Salazar, and the remaining fifty were equipped with old carbines and ten rounds of ammunition apiece. Our commanding officer was Lieutenant-Colonel Petronilo Hernandez, who had been six years a Major in the Federal army until the murder of Madero drove him to the other side. He was a brave, good-hearted little man, with twisted shoulders, but years of official army red tape had unfitted him to handle troops like these. Every morning he issued an Order of the Day, distributing guards, posting sentinels, and naming the officer on duty. Nobody ever read it. Officers in that army have nothing to do with the disciplining or ordering of soldiers. They are officers because they have been brave, and their job is to fight at the head of their troop—that's all. The soldiers all look up to some one General, under whom they are recruited, as to their feudal lord. They call themselves his *gente*—his people; and an officer of anybody else's *gente* hasn't much authority over them. Petronilo was of Urbina's *gente;* but two-thirds of the Cadena garrison belonged to Arrieta's division. That's why there were no sentinels to the west and north. Lieutenant-Colonel Alberto Redondo guarded another pass four leagues to the south, so we thought we were safe in that direction. True, twenty-five men did outpost duty at the Puerta, and the Puerta was strong. . . .

# 8

## The Five Musketeers

THE Casa Grande of La Cadena had been sacked, of course, by Che Che Campa the year before. In the patio were corralled the officers' horses. We slept on the tiled floors of the rooms surrounding it. In the *sala* of the owner, once barbarically decorated, pegs were driven into the walls to hang saddles and bridles on, rifles and sabers were stacked against the wall, and dirty blanket rolls lay flung into the corner. At night a fire of corncobs was built in the middle of the floor, and we squatted around it, while Apolinario and fourteen-year-old Gil Tomas, who was once a *colorado*, told stories of the Bloody Three Years.

"At the taking of Durango," said Apolinario, "I was of the *gente* of Captain Borunda; he that they call the *Matador*, because he always shoots his prisoners. But when Urbina took Durango there weren't many prisoners. So Borunda, thirsty for blood, made the rounds of all the saloons. And in every one he would pick out some unarmed man and ask him if he were a Federal. 'No, señor,' the man would say. 'You deserve death because you have not told the truth!' yelled Borunda, pulling his gun. Bang!"

We all laughed heartily at this.

"That reminds me," broke in Gil, "of the time I fought with Rojas in Orozco's—(cursed be his mother!)—Revolución. An old Porfirista officer deserted to our side, and Orozco sent him out to teach the *colorados* (animals!) how to drill. There was one droll fellow in our company. Oh! he had a fine sense of humor. He pretended he was too stupid to learn the manual of arms. So this cursed old Huertista—(may he fry in hell!)—made him drill alone.

" 'Shoulder arms!' The *compañero* did it all right.

" 'Present arms!' Perfectly.

" 'Port arms!' He acted like he didn't know how, so the old fool went around and took hold of the rifle.

" '*This* way!' says he, pulling on it.

" 'Oh!' says the fellow, '*that way!*' And he let him have the bayonet right in the chest. . . ."

After that Fernando Silveyra, the paymaster, recounted a few anecdotes of the *curas*, or priests, that sounded exactly like Touraine in the thirteenth century, or the feudal rights of landlords over their women tenants before the French Revolution. Fernando ought to have known, too, for he was brought up for the Church. There must have been about twenty of us sitting around that fire, all the way from the most miserably poor peon in the Tropa up to First Captain Longinos Güereca. There wasn't one of these men who had any religion at all, although once they had all been strict Catholics. But three years of war have taught the Mexican people many things. There will never be another Porfirio Diaz; there will never be another Orozco Revolution; and the Catholic Church in Mexico will never again be the voice of God.

Then Juan Santillanes, a twenty-two-year-old *subteniente*, who seriously informed me that he was descended from the great Spanish hero, Gil Blas, piped up the ancient disreputable ditty, which begins:

*I am Count Oliveros*
*Of the Spanish artillery. . . .*

Juan proudly displayed four bullet wounds. He had killed a few defenseless prisoners with his own gun, he said; giving promise of growing up to be *muy matador* (a great killer) some day. He boasted of being the strongest and bravest man in the army. His idea of humor seemed to be breaking eggs into the pocket of my coat. Juan was very young for his years, but very likable.

But the best friend I had beside 'Gino Güereca was Subteniente Luis Martinez. They called him *Gachupine*—the contemptuous name for Spaniards—because he might have stepped out of a portrait of some noble Spanish youth by Greco. Luis was pure race—sensitive, gay and high-spirited. He was only twenty, and had never been in battle. Around the contour of his face was a faint black beard.

He fingered it, grinning. "Nicanor and I made a bet that we wouldn't shave until we took Torreon. . . ."

Luis and I slept in different rooms. But at night, when the fire had gone out and the rest of the fellows were snoring, we sat at each other's blankets—one night in his cuartel, the one next to mine—talking about the world, our girls, and what we were going to be and to do when we really got at it. When the war was over, Luis was coming to the United States to visit me; and then we were both coming back to Durango City to visit the Martinez family. He showed me the photograph of a little baby, proudly boasting that he was an uncle already. "What will you do when the bullets begin to fly?" I asked him.

"*Quien sabe?*" he laughed. "I guess I'll run!"

It was late. The sentinel at the door had long since gone to sleep. "Don't go," said Luis, grabbing my coat. "Let's gossip a little longer. . . ."

'GINO, Juan Santillanes, Silveyra, Luis, Juan Vallejo and I rode up the arroyo to bathe in a pool that was rumored to be there. It was a scorched river bed filled with white-hot sand, rimmed with dense mesquite and cactus. Every kilometer the hidden river showed itself for a little space, only to disappear at a crackling white rim of alkali. First came the horse pool, the troopers and their wretched ponies gathered around it; one or two squatting on the rim, scooping water up against the animals' sides with calabashes. . . . Above them kneeled the women at their eternal laundry on the stones. Beyond that the ancient path from the hacienda cut across, where the never-ending line of black-shawled women moved with water-jars on their heads. Still farther up were women bathers, wrapped round and round with yards of pale blue or white cotton, and naked brown babies splashing in the shallows. And, last of all, naked brown men, with sombreros on and bright-colored serapes draped over their shoulders, smoked their *hojas*, squatting on the rocks. We flushed a coyote up there, and scrambled steeply up to the desert, pulling at our revolvers. There he went! We spurred into the chaparral on the dead run, shooting and yelling. But of course he got away. And later, much later, we found the mythical pool—a cool, deep basin worn in the solid rock, with green weeds growing on the bottom.

When we got back, 'Gino Güereca became greatly excited, because his new *tordillo* horse had come from Bruquilla—a four-year-old stallion that his father had raised for him to ride at the head of his company.

"If he is dangerous," announced Juan Santillanes, as we hurried out, "I want to ride him first. I *love* to subdue dangerous horses!"

A mighty cloud of yellow dust filled all the corral, rising high into the still air. Through it appeared the dim chaotic shapes of many running horses. Their hoofs made dull thunder. Men were vaguely visible, all braced legs and swinging arms, handkerchiefs bound over their faces; wide-spreading rope coils lifted, circling. The big gray felt the loop tighten on his neck. He trumpeted and plunged; the *vaquero* twisted the rope around his hip, lying back almost to the ground, feet plowing the dirt. Another noose gripped the horse's hind legs—and he was down. They put a saddle on him and a rope halter.

"Want to ride him, Juanito?" grinned 'Gino.

"After you," answered Juan with dignity. "He's your horse...."

But Juan Vallejo already was astride, shouting to them to loose the ropes. With a sort of squealing roar, the *tordillo* struggled up, and the earth trembled to his furious fight.

WE dined in the ancient kitchen of the hacienda, sitting on stools around a packing box. The ceiling was a rich, greasy brown, from the smoke of generations of meals. One entire end of the room was taken up by immense adobe stoves, ovens, and fireplaces, with four or five ancient crones bending over them, stirring pots and turning *tortillas*. The fire was our only light, flickering strangely over the old women; lighting up the black wall, up which the smoke fled, to wreathe around the ceiling and finally pour from the window. There were Colonel Petronilo, his mistress, a strangely beautiful peasant woman with a pock-marked face, who always seemed to be laughing to herself about something; Don Tomas, Luis Martinez, Colonel Redondo, Major Salazar, Nicanor, and I. The Colonel's mistress seemed uncomfortable at the table; for a Mexican peasant woman is a servant in her house. But Don Petronilo always treated her as if she were a great lady.

Redondo had just been telling me about the girl he was going to marry. He showed me her picture. She was even then on her way to Chihuahua to get her wedding dress. "As soon as we take Torreon," he said.

"*Oiga, señor!*" Salazar touched me on the arm. "I have found out who you are. You are an agent of American businessmen who have vast interests in Mexico. I know *all* about American business. You are an agent of the trusts. You come down here to spy upon the movement of our troops, and then you will secretly send them word. Is it not true?"

"How could I secretly send anybody any word from here?" I asked. "We're four days' hard ride from a telegraph line."

"Ah, *I* know," he grinned cunningly, wabbling a finger at me. "I know many things; I have much in the head." He was standing up now. The Major suffered badly from gout; his legs were wrapped in yards and yards of woolen bandages, which made them look like *tamales*. "I know *all* about business. I have studied much in my youth. These American trusts are invading Mexico to rob the Mexican people——"

"You're mistaken, Major," interrupted Don Petronilo sharply. "This señor is my friend and my guest."

"Listen, *mi Coronel*," Salazar burst out with unexpected violence. "This señor is a spy. All Americans are Porfiristas and

Huertistas. Take this warning before it is too late. I have much in the head. I am a very smart man. Take this gringo out and shoot him—at once. Or you will regret it."

A clamor of voices burst out all together from the others, but it was interrupted by another sound—a shot, and then another, and men shouting.

Came a trooper running. "Mutiny in the ranks!" he cried. "They won't obey orders!"

"Who won't?" snapped Don Petronilo.

"The *gente* of Salazar!"

"Bad people!" exclaimed Nicanor as we ran. "They were *colorados* captured when we took Torreon. Joined us so we wouldn't kill 'em. Ordered out tonight to guard the Puerta!"

"Till tomorrow," said Salazar at this point, "I'm going to bed!"

The peons' houses at La Cadena, where the troops were quartered, enclosed a great square, like a walled town. There were two gates. At one we forced our way through a mob of women and peons fighting to get out. Inside, there were dim lights from doorways, and three or four little fires in the open air. A bunch of frightened horses crowded one another in a corner. Men ran wildly in and out of their cuartels, with rifles in their hands. In the center of the open space stood a group of about fifty men, mostly armed, as if to repel an attack.

"Guard those gates!" cried the Colonel. "Don't let anybody out without an order from me!" Then running troops began to mass at the gates. Don Petronilo walked out alone into the middle of the square.

"What's the trouble, *compañeros?*" he asked quietly.

"They were going to kill us all!" yelled somebody from the darkness. "They wanted to escape! They were going to betray us to the *colorados!*"

"It's a lie!" cried those in the center. "We are not Don Petronilo's *gente*! Our *jefe* is Manuel Arrieta!"

Suddenly Longinos Güereca, unarmed, flashed by us and fell upon them furiously, wrenching away their rifles and throwing them far behind. For a moment it looked as if the rebels would turn on him, but they did not resist.

"Disarm them!" ordered Don Petronilo. "And lock them up!"

They herded the prisoners into one large room, with an armed guard at the door. And long after midnight I could hear them hilariously singing.

That left Don Petronilo with a hundred effectives, some extra horses with running sores on their backs, and two thousand rounds of ammunition, more or less. Salazar took himself off in the morning, after recommending that all his *gente* be shot; he was evidently greatly relieved to be rid of them. Juan Santillanes was in favor of execution, too. But Don Petronilo decided to send them to General Urbina for trial.

# The Last Night

The days at La Cadena were full of color. In the cold dawn, when the river pools were filmed with ice, a trooper would gallop into the great square with a plunging steer at the end of his rope. Fifty or sixty ragged soldiers, only their eyes showing between serapes and big sombreros, would begin an amateur bullfight, to the roaring delight of the rest of the *compañeros*. They waved their blankets, shouting the correct bullfight cries. One would twist the infuriated animal's tail. Another, more impatient, beat him with the flat of a sword. Instead of banderillas, they stuck daggers into his shoulder—his hot blood spattering them as he charged. And when at last he was down and the merciful knife in his brain, a mob fell upon the carcase, cutting and ripping, and bearing off chunks of raw meat to their cuartels. Then the white, burning sun would rise suddenly behind the Puerta, stinging your hands and face. And the pools of blood, the faded patterns of the serapes, the far reaches of umber desert glowed and became vivid. . . .

Don Petronilo had confiscated several coaches in the campaign. We borrowed them for many an excursion—the five of us. Once it was a trip to San Pedro del Gallo to see a cockfight, appropriately enough. Another time 'Gino Güereca and I went to see the fabulously rich lost mines of the Spaniards, which he knew. But we never got past Bruquilla—just lounged in the shade of the trees and ate cheese all day.

Late in the afternoon the Puerta guard trotted out to their post, the late sun soft on their rifles and cartridge belts; and long after dark the detachment relieved came jingling in out of the mysterious dark.

The four peddlers whom I had seen in Santo Domingo arrived that night. They had four burro loads of *macuche* to sell the soldiers.

"It's Meester!" they cried, when I came down to their little fire. "*Que tal*, Meester? How goes it? Aren't you afraid of the *colorados?*"

"How is business?" I asked, accepting the heaped-up handful of *macuche* they gave me.

They laughed uproariously at this.

"Business! Far better for us if we had stayed in Santo Domingo! *This* Tropa couldn't buy one cigarro if they clubbed their money! . . ."

One of them began to sing that extraordinary ballad, "The Morning Song to Francisco Villa." He sang one verse, and then the next man sang a verse, and so on around, each man composing a dramatic account of the deeds of the Great Captain. For half an hour I lay there, watching them, as they squatted between their knees, serapes draped loosely from their shoulders, the firelight red on their simple, dark faces. While one man sang the others stared upon the ground, wrapt in composition.

> *Here is Francisco Villa*
> *With his chiefs and his officers,*
> *Who come to saddle the shorthorns*
> *Of the Federal Army.*
>
> *Get ready now, colorados,*
> *Who have been talking so loud,*
> *For Villa and his soldiers*
> *Will soon take off your hides!*
>
> *Today has come your tamer,*
> *The Father of Rooster Tamers,*
> *To run you out of Torreon—*
> *To the devil with your skins!*

> *The rich with all their money*
> *Have already got their lashing,*
> *As the soldiers of Urbina*
> *Can tell, and those of Maclovio Herrera.*
>
> *Fly, fly away, little dove,*
> *Fly over all the prairies,*
> *And say that Villa has come*
> *To drive them all out forever.*
>
> *Ambition will ruin itself,*
> *And justice will be the winner,*
> *For Villa has reached Torreon*
> *To punish the avaricious.*
>
> *Fly away, Royal Eagle,*
> *These laurels carry to Villa,*
> *For he has come to conquer*
> *Bravo and all his colonels.*
>
> *Now you sons of the Mosquito,*
> *Your pride will come to an end,*
> *If Villa has come to Torreon,*
> *It is because he could do it!*
>
> *Viva Villa and his soldiers!*
> *Viva Herrera and his gente!*
> *You have seen, wicked people,*
> *What a brave man can do.*
>
> *With this now I say good-bye;*
> *By the Rose of Castile,*
> *Here is the end of my rhyme*
> *To the great General Villa!*

After a while I slipped away; I doubt if they even saw me go. They sang around their fire for more than three hours.

But in our cuartel there was other entertainment. The room was full of smoke from the fire on the floor. Through it I dimly made out some thirty or forty troopers squatting or sprawled at full length—perfectly silent as Silveyra read aloud a proclamation from the Governor of Durango forever condemning the lands of the great haciendas to be divided among the poor.

* * *

He read:

> Considering: that the principal cause of discontent among the people in our State, which forced them to spring to arms in the year 1910, was the absolute lack of individual property; and that the rural classes have no means of subsistence in the present, nor any hope for the future, except to serve as peons on the haciendas of the great land owners, who have monopolized the soil of the State;
>
> Considering: that the principal branch of our national riches is agriculture, and that there can be no true progress in agriculture without that the majority of farmers have a personal interest in making the earth produce. . . .
>
> Considering, finally: that the rural towns have been reduced to the deepest misery, because the common lands which they once owned have gone to augment the property of the nearest hacienda, especially under the Dictatorship of Diaz; with which the inhabitants of the State lost their economic, political, and social independence, then passed from the rank of citizens to that of slaves, without the Government being able to lift the moral level through education, because the hacienda where they lived is private property. . . .
>
> Therefore, the Government of the State of Durango declares it a public necessity that the inhabitants of the towns and villages be the owners of agricultural lands. . . .

When the paymaster had painfully waded through all the provisions that followed, telling how the land was to be applied for, etc., there was a silence.

"That," said Martinez, "is the Mexican Revolución."

"It's just what Villa's doing in Chihuahua," I said. "It's great. All you fellows can have a farm now."

An amused chuckle ran around the circle. Then a little, bald-headed man, with yellow, stained whiskers, sat up and spoke.

"Not us," he said, "not the soldiers. After a Revolución is done it wants no more soldiers. It is the *pacificos* who will get the land—those who did not fight. And the next generation. . . ." He paused and spread his torn sleeves to the fire. "I was a schoolteacher," he explained, "so I know that Revoluciones, like Republics, are ungrateful. I have fought three years. At the end of the first Revolución that great man, Father Madero, invited his soldiers to the

Capital. He gave us clothes, and food, and bullfights. We returned to our homes and found the greedy again in power."

"I ended the war with forty-five pesos," said a man.

"You were lucky," continued the schoolmaster. "No, it is not the troopers, the starved, unfed, common soldiers who profit by the Revolución. Officers, yes—some—for they get fat on the blood of the Patria. But we—no."

"What on earth are you fighting for?" I cried.

"I have two little sons," he answered. "And *they* will get their land. And they will have other little sons. They, too, will never want for food. . . ." The little man grinned. "We have a proverb in Guadalajara: 'Do not wear a shirt of eleven yards, for he who wants to be a Redeemer will be crucified.' "

"*I've* got no little son," said fourteen-year-old Gil Tomas, amid shouts of laughter. "I'm fighting so I can get a thirty-thirty rifle from some dead Federal, and a good horse that belonged to a millionaire."

Just for fun I asked a trooper with a photo button of Madero pinned to his coat who that was.

"*Pues, quien sabe, señor?*" he replied. "My captain told me he was a great saint. I fight because it is not so hard as to work."

"How often are you fellows paid?"

"We were paid three pesos just nine months ago tonight," said the schoolmaster, and they all nodded. "We are the real volunteers. The *gente* of Villa are professionals."

Then Luis Martinez got a guitar and sang a beautiful little love song, which he said a prostitute had made up one night in a *bordel*.

The last thing I remember of that memorable night was 'Gino Güereca lying near me in the dark, talking.

"Tomorrow," he said, "I shall take you to the lost gold mines of the Spaniards. They are hidden in a cañon in the western mountains. Only the Indians know of them—and I. The Indians go there sometimes with knives and dig the raw gold out of the ground. We'll be rich. . . ."

# 10

## The Coming of the Colorados

Before sunrise next morning, Fernando Silveyra, fully dressed, came into the room and said calmly to get up, that the *colorados* were coming. Juan Vallejo laughed: "How many, Fernando?"

"About a thousand," he answered in a quiet voice, rummaging for his bandolier.

The patio was unusually full of shouting men saddling horses. I saw Don Petronilo, half dressed, at his door, his mistress buckling on his sword. Juan Santillanes was pulling at his trousers with furious haste. There was a steady rattle of clicks as cartridges slipped into rifles. A score of soldiers ran to and fro aimlessly, asking everyone where something was.

I don't think we any of us really believed it. The little square of quiet sky over the patio gave promise of another hot day. Roosters crowed. A cow that was being milked bellowed. I felt hungry.

"How near are they?" I asked.

"Near."

"But the outpost—the guard at the Puerta?"

"Asleep," Fernando said, as he strapped on his cartridge belt.

Pablo Arriola clanked in, crippled by his big spurs.

"A little bunch of twelve rode up. Our men thought it was only the daily reconnaissance. So after they drove them back, the Puerta guard sat down to breakfast. Then Argumedo himself and hundreds—hundreds———"

"But twenty-five could hold that pass against an army until the rest got there. . . ."

"They're already past the Puerta," said Pablo, shouldering his saddle. He went out.

69

"The————!" swore Juan Santillanes, spinning the chambers of his revolver. "Wait till I get at them!"

"Now Meester's going to see some of those shots he wanted," cried Gil Tomas. "How about it, Meester? Feel scared?"

Somehow the whole business didn't seem real. I said to myself, "You lucky devil, you're actually going to see a fight. That will round out the story." I loaded my camera and hurried out in front of the house.

There was nothing much to see there. A blinding sun rose right in the Puerta. Over the leagues and leagues of dark desert to the east nothing lived but the morning light. Not a movement. Not a sound. Yet somewhere out there a mere handful of men were desperately trying to hold off an army.

Thin smoke floated up in the breathless air from the houses of the peons. It was so still that the grinding of *tortilla* meal between two stones was distinctly audible—and the slow, minor song of some woman at her work way around the Casa Grande. Sheep were maaing to be let out of the corral. On the road to Santo Domingo, so far away that they were mere colored accents in the desert, the four peddlers sauntered behind their burros. Little knots of peons were gathered in front of the hacienda, pointing and looking east. And around the gate of the big enclosure where the soldiers were quartered a few troopers held their horses by the bridle. That was all.

Occasionally the door of the Casa Grande vomited mounted men—two or three at a time—who galloped down the Puerta road with their rifles in their hands. I could follow them as they rose and fell over the waves of the desert, growing smaller all the time, until they mounted the last roll—where the white dust they kicked up caught the fierce light of the sun, and the eye couldn't stand it. They had taken my horse, and Juan Vallejo didn't have one. He stood beside me, cocking and firing his empty rifle.

"Look!" he shouted suddenly. The western face of the mountains that flanked the Puerta was in shadow still. Along their base, to the north and to the south, too, wriggled little thin lines of dust. They lengthened out—oh so slowly. At first there was only one in each direction; then two others began, farther down, nearer, advancing relentlessly, like raveling in a stocking—like a crack in thin glass. The enemy, spreading wide around the battle, to take us in the flank!

Still the little knots of troopers poured from the Casa Grande, and spurred away. Pablo Arriola went, and Nicanor, waving to me brightly as they passed. Longinos Güereca rocketed out on his great *tordillo* horse, yet only half broken. The big gray put down his head and buck-jumped four times across the square.

"Tomorrow for the mines," yelled 'Gino over his shoulder. "I'm very busy today—very rich—the lost mines of———" But he was too far away for me to hear. Martinez followed him, shouting to me with a grin that he felt scared to death. Then others. It made about thirty so far. I remember that most of them wore automobile goggles. Don Petronilo sat his horse, with field glasses to his eyes. I looked again at the lines of dust—they were curving slowly down, the sun glorifying them—like scimitars.

Don Tomas galloped past, Gil Tomas at his heels. But someone was coming. A little running horse appeared on the rise, headed our way, the rider outlined in a radiant dust. He was going at furious speed, dipping and rising over the rolling land. . . . And as he spurred wildly up the little hill where we stood, we saw a horror. A fan-shaped cascade of blood poured from the front of him. The lower part of his mouth was quite shot away by a soft-nosed bullet. He reined up beside the colonel, and tried earnestly, terribly, to tell him something; but nothing intelligible issued from the ruin. Tears poured down the poor fellow's cheeks. He gave a hoarse cry, and, driving his spurs deep in his horse, fled up the Santo Domingo road. Others were coming, too, on the dead run—those who had been the Puerta guard. Two or three passed right through the hacienda without stopping. The rest threw themselves upon Don Petronilo, in a passion of rage. "More ammunition!" they cried. "More cartridges!"

Don Petronilo looked away. "There isn't any!" The men went mad, cursing and hurling their guns on the ground.

"Twenty-five more men at the Puerta," shouted the Colonel.

In a few minutes half of the new men galloped out of their cuartel and took the eastern road. The near ends of the dust lines were now lost to view behind a swell of ground.

"Why don't you send them all, Don Petronilo?" I yelled.

"Because, my young friend, a whole company of *colorados* is riding down that arroyo. You can't see them from there, but I can."

He had no sooner spoken than a rider whirled around the corner of the house, pointing back over his shoulder to the south, whence he had come.

"They're coming that way, too," he cried. "Thousands! Through the other pass! Redondo had only five men on guard! They took them prisoner and got into the valley before he knew it!"

"*Valgame Dios!*" muttered Don Petronilo.

We turned south. Above the umber rise of desert loomed a mighty cloud of white dust, shining in the sun, like the biblical pillar of smoke.

"The rest of you fellows get out there and hold them off!" The last twenty-five leaped to their saddles and started southward.

Then suddenly the great gate of the walled square belched men and horses—men without rifles. The disarmed *gente* of Salazar! They milled around as if in a panic. "Give us our rifles!" they shouted. "Where's our ammunition?"

"Your rifles are in the cuartel," answered the Colonel, "but your cartridges are out there killing *colorados!*"

A great cry went up. "They've taken away our arms! They want to murder us!"

"How can we fight, man? What can we do without rifles?" screamed one man in Don Petronilo's face.

"Come on, *compañeros*! Let's go out and strangle 'em with our hands, the—*colorados!*" yelled one. Five struck spurs into their horses, and sped furiously toward the Puerta—without arms, without hope. It was magnificent!

"We'll all get killed!" said another. "Come on!" And the other forty-five swept wildly out on the road to Santo Domingo.

The twenty-five recruits that had been ordered to hold the southern side had ridden out about half a mile, and there stopped, seeming uncertain what to do. Now they caught sight of the disarmed fifty galloping for the mountains.

"The *compañeros* are fleeing! The *compañeros* are fleeing!"

For a moment there was a sharp exchange of cries. They looked at the dust cloud towering over them. They thought of the mighty army of merciless devils who made it. They hesitated, broke—and fled furiously through the chaparral toward the mountains.

I suddenly discovered that I had been hearing shooting for some time. It sounded immensely far away—like nothing so much as a clicking typewriter. Even while it held our attention it grew. The little trivial pricking of rifles deepened and became serious. Out in front now it was practically continuous—almost the roll of a snare drum.

Don Petronilo was a little white. He called Apolinario and told him to harness the mules to the coach.

"If anything happens that we get the worst of it," he said lightly to Juan Vallejo, "call my woman and you and Reed go with her in the coach. Come on, Fernando—Juanito!" Silveyra and Juan Santillanes spurred out; the three vanished toward the Puerta.

We could see them now, hundreds of little black figures riding everywhere through the chaparral; the desert swarmed with them. Savage Indian yells reached us. A spent bullet droned overhead, then another; then one unspent, and then a whole flock singing fiercely. Thud! went the adobe walls as bits of clay flew. Peons and their women rushed from house to house, distracted with fear. A trooper, his face black with powder and hateful with killing and terror, galloped past, shouting that all was lost. . . .

Apolinario hurried out the mules with their harness on their backs, and began to hitch them to the coach. His hands trembled. He dropped a trace, picked it up, and dropped it again. He shook all over. All at once he threw the harness to the ground and took to his heels. Juan and I rushed forward. Just then a stray bullet took the off mule in the rump. Nervous already, the animals plunged wildly. The wagon tongue snapped with the report of a rifle. The mules raced madly north into the desert.

And then came the rout, a wild huddle of troopers all together, lashing their terrified horses. They passed us without stopping, without noticing, all blood and sweat and blackness. Don Tomas, Pablo Arriola, and after them little Gil Tomas, his horse staggering and falling dead right in front of us. Bullets whipped the wall on all sides of us.

"Come on, Meester!" said Juan. "Let's go!" We began to run. As I panted up the steep opposite bank of the arroyo, I looked back. Gil Tomas was right behind me, with a red- and black-checked serape round his shoulders. Don Petronilo came in sight, shooting back over his shoulder, with Juan Santillanes at his side. In front raced Fernando Silveyra, bending low over his horse's neck. All around the hacienda was a ring of galloping, shooting, yelling men; and as far as the eye could reach, on every rise of the desert, came more.

## 11

---

# Meester's Flight

J UAN Vallejo was already far ahead, running doggedly with his rifle in one hand. I shouted to him to turn off the high road, and he obeyed, without looking back. I followed. It was a straight path through the desert toward the mountains. The desert was as bald as a billiard table here. We could be seen for miles. My camera got between my legs. I dropped it. My overcoat became a terrible weight. I shook it off. We could see the *compañeros* fleeing wildly up the Santo Domingo road. Beyond them unexpectedly appeared a wave of galloping men—the flanking party from the south. The shooting broke out again—and then pursuers and pursued vanished around the corner of a little hill. Thank God the path was diverging from the road!

I ran on—ran and ran and ran, until I could run no more. Then I walked a few steps and ran again. I was sobbing instead of breathing. Awful cramps gripped my legs. Here there was more chaparral, more brush, and the foothills of the western mountains were near. But the entire length of the path was visible from behind. Juan Vallejo had reached the foothills, half a mile ahead. I saw him crawling up a little rise. Suddenly three armed horsemen swept in behind him, and raised a shout. He looked around, threw his rifle far into the brush, and fled for his life. They shot at him, but stopped to recover the rifle. He disappeared over the crest, and then they did, too.

I ran. I wondered what time it was. I wasn't very frightened. Everything still was so unreal, like a page out of Richard Harding Davis. It just seemed to me that if I didn't get away I wouldn't be doing my job well. I kept thinking to myself: "Well, this is certainly an experience. I'm going to have something to write about."

Then came yells and hoofs drumming in the rear. About a hundred yards behind ran little Gil Tomas, the ends of his gay serape flying out straight. And about a hundred yards behind him rode two black men with crossed bandoliers and rifles in their hands. They shot. Gil Tomas raised a ghastly little Indian face to me, and ran on. Again they shot. One bullet z-z-z-m-m-d by my head. The boy staggered, stopped, wheeled, and doubled suddenly into the chaparral. They turned after him. I saw the foremost horse's hoofs strike him. The *colorados* jerked their mounts to their haunches over him, shooting down again and again. . . .

I ran into the chaparral, topped a little hill, tripped on a mesquite root, fell, rolled down a sandy incline, and landed in a little arroyo. Dense mesquite covered the place. Before I could stir the *colorados* came plunging down the hillside. "There he goes!" they yelled, and, jumping their horses over the arroyo not ten feet from where I lay, galloped off into the desert. I suddenly fell asleep.

I COULDN'T have slept very long, for when I woke the sun was still in about the same place, and a few scattered shots could be heard way to the west, in the direction of Santo Domingo. I stared up through the brush tangle into the hot sky, where one great vulture slowly circled over me, wondering whether or not I was dead. Not twenty paces away a barefooted Indian with a rifle crouched on his motionless horse. He looked up at the vulture, and then searched the face of the desert. I lay still. I couldn't tell whether he was one of ours or not. After a little time he jogged slowly north over a hill and disappeared.

I waited about half an hour before crawling out of the arroyo. In the direction of the hacienda they were still shooting—making sure of the dead, I afterward learned. I couldn't see it. The little valley in which I was ran roughly east and west. I traveled westward, toward the Sierra. But it was still too near the fatal path. I stooped low and ran up over the hill, without looking back. Beyond was another, higher, and then another still. Running over the hills, walking in the sheltered valleys, I bore steadily north-west, toward the always nearing mountains. Soon there were no more sounds. The sun burned fiercely down, and the long ridges of desolate country wavered in the heat. High chaparral tore my clothes and face. Underfoot were cactuses, century plants, and the murderous *espadas*, whose long, interlaced spikes slashed my boots, drawing blood at every step; and beneath them sand and jagged stones. It was terrible going. The big still forms of Spanish bayonet, astonishingly like men, stood up all around the skyline. I stood stiffly for a moment on the top of a high hill, in a clump of them, looking back. The hacienda was already so far away that it was only a white blur in the immeasurable reaches of the desert. A thin line of dust moved from it toward the Puerta—the *colorados* taking back their dead to Mapimi.

Then my heart gave a jump. A man was coming silently up the valley. He had a green serape over one arm, and nothing on his head but a blood-clotted handkerchief. His bare legs were covered with blood from the *espadas*. He caught sight of me all of a sudden and stood still; after a pause he beckoned. I went down to where he was; he never said a word, but led the way back down the valley. About a hundred yards farther he stopped and pointed. A dead horse sprawled in the sand, its stiff legs in the air; beside it lay a man, disemboweled by a knife or a sword—evidently a *colorado*, because his cartridge belt was almost full. The man with the green serape produced a wicked-looking dagger, still ruddy with blood, fell on his knees, and began to dig among the *espadas*. I brought rocks. We cut a branch of mesquite and made a cleft cross out of it. And so we buried him.

"Where are you bound, *compañero*?" I asked.

"For the sierra," he answered. "And you?"

I pointed north, where I knew the Güerecas' ranch lay.

"The Pelayo is over that way—eight leagues."

"What is the Pelayo?"

"Another hacienda. There are some of ours at the Pelayo, I think. . . ."

We parted with an *adios*.

For hours I went on, running over the hilltops, staggering

through the cruel *espadas*, slipping down the steep sides of dried river beds. There was no water. I hadn't eaten or drunk. It was intensely hot.

About eleven I rounded the shoulder of a mountain and saw the small gray patch that was Bruquilla. Here passed the Camino Real, and the desert lay flat and open. A mile away a tiny horseman jogged along. He seemed to see me; he pulled up short and looked in my direction a long time. I stood perfectly motionless. Pretty soon he went on, getting smaller and smaller, until at last there was nothing but a little puff of dust. There was no other sign of life for miles and miles. I bent low and ran along the side of the road, where there was no dust. Half a league westward lay the Güerecas' house, hidden in the gigantic row of alamo trees that fringed its running brook. A long way off I could see a little red spot on the top of the low hill beside it; when I came nearer, I saw it was father Güereca, staring toward the east. He came running down when he saw me, clenching his hands.

"What has passed? What has passed? Is it true that the *colorados* have taken the Cadena?"

I told him briefly what had happened.

"And Longinos?" he cried, wrenching at my arm. "Have you seen Longinos?"

"No," I said. "The *compañeros* all retreated to Santo Domingo."

"You must not stay here," said the old man, trembling.

"Let me have some water—I can hardly speak."

"Yes, yes, drink. There is the brook. The *colorados* must not find you here." The old man looked around with anguish at the little rancho he had fought so hard to gain. "They would destroy us all."

Just then the old mother appeared in the doorway.

"Come here, Juan Reed," she cried. "Where is my boy? Why doesn't he come? Is he dead? Tell me the truth!"

"Oh, I think they all got away all right," I told her.

"And you! Have you eaten? Have you breakfasted?"

"I haven't had a drop of water since last night, nor any food. And I came all the way from La Cadena on foot."

"Poor little boy! Poor little boy!" she wailed, putting her arms around me. "Sit down now, and I will cook you something."

Old Güereca bit his lip in an agony of apprehension. Finally hospitality won.

"My house is at your orders," he muttered. "But hurry! Hurry! You must not be seen here! I will go up on the hill and watch for dust!"

I drank several quarts of water and ate four fried eggs and some cheese. The old man had returned and was fidgeting around.

"I sent all my children to Jarral Grande," he said. "We heard this morning. The whole valley is fleeing to the mountains. Are you ready?"

"Stay here," invited the Señora. "We will hide you from the *colorados* until Longinos comes home!"

Her husband screamed at her. "Are you mad? He mustn't be found here! Are you ready now? Come on then!"

I limped along down through a burnt, yellow cornfield. "Follow this path," said the old man, "through those two fields and the chaparral. It will take you to the highroad to the Pelayo. May you go well!" We shook hands, and a moment later I saw him shuffling back up the hill with flapping sandals.

I crossed an immense valley covered with mesquite as high as my head. Twice horsemen passed, probably only *pacificos*, but I took no chances. Beyond that valley lay another, about seven miles long. Now there were bare mountains all around, and ahead loomed a range of fantastic white, pink, and yellow hills. After about four hours, with stiff legs and bloody feet, a backache and a spinning head, I rounded these and came in sight of the alamo trees and low adobe walls of the Hacienda del Pelayo.

The peons gathered around, listening to my story.

"*Que carrai-i-i-i!*" they murmured. "But it is impossible to walk from La Cadena in one day! *Pobrecito!* You must be tired! Come now and eat. And tonight there will be a bed."

"My house is yours," said Don Felipe, the blacksmith. "But are you quite sure the *colorados* are not coming this way? The last time they paid us a visit" (he pointed to the blackened walls of the Casa

Grande), "they killed four *pacificos* who refused to join them." He put his arm through mine. "Come now, *amigo*, and eat."

"If there were only some place to bathe first!"

At this they smiled and led me behind the hacienda, along a little stream overhung with willows, whose banks were the most vivid green. The water gushed out from under a high wall, and over that wall reared the gnarled branches of a giant alamo. We entered a little door; there they left me.

The ground inside sloped sharply up, and the wall—it was faded pink—followed the contour of the land. Sunk in the middle of the enclosure was a pool of crystal water. The bottom was white sand. At one end of the pool the water fountained up from a hole in the bottom. A faint steam rose from the surface. It was *hot* water.

There was a man already standing up to his neck in the water, a man with a circle shaved on the top of his head.

"Señor," he said, "are you a Catholic?"

"No."

"Thank God," he returned briefly. "We Catholics are liable to be intolerant. Are you a Mexican?"

"No, señor."

"It is well," he said, smiling sadly. "I am a priest and a Spaniard. I have been made to understand that I am not wanted in this beautiful land, señor. God is good. But He is better in Spain than He is in Mexico. . . ."

I let myself slowly down into the pellucid, hot depths. The pain and the soreness and the weariness fled shuddering up my body. I felt like a disembodied spirit. Floating there in the warm embrace of that marvelous pool, with the crooked gray branches of the alamo above our heads, we discussed philosophy. The fierce sky cooled slowly, and the rich sunlight climbed little by little up the pink wall.

Don Felipe insisted that I sleep in his house, in his bed. This bed consisted of an iron frame with loose wooden slats stretched across it. Over these was laid one tattered blanket. My clothing covered me. Don Felipe, his wife, his grown son and daughter, his two small infants, all of whom had been accustomed to use the bed, lay down upon the soft floor. There were also two sick persons in the room—a very old man covered with red spots, too far gone to speak, and a boy with extraordinarily swollen tonsils. Occasionally a centenarian hag entered and ministered unto the patients. Her method of treatment was simple. With the old man she merely heated a piece of iron at the candle and touched the spots. For the boy's case she made a paste of corn meal and lard, and gently rubbed his elbows with it, loudly saying prayers. This went on at intervals all night. Between treatments the babies would wake up at intervals and insist upon being nursed. . . . The door was shut early in the evening, and windows there were none.

Now all this hospitality meant a real sacrifice to Don Felipe, especially the meals, at which he unlocked a tin trunk and brought me with all reverence his precious sugar and coffee. He was, like all peons, incredibly poor and lavishly hospitable. The giving up of his bed was a mark of the highest honor, too. But when I tried to pay him in the morning he wouldn't hear of it.

"My house is yours," he repeated. " 'A stranger might be God,' as we say."

Finally I told him that I wanted him to buy me some tobacco, and he took the money. I knew then that it would go to the right place, for a Mexican can be trusted never to carry out a commission. He is delightfully irresponsible.

At six o'clock in the morning I set out for Santo Domingo in a two-wheeled cart driven by an old peon named Froilan Mendarez. We avoided the main road, jolting along by a mere track that led behind a range of hills. After we'd traveled for about an hour, I had an unpleasant thought.

"What if the *compañeros* fled beyond Santo Domingo and the *colorados* are there?"

"What indeed?" murmured Froilan, chirruping to the mule.

"But if they are, what'll we do?"

Froilan thought a minute. "We might say we were cousins to President Huerta," he suggested, without a smile. Froilan was a barefooted peon, his face and hands incredibly damaged by age and dirt; I was a ragged gringo. . . .

We jogged on for several hours. At one place an armed man

started out of the brush and hailed us. His lips were split and leathery with thirst. The *espadas* had slashed his legs terribly. He had escaped over the Sierra, climbing and slipping all night. We gave him all the water and food we had, and he went on toward the Pelayo.

Long after noon our cart topped the last desert rise, and we saw sleeping below us the long spread-out hacienda of Santo Domingo, with its clump of tall alamos like palm trees around the oasis-like spring. My heart was in my mouth as we drove down. In the big *ribota* court the peons were playing hand ball. Up from the spring moved the long line of water carriers. A fire sent up thin smoke among the trees.

We came upon an aged peon carrying fagots. "No," he said, "there had been no *colorados*. The Maderistas? Yes, they had come last night—hundreds of them, all running. But at dawn they had gone back to La Cadena to 'lift the fields' (bury the dead)."

From around the fire under the alamos came a great shout: "The Meester! Here comes the Meester! *Que tal, compañero?* How did you escape?" It was my old friends, the peddlers. They crowded around eagerly, questioning, shaking my hand, throwing their arms around me.

"Ah, but that was close! *Carramba*, but I was lucky! Did I know that Longinos Güereca was killed? Yes, but he shot six *colorados* before they got him. And Martinez also, and Nicanor, and Redondo."

I felt sick. Sick to think of so many useless deaths in such a petty fight. Blithe, beautiful Martinez; 'Gino Güereca, whom I had learned to love so much; Redondo, whose girl was even then on her way to Chihuahua to buy her wedding dress; and jolly Nicanor. It seems that when Redondo found that his flank had been turned his troop deserted him; so he galloped alone toward La Cadena, and was caught by three hundred *colorados*. They literally shot him to pieces. 'Gino, and Luis Martinez, and Nicanor, with five others, held the eastward side of the hacienda unaided until their cartridges were gone, and they were surrounded by a ring of shooting men. Then they died. The *colorados* carried off the Colonel's woman.

"But there's a man who's been through it all," said one of the peddlers. "He fought till his last cartridge was gone, and then cut his way through the enemy with a saber."

I looked around. Surrounded by a ring of gaping peons, his lifted arm illustrating the great deed, was—Apolinario! He caught sight of me, nodded coldly, as to one who has run from the fight, and went on with his recital.

ALL through the long afternoon Froilan and I played *ribota* with the peons. It was a drowsy, peaceful day. A gentle wind rustled the high branches of the great trees, and the late sun, from behind the hill that is back of Santo Domingo, warmed with color their lofty tops.

It was a strange sunset. The sky became overcast with light cloud toward the end of the afternoon. First it turned pink, then scarlet, then of a sudden the whole firmament became a deep, bloody red.

An immense drunken man—an Indian about seven feet tall—staggered out in the open ground near the *ribota* court with a violin in his hand. He tucked it under his chin and sawed raggedly on the strings, staggering to and fro as he played. Then a little one-armed dwarf sprang out of the crowd of peons and began to dance. A dense throng made a circle around the two, roaring with mirth.

And just at that moment there appeared against the bloody sky, over the eastern hill, the broken, defeated men—on horseback and on foot, wounded and whole, weary, sick, disheartened, reeling and limping down to Santo Domingo. . . .

# Elizabetta

So, against a crimson sky, the beaten, exhausted soldiers came down the hill. Some rode, their horses hanging weary heads—occasionally two on a horse. Others walked, with bloody bandages around their foreheads and arms. Cartridge belts were empty, rifles gone. Their hands and faces were foul with sweaty dirt and stained still with powder. Beyond the hill, across the twenty-mile arid waste that lay between us and La Cadena, they straggled. There were not more than fifty left, including the women—the rest had dispersed in the barren mountains and the folds of the desert—but they stretched out for miles; it took hours for them to arrive.

Don Petronilo came in front, with lowered face and folded arms, the reins hanging loose upon the neck of his swaying, stumbling horse. Right behind him came Juan Santillanes, gaunt and white, his face years older. Fernando Silveyra, all rags, dragged along at his saddle. As they waded the shallow stream they looked up and saw me. Don Petronilo weakly waved his hand; Fernando shouted, "Why, there's Meester! How did you escape? We thought sure they had shot you."

"I ran a race with the goats," I answered. Juan gave a laugh. "Scared to death, eh?"

The horses thrust eager muzzles into the stream, sucking fiercely. Juan cruelly spurred across, and we fell into each other's arms. But Don Petronilo dismounted in the water, dully as if in a dream, and, wading up to the tops of his boots, came to where I was.

He was weeping. His expression didn't change, but slow, big tears fell silently down his cheeks.

"The *colorados* captured his wife!" murmured Juan in my ear.

I was filled with pity for the man.

"It is a terrible thing, *mi Coronel,*" I said gently, "to feel the responsibility for all these brave fellows who died. But it was not your fault."

"It is not that," he replied slowly, staring through tears at the pitiful company crawling down from the desert.

"I, too, had many friends who died in the battle," I went on. "But they died gloriously, fighting for their country."

"I do not weep for them," he said, twisting his hands together. "This day I have lost all that is dear to me. They took my woman who was mine, and my commission and all my papers, and all my money. But I am wrenched with grief when I think of my silver spurs inlaid with gold, which I bought only last year in Mapimi!" He turned away, overcome.

And now the peons began to come down from their houses, with pitying cries and loving offers. They threw their arms around the soldiers' necks, assisting the wounded, patting them shyly on the shoulders and calling them "brave." Desperately poor themselves, they offered food, and beds, and fodder for the horses, inviting them to stay at Santo Domingo until they should become well. I already had a place to sleep. Don Pedro, the chief goatherd, had given me his room and his bed in a gush of warm-hearted generosity, and had removed himself and his family to the kitchen. He did so without hope of recompense, for he thought I had no money. And now everywhere men, women and children left their houses to make way for the defeated and weary troops.

Fernando, Juan and I went over and begged some tobacco from the four peddlers camped under the trees beside the spring. They had made no sales for a week, and were almost starving, but they loaded us lavishly with *macuche.* We talked of the battle, lying there on our elbows watching the shattered remnants of the garrison top the hill.

"You have heard that 'Gino Güereca fell," said Fernando. "Well, I saw him. His big gray horse that he rode for the first time was terrified by the bridle and saddle. But once he came where the bullets were flying and the guns roaring, he steadied at once. Pure race, that horse. . . . His fathers must have been all warriors. Around 'Gino were four or five more heroes, with almost all their cartridges gone. They fought until on the front and on both sides double galloping lines of *colorados* closed in. 'Gino was standing beside his horse—suddenly a score of shots hit the animal all at once, and he sighed and fell over. The rest ceased firing in a sort of panic. 'We're lost!' they cried. 'Run while there is yet a chance!' 'Gino shook his smoking rifle at them. 'No,' he shouted. 'Give the *compañeros* time to get away!' Shortly after that they closed around him, and I never saw him until we buried his body this morning. . . . It was the devil's hell out there. The rifles were so hot you couldn't touch the barrels, and the whirling haze that belched out when they shot twisted everything like a mirage. . . ."

Juan broke in. "We rode straight out toward the Puerta when the retreat began, but almost immediately we saw it was no use. The *colorados* broke over our little handfuls of men like waves of the sea. Martinez was just ahead. He never had a chance even to fire his gun—and this was his first battle, too. They hit him as he rode. . . . I thought how you and Martinez loved each other. You used to talk together at night so warmly, and never wished to leave each other to sleep. . . ."

Now the tall, naked tops of the trees had dulled with the passing of the light, and seemed to stand still among the swarming stars in the deep dome overhead. The peddlers had kindled their tiny fire; the low, contented murmur of their gossip floated to us. Open doors of the peons' huts shed wavering candlelight. Up from the river wound a silent line of black-robed girls with water-jars on their heads. Women ground their corn meal with a monotonous stony scraping. Dogs barked. Drumming hoofs marked the passing of the *caballada* to the river. Along the ledge in front of Don Pedro's house the warriors smoked and fought the battle over again, stamping around and shouting descriptive matter. "I took my rifle by the barrel and smashed in his grinning face, just as——" some one was narrating, with gestures. The peons squatted around, breathlessly listening. . . . And still the ghastly procession of the defeated straggled down the road and across the river.

It was not yet quite dark. I wandered down to the bank to watch them, in the vague hope of finding some of my *compadres* who were still reported missing. And it was there that I first saw Elizabetta.

There was nothing remarkable about her. I think I noticed her chiefly because she was one of the few women in that wretched company. She was a very dark-skinned Indian girl, about twenty-five years old, with the squat figure of her drudging race, pleasant features, hair hanging forward over her shoulders in two long plaits, and big, shining teeth when she smiled. I never did find out whether she had been just a peon woman working around La Cadena when the attack had come, or whether she was a *vieja*—a camp follower of the army.

Now she was trudging stolidly along in the dust behind Captain Felix Romero's horse—and had trudged so for thirty miles. He never spoke to her, never looked back, but rode on unconcernedly. Sometimes he would get tired of carrying his rifle and hand it back to her to carry, with a careless "Here! Take this!" I found out later that when they returned to La Cadena after the battle to bury the dead he had found her wandering aimlessly in the hacienda, apparently out of her mind; and that, needing a woman, he had ordered her to follow him. Which she did, unquestioningly, after the custom of her sex and country.

Captain Felix let his horse drink. Elizabetta halted, too, kneeled and plunged her face into the water.

"Come on," ordered the Captain. "*Andale!*" She rose without a word and waded through the stream. In the same order they climbed the near bank, and there the Captain dismounted, held out his hand for the rifle she carried, and said, "Get me my supper!" Then he strolled away toward the houses where the rest of the soldiers sat.

Elizabetta fell upon her knees and gathered twigs for her fire. Soon there was a little pile burning. She called a small boy in the harsh, whining voice that all Mexican women have, "*Aie! chamaco!* Fetch me a little water and corn that I may feed my man!" And, rising upon her knees above the red glow of the flames, she shook down her long, straight black hair. She wore a sort of blouse of faded light blue rough cloth. There was dried blood on the breast of it.

"What a battle, señorita!" I said to her.

Her teeth flashed as she smiled, and yet there was a puzzling vacancy about her expression. Indians have mask-like faces. Under it I could see that she was desperately tired and even a little hysterical. But she spoke tranquilly enough.

"Perfectly," she said. "Are you the gringo who ran so many miles with the *colorados* after you shooting?" And she laughed— catching her breath in the middle of it as if it hurt.

The *chamaco* shambled up with an earthen jar of water and an armful of corn-ears that he tumbled at her feet. Elizabetta unwound from her shawl the heavy little stone trough that Mexican women carry, and began mechanically husking the corn into it.

"I do not remember seeing you at La Cadena," I said. "Were you there long?"

"Too long," she answered simply, without raising her head. And then suddenly, "Oh, but this war is no game for women!" she cried.

Don Felix loomed up out of the dark, with a cigarette in his mouth.

"My dinner," he growled. "Is it *pronto*?"

"*Luego, luego!*" she answered. He went away again.

"Listen, señor, whoever you are!" said Elizabetta swiftly, looking up to me. "My lover was killed yesterday in the battle. This man is my man, but, by God and all the Saints, I can't sleep with him this night. Let me stay then with you!"

There wasn't a trace of coquetry in her voice. This blundering, childish spirit had found itself in a situation it couldn't bear, and had chosen the instinctive way out. I doubt if she even knew herself why the thought of this new man so revolted her, with her lover scarcely cold in the ground. I was nothing to her, nor she to me. That was all that mattered.

I assented, and together we left the fire, the Captain's neglected corn spilling from the stone trough. And then we met him a few feet into the darkness.

"My dinner!" he said impatiently. His voice changed. "Where are you going?"

"I'm going with this señor," Elizabetta answered nervously. "I'm going to stay with him——"

"You——" began Don Felix, gulping. "You are my woman. *Oiga*, señor, this is my woman here!"

"Yes," I said. "She is your woman. I have nothing to do with her. But she is very tired and not well, and I have offered her my bed for the night."

"This is very bad, señor!" exclaimed the Captain, in a tightening voice. "You are the guest of this Tropa and the Colonel's friend, but this is my woman and I want her——"

"Oh!" Elizabetta cried out. "Until the next time, señor!" She caught my arm and pulled me on.

We had been living in a nightmare of battle and death—all of us. I think everybody was a little dazed and excited. I know I was.

By this time the peons and soldiers had begun to gather around us, and as we went on the Captain's voice rose as he retailed his injustice to the crowd.

"I shall appeal to the Colonel," he was saying. "I shall tell the Colonel!" He passed us, going toward the Colonel's cuartel, with averted, mumbling face.

"*Oiga, mi Coronel!*" he cried. "This gringo has taken away my woman. It is the grossest insult!"

"Well," returned the Colonel calmly, "if they both want to go, I guess there isn't anything we can do about it, eh?"

The news had traveled like light. A throng of small boys followed us close behind, shouting the joyful indelicacies they shout behind rustic wedding parties. We passed the ledge where the soldiers and the wounded sat, grinning and making rough, genial remarks as at a marriage. It was not coarse or suggestive, their banter; it was frank and happy. They were honestly glad for us.

As we approached Don Pedro's house we were aware of many candles within. He and his wife and daughter were busy with brooms, sweeping and resweeping the earthen floor, and sprinkling it with water. They had put new linen on the bed, and lit the rush candle before the table altar of the Virgin. Over the doorway hung a festoon of paper blossoms, faded relics of many a Christmas Eve celebration—for it was winter, and there were no real flowers.

Don Pedro was radiant with smiles. It made no difference who we were, or what our relation was. Here were a man and a maid, and to him it was a bridal.

"May you have a happy night," he said softly, and closed the door. The frugal Elizabetta immediately made the rounds of the room, extinguishing all the candles but one.

And then, outside, we heard music beginning to tune up. Someone had hired the village orchestra to serenade us. Late into the night they played steadily, right outside our door. In the next house we heard them moving chairs and tables out of the way; and just before I went to sleep they began to dance there, economically combining a serenade with a *baile*.

Without the least embarrassment, Elizabetta lay down beside me on the bed. Her hand reached for mine. She snuggled against my body for the comforting human warmth of it, murmured, "Until morning," and went to sleep. And calmly, sweetly, sleep came to me. . . .

When I woke in the morning she was gone. I opened my door and looked out. Morning had come dazzlingly, all blue and gold—a heaven of flame-trimmed big white clouds and windy sky, and the desert brazen and luminous. Under the ashy bare trees the peddlers' morning fire leaped horizontal in the wind. The black women, with wind-folded draperies, crossed the open ground to the river in single file, with red water-jars on their heads. Cocks crew, goats clamored for milking, and a hundred horses drummed up the dust as they were driven to water.

Elizabetta was squatted over a little fire near the corner of the house, patting *tortillas* for the Captain's breakfast. She smiled as I came up, and politely asked me if I had slept well. She was quite contented now; you knew from the way she sang over her work.

Presently the Captain came up in a surly manner and nodded briefly to me.

"I hope it's ready now," he grunted, taking the *tortillas* she gave him. "You take a long time to cook a little breakfast. *Carramba!* Why is there no coffee?" He moved off, munching. "Get ready," he flung back over his shoulder. "We go north in an hour."

"Are you going?" I asked curiously. Elizabetta looked at me with wide-open eyes.

"Of course I am going. *Seguro!* Is he not my man?" She looked after him admiringly. She was no longer revolted.

"He is my man," she said. "He is very handsome, and very brave. Why, in the battle the other day——"

Elizabetta had forgotten her lover.

# FRANCISCO VILLA

**1**

# Villa Accepts a Medal

It was while Villa was in Chihuahua City, two weeks before the advance on Torreon, that the artillery corps of his army decided to present him with a gold medal for personal heroism on the field.

In the audience hall of the Governor's palace in Chihuahua, a place of ceremonial, great luster chandeliers, heavy crimson portières, and gaudy American wallpaper, there is a throne for the governor. It is a gilded chair, with lion's claws for arms, placed upon a dais under a canopy of crimson velvet, surmounted by a heavy, gilded, wooden cap, which tapers up to a crown.

The officers of artillery, in smart blue uniforms faced with black velvet and gold, were solidly banked across one end of the audience hall, with flashing new swords and their gilt-braided hats stiffly held under their arms. From the door of that chamber, around the gallery, down the state staircase, across the grandiose inner court of the palace, and out through the imposing gates to the street, stood a double line of soldiers, with their rifles at present arms. Four regimental bands grouped in one wedged in the crowd. The people of the capital were massed in solid thousands on the Plaza de Armas before the palace.

"*Ya viene!*" "Here he comes!" "Viva Villa!" "Viva Madero!" "Villa, the Friend of the Poor!"

The roar began at the back of the crowd and swept like fire in heavy growing crescendo until it seemed to toss thousands of hats above their heads. The band in the courtyard struck up the Mexican national air, and Villa came walking down the street.

He was dressed in an old plain khaki uniform, with several but-

95

tons lacking. He hadn't recently shaved, wore no hat, and his hair had not been brushed. He walked a little pigeon-toed, humped over, with his hands in his trousers pockets. As he entered the aisle between the rigid lines of soldiers he seemed slightly embarrassed, and grinned and nodded to a *compadre* here and there in the ranks. At the foot of the grand staircase, Governor Chao and Secretary of State Terrazzas joined him in full-dress uniform. The band threw off all restraint, and, as Villa entered the audience chamber, at a signal from someone in the balcony of the palace, the great throng in the Plaza de Armas uncovered, and all the brilliant crowd of officers in the room saluted stiffly.

It was Napoleonic!

Villa hesitated for a minute, pulling his mustache and looking very uncomfortable, finally gravitated toward the throne, which he tested by shaking the arms, and then sat down, with the Governor on his right and the Secretary of State on his left.

Señor Bauche Alcalde stepped forward, raised his right hand to the exact position which Cicero took when denouncing Catiline, and pronounced a short discourse, indicting Villa for personal bravery on the field on six counts, which he mentioned in florid detail. He was followed by the Chief of Artillery, who said: "The army adores you. We will follow you wherever you lead. You can be what you desire in Mexico." Then three other officers spoke in the high-flung, extravagant periods necessary to Mexican oratory. They called him "The Friend of the Poor," "The Invincible General," "The Inspirer of Courage and Patriotism," "The Hope of the Indian Republic." And through it all Villa slouched on the throne, his mouth hanging open, his little shrewd eyes playing around the room. Once or twice he yawned, but for the most part he seemed to be speculating, with some intense interior amusement, like a small boy in church, what it was all about. He knew, of course, that it was the proper thing, and perhaps felt a slight vanity that all this conventional ceremonial was addressed to him. But it bored him just the same.

Finally, with an impressive gesture, Colonel Servín stepped forward with the small pasteboard box which held the medal. General Chao nudged Villa, who stood up. The officers applauded violently; the crowd outside cheered; the band in the court burst into a triumphant march.

Villa put out both hands eagerly, like a child for a new toy. He could hardly wait to open the box and see what was inside. An expectant hush fell upon everyone, even the crowd in the square. Villa looked at the medal, scratching his head, and, in a reverent silence, said clearly: "This is a hell of a little thing to give a man for all that heroism you are talking about!" And the bubble of Empire was pricked then and there with a great shout of laughter.

They waited for him to speak—to make a conventional address of acceptance. But as he looked around the room at those brilliant, educated men, who said that they would die for Villa, the peon, and meant it, and as he caught sight through the door of the ragged soldiers, who had forgotten their rigidity and were crowding eagerly into the corridor with eyes fixed eagerly on the *compañero* that they loved, he realized something of what the Revolution signified.

Puckering up his face, as he did always when he concentrated intensely, he leaned across the table in front of him and poured out, in a voice so low that people could hardly hear: "There is no word to speak. All I can say is my heart is all to you." Then he nudged Chao and sat down, spitting violently on the floor; and Chao pronounced the classic discourse.

# 2

## The Rise of a Bandit

Villa was an outlaw for twenty-two years. When he was only a boy of sixteen, delivering milk in the streets of Chihuahua, he killed a government official and had to take to the mountains. The story is that the official had violated his sister, but it seems probable that Villa killed him on account of his insufferable insolence. That in itself would not have outlawed him long in Mexico, where human life is cheap; but once a refugee he committed the unpardonable crime of stealing cattle from the rich *hacendados*. And from that time to the outbreak of the Madero revolution the Mexican government had a price on his head.

Villa was the son of ignorant peons. He had never been to school. He hadn't the slightest conception of the complexity of civilization, and when he finally came back to it, a mature man of extraordinary native shrewdness, he encountered the twentieth century with the naïve simplicity of a savage.

It is almost impossible to procure accurate information about his career as a bandit. There are accounts of outrages he committed in old files of local newspapers and government reports, but those sources are prejudiced, and his name became so prominent as a bandit that every train robbery and holdup and murder in northern Mexico was attributed to Villa. But an immense body of popular legend grew up among the peons around his name. There are many traditional songs and ballads celebrating his exploits—you can hear the shepherds singing them around their fires in the mountains at night, repeating verses handed down by their fathers or composing others extemporaneously. For instance, they tell the story of how Villa, fired by the story of the misery of the peons on the Hacienda of Los Alamos, gathered a small army and descended upon the Big House, which he looted, and distributed the spoils among the poor people. He drove off thousands of cattle from the Terrazzas range and ran them across the border. He would suddenly descend upon a prosperous mine and seize the bullion. When he needed corn he captured a granary belonging to some rich man. He recruited almost openly in the villages far removed from the well-traveled roads and railways, organizing the outlaws of the mountains. Many of the present rebel soldiers used to belong to his band and several of the Constitutionalist generals, like Urbina. His range was confined mostly to southern Chihuahua and northern Durango, but it extended from Coahuila right across the Republic to the State of Sinaloa.

His reckless and romantic bravery is the subject of countless poems. They tell, for example, how one of his band named Reza was captured by the rurales and bribed to betray Villa. Villa heard of it and sent word into the city of Chihuahua that he was coming for Reza. In broad daylight he entered the city on horseback, took ice cream on the Plaza—the ballad is very explicit on this point—and rode up and down the streets until he found Reza strolling with his sweetheart in the Sunday crowd on the Paseo Bolivar, where he shot him and escaped. In time of famine he fed whole districts, and took care of entire villages evicted by the soldiers under Porfirio Diaz's outrageous land law. Everywhere he was known as The Friend of the Poor. He was the Mexican Robin Hood.

In all these years he learned to trust nobody. Often in his secret journeys across the country with one faithful companion he camped in some desolate spot and dismissed his guide; then, leaving a fire burning, he rode all night to get away from the faithful companion. That is how Villa learned the art of war, and in the field today, when the army comes into camp at night, Villa flings the bridle of his horse to an orderly, takes a serape over his shoulder, and sets out for the hills alone. He never seems to sleep. In the dead of night he will appear somewhere along the line of outposts to see if the sentries are on the job; and in the morning he returns from a totally different direction. No one, not even the most trusted officer of his staff, knows the last of his plans until he is ready for action.

WHEN Madero took the field in 1910, Villa was still an outlaw. Perhaps, as his enemies say, he saw a chance to whitewash himself; perhaps, as seems probable, he was inspired by the Revolution of the peons. Anyway, about three months after they rose in arms, Villa suddenly appeared in El Paso and put himself, his band, his knowledge of the country and all his fortune at the command of Madero. The vast wealth that people said he must have accumulated during his twenty years of robbery turned out to be 363 silver *pesos*, badly worn. Villa became a Captain in the Maderista army, and as such went to Mexico City with Madero and was made honorary general of the new *rurales*. He was attached to Huerta's army when it was sent north to put down the Orozco Revolution. Villa commanded the garrison of Parral, and defeated Orozco with an inferior force in the only decisive battle of the war.

Huerta put Villa in command of the advance, and let him and the veterans of Madero's army do the dangerous and dirty work while the old line Federal regiments lay back under the protection of their artillery. In Jimenez Huerta suddenly summoned Villa before a court-martial and charged him with insubordination—claiming to have wired an order to Villa in Parral, which order Villa said he never received. The court-martial lasted fifteen minutes, and Huerta's most powerful future antagonist was sentenced to be shot.

Alfonso Madero, who was on Huerta's staff, stayed the execution, but President Madero, forced to back up the orders of his commander in the field, imprisoned Villa in the penitentiary of the capital. During all this time Villa never wavered in his loyalty to Madero—an unheard-of thing in Mexican history. For a long time he had passionately wanted an education. Now he wasted no time in regrets or political intrigue. He set himself with all his force to learn to read and write. Villa hadn't the slightest foundation to work upon. He spoke the crude Spanish of the very poor—what is called *pelado*. He knew nothing of the rudiments or philosophy of language; and he started out to learn those first, because he always must know the *why* of things. In nine months he could write a very fair hand and read the newspapers. It is interesting now to see him read, or, rather, hear him, for he has to drone the words aloud like a small child. Finally, the Madero government connived at his escape from prison, either to save Huerta's face because Villa's friends had demanded an investigation, or because Madero was convinced of his innocence and didn't dare openly to release him.

From that time to the outbreak of the last revolution, Villa lived in El Paso, Texas, and it was from there that he set out, in April, 1913, to conquer Mexico with four companions, three led horses, two pounds of sugar and coffee, and a pound of salt.

There is a little story connected with that. He hadn't money enough to buy horses, nor had any of his companions. But he sent two of them to a local livery stable to rent riding horses every day for a week. They always paid carefully at the end of the ride, so when they asked for eight horses the livery stable man had no hesitation about trusting them with them. Six months later, when Villa came triumphantly into Juarez at the head of an army of four thousand men, the first public act he committed was to send a man with double the price of the horses to the owner of the livery stable.

He recruited in the mountains near San Andres, and so great was his popularity that within one month he had raised an army of three thousand men; in two months he had driven the Federal garrisons all over the State of Chihuahua back into Chihuahua City; in six months he had taken Torreon; and in seven and a half Juarez had fallen to him, Mercado's Federal army had evacuated Chihuahua, and Northern Mexico was almost free.

# 3

# A Peon in Politics

Villa proclaimed himself military governor of the State of Chihuahua, and began the extraordinary experiment—extraordinary because he knew nothing about it—of creating a government for 300,000 people out of his head.

It has often been said that Villa succeeded because he had educated advisers. As a matter of fact, he was almost alone. What advisers he had spent most of their time answering his eager questions and doing what he told them. I used sometimes to go to the Governor's palace early in the morning and wait for him in the Governor's chamber. About eight o'clock Sylvestre Terrazzas, the Secretary of State, Sebastian Vargas, the State Treasurer, and Manuel Chao, then Interventor, would arrive, very bustling and busy, with huge piles of reports, suggestions and decrees which they had drawn up. Villa himself came in about eight-thirty, threw himself into a chair, and made them read out loud to him. Every minute he would interject a remark, correction or suggestion. Occasionally he waved his finger back and forward and said: *"No sirve."* When they were all through he began rapidly and without a halt to outline the policy of the State of Chihuahua, legislative, financial, judicial, and even educational. When he came to a place that bothered him, he said: "How do they do that?" And then, after it was carefully explained to him: "Why?" Most of the acts and usages of government seemed to him extraordinarily unnecessary and snarled up. For example, his advisers proposed to finance the Revolution by issuing State bonds bearing 30 or 40 percent interest. He said, "I can understand why the State should pay something to people for the rent of their

money, but how is it just to pay the whole sum back to them three
or four times over?" He couldn't see why rich men should be
granted huge tracts of land and poor men should not. The whole
complex structure of civilization was new to him. You had to be a
philosopher to explain anything to Villa; and his advisers were
only practical men.

There was the financial question. It came to Villa in this way. He
noticed, all of a sudden, that there was no money in circulation.
The farmers who produced meat and vegetables refused to come
into the city markets any more because no one had any money to
buy from them. The truth was that those possessing silver or
Mexican bank notes buried them in the ground. Chihuahua not
being a manufacturing center, and the few factories there having
closed down, there was nothing which could be exchanged for
food. So, like a blight, the paralysis of the production of food
began all at once and actual starvation stared at the town populations. I remember hearing vaguely of several highly elaborate
plans for the relief of this condition put forward by Villa's advisers. He himself said: "Why, if all they need is money, let's print
some." So they inked up the printing press in the basement of the
Governor's palace and ran off two million pesos on strong paper,
stamped with the signatures of government officials, and with
Villa's name printed across the middle in large letters. The counterfeit money, which afterward flooded El Paso, was distinguished from the original by the fact that the names of the
officials were signed instead of stamped.

This first issue of currency was guaranteed by absolutely nothing but the name of Francisco Villa. It was issued chiefly to revive
the petty internal commerce of the State so that the poor people
could get food. And yet almost immediately it was bought by the
banks of El Paso at 18 to 19 cents on the dollar because Villa
guaranteed it.

Of course he knew nothing of the accepted ways of getting his
money into circulation. He began to pay the army with it. On
Christmas Day he called the poor people of Chihuahua together
and gave them $15 apiece outright. Then he issued a short de-

cree, ordering the acceptance of his money at par throughout the State. The succeeding Saturday the marketplaces of Chihuahua and the other nearby towns swarmed with farmers and with buyers.

Villa issued another proclamation, fixing the price of beef at seven cents a pound, milk at five cents a quart, and bread at four cents a loaf. There was no famine in Chihuahua. But the big merchants, who had timidly reopened their stores for the first time since his entry into Chihuahua, placarded their goods with two sets of price marks—one for Mexican silver money and bank bills, and the other for "Villa money." He stopped that by another decree, ordering sixty days' imprisonment for anybody who discriminated against his currency.

But still the silver and bank bills refused to come out of the ground, and these Villa needed to buy arms and supplies for his army. So he simply proclaimed to the people that after the tenth of February Mexican silver and bank bills would be regarded as counterfeit, and that before that time they could be exchanged for his own money at par in the State Treasury. But the large sums of the rich still eluded him. Most of the financiers declared that it was all a bluff, and held on. But lo! on the morning of February tenth, a decree was pasted up on the walls all over Chihuahua City, announcing that from that time on all Mexican silver and bank notes were counterfeit and could not be exchanged for Villa money in the Treasury, and anyone attempting to pass them was liable to sixty days in the penitentiary. A great howl went up, not only from the capitalists, but from the shrewd misers of distant villages.

About two weeks after the issue of this decree, I was taking lunch with Villa in the house which he had confiscated from Manuel Gomeros and used as his official residence. A delegation of three peons in sandals arrived from a village in the Tarahumare to protest against the Counterfeit Decree.

"But, *mi General*," said the spokesman, "we did not hear of the decree until today. We have been using bank bills and silver in our village. We had not seen your money, and we did not know. . . ."

"You have a good deal of money?" interrupted Villa suddenly.
"Yes, *mi General.*"
"Three or four or five thousand, perhaps?"
"More than that, *mi General.*"
"Señores," Villa squinted at them ferociously, "samples of my money reached your village within twenty-four hours after it was issued. You decided that my government would not last. You dug holes under your fireplaces and put the silver and bank notes there. You knew of my first proclamation a day after it was posted up in the streets of Chihuahua, and you ignored it. The Counterfeit Decree you also knew as soon as it was issued. You thought there was always time to change if it became necessary. And then you got frightened, and you three, who have more money than anyone else in the village, got on your mules and rode down here. Señores, your money is counterfeit. You are poor men!"

"*Valgame Dios!*" cried the oldest of the three, sweating profusely.

"But we are ruined, *mi General!*—I swear to you—We did not know—We would have accepted—There is no food in the village———"

The General in Chief meditated for a moment.

"I will give you one more chance," he said, "not for you, but for the poor people of your village who can buy nothing. Next Wednesday at noon bring all your money, every cent of it, to the Treasury, and I will see what can be done."

To the perspiring financiers who waited hat in hand out in the hall, the news spread by word of mouth; and Wednesday at high noon one could not pass the Treasury door for the eager mob gathered there.

Villa's great passion was schools. He believed that land for the people and schools would settle every question of civilization. Schools were an obsession with him. Often I have heard him say: "When I passed such and such a street this morning I saw a lot of kids. Let's put a school there." Chihuahua has a population of under 40,000 people. At different times Villa established over fifty schools there. The great dream of his life has been to send his son to school in the United States, but at the opening of the term in February he had to abandon it because he didn't have money enough to pay for a half year's tuition.

No sooner had he taken over the government of Chihuahua than he put his army to work running the electric light plant, the street railways, the telephone, the water works and the Terrazzas flour mill. He delegated soldiers to administer the great haciendas which he had confiscated. He manned the slaughterhouse with soldiers, and sold Terrazzas's beef to the people for the government. A thousand of them he put in the streets of the city as civil police, prohibiting on pain of death stealing, or the sale of liquor to the army. A soldier who got drunk was shot. He even tried to run the brewery with soldiers, but failed because he couldn't find an expert maltster. "The only thing to do with soldiers in time of peace," said Villa, "is to put them to work. An idle soldier is always thinking of war."

In the matter of the political enemies of the Revolution he was just as simple, just as effective. Two hours after he entered the Governor's palace the foreign consuls came in a body to ask his protection for 200 Federal soldiers who had been left as a police force at the request of the foreigners. Before answering them, Villa said suddenly: "Which is the Spanish consul?" Scobell, the British vice-consul, said: "I represent the Spaniards." "All right!" snapped Villa. "Tell them to begin to pack. Any Spaniard caught within the boundaries of this State after five days will be escorted to the nearest wall by a firing squad."

The consuls gave a gasp of horror. Scobell began a violent protest, but Villa cut him short.

"This is not a sudden determination on my part," he said; "I have been thinking about this since 1910. The Spaniards must go."

Letcher, the American consul, said: "General, I don't question your motives, but I think you are making a grave political mistake in expelling the Spaniards. The government at Washington will hesitate a long time before becoming friendly to a party which makes use of such barbarous measures."

"Señor Consul," answered Villa, "we Mexicans have had three

hundred years of the Spaniards. They have not changed in character since the *Conquistadores*. They disrupted the Indian empire and enslaved the people. We did not ask them to mingle their blood with ours. Twice we drove them out of Mexico and allowed them to return with the same rights as Mexicans, and they used these rights to steal away our land, to make the people slaves, and to take up arms against the cause of liberty. They supported Porfirio Diaz. They were perniciously active in politics. It was the Spaniards who framed the plot that put Huerta in the palace. When Madero was murdered the Spaniards in every State in the Republic held banquets of rejoicing. They thrust on us the greatest superstition the world has ever known—the Catholic Church. They ought to be killed for that alone. I consider we are being very generous with them."

Scobell insisted vehemently that five days was too short a time, that he couldn't possibly reach all the Spaniards in the State by that time; so Villa extended the time to ten days.

The rich Mexicans who had oppressed the people and opposed the Revolution, he expelled promptly from the State and confiscated their vast holdings. By a simple stroke of the pen the 17,000,000 acres and innumerable business enterprises of the Terrazzas family became the property of the Constitutionalist government, as well as the great lands of the Creel family and the magnificent palaces which were their town houses. Remembering, however, how the Terrazzas exiles had once financed the Orozco Revolution, he imprisoned Don Luis Terrazzas, Jr., as a hostage in his own house in Chihuahua. Some particularly obnoxious political enemies were promptly executed in the penitentiary. The Revolution possesses a black book in which are set down the names, offenses, and property of those who have oppressed and robbed the people. The Germans, who had been particularly active politically, the Englishmen and Americans, he does not yet dare to molest. Their pages in the black book will be opened when the Constitutionalist government is established in Mexico City; and there, too, he will settle the account of the Mexican people with the Catholic Church.

· · ·

VILLA knew that the reserve of the Banco Minero, amounting to about $500,000 gold, was hidden somewhere in Chihuahua. Don Luis Terrazzas, Jr., was a director of that bank. When he refused to divulge the hiding-place of the money, Villa and a squad of soldiers took him out of his house one night, rode him on a mule out into the desert, and strung him up to a tree by the neck. He was cut down just in time to save his life, and led Villa to an old forge in the Terrazzas iron works, under which was discovered the reserve of the Banco Minero. Terrazzas went back to prison badly shaken, and Villa sent word to his father in El Paso that he would release the son upon payment of $500,000 ransom.

**4**

# The Human Side

Villa has two wives, one a patient, simple woman who was with him during all his years of outlawry, who lives in El Paso, and the other a cat-like, slender young girl, who is the mistress of his house in Chihuahua. He is perfectly open about it, though lately the educated, conventional Mexicans who have been gathering about him in ever-increasing numbers have tried to hush up the fact. Among the peons it is not only not unusual but customary to have more than one mate.

One hears a great many stories of Villa's violating women. I asked him if that were true. He pulled his mustache and stared at me for a minute with an inscrutable expression. "I never take the trouble to deny such stories," he said. "They say I am a bandit, too. Well, you know my history. But tell me; have you ever met a husband, father or brother of any woman that I have violated?" He paused: "Or even a witness?"

It is fascinating to watch him discover new ideas. Remember that he is absolutely ignorant of the troubles and confusions and read-justments of modern civilization. "Socialism," he said once, when I wanted to know what he thought of it: "Socialism—is it a thing? I only see it in books, and I do not read much." Once I asked him if women would vote in the new Republic. He was sprawled out on his bed, with his coat unbuttoned. "Why, I don't think so," he said, startled, suddenly sitting up. "What do you mean—vote? Do you mean elect a government and make laws?" I said I did and that women already were doing it in the United States. "Well," he said, scratching his head, "if they do it up there I don't see that they shouldn't do it down here." The idea seemed to amuse him enormously. He rolled it over and over in his mind, looking at me and away again. "It may be as you say," he said, "but I have never thought about it. Women seem to me to be things to protect, to love. They have no sternness of mind. They can't consider anything for its right or wrong. They are full of pity and softness. Why," he said, "a woman would not give an order to execute a traitor."

"I am not so sure of that, *mi General*," I said. "Women can be crueller and harder than men."

He stared at me, pulling his mustache. And then he began to grin. He looked slowly to where his wife was setting the table for lunch. "*Oiga*," he said, "come here. Listen. Last night I caught three traitors crossing the river to blow up the railroad. What shall I do with them? Shall I shoot them or not?"

Embarrassed, she seized his hand and kissed it. "Oh, I don't know anything about that," she said. "You know best."

"No," said Villa. "I leave it entirely to you. Those men were going to try to cut our communications between Juarez and Chihuahua. They were traitors—Federals. What shall I do? Shall I shoot them or not?"

"Oh, well, shoot them," said Mrs. Villa.

Villa chuckled delightedly. "There is something in what you say," he remarked, and for days afterward went around asking the cook and the chambermaids whom they would like to have for President of Mexico.

He never missed a bullfight, and every afternoon at four o'-clock he was to be found at the cockpit, where he fought his own birds with the happy enthusiasm of a small boy. In the evening he played faro in some gambling hall. Sometimes in the late morning he would send a fast courier after Luis Leon, the bullfighter, and telephone personally to the slaughterhouse, asking if they had any fierce bulls in the pen. They almost always did have, and we would all get on horseback and gallop through the streets about a mile to the big adobe corrals. Twenty cowboys cut the bull out of the herd, threw and tied him and cut off his sharp horns, and then Villa and Luis Leon and anybody else who wanted to would take the professional red capes and go down into the ring; Luis Leon with professional caution, Villa as stubborn and clumsy as the bull, slow on his feet, but swift as an animal with his body and arms. Villa would walk right up to the pawing, infuriated animal, and, with his double cape, slap him insolently across the face, and, for half an hour, would follow the greatest sport I ever saw. Sometimes the sawed-off horns of the bull would catch Villa in the seat of the trousers and propel him violently across the ring; then he would turn and grab the bull by the head and wrestle with him with the sweat streaming down his face until five or six *compañeros* seized the bull's tail and hauled him plowing and bellowing back.

Villa never drinks nor smokes, but he will outdance the most ardent *novio* in Mexico. When the order was given for the army to advance upon Torreon, Villa stopped off at Camargo to be best man at the wedding of one of his old *compadres*. He danced steadily without stopping, they said, all Monday night, all Tuesday, and all Tuesday night, arriving at the front on Wednesday morning with bloodshot eyes and an air of extreme lassitude.

# The Funeral of Abram Gonzales

THE fact that Villa hates useless pomp and ceremony makes it more impressive when he does appear on a public occasion. He has the knack of absolutely expressing the strong feeling of the great mass of the people. In February, exactly one year after Abram Gonzales was murdered by the Federals at Bachimba Cañon, Villa ordered a great funeral ceremony to be held in the City of Chihuahua. Two trains, carrying the officers of the army, the consuls and representatives of the foreign colony, left Chihuahua early in the morning to take up the body of the dead Governor from its resting-place under a rude wooden cross in the desert. Villa ordered Major Fierro, his Superintendent of Railroads, to get the trains ready—but Fierro got drunk and forgot; and when Villa and his brilliant staff arrived at the railway station the next morning the regular passenger train to Juarez was just leaving and there was no other equipment on hand. Villa himself leaped on to the already moving engine and compelled the engineer to back the train up to the station. Then he walked through the train, ordering the passengers out, and switched it in the direction of Bachimba. They had no sooner started than he summoned Fierro before him and discharged him from the superintendency of the railroads, appointing Calzado in his place, and ordered the latter to return at once to Chihuahua and be thoroughly informed about the railroads by the time he returned. At Bachimba Villa stood silently by the grave with the tears rolling down his cheeks. For Gonzales had been his close friend. Ten thousand people stood in the heat and dust at Chihuahua railway station when the funeral train arrived, and poured weeping through the narrow streets behind the army, at the head of which walked Villa beside the hearse. His automobile was waiting, but he angrily refused to ride, stumbling stubbornly along in the dirt of the streets with his eyes on the ground.

THAT night there was a *velada* in the Theater of the Heroes, an immense auditorium packed with emotional peons and their women. The ring of boxes was brilliant with officers in their full dress, and wedged behind them up the five high balconies were the ragged poor. Now, the *velada* is an entirely Mexican institution. First there comes a speech, then a "recitation" on the piano, then a speech, followed by a patriotic song rendered by a chorus of awkward little Indian girls from the public school with squeaky voices, another speech, and a soprano solo from "Trovatore" by the wife of some government official, still another speech, and so on for at least five hours. Whenever there is a prominent funeral, or a national holiday, or a President's anniversary, or, in fact, an occasion of the least importance, a *velada* must be held. It is the conventional and respectable way of celebrating anything. Villa sat in the left-hand stage box and controlled the proceedings by tapping a little bell. The stage itself was brilliantly hideous with black bunting, huge masses of artificial flowers, abominable crayon portraits of Madero, Piño Suarez and the dead Governor, and red, white and green electric lights. At the foot of all this was a very small, plain, black wooden box which held the body of Abram Gonzales.

The *velada* proceeded in an orderly and exhausting manner for about two hours. Local orators, trembling with stage fright, mouthed the customary Castilian extravagant phrases, and little girls stepped on their own feet and murdered Tosti's "Goodbye." Villa, with his eyes riveted on that wooden box, never moved nor spoke. At the proper time he mechanically tapped the little bell, but after a while he couldn't stand it any longer. A large fleshy Mexican was in the middle of Handel's "Largo" on the grand piano, when Villa stood erect. He put his foot on the railing of the box and leaped to the stage, kneeled, and took up the coffin in his arms. Handel's "Largo" petered out. Silent astonishment paralyzed the audience. Holding the black box tenderly in his arms as a mother with her baby, not looking at anyone, Villa started down the steps of the stage and up the aisle. Instinctively, the house rose; and as he passed out through the swinging doors they followed on silently behind him. He strode down between the lines of waiting soldiers, his sword banging on the floor, across the dark square to the Governor's palace; and, with his own hands, put the coffin on the flower-banked table waiting for it in the audience hall. It had been arranged that four generals in turn should stand the death watch, each for two hours. Candles shed a dim light over the table and the surrounding floor, but the rest of the room was in darkness. A dense mass of silent, breathing people packed the doorway. Villa unbuckled his sword and threw it clattering into a corner. Then he took his rifle from the table and stood the first watch.

# 6

## Villa and Carranza

IT seems incredible to those who don't know him, that this remarkable figure, who has risen from obscurity to the most prominent position in Mexico in three years, should not covet the Presidency of the Republic. But that is in entire accordance with the simplicity of his character. When asked about it he answered as always with perfect directness, just in the way that you put it to him. He didn't quibble over whether he could or could not be President of Mexico. He said: "I am a fighter, not a statesman. I am not educated enough to be President. I only learned to read and write two years ago. How could I, who never went to school, hope to be able to talk with the foreign ambassadors and the cultivated gentlemen of the Congress? It would be bad for Mexico if an uneducated man were to be President. There is one thing that I will not do—and that is to take a position for which I am not fitted. There is only one order of my *Jefe* (Carranza) which I would refuse to obey—if he would command me to be a President or a Governor." On behalf of my paper I had to ask him this question five or six times. Finally he became exasperated. "I have told you many times," he said, "that there is no possibility of my becoming President of Mexico. Are the newspapers trying to make trouble between me and my Jefe? This is the last time that I will answer that question. The next correspondent that asks me I will have him spanked and sent to the border." For days afterward he went around grumbling humorously about the *chatito* (pug nose) who kept asking him whether he wanted to be President of Mexico. The idea seemed to amuse him. Whenever I went to see him after that he used to say, at the end of our talk: "Well, aren't you going to ask me today whether I want to be President?"

HE never referred to Carranza except as "my Jefe," and he obeyed implicitly the slightest order from "the First Chief of the Revolution." His loyalty to Carranza was perfectly obstinate. He seemed to think that in Carranza were embodied the entire ideals of the Revolution. This, in spite of the fact that many of his advisers tried to make him see that Carranza was essentially an aristocrat and a reformer, and that the people were fighting for more than reform.

Carranza's political program, as set forth in the plan of Guadelupe, carefully avoids any promise of settlement of the land question, except a vague endorsement of Madero's plan of San Luis Potosi, and it is evident that he does not intend to advocate any radical restoration of the land to the people until he becomes provisional president—and then to proceed very cautiously. In the meantime he seems to have left it to Villa's judgment, as well as all other details of the conduct of the Revolution in the north. But Villa, being a peon, and feeling with them, rather than consciously reasoning it out, that the land question is the real cause of the Revolution, acted with characteristic promptness and directness. No sooner had he settled the details of government of Chihuahua State, and appointed Chao his provisional governor, than he issued a proclamation, giving sixty-two and one-half acres out of the confiscated lands to every male citizen of the State, and declaring these lands inalienable for any cause for a period of ten years. In the State of Durango the same thing has happened and as other states are free of Federal garrisons, he will pursue the same policy.

# The Rules of War

On the field, too, Villa had to invent an entirely original method of warfare, because he never had a chance to learn anything of accepted military strategy. In that he is without the possibility of any doubt the greatest leader Mexico has ever had. His method of fighting is astonishingly like Napoleon's. Secrecy, quickness of movement, the adaptation of his plans to the character of the country and of his soldiers—the value of intimate relations with the rank and file, and of building up a tradition among the enemy that his army is invincible, and that he himself bears a charmed life—these are his characteristics. He knew nothing of accepted European standards of strategy or of discipline. One of the troubles of the Mexican Federal army is that its officers are thoroughly saturated with conventional military theory. The Mexican soldier is still mentally at the end of the eighteenth century. He is, above all, a loose, individual, guerrilla fighter. Red tape simply paralyzes the machine. When Villa's army goes into battle he is not hampered by salutes, or rigid respect for officers, or trigonometrical calculations of the trajectories of projectiles, or theories of the percentage of hits in a thousand rounds of rifle fire, or the function of cavalry, infantry and artillery in any particular position, or rigid obedience to the secret knowledge of its superiors. It reminds one of the ragged Republican army that Napoleon led into Italy. It is probable that Villa doesn't know much about those things himself. But he does know that guerrilla fighters cannot be driven blindly in platoons around the field in perfect step, that men fighting individually and of their own free will are braver than long volleying rows in the trenches, lashed to it by officers with the flat of their swords. And where the fighting is fiercest—when a ragged mob of fierce brown men with hand bombs and rifles rush the bullet-swept streets of an ambushed town—Villa is among them, like any common soldier.

Up to his day, Mexican armies had always carried with them hundreds of the women and children of the soldiers; Villa was the first man to think of swift forced marches of bodies of cavalry, leaving their women behind. Up to his time no Mexican army had ever abandoned its base; it had always stuck closely to the railroad and the supply trains. But Villa struck terror into the enemy by abandoning his trains and throwing his entire effective army upon the field, as he did at Gomez Palacio. He invented in Mexico that most demoralizing form of battle—the night attack. When, after the fall of Torreon last September, he withdrew his entire army in the face of Orozco's advance from Mexico City and for five days unsuccessfully attacked Chihuahua, it was a terrible shock to the Federal General when he waked up one morning and found that Villa had sneaked around the city under cover of darkness, captured a freight train at Terrazzas and descended with his entire army upon the comparatively undefended city of Juarez. It wasn't fair! Villa found that he hadn't enough trains to carry all his soldiers, even when he had ambushed and captured a Federal troop train, sent south by General Castro, the Federal commander in Juarez. So he telegraphed that gentleman as follows, signing the name of the Colonel in command of the troop train: "Engine broken down at Moctezuma. Send another engine and five cars." The unsuspecting Castro immediately dispatched a new train. Villa then telegraphed him: "Wires cut between here and Chihuahua. Large force of rebels approaching from south. What shall I do?" Castro replied: "Return at once." And Villa obeyed, telegraphing cheering messages at every station along the way. The Federal commander got wind of his coming about an hour before he arrived, and left, without informing his garrison, so that, outside of a small massacre, Villa took Juarez almost without a shot. And with the border so near he managed to smuggle across enough ammunition to equip his almost armless forces and a week later sallied out and routed the pursuing Federal forces with great slaughter at Tierra Blanca.

GENERAL Hugh L. Scott, in command of the American troops at Fort Bliss, sent Villa a little pamphlet containing the Rules of War adopted by the Hague Conference. He spent hours poring over it. It interested and amused him hugely. He said: "What is this Hague Conference? Was there a representative of Mexico there? Was there a representative of the Constitutionalists there? It seems to me a funny thing to make rules about war. It's not a game. What is the difference between civilized war and any other kind of war? If you and I are having a fight in a *cantina* we are not going to pull a little book out of our pockets and read over the rules. It says here that you must not use lead bullets; but I don't see why not. They do the work."

For a long time afterward he went around popping questions at his officers like this: "If an invading army takes a city of the enemy, what must you do with the women and children?"

As far as I could see, the Rules of War didn't make any difference in Villa's original method of fighting. The *colorados* he executed wherever he captured them; because, he said, they were peons like the Revolutionists and that no peon would volunteer against the cause of liberty unless he were bad. The Federal officers also he killed, because, he explained, they were educated men and ought to know better. But the Federal common soldiers he set at liberty because most of them were conscripts, and thought that they were fighting for the Patria. There is no case on record where he wantonly killed a man. Anyone who did so he promptly executed—except Fierro.

Fierro, the man who killed Benton, was known as "The Butcher" throughout the army. He was a great handsome animal, the best and cruellest rider and fighter, perhaps, in all the revolutionary forces. In his furious lust for blood Fierro used to shoot down a hundred prisoners with his own revolver, only stopping long enough to reload. He killed for the pure joy of it. During two weeks that I was in Chihuahua, Fierro killed fifteen inoffensive citizens in cold blood. But there was always a curious relationship between him and Villa. He was Villa's best friend; and Villa loved him like a son and always pardoned him.

But Villa, although he had never heard of the Rules of War, carried with his army the only field hospital of any effectiveness that any Mexican army has ever carried. It consisted of forty boxcars enameled inside, fitted with operating tables and all the latest appliances of surgery, and manned by more than sixty doctors and nurses. Every day during the battle shuttle trains full of the desperately wounded ran from the front to the base hospitals at Parral, Jimenez and Chihuahua. He took care of the Federal wounded just as carefully as of his own men. Ahead of his own supply train went another train, carrying two thousand sacks of flour, and also coffee, corn, sugar, and cigarettes to feed the entire starving population of the country around Durango City and Torreon.

The common soldiers adore him for his bravery and his coarse, blunt humor. Often I have seen him slouched on his cot in the little red caboose in which he always traveled, cracking jokes familiarly with twenty ragged privates sprawled on the floor, chairs and tables. When the army was entraining or detraining, Villa personally would be on hand in a dirty old suit, without a collar, kicking mules in the stomach and pushing horses in and out of the stock cars. Getting thirsty all of a sudden, he would grab some soldier's canteen and drain it, in spite of the indignant protests of its owner; and then tell him to go over to the river and say that Pancho Villa said that he should fill it there.

# 8

## The Dream of Pancho Villa

IT might not be uninteresting to know the passionate dream—the vision which animates this ignorant fighter, "not educated enough to be President of Mexico." He told it to me once in these words: "When the new Republic is established there will never be any more army in Mexico. Armies are the greatest support of tyranny. There can be no dictator without an army.

"We will put the army to work. In all parts of the Republic we will establish military colonies composed of the veterans of the Revolution. The State will give them grants of agricultural lands and establish big industrial enterprises to give them work. Three days a week they will work and work hard, because honest work is more important than fighting, and only honest work makes good citizens. And the other three days they will receive military instruction and go out and teach all the people how to fight. Then, when the Patria is invaded, we will just have to telephone from the palace at Mexico City, and in half a day all the Mexican people will rise from their fields and factories, fully armed, equipped and organized to defend their children and their homes.

"My ambition is to live my life in one of those military colonies among my *compañeros* whom I love, who have suffered so long and so deeply with me. I think I would like the government to establish a leather factory there where we could make good saddles and bridles, because I know how to do that; and the rest of the time I would like to work on my little farm, raising cattle and corn. It would be fine, I think, to help make Mexico a happy place."

# PART III

# JIMENEZ AND POINTS WEST

# 1

## Doña Luisa's Hotel

I WENT south from Chihuahua on a troop train bound for the advance near Escalon. Attached to the five freight cars, filled with horses and carrying soldiers on top, was a coach in which I was allowed to ride with two hundred noisy *pacificos*, male and female. It was gruesomely suggestive: car windows smashed, mirrors, lamps and plush seats torn out, and bullet holes after the manner of a frieze. The time of our departure was not fixed, and no one knew when the train would arrive. The railroad had just been repaired. In places where there had once been bridges we plunged into arroyos and snorted up the farther bank on a rickety new-laid track that bent and cracked under us. All day long the roadside was lined with immense distorted steel rails, torn up with a chain and a backing engine by the thorough Orozco last year. There was a rumor that Castillo's bandits were planning to blow us up with dynamite sometime during the afternoon. . . .

Peons with big straw sombreros and beautifully faded serapes, Indians in blue working clothes and cowhide sandals, and squat-faced women with black shawls around their heads, and squalling babies—packed the seats, aisles and platforms, singing, eating, spitting, chattering. Occasionally there staggered by a ragged man with a cap labeled "conductor" in tarnished gold letters, very drunk, embracing his friends and severely demanding the tickets and safe conducts of strangers. I introduced myself to him by a small present of United States currency. He said, "Señor, you may travel freely over the Republic henceforth without payment. Juan Algomero is at your orders." An officer smartly uniformed, with a sword at his side, was at the rear of the car. He was bound for the front, he said, to lay down his life for his country. His only baggage consisted of four wooden bird cages full of meadow larks. Farther to the rear two men sat across the aisle from each other, each with a white sack containing something that moved and clucked. As soon as the train started these bags were opened to disgorge two large roosters, who wandered up and down the aisles eating crumbs and cigarette butts. The two owners immediately raised their voices. "Cockfight, señores! Five pesos on this valiant and handsome rooster. Five pesos, señores!" The males at once deserted their seats and rushed clamoring toward the center of the car. Not one of them appeared to lack the necessary five dollars. In ten minutes the two promoters were kneeling in the middle of the aisle, throwing their birds. And, as we rattled along, swaying from side to side, swooping down into the gullies and laboring up the other bank, a whirling mass of feathers and flashing steel rolled up and down the aisle. That over, a one-legged youth stood up and played "Whistling Rufus" on a tin flute. Someone had a leather bottle of *tequila*, of which we all took a swig. From the rear of the car came shouts of *"Vamonos a bailar! Come on and dance!"* And in a moment five couples, all men, of course, were madly two-stepping. A blind old peasant was assisted to climb upon his seat, where he quaveringly recited a long ballad about the heroic exploits of the great General Maclovio Herrera. Everybody was silently attentive and showered pennies into the old man's sombrero. Occasionally there floated back to us the singing of the soldiers on the boxcars in front and the sound of their shots as they caught sight of a coyote galloping through the mesquite. Then everybody in our car would make a rush for the windows, pulling at their revolvers, and shoot fast and furiously.

All the long afternoon we ambled slowly south, the western rays of the sun burning as they struck our faces. Every hour or so we stopped at some station, shot to pieces by one army or the other during the three years of Revolution; there the train would be besieged by vendors of cigarettes, pine nuts, bottles of milk, *camotes*, and *tamales* rolled in cornhusks. Old women, gossiping, descended from the train, built themselves a little fire and boiled coffee. Squatting there, smoking their cornhusk cigarettes, they told one another interminable love stories.

It was late in the evening when we pulled into Jimenez. I shouldered through the entire population, come down to meet the train, passed between the flaring torches of the little row of candy booths, and went along the street, where drunken soldiers alternated with painted girls, walking arm in arm, to Doña Luisa's Station Hotel. It was locked. I pounded on the door and a little window opened at the side, showing an incredibly ancient woman's face, crowned with straggly white hair. This being squinted at me through a pair of steel spectacles and remarked, "Well, I guess you're all right!" Then there came a sound of bars being taken down, and the door swung open. Doña Luisa herself, a great bunch of keys at her belt, stood just inside. She held a large Chinaman by the ear, addressing him in fluent and profane Spanish. "*Chango!*" she said. "What do you mean by telling a guest at this hotel that there wasn't any more hot cakes? Why didn't you make some more? Now take your dirty little bundle and get out of here!" With a final wrench she released the squealing Oriental. "These damn heathen," she announced in English, "the nasty beggars! I don't take any lip from a dirty Chinaman who can live on a nickel's worth of rice a day!" Then she nodded apologetically toward the door. "There's so many damned drunken generals around today that I've got to keep the door locked. I don't want the —————— ————Mexican————s in here!"

Doña Luisa is a small, dumpy American woman more than eighty years of age—a benevolent New-England grandmother sort of person. For forty-five years she has been in Mexico, and thirty or more years ago, when her husband died, she began to keep the Station Hotel. War and peace make no difference to her. The American flag flies over the door and in her house she alone is boss. When Pascual Orozco took Jimenez, his men began a drunken reign of terror in the town. Orozco himself—Orozco the invincible, the fierce, who would as soon kill a person as not—

came drunk to the Station Hotel with two of his officers and several women. Doña Luisa planted herself across the doorway—alone—and shook her fist in his face. "Pascual Orozco," she cried, "take your disreputable friends and go away from here. I'm keeping a decent hotel!" And Orozco went. . . .

# 2

## Duello a la Frigada

I WANDERED up the mile-long, incredibly dilapidated street that leads to the town. A streetcar came past, drawn by one galloping mule and bulging with slightly intoxicated soldiers. Open surreys full of officers with girls on their laps rolled along. Under the dusty, bare alamo trees each window held its señorita, with a blanket-wrapped *caballero* in attendance. There were no lights. The night was dry and cold and full of a subtle exotic excitement; guitars twanged, snatches of song and laughter and low voices, and shouts from distant streets, filled the darkness. Occasionally little companies of soldiers on foot came along, or a troop of horsemen in high sombreros and serapes jingled silently out of the blackness and faded away again, bound probably for the relief of guard.

In one quiet stretch of street near the bull ring, where there are no houses, I noticed an automobile speeding from the town. At the same time a galloping horse came from the other direction, and just in front of me the headlights of the machine illumined the horse and his rider, a young officer in a Stetson hat. The automobile jarred to a grinding stop and a voice from it cried, *"Haltoie!"*

"Who speaks?" asked the horseman, pulling his mount to its haunches.

"I, Guzman!" and the other leaped to the ground and came into the light, a coarse, fat Mexican, with a sword at his belt.

*"Como le va, mi Capitan?"* The officer flung himself from his horse. They embraced, patting each other on the back with both hands.

"Very well. And you? Where are you going?"

"To see Maria."

The captain laughed. "Don't do it," he said, "I'm going to see Maria myself, and if I see you there I shall certainly kill you."

"But I am going just the same. I am as quick with my pistol as you, señor."

"But you see," returned the other mildly, "we both cannot go!"

"Perfectly!"

"*Oiga!*" said the captain to his chauffeur. "Turn your car so as to throw the light evenly along the sidewalk. . . . And now we will walk thirty paces apart and stand with our backs turned until you count three. Then the man who first puts a bullet through the other man's hat wins. . . ."

Both men drew immense revolvers and stood a moment in the light, spinning the chambers.

"*Listo!* Ready!" cried the horseman.

"Hurry it," said the captain. "It is a bad thing to balk love."

Back to back, they had already begun to pace the distance.

"One!" shouted the chauffeur.

"Two!"

But quick as a flash the fat man wheeled in the trembling, uncertain light, threw down his lifted arm, and a mighty roar went soaring slowly into the heavy night. The Stetson of the other man, whose back was still turned, took an odd little leap ten feet beyond him. He spun around, but the captain was already climbing into his machine.

"*Bueno!*" he said cheerfully. "I win. Until tomorrow then, *amigo!*" And the automobile gathered speed and disappeared down the street. The horseman slowly went to where his hat lay, picked it up and examined it. He stood a moment, meditating, and then deliberately mounted his horse and he also went away. I had already started some time before. . . .

In the plaza the regimental band was playing "El Pagare," the song which started Orozco's Revolution. It was a parody of the original, referring to Madero's payment of his family's $750,000 war claims as soon as he became president, that spread like wild-fire over the Republic, and had to be suppressed with police and soldiers. "El Pagare" is even now taboo in most revolutionary cir-cles, and I have heard of men being shot for singing it; but in Jimenez at this time the utmost license prevailed. Moreover, the Mexicans, unlike the French, have absolutely no feeling for sym-bols. Bitterly antagonistic sides use the same flag; in the plaza of almost every town still stand eulogistic statues of Porfirio Diaz; even at officers' mess in the field I have drunk from glasses stamped with the likeness of the old dictator, while Federal army uniforms are plentiful in the ranks.

But "El Pagare" is a swinging, glorious tune, and under the hundreds of little electric light globes strung on the plaza a dou-ble procession marched gaily round and round. On the outside, in groups of four, went the men, mostly soldiers. On the inside, in the opposite direction, the girls walked arm in arm. As they passed they threw handfuls of confetti at one another. They never talked to one another, never stopped; but as a girl caught a man's fancy, he slipped a lover's note into her hand as she went by, and she answered with a smile if she liked him. Thus they met, and later the girl would manage to let the *caballero* know her address; this would lead to long talks at her window in the darkness, and then they would be lovers. It was a delicate business, this handing of notes. Every man carried a gun, and every man's girl was his jealously guarded property. It was a killing matter to hand a note to someone else's girl. The close-packed throng moved gaily on, thrilling to the music. . . . Beyond the plaza gaped the ruins of Marcos Russek's store, which these same men had looted less than two weeks before, and at one side the ancient pink cathedral towered among its fountains and great trees, with the iron and glass illuminated sign, "Santo Cristo de Burgos," shining above the door.

There, at the side of the plaza, I came upon a little group of five Americans huddled upon a bench. They were ragged beyond be-lief, all except a slender youth in leggings and a Federal officer's uniform, who wore a crownless Mexican hat. Feet protruded from their shoes, none had more than the remnants of socks, all were unshaven. One mere boy wore his arm in a sling made out of a torn blanket. They made room for me gladly, stood up, crowded around, cried how good it was to see another American among all these damned greasers.

"What are you fellows doing here?" I asked.

"We're soldiers of fortune!" said the boy with the wounded arm.

"Aw—!" interrupted another. "Soldiers of—!"

"Ye see it's this way," began the soldierly looking youth. "We've been fighting right along in the Brigada Zaragosa—was at the battle of Ojinaga and everything. And now comes an order from Villa to discharge all the Americans in the ranks and ship 'em back to the border. Ain't that a hell of a note?"

"Last night they gave us our honorable discharges and threw us out of the cuartel," said a one-legged man with red hair.

"And we ain't had any place to sleep and nothing to eat—" broke in a little gray-eyed boy whom they called the Major.

"Don't try and panhandle the guy!" rebuked the soldier indignantly. "Ain't we each going to get fifty Mex in the morning?"

We adjourned for a short time to a nearby restaurant, and when we returned I asked them what they were going to do.

"The old U.S. for mine," breathed a good-looking black Irishman who hadn't spoken before. "I'm going back to San Fran and drive a truck again. I'm sick of greasers, bad food and bad fighting."

"I got two honorable discharges from the United States army," announced the soldierly youth proudly. "Served through the Spanish War, I did. I'm the only soldier in this bunch." The others sneered and cursed sullenly. "Guess I'll reënlist when I get over the border."

"Not for mine," said the one-legged man. "I'm wanted for two murder charges—I didn't do it, swear to God I didn't—it was a frame-up. But a poor guy hasn't got a chance in the United States. When they ain't framing up some fake charge against me, they jail me for a 'vag.' I'm all right though," he went on earnestly. "I'm a hard-working man, only I can't get no job."

The Major raised his hard little face and cruel eyes. "I got out of a reform school in Wisconsin," he said, "and I guess there's some cops waiting for me in El Paso. I always wanted to kill somebody with a gun, and I done it at Ojinaga, and I ain't got a bellyful yet. They told us we could stay if we signed Mex citizenship papers; I guess I'll sign tomorrow morning."

"The hell you will," cried the others. "That's a rotten thing to do. Suppose we get Intervention and you have to shoot against your own people. You won't catch me signing myself away to be a greaser."

"That's easy fixed," said the Major. "When I go back to the States I leave my name here. I'm going to stay down here till I get enough of a stake to go back to Georgia and start a child-labor factory."

The other boy had suddenly burst into tears. "I got my arm shot through in Ojinaga," he sobbed, "and now they're turning me loose without any money, and I can't work. When I get to El Paso the cops'll jail me and I'll have to write my dad to come and take me home to California. I run away from there last year," he explained.

"Look here, Major," I advised, "you'd better not stay down here if Villa wants Americans out of the ranks. Being a Mexican citizen won't help you if Intervention comes."

"Perhaps you're right," agreed the Major thoughtfully. "Aw, quit your bawling, Jack! I guess I'll beat it over to Galveston and get on a South American boat. They say there's a revolution started in Peru."

The soldier was about thirty, the Irishman twenty-five, and the three others somewhere between sixteen and eighteen.

"What did you fellows come down here for?" I asked.

"Excitement!" answered the soldier and the Irishman, grinning. The three boys looked at me with eager, earnest faces, drawn with hunger and hardship.

"Loot!" they said simultaneously. I cast an eye at their dilapidated garments, at the throngs of tattered volunteers parading around the plaza, who hadn't been paid for three months, and restrained a violent impulse to shout with mirth. Soon I left them, hard, cold misfits in a passionate country, despising the cause for which they were fighting, sneering at the gaiety of the irrepressible Mexicans. And as I went away I said, "By the way; what company did you fellows belong to? What did you call yourselves?"

The red-haired youth answered, "The Foreign Legion!" he said.

I want to say right here that I saw few soldiers of fortune except one—and he was a dry-as-dust scientist studying the action of high explosives in field guns—who would not have been tramps in their own country.

It was late night when I finally got back to the hotel. Doña Luisa went ahead to see to my room, and I stopped a moment in the bar. Two or three soldiers, evidently officers, were drinking there—one pretty far gone. He was a pock-marked man with a trace of black mustache; his eyes couldn't seem to focus. But when he saw me he began to sing a pleasant little song:

> *Yo tengo un pistole*
> *Con manago de marfil*
> *Para matar todos los gringos*
> *Qui viennen por ferrocarril!*

> (I have a pistol
> With a marble handle
> With which to kill all the Americans
> Who come by railroad!)

I thought it diplomatic to leave, because you can never tell what a Mexican will do when he's drunk. His temperament is much too complicated.

Doña Luisa was in my room when I got there. With a mysterious finger to her lips she shut the door and produced from beneath her skirt a last year's copy of the *Saturday Evening Post,* in an incredible state of dissolution. "I got it out of the safe for you," she said. "The damn thing's worth more than anything in the house. I've been offered fifteen dollars for it by Americans going out to the mines. You see we haven't had any American magazines in a year now."

# Saved by a Wrist Watch

AFTER that what could I do but read the precious magazine, although I had read it before. I lit the lamp, undressed, and got into bed. Just then came an unsteady step on the gallery outside and my door was flung violently open. Framed in it stood the pock-marked officer who had been drinking in the bar. In one hand he carried a big revolver. For a moment he stood blinking at me malevolently, then stepped inside and closed the door with a bang.

"I am Lieutenant Antonio Montoya, at your orders," he said. "I heard there was a gringo in this hotel and I have come to kill you."

"Sit down," said I politely. I saw he was drunkenly in earnest. He took off his hat, bowed politely and drew up a chair. Then he produced another revolver from beneath his coat and laid them both on the table. They were loaded.

"Would you like a cigarette?" I offered him the package. He took one, waved it in thanks, and lit it at the lamp. Then he picked up the guns and pointed them both at me. His fingers tightened slowly on the triggers, but relaxed again. I was too far gone to do anything but just wait.

"My only difficulty," said he, lowering his weapons, "is to determine which revolver I shall use."

"Pardon me," I quavered, "but they both appear a little obsolete. That Colt forty-five is certainly an 1895 model, and as for the Smith and Wesson, between ourselves it is only a toy."

"True," he answered, looking at them a little ruefully. "If I had only thought I would have brought my new automatic. My apologies, señor." He sighed and again directed the barrels at my chest, with an expression of calm happiness. "However, since it is so, we must make the best of it." I got ready to jump, to duck, to scream. Suddenly his eye fell upon the table, where my two-dollar wrist watch was lying.

"What is that?" he asked.

"A watch!" Eagerly I demonstrated how to fasten it on. Unconsciously the pistols slowly lowered. With parted lips and absorbed attention he watched it delightedly, as a child watches the operation of some new mechanical toy.

"Ah," he breathed. *"Que esta bonita!* How pretty!"

"It is yours," said I, unstrapping it and offering it to him. He looked at the watch, then at me, slowly brightening and glowing with surprised joy. Into his outstretched hand I placed it. Reverently, carefully, he adjusted the thing to his hairy wrist. Then he rose, beaming down upon me. The revolvers fell unnoticed to the floor. Lieutenant Antonio Montoya threw his arms around me.

"Ah, *compadre!*" he cried emotionally.

THE next day I met him at Valiente Adiana's store in the town. We sat amicably in the back room drinking native *aguardiente*, while Lieutenant Montoya, my best friend in the entire Constitutionalist army, told me of the hardships and perils of the campaign. For three weeks now Maclovio Herrera's brigade had lain at Jimenez under arms, waiting the emergency call for the advance on Torreon.

"This morning," said Antonio, "the Constitutionalist spies intercepted a telegram from the Federal commander in Zacatecas City to General Velasco in Torreon. He said that upon mature judgment he had decided that Zacatecas was an easier place to attack than to defend. Therefore he reported that his plan of campaign was this. Upon the approach of the Constitutionalist forces he intended to evacuate the city and then take it again."

"Antonio," I said, "I am going a long journey across the desert tomorrow. I am going to drive to Magistral. I need a *mozo*. I will pay three dollars a week."

" *'Sta bueno!*" cried Lieutenant Montoya. "Whatever you wish, so that I can go with my *amigo!*"

"But you are on active service," said I. "How can you leave your regiment?"

"Oh, that's all right," answered Antonio. "I won't say anything about it to my colonel. They don't need me. Why, they've got five thousand other men here."

# 4

## Symbols of Mexico

In the early dawn, when yet the low gray houses and the dusty trees were stiff with cold, we laid a bull whip on the backs of our two mules and rattled down the uneven streets of Jimenez and out into the open country. A few soldiers, wrapped to the eyes in their serapes, dozed beside their lanterns. There was a drunken officer sleeping in the gutter.

We drove an ancient buggy, whose broken pole was mended with wire. The harness was made of bits of old iron, rawhide and rope. Antonio and I sat side by side upon the seat, and at our feet dozed a dark, serious-minded youth named Primitivo Aguilar. Primitivo had been hired to open and shut gates, to tie up the harness when it broke, and to keep watch over wagon and mules at night, because bandits were reported to infest the roads.

The country became a vast fertile plain, cut up by irrigating ditches which were overshadowed by long lines of great alamo trees, leafless and gray as ashes. Like a furnace door, the white-hot sun blazed upon us, and the far-stretched barren fields reeked a thin mist. A cloud of white dust moved with us and around us. By the church of the Hacienda San Pedro we stopped and dickered with an aged peon for a sack of corn and straw for the mules. Farther along was an exquisite low building of pink plaster, set back from the road in a grove of green willows. "That?" said Antonio. "Oh, that is nothing but a flour mill." We had lunch in the long whitewashed, dirt-floored room of a peon's house at another great hacienda, whose name I forget, but which I know had once belonged to Luis Terrazzas and was now the confiscated property of the Constitutionalist government. And that night we made

138

camp beside an irrigation ditch miles from any house, in the middle of the bandit territory.

After a dinner of chopped-up meat and peppers, *tortillas*, beans and black coffee, Antonio and I gave Primitivo his instructions. He was to keep watch beside the fire with Antonio's revolver and, if he heard anything, was to wake us. But on no account was he to go to sleep. If he did we would kill him. Primitivo said, *"Si, señor,"* very gravely, opened his eyes wide, and gripped the pistol. Antonio and I rolled up in our blankets by the fire.

I must have gone to sleep at once, because when I was wakened by Antonio's rising, my watch showed only half an hour later. From the place where Primitivo had been placed on guard came a series of hearty snores. The lieutenant walked over to him.

"Primitivo!" he said.

No answer.

"Primitivo, you fool!" Our sentinel stirred in his sleep and turned over with noises indicative of comfort.

"Primitivo!" shouted Antonio, violently kicking him.

He gave absolutely no response.

Antonio drew back and launched a kick at his back that lifted him several feet into the air. With a start Primitivo woke. He started up alertly, waving the revolver.

*"Quien vive?"* cried Primitivo.

THE next day took us out of the lowlands. We entered the desert, winding over a series of rolling plains, sandy and covered with black mesquite and here and there an occasional cactus. Now we began to see beside the road those sinister little wooden crosses that the country people erect on the spot where some man died a violent death. Around the horizon barren purple mountains hemmed us in. To the right, across a vast dry valley, a white and green and gray hacienda stood like a city. An hour later we passed the first of those great fortified square ranchos that one comes across once a day lost in the folds of this tremendous country. Night gathered straight above in the cloudless zenith, while all the skyline still was luminous with clear light, and then the day snuffed out, and stars burst out in the dome of heaven like a rocket. Antonio and Primitivo, in that queer harsh Mexican harmony which sounds like nothing so much as a fiddle with frazzled strings, sang *"Esperanza"* as we jogged along. It grew cold. For leagues and leagues around was a blasted land, a country of death. It was hours since we had passed a house.

Antonio claimed to know of a water-hole somewhere vaguely ahead. But toward midnight, which was black and without moon, we discovered that the road upon which we were traveling suddenly petered out in a dense mesquite thicket. Somewhere we had turned off the *Camino Real.* It was late and the mules were worn out. There seemed nothing for it but a "dry camp," for so far as we knew there was no water anywhere near.

Now we had unharnessed the mules and fed them, and were lighting our fire, when somewhere in the dense thicket of chaparral stealthy footsteps sounded. They moved a space and then were still. Our little blaze of greasewood crackled fiercely, lighting up a leaping, glowing radius of about ten feet. Beyond that all was black.

Primitivo made one backward leap into the shelter of the wagon; Antonio drew his revolver, and we froze beside the fire. The sound came again.

"Who lives?" said Antonio. There was a little shuffling noise out in the brush, and then a voice.

"What party are you?" it asked hesitantly.

"Maderistas," answered Antonio. "Pass!"

"It is safe for *pacíficos*?" queried the invisible one.

"On my word," I cried. "Come out that we may see you."

At that very moment two vague shapes materialized on the edge of the firelight glow, almost without a sound—two peons, we saw as soon as they came close, wrapped tightly in their torn blankets. One was an old, wrinkled, bent man wearing homemade sandals, his trousers hanging in rags upon his shrunken legs; the other a very tall, barefooted youth, with a face so pure and so simple as to almost verge upon idiocy. Friendly, warm as sunlight, eagerly curious as children, they came forward, holding out their hands.

We shook hands with each of them in turn, greeting them with elaborate Mexican courtesy.

"Good evening, friend. How are you?"

"Very well, *gracias*. And you?"

"Well, *gracias*. And how are all your people?"

"Well, thanks. And yours?"

"Well, thanks. What have you of new here?"

"*Nada*. Nothing. And you?"

"Nothing. Sit down."

"Oh, thanks, but I am well standing."

"Sit down. Sit down."

"A thousand thanks. Excuse us for a moment."

They smiled and faded away once more into the thicket. In a minute they reappeared, with great armfuls of dried mesquite branches for our fire.

"We are *rancheros*," said the elder, bowing. "We keep a few goats, and our houses are at your orders, and our corrals for your mules, and our small stock of corn. Our *ranchitos* are very near here in the mesquite. We are very poor men, but we hope you will do us the honor of accepting our hospitality." It was an occasion for tact.

"A thousand times many thanks," said Antonio politely, "but we are, unfortunately, in great haste and must leave early. We would not like to disturb your household at that hour."

They protested that their families and their houses were entirely ours, to be used as we saw fit with the greatest delight on their part. I do not remember how we finally managed to evade the invitation without wounding them, but I do recall that it took half an hour of courteous talking. For we knew, in the first place, that we would be unable to leave for hours in the morning if we accepted, because Mexican manners are that haste to leave a house signifies dissatisfaction with the entertainment; and then, too, one could not pay for one's lodging, but would have to bestow a handsome present upon the hosts—which we could none of us afford.

At first they politely refused our invitation to dine, but after much urging we finally persuaded them to accept a few *tortillas* and *chile*. It was ludicrous and pitiful to see how wretchedly hungry they were, and how they attempted to conceal it from us.

After dinner, when they had brought us a bucket of water out of sheer kindly thoughtfulness, they stood for a while by our fire, smoking our cigarettes and holding out their hands to the blaze. I remember how their serapes hung from their shoulders, open in front so the grateful warmth could reach their thin bodies—and how gnarled and ancient were the old man's outstretched hands, and how the ruddy light glowed upon the other's throat, and kindled fires in his big eyes. Around them stretched the desert, held off only by our fire, ready to spring in upon us when it should die. Above the great stars would not dim. Coyotes wailed somewhere out beyond the firelight like demons in pain. I suddenly conceived these two human beings as symbols of Mexico—courteous, loving, patient, poor, so long slaves, so full of dreams, so soon to be free.

"When we saw your wagon coming here," said the old man, smiling, "our hearts sank within us. We thought you were soldiers, come perhaps, to take away our last few goats. So many soldiers have come in the last few years—so many. It is mostly the Federals—the Maderistas do not come unless they are hungry themselves. Poor Maderistas!"

"Ay," said the young man, "my brother that I loved very much died in the eleven days' fighting around Torreon. Thousands have died in Mexico, and still more thousands shall fall. Three years—it is long for war in a land. Too long!" The old man murmured, *"Valgame Dios!"* and shook his head. "But there shall come a day—"

"It is said," remarked the old man quaveringly, "that the United States of the North covets our country—that gringo soldiers will come and take away my goats in the end. . . ."

"That is a lie," exclaimed the other, animated. "It is the rich Americanos who want to rob us, just as the rich Mexicans want to rob us. It is the rich all over the world who want to rob the poor."

The old man shivered and drew his wasted body nearer to the fire. "I have often wondered," said he mildly, "why the rich, having so much, want so much. The poor, who have nothing, want so very little. Just a few goats. . . ."

His *compadre* lifted his chin like a noble, smiling gently. "I have never been out of this little country here—not even to Jimenez," he said. "But they tell me that there are many rich lands to the north and south and east. But this is my land and I love it. For the years of me, and my father and my grandfather, the rich men have gathered the corn and held it in their clenched fists before our mouths. And only blood will make them open their hands to their brothers."

The fire died down. At his post slept the alert Primitivo. Antonio stared into the embers, a faint glorified smile upon his mouth, his eyes shining like stars.

"*Adio!*" he said suddenly, as one who sees a vision. "When we get into Mexico City what a *baile* shall be held! How drunk I shall get! . . ."

# PART IV

## A PEOPLE IN ARMS

# 1

## "On to Torreon!"

At Yermo there is nothing but leagues and leagues of sandy desert, sparsely covered with scrubby mesquite and dwarf cactus, stretching away on the west to jagged, tawny mountains, and on the east to a quivering skyline of plain. A battered water tank, with too little dirty alkali water, a demolished railway station shot to pieces by Orozco's cannon two years before, and a switch track compose the town. There is no water to speak of for forty miles. There is no grass for animals. For three months in the spring bitter, parching winds drive the yellow dust across it.

Along the single track in the middle of the desert lay ten enormous trains, pillars of fire by night and of black smoke by day, stretching back northward farther than the eye could reach. Around them, in the chaparral, camped nine thousand men without shelter, each man's horse tied to the mesquite beside him, where hung his one serape and red strips of drying meat. From fifty cars horses and mules were being unloaded. Covered with sweat and dust, a ragged trooper plunged into a cattle car among the flying hoofs, swung himself upon a horse's back, and jabbed his spurs deep in, with a yell. Then came a terrific drumming of frightened animals, and suddenly a horse shot violently from the open door, usually backward, and the car belched flying masses of horses and mules. Picking themselves up, they fled in terror, snorting through wide nostrils at the smell of the open. Then the wide, watchful circle of troopers turned *vaqueros* lifted the great coils of their lassoes through the choking dust, and the running animals swirled round and round upon one another in a panic. Officers, orderlies, generals with their staffs, soldiers with halters,

147

hunting for their mounts, galloped and ran past in inextricable confusion. Bucking mules were being harnessed to the caissons. Troopers who had arrived on the last trains wandered about looking for their brigades. Way ahead some men were shooting at a rabbit. From the tops of the boxcars and the flatcars, where they were camped by hundreds, the *soldaderas* and their half-naked swarms of children looked down, screaming shrill advice and asking everybody in general if they had happened to see Juan Moñeros, or Jesus Hernandez, or whatever the name of their man happened to be. . . . One man trailing a rifle wandered along shouting that he had had nothing to eat for two days and he couldn't find his woman who made his *tortillas* for him, and he opined that she had deserted him to go with some——of another brigade. . . . The women on the roofs of the cars said, *"Valgame Dios!"* and shrugged their shoulders; then they dropped him down some three-days-old *tortillas*, and asked him, for the love he bore Our Lady of Guadelupe, to lend them a cigarette. A clamorous, dirty throng stormed the engine of our train, screaming for water. When the engineer stood them off with a revolver, telling them there was plenty of water in the water train, they broke away and aimlessly scattered, while a fresh throng took their places. Around the twelve immense tank cars, a fighting mass of men and animals struggled for a place at the little faucets ceaselessly pouring. Above the place a mighty cloud of dust, seven miles long and a mile wide, towered up into the still, hot air, and, with the black smoke of the engines, struck wonder and terror into the Federal outposts fifty miles away on the mountains back of Mapimi.

When Villa left Chihuahua for Torreon, he closed the telegraph wires to the north, stopped train service to Juarez, and forbade on pain of death that anyone should carry or send news of his departure to the United States. His object was to take the Federals by surprise, and it worked beautifully. No one, not even Villa's staff, knew when he would leave Chihuahua; the army had delayed there so long that we all believed it would delay another two weeks. And then Saturday morning we woke to find the telegraph and railway cut, and three huge trains, carrying the Brigada

Gonzales-Ortega, already gone. The Zaragosa left the next day, and Villa's own troops the following morning. Moving with the swiftness that always characterizes him, Villa had his entire army concentrated at Yermo the day afterward, without the Federals knowing that he had left Chihuahua.

There was a mob around the portable field telegraph that had been rigged up in the ruined station. Inside, the instrument was clicking. Soldiers and officers indiscriminately choked up the windows and the door, and every once in a while the operator would shout something in Spanish and a perfect roar of laughter would go up. It seemed that the telegraph had accidentally tapped a wire that had not been destroyed by the Federals—a wire that connected with the Federal military wire from Mapimi to Torreon.

"Listen!" cried the operator. "Colonel Argumedo in command of the *cabecillos colorados* in Mapimi is telegraphing to General Velasco in Torreon. He says that he sees smoke and a big dust cloud to the north, and thinks that some rebel troops are moving south from Escalon!"

Night came, with a cloudy sky and a rising wind that began to lift the dust. Along the miles and miles of trains, the fires of the *soldaderas* flared from the tops of the freight cars. Out into the desert so far that finally they were mere pinpoints of flame stretched the innumerable campfires of the army, half obscured by the thick, billowing dust. The storm completely concealed us from Federal watchers. "Even God," remarked Major Leyva, "even God is on the side of Francisco Villa!" We sat at dinner in our converted boxcar, with young, great-limbed, expressionless General Maximo Garcia and his brother, the even huger red-faced Benito Garcia, and little Major Manuel Acosta, with the beautiful manners of his race. Garcia had long been holding the advance at Escalon. He and his brothers—one of whom, José Garcia, the idol of the army, had been killed in battle but a short four years ago—were wealthy *hacendados*, owners of immense tracts of land. They had come out with Madero. . . . I remember that he brought us a jug of whiskey, and refused to discuss the

Revolution, declaring that he was fighting for better whiskey! As I write this comes a report that he is dead from a bullet wound received in the battle of Sacramento. . . .

Out in the dust storm, on a flatcar immediately ahead of ours, some soldiers lay around their fire with their heads in their women's laps, singing "The Cockroach," which tells in hundreds of satirical verses what the Constitutionalists would do when they captured Juarez and Chihuahua from Mercado and Orozco.

Above the wind one was aware of the immense sullen murmur of the host, and occasionally some sentry challenged in a falsetto howl: *"Quien vive?"* And the answer: *"Chiapas!" "Que gente?" "Chao!"* . . . Through the night sounded the eerie whistle of the ten locomotives at intervals as they signaled back and forth to one another.

# 2

## The Army at Yermo

$A_T$ dawn next morning General Toribio Ortega came to the car for breakfast—a lean, dark Mexican, who is called "The Honorable" and "The Most Brave" by the soldiers. He is by far the most simple-hearted and disinterested soldier in Mexico. He never kills his prisoners. He has refused to take a cent from the Revolution beyond his meager salary. Villa respects and trusts him perhaps beyond all his Generals. Ortega was a poor man, a cowboy. He sat there, with his elbows on the table, forgetting his breakfast, his big eyes flashing, smiling his gentle, crooked smile, and told us why he was fighting.

"I am not an educated man," he said. "But I know that to fight is the last thing for any people. Only when things get too bad to stand, eh? And, if we are going to kill our brothers, something fine must come out of it, eh? You in the United States do not know what we have seen, we Mexicans! We have looked on at the robbing of our people, the simple, poor people, for thirty-five years, eh? We have seen the *rurales* and the soldiers of Porfirio Diaz shoot down our brothers and our fathers, and justice denied to them. We have seen our little fields taken away from us, and all of us sold into slavery, eh? We have longed for our homes and for schools to teach us, and they have laughed at us. All we have ever wanted was to be let alone to live and to work and make our country great, and we are tired—tired and sick of being cheated. . . ."

Outside in the dust, that whirled along under a sky of driving clouds, long lines of soldiers on horseback stood in the obscurity, while their officers passed along in front, peering closely at cartridge belts and rifles.

151

"Geronimo," said a Captain to one trooper, "go back to the ammunition train and fill up the gaps in your *cartouchera*. You fool, you've been wasting your cartridges shooting coyotes!"

Across the desert westward toward the distant mountains rode strings of cavalry, the first to the front. About a thousand went, in ten different lines, diverging like wheel spokes; the jingle of their spurs ringing, their red-white-and-green flags floating straight out, crossed bandoliers gleaming dully, rifles flopping across their saddles, heavy, high sombreros and many-colored blankets.

Behind each company plodded ten or twelve women on foot, carrying cooking utensils on their heads and backs, and perhaps a pack mule loaded with sacks of corn. And as they passed the cars they shouted back to their friends on the trains.

"*Poco tiempo California!*" cried one.

"Oh! there's a *colorado* for you!" yelled another. "I'll bet you were with Salazar in Orozco's Revolution. Nobody ever said '*Poco tiempo California*' except Salazar when he was drunk!"

The other man looked sheepish. "Well, maybe I was," he admitted. "But wait till I get a shot at my old *compañeros*. I'll show you whether I'm a Maderista or not!"

A little Indian in the rear cried: "I know how much of a Maderista you are, Luisito. At the first taking of Torreon, Villa gave you the choice of turning your coat or getting a *cabronasso* or *balasso* through the head!" And, joshing and singing, they jogged southwest, became small, and finally faded into the dust.

Villa himself stood leaning against a car, hands in his pockets. He wore an old slouch hat, a dirty shirt without a collar, and a badly frayed and shiny brown suit. All over the dusty plain in front of him men and horses had sprung up like magic. There was an immense confusion of saddling and bridling—a cracked blowing of tin bugles. The Brigada Zaragosa was getting ready to leave camp—a flanking column of two thousand men who were to ride southeast and attack Tlahualilo and Sacramento. Villa, it seemed, had just arrived at Yermo. He had stopped off Monday night at Camargo to attend the wedding of a *compadre*. His face was drawn into lines of fatigue.

"*Carramba!*" he was saying with a grin, "we started dancing

Monday evening, danced all night, all the next day, and last night, too! What a *baile*! And what *muchachas*! The girls of Camargo and Santa Rosalia are the most beautiful in Mexico! I am worn out—*rendido*! It was harder work than twenty battles. . . ."

Then he listened to the report of some staff officer who dashed up on horseback, gave a concise order without hesitating, and the officer rode off. He told Señor Calzado, General Manager of the Railroad, in what order the trains should proceed south. He indicated to Señor Uro, the Quartermaster-general, what supplies should be distributed from the troop trains. To Señor Munoz, Director of the Telegraph, he gave the name of a Federal captain surrounded by Urbina's men a week before and killed with all his men in the hills near La Cadena, and ordered him to tap the Federal wire and send a message to General Velasco in Torreon purporting to be a report from this Captain from Conejos, and asking for orders. . . . He seemed to know and order everything.

We had lunch with General Eugenio Aguirre Benavides, the quiet, cross-eyed little commander of the Zaragosa Brigade, a member of one of the cultivated Mexican families that gathered around Madero in the first Revolution; with Raul Madero, brother of the murdered President, second in command of the Brigade, who is a graduate of an American University, and looks like a Wall Street bond salesman; with Colonel Guerra, who went through Cornell, and Major Leyva, Ortega's nephew, a historic fullback on the Notre Dame football team. . . .

In a great circle, ready for action, the artillery was parked, with caissons open and mules corralled in the center. Colonel Servin, commander of the guns, sat perched high up on an immense bay horse, a ridiculous tiny figure, not more than five feet tall. He was waving his hand and shouting a greeting across to General Angeles, Carranza's Secretary of War—a tall, gaunt man, bareheaded, in a brown sweater, with a war map of Mexico hanging from his shoulder—who straddled a small burro. In the thick dust clouds, sweating men labored. The five American artillery men had squatted down in the lee of a cannon, smoking. They hailed me with a shout:

"Say, bo! What in hell did we ever get into this mess for?

Nothing to eat since last night—work twelve hours—say, take our pictures, will you?"

There passed by with a friendly nod the little Cockney soldier that had served with Kitchener, and then the Canadian Captain Treston, bawling for his interpreter, so that he could give his men some orders about the machine guns; and Captain Marinelli, the fat Italian soldier of fortune, pouring an interminable and unintelligible mixture of French, Spanish and Italian into the ear of a bored Mexican officer. Fierro rode by, cruelly roweling his horse with the bloody mouth—Fierro, the handsome, cruel and insolent—The Butcher they called him, because he killed defenseless prisoners with his revolver, and shot down his own men without provocation.

Late in the afternoon the Brigada Zaragosa rode away southeast over the desert, and another night came down.

The wind rose steadily in the darkness, growing colder and colder. Looking up at the sky, which had been ablaze with polished stars, I saw that all was dark with cloud. Through the roaring whirls of dust a thousand thin lines of sparks from the fires streamed southward. The coaling of the engines' fire boxes made sudden glares along the miles of trains. At first we thought we heard the sound of big guns in the distance. But all at once, unexpectedly, the sky split dazzlingly open from horizon to horizon, thunder fell like a blow, and the rain came level and thick as a flood. For a moment the human hum of the army was silenced. All the fires disappeared at once. And then came a vast shout of anger and laughter and discomfiture from the soldiers out on the plain, and the most amazing wail of misery from the women that I have ever heard. The two sounds only lasted a minute. The men wrapped themselves in their serapes and sank down in the shelter of the chaparral; and the hundreds of women and children exposed to the cold and the rain on the flatcars and the tops of the boxcars silently and with Indian stoicism settled down to wait for dawn. In General Maclovio Herrera's car ahead was drunken laughter and singing to a guitar. . . .

. . .

DAYBREAK came with a sound of all the bugles in the world blowing; and looking out of the car door I saw the desert for miles boiling with armed men saddling and mounting. A hot sun popped over the western mountains, burning in a clear sky. For a moment the ground poured up billowing steam, and then there was dust again, and a thirsty land. There might never have been rain. A hundred breakfast fires smoked from the car tops, and the women stood turning their dresses slowly in the sun, chattering and joking. Hundreds of little naked babies danced around, while their mothers lifted up their little clothes to the heat. A thousand joyous troopers shouted to each other that the advance was beginning; away off to the left some regiment had given away to joy, and was shooting into the air. Six more long trains had come in during the night, and all the engines were whistling signals. I went forward to get on the first train out, and as I passed the car of Trinidad Rodriguez, a harsh, feminine voice cried: "Hey, kid! Come in and get some breakfast." Leaning out of the door were Beatrice and Carmen, two noted Juarez women that had been brought to the front by the Rodriguez brothers. I went in and sat down at the table with about twelve men, several of them doctors in the hospital train, one French artillery captain, and an assortment of Mexican officers and privates. It was an ordinary freight boxcar like all the private cars, with windows cut in the walls, partitions built to shut out the Chinese cook in the kitchen, and bunks arranged across sides and end. Breakfast consisted of heaping platters of red meat with *chile*, bowls of *frijoles*, stacks of cold flour *tortillas*, and six bottles of Monopole Champagne. Carmen's complexion was bad, and she was a little stupid from the gastronomic combination, but Beatrice's white, colorless face and red hair cut Buster Brown fashion fairly radiated a sort of malicious glee. She was a Mexican, but talked Tenderloin English without an accent. Jumping up from the table, she danced around it, pulling the men's hair. "Hello, you damned gringo," she laughed at me. "What are you doing here? You're going to get a bullet in you if you don't get careful!"

A morose young Mexican, already a little drunk, snapped at her furiously in Spanish: "Don't you talk to him! Do you understand? I'll tell Trinidad how you asked the gringo in to breakfast, and he'll have you shot!"

Beatrice threw back her head and roared. "Did you hear what he said? He thinks he owns me, because he once stayed with me in Juarez! . . . My God!" she went on. "How funny it seems to travel on the railroad and not have to buy a ticket!"

"Look here, Beatrice," I asked her, "we may not have such an easy time of it down here. What will you do if we get licked?"

"Who, me?" she cried. "Why, I guess it won't take me long to get friends in the Federal army. I'm a good mixer!"

"What is she saying? What do you say?" asked the others in Spanish.

With the most perfect insolence Beatrice translated for them. And in the midst of the uproar that followed I left. . . .

# 3

## First Blood

T HE water train pulled out first. I rode on the cowcatcher of the engine, which was already occupied by the permanent home of two women and five children. They had built a little fire of mesquite twigs on the narrow iron platform, and were baking *tortillas* there; over their heads, against the windy roar of the boiler, fluttered a little line of wash. . . .

It was a brilliant day, hot sunshine alternating with big white clouds. In two thick columns, one on each side of the train, the army was already moving south. As far as the eye could reach, a mighty double cloud of dust floated over them; and little straggling groups of mounted men jogged along, with every now and then a big Mexican flag. Between slowly moved the trains; the pillars of black smoke from their engines, at regular intervals, growing smaller, until over the northern horizon only a dirty mist appeared.

I went down into the caboose to get a drink of water, and there I found the conductor of the train lying in his bunk reading the Bible. He was so interested and amused that he didn't notice me for a minute. When he did he cried delightedly: *"Oiga*, I have found a great story about a chap called Samson who was *muy hombre*—a good deal of a man—and his woman. She was a Spaniard, I guess, from the mean trick she played on him. He started out being a good Revolutionist, a Maderista, and she made him a *pelon!"*

Pelon means literally "cropped head," and is the slang term for a Federal soldier, because the Federal army is largely recruited from the prisons.

Our advance guard, with a telegraph field operator, had gone on to Conejos the night before, and they met the train in great excitement. The first blood of the campaign had been spilt; a few *colorados* scouting northward from Bermejillo had been surprised and killed just behind the shoulder of the big mountain which lies to the east. The telegrapher also had news. He had again tapped the Federal wire, and sent to the Federal commander in Torreon, signing the dead Captain's name and asking for orders, since a large force of rebels seemed to be approaching from the north. General Velasco replied that the Captain should hold Conejos and throw out outposts to the north, to try and discover how large the force was. At the same time the telegrapher had heard a message from Argumedo, in command at Mapimi, saying that the entire north of Mexico was coming down on Torreon, together with the gringo army!

Conejos was just like Yermo, except that there was no water tank. A thousand men, with white-bearded old General Rosalio Hernandez riding ahead, went out almost at once, and the repair train followed them a few miles to a place where the Federals had burned two railroad bridges a few months before. Out beyond the last little bivouac of the immense army spread around us, the desert slept silently in the heat waves. There was no wind. The men gathered with their women on the flatcars, guitars came out, and all night hundreds of singing voices came from the trains.

THE next morning I went to see Villa in his car. This was a red caboose with chintz curtains on the windows, the famous little caboose which Villa has used in all his journeys since the fall of Juarez. It was divided by partitions into two rooms—the kitchen and the General's bedroom. This tiny room, ten by twenty feet, was the heart of the Constitutionalist army. There were held all the councils of war, and there was scarcely room enough for the fifteen Generals who met there. In these councils the vital immediate questions of the campaign were discussed, the Generals decided what was to be done—and then Villa gave his orders to suit himself. It was painted a dirty gray. On the walls were tacked photographs of showy ladies in theatrical poses, a large picture of Carranza, one of Fierro, and a picture of Villa himself. Two double-width wooden bunks folded up against the wall, in one of which Villa and General Angeles slept, and in the other José Rodriguez and Doctor Raschbaum, Villa's personal physician. That was all. . . .

"*Que desea, amigo?* What do you want?" said Villa, sitting on the end of the bunk in blue underclothes. The troopers who lounged around the place lazily made way for me.

"I want a horse, *mi General.*"

"*Ca-r-r-r-ai-i,* our friend here wants a horse!" grinned Villa sarcastically amid a burst of laughter from the others. "Why, you correspondents will be wanting an automobile next! *Oiga,* señor reporter, do you know that about a thousand men in my army have no horses? Here's the train. What do you want a horse for?"

"So I can ride with the advance."

"No," he smiled. "There are too many *balassos*—too many bullets flying in the advance. . . ."

He was hurrying into his clothes as he talked, and gulping coffee from the side of a dirty tin coffee pot. Somebody handed him his gold-handled sword.

"No!" he said contemptuously. "This is to be a fight, not a parade. Give me my rifle!"

He stood at the door of his caboose for a moment, thoughtfully looking at the long lines of mounted men, picturesque in their crossed cartridge belts and varied equipment. Then he gave a few quick orders and mounted his big stallion.

"*Vamonos!*" cried Villa. The bugles brayed and a subdued silver clicking ringing sounded as the companies wheeled and trotted southward in the dust. . . .

And so the army disappeared. During the day we thought we heard cannonading from the southwest, where Urbina was reported to be coming down from the mountains to attack Mapimi. And late in the afternoon news came of the capture of

Bermejillo, and a courier from Benavides said that he had taken Tlahualilo.

We were in a fever of impatience to be off. About sundown Señor Calzado remarked that the repair train would leave in an hour, so I grabbed a blanket and walked a mile up the line of trains to it.

**4**

# On the Cannon Car

T HE first car of the repair train was a steel-encased flatcar, upon which was mounted the famous Constitutionalist cannon "El Niño," with an open caisson full of shells behind it. Behind that was an armored car full of soldiers, then a car of steel rails, and four loaded with railroad ties. The engine came next, the engineer and fireman hung with cartridge belts, their rifles handy. Then followed two or three boxcars full of soldiers and their women. It was a dangerous business. A large force of Federals were known to be in Mapimi, and the country swarmed with their outposts. Our army was already far ahead, except for five hundred men who guarded the trains at Conejos. If the enemy could capture or wreck the repair train the army would be cut off without water, food or ammunition. In the darkness we moved out. I sat upon the breech of "El Niño," chatting with Captain Diaz, the commander of the gun, as he oiled the breech lock of his beloved cannon and curled his vertical mustachios. In the armored recess behind the gun, where the Captain slept, I heard a curious, subdued rustling noise.

"What's that?"

"Eh?" cried he nervously. "Oh, nothing, nothing!"

Just then there emerged a young Indian girl with a bottle in her hand. She couldn't have been more than seventeen, very lovely. The Captain shot a glance at me, and suddenly whirled around.

"What are you doing here?" he cried furiously to her. "Why are you coming out here?"

"I thought you said you wanted a drink," she began.

I perceived that I was one too many, and excused myself. They

161

hardly noticed me. But as I was climbing over the back of the car I couldn't help stopping and listening. They had gone back to the recess, and she was weeping.

"Didn't I tell you," stormed the Captain, "not to show yourself when there are strangers here? I will not have every man in Mexico looking at you. . . ."

I stood on the roof of the rocking steel car as we nosed slowly along. Lying on their bellies on the extreme front platform, two men with lanterns examined each foot of the track for wires that might mean mines planted under us. Beneath my feet the soldiers and their women were having dinner around fires built on the floor. Smoke and laughter poured out of the loopholes. . . . There were other fires aft, brown-faced, ragged people squatting at them, on the car tops. Overhead the sky blazed stars, without a cloud. It was cold. After an hour of riding we came to a piece of broken track. The train stopped with a jar, the engine whistled, and a score of torches and lanterns jerked past. Men came running. The flares clustered bobbing together as the foremen examined the damage. A fire sprang up in the brush, and then another. Soldiers of the train guard straggled by, dragging their rifles, and formed impenetrable walls around the fires. Iron tools clanged, and the "Wai-hoy!" of men shoving rails off the flatcar. A Chinese dragon of workmen passed with a rail on their shoulders, then others with ties. Four hundred men swarmed upon the broken spot, working with extraordinary energy and good humor, until the shouts of gangs setting rails and ties, and the rattle of sledges on spikes, made a continuous roar. It was an old destruction, probably a year old, made when these same Constitutionalists were retreating north in the face of Mercado's Federal army, and we had it all fixed in an hour. Then on again. Sometimes it was a bridge burned out, sometimes a hundred yards of track twisted into grapevines by a chain and a backing engine. We advanced slowly. At one big bridge that it would take two hours to prepare, I built by myself a little fire in order to get warm. Calzado came past, and hailed me. "We've got a handcar up ahead," he said, "and we're going along down and see the dead men. Want to come?"

"What dead men?"

"Why, this morning an outpost of eighty *rurales* was sent scouting north from Bermejillo. We heard about it over the wire and informed Benavides on the left. He sent a troop to take them in the rear, and drove them north in a running fight for fifteen miles until they smashed up against our main body and not one got out alive. They're scattered along the whole way just where they fell."

In a moment we were speeding south on the handcar. At our right hand and our left rode two silent, shadowy figures on horseback—cavalry guards, with rifles ready under their arms. Soon the flares and fires of the train were left behind, and we were enveloped and smothered in the vast silence of the desert.

"Yes," said Calzado, "the *rurales* are brave. They are *muy hombres*. *Rurales* are the best fighters Diaz and Huerta ever had. They never desert to the Revolution. They always remain loyal to the established government. Because they are police."

It was bitter cold. None of us talked much.

"We go ahead of the train at night," said the soldier at my left, "so that if there are any dynamite bombs underneath——"

"We could discover them and dig them out and put water in them, *carramba!*" said another sarcastically. The rest laughed. I began to think of that, and it made me shiver. The dead silence of the desert seemed an expectant hush. One couldn't see ten feet from the track.

"*Oiga!*" shouted one of the horsemen. "It was just here that one lay." The brakes ground and we tumbled off and down the steep embankment, our lanterns jerking ahead. Something lay huddled around the foot of a telegraph pole—something infinitely small and shabby, like a pile of old clothes. The *rurale* was upon his back, twisted sideways from his hips. He had been stripped of everything of value by the thrifty rebels—shoes, hat, underclothing. They had left him his ragged jacket with the tarnished silver braid, because there were seven bullet holes in it; and his trousers, soaked with blood. He had evidently been much bigger when alive, the dead shrink so. A wild red beard made the pallor of his face grotesque, until you noticed that under it and the dirt, and the long lines of sweat of his terrible fight and hard riding, his mouth was gently and serenely open as if he slept. His brains had been blown out.

"*Carrai!*" said one guard. "There was a shot for the dirty goat! Right through the head!"

The others laughed. "Why, you don't think they shot him there in the fight, do you, *pendeco?*" cried his companion. "No, they *always* go around and make sure afterward——"

"Hurry up! I've found the other," shouted a voice off in the darkness.

We could reconstruct this man's last struggle. He had dropped off his horse, wounded—for there was blood on the ground—into a little dry arroyo. We could even see where his horse had stood while he pumped shells into his Mauser with feverish hands, and blazed away, first to the rear, where the pursuers came running with Indian yells, and then at the hundreds and hundreds of bloodthirsty horsemen pouring down from the north, with the Demon Pancho Villa at their head. He must have fought a long time, perhaps until they ringed him round with living flame—for we found hundreds of empty cartridges. And then, when the last shot was spent, he made a dash eastward, hit at every step; hid for a moment under the little railroad bridge, and ran out upon the open desert, where he fell. There were twenty bullet holes in him. They had stripped him of all save his underclothes. He lay sprawled in an attitude of desperate action, muscles tense, one fist clenched and spread across the dust as if he were dealing a blow; the fiercest exultant grin on his face. Strong, savage, until one looked closer and saw the subtle touch of weakness that death stamps on life—the delicate expression of idiocy over it all. They had shot him through the head three times—how exasperated they must have been!

Crawling south through the cold night once more. . . . A few miles and then a bridge dynamited, or a strip of track wrecked. The stop, the dancing torches, the great bonfires leaping up from the desert, and the four hundred wild men pouring furiously out and falling upon their work. . . . Villa had given orders to hurry. . . .

. . .

About two o'clock in the morning I came upon two *soldaderas* squatting around a fire, and asked them if they could give me *tortillas* and coffee. One was an old, gray-haired Indian woman with a perpetual grin, the other a slight girl not more than twenty years old, who was nursing a four-months baby at her breast. They were perched at the extreme tip of a flatcar, their fire built upon a pile of sand, as the train jolted and swayed along. Around them, backed against them, feet sticking out between them, was a great, inconglomerate mass of sleeping, snoring humans. The rest of the train was by this time dark; this was the only patch of light and warmth in the night. As I munched my *tortilla* and the old woman lifted a burning coal in her fingers to light her corn-husk cigarette, wondering where her Pablo's brigade was this night; and the girl nursed her child, crooning to it, her blue-enameled earrings twinkling—we talked.

"Ah! it is a life for us *viejas*," said the girl. "*Adio*, but we follow our men out in the campaign, and then do not know from hour to hour whether they live or die. I remember well when Filadelfo called to me one morning in the little morning before it was light—we lived in Pachuca—and said: 'Come! we are going out to fight because the good Pancho Madero has been murdered this day!' We had only been loving each other eight months, too, and the first baby was not born.... We had all believed that peace was in Mexico for good. Filadelfo saddled the burro, and we rode out through the streets just as light was coming, and into the fields where the farmers were not yet at work. And I said: 'Why must I come?' And he answered: 'Shall I starve, then? Who shall make my *tortillas* for me but my woman?' It took us three months to get north, and I was sick and the baby was born in a desert just like this place, and died there because we could not get water. That was when Villa was going north after he had taken Torreon."

The old woman broke in: "Yes, and all that is true. When we go so far and suffer so much for our men, we are cruelly treated by the stupid animals of Generals. I am from San Luis Potosí, and my man was in the artillery of the Federación when Mercado came north. All the way to Chihuahua we traveled, the old fool of a Mercado grumbling about transporting the *viejas*. And then he ordered his army to go north and attack Villa in Juarez, and he forbade the women to go. Is that the way you are going to do, *desgraciado?* I said to myself. And when he evacuated Chihuahua and ran away with my man to Ojinaga, I just stayed right in Chihuahua and got a man in the Maderista army when it came in. A nice handsome young fellow, too—much better than Juan. I'm not a woman to stand being put upon."

"How much are the *tortillas* and coffee?" I asked.

They looked at each other, startled. Evidently they had thought me one of the penniless soldiers on the train.

"What you would like," said the young woman faintly. I gave them a peso.

The old woman exploded in a torrent of prayer. "God, his sainted Mother, the Blessed Niño and Our Lady of Guadelupe have sent this stranger to us tonight! Here we had not a centavo to buy coffee and flour with. . . ."

I suddenly noticed that the light of our fire had paled, and looked up in amazement to find it was dawn. Just then a man came running along the train from up front, shouting something unintelligible, while laughter and shouts burst out in his wake. The sleepers raised their curious heads and wanted to know what was the matter. In a moment our inanimate car was alive. The man passed, still yelling something about "*padre,*" his face exultant with some tremendous joke.

"What is it?" I asked.

"Oh!" cried the old woman. "His woman on the car ahead has just had a baby!"

Just in front of us lay Bermejillo, its pink and blue and white plastered adobe houses as delicate and ethereal as a village of porcelain. To the east, across a still, dustless desert, a little file of sharp-cut horsemen, with a red-white-and-green flag over them, were riding into town. . . .

# 5

## At the Gates of Gomez

W E had taken Bermejillo the afternoon before—the army breaking into a furious gallop five kilometers north of the town and pouring through it at top speed, driving the unprepared garrison in a rout southward—a running fight that lasted five miles, as far as the Hacienda of Santa Clara—and killing a hundred and six *colorados*. Within a few hours afterward Urbina came in sight above Mapimi, and the eight hundred *colorados* there, informed of the astonishing news that the entire Constitutionalist army was flanking them on their right evacuated the place, and fled hotly to Torreon. All over the country the astounded Federals were falling back in a panic upon the city.

Late in the afternoon a dumpy little train came down the narrow-gauge track from the direction of Mapimi, and from it proceeded the loud strains of a string orchestra of ten pieces playing *"Recuerdos* of Durango"—to which I had so often *baile*'d with the Tropa. The roofs, doors and windows were packed with Mexicans, singing and beating time with their heels, as they fired their rifles in a sort of salute upon entering the town. At the station this curious equipage drew up, and from it proceeded—who but Patricio, General Urbina's fighting stage-driver at whose side I had so often ridden and danced! He threw his arms around me, yelling: "Juanito! Here is Juanito, *mi General!*" In a minute we were asking and answering each other a million questions. Did I have the photographs I took of him? Was I going to the battle of Torreon? Did he know where Don Petronilo was? And Pablo Seañes? And Raphaelito? And right in the midst of it somebody shouted, "Viva Urbina!" and the old General himself stood at the top of the steps—the lion-hearted hero of Durango. He was lame, and leaned upon two soldiers. He held a rifle in his hand—an old, discarded Springfield, with the sights filed down—and wore a double cartridge belt around his waist. For a moment he remained there, absolutely expressionless, his small, hard eyes boring into me. I thought he did not recognize me, when all at once his harsh, sudden voice shot out: "That's not the camera you had! Where's the other one?"

I was about to reply when he interrupted: "I know. You left it behind you in La Cadena. Did you run very fast?"

"Yes, *mi General.*"

"And you've come down to Torreon to run again?"

"When I began to run from La Cadena," I remarked, nettled, "Don Petronilo and the troops were already a mile away."

He didn't answer, but came haltingly down the steps of the car, while a roar of laughter went up from the soldiers. Coming up to me he put a hand over my shoulder and gave me a little tap on the back. "I'm glad to see you, *compañero,*" he said. . . .

Across the desert the wounded had begun to straggle in from the battle of Tlahualilo to the hospital train, which lay far up near the front of the line of trains. On the flat barren plain, as far as I could see, there were only three living things in sight: a limping, hatless man, with his head tied up in a bloody cloth; another staggering beside his staggering horse; and a mule mounted by two bandaged figures far behind them. And in the still hot night we could hear from our car groans and screams. . . .

LATE Sunday morning we were again on "El Niño" at the head of the repair train, moving slowly down the track abreast of the army. "El Chavalito," another cannon mounted on a flatcar, was coupled behind, then came two armored cars, and the workcars. This time there were no women. The army wore a different air, winding along in two immense serpents each side of us—there was little laughter or shouting. We were close now, only eighteen miles from Gomez Palacio, and no one knew what the Federals planned to do. It seemed incredible that they would let us get so close without making one stand. Immediately south of Bermejillo we entered a new land. To the desert succeeded fields bordered with irrigation ditches, along which grew immense green alamos, towering pillars of freshness after the baked desolation we had just passed through. Here were cotton fields, the white tufts unpicked and rotting on their stalks; cornfields with sparse green blades just showing. Along the big ditches flowed swift, deep water in the shade. Birds sang, and the barren western mountains marched steadily nearer as we went south. It was summer—hot, moist summer, such as we have at home. A deserted cotton gin lay on our left, hundreds of white bales tumbled in the sun, and dazzling heaps of cottonseed left just as the workmen had piled it months before. . . .

At Santa Clara the massed columns of the army halted and began to defile to left and right, thin lines of troops jogging out under the checkered sun and shade of the great trees, until six thousand men were spread in one long single front, to the right over fields and through ditches, beyond the last cultivated field, across the desert to the very base of the mountains; to the left over the roll of the flat world. The bugles blared faintly and near, and the army moved forward in a mighty line across the whole country. Above them lifted a five-mile-wide golden dust-glory. Flags flapped. In the center, level with them, came the cannon car, and beside that Villa rode with his staff. At the little villages along the way the big-hatted, white-bloused *pacificos* stood in silent wonder, watching this strange host pass. An old man drove his goats homeward. The foaming wave of troopers broke upon him, yelling with pure mischief, and all the goats ran in different directions. A mile of army shouted with laughter—the dust rolled up from their thousand hoofs, and they passed. At the village of Brittingham the great line halted, while Villa and his staff galloped up to the peons watching from their little mound.

"*Oyez!*" said Villa. "Have any troops passed through here lately?"

"*Si*, señor!" answered several men at once. "Some of Don Carlo Argumedo's *gente* went by yesterday pretty fast."

"Hum," Villa meditated. "Have you seen that bandit Pancho Villa around here?"

"No, señor!" they chorused.

"Well, he's the fellow I'm looking for. If I catch that *diablo* it will go hard with him!"

"We wish you all success!" cried the *pacificos*, politely.

"You never saw him, did you?"

"No, God forbid!" they said fervently.

"Well!" grinned Villa. "In the future when people ask if you know him you will have to admit the shameful fact! I am Pancho Villa!" And with that he spurred away, and all the army followed. . . .

# 6

# The Compañeros Reappear

Such had been the surprise of the Federals, and they had fled in such a hurry, that for many miles the railroad was intact. But toward afternoon we began to find little bridges burned and still smoking, and telegraph poles cut down with an axe—badly and hastily done bits of destruction that were easily repaired. But the army had got far ahead, and by nightfall, about eight miles from Gomez Palacio, we reached the place where eight solid miles of torn-up track began. There was no food on our train. We had only a blanket apiece; and it was cold. In the flare of torches and fires, the repair gang fell upon their work. Shouts and hammering steel, and the thud of falling ties. . . . It was a black night, with a few dim stars. We had settled down around one fire, talking and drowsing, when suddenly a new sound smote the air—a sound heavier than hammers, and deeper than the wind. It shocked—and was still. Then came a steady roll, as of distant drums, and then shock! shock! The hammers fell, voices were silent, we were frozen. Somewhere ahead, out of sight, in the darkness—so still it was that the air carried every sound—Villa and the army had flung themselves upon Gomez Palacio, and the battle had begun. It deepened steadily and slowly, until the booffs of cannon fell echoing upon each other, and the rifle fire rippled like steel rain.

"*Andale!*" screamed a hoarse voice from the roof of the cannon car. "What are you doing? Get at that track! Pancho Villa is waiting for the trains!"

And, with a yell, four hundred raging maniacs flung themselves upon the break. . . .

I remember how we besought the Colonel in command to let

171

us go to the front. He would not. Orders were strict that no one should leave the trains. We pled with him, offered him money, almost got on our knees to him. Finally he relented a little.

"At three o'clock," he said, "I'll give you the sign and counter-sign and let you go."

We curled miserably about a little fire of our own, trying to sleep, trying at least to get warm. Around us and ahead the flares and the men danced along the ruined track; and every hour or so the train would creep forward a hundred feet and stop again. It was not hard to repair—the rails were intact. A wrecker had been hitched to the right-hand rail and the ties twisted, splintered, torn from their bed. Always the monotonous and disturbing furious sound of battle filtered out of the blackness ahead. It was so tiresome, so much the same, that sound; and yet I could not sleep. . . .

About midnight one of our outposts galloped from the rear of the trains to report that a large body of horsemen had been challenged coming from the north, who said they were Urbina's *gente* from Mapimi. The Colonel didn't know of any body of troops that were to pass at that time of night. In a minute everything was a fury of preparation. Twenty-five armed and mounted men galloped like mad to the rear, with orders to stop the newcomers for fifteen minutes—if they were Constitutionalists, by order of the Colonel; if not, by holding them off as long as possible. The workmen were hurried back to the train and given their rifles. The fires were put out, the flares—all but ten—extinguished. Our guard of two hundred slipped silently into the thick brush, loading their rifles as they went. On either side of the track the Colonel and five of his men took up their posts, unarmed, with torches held high over their heads. And then, out of the thick blackness, the head of the column appeared. It was made up of different men from the well-clothed, well-equipped, well-fed soldiers of Villa's army. These were ragged, gaunt people, wrapped in faded, tattered serapes, without shoes on their feet, crowned with the heavy, picturesque sombreros of the back-country. Lasso ropes hung coiled at their saddles. Their mounts were the lean, hard, half-savage ponies of the Durango mountains. They rode sullenly, contemptuous of us. They neither knew the countersign nor cared to know it. And as they rode, whole files sang the monotonous, extemporaneous ballads that the peons compose and sing to themselves as they guard the cattle at night on the great upland plains of the north.

And, suddenly, as I stood at the head of the line of flares, a passing horse was jerked to his haunches, and a voice I knew cried: "Hey! Meester!" The enfolding serape was cast high in the air, the man fell from his horse, and in a moment I was clasped in the arms of Isidro Amaya. Behind him burst forth a chorus of shouts: "*Que tal!* Meester! O Juanito, how glad we are to see you! Where have you been? They said you were killed in La Cadena! Did you run fast from the *colorados*? *Mucha susto*, eh?" They threw themselves to the ground, clustering around, fifty men reaching at once to pat me on the back; all my dearest friends in Mexico— the *compañeros* of La Tropa and the Cadena!

The long file of men, blocked in the darkness, raised a chorus of shouts: "Move on! *Vamonos!* What's the matter? Hurry up! We can't stay here all night!" And the others yelled back: "Here's Meester! Here's the gringo we were telling you about who danced the *jota* in La Zarca! Who was in La Cadena!" And then the others crowded forward too.

There were twelve hundred of them. Silently, sullenly, eagerly, sniffing the battle ahead, they defiled between the double line of high-held torches. And every tenth man I had known before. As they passed the Colonel shouted to them: "What is the countersign? Turn your hats up in front! Do you know the countersign?" Hoarsely, exasperatedly, he bawled at them. Serenely and insolently they rode by, without paying the least attention to him. "To hell with the countersign!" they hooted, laughing at him. "We don't need any countersign! They'll know well enough which side we're on when we begin to fight!"

For hours, it seemed, they jogged past, fading into the darkness, their horses with nervous heads turned to catch the sound of the guns, the men with glowing eyes fixed on the darkness ahead—rode into battle with their ancient Springfield rifles that had seen service for three years, with their meager ten rounds of ammunition. And when they had all gone the battle seemed to brighten and quicken with new life. . . .

# The Bloody Dawn

THE steady noise of battle filled all the night. Ahead torches danced, rails clanged, sledges drummed on the spikes, the men of the repair gang shouted in the frenzy of their toil. It was after twelve. Since the trains had reached the beginning of the torn track we had made half a mile. Now and then a straggler from the main body came down the line of trains, shuffled into the light with his heavy Mauser awry across his shoulders, and faded into the darkness toward the debauch of sound in the direction of Gomez Palacio. The soldiers of our guard, squatting about their little fires in the fields, relaxed their tense expectancy; three of them were singing a little marching song, which began:

> *I don't want to be a Porfirista,*
> *I don't want to be an Orozquista,*
> *But I want to be a volunteer in the army Maderista!*

Curious and excited, we hurried up and down the trains, asking people what they knew, what they thought. I had never heard a real killing-sound before, and it made me frantic with curiosity and nervousness. We were like dogs in a yard when a dogfight is going on outside. Finally the spell snapped and I found myself desperately tired. I fell into a dead sleep on a little ledge under the lip of the cannon, where the laborers tossed their wrenches and sledge-hammers and crowbars when the train moved forward a hundred feet, and piled on themselves with shouts and horseplay.

In the coldness of before dawn I woke with the Colonel's hand on my shoulder.

"You can go now," he said. "The sign is 'Zaragosa' and the countersign 'Guerrero.' Our soldiers will be recognized by their hats pinned up in front. May you go well!"

It was bitter cold. We threw our blankets around us, serape fashion, and trudged down past the fury of the repair gang as they hammered at it under the leaping flares—past the five armed men slouching around their fire on the frontier of the dark.

"Are you off to the battle, *compañeros?*" cried one of the gang. "Look out for the bullets!" At that they all laughed. The sentries cried, "*Adios!* Don't kill them all! Leave a few *pelones* for us!"

Beyond the last torch, where the torn track was wrenched and tumbled about on the uprooted roadbed, a shadowy figure waited for us.

"*Vamonos* together," he said, peering at us. "In the dark three are an army." We stumbled along over the broken track, silently, just able to make him out with our eyes. He was a little dumpy soldier with a rifle and a half-empty cartridge belt over his breast. He said that he had just brought a wounded man from the front to the hospital train and was on his way back.

"Feel this," he said, holding out his arm. It was drenched. We could see nothing.

"Blood," he continued unemotionally. "His blood. He was my *compadre* in the Brigada Gonzales-Ortega. We went in this night down there and so many, so many——We were cut in half."

It was the first we had heard, or thought, of wounded men. All of a sudden we heard the battle. It had been going on steadily all the time, but we had forgotten—the sound was so monstrous, so monotonous. Far rifle fire came like the ripping of strong canvas, the cannon shocked like pile drivers. We were only six miles away now.

Out of the darkness loomed a little knot of men—four of them—carrying something heavy and inert in a blanket slung between. Our guide threw up his rifle and challenged, and his answer was a retching groan from the blanket.

"*Oiga compadre,*" lisped one of the bearers huskily. "Where, for the love of the Virgin, is the hospital train?"

"About a league——"

"*Valgame Dios!* How can we. . . ."

"Water! Have you any water?"

They stood with the blanket taut between them, and something fell from it, drip, drip, drip, on the ties.

That awful voice within screamed once, "To drink!" and fell away to a shuddering moan. We handed our canteens to the bearers—and silently, bestially, they drained them. The wounded man they forgot. Then, sullen, they pitched on. . . .

Others appeared, singly, or in little groups. They were simply vague shapes staggering in the night, like drunkards, like men incredibly tired. One dragged between two walkers, his arms around their shoulders. A mere boy reeled along with the limp body of his father on his back. A horse passed with his nose to the ground, two bodies flopping sideways across the saddle, and a man walking behind and beating the horse on the rump, cursing shrilly. He passed, and we could hear his falsetto fading dissonantly in the distance. Some groaned, with the ugly, deadened groan of uttermost pain; one man, slouched in the saddle of a mule, screamed mechanically every time the mule took a step. Under two tall cottonwood trees beside an irrigation ditch a little fire glowed. Three sleepers with empty cartridge belts sprawled snoring on the uneven ground; beside the fire sat a man holding with both hands his leg straight out to the warmth. It was a perfectly good leg as far as the ankle—there it ended in a ragged, oozing mess of trousers and shattered flesh. The man simply sat looking at it. He didn't even stir as we came near, and yet his chest rose and fell with calm breathing, and his mouth was slightly open as if he were daydreaming. By the side of the ditch knelt another. A soft lead bullet had entered his hand between the two middle fingers and then spread until it hollowed out a bloody cave inside. He had wrapped a rag around a little piece of stick and was unconcernedly dipping it in the water and gouging out the wound.

Soon we were near the battle. In the east, across the vast level country, a faint gray light appeared. The noble alamo trees, towering thickly in massy lines along the ditches to the west, burst into showers of bird song. It was getting warm, and there came the tranquil smell of earth and grass and growing corn—a calm summer dawn. Into this the noise of battle broke like something insane. The hysterical chatter of rifle fire, that seemed to carry a continuous undertone of screaming—although when you listened for it it was gone. The nervous, deadly stab—stab—stab—stab of the machine guns, like some gigantic woodpecker. The cannon booming like great bells, and the whistle of their shells. Boom—Pi-i-i-e-e-a-uuu! And that most terrible of all the sounds of war, shrapnel exploding. Crash—Whee-e-eaaa!!

The great hot sun swam up in the east through a faint smoke from the fertile land, and over the eastern barrens the heat waves began to wiggle. It caught the startlingly green tops of the lofty alamos fringing the ditch that paralleled the railroad on our right. The trees ended there, and beyond, the whole rampart of bare mountains, piled range on range, grew rosy. We were now in scorched desert again, thickly covered with dusty mesquite. Except for another line of alamos straggling across from east to west, close to the city, there were no trees in all the plain but two or three scattered ones to the right. So close we were, barely two miles from Gomez Palacio, that we could look down the torn track right into the town. We could see the black round water tank, and back of that the roundhouse, and across the track from them both the low adobe walls of the Brittingham Corral. The smokestacks and buildings and trees of La Esperanza soap factory rose clear and still, like a little city, to the left. Almost directly to the right of the railroad track, it seemed, the stark, stony peak of the Cerro de la Pila mounted steeply to the stone reservoir that crowned it, and sloped off westward in a series of smaller peaks, a spiny ridge a mile long. Most of Gomez lay behind the shoulder of the Cerro, and at its western end the villas and gardens of Lerdo made a vivid patch of green in the desert. The great brown mountains on the west made a mighty sweep around behind the two cities, and then fell away south again in folds on folds of gaunt desolation. And directly south from Gomez, stretched along the base of this range, lay Torreon, the richest city of northern Mexico.

The shooting never ceased, but it seemed to be subdued to a

subordinate place in a fantastic and disordered world. Up the track in the hot morning light straggled a river of wounded men, shattered, bleeding, bound up in rotting and bloody bandages, inconceivably weary. They passed us, and one even fell and lay motionless nearby in the dust—and we didn't care. Soldiers with their cartridges gone wandered aimlessly out of the chaparral, dragging their rifles, and plunged into the brush again on the other side of the railroad, black with powder, streaked with sweat, their eyes vacantly on the ground. The thin, subtle dust rose in lazy clouds at every footstep, and hung there, parching throat and eyes. A little company of horsemen jogged out of the thicket and drew up on the track, looking toward town. One man got down from his saddle and squatted beside us.

"It was terrible," he said suddenly. "*Carramba!* We went in there last night on foot. They were inside the water tank, with holes cut in the iron for rifles. We had to walk up and poke our guns through the holes and we killed them all—a death trap! And then the Corral! They had two sets of loopholes, one for the men kneeling down and the other for the men standing up. Three thousand *rurales* in there—and they had five machine guns to sweep the road. And the roundhouse, with three rows of trenches outside and subterranean passages so they could crawl under and shoot us in the back. . . . Our bombs wouldn't work, and what could we do with rifles? *Madre de Dios!* But we were so quick—we took them by surprise. We captured the roundhouse and the water tank. And then this morning thousands came—thousands—reinforcements from Torreon—and their artillery—and they drove us back again. They walked up to the water tank and poked their rifles through the holes and killed all of us—the sons of the devils!"

We could see the place as he spoke and hear the hellish roar and shriek, and yet no one moved, and there wasn't a sign of the shooting—not even smoke, except when a shrapnel shell burst yelling down in the first row of trees a mile ahead and vomited a puff of white. The cracking rip of rifle fire and the staccato machine guns and even the hammering cannon didn't reveal themselves at all. The flat, dusty plain, the trees and chimneys of

Gomez, and the stony hill, lay quietly in the heat. From the alamos off to the right came the careless song of birds. One had the impression that his senses were lying. It was an incredible dream, through which the grotesque procession of wounded filtered like ghosts in the dust.

# 8

## The Artillery Comes Up

OVER to the right, along the base of the line of trees, heavy dust billowed up, men shouted, whips snapped, and there was a rumble and a jangling of chains. We plunged into a little path that wound among the chaparral and emerged upon a tiny village, lost in the brush near the ditch. It was strikingly like a Chinese or Central American village: five or six adobe huts thatched with mud and twigs. It was called San Ramon, and there a little struggling knot of men swayed about every door, clamoring for coffee and *tortillas*, and waving fiat money. The *pacificos* squatted in their tiny corrals, selling *macuche* at exorbitant prices; their women sweated over the fire, hammering *tortillas* and pouring villainous black coffee. All around, in the open spaces, lay sleepers like the dead, and men with bloody arms and heads, tossing and groaning. Presently an officer galloped up, streaked with sweat, and screamed, "Get up, you fools! *Pendecos!* Wake up and get back to your companies! We're going to attack!" A few stirred and stumbled, cursing, to their weary feet—the others still slept. "*Hijos de la——!*" snapped the officer, and spurred his horse upon them, trampling, kicking. . . . The ground boiled men scrambling out of the way and yelling. They yawned, stretched, still half asleep, and sifted off slowly toward the front in an aimless way. . . . The wounded only dragged themselves listlessly to the shade of the brush.

Along the side of the ditch went a sort of wagon track, and up this the Constitutionalist artillery were arriving. One could see the gray heads of the straining mules, and the big hats of their drivers, and the circling whips—the rest was masked in dust.

Slower than the army, they had been marching all night. Past us rumbled the carriages and caissons, the long, heavy guns yellow with dust. The drivers and gunners were in fine good humor. One, an American, whose features were absolutely indistinguishable in the all-mantling mud of sweat and earth, shouted to know if they were in time, or if the town had fallen.

I answered in Spanish that there were lots of *colorados* yet to kill, and a cheer ran along the line.

"Now we'll show them something," cried a big Indian on a mule. "If we could get into their cursed town without guns, what can we do with them?"

The alamos ended just beyond San Ramon, and under the last trees Villa, General Angeles, and the staff sat on horseback at the bank of the ditch. Beyond that the ditch ran naked across the naked plain into the town, where it took water from the river. Villa was dressed in an old brown suit, without a collar, and an ancient felt hat. He was covered with dirt, and had been riding up and down the lines all night; but he bore no trace of fatigue.

When he saw us he called out, "Hello, *muchachos*! Well, how do you like it?"

"Fine, *mi General*!"

We were worn out and very dirty. The sight of us amused him profoundly; he never could take the correspondents seriously, anyway, and it seemed to him very droll that an American periodical would be willing to spend so much money just to get the news.

"Good," he said with a grin. "I'm glad you like it, because you're going to get all you want."

The first gun had now come opposite the staff and unlimbered, the gunners ripping off the canvas covers and tilting up the heavy caisson. The captain of the battery screwed on the telescopic sight and the crank of the raising-lever spun. The brass butts of heavy shells shone in gleaming rows; two men staggered under the weight of one, and rested it on the ground while the captain regulated the shrapnel timer. The breech lock crashed shut, and we ran far back. Craboom-shock! A soaring whistling Pi-i-i-e-e-eeuu! flew high after the shell, and then a tiny white smoke flowered at the foot of the Cerro de la Pila—and, minutes after, a far detonation. About a hundred yards apart, all along in front of the gun, picturesque ragged men stared motionless through their field glasses. They burst into a chorus of yells, "Too low! Too far to the right! Their guns are all along the ridge! Time it about fifteen seconds later!" Down front the rifle fire had frittered away to ragged sputtering and the machine guns were silent. Everybody was watching the artillery duel. It was about five-thirty in the morning, and already very hot. In the fields behind sounded the parched chirp of crickets; the lofty fresh tops of the alamos rustled in a high languid breeze; birds began to sing again.

Another gun wheeled into line, and the breechblock of the first clacked again. There came the snap of the trigger, but no roar. The gunners wrenched open the breech and hurled the smoking brass projectile on the grass. Bad shell. I saw General Angeles in his faded brown sweater, hatless, peering through the sight and cranking up the range. Villa was spurring his reluctant horse up to the caisson. Cra-boom-shock! Pi-i-i-e-e-eeuu! The other gun this time. We saw the shell burst higher up the stony hill this time. And then four booms floated to us, and, simultaneously, the enemy's shells, which had been exploding desultorily over the line of trees nearest the city, marched out into the open desert and leaped toward us in four tremendous explosions, each nearer. More guns had wheeled into line; others filed off to the right along a diagonal of trees, and a long line of heavy trucks, plunging mules, and cursing, shouting men choked up the dusty road to the rear. The unlimbered mules jingled back and the drivers threw themselves, exhausted, under the nearest chaparral.

The Federal shrapnel, well fired and excellently timed, was bursting now only a few hundred yards in front of our line, and the minute boom of their guns was almost incessant. Crash—Wheeeeaa! Over our heads, snapping viciously in the leafy trees, sang the rain of lead. Our guns replied spasmodically. The homemade shells, fashioned on converted mining machinery in Chihuahua, were not reliable. Galloped past stout Captain Marinelli, the Italian soldier of fortune, steering as near the newspapermen as possible, with a serious, Napoleonic look on his face.

He glanced once or twice at the camera man, smiling graciously, but the latter coldly looked away. With a workmanlike flourish he ordered the wheeling of his gun into position and sighted it himself. Just then a shell burst deafeningly about a hundred yards in front. The Federals were getting the range. Marinelli bounded away from his cannon, mounted his horse, limbered up and came galloping dramatically back with his gun rumbling along at a dead run behind. None of the other guns had retreated. Pulling up his foaming charger in front of the camera man, he flung himself to the ground and took a position. "Now," he said, "you can take my picture!"

"Go to hell," said the camera man, and a great shout of laughter went up along the line.

The high cracked note of a bugle thrilled through the racking roar. Immediately mules dragging their jangling limbers appeared, and shouting men. The caissons snapped shut.

"Going down front," shouted Colonel Servin. "Not hitting. Too far away here. . . ."

And the long-halted line snapped taut and wound out into the open desert, under the bursting shells.

# Battle

W<small>E</small> returned along the winding path through the mesquite, crossed the torn-up track, and struck out across the dusty plain southeastward. Looking back along the railroad I could see smoke and the round front of the first train miles away; and in front of it throngs of active little dots swarming on the right of way, distorted like things seen in a wavy mirror. We strode along in a haze of thin dust. The giant mesquite dwindled until it scarcely reached to our knees. To the right the tall hill and the chimneys of the town swam tranquilly in the hot sun; rifle fire had almost ceased for the moment, and only dazzling bursts of thick white smoke marked our occasional shells along the ridge. We could see our drab guns rocking down the plain, spreading along the first line of alamos, where the searching fingers of the enemy's shrapnel probed continually. Little bodies of horsemen moved here and there over the desert, and stragglers on foot, trailing their rifles.

An old peon, stooped with age and dressed in rags, crouched in the low shrub gathering mesquite twigs.

"Say, friend," we asked him, "is there any way we can get in close to see the fighting?"

He straightened up and stared at us.

"If you had been here as long as I have," said he, "you wouldn't care about seeing the fighting. *Carramba!* I have seen them take Torreon seven times in three years. Sometimes they attack from Gomez Palacio and sometimes from the mountains. But it is always the same—war. There is something interesting in it for the young, but for us old people, we are tired of war." He paused and stared out over the plain. "Do you see this dry ditch? Well, if you will get down in it and follow along it will lead you into the town." And then, as an afterthought, he added incuriously, "What party do you belong to?"

"The Constitutionalists."

"So. First it was the Maderistas, and then the Orozquistas, and now the—what did you call them? I am very old, and I have not long to live; but this war—it seems to me that all it accomplishes is to let us go hungry. Go with God, señores." And he bent again to his slow task, while we descended into the arroyo. It was a disused irrigation ditch running a little south of west, its bottom covered with dusty weeds, and the end of its straight length hidden from us by a sort of mirage that looked like a glaring pool of water. Stooped a little, so as to be hidden from the outside, we walked along, it seemed, for hours, the cracked bottom and dusty sides of the ditch reflecting the fierce heat upon us until we were faint with it. Once horsemen passed quite near on our right, their big iron spurs ringing; we crouched down until they passed, for we didn't want to take any chances. Down in the ditch the artillery fire sounded very faint and far away, but once I cautiously lifted my head above the bank and discovered that we were very near the first line of trees. Shells were bursting along it, and I could even see the belch of furious haze hurling out from the mouths of our cannon, and feel the surf of sound waves hit me like a blow when they fired. We were a good quarter of a mile in front of our artillery, and evidently making for the water tank on the very edge of the town. As we stooped again the shells passing overhead whined sharply and suddenly across the arc of sky and were cut off abruptly until the sullen echoless booff! of their explosion. There ahead, where the railroad trestle of the main line crossed the arroyo, huddled a little pile of bodies—evidently left from the first attack. Hardly one was bloody; their heads and hearts were pierced with the clean, tiny holes of steel Mauser bullets. They lay limply, with the unearthly calm, lean faces of the dead. Someone, perhaps their own thrifty *compañeros*, had stripped them of arms, shoes, hats and serviceable clothing. One sleeping soldier, squatting on the edge of the heap with his rifle across his knees, snored deeply. Flies covered him—the dead hummed with them. But the sun had not yet affected them. Another soldier leaned against the townward bank of the ditch, his feet resting on a corpse, banging methodically away at something he saw. Under the shadow of the trestle four men sat playing cards. They played listlessly, without talking, their eyes red with lack of sleep. The heat was frightful. Occasionally a stray bullet came by screaming, "Where—is-s-s-z—ye!" This strange company took our appearance as a matter of course. The sharpshooter doubled up out of range and carefully put another cartridge clip in his rifle.

"You haven't got another drop of water in that canteen, have you?" he asked. "*Adio!* we haven't eaten or drunk since yesterday!" He guzzled the water, furtively watching the card players lest they, too, should be thirsty. "They say that we are to attack the water tank and the Corral again when the artillery is in position to support us. Chi-*hua*hua *hombre!* but it was *duro* in the night! They slaughtered us in the streets there. . . ." He wiped his mouth on the back of his hand and began firing again. We lay beside him and looked over. We were about two hundred yards from the deadly water tank. Across the track and the wide street beyond lay the brown mud walls of the Brittingham Corral, innocent looking enough now, with only black dots to show the double line of loopholes.

"There are the machine guns," said our friend. "See them, those slim barrels peeping over the edge?" We couldn't make them out. Water tank, Corral and town lay sleeping in the heat. Dust hovered still in the air, making a thin haze. About fifty yards in front of us was a shallow exposed ditch, evidently once a Federal trench, for the dirt had been piled on our side. Two hundred drab, dusty soldiers lay in it now, facing townward—the Constitutionalist infantry. They were sprawled on the ground, in all attitudes of weariness; some sleeping on their backs, facing up to the hot sun; others wearily transferring the dirt with their scooped hands from rear to front. Before them they had piled up irregular heaps of rocks. Now infantry, in the Constitutionalist army, is simply cavalry without horses; all Villa's soldiers are mounted except the artillery, and those for whom horses cannot be procured.

Of a sudden the artillery in our rear boomed all together, and over our heads a dozen shells screamed toward the Cerro.

"That is the signal," said the man at our side. He clambered down into the ditch and kicked the sleeper. "Come on," he yelled. "Wake up. We're going to attack the *pelones*." The snorer groaned and opened his eyes slowly. He yawned and picked up his rifle without a word. The card players began to squabble about their winnings. A violent dispute broke out as to who owned the pack of cards. Grumbling and still arguing, they stumbled out and followed the sharpshooter up over the edge of the ditch.

Rifle fire rang along the edge of the trench in front. The sleepers flopped over on their stomachs behind their little shelters— their elbows worked vigorously pumping the guns. The hollow steel water tank resounded to the rain of thumping bullets; chips of adobe flew from the wall of the Corral. Instantly the wall bristled with shining barrels and the two awoke crackling with hidden vicious firing. Bullets roofed the heavens with whistling steel— drummed the smoking dust up until a yellow curtain of whirling cloud veiled us from the houses and the tank. We could see our friend running low along the ground, the sleepy man following, standing erect, still rubbing his eyes. Behind strung out the gamblers, squabbling yet. Somewhere in the rear a bugle blew. The sharpshooter running in front stopped suddenly, swaying, as if he had run against a solid wall. His left leg doubled under him and he sank crazily to one knee in the exposed flat, whipping up his rifle with a yell.

"—— the dirty monkeys!" he screamed, firing rapidly into the dust. "I'll show the ——! The cropped heads! The jailbirds!" He shook his head impatiently, like a dog with a hurt ear. Blood drops flew from it. Bellowing with rage, he shot the rest of his clip, and then slumped to the ground and thrashed to and fro for a minute. The others passed him with scarcely a look. Now the trench was boiling with men scrambling to their feet, like worms when you turn over a log. The rifle fire rattled shrilly. From behind us came running feet, and men in sandals, with blankets over their shoulders, came falling and slipping down the ditch, and scrambling up the other side—hundreds of them, it seemed. . . .

They almost hid from us the front, but through the dust and the spaces between running legs we could see the soldiers in the trench leap their barricade like a breaking wave. And then the impenetrable dust shut down and the fierce stabbing needle of the machine guns sewed the mighty jumble of sounds together. A glimpse through a rift in the cloud torn by a sudden hot gust of wind—we could see the first brown line of men reeling altogether like drunkards, and the machine guns over the wall spitting sharp, dull red in the sunshine. Then a man came running back out of it, the sweat streaming down his face, without a gun. He ran fast, half sliding, half falling, down into our ditch and up the other side. Other dim forms loomed up in the dust ahead.

"What is it? How is it going?" I cried.

He answered nothing, but ran on. Suddenly and terribly the monstrous crash and scream of shrapnel burst from the turmoil ahead. The enemy's artillery! Mechanically I listened for our guns. Except for an occasional boom they were silent. Our home-made shells were failing again. Two more shrapnel shells. Out of the dust cloud men came running back—singly, in pairs, in groups, a stampeding mob. They fell over us, around us— drowned us in a human flood, shouting, "To the alamos! To the trains! The Federation is coming!" We struggled up among them and ran, too, straight up the railroad track. . . . Behind us roared the shells searching in the dust, and the tearing musketry. And then we noticed that all the wide roadway ahead was filled with galloping horsemen, yelling shrill Indian cries and waving their rifles—the main column! We stood to one side as they whirled past, about five hundred of them—watched them stoop in their saddles and begin to shoot. The drumming of their horses' hoofs was like thunder.

"Better not go in there! It's too hot!" cried one of the infantry with a grin.

"Well, I'll bet I'm hotter," answered a horseman, and we all laughed. We walked tranquilly back along the railroad track, while the firing behind wound up to a continuous roar. A group of peons—*pacificos*—in tall sombreros, blankets and white cotton blouses, stood along here with folded arms, looking down the track toward town.

"Look out there, friends," joshed a soldier. "Don't stand there. You'll get hit."

The peons looked at each other and grinned feebly.

"But, señor," said one, "this is where we always stand when there is a battle."

A little farther along I came upon an officer—a German—wandering along, leading his horse by the bridle. "I cannot ride him any more," he said to me earnestly. "He is quite too tired. I am afraid he will die if he does not sleep." The horse, a big chestnut stallion, stumbled and swayed as he walked. Enormous tears trickled from his half-shut eyes and rolled down his nose. . . .

I was dead tired, reeling from lack of sleep and food and the terrible heat of the sun. About half a mile out I looked back and saw the enemy's shrapnel poking into the line of trees more frequently than ever. They seemed to have thoroughly got the range. And just then I saw the gray line of guns, limbered to their mules, begin to crawl out from the trees toward the rear at four or five different points. Our artillery had been shelled out of their positions. . . . I threw myself down to rest in the shade of a big mesquite bush.

Almost immediately a change seemed to come in the sound of the rifle fire, as if half of it had been suddenly cut off. At the same time twenty bugles shrilled. Rising, I noticed a line of running horsemen fleeing up the track, shouting something. More followed, galloping, at the place where the railroad passed beyond the trees on its way into town. The cavalry had been repulsed. All at once the whole plain squirmed with men, mounted and on foot, all running rearward. One man threw away his blanket, another his rifle. They thickened over the hot desert, stamping up the dust, until the flat was crowded with them. Right in front of me a horseman burst out of the brush, shouting, "The Federals are coming! To the trains! They are right behind!" The entire Constitutionalist army was routed! I caught up my blanket and took to my heels. A little way farther on I came upon a cannon abandoned in the desert, traces cut, mules gone. Underfoot were guns, cartridge belts and dozens of serapes. It was a rout. Coming to an open space, I saw ahead a large crowd of fleeing soldiers, without rifles. Suddenly three men on horseback swept across in front of them, waving their arms and yelling. "Go back!" they cried. "They aren't coming out! Go back for the love of God!" Two I didn't recognize. The other was Villa.

# 10

---

# Between Attacks

$A$BOUT a mile back the flight was stopped. I met the soldiers coming back, with the relieved expression of men who have feared an unknown danger and been suddenly set free from it. That was always Villa's power—he could explain things to the great mass of ordinary people in a way that they immediately understood. The Federals, as usual, had failed to take advantage of their opportunity to inflict a lasting defeat upon the Constitutionalists. Perhaps they feared an ambush like the one Villa had arranged at Mapula, when the victorious Federals sallied out to pursue Villa's fleeing army after the first attack on Chihuahua, and were repulsed with heavy slaughter. Anyway, they did not come out. The men came straggling back, hunting in the mesquite for their guns and blankets, and for other people's guns and blankets. You could hear them shouting and joking all over the plain. "*Oiga!* Where are you going with that rifle? That's my water bag! I dropped my serape right here by this bush, and now it's gone!"

"O Juan," cried one man to another, "I always told you I could beat you running!"

"But you didn't, *compadre*. I was a hundred meters ahead, flying through the air like a cannon ball! . . ."

The truth was that after riding twelve hours the day before, fighting all night, and all morning in the blazing sun, under the frightful strain of charging an entrenched force in the face of artillery and machine guns, without food, water or sleep, the army's nerve had suddenly given way. But from the time that they returned after the flight the ultimate result was never in doubt. The psychological crisis was past. . . .

Now the rifle fire had altogether ceased, and even cannon shots from the enemy were few and far between. At the ditch under the first line of trees our men entrenched themselves; the artillery had withdrawn to the second line of trees—a mile back; and under the grateful shade the men threw themselves heavily down and slept. The strain had snapped. As the sun rose toward noon the desert, hill and town throbbed silently in the intense heat. Sometimes an exchange of shots far to the right or left told where the outposts were exchanging compliments. But even that soon stopped. In the cotton and cornfields to the north, among the sprouting green things, insects chirped. The birds sang no more because of the heat. It was breathless. The leaves stirred in no wind.

Here and there little fires smoked, where the soldiers rolled *tortillas* from the scanty flour they had brought in their saddle-bags—and those who didn't have any swarmed around, begging a crumb. Everybody simply and generously divided the food. I was hailed from a dozen fires with "Hey, *compañero*, have you break-fasted? Here is a piece of my *tortilla*. Come and eat!" Rows of men lay flat on their stomachs along the irrigation ditch, scooping up the dirty water in their palms. Three or four miles back we could see the cannon car and the first two trains, opposite the big ranch of El Verjel, with the tireless repair gang hard at it in the hot sun. The provision train had not come up yet. . . .

Little Colonel Servin came by, perched on an immense bay horse, still dapper and fresh after the terrible work of the night. "I don't know what we shall do yet," he said. "Only the General knows that, and he never tells. But we shall not assault again until the Brigada Zaragosa returns. Benavides has had a hard battle over there at Sacramento—two hundred and fifty of ours killed, they say. And the General has sent for General Robles and General Contreras, who have been attacking from the south, to bring up all their men and join him here. . . . They say, though, that we are going to deliver a night attack next, so that their artillery won't be effective. . . ." He galloped on.

About midday thin columns of sluggish, dirty smoke began to rise from several points in the town, and toward afternoon a slow, hot wind brought to us the faintly sickening smell of crude oil mingled with scorched human flesh. The Federals were burning piles of the dead. . . .

We walked back to the trains and stormed General Benavides' private car in the Brigada Zaragosa train. The major in charge had them cook us something to eat in the General's kitchen. We ate ravenously, and afterward went over along the line of trees and slept for hours. Late in the afternoon we started once more for the front. Hundreds of soldiers and peons of the neighborhood, ravenously hungry, prowled around the trains, hoping to pick up discarded food, or slops, or anything at all to eat. They were ashamed of themselves, however, and affected a sauntering indolence when we passed. I remember that we sat for a while talking with some soldiers on the top of a boxcar, when a boy, crisscrossed with cartridge belts and lugging a huge rifle, came past beneath, his eyes searching the ground. A stale *tortilla*, half rotting, crunched into the dirt by many passing feet, caught his attention. He pounced upon it and bit a piece out. Then he looked up and saw us. "As if I were dying of hunger!" he said scornfully and tossed it away with contempt. . . .

DOWN in the shade of the alamos, across the ditch from San Ramon, the Canadian Captain Treston was bivouacked with his machine gun battery. The guns and their heavy tripods were unloaded from the mules, and all around lay the unlimbered fieldpieces, their animals grazing in the rich green fields, the men squatted around their fires or lying stretched out on the bank of the ditch. Treston waved an ashy *tortilla* he was munching and bawled, "Say, Reed! Please come here and interpret for me! I can't find my interpreters, and if we go into action I'll be in a hell of a fix! You see I don't know the damn language, and when I came down here Villa hired two interpreters to go around with me all the time. And I can't ever find the sons-of-guns; they always go off and leave me in a hole!"

I took part of the proffered delicacy and asked him if he thought there was any chance of going into action.

"I think we'll go in tonight as soon as it's dark," he answered. "Do you want to go along with the machine guns and interpret?" I said I did.

A ragged man near the fire, whom I had never seen before, rose and came across smiling.

"I thought when I looked at you that you seemed to be an *hombre* who hadn't tasted tobacco for a while. Will you take half my cigarette?" Before I could protest he produced a lopsided brown cigarette and tore it across in two pieces. . . .

The sun went gloriously down behind the notched purple mountains in front of us, and for a minute a clear fan of quivering light poured up the high arc of stainless sky. The birds awoke in the trees; leaves rustled. The fertile land exhaled a pearly mist. A dozen ragged soldiers, lying close together, began to improvise the air and words of a song about the battle of Torreon—a new ballad was being born. . . . Other singing came to us through the still, cool dusk. I felt my whole feeling going out to these gentle, simple people—so lovable they were. . . .

It was just after I had been to the ditch for a drink that Treston said casually: "By the way, one of our men found this floating in the ditch a little while ago. I can't read Spanish, so I didn't know what the word meant. You see the water from these ditches all comes from the river inside the town, so I thought it might be a Federal paper." I took it from his hand. It was a little folded white piece of wet paper, like the corner and front of a package. In large black letters was printed on the front, ARSENICO, and in smaller type, "*Cuidado! Veneno!*" "Arsenic. Beware! Poison!"

"Look here," I demanded, sitting up suddenly. "Have there been any sick people around here this evening?"

"That's funny you're asking," he said. "A good many of the men have had bad cramps in the stomach, and I don't feel altogether well. Just before you came a mule suddenly keeled over

and died in that next field, and a horse across the ditch. Fatigue or
sunstroke, probably. . . ."

Fortunately the ditch carried a large body of swiftly running
water, so the danger was not great. I explained to him that the
Federals had poisoned the ditch.

"My God," said Treston. "Perhaps that is what they were trying to tell me. About twenty people have come up to me and said
something about *envenenado*. What does that mean?"

"That's what it means," I answered. "Where can we get about
a quart of strong coffee?" We found a great can of it at the nearest
fire and felt better.

"O yes, we knew," said the men. "That is why we watered the
animals at the other ditch. We heard long ago. They say that ten
horses are dead down in front, and that many men are rolling very
sick on the ground."

An officer on horseback rode by, shouting that we were all to
go back to El Verjel and camp there beside the trains for the
night; that the general had said that everyone but the advance
guards were to get a good night's sleep out of the zone of fire, and
that the commissary train had come up and was just behind the
hospital train. Bugles sounded, and the men struggled up off the
ground, catching mules, fastening their harness on amid shouting
and braying and jingling, saddling horses and limbering guns.
Treston got on his pony and I walked along beside him. So there
was to be no night attack then. It was now almost dark. Across the
ditch we fell in with the shadowy forms of a company of soldiers
trotting northward, all muffling blankets and big hats and ringing
spurs. They hailed me. "Hey, *compañero*, where's your horse?" I
admitted I had none. "Jump up behind me then," chimed in five
or six altogether. One pulled up right beside me and I mounted
with him. We jogged on through the mesquite and across a dim,
lovely field. Someone began to sing and two more joined in. A
round, full moon bubbled up in the clear night.

"*Oiga*, how do you say *mula* in English?" asked my horseman.

"G—— d—— stubborn-fathead-mule," I told him. And for
days after entire strangers would stop me and ask me, with roars
of laughter, how the Americans said *mula*. . . .

Around the ranch of El Verjel the army was encamped. We rode into a field dotted with fires, where aimless soldiers wandered around in the dark, shouting to know where the Brigada Gonzales-Ortega was, or José Rodriguez's *gente*, or the *amitrailladoras*. Townward the artillery was unlimbering in a wide, alert half-circle, guns pointing south. To the east, the camp of Benavides' Brigada Zaragosa, just arrived from Sacramento, made an immense glow in the sky. From the direction of the provision train a long ant-like file of men bore sacks of flour, coffee, and packages of cigarettes. . . . A hundred different singing choruses swelled up into the night. . . .

It comes to my mind with particular vividness how I saw a poor poisoned horse suddenly double up and fall, thrashing; how we passed a man bent to the ground in the darkness, vomiting violently; how, after I had rolled up on the ground in my blankets, terrible cramps suddenly wrenched me, and I crawled out a way into the brush and didn't have the strength to crawl back. In fact, until gray dawn, I "rolled very sick on the ground."

# 11

## An Outpost in Action

Tuesday, early in the morning, the army was in motion again toward the front, straggling down the track and across the field. Four hundred raging demons sweated and hammered at the ruined track; the foremost train had made half a mile in the night. Horses were plenty that morning, and I bought one, saddle and all, for seventy-five pesos—about fifteen dollars in gold. Trotting down by San Ramon, I fell in with two wild-looking horsemen, in high sombreros, with little printed pictures of Our Lady of Guadelupe sewed on the crowns. They said they were going out to an outpost upon the extreme right wing, near the mountains above Lerdo, where their company was posted to hold a hill. Why should I want to come with them? Who was I, anyway? I showed them my pass, signed by Francisco Villa. They were still hostile. "Francisco Villa is nothing to us," they said. "And how do we know whether this is his name, written by him? We are of the Brigada Juarez, Calixto Contreras' *gente.*" But after a short consultation the taller grunted, "Come."

We left the protection of the trees, striking out diagonally across the ramparted cotton fields, due west, straight for a steep, high hill that already quivered in the heat. Between us and the suburbs of Gomez Palacio stretched a barren, flat plain, covered with low mesquite and cut by dry irrigation ditches. The Cerro de la Pila, with its murderous concealed artillery, lay perfectly quiet, except that up one side of it, so clear was the air, we could make out a little knot of figures dragging what looked like a cannon. Just outside of the nearest houses some horsemen were riding around; we immediately struck north, making a wide detour, carefully on the watch, for this intermediate ground was overrun by pickets and scouting parties. About a mile beyond, almost along the foot of the hill, ran the high road from the north to Lerdo. We reconnoitered this carefully from the brush. A peasant passed whistling, driving a flock of goats. On the very edge of this road, under a bush, was an earthen jar full of milk. Without the least hesitation the first soldier drew his revolver and shot. The jar split into a hundred pieces—milk spurting everywhere.

"Poisoned," he said briefly. "The first company stationed over here drank some of that stuff. Four died." We rode on.

Up on the hill crest a few black figures squatted, their rifles tilted against their knees. My companions waved to them, and we turned north along the bank of a little river that unrolled a narrow strip of green grass in the midst of desolation. The outpost was camped on both sides of the water, in a sort of meadow. I asked where the colonel was, and finally found him stretched out in the shade of a tent that he had made by hanging his serape over a bush.

"Get down from your horse, friend," he said. "I am glad to welcome you here. My house" (pointing quizzically to the roof of his tent) "is at your disposal. Here are cigarettes. There is meat cooking on the fire." Upon the meadow, fully saddled, grazed the horses of the troop, about fifty of them. The men sprawled on the grass in the shade of the mesquite, chatting and playing cards. This was a different breed of men from the well-armed, well-mounted, comparatively disciplined troops of Villa's army. They were simply peons who had risen in arms, like my friends of La Tropa—a tough, happy race of mountaineers and cowboys, among whom were many who had been bandits in the old days. Unpaid, ill-clad, undisciplined—their officers merely the bravest among them—armed only with aged Springfields and a handful of cartridges apiece, they had fought almost continuously for three years. For four months they, and the irregular troops of such guerrilla chiefs as Urbina and Robles, had held the advance around Torreon, fighting almost daily with Federal outposts and suffering all the hardships of the campaign, while the main army garrisoned Chihuahua and Juarez. These ragged men were the bravest soldiers in Villa's army.

I had lain there about fifteen minutes, watching the beef sizzle in the flames and satisfying the eager curiosity of a crowd as to my curious profession, when there was a sound of galloping, and a voice, "They're coming out of Lerdo! To horse!"

Half a hundred men reluctantly, and in a leisurely manner, made for their horses. The colonel rose, yawning. He stretched.

"—— —— the animals of Federals!" he growled. "They stay on our minds all the time. You never have time to think of more pleasant things. It's a shame they won't let us even eat our dinner!"

We were mounted soon, trotting down the bank of the stream. Far in front sounded the pin-pricking rifles. Instinctively, without order, we broke into a gallop; through the streets of a little village, where the *pacificos* stood on the roofs of their houses, looking off to the south, little bundles of their belongings beside them so they could flee if the battle went against us, for the Federals cruelly punish villages which have harbored the enemy. Beyond lay the stony little hill. We got off our horses, and throwing the reins over their heads, climbed on foot. About a dozen men already lay there, shooting spasmodically in the direction of the green bank of trees behind which lay Lerdo. Unseen scattering shots ripped from the blank desert between. About half a mile away small brown figures dodged around in the brush. A thin dust cloud showed where another detachment was marching slowly north in their rear.

"We already got one sure, and another one in the leg," said a soldier, spitting.

"How many do you make them out?" asked the colonel.

"About two hundred."

The colonel stood bolt upright, carelessly looking out over the sunny plain. Immediately a roll of shots swept along their front. A bullet chirped overhead. Already the men had gone to work, unordered. Each soldier picked out a smooth place to lie and piled up a little heap of stones in front to shield him. They lay down grunting, loosening their belts and taking off their coats to be perfectly comfortable; then they began slowly and methodically to shoot.

"There goes another," announced the colonel. "Yours, Pedro."

"Not Pedro's at all," interrupted another man fretfully. "I got him."

"O the devil you did," snapped Pedro. They quarreled. . . .

The firing from the desert was now pretty general, and we could see the Federals slipping toward us under the protection of every bush and arroyo. Our men fired slowly and carefully, aiming a long time before they pulled the trigger, for the months with scanty ammunition around Torreon had made them economical. But now every hill and bush along our line held a little knot of sharpshooters, and looking back on the wide flats and fields between the hill and the railroad, I saw innumerable single horsemen and squads of them spurring through the brush. In ten minutes we would have five hundred men with us.

The rifle fire along the line swelled and deepened until there was a solid mile of it. The Federals had stopped; now the dust clouds began slowly to move backward in the direction of Lerdo. The fire from the desert slackened. And then, from nowhere, we suddenly saw the broad-winged vultures sailing, serene and motionless, in the blue. . . .

THE colonel, his men and I democratically ate lunch in the shade of the village houses. Our meat was, of course, scorched, so we had to do the best we could with jerked beef and *piñole*, which seems to be cinnamon and bran, ground fine. I never enjoyed a meal so. . . . And when I left the men made up a double handful of cigarettes as a present.

Said the colonel: "*Amigo*, I am sorry that we had not time for a talk together. There are many things I want to ask you about your country—whether it is true, for example, that in your cities men have entirely lost the use of their legs and don't ride horseback in the streets, but are borne about in automobiles. I had a brother once who worked on the railroad track near Kansas City, and he told me wonderful things. But a man called him 'greaser' one day and shot him without that my brother did anything to him. Why is it your people don't like Mexicans? I like many Americans. I like you. Here is a gift for you." He unbuckled one of his huge iron spurs, inlaid with silver, and gave it to me. "But we never had any time here for talk. These————always annoy us, and then we have to get up and kill a few of them before we can have a moment's peace. . . ."

Under the alamo trees I found one of the photographers and a moving picture man. They were lying flat on their backs near a fire, around which squatted twenty soldiers, gorging ravenously flour *tortillas*, meat and coffee. One proudly displayed a silver wrist watch.

"That used to be my watch," explained the photographer. "You see we hadn't had anything to eat for two days, and when we came past here these boys called us and gave us the most magnificent feed I have ever tasted. After that I just couldn't help giving them a present!"

The soldiers had accepted the gift communally and were agreeing that each should wear it for two hours, from then on until the end of life. . . .

## 12

## Contreras' Men Assault

WEDNESDAY my friend the photographer and I were wandering across a field when Villa came by on his horse. He looked tired, dirty, but happy. Reining up in front of us, the motions of his body as easy and graceful as a wolf's, he grinned and said, "Well, boys, how is it going now?"

We answered that we were perfectly contented.

"I haven't time to worry about you, so you must be careful not to go into danger. It is bad—the wounded. Hundreds. They are brave, those *muchachos;* the bravest people in the world. But," he continued delightedly, "you must go and see the hospital train. There is something fine for you to write your papers about. . . ."

And truly it was a magnificent thing to see. The hospital train lay right behind the work train now. Forty boxcars, enameled inside, stenciled on the side with a big blue cross and the legend, "Servicio Sanitario," handled the wounded as they came from the front. They were fitted inside with the latest surgical appliances and manned by sixty competent American and Mexican doctors. Every night shuttle trains carried the seriously hurt back to the base hospitals at Chihuahua and Parral.

WE went down through San Ramon and beyond the end of the line of trees out across the desert. It was already stinging hot. In front a snake of rifle fire unfolded along the line, and then a machine gun, "spat-spat-spat!" As we emerged into the open a lone Mauser began cracking down to the right somewhere. We paid no attention to it at first, but pretty soon we noticed that there was a little plumping sound on the ground around us—puffs of dust flew up every few minutes.

"By God," said the photographer. "Some beggar's sniping at us."

Instinctively we both sprinted. The rifle shots came faster. It was a long distance across the plain. After a little we reduced it to a jog trot. Finally we walked along, with the dust spurting up as before, and a feeling that, after all, it wouldn't do any good to run. Then we forgot it. . . .

Half an hour later we crept through the brush a quarter of a mile from the outskirts of Gomez and came upon a tiny ranch of six or eight adobe huts, with a street running between. In the lee of one of the houses lounged and sprawled about sixty of Contreras' ragged fighters. They were playing cards and talking lazily. Down the street, just around the corner, which pointed straight as a die toward the Federal positions, a storm of bullets swept continually, whipping up the dust. These men had been on duty at the front all night. The countersign had been "no hats," and they were bareheaded in the broiling sun. They had had no sleep and no food, and there wasn't any water for half a mile.

"There is a Federal cuartel up ahead there that is firing," explained a boy about twelve years old. "We've got orders to attack when the artillery comes."

An old man squatting against the wall asked me where I came from. I said New York.

"Well," he said, "I don't know anything about New York, but I'll bet you don't see such fine cattle going through the streets as you see in the streets of Jimenez."

"You don't see any cattle in the streets of New York," I said.

He looked at me incredulously. "What, no cattle? You mean to tell me that they don't drive cattle through the streets up there? Or sheep?"

I said they didn't. He looked at me as if he thought I was a great liar; then he cast his eyes on the ground and thought deeply.

"Well," he pronounced finally, "then I don't want to go there! . . ."

Two skylarking boys started a game of tag; in a minute twenty full-grown men were chasing each other around in great glee. The card players had one short deck of torn cards, and at least eight people were trying to play some game and arguing about the rules at the top of their voices, or perhaps there weren't enough cards to go around. Four or five had crawled into the shade of the house, singing satirical love songs. All this time the steady infernal din up ahead never relented, and the bullets spattered in the dust like rain drops. Occasionally one of the men would slouch over, poke his rifle around the corner and fire. . . .

We stayed there about half an hour. Then two gray cannons came rocketing out of the brush behind and wheeled into position in a dry ditch seventy-five yards away on the left.

"I guess we're going in a minute," said the boy.

At that moment three men galloped up from the rear, evidently officers. They were entirely exposed to rifle fire over the roofs of the huts, but jerked up their horses with the shots yelling all around, contemptuous of them. The first to speak was Fierro, the superb great animal of a man who had murdered Benton.

He sneered down at the ragged soldiers from his saddle. "Well, this is a fine-looking crowd to take a city with," he said. "But we've got nobody else down here. Go in when you hear the bugle." Pulling cruelly on the bit, so that his big horse reared straight up and whirled on his hind legs, Fierro galloped off rearward, saying as he went, "Useless, those simple fools of Contreras——"

"Death to the Butcher!" said a man furiously. "That murderer killed my *compadre* in the streets of Durango—for no crime or insult! My *compadre* was very drunk, walking in front of the theater. He asked Fierro what time it was, and Fierro said, 'You ——! How dare you speak to me before I speak to you first——' "

But the bugle was blowing, and up they got, grabbing their guns. The tag game tried to stop, but couldn't. Furious card players were accusing each other of stealing the deck.

"*Oiga*, Fidencio!" cried one soldier. "I'll bet you my saddle I come back and you don't! This morning I won a nice bridle from Juan——"

"All right! *Muy bien!* My new pinto horse. . . ."

Laughing, joking, rollicking, they swept out of the shelter of the houses into the rain of steel. They scuttled awkwardly up the street, like little brown animals unused to running. Billowing dust veiled them and a hell of noise. . . .

# 13

---

# A Night Attack

Two or three of us had a sort of camp beside the ditch far up along the alamos. Our car, with its food supply, clothes and blankets, was still twenty miles back. Most of the time we went without meals. When we could manage to beg a few cans of sardines or some flour from the commissary train we were lucky. Wednesday one of the crowd had managed to get hold of tinned salmon, coffee, crackers and a big package of cigarettes; and as we cooked dinner Mexican after Mexican, passing on his way to the front, dismounted and joined us. After the most elaborate exchange of courtesies, in which we had to persuade our guest to eat hugely of the dinner we had painfully foraged for ourselves, and he had to comply out of politeness, he would mount and ride away without gratitude, though full of friendliness.

We stretched out on the bank in the golden twilight, smoking. The first train, headed by a flatcar upon which was mounted the cannon "El Niño," had now reached a point opposite the end of the second line of trees—scarcely a mile from town. As far as you could see ahead of her, the repair gang toiled on the track. All at once there came a terrific boom, and a little puff of smoke lifted from the front of the train. Far cheering scattered among the trees and fields. "El Niño," the darling of the army, had got within range at last. Now the Federals would sit up and take notice. She was a three-inch gun—the largest we had. . . . Later we found out that an exploratory engine had sallied forth from the Gomez roundhouse, and that a shot from "El Niño" had hit her square in the middle of the boiler and blown her up. . . .

We were to attack that night, they said, and long after dark I got on my horse, Bucephalus, and rode down front. The sign was "Herrera" and the countersign "Chihuahua number four." So as to be sure of recognition as one of "ours," the command was to pin your hat up behind. Everywhere the strictest orders had been sent out that no fires should be lit in the "zone of fire," and that anyone striking a match until the battle began should be shot by the sentries.

Bucephalus and I jogged slowly along in the moonless and absolutely silent night. Nowhere was there a light or a stir all over the vast plain before Gomez, except the far hammering of the tireless repair gang working on the track. In the town itself the electric lights shone brightly, and even a streetcar bound for Lerdo lost itself behind the Cerro de la Pila.

Then I heard a tiny murmuring of human voices in the darkness near the ditch ahead—evidently an outpost.

*"Quien vive?"* came a shout. And before I had a chance to answer, BANG! He fired. The bullet went past my head. *Biou!*

"No, no, you fool," drawled an exasperated voice. "Don't shoot as soon as you challenge! Wait until he gives the wrong answer! Listen to me, now." This time the formality was satisfactory to both sides and the officer said, *"Pase usted!"* But I could hear the original sentry growling, "Well, I don't see what difference it makes. I never hit anybody when I shoot. . . ."

Feeling my way carefully through the darkness, I stumbled into the rancho of San Ramon. I knew that the *pacificos* had all fled, so it surprised me to see light shining around the chinks of a door. I was thirsty and didn't care to trust the ditch. I called. A woman appeared, with a little brood of four babies clinging to her skirts. She brought water, and all of a sudden burst out with, "O señor, do you know where the guns of the Brigada Zaragosa are? My man is there, and I haven't seen him for seven days."

"Then you are not a *pacifico*?"

"Truly I am not," she returned indignantly, pointing to her children. "We belong to the artillery."

Down front the army lay stretched along the ditch at the foot of the first line of trees. In absolute darkness they whispered to

each other, waiting until the word of Villa to the advance guard a
quarter of a mile ahead should precipitate the first rifle shots.

"Where are your rifles?" I asked.

"This brigade is to use no rifles tonight," answered a voice.
"Over on the left, where they are to attack the entrenchments,
there are rifles. But we must capture the Brittingham Corral tonight, and rifles are no good. We are Contreras' men, the Brigada
Juarez. See, we have orders to walk up to the walls and throw
these bombs inside!" He held out the bomb. It was made of a
short stick of dynamite sewed in a strip of cowhide, with a fuse
stuck in one end. He went on: "General Robles' *gente* are over
there on the right. They, too, have *granados*, but rifles also. They
are going to assault the Cerro de la Pila. . . ."

And now down the warm, still night came suddenly the sound
of heavy firing from the direction of Lerdo, where Maclovio
Herrera was going in with his brigade. Almost simultaneously
from dead ahead rifle fire awoke sputtering. A man came down
the line with a lighted cigar glowing like a firefly in the hollow of
his hands.

"Light your cigarettes from this," he said, "and don't set fire to
your fuses until you're right up under the wall."

"Captain, *carramba*! It's going to be very, very *duro*! How shall
we know the right time?"

Another voice, deep, rough, spoke up in the dark.

"I'll tell you. Just come along with me."

A whispered, smothered shout of "Viva Villa!" burst from
them. On foot, holding a lighted cigar in one hand—for he never
smoked—and a bomb in the other, the General climbed the bank
of the ditch and plunged into the brush, the others pouring after
him. . . .

All along the line now the rifle fire roared, though down behind the trees I could see nothing of the attack. The artillery was
silent, the troops being too close together in the dark to permit
the use of shrapnel by either side. I rode back and over to the
right, where I climbed my horse up the steep ditch bank. From
there I could see the dancing tiny fires of the guns at Lerdo, and

scattered spurts like a string of jewels all along our front. Over to the extreme left a new and deeper noise told where Benavides was making a demonstration against Torreon proper with quick-firing guns. I stood tensely awaiting the attack.

It came with the force of an explosion. In the direction of the Brittingham Corral, which I could not see, the syncopated rhythm of four machine guns and a continuous inhuman blast of volleying rifles made the previous noise seem like the deepest silence. A quick glare reddened the heaven above, and then the shocking detonations of dynamite. I could imagine the yelling savages sweeping up the street against that withering flame, wavering, pausing, struggling on again, with Villa just in front, talking to them back over his shoulder, as he always did. Now more furious firing over to the right indicated that the attack against the Cerro de la Pila had reached the foot of the hill. And all at once on the far end of the ridge toward Lerdo, there were flashes. Maclovio must have taken Lerdo! Lo! All at once appeared a magical sight. Up the steep slope of the Cerro, around three sides of it, slowly rose a ring of fierce light. It was the steady flame of rifle fire from the attackers. The summit, too, streamed fire, which intensified as the ring converged toward it, raggeder now. A bright glare burst from the top—then another. A second later arrived the dreadful reports of cannon. They were opening upon the little line of climbing men with artillery! But still they rose upon the black hill. The ring of flame was broken now in many places, but it never faltered. So until it seemed to merge with the venomous spitting blaze at the summit. Then all at once it seemed to wither completely, and little single fireflies kept dropping down the slope—all that were left. And when I thought that all was lost, and marveled at the useless heroism of these peons who walked up a hill in the face of artillery, behold! The ring of flame was creeping slowly upward again. . . . That night they attacked the Cerro seven times on foot, and at every attack seven-eighths of them were killed. . . . All this time the infernal roaring and the play of red light over the Corral did not stop. Occasionally there seemed to come a lull, but it recommenced only more terribly. They assaulted the Corral eight times. . . . The morning that I entered Gomez, although the Federals had been steadily burning bodies for three days, they were so thick in the wide space before the Brittingham Corral that I could hardly ride through on horseback, and around the Cerro were seven distinct ridges of rebel dead. . . .

The wounded began creeping through the plain obscurely in the dense darkness. Their cries and groans could be distinctly heard, though the battle noise drowned every other sound—you could even hear the rustle of the bushes as they crept through, and their dragging feet on the sand. A horseman passed along the path below me, cursing furiously that he must leave the battle because his arm was broken, and weeping between curses. Then came a footman, who sat at the foot of my bank and nursed a hand, talking without cessation about all sorts of things to keep from a nervous breakdown.

"How brave we Mexicans are," he said drolly. "Killing each other like this! . . ."

I soon went back to camp, sick with boredom. A battle is the most boring thing in the world if it lasts any length of time. It is all the same. . . . And in the morning I went to get the news at headquarters. We had captured Lerdo, but the Cerro, the Corral and the cuartel were still the enemy's. All that slaughter for nothing!

# 14

# The Fall of Gomez Palacio

El Niño" was now within half a mile of the town, and the workmen of the repair gang labored on the last stretch of track under heavy shrapnel fire. The two cannon on the front of the trains bore all the brunt of their artillery, and bravely did they return the fire—so well, in fact, that after one Federal shell had killed ten workmen, "El Niño's" captain put two guns on the Cerro out of action. So the Federals left the trains alone and turned their attention to shelling Herrera out of Lerdo.

The Constitutionalist army was terribly shattered. In the four days' fighting about a thousand men had been killed and almost two thousand more wounded. Even the excellent hospital train was inadequate to handle the wounded. Out on the wide plain where we were the faint smell of dead bodies pervaded everything. In Gomez it must have been horrible. Thursday the smoke from twenty funeral pyres stained the sky. But Villa was more determined than ever. Gomez must be taken, and quickly. He didn't have ammunition or supplies enough for a siege, and, moreover, his name was a legend already with the enemy—wherever Pancho Villa appeared in battle, they had begun to believe it lost. And the effect on his own troops was most important, too. So he scheduled another night attack.

"The track is all repaired," reported Calzado, Superintendent of the Railways.

"Good," said Villa. "Bring up all the trains from the rear tonight, because we're going into Gomez in the morning!"

Night fell; breathless, silent night, with a sound of frogs along the ditches. Across the front of the town the soldiers lay waiting for the word to attack. Wounded, worn out, nervously broken, they straggled to the front, keyed up to the last notch of desperation. This night they would not be repulsed. They would take the town or die where they stood. And as nine o'clock approached, the hour at which the attack had been set, the tension became dangerous.

Nine o'clock came and passed—not a sound or movement. For some reason the order was withheld. Ten o'clock. Suddenly off to the right a volley burst from the town. All along our line awoke the answer, but after a few more volleys the Federal fire altogether ceased. From the town came other, more mysterious sounds. The electric lights went out and in the darkness there was a subtle stir and movement, indefinable. At length the order was given to advance, but as our men crept forward in the dark the front rank suddenly gave a yell, and the truth spread through the ranks and out into the country, in one triumphant shout. Gomez Palacio had been evacuated! With a great babble of voices the army poured into the town. A few scattered shots sounded where our troops caught some of the Federals looting—for the Federal army had gutted the whole town before it left. And then our army began to loot. Their shouts and drunken singing and the sounds of smashing doors reached us out on the plain. Little tongues of flame flickered up where the soldiers were burning some house that had been a fort of Federals. But the looting of the rebels was confined, as it almost always is, to food and drink, and clothes to cover them. They disturbed no private house.

The chiefs of the army winked at this. A specific order was issued by Villa stating that whatever any soldier picked up was his and could not be taken from him by an officer. Now up to this time there was not much of stealing in the army—at least so far as we were concerned. But the morning of the entry into Gomez a curious change had come over the psychology of the soldiers. I woke at our camp beside the ditch to find my horse gone. Bucephalus had been stolen in the night and I never saw him again. During breakfast several troopers dropped in to share our meal—when they had gone we missed a knife and a revolver. The truth was that everybody was looting from everybody else. So I, too, stole what I needed. There was a great gray mule grazing in the field nearby, with a rope around his neck. I put my saddle on him and rode down toward the front. He was a noble animal—worth at least four times as much as Bucephalus, as I soon discovered. Everybody I met coveted that mule. One trooper marching along with two rifles hailed me.

"*Oiga, compañero*, where did you get that mule?"

"I found him in a field," said I unwisely.

"It is just as I thought," he exclaimed. "That is my mule! Get off and give him to me at once!"

"And is this your saddle?" I asked.

"By the Mother of God, it is!"

"Then you lie about the mule, for the saddle is my own." I rode on, leaving him yelling in the road. A short distance farther on an old peon walking along suddenly ran up and threw his arms around the animal's neck.

"Ah, at last! My beautiful mule which I lost! My Juanito!" I shook him off in spite of his entreaties that at least I should pay him fifty pesos as compensation for his mule. In town a cavalryman rode across in front of me, demanding his mule at once. He was rather ugly and had a revolver. I got away by saying that I was a captain of artillery and that the mule belonged to my battery. Every few feet some owner of that mule sprang up and asked me how dared I ride his own dear Panchito, or Pedrito, or Tomasito! At last one came out of a cuartel with a written order from his colonel, who had seen the mule from his window. I showed them my pass signed by Francisco Villa. That was enough. . . .

Across the wide desert, where the Constitutionalists had fought so long, the army was winding in from every direction, in long snake-like columns, dust hanging over them. And along the track, as far as the eye could reach, came the trains, one after another, blowing triumphant whistles, crowded with thousands of women and soldiers cheering. Within the city, dawn had brought absolute quiet and order. With the entrance of Villa and his staff the looting had absolutely ceased and the soldiers again respected other people's property. A thousand were hard at work gathering up the bodies and carrying them to the edge of the city, where they were set on fire. Five hundred more policed the town. The first order issued was that any soldier caught drinking should be shot.

IN the third train was our car—the private boxcar fitted up for the correspondents, photographers and moving-picture men. At last we had our bunks, our blankets, and Fong, our beloved Chinese cook. The car was switched up near in the railway station—in the very front rank of trains. And as we gathered in its grateful interior, hot, dusty and worn out, the Federals in Torreon dropped a few shrapnel shells right close beside us. I was standing in the door of the car at the time and heard the boom of cannon, but paid no particular attention to it. Suddenly I noticed a small object in the air like an exaggerated beetle, trailing a little spiral of black smoke behind it. It passed the door of the car with a zzzzzing noise and about forty feet beyond burst with a frightful Crash—Whee-e-e-eeaa!! among the trees of a park where a company of cavalry and their women were camping. A hundred men leaped for their plunging horses in a panic and galloped frantically toward the rear, the women streaming after them. Two women had been killed, it seemed, and a horse. Blankets, food, rifles—all were discarded in the panic. Pow! Another burst on the other side of the car. They were very close. Behind us on the track twenty long trains, laden with shrilly screaming women, were trying to back out of the yards all at once, with a mighty hysterical tooting of whistles. Two or three more shells followed, then we could hear "El Niño" replying.

But the effect on the correspondents and newspapermen was peculiar. No sooner had the first shell exploded than someone produced the whiskey jug, entirely of his own impulse, and we passed it around. No one said a word, but everybody drank a stiff swig as it came his way. Every time a shell would explode nearby we would all wince and jump, but after a while we did not mind it. Then we began to congratulate each other and ourselves for being so brave as to stay by the car under artillery fire. Our courage increased as the firing grew far between and finally quit altogether, and as the whiskey grew low. Everybody forgot dinner.

I remember that in the darkness two belligerent Anglo-Saxons stood at the door of the car, challenging the soldiers who passed and abusing them in the most discourteous language. We fell out among ourselves, too, and one man almost choked a driveling old fool who was with the moving-picture outfit. Late that night we were still trying earnestly to persuade two of the boys not to sally forth without the password and reconnoiter the Federal lines at Torreon.

"Aw, what's there to be afraid of?" cried they. "A Mexican greaser hasn't any guts! One American can lick fifty Mexicans! Why, did you see how they ran this afternoon when the shells hit that grove? And how we—hic—we staid by the car?"

# PART V

CARRANZA—AN IMPRESSION

W HEN the Treaty of Peace was signed in Juarez which ended the Revolution of 1910, Francisco Madero proceeded south toward Mexico City. Everywhere he spoke to enthusiastic and triumphant throngs of peons, who acclaimed him The Liberator. In Chihuahua he addressed the people from the balcony of the Governor's palace. As he told of the hardships endured and the sacrifices made by the little band of men who had overthrown the dictatorship of Diaz forever, he was overcome with emotion. Reaching inside the room he pulled out a tall, bearded man of commanding presence, and throwing his arm about his shoulder, he said, in a voice choked with tears:

"This is a good man! Love and honor him always."

It was Venustiano Carranza, a man of upright life and high ideals; an aristocrat, descended from the dominant Spanish race; a great landowner, as his family had always been great landowners; and one of those Mexican nobles who, like a few French nobles such as Lafayette in the French Revolution, threw themselves heart and soul into the struggle for liberty. When the Madero Revolution broke out Carranza took the field in truly medieval fashion. He armed the peons who worked upon his great estates, and led them to war like any feudal overlord; and, when the Revolution was done, Madero made him Governor of Coahuila.

There he was when Madero was murdered at the Capital, and Huerta, seizing the Presidency, sent a circular letter to the Governors of the different States, ordering them to acknowledge the new dictatorship. Carranza refused even to answer the letter, declaring that he would have no dealings with a murderer and a usurper. He issued a proclamation calling the Mexican people to arms, proclaiming himself First Chief of the Revolution, and inviting the friends of liberty to rally around him. Then he marched out from his capital and took the field, where he assisted in the early fighting around Torreon.

After a short time Carranza marched his force from Coahuila, where things were happening, straight across the Republic into the State of Sonora, where nothing was happening. Villa had begun heavy fighting in Chihuahua State, Urbina and Herrera in Durango, Blanco and others in Coahuila, and Gonzales near Tampico. In times of upheaval like these it is inevitable that there shall be some preliminary squabbling over the ultimate spoils of war. Among the military leaders, however, there was no such dissension; Villa having just been unanimously elected General Chief of the Constitutionalist Army by a remarkable gathering of all the independent guerrilla leaders before Torreon—an unheard-of event in Mexican history. But over in Sonora, Maytorena and Pesquiera were already squabbling over who should be Governor of the State, and threatening revolutions against each other. Carranza's reported purpose in crossing to the west with his army was to settle this dispute. But that doesn't seem possible.

Other explanations are that he desired to secure a seaport for the Constitutionalists on the west; that he wanted to settle the Yaqui land question; and that in the quiet of a comparatively peaceful State he could better organize the provisional government of the new Republic. He remained there six months, apparently doing nothing whatever, keeping a force of more than 6,000 good fighters practically inoperative, attending banquets and bullfights, establishing and celebrating innumerable new national holidays, and issuing proclamations. His army, twice or three times as big as the disheartened garrisons of Guaymas and Mazatlan, kept up a lazy siege of those places. Mazatlan fell only a short time ago, I think; as did Guaymas. Only a few weeks ago Provisional Governor Maytorena was threatening counterrevolutions against General Alvardo, Chief of Arms of Sonora, because he would not guarantee the Governor's safety, and evidently proposing to upset the Revolution because Maytorena was uncomfortable in the palace at Hermosillo. During all that time not a word was said about any aspect of the land question, as far as I could learn. The Yaqui Indians, the expropriation of whose lands is the blackest spot in the whole black history of the Diaz régime, got nothing but a vague promise. Upon that the whole tribe joined the Revolution. But a few months later most of them went back to their homes and began again their hopeless campaign against the white man.

CARRANZA hibernated until early in the spring of this year, when, the purpose of his Sonora sojourn evidently having been accomplished, he turned his face toward the territory where the real Revolution was being fought.

Within that six months the aspect of things had entirely changed. Except for the northern part of Nuevo Leon, and most of Coahuila, northern Mexico was Constitutionalist territory almost from sea to sea, and Villa, with a well-armed, well-disciplined force of 10,000 men, was entering on the Torreon campaign. All this was accomplished almost single-handed by Villa; Carranza seems to have contributed nothing but congratulations. He had, indeed, formed a provisional government. An immense throng of opportunist politicians surrounded the First Chief, loud in their protestations of devotion to the Cause, liberal with proclamations, and extremely jealous of each other and of Villa. Little by little Carranza's personality seemed to be engulfed in the personality of his Cabinet, although his name remained as prominent as ever.

It was a curious situation. Correspondents who were with him during these months have told me how secluded the First Chief finally became. They almost never saw him. Very rarely did they speak with him. Various secretaries, officials, Cabinet members, stood between them and him—polite, diplomatic, devious gentlemen, who transmitted their questions to Carranza on paper and brought them back his answers written out, so that there would be no mistake.

But, whatever he did, Carranza left Villa strictly alone, to undergo defeats if he must, or make mistakes; so much so that Villa himself was forced to deal with foreign powers as if he were the head of the government.

There is no doubt that the politicians at Hermosillo sought in every way to make Carranza jealous of Villa's growing power in the north. In February the First Chief began a leisurely journey northward, accompanied by 3,000 troops, with the ostensible object of sending reinforcements to Villa and of making his provisional capital in Juarez when Villa left for Torreon. Two correspondents, however, who had been in Sonora, told me that the officers of this immense bodyguard believed that they were to be sent against Villa himself.

In Hermosillo Carranza had been remote from the world's new centers. No one knew but what he might be accomplishing great things. But when the First Chief of the Revolution began to move toward the American border, the attention of the world was concentrated upon him; and the attention of the world revealed so little to concentrate upon, that rumors rapidly spread of the nonexistence of Carranza; for example, one paper said that he was insane, and another alleged that he had disappeared altogether.

I was in Chihuahua at the time. My paper wired me these rumors and ordered me to go and find Carranza. It was at the immensely exciting time of the Benton murder. All the protestations and half-veiled threats of the British and American governments converged upon Villa. But by the time I had received the message Carranza and his Cabinet had arrived at the Border and broken the six months' silence in a startling way. The First Chief's declaration to the State Department was practically this:

"You have made a mistake in addressing representations in the Benton case to General Villa. They should be addressed to me as First Chief of the Revolution and head of the Provisional Constitutionalist Government. Moreover, the United States has no business to address, even to me, any representations concerning Benton, who was a British subject. I have received no envoy from the government of Great Britain. Until I do I will make no answer to the representations of any other government. Meanwhile, a thorough investigation will be made of the circumstances of Benton's death, and those responsible for it will be judged strictly according to law."

At the same time Villa received a pretty plain intimation that he was to keep out of international affairs, and Villa gratefully shut up.

THAT was the situation when I went to Nogales. Nogales, Arizona, and Nogales, Sonora, Mexico, really form one big straggling town. The international boundary runs along the middle of the street, and at a small customs-house lounge a few ragged Mexican sentries, smoking interminable cigarettes, and evidently interfering with nobody, except to collect export taxes from everything that passes to the American side. The inhabitants of the American town go across the line to get good things to eat, to gamble, to dance, and to feel free; the Mexicans cross to the American side when somebody is after them.

I arrived at midnight and went at once to a hotel in the Mexican town where the Cabinet and most of the political hangers-on of Carranza were staying; sleeping four in a room, on cots in the corridors, on the floor, and even on the stairs. I was expected. A temperamental Constitutionalist consul up the line, to whom I had explained my errand, evidently considered it of great importance; for he had telegraphed to Nogales that the entire fate of the Mexican Revolution depended upon Mr. Reed's seeing the First Chief of the Revolution immediately upon his arrival. However, everybody had gone to sleep, and the proprietor, routed out of his back office, said that he hadn't the slightest idea what the names of any of the gentlemen were or where they slept. Yes, he said, he had heard that Carranza was in town. We went around kicking doors and Mexicans until we stumbled upon an unshaven but courteous gentleman who said that he was the Collector of Customs for the whole of Mexico under the new government. He waked up in turn the Secretary of the Navy, who routed out the Secretary of the Treasury; the Secretary of the Treasury finally flushed the Secretary of Hacienda, who finally brought us to the room of the Secretary of Foreign Relations, Señor Isidro Fabela. Señor Fabela said that the First Chief had retired and couldn't see me; but that he himself would give me immediately a statement of just what Carranza thought about the Benton incident.

Now none of the newspapers had ever heard of Señor Fabela before. They were all clamoring to their correspondents, wanting to know who he was. He seemed to be such an important member of the provisional government, and yet his antecedents were not known at all. At different times he apparently filled most of the positions in the First Chief's Cabinet. Rather medium height and distinguished-looking, suave, courteous, and evidently very well educated, his face was decidedly Jewish. We talked for a long time, sitting on the edge of his bed. He told me what the First Chief's aims and ideals were; but in them I could discern nothing of the First Chief's personality whatever.

"Oh, yes," he said, "of course I could see the First Chief in the morning. Of course he would receive me."

But when we came right down to cases, Señor Fabela told me that the First Chief would answer no questions outright. They had all to be put in writing, he said, and submitted to Fabela first. He would then take them to Carranza and bring back his answer. Accordingly, the next morning I wrote out on paper about twenty-five questions and gave them to Fabela. He read them carefully.

"Ah!" he said, "there are many questions here that I know the First Chief will not answer. I advise you to strike them out."

"Well, if he doesn't answer them," I said, "all right. But I would like to give him a chance to see them. He could only refuse to answer them."

"No," said Fabela, politely. "You had better strike them out now. I know exactly what he will answer and what he will not. You see, some of your questions might prejudice him against answering all the rest, and you would not want that to occur, would you?"

"Señor Fabela," I said, "are you sure that you know just what Don Venustiano won't answer?"

"I know that he won't answer these," he replied, indicating four or five which dealt rather specifically with the platform of the Constitutionalist government: such as land distribution, direct elections, and the right of suffrage among the peons.

"I will bring back your answers in twenty-four hours," he said. "Now I will take you to see the Chief; but you must promise me this: that you will not ask him any questions—that you will simply go into the room, shake hands with him, and say 'How do you do,' and leave again immediately."

I promised, and, together with another reporter, followed him across the square to the beautiful little yellow municipal palace. We stood a while in the patio. The place was thronged with self-important Mexicans button-holing other self-important Mexicans who rushed from door to door with portfolios and bundles of papers. Occasionally, when the door of the Department of the Secretaryship opened, a roar of typewriters smote our ears. Officers in uniform stood about the portico waiting for orders. General Obregon, Commander of the Army of Sonora, was outlining in a loud voice the plans for his march south upon Guadalajara. He started for Hermosillo three days afterward, and marched his army four hundred miles through a friendly country in three months. Although Obregon had shown no startling capacity for leadership, Carranza had made him General-in-Chief of the Army of the North-West, with a rank equal to Villa's. Talking to him was a stout, red-haired Mexican woman in a black satin princess dress embroidered with jet, with a sword at her side. She was Colonel Ramona Flores, Chief-of-Staff to the Constitutionalist General Carrasco, who operates in Tepic. Her husband had been killed while an officer in the first Revolution, leaving her a gold mine, with the proceeds of which she had raised a regiment and taken the field. Against the wall lay two sacks of gold ingots which she had brought north to purchase arms and uniforms for her troops. Polite American concession-seekers shifted from one foot to the other, hat in hand. The ever-present arms and ammunition drummers poured into the ears of whoever would listen, praises of their guns and bullets.

Four armed sentries stood at the palace doors, and others lounged around the patio. There were no more in sight, except two who flanked a little door halfway down the corridor. These men seemed more intelligent than the others. Anybody who passed was scrutinized carefully, and those who paused at the door were questioned according to some thorough formula. Every two hours this guard was changed; the relief was in charge of a general, and a long colloquy took place before the change was effected.

"What room is that?" I asked Señor Fabela.

"That is the office of the First Chief of the Revolution," he answered.

I WAITED for perhaps an hour, and during that time I noticed that nobody entered the room except Señor Fabela and those he took with him. Finally he came over to me and said:

"All right. The First Chief will see you now."

We followed him. The soldiers on guard threw up their rifles.

"Who are these señores?" asked one.

"It's all right. They are friends," answered Fabela, and opened the door.

It was so dark within that at first we could see nothing. Over the two windows blinds were drawn. On one side was a bed, still unmade and on the other a small table covered with papers upon which stood a tray containing the remains of breakfast. A tin bucket full of ice with two or three bottles of wine stood in a corner. As our eyes became accustomed to the light, we saw the gigantic, khaki-clad figure of Don Venustiano Carranza sitting in a big chair. There was something strange in the way he sat there with his hands on the arms of the chair, as if he had been placed in it and told not to move. He did not seem to be thinking, nor to have been working—you couldn't imagine him at that table. You got the impression of a vast, inert body—a statue.

He rose to meet us, a towering figure, seven feet tall it seemed. I noticed with a kind of shock that in that dark room he wore smoked glasses, and, although ruddy and full-cheeked, I felt that he was not well—the thing you feel about tuberculous patients. That tiny, dark room, where the First Chief of the Revolution slept and ate and worked, and from which he hardly ever emerged seemed too small—like a cell.

Fabela had entered with us. He introduced us one by one to Carranza, who smiled a vacant, expressionless smile, bowed slightly, and shook our hands. We all sat down. Indicating the other reporter, who could not speak Spanish, Fabela said:

"These gentlemen have come to greet you on behalf of the great newspapers which they represent. This gentleman says that he desires to present his respectful wishes for your success."

Carranza bowed again slightly, and rose as Fabela stood up, as if to indicate that the interview was over.

"Allow me to assure the gentlemen," he said, "of my grateful acceptance of their good wishes."

Again we all shook hands; but as I took his hand I said in Spanish:

"Señor Don Venustiano, my paper is your friend and the friend of the Constitutionalists."

He stood there as before, a huge mask of a man. But as I spoke he stopped smiling. His expression remained as vacant as before, but suddenly he began to speak:

"To the United States I say the Benton case is none of your business. Benton was a British subject. I will answer to the delegates of Great Britain when they come to me with representations of their government. Why should they not come to me? England now has an Ambassador in Mexico City, who accepts invitations to dinner from Huerta, takes off his hat to him, and shakes hands with him!

"When Madero was murdered the foreign powers flocked to the spot like vultures to the dead, and fawned upon the murderer because they had a few subjects in the Republic who were petty tradesmen doing a dirty little business."

The First Chief ended as abruptly as he had begun, with the same immobility of expression, but he clenched and unclenched his hands and gnawed his mustaches. Fabela hurriedly made a move toward the door.

"The gentlemen are very grateful to you for having received

them," he said, nervously. But Don Venustiano paid no attention to him. Suddenly he began again, his voice pitched a little higher and louder:

"These cowardly nations thought they could secure advantages by standing in with the government of the usurper. But the rapid advancement of the Constitutionalists showed them their error, and now they find themselves in a predicament."

Fabela was plainly nervous.

"When does the Torreon campaign begin?" he asked, attempting to change the subject.

"The killing of Benton was due to a vicious attack on Villa by an enemy of the Revolutionists," roared the First Chief, speaking louder and louder and more rapidly; "and England, the bully of the world, finds herself unable to deal with us unless she humiliates herself by sending a representative to the Constitutionalists; so she tried to use the United States as a cat's paw. More shame to the United States," he cried, shaking his fists, "that she allowed herself to join with these infamous Powers!"

The unhappy Fabela made another attempt to dam the dangerous torrent. But Carranza took a step forward, and, raising his arm, shouted:

"I tell you that, if the United States intervenes in Mexico upon this petty excuse, intervention will not accomplish what it thinks, but will provoke a war which, besides its own consequences, will deepen a profound hatred between the United States and the whole of Latin America, a hatred which will endanger the entire political future of the United States!"

He ceased talking on a rising note, as if something inside had cut off his speech. I tried to think that here was the voice of aroused Mexico thundering at her enemies; but it seemed like nothing so much as a slightly senile old man, tired and irritated.

Then we were outside in the sunlight, with Señor Fabela agitatedly telling me not to publish what I had heard—or, at least, to let him see the dispatch.

I STAYED at Nogales a day or two longer. The next day after my interview, the typewritten paper upon which my questions had been printed was returned to me; the answers written in five different handwritings. Newspapermen were in high favor at Nogales; they were treated always with the utmost courtesy by the members of the Provisional Cabinet; but they never seemed to reach the First Chief. I tried often to get from these Cabinet members the least expression of what their plans were for the settlement of the troubles which caused the Revolution; but they seemed to have none, except a Constitutional Government. During all the times I talked with them I never detected one gleam of sympathy for, or understanding of, the peons. Now and again I surprised quarrels about who was going to fill the high posts of the new Mexican Government. Villa's name was hardly ever mentioned; when it was it was in this manner:

"We have every confidence in Villa's loyalty and obedience."

"As a fighting man Villa has done very well—very well, indeed. But he should not attempt to mingle in the affairs of Government; because, of course, you know, Villa is only an ignorant peon."

"He has said many foolish things and made many mistakes which we will have to remedy."

And scarcely a day passed but what Carranza would give out a statement from headquarters:

"There is no misunderstanding between General Villa and myself. He obeys my orders without question, as any common soldier. It is unthinkable that he would do anything else."

I SPENT a good deal of time loafing around the Municipal Palace; but I never saw Carranza again but once. It was toward sunset, and most of the Generals, drummers, and politicians had gone to dinner. I lounged on the edge of the fountain in the middle of the patio, talking with some soldiers. Suddenly the door of that little office opened, and Carranza himself stood framed in it, arms hanging loosely by his sides, his fine old head thrown back, as he stared blindly over our heads across the wall to the flaming clouds in the west. We stood up and bowed, but he didn't notice us. Walking with slow steps, he came out and went along the portico toward the door of the palace. The two guards presented arms. As he passed they shouldered their rifles and fell in behind him. At the doorway he stopped and stood there a long time, looking out on the street. The four sentries jumped to attention. The two men behind him grounded their arms and stopped. The First Chief of the Revolution clasped his hands behind his back, his fingers working violently. Then he turned, and pacing between the two guards, went back to the little dark room.

# PART VI

## MEXICAN NIGHTS

# 1

# El Cosmopolita

Eʟ Cosmopolita is Chihuahua's fashionable gambling hell. It used to be owned by Jacob La Touche—"The Turk"—a fat shambling man, who came to Chihuahua barefooted with a dancing bear twenty-five years ago, and became many times a millionaire. He owned an extravagant residence on the Paseo Bolivar, which was never called anything but "The Palace of Tears," because it was built with the proceeds of the Turk's gambling concessions, which ruined many families. But the wicked old man slunk away with Mercado's retreating Federal army; and when Villa came to Chihuahua he gave "The Palace of Tears" to General Ortega as a Christmas present, and confiscated El Cosmopolita.

Having a few idle pesos from my expense account, we used to frequent El Cosmopolita. Johnny Roberts and I stopped on our way from the hotel to take a few hot Tom-and-Jerries at a Chinese bar, run by a hoary Mongolian named Chee Lee. From there we proceeded to the gaming tables with the leisurely air of Russian Grand Dukes at Monte Carlo.

One entered first a long, low room, lighted with three smoky lanterns, where the roulette game was.

Above the table was a sign which read: *Please do not get on the roulette table with your feet.*

It was a vertical wheel, not a horizontal one, bristling with spikes which caught a flexible steel strip and finally stopped the wheel opposite a number. Each way the table extended twelve feet, always crowded with at least five rows of small boys, peons, and soldiers—excited and gesticulating, tossing a rain of small bills on the numbers and colors, and arguing violently over the winnings. Those who lost would set up terrible screams of rage as the croupier raked their money into the drawer, and often the wheel was quiet for three-quarters of an hour while some player, who had lost ten cents, exhausted his vocabulary upon the treasurer, the owner of the place and his ancestors and descendants ten generations each way, and upon God and his family, for allowing such injustice to go unpunished. Finally he would take himself off, muttering ominously: "*A ver!* We shall see!" while the others would sympathetically make way for him, murmuring: "*Ah! Que mala suerte!*"

Near where the croupier sat was a worn place in the cloth with a small ivory button in the center. And when anyone was winning largely at the wheel the croupier would press this little button, which stopped the wheel where he wished, until the winner was discouraged from playing further. This was looked upon as perfectly legitimate by all present, since, *carramba!* there is no sense in operating a gambling house at a loss!

The most amazing diversity of money was used. Silver and copper had long since been forced out of circulation in Chihuahua because of revolutionary hard times. But there were still some Mexican bank bills; besides those there was fiat money, printed on ordinary writing paper by the Constitutionalist army, and worth nothing; scrip issued by the mining companies; I. O. U.'s; notes of hand; mortgages; and a hundred different *vales* of various railroads, plantations, and public service corporations.

But the roulette table did not long interest us. There was not enough action for your money. So we shouldered our way into a small room, blue with smoke, where a perpetual poker game was going at a fan-shaped, baize-covered table. At a little recess at the straight side of the table sat the dealer; chairs were distributed around the circumference where the players sat. One played against the bank, the dealer scraping into the drawer a tenth of every pot—the house's commission. Whenever anyone began to plunge, and displayed a large wad, the dealer would give a shrill, penetrating whistle and two suave gentlemen, who were employed by the house, would come running and take a hand. There was no limit as long as you had chips, or if your stack was under-laid with bank bills. The gentleman in possession of the "buck" had the say whether it was to be draw poker (*cerrado*) or stud (*abierto*). Stud was the most fun, because a Mexican could never realize that the next card would not give him a magnificent hand, and he bet increasing amounts on every card with wildly growing excitement.

The strict rules of the American game, which so restrict free-dom of action, were absent here. Johnny and I would lift a corner of our cards as soon as they were dealt, to show each other. And when I seemed to be drawing ahead Johnny would impulsively push his whole stack over to me; with the next card Johnny's hand would seem to have more promise than mine, and I would push both stacks back to him. By the time the last card was dealt all the chips would be laying neutrally between us, and whoever had the best hand bet our entire joint capital.

Of course nobody objected to this way of playing, but to offset it the dealer would whistle shrilly to the two house players and slyly deal them each a hand off the bottom of the pack.

Meanwhile a Chinaman would be dashing madly between the table and a lunch counter across the street, bearing sandwiches, *chile con carne*, and cups of coffee to the players, who ate and drank loudly during the game, and spilled coffee and food into the jack pot.

Occasionally some player who had traveled extensively in for-eign lands got up and walked around his chair to dispel a run of bad luck; or asked for a new deck with an offhand, expensive air. The dealer would bow politely, sweep the deck into his drawer and produce another one. He had only two decks of cards in the house. Both were about a year old, and largely decorated with the meals of former players.

Of course, the American game was played. But there would sometimes enter a Mexican who was not intimately acquainted with the subtleties of the American deck. In the Mexican deck, for example, the seven, eight and nine spots are omitted. One such person, a pompous, pretentious Mexican, sat in one night just as I had called for a hand of stud. Before the dealer could whistle, the stranger had produced a great wad of money—all sorts, sizes and denominations, and bought one hundred pesos' worth of chips. The game was on. I drew three hearts in rapid succession, secured Roberts' pile, and began to play for a flush. The stranger gazed at his cards for a long time as if they were new to him. Then he flushed the deep red of intense excitement, and pushed in fifteen dollars. With the succeeding card he turned quite pale and pushed in twenty-five dollars, and when he looked at his last card he turned red again, and bet fifty dollars.

By some miracle I had filled a flush. But the man's wild betting scared me. I knew that a flush was good for almost anything in stud poker, but I couldn't keep up with that pace, so I passed the bet to him. He rose at that and protested violently.

"How do you mean 'Pass the bet'?" he cried, shaking both fists.

It was explained to him, and he subsided.

"Very well, then," he said. "Since this fifteen dollars is all I have, and you will not let me buy any more chips, I will bet everything," and he pushed it into the center.

I called him.

"What have you got?" he almost screamed, leaning trembling over the table. I spread out my flush. With an excited laugh he banged the table a great blow.

"Straight!" he cried—and turned up four, five, six, ten, Jack.

He had already reached out an arm to gather in the money when the entire table burst into a clamor.

"It is wrong!"

"It is not a straight!"

"The money belongs to the gringo!"

He lay sprawled out on the table with both arms round the pot.

"How?" he cried sharply, looking up. "It is not a straight? Look here—four, five, six, ten, knave!"

The dealer interposed:

"But it should have been four, five, six, seven, eight," he said. "In the American pack there are seven, eight and nine."

"How ridiculous!" sneered the man. "I have played cards all my life, and never, never have I seen a seven, eight or nine!"

By this time most of the roulette table throng had swarmed in at the door. They added their clamor to ours.

"Of course it is not a straight!"

"Of course it must be! Is there not four, five, six, ten, knave?"

"But the American pack is different!"

"But this is not the United States. This is Mexico!"

"Hey! Pancho!" shouted the dealer. "Go at once and notify the police!"

The situation remained the same. My opponent still lay upon the table with the jack pot in his arms. A perfect pandemonium of argument filled the place; in some cases it had developed a personal note, and hands were stealing to hips. I unobtrusively pushed my chair against the wall. Presently the Chief of Police arrived with four or five gendarmes. He was a large, unshaven man whose mustaches twisted up to his eyes; dressed in a loose, dirty uniform with red plush epaulettes. As he came in everybody began explaining to him at once. The dealer made a megaphone out of his hands and shouted through the din; the man on the table turned up a livid face, insisting shrilly that it was an outrage for gringo rules to spoil a perfectly good Mexican game like stud poker.

The chief listened, curling his mustaches, his chest swelling with the importance of being the deciding factor in an argument involving such large sums of money. He looked at me. I said nothing, but bowed politely. He returned the bow. Then, turning to his policeman he pointed a dramatic finger at the man at the table.

"Arrest this goat!" he said.

It was a fitting climax. Shrieking and protesting, the unfortunate Mexican was led into a corner, where he stood facing the table.

"The money belongs to this gentleman," continued the Chief of Police. "As for you, you evidently do not understand the rudiments of this game. I have a mind. . . ."

"Perhaps," said Roberts, politely, nudging me, "the Señor Captain would like to show the gentleman. . . . ?"

"I should be only too glad to loan him a few chips," I added, raking in the pile.

"*Oiga!*" said the Chief. "I will be glad to do so. Superlative thanks, sir!"

He drew up a chair, and, out of politeness, the buck was given to him.

"*Abierto!*" he said, with the air of an old hand.

We played. The Chief of Police won. He rattled his chips like a professional gambler, slapping the buck to his neighbor, and we played again.

"You see," said the Chief of Police, "it is easy if you observe the rules." He twisted his mustache, ruffled the cards, and pushed in twenty-five dollars. He won again.

After some time one of the policemen approached him respectfully and said:

"I beg your pardon, *mi Capitan*, but what shall we do with the prisoner?"

"Oh!" said the Chief, staring. He waved his hand casually. "Just release him and return to your stations."

Long after the last wheel had been spun on the roulette table, the lamps blown out, and the most feverish gambler ejected into the street, we sat playing in the poker room. Roberts and I were down to about three pesos apiece. We yawned and nodded with sleepiness. But the Chief of Police had his coat off and was crouched like a tiger over his cards. Now he was losing steadily. . . .

# 2

# Happy Valley

Iт happened to be the day of a fiesta, and, of course, nobody worked in Valle Allegre. The cockfight was to take place at high noon in the open space back of Catarino Cabrera's drinking shop—almost directly in front of Dionysio Aguirre's, where the long burro pack-trains rest on their mountain journeys, and the muleteers swap tales over their *tequila*. At one, the sunny side of the dry arroyo that is called a street was lined with double rows of squatting peons—silent, dreamily sucking their corn-husk cigarettes as they waited. The bibulously inclined drifted in and out of Catarino's, whence came a cloud of tobacco smoke and a strong reek of *aguardiente*. Small boys played leapfrog with a large yellow sow, and on opposite sides of the arroyo the competing roosters, tethered by the leg, crew defiantly. One of the owners, an ingratiating, business-like professional, wearing sandals and one cerise sock, stalked around with a handful of dirty bank bills, shouting:

"*Diez pesos*, señores! Only ten dollars!"

It was strange; nobody seemed too poor to bet ten dollars. It came on toward two o'clock, and still no one moved, except to follow the sun a few feet as it swung the black edge of the shadow eastward. The shadow was very cold, and the sun white hot.

On the edge of the shadow lay Ignacio, the violinist, wrapped in a tattered serape, sleeping off a drunk. He can play one tune when intoxicated—Tosti's "Good-Bye." When very drunk he also remembers fragments of Mendelssohn's "Spring Song." In fact, he is the only highbrow musician in the whole State of Durango, and possesses a just celebrity. Ignacio used to be brilliant and industrious—his sons and daughters are innumerable—but the artistic temperament was too much for him.

The color of the street was red—deep, rich, red clay—and the open space where the burros stood, olive drab; there were brown crumbling adobe walls and squat houses, their roofs heaped high with yellow cornstalks or hung with strings of red peppers. A gigantic green mesquite tree, with roots like a chicken's foot, thatched on every branch with dried hay and corn. Below, the town fell steeply down the arroyo, roofs tumbled together like blocks, with flowers and grass growing on them, blue feathers of smoke waving from the chimneys, and occasional palms sticking up between. They fell away to the yellow plain where the horse races are run, and beyond that the barren mountains crouched, tawny as lions, then faintly blue, then purple and wrinkled, notched and jagged across the fierce, bright sky. Straight down and away through the arroyo one saw a great valley, like an elephant's hide, where the heat waves buck-jumped.

A lazy smoke of human noises floated up: roosters crowing, pigs grunting, burros giving great racking sobs, the rustling crackle of dried cornstalks being shaken out of the mesquite tree, a woman singing as she mashed her corn on the stones, the wailing of a myriad of babies.

The sun fairly blistered. My friend Atanacio sat upon the sidewalk thinking of nothing. His dirty feet were bare except for sandals, his mighty sombrero was of a faded dull brick color embroidered with tarnished gold braid, and his serape was of the pottery blue one sees in Chinese rugs, and decorated with yellow suns. He rose when he saw me. We removed our hats and embraced after the Mexican fashion, patting each other on the back with one hand while we shook the other.

"*Buenas tardes, amigo,*" he murmured. "How do you seat yourself?"

"Very well, much thanks. And you? How have they treated you?"

"Delicious. Superlative thanks. I have longed to see you again."

"And your family? How are they?" (It is considered more delicate in Mexico not to ask about one's wife, because so few people are married.)

"Their health is of the best. Great, great thanks. And your family?"

"*Bien, bien!* I saw your son with the army at Jimenez. He gave me many, many remembrances of you. Would you desire a cigarette?"

"Thanks. Permit me, a light. You are in Valle Allegre many days?"

"For the fiesta only, señor."

"I hope your visit is fortunate, señor. My house is at your orders."

"Thanks. How is it that I did not see you at the *baile* last night, señor? You, who were always such a sympathetic dancer!"

"Unhappily Juanita is gone to visit her mother in El Oro, and now, therefore, I am a *platónico.* I grow too old for the señoritas."

"Ah, no, señor. A *caballero* of your age is in the prime of life. But tell me. Is it true what I hear, that the Maderistas are now at Mapimi?"

"*Si,* señor. Soon Villa will take Torreon, they say, and then it is only a matter of a few months before the Revolution is accomplished."

"I think that, yes. But tell me; I have great respect for your opinion. Which cock would you advise me to bet on?"

We approached the combatants and looked them over, while their owners clamored in our ears. They sat upon the curbing negligently herding their birds apart. It was getting toward three of the afternoon.

"But will there be a cockfight?" I asked them.

"*Quien sabe?*" drawled one.

The other murmured that possibly it would be *mañana.* It developed that the steel spurs had been forgotten in El Oro, and that a small boy had gone after them on a burro. It was six miles over the mountains to El Oro.

However, no one was in any hurry, so we sat down also. Appeared then Catarino Cabrera, the saloon keeper, and also the Constitutionalist *jefe politico* of Valle Allegre, very drunk, walking arm in arm with Don Priciliano Saucedes, the former *jefe* under the Diaz government. Don Priciliano is a fine-looking, white-haired old Castilian who used to lend money to the peons at twenty percent. Don Catarino is a former schoolmaster, an ardent Revolutionist—he lends money at a slightly less rate of usury to the same parties. Don Catarino wears no collar, but he sports a revolver and two cartridge belts. Don Priciliano during the first Revolution was deprived of most of his property by the Maderistas of the town, and then strapped naked upon his horse and beaten upon his bare back with the flat of a sword.

"*Aie!*" he says to my question. "The Revolution! I have most of the Revolution upon my back!"

And the two pass on to Don Priciliano's house, where Catarino is courting a beautiful daughter.

Then, with the thunder of hoofs, dashes up the gay and gallant young Jesus Triano, who was a Captain under Orozco. But Valle Allegre is a three days' ride from the railroad, and politics are not a burning issue there; so Jesus rides his stolen horse with impunity around the streets. He is a large young man with shining teeth, a rifle and bandolier, and leather trousers fastened up the side with buttons as big as dollars—his spurs are twice as big. They say that his dashing ways and the fact that he shot Emetario Flores in the back have won him the hand of Dolores, youngest daughter of Manuel Paredes, the charcoal contractor. He plunges down the arroyo at a gallop, his horse tossing bloody froth from the cruel curb.

Captain Adolfo Melendez, of the Constitutionalist army, slouches around the corner in a new, bottle-green corduroy uniform. He wears a handsome gilded sword which once belonged to the Knights of Pythias. Adolfo came to Valle Allegre on a two weeks' leave, which he prolonged indefinitely in order to take to himself a wife—the fourteen-year-old daughter of a village aristocrat. They say that his wedding was magnificent beyond belief, two priests officiating and the service lasting an hour more than necessary. But this may have been good economy on Adolfo's part, since he already had one wife in Chihuahua, another in Parral, and a third in Monterey, and, of course, had to placate the parents of the bride. He had now been away from his regiment three months, and told me simply that he thought they had forgotten all about him by this time.

AT half past four a thunder of cheers announced the arrival of the small boy with the steel spurs. It seems that he had got into a card game at El Oro, and had temporarily forgotten his errand.

But, of course, nothing was said about it. He had arrived, which was the important thing. We formed a wide ring in the open space where the burros stood, and the two owners began to "throw" their birds. But at the first onslaught the fowl upon which we had all bet our money spread its wings, and, to the astonishment of the assembled company, soared screaming over the mesquite tree and disappeared toward the mountains. Ten minutes later the two owners unconcernedly divided the proceeds before our eyes, and we strolled home well content.

Fidencio and I dined at Charlie Chee's hotel. Throughout Mexico, in every little town, you will find Chinamen monopolizing the hotel and restaurant business. Charlie, and his cousin Foo, were both married to the daughters of respectable Mexican villagers. No one seemed to think that strange. Mexicans appear to have no race prejudices whatever. Captain Adolfo, in a bright yellow khaki uniform and another sword, brought his bride, a faintly pretty brown girl with her hair in a bang, wearing chandelier lusters as earrings. Charlie banged down in front of each of us a quart bottle of *aguardiente*, and, sitting down at the table, flirted politely with Señora Melendez, while Foo served dinner, enlivened with gay social chatter in pidgin Mexican.

It seemed that there was to be a *baile* at Don Priciliano's that evening, and Charlie politely offered to teach Adolfo's wife a new step which he had learned in El Paso, called the Turkey Trot. This he did until Adolfo began to look sullen and announced that he didn't think he would go to Don Priciliano's, since he considered it a bad thing for young wives to be seen much in public. Charlie and Foo also tendered their regrets, because several of their countrymen were due in the village that evening from Parral, and said that they would, of course, want to raise a little Chinese hell together.

So Fidencio and I finally departed, after solemnly promising that we would return in time for the Chinese festivities after the dance.

Outside, strong moonlight flooded all the village. The jumbled roofs were so many tipped-up silvery planes, and the treetops glistened. Like a frozen cataract the arroyo fell away, and the great valley beyond lay drowned in rich, soft mist. The life sounds quickened in the dark-excited laughter of young girls, a woman catching her breath at a window to the swift, hot torrent of a man's speech as he leaned against the bars, a dozen guitars syncopating each other, a young buck hurrying to meet his *novia*, spurs ringing clear. It was cold. As we passed Cabrera's door a hot, smoky, alcoholic breath smote us. Beyond that you crossed on stepping stones the stream where the women wash their clothes. Climbing the other bank we saw the brilliant windows of Don Priciliano's house, and heard the far strains of Valle Allegre's orchestra.

Open doors and windows were choked with men—tall, dark, silent peons, wrapped to the eyes in their blankets, staring at the dance with eager and solemn eyes, a forest of sombreros.

Now Fidencio had just returned to Valle Allegre after a long absence, and as we stood on the outside of the group a tall young fellow caught sight of him, and, whirling his serape like a wing, he embraced my friend, crying:

"Happy return, Fidencio! We looked for you many months!"

The crowd swayed and rocked like a windy wheat field, blankets flapped dark against the night. They took up the cry:

"Fidencio! Fidencio is here! Your Carmencita is inside, Fidencio. You had better look out for your sweetheart! You can't stay away as long as that and expect her to remain faithful to you!"

Those inside caught the cry and echoed it, and the dance, which had just begun, stopped suddenly. The peons formed a lane through which we passed, patting us on the back with little words of welcome and affection; and at the door a dozen friends crowded forward to hug us, faces alight with pleasure.

Carmencita, a dumpy, small Indian girl, dressed in a screaming blue ready-made dress that didn't fit, stood over near the corner by the side of a certain Pablito, her partner, a half-breed youth about sixteen years old with a bad complexion. She affected to pay no attention to Fidencio's arrival, but stood dumbly, with her eyes on the ground, as is proper for unmarried Mexican women.

Fidencio swaggered among his *compadres* in true manly fashion for a few minutes, interspersing his conversation with loud virile oaths. Then, in a lordly manner, he went straight across the room to Carmencita, placed her left hand within the hollow of his right arm, and cried: "Well, now; let's dance!" and the grinning, perspiring musicians nodded and fell to.

There were five of them—two violins, a cornet, a flute and a harp. They swung into *"Tres Piedras,"* and the couples fell in line, marching solemnly round the room. After parading round twice they fell to dancing, hopping awkwardly over the rough, hard, packed-dirt floor with jingling spurs; when they had danced around the room two or three times they walked again, then danced, then walked, then danced, so that each number took about an hour.

It was a long, low room, with whitewashed walls and a beamed ceiling wattled with mud above, and at one end was the inevitable sewing machine, closed now, and converted into a sort of an altar by a tiny embroidered cloth upon which burned a perpetual rush flame before a tawdry color print of the Virgin which hung on the wall. Don Priciliano and his wife, who was nursing a baby at her breast, beamed from chairs at the other end. Innumerable candles had been heated on one side and stuck against the wall all around, whence they trailed sooty snakes above them on the white. The men made a prodigious stamping and clinking as they danced, shouting boisterously to one another. The women kept their eyes on the floor and did not speak.

I caught sight of the pimply youth glowering with folded arms upon Fidencio from his corner; and as I stood by the door, fragments of the peons' conversation floated in to me:

"Fidencio should not have stayed away so long."

"*Carramba!* See the way Pablito scowls there. He thought surely Fidencio was dead and that Carmencita was his own!"

And then a hopeful voice:

"Perhaps there will be trouble!"

The dance finally ended and Fidencio led his betrothed correctly back to her seat against the wall. The music stopped. The men poured out into the night where, in the flare of a torch, the owner of the losing rooster sold bottles of strong drink. We toasted each other boisterously in the sharp dark. The mountains around stood dazzling in the moon. And then, for the intervals between dances were very short, we heard the music erupt again, volcanically and exuberantly, into a waltz. The center of twenty curious and enthusiastic youths—for he had traveled—Fidencio strutted back into the room. He went straight to Carmencita, but as he led her out upon the floor Pablito glided up behind, pulling out a large obsolete revolver. A dozen shouts rang:

"*Cuidado,* Fidencio! Look out!"

He whirled, to see the revolver pointed at his stomach. For a moment no one moved. Fidencio and his rival looked at each other with wrathful eyes. There was a subdued clicking of automatics everywhere as the gentlemen drew and cocked their weapons, for some of them were friends of Pablito's. I heard low voices muttering:

"Porfirio! Go home and get my shotgun!"

"Victoriano! My new rifle! It lies on the bureau in mother's room."

A shoal of small boys like flying fish scattered through the moonlight to get firearms. Meanwhile, the *status quo* was preserved. The peons had squatted out of the range of fire, so that just their eyes showed above the window sills, where they watched proceedings with joyous interest. Most of the musicians were edging toward the nearest window; the harpist, however, had dropped down behind his instrument. Don Priciliano and his wife, still nursing the infant, rose and majestically made their way to some interior part of the house. It was none of their business; besides, they did not wish to interfere with the young folks' pleasure.

With one arm Fidencio carefully pushed Carmencita away, holding his other hand poised like a claw. In the dead silence he said:

"You little goat! Don't stand there pointing that thing at me if you're afraid to shoot it! Pull the trigger while I am unarmed! I am not afraid to die, even at the hand of a weak little fool who doesn't know when to use a gun!"

The boy's face twisted hatefully, and I thought he was going to shoot.

"Ah!" murmured the peons. "Now! Now is the time!"

But he didn't. After a few minutes his hand wavered, and with a curse he jammed the pistol back into his pocket. The peons straightened up again and crowded disappointedly around the doors and windows. The harpist got up and began to tune his harp. There was much thrusting back of revolvers into holsters, and the sprightly social conversation grew up again. By the time the small boys arrived with a perfect arsenal of rifles and shotguns, the dance had been resumed. So the guns were stacked in a corner.

As long as Carmencita claimed his amorous attention and there was a prospect of friction, Fidencio stayed. He swaggered among the men and basked in the admiration of the ladies, outdancing them all in speed, abandon and noise.

But he soon tired of that, and the excitement of meeting Carmencita palled upon him. So he went out into the moonlight again and up the arroyo, to take part in Charlie Chee's celebration.

As we approached the hotel we were conscious of a curious low moaning sound which seemed akin to music. The dinner table had been removed from the dining room into the street, and around the room turkey-trotted Foo and another Celestial. A barrel of *aguardiente* had been set up on a trestle in one corner, and beneath it sprawled Charlie himself, in his mouth a glass tube which syphoned up into the barrel. A tremendous wooden box of Mexican cigarettes had been smashed open on one side, the packages tumbling out upon the floor. In other parts of the room two more Chinamen slept the profound sleep of the very drunk, wrapped in blankets. The two who danced sang meanwhile their own version of a once popular ragtime song called "Dreamy Eyes." Against this marched magnificently "The Pilgrim's Chorus" from *Tannhäuser*, rendered by a phonograph set up in the kitchen. Charlie removed the glass tube from his mouth, put a thumb over it, and welcomed us with a hymn which he sang as follows:

> *Pooll for the shore, sailor,*
> *Pooll for the shore!*
> *Heed not the lowling lave*
> *But pooll for the shore!*

He surveyed us with a bleary eye, and remarked: "Bledlau! Je' Calist is wid us here toni'!"

After which he returned the syphon to his mouth.

We blended into these festivities. Fidencio offered to exhibit the steps of a new Spanish *fandango*, the way it was danced by the damned "grasshoppers" (as Mexicans call the Spaniards). He stamped bellowing around the room, colliding with the Chinamen, and roaring "La Paloma." Finally, out of breath, he collapsed upon a nearby chair, and began to descant upon the many charms of Adolfo's bride, whom he had seen for the first time that day. He declared that it was a shame for so young and blithe a spirit to be tied to a middle-aged man; he said that he himself represented youth, strength and gallantry, and was a much more fitting mate for her. He added that as the evening advanced he found that he desired her more and more. Charlie Chee, with the glass tube in his mouth, nodded intelligently at each of these statements. I had a happy thought. Why not send for Adolfo and his wife and invite them to join our festivities? The Chinamen asleep on the floor were kicked awake and their opinion asked. Since they could understand neither Spanish nor English, they answered fluently in Chinese. Fidencio translated.

"They say," he said, "that Charlie ought to be sent with the invitation."

We agreed to that. Charlie rose, while Foo took his place at the glass tube. He declared that he would invite them in the most irresistible terms, and, strapping on his revolver, disappeared. Ten minutes later we heard five shots. We discussed the matter at length, not understanding why there should be any artillery at that time of night, except that probably two guests returning from the *baile* were murdering each other before going to bed. Charlie took a long time, in the meanwhile, and we were just considering the advisability of sending out an expedition to find him when he returned.

"Well, how about it, Charlie?" I asked. "Will they come?"

"I don't think so," he replied doubtfully, swaying in the doorway.

"Did you hear the shooting?" asked Fidencio.

"Yes, very close," said Charlie. "Foo, if you will kindly get out from under that tube. . . ."

"What was it?" we asked.

"Well," said Charlie, "I knocked at Adolfo's door and said we were having a party down here and wanted him to come. He shot at me three times and I shot at him twice."

So saying, Charlie seized Foo by the leg and composedly lay down under the glass tube again.

We must have stayed there some hours after that. I remember that toward morning Ignacio came in and played us Tosti's "Good-bye," to which all the Chinamen danced solemnly around.

At about four o'clock Atanacio appeared. He burst open the door and stood there very white, with a gun in one hand.

"Friends," he said, "a most disagreeable thing has happened. My wife, Juanita, returned from her mother's about midnight on an ass. She was stopped on the road by a man muffled up in a *poncho*, who gave her an anonymous letter in which were detailed all my little amusements when I last went for recreation to Juarez. I have seen the letter. It is astonishingly accurate! It tells how I went to supper with Maria and then home with her. It tells how I took Ana to the bullfight. It describes the hair, complexion and disposition of all those other ladies and how much money I spent upon them. *Carramba!* It is exact to a cent!

"When she got home I happened to be down at Catarino's taking a cup with an old friend. This mysterious stranger appeared at the kitchen door with another letter in which he said I had three more wives in Chihuahua, which, God knows, is not true, since I only have one!

"It is not that I care, *amigos*, but these things have upset Juanita horribly. Of course, I denied these charges, but, *valgame Dios!* women are so unreasonable!

"I hired Dionysio to watch my house, but he has gone to the *baile*, and so, arousing and dressing my small son, that he may carry me word of any further outrages, I have come down to seek your help in preserving my home from this disgrace."

We declared ourselves willing to do anything for Atanacio— anything, that is, that promised excitement. We said that it was horrible, that the evil stranger ought to be exterminated.

"Who could it be?"

Atanacio replied that it was probably Flores, who had had a baby by his wife before he married her, but who had never succeeded in quite capturing her affections. We forced *aguardiente* upon him and he drank moodily. Charlie Chee was pried loose from the glass tube, where Foo took his place, and sent for weapons. And in ten minutes he returned with seven loaded revolvers of different makes.

Almost immediately came a furious pounding on the door, and Atanacio's young son flung himself in.

"Papa!" he cried, holding out a paper. "Here is another one! The man knocked at the back door, and when Mamma went to find out who it was she could only see a big red blanket covering him entirely up to the hair. He gave her a note and ran away, taking a loaf of bread off the window."

With trembling hands Atanacio unfolded the paper and read aloud:

Your husband is the father of forty-five small children in the State of Coahuila.

(Signed)    Some One Who Knows Him.

"Mother of God!" cried Atanacio, springing to his feet, in a transport of grief and rage. "It is a lie! I have always discriminated! Forward, my friends! Let us protect our homes!"

Seizing our revolvers we rushed out into the night. We staggered panting up the steep hill to Atanacio's house—sticking close together so no one would be mistaken by the others for the Mysterious Stranger. Atanacio's wife was lying on the bed weeping hysterically. We scattered into the brush and poked into the alleys around the house, but nothing stirred. In a corner of the corral lay Dionysio, the watchman, fast asleep, his rifle by his side. We passed on up the hill until we came to the edge of the town. Already dawn was coming. A never-ending chorus of roosters made the only sound, except the incredibly soft music from the *baile* at Don Priciliano's, which would probably last all that day and the next night. Afar, the big valley was like a great map, quiet, distinct, immense. Every wall corner, tree branch and grass blade on the roofs of the houses were pricked out in the wonderful clear light of before-dawn.

In the distance, over the shoulder of the red mountain, went a man covered up in a red serape.

"Aha!" cried Atanacio. "There he goes!"

And with one accord we opened up on the red blanket. There were five of us, and we had six shots apiece. They echoed fearfully among the houses and clapped from mountain to mountain, reproduced each one a hundred times. Of a sudden the village belched half-dressed men and women and children. They evidently thought that a new revolution was beginning. A very ancient crone came out of a small brown house on the edge of the village rubbing her eyes.

"*Oiga!*" she shouted. "What are you shooting at?"

"We are trying to kill that accursed man in the red blanket, who is poisoning our homes and making Valle Allegre a place unfit for a decent woman to live in!" shouted Atanacio, taking another shot.

The old woman bent her bleary eyes upon our target.

"But," she said gently, "that is not a bad man. That's only my son going after the goats."

Meanwhile, the red-blanketed figure, never even looking back, continued his placid way over the top of the mountain and disappeared.

# 3

## Los Pastores

THE romance of gold hangs over the mountains of northern Durango like an old perfume. There, it is rumored, was that mythical Ophir whence the Aztecs and their mysterious predecessors drew the red gold that Cortez found in the treasury of Moctezuma. Before the dawn of Mexican history the Indians scratched these barren hillsides with dull copper knives. You can still see the traces of their workings. And after them the Spaniards, with flashing, bright helmets and steel breastplates, filled from these mountains the lofty treasure ships of the Indies. Almost a thousand miles from the Capital, over trackless deserts and fierce stony mountains, a tiny colorful fringe of the most brilliant civilization in Europe flung itself among the canyons and high peaks of this desolate land; and so far was it from the seat of change that long after Spanish rule had disappeared from Mexico forever, it persisted here. The Spaniards enslaved the Indians of the region, of course, and the torrent-worn, narrow valleys are still sinister with legend. Almost anybody around Santa Maria del Oro can tell you stories of the old days when men were flogged to death in the mines, and the Spanish overseers lived like princes.

But they were hardly race, these mountaineers. They were always rebelling. There is a legend of how the Spaniards, finally discovering themselves alone, two hundred leagues from the seacoast, in the midst of an overwhelmingly hostile native race, attempted one night to leave the mountains. Fires sprang up on the high peaks, and the mountain villages throbbed to the sound of drums. Somewhere in the narrow defiles the Spaniards disappeared forever. And from that time, until certain foreigners secured mining concessions there, the place had an evil name. The authority of the Mexican government barely reached it.

There are two villages which were the capitals of the gold-seeking Spaniards in this region, and where the Spanish tradition is still strong: Inde, and Santa Maria del Oro, usually called El Oro. Inde, the Spaniards romantically named from their persistent dream that this new world was India; Santa Maria del Oro was called so on the same principle that one sung a *Te Deum* in honor of bloody victory—a gratefulness to heaven for the finding of red gold, Our Lady of the Gold.

In El Oro one can still see the ruins of a monastery—they call it now, vaguely, the Collegio—the pathetic little arched roofs of a row of monkish cells built of adobe, and now fast crumbling under hot suns and torrential rains. It partly surrounds what was once the patio of the cloister, and a great mesquite tree towers there over the forgotten headstone of an ancient grave, inscribed with the lordly name of Doña Isabella Guzman. Of course, everybody has entirely forgotten who Doña Isabella was, or when she died. There still stands in the public square a fine old Spanish church with a beamed ceiling. Over the door of the tiny Palacio Municipal is the almost erased carving of the arms of some ancient Spanish house.

Here is romance for you. But the inhabitants have no respect for tradition, and hardly any memory of the ancients who left these monuments. The exuberant Indian civilization has entirely obliterated all traces of the *Conquistadores*.

El Oro is noted as the gayest town of all the mountain region. There are *bailes* almost every night, and far and near it is a matter of common knowledge that El Oro is the home of the prettiest girls in Durango. In El Oro, too, they celebrate feast days with more ebullience than in other localities. All the charcoal burners and goatherds and pack-train drivers and ranchers for miles around come there on holidays—so that one feast day generally means two or three without work, since there must be one day for celebrating, and at least another for coming and returning home.

And what *Pastorellas* they have in El Oro! Once a year, on the Feast of the Santos Reyes, they perform Los Pastores all over this part of the country. It is an ancient miracle play of the kind that used to take place all over Europe in the Renaissance—the kind that gave birth to Elizabethan drama, and is now extinct everywhere in the world. It is handed down by word of mouth from mother to daughter, from the remotest antiquity. It is called "Luzbel," the Spanish for Lucifer, and depicts Perverse Man in the Midst of His Deadly Sin, Lucifer, the Great Antagonist of Souls, and the Everlasting Mercy of God Made Flesh in the Child Jesus.

In most places there is only one performance of Los Pastores. But in El Oro there are three or four on the night of the Santos Reyes, and others at different times of the year, as the spirit moves. The *cura*, or village priest, still trains the actors. The play takes place no longer in the church, however. It is added to from generation to generation, sometimes being twisted to satirize persons in the village. It has become too profane, too realistic, for the Church; but still it points the great moral of medieval religion.

Fidencio and I dined early on the night of the Santos Reyes. Afterward, he took me along the street to a narrow alleyway between adobe walls, which led through a broken place into a tiny corral behind a house hung with red peppers. Under the legs of two meditative burros scurried dogs and chickens, a pig or so, and a swarm of little naked brown children. A wrinkled old Indian hag, smoking a cigarette made of an entire cornhusk, squatted upon a wooden box. Upon our appearance she arose, muttering toothless words of greeting, lifted the lid of the box, and produced an *olla* full of new-made *aguardiente*. The distillery was in the kitchen. We paid her a silver peso, and circulated the jug among the three of us, with many polite wishes for health and prosperity. Over our heads the sunset sky yellowed and turned green, and a few large mountain stars blazed out. We heard laughter and guitars from the lower end of the town, and the uproarious shouts of the charcoal burners finishing their holiday strong. The old lady consumed much more than her share. . . .

"Oh, mother!" said Fidencio. "Where are they going to give the Pastores tonight?"

"There are many Pastores," she answered with a leer. *"Carramba!* what a year it is for Pastores! There is one in the school-house, and another back of Don Pedro's, and another in the *casa* of Don Mario, and still another in the house of Perdita, who was married to Tomas Redondo, who was killed last year in the mines; may God have mercy on his soul!"

"Which will be the best?" demanded Fidencio, kicking a goat which was trying to enter the kitchen.

*"Quien sabe?"* she shrugged vaguely. "Were my old bones not so twisted I would go to Don Pedro's. But I would be disappointed. There are no Pastores nowadays such as the ones we used to give when I was a girl."

We went, then, to Don Pedro's, down a steep, uneven street, stopped every few feet by boisterous bankrupts who wanted to know where a man could establish credit for liquor. Don Pedro's was a considerable house, for he was the village rich man. The open square which his buildings enclosed would have been a corral ordinarily; but Don Pedro could afford a patio, and it was full of fragrant shrubs and barrel cacti—a rude fountain pouring from an old iron pipe in the center. The entrance to this was a narrow, black archway, in which sat the town orchestra playing. A pine torch was stuck by its pitch against the outside wall, and under this a man took up fifty-cent pieces for the entrance fee. We watched for some time, but nobody seemed to be paying anything. A clamorous mob stood around him, pleading special privilege—that *they* ought to get in free. One was Don Pedro's cousin; another his gardener; a third had married the daughter of his mother-in-law by his first marriage, one woman insisted that she was the mother of a performer. There were other entrances at which no guardian stood; and through these, when they found themselves unable to cajole the gentleman at the main door, the crowd placidly sifted. We paid our money amid an awed silence and entered.

White, burning moonlight flooded the place. The patio sloped upward along the side of the mountain, where there was no wall to stop the view of great planes of shining upland, tilted to meet the shallow jade sky. To the low roof of the house a canopy of canvas drooped out over a flat place, supported by slanting poles, like the pavilion of a Bedouin king. Its shadow cut the moonlight blacker than night. Six torches stuck in the ground around the outside of the place sent up thin lines of pitchy smoke. There was no other light under the canopy, except the restless gleams of innumerable cigarettes. Along the wall of the house stood black-robed women with black mantillas over their heads, the menfolks squatting at their feet. Wherever there was space between their knees were children. Men and women alike smoked their cigarros, handing them placidly down so that the little ones might take a puff. It was a quiet audience, speaking little and softly, perfectly content to wait, watching the moonlight in the patio, and listening to the music, which sounded far away in the arch. A nightingale burst into song somewhere among the shrubs, and all of us fell ecstatically silent, listening to it. Small boys were dispatched to tell the band to stop while the song went on. That was very exciting.

During all this time there was no sign whatever of the performers. I don't know how long we sat there, but nobody made any comment on the fact. The audience was not there primarily to see the Pastores; it was there to see and hear whatever took place, and everything interested it. But being a restless, practical Westerner, alas! I broke the charmed silence to ask a woman next to me when the play would begin.

"Who knows?" she answered tranquilly.

A newcomer, after turning my question and the answer over in his mind, leaned across.

"Perhaps tomorrow," he said. I noticed that the band was playing no longer. "It appears," he continued, "that there are other Pastores at Doña Perdita's house. They tell me that those who were to have performed here have gone up there to see them. And the musicians have also gone up there. For the past half-hour I have been considering seriously going up there myself."

We left him, still considering seriously; the rest of the audience had settled down for an evening of pleasant gossip, having apparently forgotten the Pastores altogether. Outside, the ticket-taker with our peso had long since gathered his companions to him and sought the pleasing hilarity of a cantina.

And so we strolled slowly up the street toward the edge of town where the whitewashed plaster walls of rich men's houses give way to the undecorated adobes of the poor. There all pretense of streets ended, and we went along burro paths between huts scattered according to their owner's whims, through dilapidated corrals to the house of the widow of Don Tomas. It was built of sun-dried mud bricks, jutting part way into the mountain itself, and looked as the stable of Bethlehem must have looked. As if to carry out the analogy, a great cow lay in the moonlight just beneath the window, breathing and chewing her cud. Through the window and the door, over a throng of heads, we could see candlelight playing on the ceiling and hear a whining chant sung by girlish voices, and the beat of crooks keeping time on the floor with jingling bells.

It was a low, dirt-floored, whitewashed room, raftered and wattled with mud above, like any peasant dwelling in Italy or Palestine. At the end farthest from the door was a little table heaped with paper flowers where two tall church candles burned. Above it, on the wall, hung a chromo of the Virgin and Child. And in the middle of the flowers was set a tiny wooden model of a cradle in which lay a leaden doll to represent the Infant Jesus. All the rest of the room, except for a small space in the middle of the floor, was packed with humanity; a fringe of children sitting cross-legged around the stage, half-grownups and girls kneeling, and behind them, until they choked the doorway, blanketed peons with their hats off, eager and curious. By some exquisite chance, a woman sat next to the altar, her breast exposed as she nursed her baby. Other women with their babies stood along the wall on both sides of her, except for a narrow, curtained entrance into another room where we could hear the giggling of the performers.

"Has it begun?" I asked a boy next to me.

"No," he answered, "they just came out to sing a song to see if the stage was big enough."

It was a merry, noisy crowd, bandying jokes and gossip across each other's heads. Many of the men were exhilarated with *aguardiente*, singing snatches of ribald songs with their arms around each other's shoulders, and breaking out every now and then into fierce little quarrels that might have led to anything—for they were all armed. And right in the middle of everything a voice said: "S-s-sh! They are going to begin now!"

The curtain was lifted, and Lucifer, hurled from Heaven because of his invincible pride, stood before us. It was a young girl—all the performers are girls, in distinction to the pre-Elizabethan miracle plays, where the actors were boys. She wore a costume whose every part had been handed down from immeasurable antiquity. It was red, of course—red leather—the conventional medieval color for devils. But the exciting thing about it was that it was evidently the traditional rendering of the uniform of a Roman legionary (and the Roman soldiers who crucified Christ were considered a little less than devils in the Middle Ages). She wore a wide, skirted doublet of red leather, under which were scalloped trousers, falling almost to the shoe tops. There doesn't seem to be much connection here until you remember that the Roman legionaries in Britain and in Spain wore leather trousers. Her helmet was greatly distorted, because feathers and flowers had been fastened to it; but underneath you could trace the resemblance to the Roman helmet. A cuirass covered her breast and back; instead of steel it was made of small mirrors. And a sword hung at her side. Drawing the sword, she strutted about, pitching her voice to imitate a man's:

> *Yo soy luz; ay en mi nombre se ve!*
> *Pues con la luz*
> *Que baje*
> *Todo el abismo encendi—*

A splendid soliloquy of Lucifer hurled from heaven:

"Light am I, as my name proclaims—and the light of my fall kindled all the great abyss. Because I would not humble myself, I, who was the Captain General, be it known to all men, am today the accursed of God. . . . To thee, O mountains, and to thee, O sea, I will make my complaint, and thus—alas!—relieve my over-burdened breast. . . . Cruel fortune, why art thou so inflexibly severe? . . . I who yesterday dwelt serene in yonder starry vault am today disinherited, abandoned. Because of my mad envy and ambition, because of my rash presumption, gone is my palace of yesterday, and today finds me sad among these mountains, mute witnesses of my grievous and pitiful state. . . . O mountains! happy art thou!—happy art thou in all, whether bleak and bare, or gay with leafy verdure! O ye swift brooks flowing free, behold me! . . ."

"Good! good!" said the audience.

"That's the way Huerta is going to feel when the Maderistas enter Mexico City!" shouted one irrepressible revolutionist, amid laughter.

"Behold me in my affliction and guilt——" continued Luzbel.

Just then a large dog came through the curtain, cheerfully wagging his tail. Immensely pleased with himself, he nosed among the children, licking a face here and there. One baby slapped him violently, and the dog, hurt and astonished, made a rush between Lucifer's legs in the midst of that sublime peroration. A second time Lucifer fell, and, rising amid the wild hilarity of the house, laid about her with her sword. At least fifty of the audience descended upon the dog and ejected him howling, and the play went on.

Laura, married to Arcadio, a shepherd, appeared singing at the door of her cottage—that is to say, through the curtain. . . .

"How peacefully falls the light of the moon and the stars this supremely beautiful night! Nature appears to be on the point of revealing some wonderful secret. The whole world is at peace, and all hearts, methinks, are overflowing with joy and contentment. . . . But—who is this—of such pleasing presence and fascinating figure?"

Lucifer prinked and strutted, avowing with Latin boldness his love for her. She replied that her heart was Arcadio's; but the Arch-devil dwelt upon her husband's poverty, and himself promised her riches, towering palaces, jewels and slaves.

"I feel that I am beginning to love thee," said Laura. "Against my will—I cannot deceive myself——"

At this point there was smothered laughter in the audience: "Antonia! Antonia!" said everybody, grinning and nudging. "That's just the way Antonia left Enrique! I always thought the Devil was in it!" remarked one of the women.

But Laura had pangs of conscience about poor Arcadio. Lucifer insinuated that Arcadio was secretly in love with another, and that settled it.

"So that thou mayst not be troubled," Laura said calmly, "and, so that I may be free from him, I shall even watch for an opportunity to kill him."

This was a shock, even to Lucifer. He suggested that it would be better to make Arcadio feel the pangs of jealousy, and in an exultant aside remarked with satisfaction that "her feet are already in the direct pathway to Hell."

The women, apparently, felt a good deal of satisfaction at this. They nodded virtuously to one another. But one young girl leaned over to another, and, sighing, said:

"Ah! But it must be wonderful to love like that!"

Arcadio returned, to be reproached by Laura with his poverty. He was accompanied by Bato, a combination of Iago and Autolycus, who attended the dialogue between the shepherd and his wife with ironical asides. By means of the jeweled ring that Lucifer had given Laura, Arcadio's suspicions were aroused, and, when Laura had left him in haughty insolence, he gave vent to his feelings:

"Just when I was happy in her fidelity, she with cruel reproaches embitters my heart! What shall I do with myself?"

"Look for a new mate," said Bato.

That being rejected, Bato gave the following modest prescription for settling the difficulty:

"Kill her without delay. This done, take her skin and carefully fold it away. Shouldst thou marry again, let the bride's sheet be that skin, and thus prevent another jilting. To still further strengthen her virtue, tell her gently but firmly: 'Sweetheart, this thy sheet was once my wife; see that thou dost carry thyself circumspectly lest thou, too, come to the same end. Remember that I am a hard and peevish man who does not stick at trifles.' "

At the beginning of this speech the men began to snicker, and when it ended they were guffawing loudly. An old peon, however, turned furiously on them:

"There is a proper prescription!" he said. "If that were done more often there would not be so many domestic troubles."

But Arcadio didn't seem to see it, and Bato recommended the philosophic attitude.

"Stop thy complaining and leave Laura to her lover. Free thus from obligations, thou wilt become rich, and be able to eat well, dress well, and truly enjoy life. The rest matters but little. . . . Seize, therefore, this opportunity toward thine own good fortune. And do not forget, I beg thee, once thy fortune is made, to regale this meager paunch of mine with good cheer."

"Shame!" cried the woman, clucking. "How false!" "The *desgraciado!*" A man's voice piped up: "There is some truth in that, señoras! If it weren't for the women and children we all might be able to dress in fine clothes and ride upon a horse."

A fierce argument grew up around this point.

Arcadio lost patience with Bato, and the latter plaintively said: "If thou hast any regard for poor Bato, let us go to supper."

Arcadio answered firmly, not until he had unburdened his heart.

"Unburden and welcome," said Bato, "until thou art tired. As for me, I shall put such a knot in my tongue that even shouldst thou chatter like a parrot I shall be mute." He seated himself on a large rock and pretended to sleep; and then for fifteen minutes Arcadio unburdened himself to the mountains and the stars.

"Oh, Laura, inconstant, ungrateful and inhuman, why hast thou caused me such woe? Thou hast wounded my faith and my honor and hast put my soul in torment. Why dost thou mock my ardent love? Oh, thou steep stills and towering mountains, help me to express my woe! And thou, stern, immovable cliffs, and thou, silent woods, help me to ease my heart of its pain. . . ."

Amid heartfelt and sympathetic silence the audience mourned with Arcadio. A few women sobbed openly.

Finally Bato could stand it no longer.

"Let us go to supper," he said. "Better it is to suffer a little at a time!"

A perfect gale of laughter cut off the end of the sentence.

Arcadio: "To thee only, Bato, have I confided my secret."

Bato (aside): "I do not believe I can keep it! Already my mouth itches to tell it. This fool will learn that 'a secret and a pledge to none should be entrusted.' "

Enter a group of shepherds with their shepherdesses, singing. They were dressed in their feminine Sunday best with flowery summer hats, and carried enormous wooden apostolic crooks, hung with paper flowers and strings of bells.

> *Beautiful is this night beyond compare—*
> *Beautiful and peaceful as never before,*
> *And happy the mortal who beholds it.*
> *Everything proclaims that the Son of God,*
> *The Word Divine made human flesh,*
> *Will soon be born in Bethlehem*
> *And mankind's ransom be complete.*

Then followed a dialogue between ninety-year-old, miserly Fabio and his sprightly young wife, to which all present contributed, upon the subject of the great virtues of women and the great failings of men.

The audience joined violently in the discussion, hurling the words of the play back and forward—men and women drawing together in two solid hostile bodies. The women were supported by the words of the play, but the men had the conspicuous example of Laura to draw from. It passed soon into an argument about the virtues and failings of certain married couples in El Oro. The play suspended for some time.

———Bras, one of the shepherds, stole Fabio's wallet from between his knees as he slept. Then came gossip and backbiting. Bato forced Bras to share with him the contents of the stolen wallet, which they opened, to find none of the food they expected. In their disappointment, both declared their willingness to sell their souls to the Devil for a good meal. Lucifer overheard the declaration and attempted to bind them to it. But after a battle of wits between the rustics and the Devil—the audience solid to a man against the underhanded tactics of Lucifer—it was decided by a throw of the dice, at which the Devil lost. But he had told them where food could be obtained, and they went for it. Lucifer cursed God for interfering in behalf of two worthless shepherds. He marveled that "a hand mightier than Lucifer's has been stretched out to save." He wondered at the Everlasting Mercy toward worthless Man, who has been a persistent sinner down the ages, while he, Lucifer, had felt God's wrath so heavily. Sweet music was suddenly heard—the shepherds singing behind the curtain—and Lucifer mused upon Daniel's prophecy that "the Divine Word shall be made Flesh." The music continued, announcing the birth of Christ among the shepherds. Lucifer, enraged, swore that he would use all his power to the end that all mortals shall at some time "taste Hell," and commanded Hell to open and receive him "in its center."

At the birth of Christ the spectators crossed themselves, the women muttering prayers. Lucifer's impotent raging against God was greeted with shouts of "Blasphemy! Sacrilege! Death to the Devil for insulting God!"

Bras and Bato returned, ill from overeating, and, believing they were about to die, called wildly for help. Then the shepherds and shepherdesses came in, singing and pounding the floor with their crooks, as they promised they would cure them.

At the beginning of Act II, Bato and Bras, fully restored to health, were discovered again plotting to steal and eat the provisions laid by for a village festival, and as they went out to do so Laura appeared, singing of her love for Lucifer. Heavenly music was heard, rebuking her for her "adulterous thoughts," whereupon she renounced all desire for guilty love and declared that she would be content with Arcadio.

The women of the audience rustled and nodded and smiled at these exemplary sentiments. Sighs of relief were heard all over the house that the play was coming out right.

But just afterward the sound of a falling roof was heard, and

Comic Relief, in the persons of Bras and Bato, entered, carrying a basket of food and a bottle of wine. Everybody brightened up at the appearance of these beloved crooks; anticipatory mirth went around the room. Bato suggested that he eat his half while Bras stood guard, whereupon Bato ate Bras's share, too. In the midst of the quarrel that followed, before they could hide the traces of their guilt, the shepherds and shepherdesses came back in search of the thief. Many and absurd were the reasons invented by Bato and Bras to explain the presence of the food and drink, which they finally managed to convince the company was of diabolical origin. To further cover their traces they invited the others to eat what is left.

This scene, the most comic of the whole play, could hardly be heard for the roars of laughter that interrupted every speech. A young fellow reached over and punched a *compadre*.

"Do you remember how we got out of it when they caught us milking Don Pedro's cows?"

Lucifer returned, and was invited to join the feast. He incited them maliciously to continue discussion of the robbery, and little by little to place the blame upon a stranger whom they all agreed having seen. Of course they meant Lucifer, but, upon being invited to describe him, they depicted a monster a thousand times more repulsive than the reality. None suspected that the apparently amiable stranger seated in their midst was Lucifer.

How Bato and Bras were at last discovered and punished, how Laura and Arcadio were reconciled, how Fabio was rebuked for his avariciousness and saw the error of his ways, how the Infant Jesus was shown lying in his manger, with the three strongly individualized Kings out of the East, how Lucifer was finally discovered and cast back into hell—I have not space here to describe.

The play lasted for three hours, absorbing all the attention of the audience. Bato and Bras—especially Bato—received their enthusiastic approbation. They sympathized with Laura, suffered with Arcadio, and hated Lucifer with the hatred of gallery gods for the villain in the melodrama. Only once was the play interrupted, when a hatless youth rushed in and shouted:

"A man has come from the army, who says that Urbina has taken Mapimi!"

Even the performers stopped singing—they were pounding the floor with jingling crooks at the time—and a whirlwind of questions beat upon the newcomer. But in a minute the interest passed, and the shepherds took up their song where they had dropped it.

When we left Doña Perdita's house, about midnight, the moon had already gone behind the western mountains, and a barking dog was all the noise in the dark sharp night. It flashed upon me, as Fidencio and I went home with our arms about each other's shoulders, that this was the kind of thing which had preceded the Golden Age of the Theater in Europe—the flowering of the Renaissance. It was amusing to speculate what the Mexican Renaissance would have been if it had not come so late.

But already around the narrow shores of the Mexican Middle Ages beat the great seas of modern life—machinery, scientific thought, and political theory. Mexico will have to skip for a time her Golden Age of Drama.

# The War in Eastern Europe

Illustrations by
Boardman Robinson

HALF-SAVAGE GIANTS DRESSED IN THE ANCIENT
PANOPLY OF THAT CURIOUS SLAVIC PEOPLE
WHOSE MAIN BUSINESS IS WAR.

# Preface

W HEN war broke out in August, 1914, I went immediately to Europe as correspondent of the *Metropolitan Magazine*, visiting England, France, Switzerland, Italy, Germany, and Belgium, and seeing fighting with three armies. I returned to New York in February, 1915; and a month later, Boardman Robinson and I started for Eastern Europe. This book is a record of that second trip.

It was to be a three-months' flying journey: we were going to see Italy enter the war, Venice destroyed by the Austrians; be in Serbia in time for the last stand of the Serbs; watch Rumania plunge into the conflict; stand by at the fall of Constantinople; accompany the Russian steam-roller to Berlin; and spend a month in the Caucasus reporting barbarically colored battles between Cossacks and Turks.

As a matter of fact, we were gone seven months and didn't see one of these grand dramatic climaxes. Except for getting mixed up with the great Russian retreat, and flitting through the Balkans at the beginning of the German drive, it was our luck everywhere to arrive during a comparative lull in the hostilities. And for that very reason, perhaps, we were better able to observe the more normal life of the Eastern nations, under the steady strain of long-drawn-out warfare. In the excitement of sudden invasion, desperate resistance, capture and destruction of cities, men seem to lose their distinctive personal or racial flavor, and become alike in the mad democracy of battle. As we saw them, they had settled down to war as a business, had begun to adjust themselves to this new way of life and to talk and think of other things.

When we arrived in Italy, the most disappointing calm prevailed; but alarming rumors of the imminent capture of Constantinople caused us to drop everything and sail for Dedeagatch. At Salonika, however, the news from Turkey was so disconcertingly placid that we left the ship there and made a trip into Serbia, then devastated by typhus, and slowly recovering from the frightful consequences of the last Austrian invasion.

At the news of Rumanian mobilization we made for Bucarest hotfoot—to find much smoke but little fire.

Constantinople held. So we decided to make a short dash into Russia, and return when things grew interesting at the Dardanelles. The Russian ambassador in Bucarest was polite but vague; we must go to Petrograd, he said, and through our ambassadors formally request permission to go to the front. However, the arrival of three disgusted correspondents who had acted on this advice and cooled their heels in Petrograd for three months, rather discouraged us. The Russian retreat from the Carpathians had begun, and there was fighting near Czernowitz on the north, where the Russian, Austrian, and Rumanian frontiers meet. The American minister in Bucarest kindly gave us a list of American citizens to look up as we passed; and armed with this slender excuse, we crossed the river Pruth in a small boat at night, and landed at the Russian front.

It was unprecedented. The orders were very strict that no correspondents should be allowed in these regions, but the orders specified correspondents coming from the north. We came from the south, and so, not knowing what to do with us, they sent us north. We traveled behind the Russian front through Bucovina, Galicia, and Poland—where we spent two weeks in prison. Finally released, we went to Petrograd and found ourselves out of the frying-pan but in the fire. It seems that by this time the powers that be had made up their minds to shoot us. The American embassy washed its hands of me; but Robinson, a Canadian by birth, went to the British embassy—and the British embassy finally freed us both and got us out of Russia. Needless to say, we did not go to the Caucasus.

Once more in Bucarest, I determined to see Constantinople, which seemed calmer and safer than ever. Robinson could not go because he had a British passport. Enver Pasha first promised me that I should go to the Gallipoli front; but after two weeks' waiting he said that no more Americans would be allowed with the army, because one correspondent had gone back to Paris and there published a description of the Turkish forts. About this same time I was unofficially notified that I had better leave Turkey, because the police had seen me talking with too many Armenians.

At the Bulgarian frontier I was halted and told to return to Turkey, as my passport was not properly viséd. I had no money. The surly Bulgarian chief of police wouldn't communicate with the American embassy nor allow me to do so. So when the train for Sofia pulled out, I jumped aboard, riding the rods, the blind baggage, and the train top, and escaping into the fields when the train was halted and searched by soldiers.

At Bucarest I met Robinson, and together we went to Bulgaria, then on the brink of war. When the mobilization was declared we fled to Serbia—first, because Robinson was a Britisher, and, second, because I was informed by the Press Bureau that correspondents would not be allowed with the army.

In Serbia, however, we were sure of a warm welcome. But we discovered that the Serbians had all read our first two articles about themselves, and did not like them. We were told, in fact, that when hostilities commenced we would probably be expelled from the country. By that time we had had enough of the Balkans, so we went anyway.

Apparently nothing was doing in Salonika. We stayed there four or five days, but there were no more rumors than usual, and we didn't know whether anything would ever happen or not. So at length we took ship for Italy and home.

Of course we left at exactly the moment when the German and Austrian armies invaded Serbia, Bulgaria attacked her from the rear, and the English and French troops were only six hours' sail from Salonika. But we abandoned the warring nations to their respective fates and headed for New York, arriving toward the last of October.

As I look back on it all, it seems to me that the most important thing to know about the war is how the different peoples live; their environment, tradition, and the revealing things they do and say. In time of peace, many human qualities are covered up which come to the surface in a sharp crisis; but on the other hand, much of personal and racial quality is submerged in time of great public stress. And in this book Robinson and I have simply tried to give our impressions of human beings as we found them in the countries of Eastern Europe, from April to October, 1915.

J. R.

New York, March 20, 1916.

# Contents

# Illustrations

# PART I

# SALONIKA

# The Coveted City

T HE English spy counted his change and remonstrated with the Italian waiter, who reluctantly produced the rest—penny by penny—whining: "Ah, *signore*! I am so poor man! I serve you well! You take all."

"It was a week before the declaration of war," continued the Englishman, unheeding. "The British embassy sent me to discover the whereabouts of two Turkish army corps that had gone to Asia Minor. I took a boat to Kili on the Black Sea, and travelled twelve days by cart. Whenever I got to a village I represented myself as a British commercial agent looking for new trade routes. I talked to the Turks for hours about rice, wheat, roads, and Calcutta gunnies—you have no idea what a bore Calcutta gunnies become—and then I went out to find what I could find. When I discovered something interesting I wired to the British embassy in Constantinople—in terms of Calcutta gunnies. I found the army corps; they were headed for Armenia and going fast. The declaration of war caught me at Pera. I got out travelling overland in a cart—with an American passport."

In the silence that followed, the brazen clatter of forty Poles dominated everything. They were largely women and children returning from Europe by way of Salonika, Nish, Sofia, and Bucarest—the only line then open to Warsaw. There were Russians on board, too, an Austrian or so, a German with Heidelberg *schmizzes* on his cheek, who talked Italian with a broad Teutonic accent and passed for a Neapolitan; a Parisian, mistress and all, a French correspondent dressed like *Rudolph* in *La Bohème*, a Bulgarian diplomat who manipulated a tortoise-shell lorgnon, and a fringe of nondescript Balkanians whose nationality it was impossible to determine.

The good ship *Torino*, three days out from Brindisi, was nosing up the Greek coast beyond Piræus. As we sat at coffee we could see through the port the tawny promontory of Sunium cleaving the blue Ægean, drenched in white sunlight, the ruined temple on its summit delicately yellow against great barren mountains. Off to starboard misty islands lay like blue clouds on the sea, and between them beat wide-flung, slanting double sails like the spread wings of gulls—white-and-red—on brightly colored ships with proud sterns and stems, curving amidships deep to the water, with black bull-hides stretched along their waists to keep out the spray.

Where would the war break next? Rumania was calling reserves to the colors. Italy trembled on the brink. Everybody kept up an incessant and anxious discussion as to whether Greece and Bulgaria would intervene, and on what side. For at any moment they might be cut off from home and condemned to perpetual wandering on neutral seas; they might be captured on landing and penned into concentration camps; they might be taken off the ship as alien enemies by a hostile cruiser. It was extraordinary how these people, used to comfortable lives in civilized and peaceful Europe, adapted themselves without astonishment to mediæval conditions of travel. From plague-ridden Salonika they would take a sixty-hour railway trip in wooden third-class carriages through typhus-ridden Serbia, across the Bulgarian border where lawless bands of *comitadjis* were raiding and killing along the railway line; then Sofia, where the quarantine authorities penned them like cattle in the cars during the six hours of halt, and to that hostile frontier where the Rumanian and Bulgarian armies watched each other jealously across the Danube; a day or two days more to Russia, and then the dreadful uncertainty of slow military trains crawling across country threatened by the advancing Austrians.

An Armenian merchant from Constantinople was speaking now. He introduced himself as a graduate of the American mission

The French correspondent
and Bulgarian diplomat.

OLYMPUS AND SALONIKA.

school—Roberts College—which they say in the East produces more unscrupulous politicians and financial geniuses than any other institution in the world. Waving a cigar clutched in stubby fingers covered with jewels, he gave his personal views about the Turks, on whose religious prejudices he had battened for years.

"Yes, I am a Turkish subject," he said, "and my family for generations. They are fine people, the Turks—hospitable, kindly, and honest. I have nothing with which to reproach them, but, of course, I am for the Allies. When England holds the Dardanelles—ah, then there will be good business! Then there will be much money to be made!"

We passed a sloping headland where squat, red-tiled Turkish villages straggled up green hillsides, each with its brace of slender, gray minarets. Ahead, the muddy waters of the Gulf of Salonika opened wide against far views of long hills that crumpled into jagged mountains northward—the Balkans!

White distant walls, round towers, and a row of dazzling buildings edged the bay, and little by little a gray and yellow city grew from the barren landscape, climbing a steep hill wide-spread from the sea, a city of broad, irregular tiled roofs, round domes, spiked with a hundred minarets, encircled by the great crenellated wall that was built in the days of the Latin Kingdom—Salonika, the Eastern gate of war!

A big French war-ship was moored to the docks. Her cranes swung slowly, lowering the cannons from her turrets to the shore, where swarms of French sailors worked, hammering at the pale flames of forges.

Our Armenian friend pointed to them with a smile. "She is from the Dardanelles," he explained; "when I passed, nine days ago, she was here. And they call Salonika a neutral port!"

Offshore drifted to us the cries of Arabian porters, the shouts of the bazaar, strange minor chants of sailors from the coasts of Asia Minor and the Black Sea as they hoisted their lateen sails on ships painted at the bows with eyes, whose shape was older than history; a *muezzin* calling the faithful to prayer; the braying of donkeys; pipes and drums playing squealing dance-music from some latticed house far up in the Turkish quarter. Swarms of rainbow-colored boats manned by swarthy, barefooted pirates jostled each other in a roar of shrill squabbling two hundred yards away.

A skiff, carrying a big Greek flag, brought the medical officer. He bounded up the ladder shouting: "No one ashore who wants to come back. The city is quarantined—plague—" And now at our masthead the yellow flag fluttered down, and the gay-colored boats broke racing over the sea; in every boat half-naked brown men in fezzes and turbans stood urging them on with shouts, cursing furiously at their rivals. A big dory with the Russian flag astern drew under our counter; upright in it stood a giant Cossack in a long cloak of deep red, edged with fur. A high fur cap, barred on the top with red-and-gold, crowned his great head; he had silver baldrics, an enormous curved silver sword, and silver-hilted pistols in his belt. Another boat bore the Bulgarian flag, and the *kavas* of the Bulgarian consulate in deep blue, slung with silver ropes and tassels. We stumbled down the gangway, dragging our baggage as well as we could, and were seized by twenty rapacious hands, torn this way and that, until the strongest boatman filled his craft and shot away with a triumphant shout. The south wind was rising; as we pulled out from the lee of the ship, short yellow-green waves broke on our quarter and drenched us. Then we were paying exorbitant landing-taxes, and fighting our way to the street.

Rubber-tired, luxurious cabs, driven by turbaned Arabs, carried the veiled ladies of Turkish harems between highly modern street-cars; porters, in the immemorial breech-clout and pack-sack that Sindbad the Sailor wore, trotted by under the weight of typewriters and phonographs. So we entered Salonika, where Pierre Loti met Aziyadé, where East and West do finally stand face to face.

THIS was the ancient Thessalonika. Here Alexander launched his fleets. She has been one of the free cities of the Roman Empire; a Byzantine metropolis second only to Constantinople, and the last stronghold of that romantic Latin Kingdom, where the broken wreck of the Crusaders clung desperately to the Levant they had won and lost. Huns and Slavs and Bulgars besieged her; Saracens and Franks stormed that crumbling yellow wall, massacred and looted in those twisting streets; Greeks, Albanians, Romans, Normans, Lombards, Venetians, Phœnicians, and Turks succeeded each other as her rulers, and St. Paul bored her with visits and epistles. Austria almost won Salonika in the middle of the Second Balkan War, Serbia and Greece broke the Balkan Alliance to keep her, and Bulgaria plunged into a disastrous war to gain her.

Salonika is a city of no nations and of all nations—a hundred cities, each with its separate race, customs, and language. Halfway up the steep hill lie the tortuous streets and overhanging latticed balconies of the Turkish town; northwest is the tumble-down quarter of the Bulgarians; the Rumanians live below, and the Serbs nearer the bay. Grouped around the site of the Hippodrome to the east are pure Greeks, with Hellenic and Byzantine traditions unbroken for fifteen hundred years, and westward dwell the Albanians, that mysterious people who are supposed to have fled west from Asia at the break-up of the Hittite kingdoms.

But all the center of the city is a great community of Spanish Jews expelled from Spain by Ferdinand and Isabella. They speak fifteenth-century Spanish, written in Hebrew characters, and the language of the synagogue is Spanish, too; but half of them turned Mohammedan centuries ago to please the Turks, their masters, and now that the Turk is gone they live in a maze of mystical sects, practising black magic and an ever-changing mixture of all religions.

The men still wear the flapping slippers, long gabardine, and tall felt hat wound with a turban. The women are dressed in rich, flowered skirts, fine white waists covered by soft silk jackets edged with fur, gold beads and earrings, and green silk bonnets to hide their hair, embroidered with pearls, heavy with brass ornaments, and crossed with bright-colored ribbons that indicate whether they are maidens, wives, or widows. Their houses, too, are different. It might be a sunny corner of the rich Spanish *judería* of Toledo five hundred years ago.

All the tongues of the Western World are spoken on the narrow, tumultuous, crowded streets; Spanish is the commercial language among the natives; French is the international language; the Teutonic drive eastward has made German current; Italian is the polite language of the upper classes; Arabic and Turkish must be understood, for the servants are Arabs and Turks; Greek is universal, and Serbian, Albanian, and Bulgarian are common, for Salonika was long the port of all the Balkans.

One night we sat drinking our *mastica*, a kind of Greek absinth, in a local music-hall. First on the programme was a Greek *chanteuse* who sang Rumanian love-songs in Spanish; Russian dancers followed her, and a German monologist from Vienna, who spoke French. There was an American tramp comedian, who wore a set of seven vests with witty remarks on the back as he took each one off—and they were printed in Hebrew characters.

ON the *Place de la Liberté* at sundown little marble-topped tables overflow from the cafés to the middle of the street, and there, to the music of a Greek military band, drink and promenade the picturesque riff-raff that history and war has poured into Salonika. Besides Greeks, there are French, English, Russian, and Serbian officers in full uniform bearing swords, elegant young men exiled from Belgrade by war and pestilence, barbaric *kavases* from all the consulates—jostling the bare-legged porters, fishermen out of the "Arabian Nights," Greek priests, Mussulman *hadjis*, Jewish rabbis with the holy hat and reverend beard, veiled women, Turks, and German spies. Northward the Street of Liberty leads to the *Tcharshee*—the roaring bazaar, where, in the gloom, cross-legged Turks finger old amber and flawed emeralds and stuffs from Bokhara and Samarcand. Down the narrow, roofed-over street to the left, ablaze with clashing colors of Oriental patterns and crazy windows heaped with dusty piles of old gold and cracked turquoises, lies the Street of the Silversmiths, where bearded old men squat on high benches in their coops, hammering lumps of raw silver. Late in the afternoon a shouting tumult fills all the bazaar alleys: cries of Arab porters staggering under bales and boxes, a servant clearing the way for some rich farmer from the country, robed all in white linen, with a chain of rough gold beads around his neck, and mounted on a mule caparisoned in red and blue; lemonade-sellers in fezzes, with carved brass ewers on their backs and brass cups clanging at their waists, shop-keepers squabbling from sidewalk to sidewalk, newsboys shouting the latest extra.

Along the street that was once a part of the great Roman road from the Adriatic to the East, beyond the ruins of that marble arch carved with Greek warriors, elephants, camels, and strange peoples beyond the Indus, we lost ourselves in a maze of tortuous alleys. There we came suddenly upon a little irregular-shaped open market, squeezed between huddling shops and houses. Under enormous spreading plantain-trees was an indescribable tangle of little booths canopied with rags, where gold and blue and silver fish lay on green leaves, amid baskets of eggs, and piles of green and brown vegetables, and masses of red peppers. Bundles of chickens hung from tree-trunks, squawking feebly, pigs tethered by the legs squealed, and Macedonian farmers in white linen embroidered in colored yarns, Jewish women gleaming in silk of pale shades, Turks, and gypsies, bargained, quarrelled, stole vegetables when the marketman's back was turned—staggered from the throng with high-heaped baskets on their heads.

We ordered coffee in a dirty little Greek café overlooking the market. There was a Greek soldier there who stared at us for a long time, then finally came over.

"Where you from?" he asked. "What you doing?"

We told him. His face lighted up and he reached out a hand to both of us. "I been eight years in America," he said. "My brother has a candy-store in Mason City, Iowa; I been everywhere—Kansas, Colorado, New York, Illinois—I work in a shoe-shine parlor in Springfield, Illinois."

"Are you going back?" we asked.

"Sure I go back!" he cried, grinning. "I came here to fight in the Balkan War, and now I have only three months more to serve in the army—then I am free! I go back to the free country, the fine country, my country—America."

"Have a drink," we said.

He shook his head: "No, you have a drink with me. This is my father's restaurant. Americans always treat me good when I go to America, so I like to treat Americans. My name is Constantine Chakiris."

Two other soldiers came up and sat down. They carried on an eager conversation with Constantine, and finally spoke to us, a perfect torrent of excited words.

"These boys not speak English," said Constantine; "but this man, he has six brothers in America, and this man has a sister and his father. They both say America the great, strong country—we go to America after the war."

"Do you want Greece to go to war?" we asked.

"No." He shook his head. "Macedonia don't want war; we want peace in Greece."

"What do you think of Venezelos?"

He laughed: "Venezelos wants war. If I was for Venezelos, I would be killed now. We love Venezelos; he made us free. But we don't want war. The King? Oh, we don't mind him, he is nothing.

"We in New Greece are very ignorant about politics. We have never voted yet, so how can we know about politics? Oh, I love America!" he went on ecstatically. "In America I am just like brothers with all my friends; here there is no life for a man—he can win no money." He paused for a moment. "We are Macedonians," he finished; "we are children of Alexander the Great."

As we went home through the dark street in the evening, two other Greek soldiers passed us. As they got behind us, one of them turned round. "I bet those two guys are Americans," he said.

"Hello, Bill!" we shouted.

"Hello!" They came back. "I know you are Americans. I live seven years in the States—two years more I got to serve in the army, then I go back."

"Do you fellows want Greece to go to war?" we asked.

"Sure we want Greece to go to war! We conquer Constantinople. Our King—he is named Constantine, and once Constantinople was Greek! You remember? We will go back to Constantinople with Constantine. Fight! Sure we like to fight—fight Serbia, Bulgaria, Rumania, Italy—all!"

"Where are you from?"

"We are from Sparta!"

As we strolled up and down the city day after day, scores of people shouted to us in broad American—soldiers, shopkeepers, and even newsboys. Below the hotel was a plush-upholstered shoe-shining parlor presided over by a Greek with fierce mustache.

"Hello, boys!" he said; "glad to see you. This place is a branch of George's place on Forty-Second Street, New York. George, he is my brother." And he refused to allow us to pay for our shine.

The shops were full of American shoes with knobs on the toes, American college clothes with humps of padding on the shoulders and buttons in unexpected places, American dollar watches, and American safety-razors.

Apparently the entire masculine Greek population of Salonika had been to America. "America, the free country where you get rich! Yes, we are Greeks. We are proud to be Greeks," with a shrug; "but a man cannot live in Greece." And they are all going back when the war is over, and their military service done.

In Serbia, Bulgaria, and Rumania we met others who had been to America and caught the fever. That fierce irrational feeling called patriotism was strong in them—they loved their country and would die for it—but they could not live in it. They had tasted blood; they had experienced a civilization where the future of a new world is still an untried adventure.

# The Eastern Gate of War

By here passed the American Red Cross units, the foreign Medical Missions, on their way to typhus-stricken Serbia—veteran doctors and big, robust nurses laughing at the danger and boasting what they would do; and by here the gaunt, shaking survivors drifted back to tell how their comrades died.

Still they came. While we were in Salonika three new British expeditions passed through, one hundred and nineteen strong. Fresh young girls, untrained and unequipped, without the slightest idea what they must face, explored the colorful streets and the bazaars.

"No, I never had any experience in nursing," said one; "but one just nurses, doesn't one?"

A British Royal Army Medical Corps lieutenant who heard her shook his head in despair.

"The damned fools in England to let them come!" he cried. "It is almost certain death. And they are worse than useless, you know. They are the first to fall sick, and then we have to look after them."

Of course, there was a new rumor every five minutes. Day and night ephemeral newspapers flooded the streets and cafés with huge scareheads reading:

"CONSTANTINOPLE FALLS!"
"FORTY THOUSAND ENGLISH SLAUGHTERED
ON THE PENINSULA!"
"TURKISH REVOLUTIONISTS MASSACRE THE
GERMANS!"

One evening an excited mob of soldiers with flags swept cheering along the sea-wall shouting: "Greece declares war!"

Spies infested the city. Germans with shaved heads and sword-cuts all over their faces pretending to be Italians; Austrians in green Tyrolean hats passing as Turks; stupid-mannered Englishmen who sat drinking and talking in the cafés, eavesdropping the conversation in six languages that went on about them; exiled Mohammedans of the Old Turk party plotting in corners, and Greek secret-service men who changed their clothes fourteen times a day and altered the shape of their mustaches.

Occasionally out of the East a French or British war-ship grew slowly from the flat world of the sea, moored at the docks, and made repairs. Then the city was full of drunken sailors day and night.

For Salonika was anything but neutral. Besides the army officers on the streets, every day saw the arrival of British ships full of ammunition for the Serbian front. Every day cars loaded with English, French, and Russian cannon disappeared into the somber mountains northward. We saw the English gunboat on its special car begin the long journey to the Danube. And through this port went the French airplanes, with their hundred pilots and *mécaniciens;* and the British and Russian marines.

And all day long the refugees poured in; political exiles from Constantinople and Smyrna, Europeans from Turkey, Turks who feared the grand smash-up when the empire should fall, Greeks of the Levant. From Lemnos and Tenedos the refugee-boats carried the plague brought there by the Indian troops—even now it was spreading in the crowded lower quarters of the town. Always you could see pitiful processions crawling through the streets—men, women, and children with bloody feet limping beside broken-down wagons filled with the dilapidated furniture of some wretched peasant's hut. Hundreds of Greek popes from the monasteries of Asia Minor shuffled by, their threadbare black robes and high hats yellow with dust, their feet bound with rags, and all their possessions in a gunny sack over their shoulders. In trampled courtyards of old mosques, under pillared porticos painted red and blue, half-veiled women with black shawls on their heads crowded, staring vacantly into space or weeping quietly for their men, who had been taken for the army; the children played among the weed-grown tombs of the *hadjis;* their scanty bundles of belongings lay heaped in the corners.

LATE one night we walked through the deserted quarter of docks and warehouses, so filled with shouting movement by day. From a faintly lighted window came the sound of pounding and singing, and we peered through the grimy pane. It was a water-front saloon, a low-vaulted room with a floor of hard-packed earth, rough table and stools, piles of black bottles, barrel-ends and one smoking lamp hung crazily from the ceiling. At the table sat eight men, whining a wavering Oriental song, and beating time with their glasses. Suddenly one caught sight of our faces at the window; they halted, leaped to their feet. The door flew open— hands reached out and pulled us in.

"*Entrez! Pasen Ustedes! Herein! Herein!*" shouted the company, crowding eagerly about as we entered the room. A short, bald-headed man with a wart on his nose pumped our hands up and down, babbling in a mixture of languages: "To drink! To drink! What will you have, friends?"

"But *we* invite *you*—" I began.

"This is my shop! Never shall a stranger pay in my shop! Wine? Beer? *Mastica?*"

"Who are you?" asked the others. "French? English? Ah— Americans! I have a cousin—his name Georgopoulos—he live in California. You know him?"

One spoke English, another harsh maritime French, a third Neapolitan, a fourth Levantine Spanish, and still another pidgin-German; all knew Greek, and the strange patois of the Mediterranean sailor. The fortunes of war had swept them from the four corners of the Middle World into this obscure backwater on the Salonika docks.

"It is strange," said the man who spoke English. "We met here by chance—not one of us has ever known the other before. And we are all seven carpenters. I am a Greek from Kili on the Black Sea, and he is a Greek, and he, and he—from Ephesus, and Er-

REFUGEE PRIESTS. (SALONIKA.)

*Greek popes shuffled by—their threadbare black robes and high hats yellow with dust.*

zeroum, and Scutari. This man is an Italian—he lives in Aleppo, in Syria—and this one a Frenchman of Smyrna. Last night we were sitting here just like now, and he looked in at the window like you did."

The seventh carpenter, who had not spoken, said something that sounded like a German dialect. The proprietor translated: "This man is Armenian. He says all his family is killed by the Turks. He tries to tell you in the German he learned working on the Bagdad Railway!"

"Back there," cried the Frenchman, "I leave my wife and two kids! I go away hiding on a fisherboat——"

"God knows where is my brother." The Italian shook his head. "The soldiers took him. We could not both escape."

Now the master of the house brought liquor, and we raised our glasses to his beaming countenance.

"He is like that," the Italian explained with gestures. "We have no money. He gives us food and drink, and we sleep here on the floor, poor refugees. God will certainly reward his charity!"

"Yes. Yes. God will reward him," assented the others, drinking. The proprietor crossed himself elaborately, after the complicated fashion of the Orthodox Church.

"God knows I am fond of company," he said. "And one cannot turn away destitute men in times like these, especially men of pleasing talents. Besides, a carpenter gains good wages when he works, and then I shall be repaid."

"Do you want Greece to go to war?" we asked.

"No!" cried some; others moodily shook their heads.

"It is like this," the English-speaking Greek said slowly: "This war has driven us from our homes and our work. Now there is no work for a carpenter. War is a tearing down and not a building up. A carpenter is for building up——" He translated to the silent audience, and they growled applause.

"But how about Constantinople?"

"Constantinople for Greece! Greek Constantinople!" shouted two of the carpenters. But the others broke into violent argument.

The Italian rose and lifted his glass. "*Eviva* Constantinople In-

"THE SEVEN JOLLY CARPENTERS." (SALONIKA.)

ternazionale!" he cried. With a cheer everybody rose. "Constantinople Internazionale!"

"Come," said the proprietor, "a song for the strangers!"

"What was that you were singing when we came?" demanded Robinson.

"That was an Arab song. Now let us sing a real Turkish song!" And throwing back their heads, the company opened their noses in a whining wail, tapping with stiff fingers on the table while the glasses leaped and jingled.

"More to drink!" cried the excited innkeeper. "What is song without drink?"

"God will reward him!" murmured the seven carpenters in voices husky with emotion.

The Italian had a powerful tenor voice; he sang "*La donna è mobile*," in which the others joined with Oriental improvisations. An American song was called for, and Robinson and I obliged with "John Brown's Body"—which was encored four times.

Later dancing displaced music. In the flickering light of the fast-expiring lamp the proprietor led a stamping trio in the *kolo*, racial dance of all the Balkan peoples. Great boots clumped stiffly down, arms waved, fingers snapped, ragged clothes fluttered in brown shadow and yellow radiance. . . . Followed an Arab measure, all swaying bodies and syncopated gliding steps, and slow twirlings with closed eyes. At an early hour of the morning we were giving the company lessons in the "boston," and the turkey trot. . . . And so ended the adventure of the Seven Carpenters of Salonika.

TOWARD evening we would wander through the shouting *Tcharshee*, past the Prefecture—where the sentries wore white ballet-skirts and turned-up slippers ornamented with green pompoms—and climb the steep, crooked streets of the Turkish town. Past the little pink mosque on the corner, with its tall cypress and gray minaret; through streets overhung with *shahnichars*, behind which mysterious women tittered and rustled—no doubt all mysteriously beautiful. There were glimpses into the interior of *hans*, long trains of laden donkeys entering and leaving, pack-saddles piled in corners, Turks and peasants sitting cross-legged in the shade over their coffee. Sharp, black shadows fell across the cobbled courtyard, and women passed brightly into sunlight carrying painted earthen water-jars on their shoulders. Beyond was the Turkish market, with its leisurely, quiet crowd. Along the sides of a street thronged with booths of meat-sellers, the baskets of the fish-merchants, heaps of vegetables, and droves of chickens, were the cafés where the traders sat smoking their *chibouks*. Here one saw *hadjis*, holy men in green turbans who had made the pilgrimage to Mecca, dancing dervishes in tall gray hats and long, flaring robes of ash-color, the dull reds and sheepskins and cream-colored linens of farmers from the villages, and beardless eunuchs following veiled ladies of the seraglio.

Still farther on the cobbled street rose sharply into tranquillity. Here the latticed windows whispered, and only the occasional donkey of a street vender passed—rarely women with hidden faces going to the fountain with jugs on their hips. Unexpectedly, the climbing way broadened out in an irregular little open place, shaded by an immense and ancient tree, where two or three tiny cafés sheltered each its meditative, smoking Turks, and others squatted along the curb, speaking slowly with soft voices. They looked at us incuriously, indifferently, and turned away again to their own affairs.

Still upward, until the great yellow wall loomed overhead, all its deep crenellations sharp outlined against the warm afternoon blue. We passed through a breech where the inhabitants had for centuries taken the stone for their houses, and looked out upon the summits of green hills, far-lying meadows where sheep pastured. At the edge of the world northward loomed the purple mountains, behind which war and pestilence raged. Nearer at hand, slanting black gypsy tents were scattered, and in a far green pocket of earth leaping barelegged men in red trousers and yellow turbans played ball. Tinkling mule-trains, with linen-clad peasants strolling behind, moved along faint tracks to unseen villages somewhere over the rim of the horizon.

From a little hut built against the base of the great wall came an old Turk. He bowed to us, and returning, brought two wooden chairs. We saw him no more until we rose to go away, when he reappeared, bowed to us, and took the chairs. I tried to give him some money; he only shook his head, smiling, and said something we didn't understand. . . .

Now the sun low in the west flooded the green, cloudless sky with waves of yellow light. We went along a beaten path that wound between miserable houses built of flints, and came to an open space where the magnificent panorama of the tumbled city fell away to the sea. Dull-red plains of roofs, jutting balconies, round white domes, spires, bulbous Greek towers, minarets spiring delicately beside lofty cypresses; the squealing roar of an Oriental town mounting from hidden streets. At the water's edge stood the round white tower of the Venetian wall, and beyond spread a sea the color of cloudy Chinese jade, spotted with slanting sails, yellow, white, and red. Southward, barring the gulf, the rugged Greek mainland towered into the mighty range of Mount Olympus, covered with snow and ever veiled with a cloud. To the right, the golden city-wall plunged magnificently down into the valley, and up the slope of the hill, dwindling westward for miles. The silver Vardar wound flatly through its willowy plain; farther yet were the swamps where Bulgarian *comitadjis*, fighting to make Macedonia free, once held at bay a Turkish army corps; and at the far end of vision, the sharp Thessalian mountains.

Dusk fell swiftly. For a moment the high white crest of Olympus glowed an unearthly pink, slowly fading. In the deep sky there were suddenly millions of stars; a crescent moon brightened halfway up the night. Below us, the *muezzins* came out on the parapets of seventeen minarets with tiny yellow lanterns, and pulled them jiggling up the halyards. From where we stood we could hear their high dissonant voices shouting the shrill call of the faithful to prayer:

"God is great! God is great! God is great! God is great! I bear witness that there is no other god but God! I bear witness that there is no other god but God! I bear witness that Mohammed is the apostle of God! I bear witness that Mohammed is the apostle of God! Come to prayer, come to prayer! Come to salvation, come to salvation! Prayer is better than sleep. . . ."

· · ·

Now the Turkish town shrinks, and the quiet flow of Turkish life weakens, year by year, before the mounting flood of busy, inquisitive Greeks. Mosque after mosque falls to ruin, and every month sees voiceless and deserted some minaret where the *muezzin* called to prayer each sunset for centuries. Mecca has become distant and powerless, and whatever the result of the war, Stamboul will never again rule Salonika; the Turks of Salonika are dying out. And the city itself is dying—in the loss of her hinterland, in the fevers that sweep her periodically from the low-lying Vardar, the silt that slowly chokes her magnificent harbor, the voracious channel of the river that already eats into the town. Soon Salonika will no longer be worth a war.

# PART II

## SERBIA

# The Country of Death

W E rubbed ourselves from head to foot with camphorated oil, put kerosene on our hair, filled our pockets with moth-balls, and sprinkled naphthaline through our baggage; and boarded a train so saturated with formalin that our eyes and lungs burned as with quicklime. The Americans from the Standard Oil office in Salonika strolled down to bid us a last farewell.

"Too bad," said Wiley. "So young, too. Do you want the remains shipped home, or shall we have you buried up there?"

These were the ordinary precautions of travellers bound for Serbia, the country of the typhus—abdominal typhus, recurrent fever, and the mysterious and violent spotted fever, which kills fifty per cent of its victims, and whose bacillus no man had then discovered. Most doctors thought it was carried by clothing lice, but the British R. A. M. C. lieutenant who travelled with us was sceptical.

"I've been up there three months," he said, "and I've long ago stopped taking any precautionary measures whatever except a daily bath. As for the lice—one gets used to spending a quiet evening picking them off one." He snorted at the naphthaline. "They're really quite fond of it, you know. The truth about the typhus is that no one knows anything about it at all, except that about one-sixth of the Serbian nation is dead of it. . . ."

Already the warm weather and the cessation of the spring rains had begun to check the epidemic—and the virus was weaker. Now there were only a hundred thousand sick in all Serbia, and only a thousand deaths a day—besides cases of the dreadful post-typhus gangrene. In February it must have been ghastly—hundreds dying and delirious in the mud of the streets for want of hospitals.

The foreign medical missions had suffered heavily. Half a hundred priests succumbed after giving absolution to the dying. Out of the four hundred odd doctors with which the Serbian army began the war, less than two hundred were left. And the typhus was not all. Smallpox, scarlet fever, scarlatina, diphtheria raged along the great roads and in far villages, and already there were cases of cholera, which was sure to spread with the coming of the summer in that devastated land; where battle-fields, villages, and roads stank with the lightly buried dead, and the streams were polluted with the bodies of men and horses.

Our lieutenant belonged to the British Army Medical Mission, sent to fight the cholera. He was dressed in full service uniform, and carried a huge sword which got between his legs and embarrassed him frightfully.

"I don't know what to do with the bally thing," he cried, hurling it into a corner. "We don't wear swords in the army any more. But we have to out here, because the Serbians won't believe you're an officer unless you carry a sword. . . ."

As we crawled slowly up between barren hills along the yellow torrent of the Vardar, he told us how the English had persuaded the Serbian Government to stop all train service for a month, in order to prevent the spread of disease; then they ordered sanitary improvements in the filthy towns, compelled anticholera vaccination, and began to disinfect whole sections of the population. The Serbians sneered—these English were evidently cowards. When Colonel Hunter, unable to secure decent quarters, threatened the authorities that if one of his men died of typhus he would abandon Serbia, a storm of irony burst. Colonel Hunter was a coward! And the Americans were cowards, too, when, with half their units infected, they abandoned Gievgieli. To the Serbians, the taking of preventive measures was a proof of timidity. They regarded the immense ravages of the epidemic with a sort of gloomy pride—as mediæval Europe regarded the Black Death.

. . .

PRECAUTIONS AGAINST THE TYPHUS. (NISH.)

THE gorge of the Vardar, as if it were a sterile frontier between Greek Macedonia and the high valleys of New Serbia, broadened out into a wide valley rimmed with stony hills, beyond which lay mountains still higher, with an occasional glimpse of an abrupt snow peak. From every canyon burst rapid mountain streams. In this valley the air was hot and moist; irrigation ditches, lined with great willows, struck off from the river, across fields of young to-bacco-plants, acres upon acres of mulberry-trees, and ploughed land of heavy, rich clay that looked like cotton country. Here every field, every shelf of earth, was cultivated. Higher up, on bare slopes among the rocks, sheep and goats pastured, tended by bearded peasants with huge crooks, clad in sheepskin coats, spinning wool and silk on wooden distaffs. Irregular, white, red-roofed villages meandered along rutted spaces where squat little oxen and black water-buffaloes dragged creaking carts. Here and there was the galleried *konak* of some wealthy Turk of the old régime, set in yellow-green towering willows, or flowering almond-trees heavy with scent; and over the tumbled little town a slender gray minaret, or the dome of a Greek church.

All sorts of people hung about the stations—men turbaned and fezzed and capped with conical hats of brown fur, men in Turkish trousers, or in long shirts and tights of creamy homespun linen, their leather vests richly worked in colored wheels and flowers, or in suits of heavy brown wool ornamented with patterns of black braid, high red sashes wound round and round their waists, leather sandals sewed to a circular spout on the toe and bound to the calf with leather ribbons wound to the knees; women with the Turkish *yashmak* and bloomers, or in leather and woollen jackets embroidered in bright colors, waists of the raw silk they weave in the villages, embroidered linen underskirts, black aprons worked in flowers, heavy overskirts woven in vivid bars of color and caught up behind, and yellow or white silk kerchiefs on their heads. Many wore a black kerchief—the only sign of mourning. And always and everywhere gypsies—the men in a kind of bright turban, the women with gold pieces for earrings and patches and scraps of gay rags for dresses, barefooted—shuffling along the

*Graves along the Vardar.*

*An old soldier.*

*Refugees.*

*Peasant.*

*Soldier.*

SERBIA—NISH.

roads beside their caravans, or lounging about the rakish black tents of their camps.

A tall, bearded man in black introduced himself in French as a Serbian secret-service officer whose job was to keep us under observation. Once a dapper young officer came aboard and questioned him, nodding to us. The other responded.

"*Dobra!* Good!" he said, clicking his heels and saluting.

"That station," remarked the secret-service man as the train moved on again, "is the frontier. We are now in Serbia."

We caught a glimpse of several big, gaunt men lounging on the platform, rifles with fixed bayonets slung at their shoulders, without any uniform except the soldier's *kepi*.

"What would you?" shrugged our friend, smiling. "We Serbians have no longer any uniforms. We have fought four wars in three years—the First and Second Balkan Wars, the Albanian revolt, and now this one. . . . For three years our soldiers have not changed their clothes."

Now we were passing along a narrow field planted with small wooden crosses, that might have been vine poles, spaced about three feet apart; they marched beside the train for five minutes.

"The typhus cemetery of Gievgieli," he said laconically. There must have been thousands of those little crosses, and each marked a grave!

There came in sight a great, tramped-down space on a hillside beyond, honeycombed with burrows leading into the brown earth, and humped into round hutches of heaped-up mud. Men crawled in and out of the holes, ragged, dirty fellows in every variety of half-uniform, with rifle-belts crisscrossed over their breasts like Mexican revolutionists. Between were stacked rifles, and there were cannon with ox-yoke limbers and half a hundred springless ox-carts ranged along the side, while farther on the hobbled oxen grazed. Below the mud huts, at the bottom of the hill, men were drinking from the yellow river that poured down from a score of infected villages up the valley. Around a fire squatted twenty or more, watching the carcass of a sheep turn in the flames.

"This regiment has come to guard the frontier," explained our

**THE SENTRY.**
*Hollow-cheeked, filthy, and starved-looking.*

friend. "It was here that the Bulgarian *comitadjis* tried to break through and cut the railroad last week. At any moment they might come again. . . . Is the Bulgarian Government responsible, or did the Austrians pay them? One can never tell, in the Balkans."

And now, every quarter mile we passed a rude hut made of mud and twigs, before which stood a ragged, hollow-cheeked soldier, filthy and starved-looking, but with his rifle at present arms. All over Serbia one saw these men—the last desperate gleaning of the country's manhood—who live in the mud, with scanty food and miserable clothing, guarding the long-deserted railroad tracks.

At first there seemed no difference between this country and Greek Macedonia. The same villages, a little more unkempt— tiles gone from the roofs, white paint chipped from the walls; the same people, but fewer of them, and those mostly women, old men, and children. But soon things began to strike one. The mulberry-trees were neglected, the tobacco-plants were last year's, rotting yellow; corn-stalks stood spikily in weedy fields unturned for twelve months or more. In Greek Macedonia, every foot of arable land was worked; here only one field out of ten showed signs of cultivation. Occasionally we saw two oxen, led by a woman in bright yellow head-dress and brilliantly colored skirt, dragging a wooden plough carved from a twisted oak limb, which a soldier guided, his rifle slung from his shoulder.

The secret-service man pointed to them. "All the men of Serbia are in the army—or dead—and all the oxen were taken by the government to draw the cannon and the trains. But since December, when we drove the Austrians out, there has been no fighting. So the government sends the soldiers and the oxen over Serbia, wherever they are wanted, to help with the ploughing."

Sometimes, in details like these, there flashed before our imaginations a picture of this country of the dead: with two bloody wars that swept away the flower of its youth, a two months' hard guerilla campaign, then this fearful struggle with the greatest military power on earth, and a devastating plague on top of that. Yet from the ruins of a whole people, imperial ambitions were already springing, which might one day threaten all southern Europe.

Gievgieli shares with Valievo the distinction of being the worst plague-spot in Serbia. Trees, station, and buildings were splashed and spattered with chloride of lime, and armed sentries stood guard at the fence, where a hundred ragged people pressed murmuring—for Gievgieli was quarantined. We stared through the fence at a wide, rough street of cobbles and mud, flanked by one-story buildings white with disinfectant; at almost every door flapped a black flag, the sign of death in the house.

A stout, mustached man in a dirty collar, spotted clothing, and a smutty Panama pulled down over his eyes stood on the platform, surrounded by a dense circle of soldiers. He held a small wild flower on high, and addressed the secret-service man volubly and excitedly.

"See!" he cried. "This flower I found in that field beyond the river. It is very curious! I do not know this flower! It is evidently of the family of the *orchidæ*!" He scowled and fixed the secret-service man with a menacing eye. "Is it not of the family of the *orchidæ*?"

"It has certain characteristics, indeed," said the other timidly. "This tongue. . . . But the pistil——"

The fat man shook the flower. "Nonsense! It is of the family of the *orchidæ*!"

The soldiers round about broke into a hum of argument: "*Da! Orchida!*" "*Ne je orchida!*" "But it is evidently an orchid!" "What do *you* know of orchids, George Georgevitch? At Ralya, where you come from, they haven't even grass!" There was a laugh at this. Above it rose the fat man's voice, insistent, passionate: "I tell you it is an orchid! It is a new kind of orchid! It is unknown to the science of botany——"

Robinson caught the infection of the argument. "Orchid?" he said to me with a sneer. "Of course it's not an orchid!"

"It *is* an orchid!" I returned hotly. "It is formed very like the lady's-slippers that we see in American woods——"

The fat man wheeled around and erupted into broken English, glaring at us. "Yes, yes!" he said eagerly. "The same. Are you Americans? I have been in America. I have tramped through Kansas and Missouri, working on the farms of wheat. I have walked

THE GOVERNMENT SENDS THE SOLDIERS AND THE OXEN ALL OVER SERBIA
TO HELP WITH THE PLOUGHING.

through the Panhan'le of Texas, with work at the cattle-ranch. I am on foot gone through Seattle to San Francisco, to Sacramento, crossing the Sierras and the desert to Yuma in Arizona—you know Yuma? No? I am studying all kind of farming from first-hand for to apply these experiences to Serbian farms. My name is Lazar Obichan. I am an Agro-Geolog, and secretary in Department of Agriculture in government at Belgrade. Yes." He cleared his throat, waved his elbows to make a space in the crowd, and seized us each by a lapel.

"I am sent here to study soil, climate, and crop conditions of New Serbia. I am an expert. I have invented a new method to tell what can be grown in any soil, in any country. It is automatic, simple, can be appli' by anybody—a new science. Listen! You give me the humidity—I put her *there*." He poked Robinson stiffly in the shoulder-blade. "Then you give me the mean temperatoor—I put him *there*." A jab near Robinson's kidney. "From humidity I draw a vertical line straight down, isn't it? From mean temperatoor I draw horizontal line straight across." He suited the action to the word, furrowing the artist's diaphragm. His voice rose. "Until the two lines meet! And the point where they meet, there is the figure which gives the evaporation for one day!" He poked us simultaneously in the chest to emphasize each word, and repeated: "The Evaporation for One Day!" He threw both hands up and beamed upon us, pausing to allow this to sink in. We were impressed.

"But that is not all I have in my mind," he went on heavily. "There is a vast commercial and financial scheme—immense! Listen! After this war Serbia she will need much money, much foreign capitals. From where will he come? From England? No. England will need all at home. France and Russia will be absolute exhausticated. No capitals from Europe. Where then? I tell you. From America. America is rich. I have been in her and I know how rich. Listen! We will establish a Serbian-American Bank with American capitals and American managers. It will sit in Belgrade. It will lend money to Serbians—big profit! Serbian law allows to charge twelve per cent interest—twelve per cent! It will loan to farmers at big interest. It will buy land from poor people, split up in small pieces and sell back at four hundred per cent profit. Serbians poor now, will sell land cheap—but Serbians need land, must have land. We are bankrupted here now—you can buy—how do you say?—you can buy all Serbia for a music! Then these bank, she will open in Belgrade a permanent exhibition of American products and take orders—American shoes, American machines, American cloth—and in New York she will open one of Serbian products and take orders. Make money—big! You shall write about in your papers. If you have capitals put in these bank!"

On the station a bell was ringing. The station-master blew a horn, the engine whistled, the train began to move. We tore our lapels from Mr. Obichan's thumbs and ran. He raced along with us, still talking.

"Serbia is very rich country in natural resources," he shouted. "Here there is soil for cotton, tobacco, silk—very fine alluvial lands. Southern slopes of hills for vineyards! Farther up in mountains wheat, plums, peaches, apples. In the Machva prunes—" We swung on board. "Minerals—" he yelled after us. "Gold—copper—Labor cheap—" And then we lost his voice. Later on we asked a Serbian official about him.

"Lazar Obichan?" he said. "Yes, we know him. He is under observation—suspected of selling military secrets to the Austrian Government!"

Late in the afternoon we halted on a siding to let a military train pass—twelve open flat cars packed with soldiers, in odds and ends of uniforms, wrapped in clashing and vividly colored blankets. It had begun to rain a little. A gypsy fiddler played wildly, holding his one-stringed violin before him by the throat, which was carved rudely to represent a horse's head; and about him lay the soldiers, singing the newest ballad of the Austrian defeat:

> "The Swabos* came all the way to Ralya,
> But no further came they—
>     Hey, *Kako to?*
>     Yoy, *Sashto to?*

*Swabos—Austrians.

"They won't soon forget Rashko Pol,
For there they met the Serbs!
 Hey, how was that?
 Yoy, why was that?

"And now the Swabos know
How the Serbs receive intruders!
 Hey, *Tako to!*
 Yoy, *that* was how!"

Every regiment has two or three gypsies, who march with the troops, playing the Serbian fiddle or the bagpipes, and accompany the songs that are composed incessantly by the soldiers—love-songs, celebrations of victory, epic chants. And all through Serbia they are the musicians of the people, travelling from one country festa to another, playing for dancing and singing. Strange substitution! The gypsies have practically replaced the old-time travelling bards, the *goosslari*, who transmitted from generation to generation through the far mountain valleys the ancient national epics and ballads. And yet they alone in Serbia have no vote. They have no homes, no villages, no land—only their tents and their dilapidated caravans.

We tossed some packages of cigarettes among the soldiers in the cars. For a moment they didn't seem to understand. They turned them over and over, opened them, stared at us with heavy, slow, flat faces. Then light broke—they smiled, nodding to us. "*Fala,*" they said gently. "*Fala lepo!* Thanks beautifully!"

# The War Capital

N ISH. We took a tumble-down cab—whose bottom-board immediately fell out—attached to two dying horses and driven by a bandit in a high fur cap, and jolted up a wide street paved with mud and wide-set sharp cobbles. Round about the city the green hills rose, beautiful with new leaves and with every flowering fruit-tree, and over the wide-flung Turkish roofs, and the few mean plaster buildings in the European style, loomed the bulbous Greek domes of the cathedral. Here and there was the slender spire of a minaret, crisscrossed with telephone-wires. The street opened into a vast square, a sea of mud and cobbles bounded by wretched huts, across which marched steel poles carrying hundreds of wires and huge modern arc-lights. At one side an ox lay on his back, feet clewed up to a wooden beam, while peasants shod him with solid iron plates, as they had done it for half a thousand years.

Austrian prisoners in uniform wandered freely everywhere, without a guard. Some drove wagons, others dug ditches, and hundreds loitered up and down in idleness. We learned that by paying fifty *denars* to the government, you could have one for a servant. All the legations and consulates were manned with them. And the prisoners were glad to be servants, for there was no decent place for them to live, and scanty food. Now and then an Austrian officer passed along, in full uniform and with his sword.

"Escape?" said one government official we interrogated. "No, they do not try. The roads are meters deep in mud, the villages are depopulated and full of disease, there is no food. . . . It is difficult enough to travel by train in Serbia—on foot it would be impossible. And there are the guards all along the frontier. . . ."

We passed a big hospital where pale prisoners leaned from the windows upon dirty blankets, dragged themselves in and out of the doors, and lay propped up on piles of drying mud along the road. These were only survivors; for out of the sixty thousand Austrians captured in the war, twelve thousand were already dead of typhus.

Beyond the square was the street again, between rough one-story houses, and we were in the marketplace. A dull roar rose from the haggling of hundreds of peasants in ten different national costumes—homespun linen embroidered with flowers, high fur hats, fezzes, turbans, and infinite varieties and modifications of Turkish trousers. Pigs squealed, hens squawked; underfoot were heaped baskets of eggs and herbs and vegetables and red peppers; majestic old men in sheepskins shuffled along with lambs in their arms. Here was the center of the town. There were two or three restaurants and foul-smelling cafés, the dingy Hotel Orient, the inevitable American shoestore, and amid cheap little shops, sudden windows ablaze with expensive jewelry and extravagant women's hats.

Along the sidewalks elbowed a multitude of strangely assorted people: gypsies, poverty-stricken peasants, gendarmes with great swords, in red and blue uniforms, tax-collectors dressed like generals, also with swords, smart army officers hung with medals, soldiers in filthy tatters, their feet bound with rags—soldiers limping, staggering on crutches, without arms, without legs, discharged from the overcrowded hospitals still blue and shaking from the typhus—and everywhere the Austrian prisoners. Government officials hurried by with portfolios under their arms. Fat Jewish army contractors hobnobbed with political hangers-on over maculate café tables. Women government clerks, wives and mistresses of officers, society ladies, shouldered the peasant women in their humped-up gay skirts and high-colored socks. The government from Belgrade had taken refuge in Nish, and a mountain village of twenty thousand inhabitants had become a city of one hundred and twenty thousand—not counting those who died.

For the typhus had swept the town, where people were living six and ten in a room, until everywhere the black flags flapped in long, sinister vistas, and the windows of the cafés were plastered with black paper death-notices.

We crossed the muddy Nishava River on the bridge which leads to the heavy, arabesqued gate of the ancient Turkish citadel, which was Roman before the Turks, and where Constantine the Great was born. On the grass along the foot of the great wall sprawled hundreds of soldiers, sleeping, scratching themselves, stripping and searching their bodies for lice, tossing and twisting in fever. Everywhere about Nish, wherever there was a spot of worn grass, the miserable people clustered, picking vermin from each other.

The stench of the city was appalling. In the side streets open sewers trickled down among the cobbles. Some sanitary measures had been taken—such as the closing of cafés and restaurants from two o'clock until six every day in order to disinfect them—but still it was an even chance of typhus if you stayed in a hotel or public building. Luckily the hospitable American vice-consul, Mr. Young, took us in at the consulate and introduced us at the Diplomatic Club, which had dining-rooms over an abandoned restaurant, and where good food was to be got when half the town was starving. The entrance was through a pigsty, after stepping across an open sewer; and when you opened the club-room door, your astonished eyes encountered tables, decorated with flowers and covered with silver and snowy linen, and a head waiter in smart evening dress, an Austrian prisoner by the name of Fritz, who had been head waiter at the Carlton in London before the war. To see the British minister sail majestically past the pigsty and mount the club stairs as if it were Piccadilly was a thing worth coming miles for.

Such was Nish, as we first saw it. Two weeks later we returned, after the rains had altogether ceased, and the hot sun had dried

DISCHARGED FROM A TYPHUS HOSPITAL.

the streets. It was a few days after the feast of St. George, which marks the coming of the spring in Serbia. On that day all Serbia rises at dawn and goes out into the woods and fields, gathering flowers and dancing and singing and feasting all day. And even here, in this filthy, overcrowded town, with the tragic sadness of war and pestilence over every house, the streets were a gay sight. The men peasants had changed their dirty heavy woollens and sheepskins for the summer suit of embroidered dazzling linen. All the women wore new dresses and new silk kerchiefs, decorated with knots of ribbon, with leaves and flowers—even the ox-yokes and the oxen's heads were bound with purple lilac branches. Through the streets raced mad young gypsy girls in Turkish trousers of extravagant and gorgeous colors, their bodices gleaming with gold braid, gold coins hung in their ears. And I remember five great strapping women with mattocks over their shoulders, who marched singing down the middle of the road to take their dead men's places in the work of the fields.

WE were received by Colonel Soubotitch, chief of the Red Cross, in his headquarters. He described the terrible lack of all medical necessities in Serbia, and painted us a graphic picture of people dying in the streets of Nish only a month before. I noticed a handsome peasant blanket on his bed.

"My mother wove that for me," he said simply, "in the village where I live. She is a peasant. We are all peasants in Serbia—that is our pride. Voyvoda Putnik, commander-in-chief of the army, is a poor man; his father was a peasant. Voyvoda Michitch, who won the great battle that hurled the Austrian army from our country, is a peasant. Many of the deputies to the Skouptchina, our parliament, are peasants, who sit there in peasant dress." He stared at the bed. "And on that bed, on that very blanket which you so admired, I stood here where I now stand and watched my son die of the typhus, two months ago. What will you? We must do our duty. . . ."

He threw back his shoulders with a visible effort. "So you want to see a typhus hospital? Ah, they are not interesting now. The

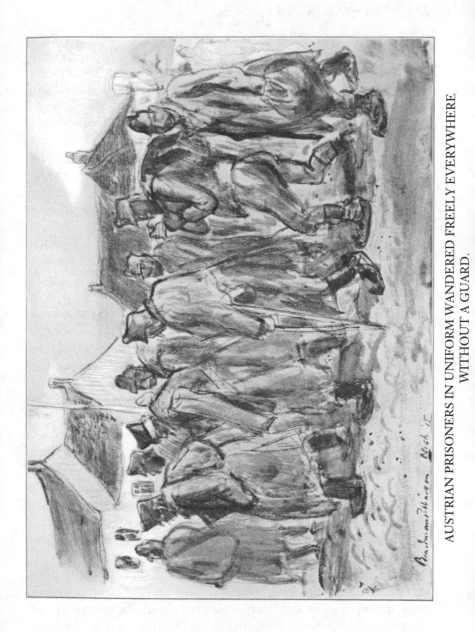

AUSTRIAN PRISONERS IN UNIFORM WANDERED FREELY EVERYWHERE
WITHOUT A GUARD.

worst is over. But I will give you a letter to Stanoievitch, at Chere Kula."

We drove to Chere Kula, a mile out of town, late one somber afternoon in the pouring rain. The name is Turkish, meaning "Mound of Skulls"; it is literally a tower of skulls of Serbian warriors, erected near the site of a great battle fought more than a century ago, as a monument to the Turkish victory. Lieutenant Stanoievitch, in command of the hospital, unlocked the Greek chapel which the Serbians have built over the holy spot. In the dim light it loomed there, completely filling the chapel, a great round tower of clay with a few grinning heads still embedded in it, and draped with wreaths of faded flowers.

Around this sinister memorial were grouped the brick buildings of the typhus hospital, and the wooden barracks where the overflow was lodged. The wind set our way, carrying the stench of bodies sweating with fever, of sick men eating, of the rotting of flesh. We entered a barrack, along whose walls cots lay touching each other, and in the feeble light of two lanterns we could see the patients writhing in their dirty blankets, five and six crowded into two beds. Some sat up, apathetically eating; others lay like the dead; still others gave short, grunting moans, or shouted suddenly in the grip of delirium. The hospital orderlies, who slept in the same room, were all Austrian prisoners.

"I have been put in charge of this hospital only three days," said the lieutenant. "Before I came it was pretty bad. Now we have only twenty deaths a day. There are eight hundred patients—you see, we have no room for even these."

We passed through fetid ward after fetid ward, smelling of decomposition and death, until we were wrung with the helplessness of these big men, and our stomachs were turned with the stench.

Later, we dined with Stanoievitch and his staff of young doctors and medical students. The good red wine of the country went around, and in a gay and lively argument about the war we forgot for a moment the poor devils dying on the other side of the wall. Stanoievitch, flushed with wine, was boasting of how the Serbians had smashed the Austrian army.

A HOSPITAL AT NISH.
*In the feeble light of two lanterns we could see the patients writhing
in their dirty blankets.*

"What are these French and English doing?" he cried impatiently. "Why do they not beat the Germans? What they need there are a few Serbians to show them how to make war. We Serbians know that all that is needed is the willingness to die—and the war would soon be over . . . !"

# Toward the Front

---

Next morning early we were on our way to Kraguijevatz, the
army headquarters. Our train was loaded with ammunition and
American flour for the army at the front, and we carried five cars
full of soldiers, in sheepskins, peasant dress, and Austrian uniforms picked up in the rout of December—one man even wore a
German casque. They sang an interminable ballad to a minor air,
about how old King Peter went to the trenches during the battle
of Kolubara River:

> "Kral Peter rose from his bed one morning
> And said to his dearly beloved son, Prince Alexander,
> 'O brave, courageous Prince, my son
> Who leads so well the army of Serbia,
> The Swabos have passed Kroupaign,—
> Their powerful hosts, like the rushing Morava,
> Have passed Valievo. . . .
> I shall go forth to conquer or to die with them!'
> He girt upon him his bright sword. . . ."

The railway line paralleled the Morava River. Here all was
green, and in the black loam of the fields women were ploughing
with oxen, and winding wool on distaffs as they ploughed. White,
low, tiled houses, their balconies overhung with graceful Turkish
arches, their corners painted in colored lozenges, lay hidden amid
plum and apple trees in bloom. Beyond them stretched meadows
under water, where thousands of frogs made a gigantic croaking
chorus, audible above the roaring of the train—for the Morava
was in flood. We passed Teshitza, Bagrdan, Dedrevatz, Lapovo,

smelling of formalin and spattered with sinister white—pest-holes all.

At Kraguijevatz we were met by a delegate from the Press Bureau, erstwhile lecturer on comparative literature at the University of Belgrade. He was a large-featured, absent-minded young man with fat knees incased in pearl riding-breeches, a bright-green felt hat over one ear, and a naughty twinkle in his eye. Within two hours we were calling him "Johnson," which is a literal translation of his name.

Johnson knew every one, and every one knew him. He kept up a running scandalous comment on the people that we passed, and would halt the cab for long periods while he got out and exchanged the latest spicy gossip with some friend. Finally, we would shout to him: "For Heaven's sake, Johnson, hurry up!"

"Excuse me, sair!" he would respond solemnly. "You must have patience. Thees is war-time!"

We found the chief of the Press Bureau, former professor of public law at the University of Belgrade, hard at work reading a novel of George Meredith. Johnson explained that the Press Bureau was a very important and active organization.

"We make here many jokes about prominent people, epigrams, and rhymes. For instance, one of the conspirators in the assassination of the Archduke Ferdinand was an officer of the Serbian army during the retreat. He feared that he would be recognized if taken prisoner, so he shaved his beard. In the Press Bureau we have made a sonnet about him, in which we said that it was in vain to shave his beard when he could not shave his prominent nose! Yes, sair. In the Press Bureau we make sometimes two hundred sonnets a day."

Johnson was a dramatist of note. He had transplanted to the Serbian stage the *Comédie Rosse* of the Théâtre Antoine, and had been ostracized by respectable society. "Because," he explained, "my play was obscene. But it was true to Serbian life, and that is the ideal of art, don't you think?"

Johnson was saturated with European culture, European smartness, cynicism, modernism; yet scratch the surface and you found the Serb; the strong, virile stock of a young race not far removed from the half-savagery of a mountain peasantry, intensely patriotic and intensely independent.

But many Serbian "intellectuals" are like the city of Belgrade, where only three years ago the peasants drove their creaking ox-carts along unpaved streets deep in mud, between one-story houses like the houses of Nish—and which now puts on the buildings, the pavements, the airs and vices of Paris and Vienna. They affect modern art, modern music, the tango and fox-trot. They ridicule the songs and costumes of the peasants.

Sometimes these affectations are laughable. We rode during all one day on horseback over the battlefield of Goutchevo Mountain with a young officer—also of the university faculty—who had lived for three years the life of a fighting nomad, such as no Englishman, Frenchman, or German could have endured. He had gone through the terrible retreat, and still more terrible attack of that winter campaign, sleeping out in the rain or in huts full of vermin, eating the coarse food of the peasants or no food, and thriving on it.

"I am so fond of the country," he said as we rode along. "It is so pastoral, don't you think? I am always reminded of Beethoven's Pastoral Symphony when I am in the country." He whistled a few bars abstractedly. "No, I made a mistake. That is the Third, isn't it?"

We discovered afterward that his father was a peasant, and all his forebears since the Serbs first came down from the plains of Hungary had been peasants, and had lived in this "country" which reminded him only of Beethoven!

And in Serbia they are still sensitive about Shaw's "Arms and the Man." . . .

We dined at the general staff mess, in the rude throne-room of the palace of Milan Obrenovitch, first of the Serbian kings; his gaudy red-plush-and-gilt throne still stands there, and on the walls are pictures of Milosh Obilich and the other heroes of Serbia's stormy history, and of the Serbian *comitadji* leaders who died by the hands of the Turks in Macedonia in the years before the Balkan War.

*Serbian officers.*

*Sketched from the saddle.*

*Sick refugees lying in the road.*

ALONG THE ROAD.

"This palace is one of our oldest national monuments," said Johnson. "It was built more than fifty years ago."

Astonishing, the youth of the kingdom of Serbia. Less than a hundred years have passed since she emerged as a free state from five centuries of Turkish domination—and in that time what a history she has had!

The secret dream of every Serb is the uniting of all the Serbian peoples in one great empire: Hungarian Croatia, identical in race and spoken language—Dalmatia, home of Serbian literature—Bosnia, fountain-head of Serbian poetry and song—Montenegro, Herzegovina, and Slovenia. An empire fifteen millions strong, reaching from Bulgaria to the Adriatic, and from Trieste, east and north, far into the plains of Hungary, which will liberate the energies of the fighting, administrative people of the kingdom of Serbia, penned in their narrow mountain valleys, to the exploitation of the rich plains country, and the powerful life of ships at sea.

Every peasant soldier knows what he is fighting for. When he was a baby, his mother greeted him, "Hail, little avenger of Kossovo!" (At the battle of Kossovo, in the fourteenth century, Serbia fell under the Turks.) When he had done something wrong, his mother reproved him thus: "Not that way will you deliver Macedonia!" The ceremony of passing from infancy to boyhood was marked by the recitation of an ancient poem:

*"Ja sam Serbin,"*

it began,

"I am a Serbian, born to be a soldier,
Son of Iliya, of Milosh, of Vasa, of Marko."

(National heroes, whose exploits here followed at length)

"My brothers are numerous as grapes in the vineyard,
But they are less fortunate than I, a son of free Serbia!
Therefore must I grow quickly, learn to sing and shoot,
That I may hasten to help those who wait for me!"

"A LITTLE AVENGER OF KOSSOVO."

And in the Serbian schools the children are taught not only the geography of old Serbia, but of all the Serbian lands, *in the order of their redemption*—first Macedonia, then Dalmatia, Bosnia, Herzegovina, Croatia, Banat, and Batchka!

Now Kossovo is avenged and Macedonia delivered, within the lifetime of these soldiers who listened to their mothers and never forgot their "brothers, numerous as grapes in the vineyard." But even while we were in Serbia, other complications threatened.

"What if Italy takes Dalmatia?" I asked a government official.

"It is very exasperating," he replied, "for it means that after we have recovered from this war we must fight again!"

An old officer that we met later said, with a sort of holy enthusiasm: "We thought that this dream of a great Serbia would come true—but many years in the future, many years. And here it is realized in our time! This is something to die for!"

And the boy who sang "Son of Free Serbia" has made his country one of the most democratic in the world. It is governed by the Skouptchina, a one-chamber parliament elected by universal suffrage and proportional representation—the Senate, derisively known as the "Museum," was abolished in 1903. King Alexander tried to rule autocratically, and they murdered him; the present King is strictly a figurehead, limited by a liberal constitution. There is no aristocracy in Serbia. Only the King's brother and the King's sons are princes, and to the Crown Prince Regent the ultra-democrats and Socialists refuse even that title, referring to him always as the "Manifest-Signer." Queen Draga attempted to establish an order of nobility, "but," as Johnson said, laughing, "we keelled her!"

The great landlords of Rumania are unknown in Serbia. Here every peasant has a right to five acres of land, inalienable for debt or taxes; he joins fields with his sons and daughters and nephews and nieces, until all through Serbia there exist co-operative estates known as *zadrougas*, where generations of one family, with its ramifications, live together in communal ownership of all their property. And as yet there is no industrial population in Serbia, and few rich men.

. . .

THAT night we heard the dramatic story of the great Serbian victory of December. Twice the Austrians invaded the country, and twice were hurled back, and the streets of Valievo groaned with wounded lying in the rain. But the second time the enemy held Shabatz, Losnitza, and the two rich provinces of Machva and Podrigna, and the heights of Goutchevo. The Serbians could not dislodge them from their strongly intrenched positions. And then, in the bitter weather of December, the Austrians began the third invasion with five hundred thousand men against two hundred and fifty thousand. Pouring across the frontier at three widely separated points, they broke the Serbian lines and rolled the little army back among its mountains. Belgrade was abandoned to the enemy. Twice the Serbians made a desperate stand, and twice they were forced to fall back. Ammunition began to fail—the cannon had less than twenty shells apiece. The enemy passed Krupaign and Valievo and was within forty-five miles of Kraguijevatz, headquarters of the Serbian general staff.

And then, at the last minute, something happened. New supplies of ammunition arrived from Salonika, and the younger officers revolted against their more cautious elders, shouting that it was as well to die attacking as to be slaughtered in the trenches. General Michitch ordered an offensive. The beaten Serbians, rushing from their trenches, fell upon the leisurely Austrian columns coming along narrow mountain defiles to attack. Caught on the march, burdened with big guns and heavy baggage-trains on roads almost impassable from mud, the Austrians resisted furiously, but were forced to recoil. The line was broken. Their center, smashed by Michitch and the first army, broke and fled in panic across the country, abandoning baggage, ammunition, and guns, and leaving behind thousands of dead and wounded, and hospitals crammed with men raving with typhus. This is how the typhus, beginning somewhere up in the plains of Hungary, entered Serbia with the Austrian army. For a time the left wing tried to hold Belgrade, but the exultant, ragged Serbians drove them literally into the River Save and shot them as they swam across.

This great battle, which Voyvoda Michitch reported laconically with the proud telegram, "There remain no Austrian soldiers on Serbian soil except prisoners," has been given no name. Some call it the Battle of Kolubara River and others the Battle of Valievo. But it is, perhaps, the most wonderful feat of arms in all the great World War.

At the right hand of the colonel sat a pope in the long black robes of the Greek Church. He was not unctuous and sly like the Greeks, however—a great ruddy man who laughed uproariously and drank his wine with the officers. These Serbian priests are remarkable people. They are the teachers, the transmitters of patriotism among the peasants. They are elected to the Skouptchina as deputies of districts.

"Why not?" he said in French. "In Serbia there is no Clerical party. We are all one here—eh?" He turned to the colonel, who nodded. "I have now been fighting in the army for three years— not as a priest, but as a Serbian soldier. Yes, we are the State Church, but the government also subsidizes the Protestant and Catholic Churches, and even the Mohammedan *hadjis*. Why, it is really extraordinary. The government pays the Mohammedan *mufti* thirty thousand *denars* a year, and the metropolitan of the Serbian Church only gets twenty thousand! Our people do not forget that Milan Obrenovitch proclaimed the revolution against the Turks at a village church, with a pope at his side. We are Serbs and men first, and priests afterward." He laughed. "Have you heard the story of how the Serbian bishop, Duchitch, shocked the Bishop of London? No? Well, they dined together in England.

" 'You are fortunate,' said the Bishop of London, 'in your people. I am told they are very devout.'

" 'Yes,' said Mr. Duchitch, 'in Serbia we do not trust too much to God. We prayed God five centuries to free us from the Turks, and finally took guns and did it ourselves!' "

IT was midnight when we took the train for Belgrade, less than a hundred kilometers away, but by morning we were still far from the city. We crawled slowly along, waiting hours on sidings for the passing of trains going north laden with soldiers and with supplies, and empty trains going south; for we were now within the lines of the Army of the Danube, and on the main military artery serving fifty thousand men. It was a region of high, rolling hills, and here and there a loftier mountain crowned with the ruined castle of some Dahee overlord, dating from Turkish days. There was no longer any pretense of cultivation. Hillside after hillside hollowed into caves or covered with huts of mud and straw housed the ragged regiments; trenches gashed in the sloping meadows crisscrossed that hard-fought ground—and in spots where the battle had been particularly fierce, the jagged stumps of great oak-trees stood branchless and leafless, stripped bare by the hail of shells and rifle-bullets.

The railway-station of Belgrade had been destroyed in the bombardment, and one by one the searching Austrian cannon had wrecked the nearer stations, so we were forced to leave the train at Rakovitza, six miles out, and drive to the city. The road wound through a beautiful, fertile valley, with white villas and farmhouses smothered in thick blooming chestnuts. Nearer town we entered the shaded road of an immense park, where in summer the fashionable world of Belgrade comes to show its smartest carriages and its newest gowns. Now the roads were weedy, the lawns dusty and unkempt. A shell had wrecked the summer pavilion. Under the big trees at the edge of an ornamental fountain a troop of cavalry was picketed, and a little farther on the tennis-court had been disembowelled to make emplacements for two French cannon—the French sailors of the gun crew, lying around on the grass, shouted gayly to us.

Our carriage had taken a left-hand road, leading toward the River Save, when suddenly a distant deep booming fell upon our ears. It was like nothing else in the world, the double boom of big cannon, and the shrill flight of shells. And now, nearer at hand, off to the left, other great guns answered. A two-horsed cab, its horses galloping, appeared around a turn ahead, and a fat officer leaned out as he passed us.

"Don't go that way!" he shouted. "*Putzaiyu!* They are firing on the road! The English batteries are replying!"

We turned around and took a long détour that led around to the right. For about a quarter of an hour the far shooting con-

TROOP-TRAINS MOVING NORTH THROUGH A REGION OF HIGH, ROLLING HILLS.

tinued—then it ceased. A deep, steady humming had been growing more and more audible for some time, filling all the air. Suddenly there came the heavy, sharp crack of a detonation over our heads. We looked up. There, immeasurably high, gleaming like a pale dragon-fly in the sun, an aeroplane hovered. Her lower planes were painted in concentric circles of red and blue. "French!" said Johnson. She was already turning slowly toward the east and south. Behind her, not more than a hundred yards it seemed, the white puff of an exploding shrapnel slowly flowered. Even as we looked, another distant gun spoke, and another, and the shells leaped after her as she drifted out of our vision behind the trees.

We crawled up a steep hill and descended the other side along a straight, white, unpaved road. In front of us, perched on a high headland between the Danube and the Save, was Belgrade, the *Beograd* of the Serbians, the White City which was ancient when they first came down from the Hungarian mountains, and yet is one of the youngest of the world's cities. Down at the bottom of the hill a long double file of Austrian prisoners, dusty with the long march from Rackovitza, stood patiently in the sun while two Serbian officers questioned them.

"Of what race are you?"

"I am a Serb from Bosnia, *gospodine*," answered the prisoner, grinning.

"And you?"

"Kratti" (Croat) "of the mountains."

"Well, brothers," said the officer, "this is a nice thing for you to be fighting for the Swabos!"

"Ah!" answered the Croat. "We asked permission to fight with you, but they wouldn't let us." Every one laughed.

"And what race are you?"

"Italiano from Trieste."

"Tchek."

"I am Magyar!" growled a sullen-faced, squat man with a look of hate.

"And you?"

"I am Rumaniassi" (Rumanian), said the last man proudly.

A few hundred yards farther along was a great shed stored with all sorts of provisions, fodder, hay, and grain for the army. Here in the hot sun the Austrian prisoners were sweating at their work of loading ox-carts with sacks of flour, their uniforms, hands, and faces caked with white meal. A sentry with a bayonetted rifle walked up and down in front of them, and as he walked he chanted:

"God bless my grandfather, Vladislav Wenz, who came to settle in Serbia forty years ago. If he hadn't, I would now be packing flour with these prisoners!"

# Belgrade Under the Austrian Guns

OUR carriage rattled, echoing through silent Belgrade. Grass and weeds pushed between the cobbles, untravelled now for half a year. The sound of guns had entirely ceased. A hot sun blazed down, dazzling on the white walls of the houses, and a little warm wind whirled spirals of white dust from the unpaved roadway; it was hard to imagine that the Austrian big guns dominated us, and that any moment they might bombard the city, as they had a dozen times before. Everywhere were visible the effects of artillery fire. Great holes fifteen feet in diameter gaped in the middle of the street. A shell had smashed the roof of the Military College and exploded within, shattering all the windows; the west wall of the War Office had sloughed down under a concentrated fire of heavy guns; the Italian legation was pitted and scarred by shrapnel, and the flag hung ragged from its broken pole. Doorless private houses, with roofs cascading to the sidewalks, showed window-frames swinging idly askew without a pane of glass. Along that crooked boulevard which is Belgrade's main and the only paved street, the damage was worse. Shells had dropped through the roof of the Royal Palace and gutted the interior. As we passed, a draggled peacock, which had once adorned the Royal Gardens, stood screaming in a ruined window, while a laughing group of soldiers clustered on the sidewalk underneath imitating it. Hardly anything had escaped that hail of fire—houses, sheds, stables, hotels, restaurants, shops, and public buildings—and there were many fresh ruins from the latest bombardment, only ten days before. A five-story office-building with the two top floors blown off by a 30.5-centimeter shell exhibited a half section of a room—an iron bed hanging perilously in the air, and flowered wall-paper decorated with framed pictures, untouched by the freak of the explosion. The University of Belgrade was only a mass of yawning ruins. The Austrians had made it their special target, for there had been the hotbed of Pan-Serbian propaganda, and among the students was formed the secret society whose members murdered the Archduke Franz Ferdinand.

We met an officer who belonged to this society—a classmate of the assassin. "Yes," he said, "the government knew. It tried to discourage us, but it could do nothing. Of course the government did not countenance our propaganda." He grinned and winked. "But how could it prevent? Our constitution guarantees the freedom of assemblies and organizations. . . . We are a free country!"

Johnson was unmoved by the wreck.

"For years we have been cramped and inconvenienced in that old building," he explained. "But the University was too poor to build again. Now we shall demand in the terms of peace one of the German universities—libraries, laboratories, and all complete. They have many, and we have only one. We have not yet decided whether to ask for Heidelberg or Bonn. . . ."

Already people were beginning to drift back to the city which they had deserted six months before, at the time of the first bombardment. Every evening, toward sundown, the streets became more and more crowded. A few stores timidly opened, some restaurants, and the cafés where the true Belgradian spends all his time sipping beer and watching the fashionable world pass. Johnson kept up a flow of comment on the people who sat at tables, or went by along the street.

"You see that little, important-looking man with the glasses? He is Mr. R——, who is very ambitious and thinks himself a great man. He is editor of an insignificant newspaper called *La Dépêche*, which he published here every day under the bombardment, and imagined himself a great hero. But there is a little song about him which is sung all over Belgrade:

" 'An Austrian cannon-ball flew through the air.
It said: "Now I shall destroy Belgrade, the White City";

LOOKING TOWARD AUSTRIA.

But when it saw that it would hit R——
It held its nose, crying "Phoot!"—and went the other way!' "

In the corner a stout, dirty man with the look of a Jewish politician was holding forth to a crowd.

"That is S——, editor of the *Mali Journal*. There are three brothers, one of them a trick bicycle-rider. This man and the other brother founded a little paper here which lived by blackmailing prominent people. They were desperately poor. No one would pay the blackmail. So they published every day for two weeks a photograph of the bicycle-rider with his bare legs, bare arms, and medals on his chest, so that some heiress with millions of *denars* would become enamored of his beautiful physique and marry him!"

We visited the ancient Turkish citadel which crowns the abrupt headland towering over the junction of the Save and the Danube. Here, where the Serbian guns had been placed, the Austrian fire had fallen heaviest; hardly a building but had been literally wrecked. Roads and open spaces were pitted with craters torn by big shells. All the trees were stripped. Between two shattered walls we crawled on our bellies to the edge of the cliff overlooking the river.

"Don't show yourselves," cautioned the captain who had us in charge. "Every time the Swabos see anything moving here, they drop us a shell."

From the edge there was a magnificent view of the muddy Danube in flood, inundated islands sticking tufts of tree tops above the water, and the wide plains of Hungary drowned in a yellow sea to the horizon. Two miles away, across the Save, the Austrian town of Semlin slept in radiant sunlight. On that low height to the west and south were planted the invisible threatening cannon. And beyond, following southwest the winding Save as far as the eye could see, the blue mountains of Bosnia piled up against the pale sky. Almost immediately below us lay the broken steel spans of the international railway bridge which used to link Constantinople to western Europe—plunging prodigiously from their massive piers into the turbid yellow water. And upstream still was the half-sunken island of Tzigalnia, where the Serbian advance-guards lay in their trenches and sniped the enemy on another island four hundred yards away across the water. The captain pointed to several black dots lying miles away up the Danube behind the shoulder of Semlin.

"Those are the Austrian monitors," he said. "And that low black launch that lies close in to shore down there to the east, she is the English gunboat. Last night she stole up the river and torpedoed an Austrian monitor. We expect the city to be bombarded any minute now. The Austrians usually take it out on Belgrade."

But the day passed and there was no sign from the enemy, except once when a French aeroplane soared up over the Save. Then white shrapnel cracked over our heads, and long after the biplane had slanted down eastward again, the guns continued to fire, miles astern.

"They have learned their lesson," said Johnson complacently. "The last time they bombarded Belgrade, they were answered by the big English, French, and Russian naval guns, which they did not know were here. We bombarded Semlin and silenced two Austrian positions."

WE made the tour of the foreign batteries with the captain next day. The French guns and their marines were posted among trees on the top of a high, wooded hill overlooking the Save. They were served by French marines. Farther along Russian sailors lolled on the grass about their heavy cannon, and on the sloping meadows back of Belgrade lay the British, guarding the channel of the Danube against the Austrian supply-boats which were moored above Semlin, waiting for a chance to slip past down the Danube, with guns and ammunition for the Turks. The Serbian batteries were a queer mixture of ordnance; there were old field-guns made by Creusot in France for the First Balkan War, ancient bronze pieces cast for King Milan in the Turkish War, and all kinds and calibers captured from the Austrians—German field-guns, artillery manufactured in Vienna for the Sultan, ornamented with Turkish symbols, and new cannon ordered by Yuan Shi Kai, their breeches covered with Chinese characters.

Our window looked out over the roofs of the city to the broad current of the Save, and the sinister highland beyond where the enemy's guns were. At night the great Austrian search-light would flare suddenly upon the stream and the city, blinding; sparks would leap and die among the trees of the river islands, and we would hear the pricking rifle-fire where the outposts lay in mud with their feet in the water, and killed each other in the dark. One night the English batteries roared behind the town, and their shells whistled over our heads as they drove back the Austrian monitors who were trying to creep down the river. Then the invisible guns of the highland across the Save spat red; for an hour heavy missiles hurtled through the sky, exploding miles back about the smoking English guns—the ground shook where we stood.

"So you want to visit the trenches," said the captain. We had driven out a mile or so through the outskirts of the city that lay along the Save, always in sight of the Austrian guns. Our carriages were spaced two hundred yards apart, for two vehicles together would have drawn fire. Where we stood the shore jutted out into the flooded river behind the trees of a submerged island that screened us from the Austrian bank. "It is not very safe. We must go in a boat and pass three hundred yards of open water commanded by an Austrian cannon."

The aged launch was supposed to be armored; a heavy sheet of tin roofed her engine-pit, and thin steel plates leaned against the bulwarks. As soon as we rounded the protecting curtain of trees, the soldier who was pilot, engineer, and crew stood up and shook his fist at the point of land where the Austrian gun lay.

"Oh, cowards and sons of cowards!" he chanted. "Why do you not fire, Swabo cowards? Does the sight of unarmed Serbians cause your knees to knock together?"

This he kept up until the launch slipped out of range behind Tzigalnia, alongside a huge cargo-scow, painted black and loop-

IN THE SERB TRENCHES ON THE SAVE, TWO HUNDRED YARDS FROM THE AUSTRIANS.

holed for rifles. On her bow, in large yellow letters, was *Neboysha*, which is Serbian for "Dreadnought."

"That is the Serbian navy," laughed the captain. "With her we have fought a great battle. In January, one dark night, we filled her full of soldiers and let her float down the river. That is how we captured this island."

From the *Neboysha* a precarious plank footbridge on floating logs led between half-submerged willow-trees to a narrow strip of land not more than ten feet wide and two hundred yards long. Here the soldiers had dug their rude rifle-pits, and here they lay forward on the muddy embankment, unshaven, unwashed, clothed in rags, and gaunt with scanty, bad food. From head to foot they were the color of mud, like animals. Many of the trenches were below the flood level, and held water; you could see where, only two days before, the river had risen until it was up to the men's waists. We could not walk along the line of trenches— soldiers poled us up and down in little scows.

A score of shaggy, big men in fur caps, with rifle-belts crossed over their chests and hand bombs slung at their shoulders, were at work under an armed guard, surlily digging trenches. These were *comitadjis*, the captain said—irregular volunteers without uniform, drawn from the half-bandits, half-revolutionists, who had been making desperate guerilla war against Turks, Bulgarians, and Greeks in Macedonia for years.

"They are under arrest," he explained. "They refused to dig trenches or work on the roads. 'We have come to fight the Swabos,' they said, 'not to dig ditches. We are warriors, not laborers!' "

Removing our hats, we peered cautiously through the gaps made for the rifles; a similar barren neck of land appeared about four hundred yards away through the tree tops rising from the water—for all this had once been land—where the Austrians lay. A blue peaked cap bobbed cautiously up—the soldier beside me grunted and fired. Almost immediately there was a scattering burst of shots from the enemy. Bullets whined close over our heads, and from the trees green leaves showered down.

. . .

**DODGING SHRAPNEL ON THE SAVE.**

*Something screamed over our heads and the roof of a building on the shore heaved up with a roar.*

OUR boatman thrust off from the *Neboysha* and headed the launch up-stream before he rounded into the channel swept by the Austrian artillery, a quarter of a mile away.

"We will go closer," said he; "perhaps it will tempt them."

The clumsy, chugging boat swept clear. He stood up in the stern, cupped his hands, and bellowed a satirical verse that the soldiers sang:

> "The Emperor Nicholas rides a black horse,
> The Emperor Franz Joseph rides a mule—
> And he put the bridle on the tail instead of the head,
> So now is the end of Austria!"

Hardly had he finished—the boat was within fifty yards of the sheltering island—when a sudden detonation stunned us. We hit the bottom of the boat with one simultaneous thud just as something screamed three yards over our heads, and the roof of a building on the shore heaved up with a roar, filling the air with whistling fragments of tiles and lead pellets—shrapnel.

"Whoop!" shouted the steersman. "There's enough black balls to defeat any candidate!"

Now we were behind the sheltering trees. A rowboat full of soldiers put off from the bank, paddling frantically.

"Don't go out there!" cried the captain to them. "They are firing!"

"That's why we're going!" they cried altogether, like children. "Perhaps they'll take a shot at us!" They rounded the island with shouts and a prodigious splashing of oars. . . .

Lunch was ready in the ruins of a great sugar factory, where the colonel in command of the island had his headquarters. To get to it, we crossed a bridge of planks laid on a quaking marsh of brown sugar—tons and tons of it, melted when the Austrian shells had set fire to the place.

The colonel, two captains, four lieutenants, a corporal, and two privates sat down with us. In Serbia the silly tradition that familiarity between officers and men destroys discipline apparently does not exist. Many times in restaurants we noticed a private or a non-commissioned officer approach a table where officers sat, salute stiffly, and then shake hands all around and sit down. And here the sergeant who waited on table took his place between us to drink his coffee and was formally introduced.

One of the privates had been secretary of the Serbian National Theatre before the war. He told us that the charter required fifty performances of Shakespeare a season, and that the Serbians preferred *Coriolanus* to all the other plays.

"*Hamlet*," he said, "was very popular. But we have not played it here for fifteen years, for the only actor who could do the part died in 1900."

# Along the Battle-Line

A THOUSAND feet up two French aeroplanes hummed slowly west, translucent in the clear morning sunlight. Below and to the left lazy shrapnel burst. The sound of the explosions and the humming of the motors drifted down, minutes later. Our carriages crawled up a hill strewn with villas hidden in new verdure and flowering fruit-trees; and, looking back, we had a last view of Belgrade, the White City, on her headland, and the Austrian shore. Then we plunged into a winding, rutted lane that wandered up beneath trees which met overhead—past low, white peasant houses roofed with heavy Turkish tiles, and fields where women in embroidered leather vests and linen skirts tramped the furrows, leading oxen lent by the army, and followed by soldiers who guided the wooden ploughs. Long strips of homespun linen hung from hedge and fence, bleaching in the sun. Except for the soldiers, the country was destitute of men.

We turned inland, along country roads that were little more than tracks—now one could not use the main road along the Save, for it lay directly under the guns of the Austrian trenches, three hundred yards away across the river. Many times the driver lost the way. We forded rapid mountain streams that washed to the wagon-bed, sank to the hubs in muddy sloughs, crept through winding, deep ravines along the dried beds of torrents, and rattled down steep hills through groves of immense oaks, where droves of half-wild pigs fled squealing before the horses. Once we passed three huge tombstones taller than a man, crowned with the carved turbans that ornament the cenotaphs of the *hadjis*. Immense scimitars were chiselled at their base. Johnson asked some peasants about them, but they answered "Heroes," and shrugged their shoulders. Farther on was a white stone sarcophagus lying in a hollow of the hill—the Roman tomb that once enclosed it had been broken up and carried away by the peasants, perhaps centuries ago. Then the track led through the middle of an ancient village graveyard, its moss-grown Greek crosses leaning crazily among dense brush. Everywhere along the way new crosses of stone, painted with gold, green, and red, stood under little roofs; these, Johnson explained, were the memorials of men of the neighborhood who had died in unknown places and whose bodies had never been found. Trees and grass and flowers rioted over the hills. Last year's fields were jungles of weeds. Houses with doors ajar and gaping windows lay amid untended vines. Sometimes we bumped down the wide street of a silent country village where old men dragged themselves to their doors to see us pass, and children romped with wolfish sheep-dogs in the dust, and groups of women came home from the fields with mattocks on their shoulders. This was the *rackia* country—where the native plum brandy comes from; immense orchards of prunes and plums sweetened the heavy air.

We stopped at a *mehana* or village inn to eat the lunch we had brought with us—for in all this country there was not enough food even for the inhabitants. In the dim, cool interior, with its rough wooden tables set on the earthen floor, aged peasants with the simplicity of children took off their hats with grave politeness. *"Dobar dan, gospodine!"* they greeted us. "Good day, sirs! We hope your voyage is pleasant." The gnarled old proprietor stooped over his earthen oven, making Turkish coffee in brass cups and telling how the Austrians had come.

"A soldier with a rifle and a bayonet came through this door. 'I want money,' he said; 'all you have—quick!' But I answered that I had no money. 'You must have money. Are you not an innkeeper?' Still I said I had none; then he thrust at me with his bayonet—here. You see?" He tremblingly lifted his shirt and showed a long gash, yet unhealed.

. . .

"Typhus!" Johnson pointed to the fences before the houses on each side of the road. Almost every one was marked with a painted white cross, sometimes two or three. "Every cross means a case of typhus in the house." In half a mile I counted more than a hundred. It seemed as if this buoyant, fertile land held nothing but death or the memorials of death.

Late in the afternoon we topped a hill and saw again the widespread Save flooding all its valley, and beyond, foothills piling greenly up to the Bosnian mountains, range behind range. Here the river made a great bend, and half concealed in the middle of a wooded plain that seemed entirely under water lay red roofs, white swollen towers and thin minarets—Obrenovatz. We drove down the hill and joined the main road, which rose just above the flood level, like a causeway through wastes of water. In the marshes on either side sacred white storks were solemnly fishing. The ground rose a little in a sort of island at the center of the flooded country; we rattled along the rocky, unpaved street of a white little Serbian town, low houses set in clumps of green, with double windows to keep out the vampires.

They led us with much ceremony to the house of Gaia Matitch, the postmaster, a nervous, slight man with a sweet smile, who welcomed us at his door. His wife stood beside him, fluttered, anxious, and bursting with the importance of entertaining strangers. The entire family waved us before them into their bedroom, which they had ornamented with the whitest linen, the gayest embroideries, and vases full of flowers from the marsh. Two officers from the divisional headquarters stood around racking their brains for things to make us comfortable; a little girl brought plates of apples and preserved plums and candied oranges; soldiers fell on their knees and pulled at our boots, and another stood by the wash-stand waiting to pour water over our hands; Gaia Matitch himself wandered in and out of the room, a bottle of *rackia* in his hand, offering us a drink, tidying the chairs and tables, shouting shrill, exasperated orders to the servants.

"We are greatly honored," he managed to convey, in a mixture of garbled French, German, and English. "In Serbia it is the highest honor for a stranger to visit one's house."

This beautiful Serbian hospitality to foreigners we experienced many times. Once, I remember we were in a strange town where for weeks no new supplies had come in, and there was no tobacco. We went to a shop to try to find some cigarettes.

"Cigarettes?" said the shopkeeper, throwing up his hands. "Cigarettes are worth double their weight in gold." He looked at us for a moment. "Are you strangers?" We said we were. Whereupon, he unlocked an iron safe and handed us each a package of cigarettes. "The charge is nothing," he said: "You are foreigners."

Our friend Matitch, with the tears standing in his eyes, pointed to two photographs on the wall—one of an old man with a white beard, and the other of a young girl.

"This man is my father," he said. "He was seventy-seven years old. When the Austrians took Shabatz they sent him to Buda-Pesth as a prisoner of war, and he is dead there in Hungary. As for my sister here, they took her also—and since August I have heard nothing. I know not whether she is living or dead."

Here we first began to hear of Austrian atrocities along the western frontier. We could not believe them at first; but later, at Belgrade, at Shabatz, at Losnitza, they were repeated again and again, by those who escaped, by the families of those who were dead or in prison, by sworn statements and the Austrian official lists of prisoners sent to the Serbian Red Cross. At the taking of the border towns the Austrians herded the civil population together—women, old men, and children—and drove them into Austria-Hungary as prisoners of war. More than seven hundred were so taken from Belgrade, and fifteen hundred from Shabatz alone. The official war-prisoner lists of the Austrian Government read cynically like this: Ion Touphechitch, age 84; Darinka Antitch (woman), age 23; Georg Georgevitch, age 78; Voyslav Petronievitch, age 12; Maria Wenz, age 69. The Austrian officers said they did this because it was a punitive expedition against the Serbs, and not a war!

At the mess we heard that we must travel by night to Shabatz, for the road led along the river bank within range of the enemy's trenches. So after dinner the entire staff accompanied us back to Matitch's. Much sour native wine had been flowing, and we went arm in arm hooting and singing along the village street. When Matitch heard that we were not going to spend the night in his house, he almost wept.

"Please stay!" he cried, grasping our arms. "Isn't my house good enough for you? Is there anything you lack?"

At length, with a sigh he thrust us into the dining-room. There we sat, saying farewell, while Matitch and Mrs. Matitch brought wine and dried salt beef to make us thirsty. A courteous officer inquired from Johnson how one drank a health in French; but all he could get was *"A votre sentir!"* which he repeated over and over again. We drank Mrs. Matitch's health, at which the good woman was furiously embarrassed. We sang American songs to uproarious applause. Some one stuffed Robinson's pockets full of dried beef, which fell out of his clothes for days afterward. It got along toward midnight, and we ought to have started at ten. Of a sudden Matitch rose to his feet. *"Pobratim!"* he shouted, and all the others echoed *"Pobratim!"*

"I now make you my *pobratim*—my blood-brother," said he, glowing with friendliness. "It is the old Serbian ceremony. Your arm through mine—so!"

One by one we linked elbows and drank thus, and then threw our arms about each other's necks, and embraced loudly on both cheeks. The company roared and pounded on the table. It was done—and to this day we are *pobratim* with Gaia Matitch.

At length we were in the carriages; the drivers snapped their whips, and we were off, to shouts of *"S Bogom! Farewell! Laku Noch! Happy night!"*

There was a bright moon. As we passed the outskirts of the village, two silent, armed figures on horseback fell in behind the first carriage, riding along with us till the danger zone was passed. Now we pitched and tossed over rocks or wallowed through deep mud; again the horses were splashing in water that rose to the hubs, where the river-flood covered the road. The drivers cracked their whips no more, nor shouted—they cursed the horses in low tones, for we were now within hearing of the Austrian trenches. No sound was heard except the beat of the horses' hoofs and the creaking of the carriage. The moon sank slowly. The mounted guards vanished as mysteriously as they had come. Still we rocked on. Gently the wide, starry sky paled to dawn, and eastward, over the great mountains of Tser, where the Serbians broke the first invasion, came the white and silver dawn. Under a grassy hill crowned with an enormous white Greek church wrecked by artillery fire, a hundred ox-carts were scattered in the fields, their drivers sleeping wrapped in blankets of vivid colors, or squatting around early fires that painted their faces red. They were bound for Belgrade, a week's crawling journey away, to bring back food for the starving country where we were going.

Over the mountains leaped the sun, hot and blinding, and we rattled into the streets of Shabatz, between endless rows of smashed and gutted and empty houses, before the town was awake.

A café stood open. We made for it, and ordered coffee. Was there anything to eat? We were ravenous. The woman shook her head. "In Shabatz there is not even bread."

"Eggs!" we cried.

Johnson lazily threw up his hands. "My dear sairs! Excuse me. There is no eggs. Thees is war!"

"But I saw hens up the street," I insisted. Finally Johnson consented to ask the woman.

"There are no eggs for sale here," she replied. "But since the *gospodine* are strangers, we will *give* you some."

Shabatz had been a rich and important town, metropolis of the wealthiest department in Serbia, Machva, and the center of a great fruit, wine, wool, and silk trade. It contained twenty-five hundred houses. Some had been destroyed by the guns; twice as many more were wantonly burned, and all of them had been broken into and looted. One walked along miles and miles of streets—every house was gutted. The invaders had taken linen, pictures, children's playthings, furniture—and what was too heavy or cumbersome to move they had wrecked with axes. They

THE NIGHT RIDE TO SHABATZ.

*The drivers cursed the horses in low tones, for we were within hearing of the Austrian trenches.*

had stabled their horses in the bedrooms of fine houses. In private libraries all the books lay scattered in filth on the floor, carefully ripped from their covers. Not simply a few houses had been so treated—*every* house. It was a terrible thing to see.

At the time of the first invasion many people remained in Shabatz, trusting that they would be safe. But the soldiers were loosed like wild beasts in the city, burning, pillaging, raping. We saw the gutted Hôtel d'Europe, and the blackened and mutilated church where three thousand men, women, and children were penned up together without food or water for four days, and then divided into two groups—one sent back to Austria as prisoners of war, the other driven ahead of the army as it marched south against the Serbians. This is not unsupported rumor or hysterical accusation, as it is often in France and Belgium; it is a fact proved by a mass of sworn testimony, by hundreds of people who made that terrible march. We talked with several; one a very old woman who had been forced at the point of the bayonet to go on foot before the troops more than thirty-five miles to Valievo. Her shoes had rotted from her feet—for ten miles she walked barefoot over the stony road.

In the Prefecture we went over hundreds of reports, affidavits, and photographs, giving names, ages, addresses of the sufferers, and details of the horrible things the Austrians had done. There was one picture taken at the village of Lechnitza, showing more than a hundred women and children chained together, their heads struck off and lying in a separate heap. At Kravitza old men, women, and children were tortured and fiendishly outraged, then butchered. At Yvremovatz fifty people were herded into a cellar and burned alive. Five undefended towns were razed to the ground—forty-two villages were sacked, and the greater part of their inhabitants massacred. The typhus, brought into the country by the Austrian army, still ran riot through Shabatz and all the region. And here there were no doctors nor hospitals.

To be perfectly fair, let me say that everywhere we were told it was the Hungarians, and not the Austrian Germans, who had committed these atrocities—the Hungarians, who have always been enemies of the Serbs, in Croatia as well as here. The Austri-

THE BLACKENED AND MUTILATED CHURCH, WHERE THREE THOUSAND MEN, WOMEN, AND CHILDREN WERE PENNED UP TOGETHER WITHOUT FOOD OR WATER FOR FOUR DAYS. (SHABATZ.)

ans themselves seem to have behaved fairly well; they paid for what they took and did not bother peaceable civilians.

But the Hungarians reverted to their savage ancestors, the Huns. When they retreated from Shabatz, in December, they gathered together in the courtyard of Gachitch's pharmacy three hundred Serbian soldiers taken prisoners in battle, shot them slowly and then broke their necks. Belgium can show no horrors as black as these. . . . The cold-blooded fiends who committed them gave as an excuse that the townspeople had harbored *comitadjis*—who, they had been told by their officers, were savage bandits, to be shot on sight. But in all this region there were no *comitadjis*, nor ever had been. In the country they pretended to believe that the Serbian peasant costume was the *comitadji* uniform—and since every civilian, man, woman, and child, wore it, they butchered them all. The slaughter of the prisoners of war had no excuse.

In this once flourishing and pleasant city hardly two hundred people now lived, camping miserably in their ruined houses, without enough to eat. We wandered in the hot sun through deserted streets, past the square where once the great market of all northwest Serbia had been held, and the peasants had gathered in their bright dress from hundreds of kilometers of rich mountain valleys and fertile plains. It was market-day. A few miserable women in rags stood mournfully by their baskets of sickly vegetables. And on the steps of the gutted Prefecture sat a young man whose eyes had been stabbed out by Hungarian bayonets. He was tall and broad-shouldered, with ruddy cheeks—dressed in the dazzling homespun linen of the peasant's summer costume, and in his hat he wore yellow dandelions. He played a melancholy tune upon a horse-headed Serbian fiddle and sang:

"I am sad, for I have lost the sight of the sun and the green fields and the blossoming plum-trees. God's blessing to you who have given me a *grosh* (four cents). Blessing to all who are about to give——"

The prefect pointed to the broken buildings. "When the war is finished we shall make a new Shabatz," he said. "The government has already ordered that no one shall repair the old ruined houses. They must be rebuilt entirely new."

# A Nation Exterminated

Next morning we boarded the train of the narrow-gauge railroad which taps the richest part of the Machva, and connects the valley of the Drina with the valley of the Save. Four box-cars followed our carriage, crammed with miserable refugees, chiefly women and children—returning to the homes from which they had fled, destitute and on foot, six months ago, before the Austrian scourge. We went slowly along a vast fertile plain, white with fruit orchards in bloom and green with tall grass and new foliage, between uncultivated fields rank with weeds, and past white houses blackened with fire. All this country had been burned, looted, and its people murdered. Not an ox was seen, and for miles not a man. We passed through little towns where grass grew in the streets and not a single human being lived. Sometimes the train would halt to let the refugees descend; they stood there beside the track, all their possessions in sacks over their shoulders, gazing silently at the ruins of their homes. . . .

The prefect came with us, stopping the train for an hour or so at different villages, to show us the sights. So we visited Prnjavor, once a rich little place of three thousand people, now a waste of burned and smashed dwellings. At the station was a tall, rugged old farmer in peasant costume of rough brown wool, who was introduced to us as Mr. Samourovitch, deputy to the Skouptchina. He pointed down into a pool of muddy water beside the railroad track, from which emerged the top of a heap of earth, crowned with two wooden crosses.

"That is the grave of my old father and mother," he said without emotion, "the Swabos shot them for *comitadjis.*" We walked

359

on into the town, to a place where once a house stood, that now was a black heap of ashes and burnt timbers. "In this place," he went on, "the Hungarians gathered together a hundred citizens of Prnjavor—they could not cram them all into the house, so they made the rest stand close and bound them to it with ropes— and then they set fire to the house, and shot those who tried to escape. . . . This long, low pile of dirt is their grave." The story seemed too horrible for any possibility, and I made particular inquiries about it. But it was literally true. Swiss doctors examined the spot and took photographs of the bodies before they were buried; they were all old people, women, and children.

Stagnant pools from the recent rains, covered with green slime, stood in the streets. A smell of decaying bodies and neglected filth was in the air. Before almost every house at least one sinister white cross was painted on the fence to show where typhus was or had been. In the dooryard of one place, where the grass had been dug up to make one huge grave for many people, a wrinkled, limping woman stood surrounded by nine children, all under fifteen. Two were almost unable to stand, dead-white and shaking from some fever; three others, one only a baby, were covered with huge running sores and scabs. The woman pointed to the grave-mound.

"I have lost every one but these—there are my husband and my sister and my father, and my brother-in-law and his wife. And we have nothing fit to feed these sick children. The condensed milk that the government sends for the children—the president of the town gives it only to his political constituents, the dishonest Socialist!"

This woman and her children, living in miserable squalor, were all that remained of a powerful *zadrouga*. Two long, one-story white houses, fronting on the street where it turned at right angles, embraced a sort of patio, carpeted with long grass and wild flowers, and shaded by an ancient oak. The entrance to the houses was from the garden, and there was another house behind, with offices, stables, and the *rackia* distillery, where the family made its own plum brandy. Here lived three generations, the women with their husbands, the men with their wives, and each

couple with its children—not to mention cousins, aunts, uncles—
more than forty people in all, who shared their land and all their
property in common. The buildings were wrecked and burned; of
the people, some had died in battle, others had been murdered by
the Hungarians, and the typhus had done the rest.

"They did terrible things," said old Samourovitch as we walked
back to the train. "We are happy that we paid the Austrians for all
this by beating them so badly in December." This extraordinary
lack of bitterness we found everywhere in Serbia; the people
seemed to think that the smashing Austrian defeat revenged them
for all those black enormities, for the murder of their brothers,
for the bringing of the typhus.

Through meadows gorgeous with purple larkspur and butter-
cups, through orchards heavy with peach, apple, cherry, and plum
blossoms we went; here the Turkish influence entirely died out,
and the mud houses became entirely Serb—capped no longer
with red tiles, but with peaked roofs of rough wooden shingles.
Then appeared once more over the westward plain the green
Bosnian mountains, and we were at Losnitza—again under the
Austrian guns across the Drina.

There was a typhus hospital, which we visited. It had once been
a school. As the Serbian doctor opened the doors of room after
room, a sickening stench of dirt, filthy clothing and airlessness
came out. The windows were all closed. The sick—mostly soldiers in the wreck of their uncleaned uniforms—lay packed
closely shoulder to shoulder upon foul straw spread on the floor.
There was no sign of disinfectant. Some leaned weakly on their
elbows, scratching feebly for vermin; others tossed and chattered
in delirium, and others lay whitely still, their eyes half open, like
the dead.

"It gets better every day," said the doctor, rubbing his hands.
"Two weeks ago we had four hundred here—now there are only
eighty-six. . . ." He glanced meditatively at the sick men, jammed
so close together that they almost lay upon one another. "Then
we were *crowded.*"

At dusk we sat at a café table in the great square of Losnitza,
drinking Turkish coffee and eating black bread and *kaymak*—de-

licious yellow cheese-butter. In the dim evening light oxen kneeled by their carts, and peasants all in white linen stood in bright groups, talking. From ten different doors of drinking-shops about the immense space, floods of yellow light poured, and there came bursts of violin music and singing. We got up and strolled over to one; the proprietress, a scrawny woman with yellow hair, caught sight of us, and raised a shrill yell: "Why do you stand there in the street? Why do you not come here and sit at my tables? I have all sorts of good wine, beer, and *koniak!*" We meekly obeyed.

"We are Americans," I explained as best I could, "and we do not know your language."

"That's no reason why you can't drink!" she cried brazenly, and slapped me on the back. "I don't care what language you drink in!"

Inside two gypsies were playing, one a fiddle and the other a cornet, while an old peasant, his head thrown back, intoned through his nose the ballad of the Bombardment of Belgrade:

### THE BOMBARDMENT OF BELGRADE

"A dream had Madame Georgina,
The faithful spouse of Nicola Pachitch
The well-known Serbian prime minister;
In her palace in the center of Belgrade
She had a dream, and this was her dream:

"Northward the earth trembles—
Trembled Srem, Batchka and Hungary—
And a terrible darkness
Rolls south upon Belgrade,
The White City that rides the waters.
Athwart the gloom lightnings cross,
And thunder follows after,
Smiting the houses and the palaces,
Wrecking the villas and hotels
And the fine shops of Belgrade.
From the Save and the Danube
Soar the roaring water-dragons—
Spitting thunder and lightnings

Over Belgrade, the White City;
Blasting houses and streets,
Reducing to ruin hotels and palaces,
Smashing the wooden pavements,
Burning the pretty shops,
And upsetting churches and chapels;
Everywhere the screams of children and invalids—
Everywhere the cries of old women and old men!
As if the last terrible Day of Judgment
Broke over Belgrade!

"Then in the night Madame Georgina awoke,
Asking herself what had happened,
And began to weep,
For she knew not how to interpret her dream.
Then awoke Nicola Pachitch also
And addressed his faithful spouse:

" 'What is the matter with thee, faithful spouse,
That thou risest in the night
And wettest thy cheek with tears?
Of what art thou frightened?
Tell it me, my faithful spouse,
Whom God bless!'

"Then spoke Madame Pachitch:

" 'My master! Pachitch, Nicola!
This night have I had a terrible dream.
I have dreamed, and in my dream have seen many things,
But I cannot interpret them,
Therefore am I miserable and worried.'
And she began to tell her dream. . . ."

(Three hundred lines more, consisting mostly of accurate prophecy by Mr. Pachitch on what actually occurred.)

OVER the sharp, crumpled house roofs westward the swollen cupola of a Greek church rose black against the warm yellow sky. And there were great trees, spread like lace across the firmament, where already faint stars glittered. A thin crescent moon floated up over the shadowy Bosnian mountains, the heart and birthplace of Serbian song—dear land so long an exile. . . .

# Goutchevo and the Valley of Corpses

$B$EFORE dawn next morning we were on horseback, galloping out of Losnitza on the way to Goutchevo Mountain, which towered in a lofty series of wooded crests three thousand feet up to the south. It was the summit of Goutchevo that the Austrians seized and intrenched at the time of the second invasion. In the face of their withering fire the Serbians climbed its eastern side, foot by foot, until their trenches were also upon the narrow crest, and along a front of ten miles on top of a savage mountain was fought that strange Battle Above the Clouds which lasted fifty-four days, and ended with the retirement of the Serbs, only because the third invasion had broken their lines down by Krupaign. After the rout at Valievo the Austrians abandoned Goutchevo without a stand.

The genial young captain who escorted us had once been a *comitadji* officer, sent by the government to organize revolt—first in Macedonia, and then in Austrian Bosnia and Herzegovina.

"Before we volunteered for *comitadji* service," he said, "we were sent to the universities in Berlin and Vienna to study the organization of revolutions, particularly of the Italian *Risorgimento.* . . ."

Our road turned to rough country way, deep in mud, then to a mere track where only mules and pedestrians could pass—winding upward through immense oaks and ashes, lost in swift mountain brooks and choked with brush. An hour's hard climb brought us to the summit of the first mountain, from which we could see the precipitous peak of Eminove Vode—"Waters of Emin," as the old Turks named it—rising tremendous from the little valley that lay between, and splendid with the vivid green of young leaves, and great shining knobs of black rock.

In the high valley of the hills the white houses of a village lay half hidden in a sea of riotous plum blossoms. Their windows gaped wide—their doors swung idly to and fro. Behind some wall which we could not see a feminine voice was wailing shrilly, flatly, with hysterical catches, the monotonous song of mourning for the dead. The captain pulled up his horse and hallooed loudly—finally a thin, gaunt woman came slowly through the orchard.

"Have you *rackia*, sister?"

"*Ima*. I have." She went back and returned with a stone jug and a long-necked vase for us to drink from.

"What is this place?"

"It is the Rich Village of the Rackia-Makers."

"Where are all the people?"

"They are dead, of the spotted heat (typhus)."

We spurred forward through the golden silence, heavy with the scent of the plum-trees and with humming bees. The wailing died behind. Here the travelled road ended, and beyond was a mountain path untravelled save by hunters and the goatherds of high Goutchevo, but now scarred and rutted by the feet of thousands, and the passage of heavy bodies dragged through the rocks and brush.

"By here the army climbed Goutchevo," said the captain, "and those marks are the marks of cannon that we took up there." He pointed to the towering height of Eminove Vode. "Horses were no good here—and the oxen fell dead of fatigue. So we pulled them up by men—a hundred and twenty to each gun."

The path wound upward along the flank of the mountain and through a leaping stream which we waded. Here it ceased; but on the other side the deeply scored hillside rose almost straight for five hundred feet. We dismounted and led the stumbling, winded mountain horses, zigzagging from shelf to shelf of earth and crumbling rock.

"It took them three days to haul the cannon up here," panted the captain.

Resting and walking, and for level spaces riding a short dis-

THE WOMAN OF GOUTCHEVO MOUNTAIN.

tance, we climbed up through the forest of the mounting crest perhaps a thousand feet higher, over ground strewn with brass cartridge-shells, trace-leathers, bits of Serbian uniforms, and the wheels of shattered cannon limbers. Everywhere in the woods were deserted huts thatched with leaves and the branches of trees, and caves in the ground, where the Serbian army had lived for two months in the snow. Higher up we noticed that the lower parts of the trees were covered with leaves, but that their tops were as if dead; slowly as we climbed the dead part descended, until half the forest lifted gaunt, broken spikes where the vicious hail of bullets had torn off their tops—and then came trees naked of branches. We crossed two lines of deep trenches, and emerged on the bare summit of Goutchevo, which had also once been wooded, but where now nothing but jagged stumps studded with glistening lead remained.

On one side of this open space were the Serbian trenches, on the other side the Austrian. Barely twenty yards separated the two. Here and there both trenches merged into immense pits, forty feet around and fifty feet deep, where the enemy had undermined and dynamited them. The ground between was humped into irregular piles of earth. Looking closer, we saw a ghastly thing: from these little mounds protruded pieces of uniform, skulls with draggled hair, upon which shreds of flesh still hung; white bones with rotting hands at the end, bloody bones sticking from boots such as the soldiers wear. An awful smell hung over the place. Bands of half-wild dogs slunk at the edge of the forest, and far away we could see two tearing at something that lay half-covered on the ground. Without a word the captain pulled out his revolver and shot. One dog staggered and fell thrashing, then lay still—the other fled howling into the trees; and instantly from the depths of the wood all around came a wolfish, eerie howling in answer, dying away along the edge of the battle-field for miles.

We walked on the dead, so thick were they—sometimes our feet sank through into pits of rotting flesh, crunching bones. Little holes opened suddenly, leading deep down and swarming with gray maggots. Most of the bodies were covered only with a film of earth, partly washed away by the rain—many were not buried at all. Piles of Austrians lay as they had fallen in desperate charge, heaped along the ground in attitudes of terrible action. Serbians were among them. In one place the half-eaten skeletons of an Austrian and a Serbian were entangled, their arms and legs wrapped about each other in a death-grip that could not even now be loosened. *Behind* the front line of Austrian trenches was a barbed-wire barricade, significant of the spirit of the men pinned in that death-trap—for they were mostly Serbians from the Austrian Slav provinces, driven at the point of a revolver to fight their brothers.

For six miles along the top of Goutchevo the dead were heaped like that—ten thousand of them, said the captain. From here we could see for forty miles around—the green mountains of Bosnia across the silver Drina, little white villages and flat roads, planes of fields green and yellow with new crops and brown with ploughing, and the towers and bright houses of Austrian Svornik, gleaming among lovely trees at the bend of the river; southward in long lines that seemed to move, so living were they, lifted and broke the farther peaks of Goutchevo, along which wriggled to the end of vision the double line of trenches and the sinister field between . . .

We rode through fruit orchards heavy with blossoms, between great forests of oaks and beeches and blooming chestnuts; under high wooded hills, whose slopes broke into a hundred rippling mountain meadows that caught the sun like silk. Everywhere springs poured from the hollows, and clear streams leaped down canyons choked with verdure, from Goutchevo, which the Turks called "Mountain of Waters"—from Goutchevo, saturated with the rotting dead. All this part of Serbia was watered by the springs of Goutchevo; and on the other side they flowed into the Drina, thence into the Save and the Danube, through lands where millions of people drank and washed and fished in them. To the Black Sea flowed the poison of Goutchevo. . . .

LATE in the afternoon we descended into the main highroad to Valievo, by which the Austrian army had entered the heart of the country, and at evening, clattered down the main street of the

THE UNBURIED DEAD. (GOUTCHEVO.)

white little village of Krupaign, where the subprefect, the chief of police, the president of the town, and the officers of the divisional staff came to meet us, dressed in their best uniforms. Our dinner consisted of roast young pig torn in fragments, beer, wine, *rackia*, cognac, and *pitta smesson*, chopped meat fried in greasy pastry.

Through the warm dark of the spring evening came the squealing of bagpipes, the stamping and shuffling of feet, and short, wild shouts. We leaned from the window. Up the cobbled street marched a big gypsy with the Serbian pipes swelling under his arm, and behind him came hundreds of soldiers, hand in hand, sidling along in a sort of rough polka step—the *kolo*, which is danced all over this part of the world. They swayed along, whooping, until they reached the village square; there they formed a huge, irregular circle, with the gypsy in the middle. The tune changed to a swifter, wilder measure. The dancers flung their legs high and leaped faster in all sorts of variations—each one the specialty of a different village—and as they danced they sang a short chorus with much laughter.

"Every Sunday the peasants all over Serbia gather in their village squares and dance the *kolo*," explained the captain. "There are *kolos* for marriages, *kolos* for christenings, *kolos* for every occasion. And each political party has a separate *kolo* for elections. This one they are dancing now is the Radical *kolo* (the government in power)—and the song they are singing is the Radical song:

> " 'If you will pay my taxes for me
> Then I will vote for you! . . .' "

At a quarter to five in the morning our breakfast appeared—a glass of cognac, a glass of tea, and a tiny cup of Turkish coffee. This was to last us perhaps all day, for between here and Valievo was all devastated country. At five we climbed into an ox-cart covered over with a bowed top of matting like the roof of a prairie-schooner, so low that we could not sit up straight. The wagon was not only springless, but built so that every unevenness was magnified one hundred times and communicated to every part. And our

HIT BY A BURSTING SHELL.

route lay over the worst road in Serbia, now rendered impassable by the double passage of two great armies in the winter. The greater part of the trip consisted of a jolting crawl over huge boulders lying in bottomless mud—and eighty kilometers lie between Krupaign and Valievo.

"*Haide!*" roared the driver, lashing the horses. He was a miserably dressed soldier, dirty and covered with fleas—who soon were holding a banquet on Robinson and me. We tore down the cobbled street at a terrible pace, bouncing up to the roof with shaking bones, in the frightful clatter of the cart over the rocks.

"See those horses go!" cried the soldier, beaming with pride. "The finest horses in all Serbia! This stallion I have named Voyvoda Michitch, and the mare, I call her King Peter."

He pulled up with a flourish at the last café in the village, got down and sat down at a table, rapping loudly for a glass of wine. And there he stayed for half an hour, embracing the hostess, patting the children on the head, and sipping his wine amid an admiring circle of girls who greeted his sallies with giggles. Finally we fell furiously upon Johnson, demanding that he call the driver.

"Excuse me, sair!" returned our guide. "You must have patience. Thees is war!"

Off again at top speed, bouncing over the stones and sinking in the mud.

"I am behind time!" explained the driver. "We must hurry!"

"Well, why did you stay at that café so long?"

He stared at us with bland surprise. "Because I wanted to talk and drink!"

Finally the horses were too tired to run, and the road became so horrible that we walked, the drivers pulling at the bridles with shouts, and lashing their beasts through mire and over heaps of great stones.

All along the débris of the Austrian retreat still littered both sides of the way—hundreds of transport wagons, cannon limbers, broken guns, heaps of rusty rifles and of unshot cartridges, uniforms, caps, hairy knapsacks, and leather ammunition-belts. The road ran along the edge of a canyon through which a river fell down the valley. A sickening stench rose from it. Into this river

RIDING BEHIND VOYVODA MICHITCH AND KING PETER.

had been thrown the bodies of men and horses found dead along the line of the retreat. Here the river widened out and poured thunderously over an immense dam; and looking down, we could see the clear water running above a mass of sodden cloth and bodies bloated gray—from the falls themselves a bone stuck straight out, with strings of flesh and pieces of clothing waving in the current.

This nightmare journey continued for five hours, until we reached the hideous, ruined, looted village of Zavlaka. Faint with hunger, we besought Johnson to get something to eat. He roused himself from a light slumber and began: "Excuse me, sair! Thees is——"

"I don't care whether it's war or not!" screamed Robinson. "You get out and rustle some eggs! *Haide!*"

We got our eggs and again started. All that day we crawled down the valley, which is nothing but a fifty-mile grave of dead Austrians.

Late at night we rounded a wooded hill where the camp-fires of the first army stretched under immense oak-trees for miles, and the soldiers lay about them singing epics of the war, and found ourselves in the streets of Valievo.

Valievo had been one of the worst typhus pestholes in all Serbia. Even now, when the disease had diminished so greatly, the streets of Valievo were nothing but avenues of hospitals. We were taken to one of these.

"Now," said the Serbian doctor who was in charge, "you shall see a good Serbian hospital. You have seen the bad ones, where we were hampered by the lack of all necessities. But *my* hospital is equal to the American hospital at Belgrade."

We entered a whitewashed hall, clean as it could be made, and smelling of disinfectant. In the wards, where the patients had each his own bed and lay in clean blankets in new clean nightclothes, all the windows were open to the sun and air. The doctor put on a white blouse over his uniform, washed his hands with sublimate, and made us do the same. We were enchanted. But in the center of the hospital was an open-air court, whitewashed with lime, where the convalescents walked slowly about. At one side was a small open shed, and within lay five dead men, clothed in the filthy rags in which they had entered the hospital. They had lain there for two days, for Serbians will not bury a man until a coffin is made—and in Valievo the coffin-makers were behind with their orders. On the other side of the court were the open toilets. And the court sloped down to the middle, *where was the well for drinking water!*

Here was a horrible room full of men with posttyphus gangrene, that awful disease that follows typhus in almost fifty percent of soldier cases, in which the flesh rots away and the bones crumble. The only hope of stopping it is by amputating the afflicted part—and this room was full of men without arms and legs, of men with rotting faces and breasts. They moaned and screamed, crying, *"Kuku Mayka!* Holy Mother, help me!"* For most of them there was nothing to be done. Their flesh would slough away until it reached their hearts or brains, and death would come in dreadful agony.

We wandered around Valievo for two days, noting the sanitary measures that had been taken to stop the epidemic. They consisted largely in throwing disinfectant over everything. In the street and in every courtyard were piles of filth and garbage. Little attempt had been made to remove these; there were even new piles on top of the old—but freshly sprinkled with lime. This is the key to the Serbian attitude toward sanitation. They do not understand it—they haven't the slightest conception what it means. It is something modern, something European, something that the civilized world uses to prevent disease; so they splash disinfectant about, with a half-contemptuous sneer at people who are so cowardly as to take such precautions, and go on accumulating filth as they always have done.

We went down to the railway-station late at night, to take the train for Nish and Russia. In the light of blue electric arcs, long chains of Austrian prisoners were unloading flour to feed the desolate country until the harvests could be sown and gathered. And as we waited on the platform, I thought with wonder of these Serbians, their origin, and their destiny. They alone of all the Balkan

"HOW IS IT WITH THEE, O SERBIA, MY DEAR MOTHER?"

peoples have been one unmixed race since first they came into this country eight centuries ago—and they alone have built their own civilization, unmodified by any other. The Romans had a string of mountain fortresses through the region—they settled no colonies here. The Crusaders passed them by. They held their narrow passes against the Tartars of Bulgaria, the Dacians of Rumania, the Huns and Tcheks of the North—and long before their neighbors, with the armed help of European nations, threw off the yoke of the Turk, Serbia made herself free. When Europe imposed foreign dynasties on Bulgaria, Rumania, and Greece, Serbia was ruled by her own house. With such a stock, with such a history, with the imperialistic impulse growing daily, hourly, in the hearts of her peasant soldiers, into what tremendous conflicts will Serbia's ambition lead her!

There was a soldier standing on guard at the platform—a tall, wiry, bearded man, dressed in the fragments of a uniform and shoes with sandals of cowhide and high socks embroidered with flowers. He was leaning on an Austrian rifle, staring out over the heads of the sweating workmen to those dim mountains lost in the dark beyond. And as he looked he sang, swaying lightly to the rhythm, that most ancient Serbian ballad of all, which begins:

"How is it with thee, O Serbia, my dear mother?"

# PART III

---

# RUSSIA

# Russia's Back Door

At the end of May the Russian army, to the astonishment of the world, had covered more than two hundred miles on its stupendous retreat from the Carpathians. In Bucovina it abandoned Czernowitz before the formidable Austrian drive, and withdrew behind the River Pruth. We decided to cross the frontier where Rumanian Moldavia, Austrian Bucovina, and Russian Bessarabia meet at the bend of the river, and try to strike the Russian front in action.

From Dorohoi, the northern terminus of the Rumanian railway, it is twenty miles over the hills to the frontier. We bargained for a four-horse coach; but the chief of police of Dorohoi smiled and shook his head.

"You cannot pass the frontier without permission from the high authorities," he said; "the Rumanian custom-house is closed." He looked us over thoughtfully. "However, I am going across to Russia myself tonight, and you can come with me in my automobile if you like. I will introduce you to the commandant of Novo Sielitza, which is the headquarters of the Third Army. . . . He is a close friend of mine—I often visit him. The Russians are hospitable people. By the way, they will be grateful to you over there if you bring a little something alcoholic——"

Joyously we sallied forth and bought cognac and dismissed our coach. And just as gray evening flooded the world after a day of rain, and the clouds rolled back like curtains, piling up to golden pinnacles in a shallow green sky, our machine roared out from the dripping forest of Hertza, and we could see beyond the white walls and thatched roofs of a little village the rolling miles of hills,

381

emerald with wheat glittering wetly, black with forests, smoking
with the sweat of fat earth after rain; and farther still, to the left,
the rolling green and gold and brown country of Bucovina—to
the right, the plain beyond the Pruth, low hills and higher hills
behind—Russian Bessarabia. On the Austrian side, far away, were
visible white winding roads, dazzling villas set in green, an occasional shining town—order and prosperity; on the Russian side,
the wet tin roofs of a clump of wooden shacks, thatched huts the
color of dirt, a wandering muddy track which served as a road—
the very reverse. In all the vast landscape nothing moved, except a
mysterious black smoke slowly rising from behind the hill, which
is Czernowitz, and steam from a whistling train at Novo Sielitza.
But the air trembled with deep, lazy sound—the cannon firing
somewhere beyond vision along the Pruth.

Just ahead the river itself came in view between hills, here and
there, shining dully like old brass. We swooped down with
screaming siren through the village of Hertza, where the peasants, clad in white linen all embroidered with flowers, were gathered on the green for their evening songs and dances and lifted
their broad-brimmed hats to us—down, through vineyards and
corn-fields, to Mamornitza on the bank of the muddy river.

Over all the west the sunset made a fierce flame, edging the
toppling clouds with fire, pouring green gold over the fields. The
radiance faded; by the time we reached the riverside it was quite
dark, except for a broad red band low down in the northern sky.
Against this reared a tumble-down shed set in a barren waste of
sand, stones, and mud—where the Pruth roared in the spring
floods. But it was Russia, Holy Russia—somber, magnificent, immense, incoherent, unknown even to herself.

They had been notified at the deserted customhouse, and in a
room musty with long neglect a shabby little man viséed our passports. Escorted by two soldiers, we picked our way down to the
river, where a flat-bottomed scow lay half full of water, and a rope
fastened to the bank stretched out into the darkness—to Russia!
We couldn't see the other side, but as we swung out into the
brown current, the Rumanian shore glided astern and disappeared; for a moment we were adrift on a boundless sea, and then

CROSSING THE PRUTH IN A FLAT-BOTTOMED SCOW, HALF FULL OF WATER.

against the dim, red sky something rose and loomed—a giant soldier with a long-bayonetted rifle, the crown of his hat peaked up in front as only Russians wear it. Beside him was the shadowy form of a two-horsed carriage.

Without a word the sentry put our baggage into the carriage and we followed. He leaped to the box—we were off through deep sand, whip cracking. . . . A sudden guttural hail from the dark, and another huge soldier bulked in the night beside the carriage. Our sentry handed him a slip of paper, which he pretended to read, holding it upside down—although it was now quite dark and he quite illiterate.

"*Koracho!* Good!" he grunted and waved us on. "*Pajal'st'!*"

The last red light had faded from the sky, and we rattled through a starless gloom troubled with the confused sounds of an army at rest. Far away on our right accordions jiggled flatly, and a mighty chorus of deep voices swelled in a slow, stern song.

To the left suddenly opened a meadow bright with many fires. Horses were picketed all about—in one corner two stallions strained, screaming, at their ropes. High saddles, sleeping-rugs of rich color, brass samovars lay on the ground, and on the flames copper pots smoked. In little knots at the fires, flat-faced, swarthy men squatted, Eastern fashion, between their knees—men with Chinese eyes and cheek-bones polished like teak, robed in long caftans and crowned with towering shaggy hats of fur. The twanging, indolent sound of their speech reached us. One stood upright in the firelight, which gleamed on the silver bosses of his belt and the long curved *yataghan* inlaid with gold that hung by his side.

"*Turkmiene,*" explained the soldier on the box.

Turcomans from beyond the Caspian, from the steppes of Asia—the boiling geyser that deluged Europe with the great Mongolian invasions—the mysterious cradle of humankind. The fathers of these warriors followed Ghenghis Khan and Tamerlane and Attila. Their cousins were Sultans in Constantinople, and sat upon the Dragon Throne in Peking. One glimpse we had of them, a tiny handful in the mighty hordes that Russia is pour-

PONTOONS FOR THE PRUTH.

ing down on the West—and then we were among the ruins of Austrian Nova Sielitza, the old frontier.

Here the gaping windows of roofless houses, walls charred and toppling, immense customs warehouses crumpled with fire. The Russians had wrecked everything at the beginning of the war— what became of the people we didn't like to think. A big stucco hotel had been struck by a bursting shell; light shone from within, and big-booted soldiers in blouses stood silhouetted in the door-ways. The road we drove on was white and smooth. Shadowy horsemen jingled past, stray light catching the guardless hilts of Cossack swords. Gleaming white linen in the gloom marked Moldavian peasants shuffling along, laughing and speaking gently their Italianate dialect.

A bridge with another sentry, who waved us by when he saw the flash of white paper—now we were in Russian Novo Sielitza. Here there was no destruction; but instead of a hard road, we rocked through a wide expanse of muddy pools and dried ruts, scored with a thousand tracks. At each side of this street was a deep ditch for drainage and sewage, spanned by wooden foot-bridges. Wide, sprawling wooden houses alternated with blocks of tiny Jewish shops, swarming with squealing, whining, bargain-ing people, and emitting that stale stench that we know on New York's lower East Side. Old Jews in long overcoats, derby hats resting on their ears, scraggly beards, elbows and hands ges-ticulating—the comedy Jew in a burlesque show—filthy babies crawling in the lamplight, rows of women in Mother Hubbards and brown wigs, nursing their babies and gossiping shrill Yiddish on the door-step.

We swung into a side street, black as pitch, lined on either side by long wooden houses behind picket fences.

"Here we are," said our guide. "Now you will see a real Russian house and family."

The door popped open and a stout, bearded officer stood on the threshold holding a lamp over his head—Captain Vladimir Constantinovitch Madji, commandant of Novo Sielitza. Behind was a bristling bald-headed man with fierce white mustache and goatee, and over his shoulder appeared a grinning face like the face of a very fat little boy, smoking a cigarette, a white silk kerchief wound tightly around its forehead.

"Please! Please! *Povtim!*" said the captain in Rumanian, making gestures of welcome. "*Pajal'st'!*" cried the others in Russian.

The chief of police explained that he had brought two friends, *Amerikanska;* they burst forth into another delighted chorus of "*Povtim! Pajal'st'!*" and pushed out to look at us, talking rapid Russian.

"They speak neither Russian nor Rumanian. Only French——"

"*Entrez!*" said the captain, with an elementary accent; then in just as amateurish German: "*Kommen Sie herein, meine Herren!*"

"*Voilà! Comment! Comment! Voilà!*" the bald-headed man roared.

"It is all my brother knows of French!" explained Madji, as we entered. The fat face turned out to belong to a girl of astonishing corpulence and terrific exuberance. Puffing furiously at her cigarette, she squeezed both our hands, grasped the lapels of our coats and shook us, shouting Russian remarks, and laughing uproariously when we didn't understand.

The captain radiated hospitality. "Alexandra Alexandrovna, get the samovar!"

She ran off, bellowing orders to invisible servants. "Antonina Feodorovna! *Prinissitié samovarou!*" And in a moment she was back with a new yellow kerchief around her head, a new cigarette, puffing clouds of smoke.

Madji indicated her with his hand. "*Mon mari!* My husband!" he said in his bad French.

His brother pranced up like a little old stallion, also pointing to her; he repeated "My husband!" adding in a fierce voice: "*Très jolie! Très jolie! Très jolie!*" He said "*très jolie*" over and over again, delighted at remembering another French phrase. . . .

As to the fat girl, we never did discover whose "husband" she was. . . . And there was also Alexandra Antonovna, a solemn little girl of about thirteen with the sophisticated eyes of a grown

TURCOMANS FROM BEYOND THE CASPIAN; FROM THE STEPPES OF ASIA.

woman, like all Russian little girls; her status in the household remained a mystery, too. Anyway, it wasn't of the least importance, for this was Russia, where such things don't matter. . . .

In the dining-room we began by drinking glass after glass of tea. Boxes of cigarettes overflowed on the table. At one end sat Alexandra Alexandrovna, lighting one cigarette from another, shaking with laughter and shouting at anybody and everybody. At the other end was the old man, beaming upon us and crying: *"Voilà! Comment! Très jolie!"* Antonina the servant shuffled in and out, taking part in the general conversation, arguing every order, bringing fresh water for the samovar—on terms of perfect equality.

Robinson explained to the old man that he looked exactly like Gogol's Cossack hero, Taras Bulba. He was delighted. And from that time on we never addressed him except as "General Taras Bulba."

From time to time other officers dropped in—men in belted Russian blouses buttoned up the neck, their hair cropped close. They kissed Alexandra's hand, and made the rounds of the table, murmuring their names. Most of them spoke some French or German, and all were astonishingly frank about the situation.

"Yes, we are falling back like the devil. It is mostly because we lack munitions; but there are other things. Graft—disorganization——"

A lieutenant broke in: "Do you know the story about Colonel B——? He had a bad record in the Japanese War, but when this one broke out he was appointed chief of staff to General Ivanov. It was he who forced the beginning of the retreat from the Carpathians; when Ivanov was absent he ordered the retreat of an entire army corps—exposing the flank of the next army. There wasn't any reason for it. People say he is insane. . . . However, the thing was hushed up, and he became chief of staff to General Dimitriev and did the same thing over again! You'd think that would finish him? Ah, no! He had powerful friends in Petrograd—and now he is chief of staff to another general!"

Said another calmly: "It is like that. Advance, retreat. Advance, retreat. If we retreat now—why, then, we shall advance again."

MADJI INDICATED HER WITH HIS HAND. "MON MARI!" ["MY HUSBAND!"] HE SAID IN HIS BAD FRENCH. (BUCOVINA.)

"But how long will the war last?"

"What do we care how long it lasts?" remarked a second captain with a grin: "What do we care—so long as England gives money and the earth gives men?"

At about ten o'clock Alexandra suddenly decided to dine. She and Antonina set the table, while Taras Bulba bustled about, giving contradictory orders. For *zakouska* there were plates of sardines, smoked and raw herrings, tunny, caviar, sausage, shirred eggs, and pickles—to sharpen the appetite—washed down with seven different kinds of liquor: cognac, benedictine, kümmel, raspberry and plum brandies, and Kiev and Bessarabian wines. Afterward came great platters of corn-meal *polenta*, then chunks of pork and potatoes. We were twelve. The company began dinner with wine-glasses full of cognac followed by the others in rotation, and finished with several cups of Turkish coffee and the seven different liquors all over again. Then the samovar was brought, and we settled down to the eternal *chai*. It was midnight.

"Ah," cried an officer, "if we only had vodka now!"

"Is it really forbidden in Russia?"

"Except in the first-class restaurants of the big cities—Kiev, Odessa, Moscow. You can also get foreign drinks. But they are very expensive. . . . You see, the object of the *ukase* was to keep alcohol from the lower classes; the rich can still get it. . . ."

A young fellow named Amethystov, lieutenant in a Crimean Tartar regiment, asked us if we had heard the story of the Bismarck *Denkmal*.

"It was during the retreat from East Prussia, after Tannenberg," he said, a gentle smile lighting his blank, fanatical face, "and my regiment was at Johannisberg, where there was a bronze statue of Bismarck about twelve feet tall—like hundreds all over Germany. My Tartars wanted to pull it down and take it with them as a trophy, but the general absolutely refused to allow it. 'It would cause an international incident,' said he. As if the war weren't enough of an international incident! Well, so we stole it—pulled it down at night, stood it upright in a field furnace, and covered it over with a tarpaulin. But we couldn't hide the great bronze feet sticking out at the bottom. . . . We got it as far as

A SON OF GHENGHIS KHAN, TURCOMAN.

Tilsit—and one day the general came riding along the line, and saw the feet!

" 'Who took that thing?' he shouts. Oh, how mad he was! 'In the morning I'll find out the guilty ones, if I have to court-martial the entire regiment! It must be abandoned here—do you understand me?'

"Of course, he had a right to be angry, because we were using four army horses to pull the thing, and we'd had to abandon a lot of baggage because transport was lacking. . . .

"So that night we took Bismarck out of his cart and set him up in a field, and had a farewell celebration around him. . . . I remember we made speeches and broke champagne bottles on him. And next day, lo and behold, he was gone—stolen by a Siberian infantry regiment. . . . Who knows where he is now?" he mused. "Perhaps retreating across Galicia with the Siberians."

At the other end of the table a captain of Atamanski Cossacks, his narrow eyes glowing, was saying: "You have seen the hiltless Cossack sword?" He showed us his own. "It is terrible in their hands! They slash with a sidelong stroke—whiz! It cuts a man in half! Beautiful! But they love to kill. When prisoners surrender to them, they say always to their colonel: '*Aga!* Let us cut them! It will disgrace us to bring back babies as prisoners!' "

We tried to explain our purpose in coming, but the captain always interrupted with an expansive smile:

"You shall go where you please, my friends. Tomorrow we will arrange all that. . . . Now eat and drink, eat and drink——"

Alexandra Alexandrovna screamed pleasantries from a cloud of smoke:

"It's not polite when you come to visit friends, to talk of going away!"

"*Très jolie!*" bellowed Taras Bulba. "You shall not leave here until you have taught me to speak French, German, Spanish, Italian, and Chinese! I have a passion for languages——"

It was now one o'clock in the morning; we were worn out.

"*Voyons!*" expostulated Madji. "To sleep is a ridiculous way to pass the night. . . ."

# Life at Novo Sielitza

A PLACE had been arranged for us to sleep, and we went in a carriage driven by a soldier. In all the town there were no lights, except in occasional houses where officers were quartered. We pulled up before a crude brick house jammed between huddling Jewish shops, and waded through a puddle that smelled of sewage. The soldier pounded on the door—light grew in the chinks, and a woman's voice whined timorously. He cursed her for a Jew. *"Germanski!"* he said; "the foreigners!" chains and bolts rattled, and a wave of fetid smell rushed out. The woman was sharp-featured and bent, with a coarse brown wig set awry, cringing in the doorway, her gums bared in an obsequious smile. She led the way up a stairway that had not been cleaned since the Passover, chattering raucous Yiddish:

"Who are the noble *Herren?* What do they here? Where do they come from? Amerika!" She stopped short and peered down at us in amazement. *"Wun-der-bar!* I have friends in Amerika— Josef Hertzovici, for example. Do you know him? No, of course not. It is a big land, bigger than this. . . . How is it to live in Amerika? Much money—*hein?* And the tall houses of New Yorch. Fifty stories? *Grosser Himmel! . . .* But why do you leave Amerika and come to Russia?"

"Why do you ask?" I said. "Isn't it good to live here?"

She gave me a suspicious glance, and fell back into a whine:

"There is little gold here, noble gentlemen, and it is hard for the poor. . . . But it is very pleasant——"

She opened a door, first carefully touching a folded paper prayer tacked on the jamb, and on tiptoe motioned us to follow.

In the corner at a table sat an aged Jew in skull-cap, black robe, and heelless slippers, reading the Torah by candle-light. His bleary eyes peered down through horn spectacles, and his white beard moved to the low droning of the sacred words. He turned half around, without looking at us, and bowed with venerable dignity. . . . A most holy *Rebbe!*

Our room lay beyond, furnished with two couches of the shape and consistency of marble slabs in the morgue. True, there was clean linen, but it smelled strongly of *gefültefisch.* . . .

We had a balcony jutting out over a wide square of mud and garbage and trampled straw, where the peasants parked their springless carts when they came to town. Deep ditches surrounded it, carrying a slow stream of evil-smelling drainage, and on all sides were rows of miserable huts where the Jews lived. In that square all day long moved a dramatic pageant of races—sometimes significant, sometimes incoherent and obscure. There were subdued, gentle Moldavian peasants all in white linen, with wide-brimmed, low-crowned hats and long, curling hair falling upon their shoulders; and their wives, crowned with the round marital "pill-box" under their kerchiefs—big, free-moving creatures with stalwart legs bare to the knees. Russian *mujiks* in blouses and peaked caps clumped along with heavy boots—bearded giants with blank, simple faces, and hale, flat-faced Russian women dressed in ghastly combinations of colored kerchiefs and shirts—one wore yellow and cerise, another vermilion, apple-green, and baby-blue. Here and there the twisted, calculating face of a Russian pope, with his long hair, and a great crucifix dancing on the front of his robe. Cossacks of the Don without distinctive uniform except a broad red stripe down their trousers, silver-inlaid saber with the guardless hilt, and tufted love-lock over the left eye; pockmarked Tartars, descendants of the Golden Horde who stormed Holy Moscow—the strong men of the army—marked by a narrow red stripe; Turcomans in enormous white or black bearskins, caftans of faded violet or blue, boots with pointed toes turned up—splendid with gold chains, inlaid belts, daggers, and *yataghans.* And always Jews, Jews, Jews: bowed, thin men in rusty derbies and greasy long coats, with stringy

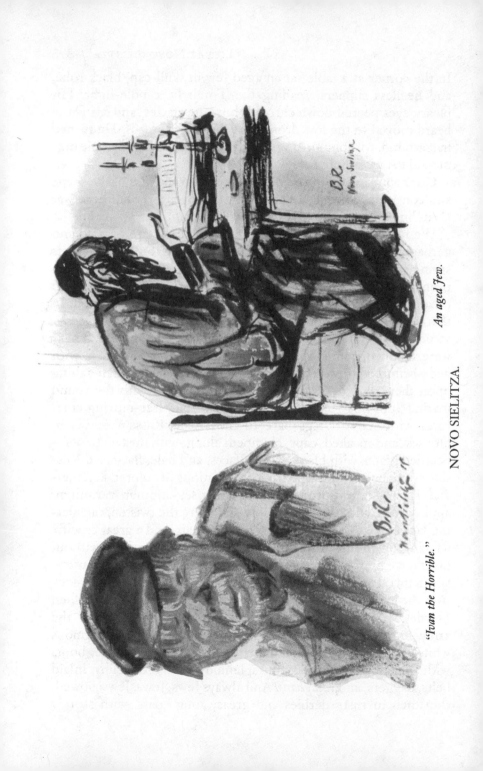

*An aged Jew.*

NOVO SIELITZA.

*"Ivan the Horrible."*

beards and crafty, desperate eyes, cringing from police, soldiers and priests, and snarling at the peasants—a hunted people, made hateful by extortion and abuse, by murderous competition in the foul, overcrowded cities of the Pale. Excitable, whining Jewesses in filthy wrappers and coarse wigs; venerable *ravs* and great scholars bent under the weight of virtuous years, with leather-bound tomes under their arms; sensitive-faced boys who passed repeating their lessons, on the way to *heder*—a race inbred and poisoned with its narrow learning, because it has been "persecuted for righteousness' sake," and butchered in the streets by men whose banner was the Cross. Jews impregnated the mass—the air smelled of Jews. . . .

Over the patched tin roofs rose the inverted green onion atop the Russian church. A blind peasant boy kneeled upright in the mud beneath our balcony, muttering prayers and crossing himself with a fluttering motion. A bawling, bargaining market was in progress in the street beyond. Police in yellow blouses, booted and spurred, strolled watchfully by, fingering the red cords that hung from their necks to their prominent revolvers—bullying Jews, hustling peasants, as is the way of police with the weak all the world over. And unnoticed by the accustomed world, the fetid air shook unceasingly with the sound of big guns, only ten miles away.

AT Madji's house the family slouched out one by one, yawning and rubbing their eyes. It was after ten o'clock. In the entry Antonina was chopping up kindling and putting it down the blazing well of the samovar—then she shook in charcoal, filled the teapot with fresh leaves, and we began again the interminable drinking of tea that keeps up all day and all night in Russian houses.

We delicately called the captain's attention to our prospects.

"Of course you may go to the front," he said. "But it is not interesting—unless you care for artillery duels. Now there is a lull in the fighting at this point. To the north it is very severe—why don't you go north?"

We jumped at the chance.

"Where do you want to go?"

Now the American Legation in Bucarest had authorized us to report on the welfare of certain American citizens in the parts of Bucovina and Galicia occupied by the Russians, and I consulted the list. No one knew exactly where the front was—but by calculating the number of miles per day which the Russians were retreating, and consulting the map, we picked out Zalezchik, a town where there were American citizens, as a place likely to be in the zone of action.

Madji took us to staff headquarters to see the general, and he readily gave permission; so the commandant made us out a pass to Zalezchik. What's more, he summoned a Jew who owned a peasant—horse, carriage, body, and soul—and bargained with him for our transportation. The price was twenty-five roubles, paid in advance—of which the peasant probably received two. And we were to start at six in the morning.

Colonel Doshdovsky, the one-armed Russian commander of all the Turcomans, wore the cross of St. George, and the first and second class of the Order of Vladimir—for he was a great hero—and his vicious Turcoman sword was covered with Persian verses inlaid with gold. With him we inspected the Turcoman camp. The warriors lived under an open shed in the field where their horses were picketed, each horse singly—for they were all savage stallions. Never had I seen such beautiful horses—lithe, strong, clean-muscled, with the arched necks and small heads of horses of race. Here and there their riders worked over them—polishing and clipping their hoofs, combing their manes, going over their glossy hides minutely with pinchers to pull out hairs longer or shorter than the others, swaddling them in blankets.

"They must furnish their own horses," said the colonel; "and their horses are their pride. The horse often represents its owner's entire fortune. If it is killed in a little skirmish of patrols, the poor fellow is ruined. Turcomans are liable for military service all their lives."

Many had taken off their long caftans, revealing the thin black undergarment, laced tight at the waist, that fell to their baggy red trousers. Others had doffed the great fur hats—and beneath was a brown head shaved bald except for a scalp-lock on the crown, covered by a little silk skull-cap. High saddles bossed with silver lay around, bundles of rich-colored cloths from Khiva and Bokhara and Samarcand, sleeping-rugs and praying-rugs whose weave and color are secrets of the dead. They wore twisted silver chains down their backs, wide sashes of brilliant silk, straight and curved daggers inlaid with precious metals, and swords in richly ornamented scabbards that perhaps Tamerlane had seen. On us they turned their slanting Mongolian eyes, indifferently, with the incurious superiority of world-conquerors, and made smiling, sardonic comments to each other. But Robinson got out his pad and sketched their portraits, and gave them away—and they crowded to pose like eager children.

All day long at Madji's tea flowed, and meals followed haphazard, and people drifted in and out. Alexandra Alexandrovna shouted and laughed and smoked incessantly, changing her kerchief twenty times. Taras Bulba insisted on learning French, Spanish, and German all at once, and blustered fiercely and ineffectually about. The captain himself was busy and distrait—there were several important matters to settle; staff-officers came in with bundles of papers and crowded his office, all talking loudly at once. There seemed to be no method. They all straggled from room to room, drinking tea and gossiping of indifferent things. Madji would determinedly seize pen and paper as if to work, then forget all about it, and come into the dining room to hear some funny story that was being shouted. A new crowd of officers were there for dinner, which happened just as unexpectedly as the night before, and half an hour later—but since we were to rise so early, we tore ourselves from those hospitable hands. Alexandra, the captain, and old Taras Bulba came to the door to say good-by. Madji beamed and wished us all good luck; Alexandra squeezed our hands with exaggerated feeling, and besought us to come back—*surely*. As for old Taras Bulba, he appeared overcome with the effort of searching for a proper French phrase. Just as we mounted the carriage he found it. His face lighted up; he assumed a rhetorical attitude, extended one arm with a superb gesture, and said sternly: "*Je vous aime—je vous adore!*"

# Breaking into Bucovina

---

Eᴀʀʟʏ the next morning we came out of our lodgings to the shrill sound of Yiddish blessings and reproaches mixed, and found the Jew smirking and rubbing his hands.

"Where's the carriage?" I asked, suspecting further extortion. The Jew pointed to a temporary scaffolding such as is used for digging artesian wells, upon which sat an incredibly discouraged-looking *mujik*. On closer inspection we discovered wheels, fastened to arbitrary places with bits of wire and rope; and apparently unattached to the structure, two aged and disillusioned horses leaned against each other.

"B-r-r-r-r-r-r!" said the *mujik* to these animals, implying that they would run away if he didn't. "B-r-r-r-r!"

We mounted, while the Jew abusively impressed upon his driver that we were to be taken to Zalezchik, through Boyan and Zastevna; he also told him to get whatever money he could out of us. . . . At the end of this tirade, the peasant rose and stolidly beat the horses with a long string fastened to a stick, shouting hoarsely: "Ugh! Eeagh! Augh!" The horses awoke, sighed, and moved experimentally—by some mechanical miracle the wheels turned, a shudder ran along our keel, and we were off!

Across the bridge into Austrian Novo Sielitza we rattled, and out upon the hard road that led frontward, slowly gaining upon and passing a long train of ox-carts driven by soldiers and loaded with cases of ammunition. Now we were in Bucovina. On the left, low fields green with young crops stretched flatly to the trees along the Pruth, beyond which rose the rich hills of Rumania; to the right the valley extended miles to cultivated rolling country.

Already the June sun poured down windless, moist heat. The driver slumped gradually into his spine, the horses' pace diminished to a merely arithmetical progression, and we crawled in a baking pall of dust like Zeus hidden in his cloud.

"Hey!" We beat upon his back. "Shake a leg, Dave!"

He turned upon us a dirty, snub-nosed face, and eyes peering through matted hair, and his mouth cracked slowly in an appalling, familiar grin—with the intelligent expression of a loaf of bread. We christened him immediately Ivan the Horrible. . . .

"Ooch!" he cried with simulated ferocity, waving the string. "Aich! Augh!"

The horses pretended to be impressed, and broke into a shuffle; but ten minutes later Ivan was again rapt in contemplation of the infinite, the horses almost stationary, and we moved in white dust. . . .

Slowly we drew near the leisurely sound of the cannon, that defined itself sharply out of the all-echoing thunder audible at Novo Sielitza. And topping a steep hill crowned with a straggling thatched village, we came in sight of the batteries. They lay on the hither side of an immense rolling hill, where a red gash in the fields dribbled along for miles. At intervals of half a minute a gun spat heavily; but you could see neither smoke nor flame—only minute figures running about, stiffening, and again springing to life. A twanging drone as the shell soared—and then on the leafy hills across the river puffs of smoke unfolding. Over there were the towers of white Czernowitz, dazzling in the sun. The village through which we passed was populous with great brown soldiers, who eyed us sullenly and suspiciously. Over a gateway hung a Red Cross flag, and along the road trickled a thin, steady stream of wounded—some leaning on their comrades, others bandaged around the head, or with their arms in slings; and peasant carts jolted by with faintly groaning heaps of arms and legs. . . .

The road slanted down until we were close to the crashing batteries. For hours we drove along behind a desultory but gigantic artillery battle. Gun after gun after gun, each in its raw pit, covered with brush to shield it from aeroplanes. Sweating men staggered under the weight of shells, moving about the shining

GUN POSITIONS IN BUCOVINA.

caissons; methodically the breech snapped home and the pointer singsonged his range; a firer jerked the lanyard—furious haze belched out, gun recoiled, shell screamed—miles and miles of great cannon in lordly syncopation.

In the very field of the artillery peasants were calmly ploughing with oxen, and in front of the roaring guns a boy in white linen drove cattle over the hill toward the pastures along the river. We met long-haired farmers, with orange poppies in their hats, unconcernedly driving to town. Eastward the world rolled up in another slow hill that bore curved fields of young wheat, running in great waves before the wind. Its crest was torn and scarred with mighty excavations, where multitudinous tiny men swarmed over new trenches and barbed-wire tangles. This was the second-line position preparing for a retreat that was sure to come. . . .

We swung northward, away from the artillery, over the bald shoulder of a powerful hill. Here the earth mounted in magnificent waves, patterned with narrow green, brown, and yellow fields that shimmered under the wind. Through valleys whose sides fell like a bird's swoop were vistas of checkered slopes and copses soft with distance. Far to the west the faint blue crinkly line of the Carpathians marched across the horizon. Tree-smothered villages huddled in the immense folds of the land—villages of clay houses unevenly and beautifully molded by hand, painted spotless white with a bright blue stripe around the bottom, and elaborately thatched. Many were deserted, smashed, and black with fire—especially those where Jews had lived. They bore marks of wanton pillage—for there had been no battle here— doors beaten in, windows torn out, and lying all about the wreckage of mean furniture, rent clothing. Since the beginning of the war the Austrians had not come here. It was Russian work. . . .

Peasants smiling their soft, friendly smile took off their hats as we went by. A gaunt man with a thin baby in his arms ran forward and kissed my hand when I gave him a piece of chocolate. Along the roadside stood hoary stone crosses inscribed with sacred verses in the old Slavonic, before which the peasants uncovered and crossed themselves devoutly. And there were rude wooden

PEASANT CARTS JOLTED BY WITH FAINTLY GROANING HEAPS OF ARMS AND
LEGS. (BUCOVINA.)

crosses, as in Mexico, to mark the spots where men had been assassinated. . . .

In a high meadow overlooking the distant river and the far-rolling plains of Bucovina we came upon a camp of Turcomans—their saddled horses staked to graze and their fires burning. Cruel-faced and slant-eyed, they squatted about the cook-pots or moved among the horses, barbaric notes of color in this green northern field, where, perhaps, their ancestors had camped with Attila a thousand years ago. Beyond the river cousins of theirs lay in the enemy's trenches—beyond the ethereal mountains in the west was Hungary, the rich land where the scourges of God from Asia had finally come to rest. Where the road dipped again into the valley was an old stone chapel, circular in form and surrounded by a graceful colonnade. It was now gutted, and the horses of Turcoman officers were stabled inside. . . .

At any cross-roads we always knew the right road to take, because Ivan invariably took the other. Although born and bred at Novo Sielitza, fifteen miles away, he had never travelled so far abroad. Worse, his porous memory could no longer hold the name of our destination, no matter how often he repeated it. Every little while he turned and peered at us, groaning. "Zalezchik!" we shouted in chorus, and he fell to larruping the horses with uncouth cries. He pulled up sometimes, until we pointed to a native and made signs for him to ask the way.

"Good day," mumbled Ivan. "Which is the road to——"

"The road to where, friend?" asked the man.

Ivan scratched his head.

"Where do you want to go?"

Ivan grinned sheepishly.

"Zalezchik!" we bawled—and Ivan repeated—"Ah, yes, Zalezchik!"

At noon, we zigzagged up a steep mountain into a pine forest, and met a long train of trucks coming down, loaded with the steel floats of a pontoon bridge. Big Don Cossacks on wiry ponies escorted it, their hair-tufts sticking rakishly out under their caps.

"*Aie, Barin!*" shouted one of the drivers, pointing southwest. "*Eto* Pruth? Is that the Pruth?"

I nodded.

"Two days!" he cried, patting his pontoon. "Two days we cross the river. . . . Czernowitz!"

Still they passed, clanging along the top of the mountain. We plunged down through the forest, meeting the great wagons crawling up with shouts and snapping whips. Steeper and steeper; the trees thinned, and suddenly fell away altogether, and the tremendous panorama of the valley of the Dniester opened out—squares and parallelograms and arcs of variegated color clashing and weaving in a mighty tapestry of fertile fields, great rounded folds of earth sweeping grandly like the ground swell, rambling white granges ship-like along the ribbony roads, and villages lost in the hollows. The pontoon-trucks staggered up, drawn each by eight horses and twenty soldiers who pushed, shouting in unison—for a mile down the hill the road was filled with lumbering big floats rocking from side to side, straining horses flecked with white foam, broad-shouldered men curbed with an agony of effort. . . .

Now we were entering a new land. Though the peasants still wore white linen, their head-dress changed; some wore tall round caps of black fur, others high, bell-crowned hats such as Welsh women used to wear. The Slavonic crosses gave away to tall Catholic crucifixes, decked with all the instruments of the Passion—the spear, the sponge, the gloves, the hammer. We met people who spoke no Rumanian—Polish began to replace it. Granges where whole patriarchal families had lived stood along the road—immense houses containing living-rooms, stables, barns all under one roof, with a road running through the middle of the building from front to back. It was a blasted country, seared with battle, and with the triple passing of two great armies. The trampled grain was sickly yellow in the fields; whole villages in ruins gaped empty, except for Russian soldiers, and few men were to be seen except the aged and crippled—only women and children, with furtive eyes and sunken faces. In the fields among the growing crops old trenches crumbled in, and rusty barbed-wire

DIGGING TRENCHES NEAR ZASTEVNA.

entanglements straggled through the wheat everywhere. For miles along the left side of the road gigantic new trenches and artillery positions were building in frantic haste. Thousands of soldiers swarmed over the landscape, the afternoon sun flashing on their lifted spades. Wagons loaded with tools and barbed wire impeded the road. Near Zastevna, we saw peasant women and children digging under the superintendence of non-commissioned officers, a long file of them carrying out the dirt in head baskets. Why this feverish activity here, twenty miles behind the positions occupied by the Russians only a month before?

# Zalezchik the Terrible

I⊤ was on the other side of Zastevna, where we stopped beside some ruined houses for a drink, that we saw the Austrian prisoners. They came limping along the road in the hot sun, about thirty of them, escorted by two Don Cossacks on horseback; gray uniforms white with dust, bristly faces drawn with fatigue. One man had the upper left-hand part of his face bound up, and the blood had soaked through; another's hand was bandaged, and some jerked along on improvised crutches. At a sign from the Cossacks, who dismounted, they reeled and stumbled to the side of the road, and sullenly threw themselves down in the shade. Two dark-faced men snarled at each other like beasts. The man with the wounded head groaned. He with the bandaged hand began tremblingly to unwrap the gauze. The Cossacks good-naturedly waved us permission to talk with them, and we went over with handfuls of cigarettes. They snatched at them with the avidity of smokers long deprived of tobacco—all except one haughty-faced youth, who produced a handsome case crammed with gold-tipped cigarettes, declined ours frigidly, and took one of his own, without offering any to the others.

"He is a Count," explained a simple, peasant-faced boy with awe.

The man with the wounded hand had got his bandage off at last, and was staring at his bloody palm with a sort of fascination.

"I think this had better be dressed again," said he at last, glancing diffidently at a stout, sulky-looking person who wore a Red Cross arm-band. The latter looked across with lazy contempt and shrugged his shoulders.

"We've got some bandages," I began, producing one. But one of the Cossacks came over, scowling and shaking his head at me. He kicked the Red Cross man with a look of disgust, and pointed to the other. Muttering something, the stout man fumbled angrily in his case, jerked out a bandage, and slouched across.

There were thirty of them, and among that thirty five races were represented: Tcheks, Croats, Magyars, Poles, and Austrians. One Croat, two Magyars, three Tcheks could speak absolutely not a word of any language but their own, and, of course, none of the Austrians knew a single word of Bohemian, Croatian, Hungarian, or Polish. Among the Austrians were Tyroleans, Viennese, and a half-Italian from Pola. The Croats hated the Magyars, and the Magyars hated the Austrians—and as for the Tcheks, no one would speak to them. Besides, they were all divided up into sharply defined social grades, each of which snubbed its inferiors. . . . As a sample of Franz Joseph's army the group was most illuminating.

They had been taken in a night attack along the Pruth, and marched more than twenty miles in two days. But they were all enthusiastic in praise of their Cossack guards.

"They are very considerate and kind," said one man. "When we stop for the night the Cossacks personally go around to each man, and see that he is comfortable. And they let us rest often. . . ."

"The Cossacks are fine soldiers," another broke in; "I have fought with them, and they are very brave. I wish we had cavalry like them!"

A young volunteer of the Polish legion asked eagerly if Rumania was coming in. We replied that it seemed like it, and suddenly he burst out, quivering:

"My God! My God! What can we do? How long can this awful war last? All we want is peace and quiet and rest! We are beaten— we are honorably beaten. England, France, Russia, Italy, the whole world is against us. We can lay down our arms with honor now! Why should this useless butchery go on?"

And the rest sat there, gloomily listening to him, without a word. . . .

. . .

TOWARD evening we were rattling down a steep gully between high cliffs. A stream plunged down beside the road, turning a hundred water-wheels whose mills lay shattered by artillery fire; shacks in partial ruin shouldered each other along the gully, and on top of the eastern cliff we could see disembowelled trenches and an inferno of twisted, snarled barbed wire, where the Russians had bombarded and stormed the Austrian defenses a month before. Hundreds of men were at work up there clearing away the wreckage and building new works. We rounded a corner suddenly and came out upon the bank of the Dniester, just below where the tall railroad bridge plunged into the water its tangle of dynamited girders and cables. Here the river made a huge bend, beneath earthen cliffs a hundred feet high, and across a pontoon bridge choked with artillery the once lovely town of Zalezchik lay bowered in trees. As we crossed, naked Cossacks were swimming their horses in the current, shouting and splashing, their powerful white bodies drenched with golden light. . . .

Zalezchik had been captured, burned, and looted three times by two armies, shelled for fifteen days, and the major portion of its population wiped out by both sides because it had given aid and comfort to the enemy. Night was falling when we drove into the market-place, surrounded with the shocking débris of tall houses. A sort of feeble market was going on there under miserable tilted shacks, where sad-eyed peasant women spread their scanty vegetables and loaves of bread, the center of a mob of soldiers. A few Jews slunk about the corners. Ivan demanded a hotel, but the man smiled and pointed to a tall crumbling brick wall with "Grand Hotel" painted boldly across it—all that remained. Where could we get something to eat?

"Something to eat? There is not enough food in this town to feed my wife and children."

An atmosphere of terror hung over the place—we could feel it in the air. It was in the crouching figures of the Jews, stealing furtively along the tottering walls; in the peasants as they got out of the way of our carriage, doffing their hats; in the faces of cringing children, as soldiers went by. It got dark, and we sat in the carriage, debating what to do.

An "Apteka"—apothecary shop—stood on the corner, comparatively undamaged, with a light inside. I found the druggist alone, a Jew who spoke German.

"What are you?" he asked suspiciously, peering at me.

"An American."

"There is no hotel here," he burst out suddenly. "There is no place to stay and nothing to eat. A month ago the Russians came in here—they slaughtered the Jews, and drove the women and children out there." He pointed west. "There is no place here——"

"Then," I said, "the military commandant must take care of us. Where can I find him?"

"I will send my assistant with you," he answered. His face stiffened with fear. "You will not say to them what I have told, noble *Herr*? You will not——"

The entry of two Russian soldiers interrupted him, and he rose, addressing me insolently for their benefit:

"I can't drive you out of the shop. It's a public shop. But remember, I assume no responsibility for you. I didn't ask you to come here. I don't know you." For, after all, we might be undesirable people.

We bestowed upon Ivan a two-rouble piece, which, after biting, he put away in his pocket with hoarse sounds betokening gratitude. And we left him sitting on his vehicle in the middle of the square, gazing at nothing. When we came out of the Apteka he was still there, hunched over in the same position, and an hour later, when we issued from the colonel's headquarters, he had not moved, though it was quite dark. What was passing in that swampy mind? Perhaps he was trying to remember the name of Novo Sielitza, his home—perhaps he was merely wondering how to get there. . . .

WE sat long over dinner with the genial colonel and his staff, chattering politics and gossip in intensely fragmentary German. Among other officers were a young Finnish lieutenant and an old

Cossack major with a wrinkled Mongolian face like the pictures of Li Hung Chang, who were very much excited over the sinking of the *Lusitania*, and sure that America would go to war.

"What can we do for you?" asked the colonel.

We said that we would like to visit this part of the front, if there were any fighting going on.

"That, I am afraid, is impossible from here," he regretted. "But if you will go to Tarnopol, the general commanding this army will surely give you permission. Then you must return here, and I shall be glad to accompany you myself. A train for Tarnopol leaves tonight at eleven."

Could he give us any idea what was happening along the front?

"With pleasure," said he eagerly, telling an orderly to bring the maps. He spread them out on the table. "Now here, near Zadagora, we have ten big guns placed in these positions, to stop the Austrian flanking column that is rolling up from the Pruth. Over here, near Kaluz, the Austrians imagine that we have nothing but cavalry, but in about three days we'll throw three regiments across this little stream at this point———"

I remarked that all those maps seemed to be German or Austrian maps.

"Oh, yes," he replied. "At the beginning of the war we had no maps at all of Bucovina or Galicia. We didn't even know the lay of the land until we had captured some. . . ."

# Behind the Russian Retreat

In the morning we woke stiff and cramped from the benches of our third-class car, and looked out the window upon the boundless Galician steppe, heavy with golden wheat and with ploughed land deeper than velvet; ten-mile planes of flat earth uptilted gently against horizons where giant windmills rode hull down, like ships at sea. We had made thirty miles in nine hours.

The train whistled triumphantly down long inclines, and panted up slopes where the mounting track was visible for miles and miles. Our car was full of officers making the cheerful hubbub that Russians always make together. And from the ten freight-cars full of troops behind came nasal accordion music, the slow roar of big voices singing, shouts and cheers. At little stations where the flat-faced, somberly dressed Polish peasants and their bright-kerchiefed, broad-hipped women stared stolidly at the train, hundreds of soldiers and officers with teapots jostled each other democratically around the *kipiatok*—the huge tank of boiling water you find at every Russian railway-station—and there was incessant tea. An officer of high rank, who had an orderly, set up a small brass samovar in the next compartment to ours. . . .

From a strap over his shoulder hung a gold-hilted Cossack sword, the gift of the Czar for bravery—it bore also the tassel of the Order of Vladimir. The orderly, probably a *mujik* from one of his estates, called him familiarly "Ivan Ivanovitch." Presently he came over with true Russian hospitality, and invited us in French to drink a glass of *chai*. We got to talking about the war.

"Nevertheless, it is impossible to beat Russia," said he.

414

I objected that Russia had been beaten many times.

"You mean the Japanese War. I served in Manchuria myself, and I think I can tell you why we were beaten. In the first place the peasants knew nothing of the causes of the war, and no one took the trouble to tell them. They had never heard of the Japanese. 'We are not angry with the Japanese, whoever they may be,' said the *mujiks*. 'Why should we fight them?'

"And then everything was horribly mismanaged. I have seen troops, worn out and half starved by a forty days' railway journey on insufficient food, detrained and sent into battle without an hour's rest. And there was the vodka, too, which we haven't got to reckon with to-day. Before the battle of Mukden I saw whole regiments lying in a drunken sleep on the ground. . . . It was an unpopular war—there was no patriotism among the peasants."

"And is there patriotism now?"

"Yes, they are very patriotic—they hate the Germans. You see, most of the agricultural machinery comes from Germany, and this machinery does the work of many men, driving the peasants into the factories at Petrograd and Moscow and Riga and Odessa. Then the Germans flood Russia with cheap goods which undersell Russian products—which causes our factories to shut down and throws thousands out of work. In the Baltic provinces, too, German landlords own all the soil, and the peasants live miserably. . . . Wherever in Russia they have no feeling against the Germans, we tell them these things. . . . Oh, yes, this time the Russians know why they are fighting!"

"So the peasants think that by beating the Germans they will get rid of poverty and oppression?"

He nodded good-humoredly. Robinson and I both had the same thought: if the peasants were going to beat any one, why didn't they begin at home? Afterward we discovered that they *were* beginning at home.

LATE in the morning we stopped within sight of the towers of Tarnopol, alongside a huge hospital-train which was marked with the imperial arms and bore the legend: "Sanitary Train, Gift of the Imperatrice Alexandra Feodorovna."

THE STATION AT TARNOPOL.

"Come on," said our friend, ordering his baggage out. "We had better change trains. Ours will probably stay here until afternoon."

We swung aboard the hospital-train just as it left, and found ourselves in a little car divided into two compartments by a rough board partition. Wooden bunks were folded up against the sides; in one corner was a stove covered with dirty pots and pans; trunks, a tin wash-basin on a box fastened to the wall, and clothes suspended from nails, gave it the look of a ship's forecastle.

In one compartment sat two middle-aged minor officers, and in the other a stout, comfortable-looking woman and a young girl. The two men and the women were smoking cigarettes, and throwing the butts on the maculate floor; steaming glasses of tea littered the tables; the windows were closed.

The girl spoke German and a little French; the woman was her mother, the grizzled sanitary lieutenant her father, and the second captain of engineers her uncle. Since the beginning of the war ten months ago they had been living in this car, travelling from Vilna and Kiev to the front, and back again with the wounded.

"My mother wouldn't let my father go to the war without her, and she made so much fuss that he took us both. . . . And my uncle's father-in-law is a Collegiate Assessor and a Judge in the government of Minsk, so he managed to get us this car to live in."

"Have you seen any fighting?"

"Twice," she answered. "Near Warsaw last winter a German shell struck one of our cars and blew it to pieces—there we were under artillery fire all day. And only last week, beyond Kalusz, the whole train was captured by Austrians. But they let us go again. . . . We're bound for Vilna now with a load of wounded. In two days we'll be back there. . . ."

Tea and cigarettes were forthcoming, with the customary large-hearted Russian hospitality, and we sat around while they told us of the pleasures of a perpetual travelling vacation—for all the world like their ancestors, the nomadic Russian tribes.

. . .

REFUGEES . . . WAITING STOLID AND BEWILDERED AMONG THEIR BUNDLES.

Tarnopol station was a place of vast confusion. From a long military train poured running soldiers with tin teapots to the *kipiatok*, hurtling a column of infantry that was marching across to another train. Officers shouted and cursed, beating with the flat of their swords. Engines whistled hysterically, bugles blared—calling the men back to their cars. Some hesitated and stopped, undecided whether to go forward or back; others ran faster. Around the hot-water tanks was a boiling, yelling mob. Clouds of steam rose from the pouring faucets. . . . Hundreds of peasant refugees—Poles, Moldavians, and Hungarians—squatted along the platform waiting stolid and bewildered among their bundles and rolls of bedding; for as they retreated the Russians were clearing the country of every living thing and destroying houses and crops. . . . The station-master waved futile hands in the center of a bawling crowd of officers and civilians, all flourishing passes and demanding when their various trains departed. . . .

An armed sentry at the door tried to stop us, but we pushed by. He made a half-motion with his rifle, took a step and paused irresolutely, bellowing something about passes—and we went on. A hundred spies could have entered Tarnopol. . . .

"*Na Stap!*" we cried to the cabby: "To the Staff!" Along the railroad yards on each side were mountains of sacks and boxes higher than the houses. Tarnopol was a city of solid Polish architecture, with occasional big modern German buildings, and sudden vistas of narrow busy streets lined with hundreds of shops, all painted with signs picturing the goods sold within; streets swarming with Jews in long black coats and curly brimmed black hats. Here they looked better off and less servile than in Novo Sielitza. As everywhere in Galicia and Poland, there was a smell of combined "kosher," boot-leather, and what we call "Polak"; it filled the air, tainted the food we ate, and impregnated our very bed-clothes.

Half-way down the street we met a column of soldiers marching four abreast toward the railway station, bound for the front. Less than a third had rifles.

They came tramping along with the heavy, rolling pace of booted peasants, heads up, arms swinging—bearded giants of men with dull, brick-red hands and faces, dirty-brown belted blouses, blanket-rolls over their shoulders, intrenching-tools at their belts, and great wooden spoons stuck in their boot-tops. The earth shook under their tread. Row after row of strong, blank, incurious faces set westward toward unknown battles, for reasons incomprehensible to them. And as they marched, they sang—a plain chant as simple and tremendous as a Hebrew psalm. A lieutenant at the head of the column sang one bar, the first sergeant took him up—and then like a dammed-up river burst the deep easy voice of three thousand men, flung out from great chests in a rising sudden swell of sound, like organs thundering:

> "For the last time I walk with you my friends—
> For the last time!
> And tomorrow, early in the morning,
> Will weep my mother and my brethren,
> For I am going away to the war!
> And also will weep my sweetheart,
> Whom I have loved for many, many years. . . .
> She whom I hoped one day to go with to the church. . . .
> I swear that I will love her until I die!"

They passed, and the roaring slow chorus rose and fell crashing fainter and fainter. Now we rode between interminable hospitals, where haggard, white-draped figures leaned listlessly from the windows, bleached yellow from long confinement. Soldiers crowded the streets—wounded men on crutches, old Landwehr veterans, regulars, and boys who couldn't have been more than seventeen. There were three soldiers to every civilian; though that may have been partly due to the fact that many Jews had been "expelled" when the Russians entered the town—a dark and bloody mystery that. On each corner stood an armed sentry, scrutinizing the passers-by with the menacing look of a suspicious peasant. As we drove by in our Stetson hats, knickerbockers and puttees—never before seen in that country of universal boots—they stared open-mouthed. You could read on their faces the

BLIND FOR LIFE. (KOVEL.)

painfully born doubt about us—but by that time we were blocks away.

"*Stowi!*" growled the guard before Staff headquarters, lowering his bayonet. "Stop! *Shto takoi?*"

We wanted an officer who could speak French or German.

"Are you *Niemetski?*" he asked, using the old peasant word for Germans—meaning "dumb," for the first Germans in Russia couldn't speak the language.

"We are Americans." Other soldiers gathered to listen.

"*Amerikanska!*" said one man with a cunning smile. "If you are Americans, tell me what language the Americans speak."

"They speak *Angliiski.*"

At this they all looked inquiringly at the learned soldier, who nodded. An officer appeared, looked us up and down very severely, and asked us in German who we were and what we were doing. We explained. He scratched his head, shrugged his shoulders, and disappeared. Another, a huge bearded man, bustled out now and tried us with Russian, Polish, and broken French. It was evidently a poser for him, too, for he walked vaguely up and down, pulling at his beard. Finally he dispatched several orderlies in different directions, and motioned us to follow him. We entered a large room that had evidently been a theater, for there was a stage at one end hung with a gaudily painted curtain. About thirty men in undress uniform bent over desks, laboriously writing out by hand the interminable documents of bureaucratic routine. One was cautiously experimenting with a new invention, the typewriter, which evidently none of them had ever seen before, and which caused everybody great amusement.

A young officer came out of an inside room, and began to fire stern questions in rapid French. Who were we? What were we doing here? How did we come? We told our story.

"Through Bucovina and Galicia!" he cried in astonishment. "But no civilians are permitted to enter Bucovina and Galicia!"

We produced our passes.

"You are correspondents? But don't you know that no correspondents can come to Tarnopol?"

We pointed out that in fact we were there. He seemed at a loss.

"What is your business?" said he uncertainly.

I told him that we wanted to visit the front of the Ninth Army, and to find out about certain American citizens in Galicia—at the request of the American minister in Bucarest. He ran his eye down the list of names.

"Bah! Jews!" he remarked disgustedly. "Why does your country admit Jews to citizenship? Or, if it does, why doesn't it keep them at home? Where do you want to go—Strij? Kalusz? That is not possible!"

"Ah," I said, "then Strij and Kalusz are on the first line now?" He grinned. "No. The second line—the *German* second line!" We were astounded by the rapidity of the German advance.

"It is only a question of time," he went on indifferently. "They will soon be here." And suddenly he sprang to attention. "The general!"

The thirty clerks leaped to their feet with one bound.

"Good day, my children," said a pleasant voice.

"Good day to your generalship!" shouted the clerks in unison—and sat down again to their work.

General Lichisky was a man under middle age, with a keen, smiling face. He saluted us and cordially shook hands.

"So you wish to go to the front?" he said, when the officer had explained. "I don't understand how you managed to get here—for correspondents have not been allowed in Tarnopol at all. However, your papers are perfectly satisfactory. But I cannot permit you to visit the first line; the Grand Duke has issued an order absolutely forbidding it. You had better go to Lvov—Lemberg—and see what can be done through Prince Bobrinski, governor-general of Galicia. . . . I will give you passes. In the meanwhile, you may stay here as long as your business requires it. . . ."

He detailed a young subofficer who spoke English to look after us, and ordered that we should be lodged at the hotel reserved for officers of the Staff, and dine at the mess.

We wandered about the town. Tarnopol was full of troops—regiments returning from the front for a rest, others going out, still more, fresh troops, arriving from Russia with uniforms yet unsoiled by battle; mighty singing choruses shocked and smashed against each other in a ceaseless surge of big voices. Few of the men had arms. Long wagon-trains loaded with immense quantities of flour, meat, and canned food filed toward the west—but we saw no ammunition.

A young lieutenant told us things. He had been through the Masurian Lakes disaster, and later in the Carpathians.

"Even before the retreat," he said, "we didn't have half enough rifles or ammunition. My company, for example, was stationed in two trenches—a front trench and a reserve trench. A third of my men were in the first trench, and they had rifles. All the rest had no rifles—their duty was to go forward, one by one, and pick up the rifles of those who were killed. . . ."

As we walked along, the guards on the corners gathered and looked at us, whispering, until they made up their minds that we were German spies—then they arrested us and took us to the Prefecture. There no one knew what to do with us, so we were solemnly marched to the Staff, where our friend the French-speaking officer set us free again, loading our captors with abuse. The poor guards slunk away in great bewilderment; their orders were to arrest suspicious-looking persons, and when they did so, they were threatened with the knout. At regular intervals all day we were arrested by new sets of soldiers, and the same farce gone through.

"Beasts!" shouted the officer, shaking his fist at the poor, puzzled soldiers. "Fools! I'll have you punished!"

We suggested mildly that he might give us a pass which we could show to people when they stopped us, but he said that he had no authority. . . .

Late in the afternoon we stood near the barracks, watching a long column of sullen Austrian prisoners marching in between their guards. A soldier on duty gaped for several minutes at our puttees, let his eyes slowly travel up our costumes, and finally arrested us, and took us up to a major in spectacles who stood on the corner.

He questioned us in German, and I answered. He peered suspiciously over his glasses.

"Where are your passports?"

A SOLDIER ON DUTY GAPED FOR SEVERAL MINUTES AT OUR PUTTEES. (TARNOPOL.)

I said that we had left them at the hotel.

"I think I shall take you to the Staff," said he.

"We have already been to the Staff," said I.

"Hum!" he meditated. "Then to the Police."

"What is the use of that? We've already been to the Police."

"Hum!" It was puzzling, so he changed the subject. "You are correspondents? In what countries have you been?"

"We have just come from Serbia."

"And how is it in Serbia?"

I said that the sickness was terrible there.

"Sickness!" said he. "What sickness?" He had never heard of the typhus. "Really!" he said indifferently. "Tell me; will Italy enter the war, do you think?"

"Italy has already been in the war for six weeks."

"You don't say!" he yawned. "Well, gentlemen, I must leave you. Very happy to have made your acquaintance—*sehr angenehm*. . . ." and he bowed and walked away.

No one knew when the train for Lemberg left; our officer telephoned to the quartermaster, who called up the chief of transport, who in turn asked the chief of the railway administration. The answer was that everything was so mixed up that there was no certainty—it might leave in five minutes and it might leave to-morrow morning. So we plunged again into the frightful mêlée at the station, stacked our bags against the wall, and sat down to wait. Long files of stretchers bore groaning wounded to hospital-trains, running soldiers jostled each other, officers bawled hoarsely, sweating conductors made despairing gestures about their trains blocked interminably along the tracks. A fat colonel confronted the harassed station-master, pointing to his regiment drawn up along the freight platform as far as the eye could reach.

"Where the devil is my train?" he shouted. The station-master shrugged.

There were cavalry officers in green trousers, with broad sabres; subalterns of the automobile and aeroplane corps who carried blunt, ivory-handled daggers in place of swords; Cossack *atamans* from Ural and Kuban with pointed, turned-up boots, long caftans open in front and laced at the waist, tall fur hats barred on top with gold and red, belts bossed with precious metals and silver-mounted *yataghans;* generals of various degrees of generality. There were club-footed officers, near-sighted officers who couldn't see to read, one-armed and epileptic officers. Minor officials of the postal service and the railway went by dressed like field-marshals and carrying swords. Almost every one wore a uniform with gold or silver shoulder-straps; their number and variety were bewildering. Scarcely an officer whose breast was not decorated with the gold and silver badges of the Polytechnic or the Engineering School, the bright ribbons of the Orders of Vladimir, St. George, or St. Michael; gold-hilted honor swords were frequent. And every one incessantly saluted every one else. . . .

Seven hours later we boarded the train for Lemberg, and got into a compartment with two shabby, middle-aged lieutenants who were typical of nine-tenths of the minor Russian bureaucrats. We began talking ragged German, and I asked them about the suppression of vodka.

"Vodka!" said one. "You may be sure they didn't suppress the vodka without making up the money lost in some other way. It is all very well for war-time—you know, the Revolution in 1905 was due entirely to the peasants' getting drunk on vodka—but after the war we shall have vodka again. Everybody wants vodka. They cannot stop it."

His companion asked if there were compulsory military service in America. I said no.

"Like England," he nodded. "That is all very well for you, but in Russia it wouldn't do at all. The peasants wouldn't fight."

"But I thought the people were very enthusiastic about the war?"

"Pooh!" he answered contemptuously. "The Russian peasant is a very silly person. He cannot read or write. If you asked him to volunteer, he would say that he was very comfortable where he was, and didn't care to be killed. But when you order him to go, he goes!"

I wanted to know whether there was any organized opposition to the war. The first man nodded.

"Fifteen members of the Duma—they can't execute Duma members—are in prison for sending revolutionary propaganda to the army. The men who circulated it in the ranks have all been shot. They were mostly Jews. . . ."

It took fourteen hours to go forty-five miles. We halted hours on switches to let military trains go by, and long white strings of silent cars that smelled of iodoform. Again miles and miles of wheat-fields yellowing richly—a wonderful harvest here. The country was alive with soldiers. They thronged every station; half-armed regiments slouched along the platform, waiting for their trains; trains of cavalry and their horses, trains of flat cars piled high with supplies, preceded and followed us, or passed going in the other direction. Everywhere utter disorganization—a battalion side-tracked all day without food, and farther on huge dining sheds where thousands of meals were spoiling, because the men didn't come. Engines whistled impatiently for a clear track. . . . One had an impression of vast forces hurled carelessly here and there, of indifference on a grand scale, of gigantic waste.

How different from the faultless German machine I saw at work in northern France four months after the occupation! There, too, was a problem of transporting millions of men, of hurrying them from one point to another, of carrying arms, ammunition, food, and clothing for them. But although northern France is covered with railroads and Galicia is not, the Germans had built new four-track lines plunging across country and cutting through cities, over bridges made of steel and concrete, erected in eighteen days. In German France trains were never late. . . .

# Lemberg Before the Germans Came

THE immense station at Lemberg—or Lvov in Polish—was choked with troops running and calling, with soldiers asleep on the filthy floor, with stupefied refugees wandering vaguely about. No one questioned or stopped us, though Lemberg was one of the forbidden places. We drove through the ancient and royal Polish city, between the gloomy walls of great stone buildings like Roman and Florentine palaces—once the seats of the world's proudest nobility. In little squares among the mediæval twisted streets were Gothic churches of the great period—high, thin roofs, spires of delicate stone tracery, and rich rose-windows. Immense modern German buildings bulked across the noble skyline, and there were the brilliant shops, restaurants and cafés, wide green squares of a big city. Shabby Jewish quarters encroached on the smart streets, littered with filth and populous with noisy Hebrews, but here their houses and shops were wider, they laughed more, walked more like free people than in the other places we had been. Soldiers—always soldiers—shuffling Jews, and quick, gesticulating Poles—the ugliest race in the world—thronged the sidewalks. Everywhere were wounded men in every stage of convalescence. Whole streets of houses had been turned into temporary hospitals. Never in any country during the war have I seen such vast numbers of wounded as behind the Russian front.

The Hotel Imperial was an old palace. Our room measured twenty-five feet by thirty, fourteen feet high, and the outside walls were nine feet thick. We breakfasted, lost in the wastes of this vast apartment; and then, because our pass read, "The bear-

429

ers must report immediately to the Chancellery of the governor-general of Galicia," we took our way to the ancient palace of the Polish kings, where the local Russian bureaucracy was functioning with all its clumsy ineffectualness.

A surging crowd of refugees and civilians of all sorts beat about the clerk's desk in the anteroom. Finally he took our pass, read it attentively two or three times, turned it upside down, and handed it back with a shrug of the shoulders. He paid no further attention to us. So we forced our way past several sentries into an inner office, where an officer sat writing at a desk. He looked at the pass and smiled sweetly.

"*Ya nisnayo,*" said he. "I know nothing about it."

We asked for some one who could speak French or German, and he went to find one. Three-quarters of an hour later he returned with an oldish captain who spoke some German. We explained that General Lichisky had ordered us to report to the Chancellery, and that we wanted to go to the front.

"I will show you. This way." He motioned us down a passage. We walked on for some time, and suddenly looking around, missed him. We never saw him again.

Immediately ahead was a door marked "Staff of the Governor-General," which we entered, telling the orderly that we wanted to speak to some one who understood French or German. A genial colonel promptly appeared, shaking hands and introducing himself: "Piotr Stefanovitch Verchovsky, *à votre service.*" We told our tale.

"Please wait a few minutes, gentlemen," said he, "and I will arrange your affair."

He took our pass and disappeared. Four hours later an orderly came into the room and handed me the pass, shrugging his shoulders.

"Where is Colonel Verchovsky?" we demanded.

"*Ne poniemayo!*" he muttered. "I don't understand!"

I went to the door and sent the orderly to find the colonel; and in a few minutes he appeared, polite as ever, but greatly surprised to see us still there.

"Your pass distinctly says that you must report to the Chancellery," he explained, "but I have tried in vain to find the proper department. The truth is that we are in great confusion here on account of this morning's news. I advise you to go to Prince Bobrinski's personal headquarters, and ask to speak with his aide-de-camp, Prince Troubetskoi. . . . But don't say I sent you."

There were four sets of suspicious sentries to pass on our way to the governor's. We sent in our cards, and were immediately ushered into a room full of smartly dressed officers smoking, laughing and talking, and reading newspapers. One dashing boy in a hussar uniform, surrounded by a gay circle, was telling in French a story about himself and a Polish countess whom he had met at Nice. . . . A gentle-faced, bearded pope of the Russian church, in a long, black-silk soutane, with a huge silver crucifix dangling from a silver neck-chain, paced up and down arm in arm with a bull-necked colonel covered with decorations. . . . Nothing seemed farther from this easy, pleasant-mannered company than war.

A great handsome youth with shining teeth under a heavy mustache came forward, holding out his hand.

"I'm Troubetskoi," said he in English. "How on earth did you manage to get here? It is impossible for correspondents to enter Lemberg!"

We produced quantities of passes signed by generals and their chiefs of staff.

"Americans!" he sighed, biting his lips to repress a grin. "Americans! What's the use of regulations when Americans are about? I don't understand how you found out I was here, or why you came to me."

We murmured something about having met Troubetskoi the sculptor, in New York.

"Ah yes," said he. "That is the international one. He does not speak Russian, I believe. . . . But now you are here, what can I do for you?"

"We want to go to the front." Here he shook his head doubtfully. "At least we thought the governor-general might let us visit Przemysl——"

"I'm sure he would," grinned the prince, "but for the regrettable news of this morning. The Austrians entered Przsemysl at eight o'clock!"

We had not dreamed that it would fall so soon. "Do you think they will get to Lemberg?"

"Very probably," he answered in an uninterested tone. "Neither are now of any strategic value. We are rectifying our line." Then changing the subject, he said that he would see the governor-general himself and ask what could be done for us. Would we come in the morning?

The pope, who had been listening, now asked in very good English, what part of America we were from.

"I have been in America for sixteen years," he said, smiling. "For eight years I was priest of the Greek church in Yonkers, New York. I came back for the war to help all I could. . . . Now I only wait for peace to go back yonder."

As we emerged on the street, a column of gigantic soldiers, four deep, rounded the corner with their tin buckets swinging, tramping to their kitchens for dinner. Just in front of the palace the front rank burst into song, and with a roar the following ranks joined in:

"I remember when I was a young girl,
During the army manœuvres
To my village came a young officer
With soldiers, and he said to me,
'Give me some water to drink.'
When he finished drinking, he stooped from his horse
And kissed me.
Long stood I looking after him as he went away,
And all night I could not sleep—
All night he was in my dreams. . . .
Many years after, when I was a widow
And had married off my four daughters,
To my village came an old general;
And he was broken and wounded with many wounds.
He groaned. When I looked at him my heart beat fast—
It was the same young officer, I could not mistake him:
Brave as ever—the same voice,
Brave as ever—the same eyes,

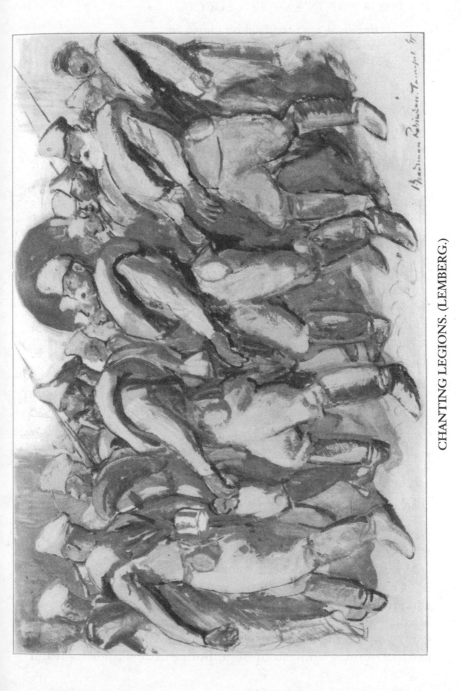

CHANTING LEGIONS. (LEMBERG.)

But many white hairs in his mustache.
And so, as many years ago, this night I cannot sleep,
And all night in my dreams I see him. . . ."

Now through all the streets poured rivers of soldiers singing.
We could see their hats flowing along the end of the avenue, over
the top of a little rise. Grand choruses met, clashing like cross-
seas in the echoing hollows between tall buildings—the city
hummed with deep melody. This was the inexhaustible strength
of Russia, the powerful blood of her veins spilled carelessly from
her bottomless fountains of manhood, wasted, lavished. The paradox of a beaten army which gathers strength, a retreating host
whose very withdrawal is fatal to the conquerors.

Our Russian money was running low, so in the morning we went
out to change our English gold. But no one wanted English gold.
Everybody asked the same question, in a low voice, peering
around to see that no soldiers were within hearing: "Have you
any Austrian money?" For already it was rumored in the city that
the Austrians were coming again.

We kept our appointment with Troubetskoi, who led us
through the ancient throne-room of the palace to the office of the
governor-general's assistant, a pleasant-mannered officer whose
coat blazed with decorations.

"Prince Troubetskoi and I have really done our best for you,"
he said with a friendly smile. "But the governor regrets that he
cannot give you permission to visit the front. For that you must
apply to the military authorities—he is simply a civil official, you
know. . . . However, I haven't a doubt that they will allow you to
go. And in that case, return here and we shall be most happy to
take care of you."

We asked where the permission was to be had.

"There are two ways. Either you may proceed to Petrograd,
and arrange matters with his Highness the Grand Duke Nicolai
Nicolaievitch through your ambassadors, or go to Cholm in Poland, which is the headquarters of General Ivanov, commander-
in-chief of the southwestern front. Both Prince Troubetskoi and

A pope.

The sceptical Colonel Bolatov.

Types of officers.

Travelling with Austrian prisoners in Bucovina.
ON THE WAY TO LEMBERG.

I think you will be more successful if you make application to General Ivanov, and his Excellency the governor-general is of the same opinion. I will give you passes which will carry you to Cholm."

At midnight we left the hotel to catch the train for Cholm, and there being no cabs in sight, an officer bound for the station called out in French that he would be happy if we would share his. His oval, half-Semitic face might have been copied from an Assyrian wall-painting—he said he was a Georgian from the Caucasus.

"The Georgian regiments have been ordered here from the Turkish front, because of their heroic conduct. The Grand Duke has done right; we Georgians are by far the bravest soldiers in the army," said he.

"Will the Austrians take Lemberg?" asked Robinson.

"Oh yes," he answered complacently: "We expect them every day now. But it doesn't matter, you know. Next winter we'll come back—or the winter after."

# An Optimistic Pilgrimage

CHOLM is not a hundred miles in an air-line from Lemberg, but there is no direct railroad between them; one must make a wide détour into Russia and back through Poland, more than three hundred miles.

We were in a compartment for four, the other two being a silent young lieutenant who lay in his berth with his boots on, smoking, and a crotchety old general invalided home. The general tried to shut tight both door and window—for the Russians share with other Continental peoples a morbid fear of fresh air. Followed a dramatic battle lasting all night, in which stalwart American manhood defied the liveried minions of the Tsar to close that window—but was finally subdued at dawn by the railroad police. . . .

White Russia. For hours we rode through an untouched wilderness of birch and pine without seeing a house or a human being, the engine's whistle alone breaking the echoing silence of the woods. Sometimes a gap in the forest gave glimpses of wide yellow plains, where black tree-stumps stood among the wheat. Wretched villages huddled around the government vodka shop— now closed—wooden huts roofed with neglected thatch, which straggled miserably beside muddy, rutted spaces populous with rooting pigs and immense flocks of geese. . . .

Great-shouldered women were working in the fields, mowing with broad strokes rhythmically abreast—probably some Female Mowers' Guild from a distant country. There were plenty of young, strong *mujiks* everywhere. They swung axes amid crashing-down trees, drove singing along the roads, and swarmed over the joists and timbers of giant miles of sheds that covered the mountainous heaps of army supplies. Yet not for an instant could we forget the war. The towns were all full of shouting soldiers; train after train whirled westward, packed with them. And as we paused on side-tracks, past glided an endless procession of white sanitary cars with pale, agonized faces peering from the windows under their bandages. Every village had its military hospital. . . .

We changed trains at Rovno, where there was a wait of nine hours. There we ran into Miroshnikov, the English-speaking subofficer who had looked after us in Tarnopol, now bound north on official business.

"Let's walk around," he proposed. "I want to show you a typical Jewish town of the Pale."

As we went along, I asked the meaning of the red, white, and blue cord that edged his shoulder-straps.

"That means I am a volunteer—exempt from compulsory service. The Russian word for 'volunteer,' " he answered the question with a grin, "is '*Volnoopredielyayoustchemusia.*' "

We gave up all hopes of learning the language. . . .

I can never forget Rovno, the Jewish town of the Pale of Settlement. It was Russian in its shabby largeness, wide streets half paved with cobbles, dilapidated sidewalks, rambling wooden houses ornamented with scroll-saw trimmings painted bright green, and the swarming uniforms of its minor officialdom. Tiny-wheeled cabs abounded, with their heavy Russian yoke, driven by hairy degenerates who wore tattered velveteen robes and bell-top hats of outrageous shape. But all the rest was Jewish. . . . The street was heaped with evil-smelling rubbish, amid slimy puddles splashed up by every passing conveyance. Clouds of bloated flies buzzed about. On both sides a multitude of little shops strangled each other, and their glaring signs, daubed with portraits of the articles for sale, made a crazy-quilt up and down as far as one could see. The greasy proprietors stood in their reeking door-ways, each one bawling to us to buy from *him*, and not from his cheating competitor across the way. Too many shops, too many cab-drivers, barbers, tailors, herded into this narrow world where alone Jews are allowed to live in Russia; and periodically augmented with the miserable throngs cleared out from the forbidden cities, where they have bribed the police to stay. In the Pale a Jew gasps for breath indeed.

How different these were from even the poorest, meanest Jews in Galician cities. Here they were a pale, stooping, inbred race, refined to the point of idiocy. Cringing men with their "sacred fringes" showing under their long coats—it was at Rovno that we first noticed the little peaked caps worn by Polish Jews—faintly bearded boys with unhealthy faces, girls prematurely aged with bitter work and eternal humiliation, grown women wrinkled and bent, in wigs and slovenly mother hubbards. People who smiled deprecatingly and hatefully when you looked at them, who stepped into the street to let Gentiles pass. And in the very center of it all, a Russian church with blue incense pouring out the open door, a glitter of gold, jewels, and candle-lighted *ikons* within, priests in stoles heavy with woven gold threads, atremble with slow, noble chanting.

For a thousand years the Russians and their Church have done their best to exterminate the Jews and their religion. With what success? Here in Rovno were thousands of Jews shut in an impregnable world of their own, scrupulously observing a religion incessantly purified, practising their own customs, speaking their own language, with two codes of morals—one for each other and the other for the Gentiles. Persecution has only engendered a poison and a running sore in the body of the Russian people. It is true what Miroshnikov said, as we drank *kvass* in a little Jewish bar—that all Jews were traitors to Russia. Of course they are.

An officer whom we had met on the train came in. He sniffed the air, bowed to us, and staring malevolently at the frightened girls who served, said distinctly: "The dirty Jews! I detest them!" and walked out.

WE were around Rovno station almost all day long, but it was not until evening that the police decided to arrest us. Among others we appealed to a pompous colonel, named Bolatov, whom we had encountered several times in the course of our travels. He was covered with high decorations, carried a gold honor sword, and had padding in his chest and dye on his ferocious mustache. We never could discover what he did on his leisurely peregrinations around the country. Miroshnikov told him that Robinson was a celebrated artist.

"We shall see!" said Bolatov cunningly. He approached Robinson. "If you are an artist," said he, "please draw my portrait."

He struck a martial attitude under the arc-light, chest expanded, hand on sword-hilt, and mustache twisted up, while Robinson drew for his life. The portrait was an outrageous flattery. Colonel Bolatov glanced at it with perfect satisfaction. He waved to the police.

"Release these gentlemen," he ordered loftily. "They are well-known journalists. . . . Would you mind signing this sketch?"

That night we slept on the benches of a troop-transport car; changed and waited seven hours at Kovel, and boarded a train bound eventually for Cholm, though no one knew when it would get there. All afternoon we crawled slowly westward through the great Polish plain—vast wheat-fields edged with a foam of red poppies, breaking like a yellow sea against cloudy promontories of trees, and archipelagoes of cheerful thatched villages. Half smothered in mighty blooming locusts were wooden stations where hospitable samovars steamed, and slow-moving, heavy-faced peasants stared motionless at the train—the men in long gray coats of coarse wool, the women gay with bright-colored skirts and kerchiefs. And late in the day, when the low sun inundated the flat world with rich mellow light, and all the red, green, and yellow glowed vividly luminous, we whistled through a sandy pine wood, and saw before us the tree-covered hill of Cholm, with its cluster of shining Greek cupolas floating like golden bubbles above the green foliage.

A new-found but already intimate friend named Captain Martinev was criticizing the army with true Russian candidness.

"—horrible waste," said he. "Let me tell you a story. In October I was with my regiment in Tilsit when the German drive on Warsaw began, and we received urgent orders to hurry to Poland. Well, from Tilsit to the nearest railroad station, Mittau, is a hundred versts. We did it in three days forced marches, arriving in

"They're German spies!"

Kubanski Cossack.

"But you are not under guard!"

CHOLM.

bad shape. Something had gone wrong—we had to wait twenty-four hours on the platform, without sleep, for it was very cold. By train we travelled two days to Warsaw, almost starving; no one had made arrangements for feeding us. When we arrived Lodz had already fallen. We got in at night and were marched across the city to another train bound for Teresa, where they were fighting. A little way out the tracks had been smashed by a shell; we detrained in the rain at two o'clock in the morning, and marched five hours to Teresa.

"At eight o'clock we reached the headquarters of the division commanded by General M——, who made such frightful mistakes in Manchuria. Our men's feet were in terrible condition; they had had practically no sleep for three nights, and hardly any food at all for two days. . . . Half an hour after we had thrown ourselves down exhausted in the rain, the general came out with his chief of staff.

" 'How many men have I here?' he asked surlily.

" 'Eight thousand.'

" 'Good. Send them to relieve the trenches.'

"Our colonel protested. 'But my men cannot go into the trenches. They must have rest and food. For five days——'

" 'Never mind!' snapped the general. 'I don't want your opinion. March!'

"The general went back to bed. We coaxed, pleaded, threatened, flogged—it was terrible to hear them beg for food and sleep—and the column staggered off to the forward trenches. . . .

"We went in at ten in the morning and stood particularly heavy fire all day—so heavy that the cook-wagons couldn't reach us until midnight, so there was nothing to eat. The Germans attacked twice in the night, so there was no sleep. Next morning heavy artillery bombarded us. The men reeled as if they were drunk, forgot to take any precautions, and went to sleep while they were shooting. The officers, with blazing eyes, muttering things like men walking in their sleep, went up and down beating the soldiers with the flat of their swords. . . . I forgot what I was doing, and so did everybody, I think; indeed, I can't remember what followed at all—but we were in there for four days and four nights. Once a night the cook-wagons brought soup and bread. At least three times a night the Germans attacked at the point of the bayonet. We retired from trench to trench, turning like beasts at bay—though we were all out of our heads. . . .

"Finally on the fifth morning they relieved us. Out of eight thousand men two thousand came back, and twelve hundred of those went to the hospital.

"But the amusing thing about it was that all the time we were being butchered out there, there were six fresh regiments held in reserve two miles away! What on earth do you suppose General M—— was thinking of?"

# Arrest à la Russe

"Cholm!" said Martinev, nodding at the window: "Next station." Somewhere among those crowded roofs and spires was the headquarters of General Ivanov, commander-in-chief of all the southwestern Russian armies, next in power to the Grand Duke Nicolai Nicolaievitch himself. At last here was a man with authority to let us visit the front. As we rattled in our cab through the twilight streets of Cholm, Robinson and I had a violent argument about the kind of battle we wanted to see; Robinson hankered for an infantry charge, and I stuck out for a ride with raiding Cossacks.

The sentry at Staff headquarters said that every one had gone for the night.

*"Loutche gostinnitza!"* we told the driver. Mechanically we looked for the Hotel Bristol, which is to be found in every city, town, and village of the Continent of Europe—but it had suffered the common decline of Hotel Bristols. The best *gostinnitza* turned out to be a three-story, lath-and-plaster structure half-way down a steep street in the crowded Jewish quarter, with a sign in Russian: "English Hotel." Of course, no one spoke English there—no English-speaking guest had ever visited the place. But a black-mustached little Pole, who bounced perspiring to answer the *"Nomernoi!"* of impatient guests, knew two phrases of French: *"Très jolie"* and *"tout de suite";* and the *Hashein* or house-master—a Jew of course—spoke Yiddish.

As we were dressing next morning appeared an officer with a shaven head, and asked us politely to accompany him to the Staff. No less than four persons, he said, had heard us speak German and reported the presence of spies at Cholm. We were ushered into a room where, at a small table, sat a pleasant-faced man who smilingly shook hands and spoke French. We gave him the passes and a card of introduction from Prince Troubetskoi.

"The governor-general of Galicia advised us to come here and ask General Ivanov for permission to go to the front."

He nodded genially. "Very good. But we must first telegraph the Grand Duke—a mere formality, you know. We'll have an answer in two or three hours at the most. In the meanwhile, please return to your hotel and wait there."

Our room was on the third floor, up under the roof, with a sloping ceiling and two dormer windows overlooking the naked, filthy dooryard of a Jewish house. Beyond were shabby, patched tin roofs of the huddled Jewish town, and rising over them the heavily wooded hill, crowned with the towers and golden domes of the monastery. A cobbled street on the right led up the hill to the gates of the monastery park, between wretched huts and tall tenements swarming with Jews. To the left the view soared over housetops to wide-flung plains that stretched forever north— patches of deep woods, fields, villages, and nearby, the railroad yards alive with shuttling trains.

We waited all day, but no one came. Before we were up next morning the bald-headed officer entered, bowing.

"The Grand Duke has not yet answered," he said evasively; "but doubtless he will in the course of the day—or maybe to-morrow."

"Maybe to-morrow!" we cried together. "I thought it was a matter of two or three hours!"

He looked everywhere but at us. "His Highness is very busy——"

"Can't his Highness spare a few minutes from planning retreats to attend to our case?"

"Have patience, gentlemen," said the officer hastily and uncomfortably. "It is only a matter of an hour or so now. I promise you that there will be no delay. . . . And now I am ordered to ask you to give me all your papers—of whatever nature."

Were we suspected of being spies? He laughed uneasily and answered no, as he made out a receipt.

"And now," said he, "I shall have to demand your word of honor not to leave the hotel until the answer comes."

"Are we under arrest?"

"Oh dear, no. You are perfectly free. But this is an important military post, you understand—" Muttering vaguely, he made off as fast as he could, to avoid answering any more questions.

Fifteen minutes later the *Hashein* walked unceremoniously into our room with three Cossacks, big fellows in tall fur hats, pointed boots, long caftans open at the chest; in each belt a silver-worked long dagger hung slantwise in front, and a long, silver-hilted Cossack sword at the side. They stared at us with expressionless faces.

"What do they want?" I asked in German.

The *Hashein* smiled conciliatingly. "Only to look at the gentlemen. . . ."

A little later when I went down-stairs one of the Cossacks was pacing up and down before our door. He drew aside to let me pass, but leaned over the stair-rail, and shouted something in Russian; another, standing in the hall below, came forward; and from the street-door I saw a third peering up.

We wrote an indignant note to General Ivanov, protesting against the Russian conception of "word of honor," and demanding a reason for such treatment. The colonel came at midnight and said that the Cossacks would immediately be withdrawn, with the general's apologies. (Next morning they *had* been withdrawn—to the bottom of the stairs, where they glowered at us suspiciously.) As for our detention, the colonel explained that that was all a very grave matter. We had entered the zone of military operations without the proper passes.

"How were we to know which passes were proper? They were signed by generals, and honored by Prince Bobrinski at Lemberg. What have we done that's wrong?"

"For one thing," said he, "you have come to Cholm, which is forbidden to correspondents. Secondly, you have discovered that Cholm is General Ivanov's headquarters, and that is a military secret."

"But the governor's adjutant——"

"I realize," he interrupted, "that some of our officials have been indiscreet. There is a great scandal about this—all the officers who sent you along have been—!" He made a suggestive movement with his hand. "But that doesn't justify you." And he escaped under a shower of argument.

SATURDAY morning our friend the shaven lieutenant appeared, looking gloomier than ever.

"I have, gentlemen, to announce to you some very disagreeable news," he began formally. "The Grand Duke has answered our telegram. He says: 'Keep the prisoners under strict guard.' "

"But what about our going to the front?"

"That is all he replied." He hurried on. "So unfortunately you will be compelled to keep to this room until further orders. The guards at the door will attend to your wants."

"Look here," said Robinson. "What's the matter with your silly Grand Duke——"

"Oh—" interjected the officer, with a shocked face.

"What are you shutting us up for? Does the Grand Duke think we're spies?"

"Well," he returned doubtfully, "you see, there are curious things, inexplicable things among your papers. In the first place, there is a list of names——"

We explained impatiently for the hundredth time that those were the names of American citizens reported to be caught by the war in the parts of Bucovina and Galicia held by the Russians, and that the American minister in Bucarest had given us the list to investigate.

The officer looked sympathetic but uncomprehending. "But many of them are Jewish names."

"But they are American citizens."

"Ah!" said he. "Do you mean to say that Jews are American citizens?" We affirmed this extraordinary fact, and he didn't contradict us—but you could see he didn't believe it.

Then he gave his orders. We were not to leave the room under any circumstances.

"Can we walk up and down the hall?"

"I am sorry,"—he shrugged his shoulders.

"This is absurd," I said. "What is the charge against us? I demand that we be allowed to telegraph our ambassadors."

He scratched his head vaguely and went out, muttering that he would ask his chief. Two Cossacks immediately mounted the stairs and began to pace up and down in the little hall outside our door; another one stood on the landing below; a fourth at the front door; and the fifth man mounted a shed in the yard of the Jewish house, three stories sheer drop below, and fixed his stolid gaze upon our window.

After consultation, Robinson and I sat down and composed a diplomatic note to the Russian Government—in English, so as to give them the trouble of translating it—formally notifying all concerned that from this date we refused to pay our hotel bill. Summoning a Cossack, we told him to take it to the Staff.

It was now about noon. Over the wide Polish plain the June sun swam slowly up, beating down on the sloping tin roof immediately over our heads. Inconceivable odors rose from the teeming filth of the Jewish quarter, converging at our window. We stripped, garment by garment, and hung out of the window gasping for air. Word had spread abroad of the illustrious captives in the top floor of the "English Hotel," and the Jewish family that inhabited the house below us swarmed out of the door, and stood gazing up at us; stooped, wrinkled old women with bleary eyes, slatternly, bewigged mothers, little girls; venerable old rabbis with long white beards, middle-aged men, thin spectacled youths, and small boys, all dressed alike in the curious peaked cap, and gabardine-like overcoat. Beyond the yard fence was a silent crowd of townspeople, almost all Jews too, staring at our window in silence. They thought we were captured German spies. The Russians considered all Jews to be traitors—indeed, who wouldn't be a traitor if he were a Jew in Russia? With what deep emotion some of them must have looked at us, who heard all day the far-shaking thunder of the German's delivering guns!

. . .

THAT night the shaven officer returned with permission for us to telegraph our ambassadors, and with General Ivanov's reply to our note: he did not know why the Grand Duke ordered us imprisoned. As for the hotel bill, that would be arranged by the government. When we told this to the *Hashein* he went dead white.

"If the Russian army pays," he cried, "I shall not then ever be paid!"

Meanwhile the telegrams disappeared into the vast unknown, and for eight days no answer came. For eight days we inhabited that malodorous chamber under the hot tin roof. It measured four strides wide by five across. We had no books except a Russian-French dictionary and the *"Jardin de Supplice,"* which exhausted their charm after the sixth perusal. Along about the fifth day the *Hashein* discovered somewhere in the town a pack of cards, and we played double-dummy bridge until even now I shriek at the sight of a card. Robinson designed me a town house and a country house to while away the time; he designed luxurious city residences for the Cossacks; he drew their portraits. I wrote verses; elaborated impossible plans of escape; planned a novel. We flirted from the window with the cook of the Jewish house below; we made speeches to the townspeople gathered in the street; we screamed curses to the surrounding air, and sang ribald songs; we walked up and down; we slept, or tried to sleep. And every day we spent a happy hour composing insulting communications to the Tsar, the Duma, the Council of Empire, the Grand Duke, General Ivanov and his Staff—which we forced a Cossack to take to headquarters.

Early in the morning appeared the *Hashein*—a young Jew with a dark, handsome, expressionless face covered by a silky brown beard—followed by a suspicious Cossack.

*"Morgen!"* he would shout at us in broken German, as we stuck our noses out of the bedclothes. *"Was wollen sie essen heute?"*

"What can we have?" we would invariably reply.

*"Spiegeleier—biftek—kartoffeln—schnitzel—brot—butter—chai."*

Day after day we took the Russian-French dictionary, and labored with him to change the diet; but he could not read Russian, and refused to understand it when we pronounced the words. So we alternated between eggs, tough steak, and veal, with always the eternal tea at least six times a day. A samovar operated on the balcony below our window, and from time to time one of us rushed to the door, pushed the Cossack out of the way, leaned over the stairs and bellowed *"Hashein!"* There was a running and calling of anxious Cossacks, doors opened and guests popped their heads out, and cries came echoing up from below.

*"Shto!"*

*"Chai!"* we bellowed. *"Dva chai—skorrie!"*

We tried to have eggs for breakfast, but the *Hashein* refused. "Eggs for lunch, eggs for dinner, but no eggs for breakfast," he announced calmly: "Eggs for breakfast are very unhealthy."

Once after an hour's labor I made him understand that we wanted bacon with our eggs. He threw up his hands in horror. "Bacon!" said he. "Yes, it can be procured; but only Gentiles eat bacon. I shall not give you bacon."

# Prison Life in Cholm

A SOTNIA of Kubanski Cossacks in reserve at Cholm had nothing to do but exercise their horses and stand guard over us. A hundred half-savage giants, dressed in the ancient panoply of that curious Slavic people whose main business is war, and who serve the Tsar in battle from their fifteenth to their sixtieth year; high fur hats, long caftans laced in at the waist and colored dull pink or blue or green, with slanting cartridge pockets on each breast, curved *yataghans* inlaid with gold and silver, daggers hilted with uncut gems, and boots with sharp toes turned up. At first, guarding prisoners was an amusing novelty to them. By day those who knew us brought their friends to look us over; and at intervals in the night, the ones who hadn't been able to come during the day stamped noisily into the room, lit the lamp, and poked us awake with their scabbards.

They were like overgrown children. Some came on guard nervously clasping their sword-hilts, and backed cautiously out again, so that we should not get behind them. Others were shy and trusting—eager to make friends; for hours they would pore over the French-Russian dictionary, spelling out their life histories. One friendly Cossack, in particular, spent most of his time with Robinson, both painfully boasting about their homes and their children. In that eight days we received the entire *sotnia* several times. They got their portraits drawn, overhauled our outfit with ceaseless curiosity, felt the material of our clothes, smoked our cigarettes, marvelled at the pictures Robinson drew of the New York sky-line, and argued interminably among themselves as to whether or not we were German spies. None of them had ever been to western Europe before, and they didn't know what to make of it.

The majority were like that—whether we were German or not made no difference to them—but one thin, evil-faced youth with a blond mustache treated us like captives of a hated enemy. When he was on duty he clumped noisily into the room without knocking, helped himself to cigarettes, and took any money he saw lying around. Sometimes when I was reading he jerked the book out of my hand. We remonstrated with Ivan; we told him in plain English to cut it out. He responded insolently in Russian. And this went on for several days.

One day Ivan entered, swaggered insolently to the table and took a handful of cigarettes—and then spat on the floor. "Get out, Ivan!" shouted Robinson. Ivan sneered in Russian. "Get out, or we'll put you out!"

The Cossack had his back to me, and the door was open. I took him suddenly around the waist from the rear, and running him to the head of the stairs, gave him a push. In a clatter of scimitars and daggers he rolled down a long flight of stairs; and rising at the bottom drew his weapons with a roar of rage and came charging up. Robinson and I held the door. Ivan thrust his sabre through the crack and waved it around, bellowing wrathfully. But the Cossacks on the landing simply leaned against the wall and shouted with laughter; so finally Ivan went away, and he never came back again. . . .

Three times a day the Cossacks rode their horses down the steep street, around the hotel and out the street to the left, and as they rode they sang a great, lifting, roaring chant, like a stern old hymn. We always leaned from the window as they passed, and when they came under us every man looked up and grinned, and raised his hand to salute—all except Ivan, who made a ferocious grimace and shook his fist at us; whereat we leaned down and shook our fists at him.

Sometimes in the breathless evening, when the Cossack in the yard below had got tired of watching and slipped off for a drink, we would climb out of our window onto the steep peaked roof and look down on the tin roofs and teeming overcrowded streets

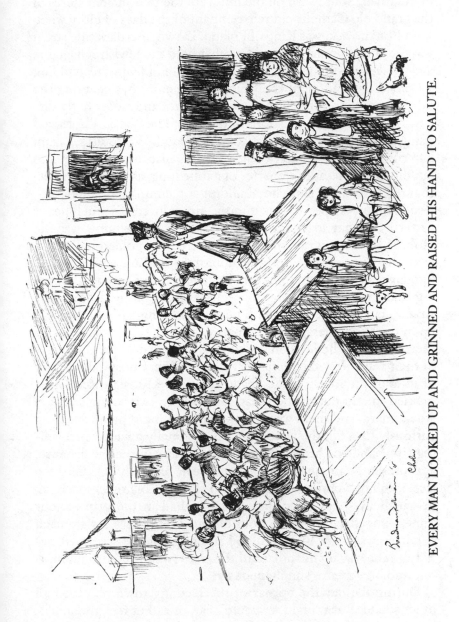

EVERY MAN LOOKED UP AND GRINNED AND RAISED HIS HAND TO SALUTE.

of the town. Southward on the hill were the two ancient spires of the grand old Catholic church, remnant of the days of glory when John Poniatowski was King of Poland. Down on a dark side street was the squat, unmarked building that held the Jewish synagogue and the *heder*—the Jewish sacred school—and from this building ascended day and night the whining drone of boys chanting the sacred books, and the deeper voices of *ravs* and *rebbes* hotly discussing the intricate questions of the law. The tide of Russia was rising and overflowing this city of old Poland. We could see from our roofs colossal military barracks and institutions—immense buildings with façades a quarter of a mile long, as they are in Petrograd; and eight churches building or completed lifted grotesque onion-shaped towers into the air, colored red and blue, or patterned in gay lozenges. Directly before our window was the Holy Hill. Above a rich mass of green trees six golden bulbs rose from the fantastic towers of the monastery, and at evening and on Sunday deep-toned and tinkly bells galloped and boomed. Morning and night we watched the priests going up and down the street—fanatic-faced men with beards and long curly hair falling upon their shoulders, dressed in gray or black silk coats falling to their feet. And the Jews on the sidewalk stepped submissively out of their way. Now the monastery was a military hospital. Groups of girls in the lovely white headdress of the Russian Red Cross hurried in and out of the great gates where two soldiers always stood guard; and there was always a silent knot of people peering curiously through the iron fence. Occasionally a wide-open yelling siren could be heard rising and deepening out of the distance, and presently an automobile would rush furiously up the steep street, full of wounded officers. Once it was a big open machine, in which the body of a huge man writhed in the grip of four nurses who were trying to hold him down. Where his stomach had been was a raw mass of blood and rags, and he screamed awfully all the way up the hill, until the trees swallowed the automobile and his screams simultaneously.

During the day the uproar of the teeming town obscured all other sound. But at night we could hear, or rather feel, the shocking thunder of the enemy's guns less than twenty miles away.

A KUBANSKI COSSACK.

. . .

IMMEDIATELY under our eyes was enacted every day the drama of Jewish life in Russia. Our Cossack guard paraded superciliously about the yard of the house below, the children making wide détours as they passed him, the young girls bringing him glasses of tea and trying to smile at his coarse familiarities, the old people stopping politely to talk with him and casting looks of hate at him behind his back. He strutted about like a lord, he the humblest slave of the Russian military machine; they cringed and curried favor with the member of the dominant race. We noticed that every two or three days all the Jews, young and old, wore upon their breasts a little paper medallion. One morning the *Hashein* came to our room with one: it was a cheap electrogravure of the Tsar's daughter, the Grand Duchess Tatiana.

"What is that?" I asked him, pointing to it.

He shrugged his shoulders in a bitter kind of way. "It is the Grand Duchess's birthday," he said.

"But I have seen the people wearing it already twice this week."

"Every two or three days," he answered, "is the Grand Duchess's birthday. At least that is what the Cossacks say. The Cossacks make every Jew buy a picture of the Grand Duchess on her birthday and wear it. It costs five rubles. We are only poor Jews, too ignorant to know what day is the Grand Duchess's birthday. But the Cossacks are Russians, and they know."

"What if you refuse to buy it?" I asked.

He drew his finger significantly across his throat and made a gurgling noise.

IT was a filthy place, that yard, full of the refuse of two Jewish houses and whatever the hotel guests threw out of their windows. A high board fence separated it from the street, with great wooden gates closed by a strong bar. The door and the lower windows of the house were also protected by heavy wooden shutters fastened from the inside. These were for defense against pogroms. Against the fence a slanting platform of planks had been erected, where all day long innumerable dirty little children climbed up and slid down, shrieking with laughter, or lay on their stomachs with their noses over the fence to watch the Cossacks ride by. Babies wailed and sprawled in the mud of the yard. From the open doors and windows ascended the odors of perpetual "kosher" cooking, the intimate smells of people too overcrowded and too poor to keep clean—the kind you meet on the lower East Side.

But every Friday at noon the house was all of a bustle, as was every Jewish house in the town, preparing for the Sabbath. All the women put on their oldest working clothes; slops were emptied into the yard, and a tin tub of steaming water stood on the doorstep, out of which bucketfuls were carried inside, whence came sounds of scrubbing, sweeping, the slap of wet mops, and the rhythmic songs of Jewish women at work. The buckets, now full of dirty water, were poured back in the tin tub, and after its contents had become brown and thick like soup, all the family receptacles were brought—pans, crockery, knives and forks, cups and glasses—and washed there. The fountain was too far away to waste water. And after that the children each filled a bucket from the tub and went in to bathe, while the rest scoured the doorjambs and the window-sills and the two stone steps below the door, swaying in unison to a minor chant.

The linen hanging on the clothes-line was taken in. A feeling of joy and release was abroad; the terrorized gloom of week-days seemed to lift. All the little Jewish shops closed early, and the men came home walking in little friendly knots like people whose work is done. Each put on his best long coat and peaked cap, his most shiny boots, and went out to join the ever-thickening steady stream of sober, black-robed people that flowed toward the synagogue.

In the house the dirty carpets were rolled up to reveal the white floor, which is always covered except on the Sabbath, and on the days of great religious feasts. And one by one the women, girls, and little children came laughing and chattering out of the purified house in their best clothes, and went out on the street, where all the other women and children were gathered, to gossip together and show off their finery.

From our window we could see a corner of the kitchen, with

the wrinkled old dowager of the house superintending the sealing of the oven; could hear the jangling of the keys being put out of sight for the Holy Day, and look full upon the dining-room table with its row of candles lit for Candle Prayer, and the Sabbath loaf covered with its doily, the wine flask, and *kiddush* cup.

The men came slowly home from synagogue, and up and down the street, in animated conversation, strolled the pale, super-refined young Jewish intellectuals, arguing delicate points of the Law as the dusk came down. The family stood silent, thick-clustered, with bowed heads hiding the table, while blessing over the wine was said, and the consecrated loaf cut—the yellow candle-light striking up along their olive skins, and the strange sharp ridges of their Oriental faces. . . . After supper the children played quietly, stiffly in their Sabbath clothes, and the women gathered in front of the houses; as the darkness grew, from every window of a Jewish house a light beamed, to show the wayfarer that the spirit of God brooded over that roof. And we could look into the windows of a long, bare room on the second story, empty during the week, where the men-folks gathered with great books spread out before them on the table, and sang together deep-toned, Oriental-sounding psalms until late into the night.

On the Sabbath the men went in the morning to the synagogue. It was a day of much visiting between houses in Sabbath clothes; of an interminable dinner that lasted the greater part of the afternoon, with gay songs sung by the whole family to clapping of hands; of dressed-up families, down to the last baby, straggling along the road that led around the base of the Holy Hill toward the open country. . . . And then night and the unsealing of the oven, the putting down of the carpets, little Yakub repeating his lessons to his teacher in a singsong wail, the opening of the shops, old clothes again, dirt, and terror.

Every day or so a tragic little procession would pass up the street that led to the prison beyond the monastery: two or three Jews in their characteristic long coats and peaked caps, shuffling along with expressionless faces and dejected drooping shoulders, preceded and followed by a great shambling soldier with a bayoneted rifle in the hollow of his arm. Many times we asked the

EVERY DAY OR SO A TRAGIC LITTLE PROCESSION WOULD PASS UP THE STREET THAT LED TO THE PRISON BEYOND THE MONASTERY.

*Hashein* about these people; but he always professed ignorance. Where were they going? "To Siberia," he would mumble, "or perhaps—" and he would gesture the pulling of a trigger. The *Hashein* was an extremely prudent person. But sometimes he stood for a long time in our room, looking from Robinson to me and back again, as if there was much to say if only he dared. Finally he shook his head, sighed, and went out past the watchful Cossack, devoutly touching the paper prayer nailed up at the door-jamb.

Toward the end we got no answer to our ultimatums, and the shaven-headed officer came no more; it was such a disagreeable job to answer our arguments! The Cossacks, too, found more entertaining business elsewhere, though they never ceased to salute and shout greetings as they rode past our window; so at last we saw only the *Hashein*, the Cossack on guard, and the two grinning and shapeless Polish servants—Fred and Annie—whom the *Hashein* underfed and overworked, as a Russian Jew will a Christian if he gets the chance.

# Further Adventures in Captivity

ONE day a postman in gaudy uniform, accompanied by several curious friends, came bowing and clicking into the room with a telegram from the American ambassador:

"You have been arrested because you entered the war zone without proper authority. The Foreign Office notifies this embassy that you will be sent to Petrograd."

That was all. Silence settled down again, and the outside world withdrew itself from our ken. One blank, monotonous day succeeded another. We were forgotten.

And then several nights later, there sounded a jingling of spurs and a light rap at our door. Two officers filed solemnly in; one a stout, perspiring little man who introduced himself as Ivanov, quartermaster of the Southwestern Army and cousin of the general, the other a thin, bald-headed epileptic with a withered arm, covered with decorations—Lieutenant Potemkin. His body and face muscles twitching with a sort of St. Vitus's dance, the latter began to talk, and after some time we discovered he was speaking an obscure dialect of English. The drift of his remarks was, that we were free.

"May we return to Bucarest?"

"Yes, gentlemans."

"How can we get to the front?"

"What does he say, what does he say?" queried the quartermaster in a squeaking voice. The lieutenant translated, and they both fell to laughing uproariously.

"I should advise you," said the lieutenant, stuttering—he was like a speaking skeleton—"I should advise you to go Petrograd

461

inquiring your ambassador the Grand Duke to petition—yes, there are diplomatical procedures." He nodded his head violently.

Robinson and I discussed the matter; perhaps if we went to Petrograd, we might yet reach the Russian front.

"If you will come quarter-general your effect documentaries are given," continued the lieutenant fluently. We accompanied him then and there, and he returned to us passports, letters, passes, and the doubtful list of Jewish citizens. We demanded a pass to Petrograd, so that we would not be arrested. He said it was not necessary; that no one would arrest us; however, upon our insisting, he made one out. And it was lucky he did, for we were arrested at least twenty times.

Mr. George T. Marye, the American ambassador, was at lunch in the hotel when I got there; a precise little man with glasses and a white mustache.

"Mr. Reed," he said in a dry, quavering voice, "I am very glad to see you in Petrograd. You have given this office a great deal of anxiety—a great deal. Now, Mr. Reed, I do not want to insist upon your misdemeanors, but my best advice is for you to leave Russia immediately by the shortest route."

"Leave Russia!" said I with considerable astonishment: "What for?"

"Why," he answered testily, "it should be perfectly evident. You have been sent here under military guard——"

"Not at all," I answered. "We were released and told that we could return to Bucarest."

"Bucarest!" said he incredulously, "but I am informed by the Foreign Office that you were to be sent here under arrest, and expelled from Russia. If this is not so, I should advise you to leave the country as fast as possible."

"But what have I done?"

"The despatches which I have received from the Foreign Office concerning you, Mr. Reed, are very alarming—very alarming indeed. The officers who examined you at the front claim to have found upon your person a false passport and letters of introduction to leaders of Jewish anti-Russian revolutionary societies. Moreover, you entered the Russian military zone without proper credentials."

"But my passport was issued in Washington," I replied, "and I had no letters to Jews of any party. All my papers were returned to me at Cholm—I have them here, if you want to see them. As for entering the army zone without credentials, I have passes from two Russian generals, the governor-general of Galicia, a letter from Prince Troubetskoi, and a commission from the American minister at Bucarest."

Mr. Marye gave me a look of utter unbelief. "Well, Mr. Reed," he said coldly, "your statement certainly does not agree with that of the Russian Government."

WHAT happened was this: The officers who arrested us at Cholm were very much embarrassed when they saw our passes. Recently, also, German spies had done effective work in that region, and they had suffered for it. They felt that they simply must catch some German spies. We were the goats. The list of Jewish-American citizens looked suspicious to the man who examined our papers; and besides, not understanding English, he couldn't read the documents. Perhaps, too, the staff at Cholm felt that they had been overzealous, and were afraid that they might be reprimanded for imprisoning an Englishman and an American. So some one invented these wild accusations and sent them to the Grand Duke, hoping that we would be done away with. That is how the Russian mind works.

As a matter of fact, we found out afterward that it had been decided to have us shot at Cholm. But the American and British ambassadors had insisted that we be sent to Petrograd.

I went to the American embassy next day to see what could be done. The first secretary intimated that I was a liar—since my statement and that of the Foreign Office did not agree.

"I understand," he said, "that you are to be expelled by way of Stockholm or Vladivostok. Meanwhile you had better remain quietly at your hotel."

"But the ambassador advised me to leave the country."

"Do not attempt to leave," said he emphatically, "on any account."

"But I must return to Bucarest!" I exclaimed. "Is this embassy going to allow me to be expelled by Stockholm or Vladivostok on false charges?"

He answered frigidly that the embassy could do nothing.

AT the British embassy, where I went with Robinson, the first secretary simply laughed. "Why, that is perfectly ridiculous!" he said. "Of course they can't expel you from Russia! Write your story, and we will act upon the facts as you state them. If Mr. Reed wants us to, we'll be glad to include him also."

In two hours a note from the British ambassador was on its way to the Foreign Office, indorsing our credentials, and guaranteeing that our motives were innocent. A day or so later I again saw Mr. Marye in the lobby of the hotel.

"What, Mr. Reed," he said sternly, "haven't you left Russia yet?"

"Your first secretary ordered me on no account to leave."

"Ah! did he?" said the ambassador uncertainly. "But I should like to see you out of the country, Mr. Reed—your case is a great worry to me!"

IN Russia the mills of God grind slowly, and they grind exceeding strange. Three weeks later, out of the clear sky came a communication to the two embassies: that Messrs. Reed and Robinson were at liberty to remain in Russia as long as they liked, but that when they departed they must leave the country by the port of Vladivostok.

"Nothing can be done—nothing," said Mr. Marye. "But I will have a talk with Mr. Sasonov."

The secretary of the British embassy was highly indignant. "Don't you go a step," he said. "The ambassador himself will protest to Mr. Sasonov immediately."

Sir George Buchanan, the British ambassador, treated the whole matter as a joke. That afternoon he was talking with the Russian Minister of Foreign Affairs.

"I think you people are very short-sighted," said Sir George. "These men have done invaluable service in the American press for the Allies, and they came to Russia to write about affairs here in a friendly way. You will simply create bad feeling against Russia in America."

"Just the same," said Sasonov, "they were very naïve to enter Russia the way they did."

"Not any more naïve than your own military authorities," retorted Sir George.

A WEEK later Mr. Marye met me in the lobby and shook me warmly by the hand.

"Well, Mr. Reed," said he, smiling, "how is your matter going on?"

"I thought you were attending to my matter, Mr. Marye," I answered. "Haven't you spoken with Mr. Sasonov?"

"I had a friendly conversation with Mr. Sasonov, who assured me that nothing could be done. Remember, Mr. Reed, it is not my fault if you get into difficulties. You recollect that I advised you frankly to leave Russia at once, and I advise you now to do so—by Vladivostok."

TEN days later we tried to escape. With a donation of thirty-five roubles the Petrograd police were persuaded to stamp our passports with the official "Free to cross the frontier"; and we left very suddenly one evening, changing cabs several times, and took the train for Kiev and Bucarest. But next morning, at Vilna, a smiling officer of *gendarmerie* came into our compartment and woke us up.

"A thousand pardons!" said he, without asking who we were or where we were going. "I am ordered by telegraph to ask you to leave the train here and return to Petrograd, and to leave Russia immediately by way of Vladivostok."

It took a day and a half to get back to Petrograd. No sooner were we in our hotel than two officers of the secret police materialized and notified us to go to headquarters and interview the chief.

Strangely enough, nothing was known there of our attempted flight. The chief, a sullen, bloated person with an evil face, read us the order which had just been received direct from his Highness the Grand Duke. It was dated three days before—a day before our escape—and said: "Mr. Boardman Robinson, British subject, and Mr. John Reed, American citizen, are herewith commanded to leave Petrograd for Vladivostok within twenty-four hours of the receipt of this; in case of non-compliance they are to be delivered to a military court martial and severely punished."

"Severely punished?" asked Robinson. "What if we are acquitted?"

"You will be severely punished," answered the chief woodenly.

In the meantime our interpreter looked up the train schedule; there was no train in the direction of Vladivostok within the twenty-four hours! Besides, our money had given out. All that didn't make any difference to the chief; he insisted that we must go, train or no train, money or no money.

Pursued by flocks of detectives in all sorts of disguises, we scurried to our respective embassies.

Mr. Marye refused to see me, but sent Mr. White, the second secretary.

"We cannot help you financially, Mr. Reed," he said coldly, "but the American consul, I believe, has a fund for destitute Americans."

In desperation I explained that we were ordered to leave for Vladivostok within twenty-four hours, and that there was no train. He replied indifferently that it was very doubtful if anything could be done. So I hurried to find Robinson.

Thank God, the British embassy had acted for us both. His Excellency the ambassador wired the British attaché on the staff of the Grand Duke to speak with his Highness. Moreover, Sir George went in person to the Foreign Office and protested in the name of his government. The secretary of foreign affairs telegraphed the Grand Duke, asking that the order be revoked; and over the telephone instructed the secret police to stop annoying us.

. . .

AN hour later the chief of police telephoned us his apologies and said that his men had been withdrawn.

Next day a Staff officer called at our hotel, and with respectful politeness presented a note from the Grand Duke's adjutant, stating that the order of expulsion was cancelled, and that we were at liberty to proceed to Bucarest when we wished.

We didn't wait, but took the next fast train south, fearing that perhaps some one might change his mind. The officer in command of the frontier put us in a corner of the station, and set four soldiers on us, who prodded our baggage inch by inch, ripped our wallets apart and the lining of our clothes, and virtually undressed us before the other passengers. All my papers and notes they confiscated, and all Robinson's sketches. But once over the frontier, on neutral ground, that seemed a small price to pay for getting free of the clumsy clutches of the Russian Army.

# The Face of Russia

W HOEVER has not travelled on the broad-gauge Russian railways does not know the delights of great cars half as wide again as American cars, berths too long and too ample, ceilings so high that you can stand in the upper berth. The train takes its smooth-rolling, leisurely way, drawn by wood-burning locomotives belching sweet-smelling birch smoke and showers of sparks, stopping long at little stations where there are always good restaurants. At every halt boys bring trays of tea glasses through the train, sandwiches, sweet cakes, and cigarettes. There are no specified hours for arriving anywhere, no fixed times for eating or sleeping. Often on a journey I have seen the dining-car come on at midnight, and everybody go in and have dinner with interminable conversation, lasting until time for breakfast. One man rents bedclothes from the porter, and disrobes in full view of the rest of the company in his compartment; others turn in on the bare mattresses; and the rest sit up drinking eternal *chai* and endlessly arguing. Windows are shut and doors. One stifles in thick cigarette smoke, and there are snores from the upper berth, and continual movement of persons getting up, going to bed, drifting in and out.

In Russia every one talks about his soul. Almost any conversation might have been taken from the pages of a Dostoievsky novel. The Russians get drunk on their talk; voices ring, eyes flash, they are exalted with a passion of self-revelation. In Petrograd I have seen a crowded café at two o'clock in the morning—of course no liquor was to be had—shouting and singing and pounding on the tables, quite intoxicated with ideas.

Outside the windows of the train the amazing country flows by, flat as a table; for hours the ancient forest marches alongside, leagues and leagues of it, untouched by the axe, mysterious and sombre. At the edge of the trees runs a dusty track along which an occasional heavy cart lumbers, its rough-coated horse surmounted by a great wooden yoke from which dangles a brass bell, the driver a great-shouldered *mujik* with a brutish face overhung with hair. Hours apart are little thatched towns, mere slashings in the primeval woods, built of untrimmed boards around the wooden church, with its bright-painted cupolas, and the government vodka shop—closed now—easily the most pretentious building in the village. Wooden sidewalks on stilts, unpaved alley-like streets that are sloughs of mud, immense piles of cordwood to burn in the engine—for all the world like a railroad town in the timber of the great Northwest. Immense women with gay-colored kerchiefs around their hair and dazzling teeth, booted giants of men in peaked caps and whiskers, and priests in long, black coats and stovepipe hats with brims. Along the platform, tall policemen much in evidence, with their yellow blouses, scarlet revolver cords, and swords. Soldiers, of course, everywhere—by the tens of thousands. . . . Then great fields breaking suddenly from the woods and stretching to the far horizon, golden-heavy with wheat with black stumps sticking up in it.

Russians are not patriotic like other races, I think. The Tsar to them is not the head of the government; he is a divinity. The government itself—the bureaucracy—commands no loyalty from the masses; it is like a separate nation imposed upon the Russian people. As a rule, they do not know what their flag looks like, and if they do it is not the symbol of Russia. And the Russian national hymn is a hymn, a half-mystical great song; but no one feels it necessary to rise and remove his hat when it is played. As a people, they have no sympathy with imperialism—they do not wish to make Russia a great country by conquest—in fact, they do not seem to realize that there is any world outside of Russia; that is why they fight so badly on an invasion of the enemy's country. But once let the enemy set foot on Russian soil, and the *mujiks* turn into savage beasts, as they did in 1812 and in 1915. Their farms, their houses, the woods and plains and holy cities are under the heel of the foreigner; that is why they fight so well on defense.

Russians seem to have a Greek feeling for the land, for the wide flat plains, the deep forests, the mighty rivers, the tremendous arch of sky that is over Russia, the churches incrusted with gold and jewels, where countless generations of their fathers have touched the ikons; for the tremendous impulses that set whole villages wandering in search of a sacred river, for the cruel hardness of the northern winter, for the fierce love and the wild gayety, and the dreadful gloom, and the myths and legends which are Russia. Once a young officer travelled with us in our compartment, and all day long he gazed out of the window at the dark woods, the vast fields, the little towns, and tears rolled down his cheeks. "Russia is a mighty mother; Russia is a mighty mother," he said over and over again. . . .

Another time it was a middle-aged civilian with a bullet head shaved close, and wide, staring, light-blue eyes that gave him the expression of a mystic.

"We Russians do not know how great we are," he said. "We cannot grasp the idea of so many millions of people to communicate with. We do not realize how much land, how much riches we have. Why, I can tell you of one, Mr. Yousoupov of Moscow, who owns more land than he knows, whose estates are greater than the territory of any German King. And no Russian realizes how many races are embraced in this nation; I myself know only thirty-nine. . . ."

Yet this vast chaotic agglomeration of barbarian races, brutalized and tyrannized over for centuries, with only the barest means of intercommunication, without consciousness of any one ideal, has developed a profound national unity of feeling and thought and an original civilization that spreads by its own power. Loose and easy and strong, it invades the life of the far-flung savage tribes of Asia; it crosses the frontiers into Rumania, Galicia, East Prussia—in spite of organized efforts to stop it. Even the English, who usually cling stubbornly to their way of living in all countries and under all conditions, are overpowered by Russia; the English colonies in Moscow and Petrograd are half Russian. And it takes hold of the minds of men because it is the most comfortable, the most liberal way of life. Russian ideas are the most exhilarating, Russian thought the freest, Russian art the most exuberant; Russian food and drink are to me the best, and Russians themselves are, perhaps, the most interesting human beings that exist.

They have a sense of space and time which fits them. In America we are the possessors of a great empire—but we live as if this was a crowded island like England, where our civilization came from. Our streets are narrow and our cities congested. We live in houses crushed up against one another, or in apartments, layer on layer; each family a little shut-in cell, self-centred and narrowly private. Russia is also a great empire; but there the people live as if they knew it were one. In Petrograd some streets are a quarter-mile broad and there are squares three-quarters of a mile across, and buildings whose façades run on uninterrupted for half a mile. Houses are always open; people are always visiting each other at all hours of the day and night. Food and tea and conversation flow interminably; every one acts just as he feels like acting, and says just what he wants to. There are no particular times for getting up or going to bed or eating dinner, and there is no conventional way of murdering a man, or of making love. To most people a Dostoievsky novel reads like the chronicle of an insane asylum; but that, I think, is because the Russians are not restrained by the traditions and conventions that rule the social conduct of the rest of the world.

This is not only true of the great cities but of the small towns, and even the villages as well. The Russian peasant cannot be taught to tell time by the clock. He is so close to the earth, so much a part of it, that machine-made time means nothing to him. But he must be regular, or his crops will not grow; so he ploughs and plants and reaps by rain, wind, snow, and the march of the seasons—and he lives according to the sun, moon, and stars. Once the peasant is driven into the cities to work in the factories he loses the driving compulsion of nature, and when he has risen above the necessity of factory hours, there is no further reason for him to live a regular life.

We saw something of life in a Russian household; samovars perpetually steaming, servants shuffling in and out with fresh water and fresh tea-leaves, laughing and joining in the perpetual clatter of conversation. In and out flowed an unbroken stream of relatives, friends, comparative strangers. There was always tea, always a long sideboard heaped with *zakouska*, always a hundred little groups telling stories, loudly arguing, laughing uproariously, always little parties of card-players. Meals occurred whenever anybody got hungry—or rather there was a perpetual meal going on. Some went to bed, others rose after a long sleep and had breakfast. Day and night it never seemed to stop.

And in Petrograd we knew some people who received callers between eleven o'clock at night and dawn. Then they went to bed, and did not get up again until evening. For three years they hadn't seen daylight—except in the white nights of summer. Many interesting characters went there; among them an old Jew who had bought immunity from the police for years, and who confided to us that he had written a history of Russian political thought in five volumes; four volumes had appeared, and had been regularly confiscated upon publication—he was now engaged upon the fifth. He was always discussing politics in a loud voice, breaking off every now and then to look out of the window to see if there were any police listening. For he had been in jail once for speaking the word "socialism." Before he began to talk he would take us into a corner and in a whisper explain that when he said "daisy," that meant "socialism"; and when he said "poppy," that meant "revolution." And then he would go ahead, striding up and down the room, and shouting all sorts of destructive doctrines.

For the Russia of melodrama and of the English popular magazines still exists. I remember seeing some prisoners on the platform of a station where our train stopped. They were huddled between the tracks: two or three young stupid-looking *mujiks* with cropped heads, a bent old man half-blind, a Jew or so, and some women, one a mere girl with a baby. Around them was a ring of police with bared swords.

"Where are they going?" I asked the conductor.

"Siberia," he whispered out of the corner of his mouth.

"What have they done?"

"Don't ask questions," he snapped nervously. "If you ask questions in Russia *that* is what happens to you!"

There were some preposterous war regulations in Petrograd. If you spoke German over the telephone you were subject to a fine of three thousand roubles, and if you were heard talking German on the street the penalty was Siberia. I have it on very good authority that two professors of Oriental languages were walking down the Morskaia, speaking ancient Armenian to each other. They were arrested, and the police swore that it was German. And from that day to this they have never again been heard of.

In spite of this, however, the fact remains that any German with money could go on living in Petrograd or Moscow, and manifest his patriotism in any way he pleased. For instance, the large German colony of Moscow gave a dinner in the city's most fashionable hotel during November, 1914, at which German songs were chanted, addresses in German delivered which consigned the Czar and his allies to purgatory, and shouts of "Hoch der Kaiser!" rent the air. Nothing whatever was done about this; but six months later the police determined to teach them a lesson without appearing at all prominent—which would have cut off their German revenues. Quantities of vodka were dug up from somewhere, the ikons taken from the churches, and, encouraged by the police, the mob started out to wreck German houses, shops, and hotels. After the first few of these had been demolished the people turned their attention to the French, English, and Russian establishments, shouting: "Down with the rich! You have speculated too long with our money!" Before the riot ended almost every great store in Moscow had been smashed and pillaged, and many wealthy Russians, men and women, torn from their automobiles and carriages and thrown into the canal. The Russian people of the upper classes did not disdain to take advantage of the situation. They sent their footmen and valets down to plunge into the riot, and take whatever silks and laces and furs they could lay their hands on. . . . As a consequence of this patriotic demonstration, the governor of the city, the governor of the province, and the chief of police were discharged from office.

How the Germans were finally removed from Moscow, is another characteristic tale of Russian methods. Did they banish them? Did they put them in detention camps? No. The police let it privately be known that if the Moscow Germans wished to leave Russia, there was a means. In Moscow, they said, it was impossible for a German to get a passport to return to his own country; but if he would go to the government of Perm, on the edge of Siberia at the base of the Ural Mountains, he could there apply for a passport and be allowed to leave. Hundreds of Germans took the hint and crowded the trains that went in the direction of Perm. They are still there.

There are four distinct sets of Russian secret police, and their main job is to supervise the regular police and to spy upon each other, besides the *dvorniks*, who act as *concierges* at your front door, and are all members of the government detective force. In times like the present, particularly, a mere suspicion is enough to send you to a military court martial, unless you have influence, or to spirit you away to Siberia.

After our arrest in Poland, when we reached Petrograd, we were dogged for weeks by municipal detectives, military secret agents, and members of the dreaded Fourth Arm—the sinister most secret police of all. But a Russian detective is easily recognizable; whatever his disguise, whether as workman, *mujik*, cab-driver, or loafer, he invariably wears patent-leather shoes and carries a silver-headed cane. A little group of them always stood in front of our hotel door, and during the long wearisome evenings we would often throw bottles at them out of the window. Whenever we took a cab to go to the American embassy, a detective detached himself from the group and followed us in another cab. And when we swung into the Nevski we would stop and wait for him to round the corner, which he did at a fast trot, thinking us far ahead, and then *we* would follow *him* for hours, to his intense discomfiture.

You cannot leave Russia without a "foreign visé" stamped on

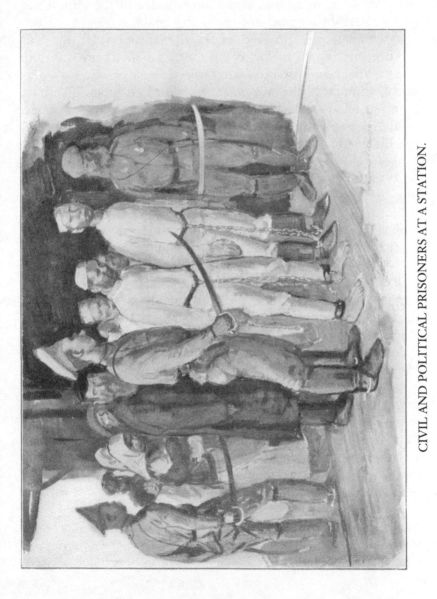

CIVIL AND POLITICAL PRISONERS AT A STATION.

your passport by the city police, permitting you to cross the frontier. We were, of course, under surveillance of the city police; nevertheless, by a present of thirty-five roubles, we got our foreign visé, and took the train for the Rumanian border. At Vilna the next morning a major of the military police came into our compartment, and without asking who we were or where we were going, announced that we must return to Petrograd. There we found secret agents of the Fourth Arm waiting for us to conduct us to the chief's headquarters. But the chief did not know that we had obtained a foreign visé, or even that we had tried to flee; he simply wanted to read us a peremptory order from the Grand Duke expelling us from Russia by way of Vladivostok for an imaginary offense.

In our hotel in Petrograd lived a squat, powerful woman who looked like an Eskimo, and had coarse hair bobbed like the roached mane of a Shetland pony. Her name was Princess ———. In the late afternoon she used to come into the tea-room, pick out a man that pleased her, and hold up her immense room-key in bald, frank invitation. This did not offend the Russians; but the hotel was full of American business men and their wives, and they complained to the manager about the scandal. The manager ordered the princess to leave the hotel; she refused. So, Russian-like, one day when she was out he took her bed apart and removed it, with every other piece of furniture, from her room. She returned to the hotel, and for several hours stamped up and down the lobby calling him every name she could think of. Then she went out. Fifteen minutes later a secret-police official drove up in an automobile, descended upon the manager, and informed him that if he ever molested that woman again he would go to Siberia. The princess was an agent of the Fourth Arm. . . .

# The National Industry

FROM Zalezchik to Tarnopol we were alone in our compartment, but in the next one were four or five shaven-headed colonels and majors, their boots highly polished, their drab blouses ablaze with decorations. Windows were closed, belts unloosened, swords hung up. On a little wooden stand was a great brass samovar, steaming, and a wooden box of cigarettes overflowing on the table. They smoked and drank tea and talked about their souls.

Moved by Russian curiosity and Russian hospitality, the major, speaking bad French, came into our compartment and introduced himself, and began telling all the military secrets he knew—where his regiment was, how many men it comprised, how it was planned to throw them across the Pruth the next night in the dark and surprise a cluster of Austrian batteries. This was not indiscretion on his part; simply, it was no fun to talk about these things to people who knew them already—and he was perfectly delighted to find strangers who seemed interested. He took us into his compartment, and the others made room, plied us with tea and cigarettes, eagerly questioned us about ourselves, our business, how much salary we got, did they drink much whiskey in America, was Newport as smart as the Riviera, and what we thought of the war. Then the original discussion was resumed, this time in broken French and German for our benefit. Each man had been telling about his first sexual experience; from that they entered upon a discussion of the psychology of sex, its relation to artistic energy, the power it had over the lives of men. . . .

Only toward evening did we discover their business. They were a commission of officers sent by General Dimitriev to discover

477

the whereabouts of seventeen million bags of flour, which were lost.

Now seventeen million bags of flour, if assembled, would loom as large as the city of Poughkeepsie; yet it had vanished. It seemed that the Russian Government had bought, caused to be ground and packed the seventeen million bags as a provision for the Southwestern Armies for the year. The flour was shipped from Kiev to Tarnopol, a distance of two hundred and thirty versts, along a line of railroad crossed only twice by other lines; and yet within that one hundred and eighty odd miles more than thirty train-loads of flour had absolutely disappeared from the face of the earth.

"But where can it have gone?" I asked.

The grizzled colonel shrugged his shoulders with a smile. "We have reason to believe," said he, "that it was sold to the Rumanians and then shipped into Austria." He sighed. "Such things will happen. . . ."

GRAFT in Russia is on such a naïvely vast scale that it becomes almost grotesque.

During the Japanese War the French Government sent fifty batteries of .75 guns to the Russian army. They were registered as having passed the frontier, but strangely enough they never officially arrived in Russia. Six months later a French military officer in Brazil signalled to his government the presence of several Creusot .75 field-pieces. Since every gun that leaves the Creusot Works is registered, the company officials were puzzled, because no guns had even been sold to the Brazilian army. Upon comparing serial numbers, however, they turned out to be the ones shipped to Russia in 1905.

I have another story from the Russian representative of a foreign ship-building concern, who told me of a battleship which he personally designed for the Russian Government at that same time. The plans were accepted, the steel contracted for, an army of working men assembled at Odessa, and in the course of time it was reported that the battleship was ready for launching. The governor of the province personally broke a champagne-bottle over her bow, and a month later she put to sea on her trial trip. Then news came that the battleship had sunk somewhere in the Black Sea. Some one was suspicious—an investigation was ordered, and it developed that *the battleship had never been built at all.*

In 1909, a French general visiting the Tsar was invited by his majesty to go down to Poland and inspect a great new modern fort which had just been built near Warsaw. The military governor to whom he applied assured him that the country was in a very unsettled condition, and that it would be unwise to visit the fort without a proper military escort—and he could not spare soldiers for that. After combating all sorts of obstructions and evasions, the general lost his temper and insisted on going to see the fort alone. There was of course no fort.

At the most serious epoch of the Russian retreat last summer, when whole divisions were annihilated because of the lack of ammunition for their cannon, I met an Englishman who had come to Russia three months before with a ship-load of shrapnel. He said it was still at Archangel—because he would not bribe the railway and ordnance officials to ship it to the front. . . .

A French steel manufacturer of Moscow contracted to furnish several million shells for the Russian artillery. Many car-loads were sent to the front, but when they arrived it was found that they did not fit the Russian cannon; so they were left behind on the retreat, and the Germans used them with entire success. Summoned before an investigating commission, the Frenchman produced his specifications, drawn up and signed by the Minister of War, Mr. Soukomlinov.

Now Mr. Soukomlinov had been a comparatively poor man before the war; but after the commencement of hostilities he began to buy large blocks of Petrograd real estate, and it was freely said by people on the inside that he had been quite simply selling military secrets to the Germans. Later he resigned under a cloud of suspicion, which must have been grave indeed, as he was one of the leaders of the Reactionaries.

I was in Petrograd when a certain colonel drove up one day in front of the establishment of a friend of mine who sold automobile tires. The colonel had fifty motor ambulances, just then in great need at the front, and he asked my friend to look them over and estimate what it would cost to put new tires on the entire fifty. The salesman named the figure.

"And how much do I get out of it?" asked the colonel.

"The customary ten per cent."

"All right, then, go ahead."

The salesman came out and looked at the tires.

"Why," he said, "you don't need new tires on these cars. They are almost new!"

"You mind your own business!" snapped the colonel. "Put those tires on, and don't talk too much about it if you know what's good for you!"

American business men selling supplies to the Russian Government had endless stories of the sublime voracity of the purchasing department. It did not make any difference how good the product—the question invariably asked was: "How much do I get?" In many cases, when the company could not afford to pay a large graft, the Russians themselves raised the prices to their own government.

Suppose you had an automobile truck to sell. It was demonstrated before a commission which made a secret report to one of the officials of the Intendancy, who summoned you to consultation. Now, by a little gift of twenty or thirty dollars you had discovered that your product had been favorably reported on, or you had arranged that it would be favorably reported on by a similar gift to the other members of the commission.

Upon entering the office of the Intendancy official, he would say: "Your automobile has been recommended very highly. But there are also other automobiles. I must consider your proposition." He would look at his watch. "Excuse me for a moment, I must run out. By the way, wouldn't you like a cigarette?" and, handing you his cigarette-case, he would leave you there. Perhaps you opened the cigarette-case and found it empty. And if you had been in Russia long you would extract from your pocket a five-hundred-rouble note, and slip it into the cigarette-box. When the officer returned he would say: "Now, about prices. What commission do I get?" You would arrange that to his satisfaction, and he would tell you to wait for his answer at your hotel.

But, of course, it was all a gamble. Somebody else might have put a thousand-rouble note in the cigarette-box. . . . There were, of course, other ways of notifying prospective salesmen that they had to "come across." For example, a number of professional "intermediaries" hung around the hotels frequented by Americans, hinting that such an official ought to be "greased," and so forth.

But the whole business was so frank and greedy that, even with the best intentions in the world, the secret police could not fail to stumble on some gigantic system of fraud every two or three days. Exposure after exposure revealed that the entire Intendancy was nothing but a mass of corruption; but the trail always led so far and so high that it had to be choked off. Princes and barons and financiers and army officers and cabinet ministers were implicated. Even the Grand Duke Serge, chief of the Department of Artillery Munitions, was suspected, and the Tsar's household was not free from calumny. Banks were seized and safe-deposit boxes broken open, and enough documents found to convict practically the whole bureaucracy. Persons high in power one day were replaced the next. Sometimes you went to the Intendancy to see an official with whom you had talked three hours previously, and found a new man in his place.

"Where is Colonel Verchovsky?" you asked.

Sometimes the newcomer replied briefly, "Siberia"; sometimes he shrugged his shoulders; and sometimes he lit a match, let it burn a little while, and then gracefully blew it out.

# A Patriotic Revolution

---

T HE war-time traveller in Russia was immediately struck with Russian commercial dependence upon Germany. In Petrograd I tried to buy an antiseptic mouth-wash. "Ah," said the drug clerk, a German himself, by the way, "all such preparations come from Germany—we cannot get them now." And so with cameras, with films, with milk-chocolate, with clothing, automobiles, typewriters. There was even no good surgeon in Petrograd, no physician who was a specialist in diseases of the intestines; the reply was: "We always send such cases to Berlin."

For the last ten years Russia has become more and more a German commercial colony. Every embarrassment of Russia was taken advantage of by Germany to increase her trade advantages in the empire; as, for example, in 1905, German interests exacted enormous concessions by overt threats of aiding the revolutionists. The Germans also crept into government offices, even into the army administration. They dictated the plans of the Russian strategic railways on the German frontier. And in the Imperial Court, in the entourage of the Tsarina—herself a German—they exercised a sinister and powerful influence.

Russian merchants, manufacturers, and bankers have long bitterly opposed the German power in their country, and this has made them enemies of the corrupt and tyrannical Russian Government—which is bound up with the Germans—and allies of the revolutionists. So in this war we have the curious spectacle of the Russian proletariat and the middle class both intensely patriotic, and both opposing the government of their country. And to

482

understand Russia now one must realize the paradox that to make war on Germany is to make war on the Russian bureaucracy.

When I was in Russia, in June, the internal struggle was at its height. A vast organization existed, even in the highest places of the government, to betray Russia to the enemy. A secret wireless station which intercepted military messages and transmitted them to Germany was discovered in a chimney of the Winter Palace itself. Besides the Soukomlinov scandal, there was also the case of General Masdeiev, who did a thriving export business in plans of Russian fortresses until somebody squealed.

After the battle of Tannenburg General Rennenkampf bitterly accused his own officers of selling him out; and in Russia they say that that was one of the reasons he was removed from command. The same thing is also said to be one of the reasons why the Grand Duke Nicholas was transferred to the Caucasus; at any rate, his bitter criticism of the Germans in the Imperial Court and the government were a matter of common knowledge.

Where does the Tsar stand in relation to all this? In Russia, the more you hear about him, the more fantastic and legendary he becomes. In Petrograd I knew an American fortune-teller who said he was a friend of the Emperor—and in proof of it produced a great platinum cigarette-case embossed with the Imperial monogram in diamonds, and with the gold relief of an outstretched hand; this, he said, the Tsar had given him in reward for his services in foretelling the fall of Warsaw. During the week before that event the Tsar had summoned him three times to Tsarskoe Selo, to read the Imperial palm and predict from its lines whether Warsaw would be taken by the Germans. The fortune-teller, who read the newspapers, said that it would. And it did.

Men who have talked with the Tsar assured me that he knew little that was going on in the empire, except what his reactionary advisers chose to tell him.

The fortune-teller had had many curious contacts with the Imperial Court. For instance, he said that several years ago he had been suddenly summoned from Vienna to Sebastopol, and taken out to the Imperial yacht, lying off the harbor; there he found a concourse of surgeons, homeopaths, faith-healers, and all sorts of quacks from every part of Europe. They had been gathered to save the life of the young Tsarovitch, who had been stabbed in the hip by a revolutionist sailor. That, said the fortune-teller, was the basis for all those later stories of the Tsarovitch's mysterious illness.

He had also run foul of Rasputin, the lay monk, that sinister figure whose power over the Tsarina, men say, is so evil and profound. The fortune-teller showed me an almost illegible scrawl of bad French which he had received the week previously, and which ran approximately as follows:

"Father Gregory Rasputin asks me to inform you that he is cognizant of your visits to Tsarskoe Selo. He has no objection to your interviewing the Emperor; but if you are summoned by the Empress, and visit her, your stay in Russia is likely to be very unpleasant."

Now, these things may not be true; but they are no more preposterous than other details of the life of that Oriental hierarchy—and no more impossible than the well-known fact that many members of the Duma came to have their palms read by this same fortune-teller on political questions.

UNDER the surface of the vast, restless sea of Russian life mighty currents rush obscurely to and fro. Crusades, revolutions, religious schisms, and tremendous popular movements go on; rarely they burst up into the light where they can be seen and judged, but one is always conscious of them. The great revolution of 1905 broke the surface, and at the outbreak of this war another revolution was ready to break, beginning with a gigantic general strike. Its sharp alarms were lost in the roar of mobilization and the barbaric pageantry of Imperial proclamations—promises by the Tsar of a more liberal government, of autonomy for Poland, of reform for the Jews. Probably the mobilization impressed the revolutionists more than the proclamations; for not only were the promises made in the Imperial manifesto of 1905 not carried out, but in some respects things were worse than they ever had been. The

Duma was in existence, but by changing the rules of procedure and using the police to terrorize provincial elections, the government had robbed it of all its hard-won prerogatives. The freedom of the press had been promised, but during the Beiliss trial that great paper, the *Russkoe Slovo*, was fined thousands of roubles for publishing reports of the proceedings. And that was a rich and powerful journal; other periodicals could not afford to publish anything at all. Free speech was promised, but you had to get a police permit for a public meeting—and in Russia the police are not very indulgent. Religious freedom was promised, and freedom of conscience; but recently the Minister of the Interior closed the Unified Catholic church in Petrograd, and others in other towns, on the ground that they violated the building code. The inviolability of the person was guaranteed and the right of trial, but never have so many people been kidnapped to Siberia, without even an accusation against them, as now.

In the face of the wholesale corruption of the purchasing department of the government, the Association of Zemstvos, or county councils, undertook to buy army supplies for the government—a job which it accomplished with real ability. This is an important fact, as the Association represented to a large extent the Russian middle class.

All this time the Duma, limited as it was, had been getting more and more frankly critical. For example, one speaker said that Russia had a government which was extraordinarily inefficient, extraordinarily corrupt, and extraordinarily traitorous. In addition, it began to name specific grafters and traitors and hinted where the trail led, and it recommended that committees of the Duma be put in charge of the buying of supplies, in conjunction with the Zemstvos, and also the manufacture of munitions. Besides all this, there was rapidly growing popular unrest manifested all over the empire. And it was the discontent of patriots that determined Russia should win the war.

On September 8 the Grand Duke Nicholas was superseded by the Tsar in command of the western front. The people looked upon this as a very doubtful move and wondered what lay back of it; for the Grand Duke was at least honest, and the Tsar had called to his pavilion at the front Mr. Soukomlinov, who was not trusted. An important Russian general stated that it meant that the Tsar was about to make a separate peace; at any rate, the ambassadors of the Entente Powers tried for three weeks to dissuade his Majesty from assuming command.

One amazing rumor generally credited by intelligent people declared that the Tsar had been forced to take command by Rasputin, who had interpreted visions of the Most High commanding that this be done. It is not improbable.

On September 15 a strike was declared by the thirty thousand workmen in the Poteelov Armament Works in Petrograd, and the next day proclamations were posted on the street corners forbidding gatherings of workmen. Members of the foreign colonies, on account of the confidential information from the War Office, began hurriedly to leave Russia. On the following morning it was reported that thirty workmen from the Poteelov Works, who had presented a petition to the Duma on the 15th, had been banished to Siberia with their families. Riots followed in which soldiers fired on the strikers, and on the same day the Tsar suddenly dissolved the Duma. In Petrograd it was known that all the members of the cabinet were opposed to the dissolution except the Reactionary premier, Goremykin. At the same time proclamations were posted calling new troops to the colors— which increased the general dissatisfaction—and on the 18th new posters appeared threatening that the strikers would be either sent to the trenches or given indefinite terms of imprisonment in Siberia, unless they returned to work on the following Tuesday, and unless thereafter they obeyed orders.

During these days spasmodic strikes on the railways caused a shortage of food and fuel in Petrograd, and severe suffering followed among the population. A cholera epidemic broke out. The papers every day published long lists of deaths, calling them euphemistically "death from stomach trouble," and the official organs announced that during the winter there would be a shortage of everything except flour.

On the 20th, news came of strikes in Kiev, Odessa, and other cities, and of the complete paralysis of the street-cars and electric-light plants in Moscow. The Association of Zemstvos and the Association of Cities sent a committee direct to the Tsar, threatening that unless he liberalized the government they would favor revolution, and declaring emphatically the absolute necessity of a liberal ministry responsible to the Duma. The Tsar refused to receive the delegation.

Is there a powerful and destructive fire working in the bowels of Russia, or is it quenched? Rigid censorship and the suppression of news within the empire make it very difficult to know; but even after the prorogation of the Duma there were wholesale dismissals of Intendancy officials, and a complete military reorganization of the western armies, and even as I write this some powerful, quiet menace, as yet vaguely defined, has forced the Tsar to reopen the Duma with Imperial pomp. And Boris Sturmer, the new premier, though a Reactionary of the worst type, has assured the Duma that "even in war time the work of internal reorganization must go on."

In the White Russian town of Rovno I had a talk with a young volunteer non-commissioned officer, who had been clerk in a Petrograd bank before the war. The revolution of 1905, he explained, was not a revolution at all; it was a gigantic scandal. It was the instinctive revolt of millions of human beings against robbery and tyranny that were absolutely absurd. "That is all over," he said hastily, for after all he belonged to the governing class. "But," he added, "after this war we shall ask for a new constitution."

"And what if they don't give it to you?" said I. "Will there be a revolution?"

"Oh, I think they will give it to us. But if not—well, we *must* have it!"

"And how about the Jews?"

"The Jews!" he cried. "What has democracy to do with the Jews? We do not want the Jews in Russia. Why don't they all go to America, or to the devil?"

# The Betrayal of the Jews

$A$T the beginning of the war French, English, and American newspapers published accounts of proclamations by the Tsar and the Grand Duke "to our faithful Jewish subjects." They were promised liberty of residence in all parts of Russia, removal of civic disabilities, freedom of worship, and, finally, the highest ranks of the army and the grades of nobility were opened to them.

On the strength of this news, which seemed significant of great, deep change, hundreds of Russian Jews returned from exile to enlist in the armies of the Tsar, and the Jewish women offered their services to the Russian Red Cross. Their reward was this: The men, disillusioned and bitter, died in the trenches defending their oppressors—and the women nurses were outraged in the hospitals by the soldiers they tended. For the truth was that no such proclamations had been issued in Russia. It was all a lie invented in London and Paris by Russian Government agents, to hoodwink the Liberal peoples of the world.

I dined with a captain of Atamanski Cossacks at headquarters in a Bessarabian village near the front. He was telling of his regiment:

"They are such impetuous fellows, the officers cannot always hold them; when they come into a village where there are Jews, for example. Ah, the rascals! When they get to killing Jews they cannot be halted!"

"Speaking of Jews," remarked an infantry captain across the table, "a very funny thing happened when my company was stationed at Brest-Litovsk. A young Jewish soldier one day was seen to kiss the hand of an old rabbi. My men were furious; they kicked and cuffed him well, and then buried his face in a pile of ordure."

Robinson protested. But the colonel at the head of the table held up his hand gravely.

"You Americans," he said, "do not understand what we have to endure from these people. The Jews are all traitors to Russia."

I remarked that that was curious, because in Austria and Germany they were entirely loyal, and in fact had subscribed the greater part of the last two Austrian war loans.

"That is different," replied the colonel firmly. "In Germany and Austria the Jews have civil rights; therefore naturally they are patriotic. In Russia, however, the Jews have no civil rights. So they betray us. So we kill them."

He seemed perfectly satisfied with this explanation, and the others did, too. . . .

For two hundred miles we travelled behind the Russian front through Bucovina and Galicia into Poland, and everywhere were evidences of the horrors inflicted on the Jews. Village after village of white-washed, brightly painted little mud houses was sacked and smashed—especially the houses where Jews had lived—by the Cossacks or the Russian soldiers. Zalezchik, where thousands of Jews had lived, was a mass of ruins, and the population had been driven out toward the enemy in front of the Russian advance. In Rovno there had been anti-Semitic riots, and in Kielze, Poland, a real old-fashioned pogrom—wholesale slaughter by the Cossacks. I have told in another place the stories of the Jew apothecary of Zalezchik and the Jew hotel-keeper in Cholm, and what a small town in the Pale of Settlement looks like. In Vilna twenty thousand Jews, men, women, and children, were torn from their homes and sent to Siberia, on the wholesale charge that they were plotting treachery. And it was in Vilna that two English war correspondents were arrested as spies and taken to the police court. They had a small black despatch-bag, which the police commanded them to open. They refused to do so. Then the police brought in a Jew with his hands bound and his back bare, and proceeded to beat him with whips.

"Do you see what we are doing with this Jew?" said the chief of police. "Well, then, you had better open that bag. . . ."

Everywhere the same old terror for the Jews, the same hate and fear of priests and Cross and the name of Jesus Christ.

On the train to Lemberg we got into a compartment with two minor officials of the postal service, who were typical of the great mass of Russian bureaucrats.

"Civil rights for the Jews!" cried one in astonishment. "You are mad! The Russian people would not allow it. As for the official ranks of the army being open to Jews, that is ridiculous. Their own men would shoot them as soon as they gave an order. I know only two Jewish officers in the Russian army, and they are detailed for clerical work in the War Department. Their fathers, you see, are rich. But they would not dare to go on active service."

# Petrograd and Moscow

MOST travellers speak of Moscow as the Heart of Russia, the real Russian city, and dismiss Petrograd as an imitation of other European capitals. But to me Petrograd seems more characteristically Russian—with its immense façades of government buildings and barracks marching along as far as the eye can reach, broad streets, and mighty open spaces. The great stone quays along the Neva, the palaces, cathedrals, and Imperial avenues paved with cobbles grew under the hands of innumerable serfs chained in a swamp by the will of a tyrant, and were cemented with their blood; for where Petrograd now sprawls for miles and miles, a city built for giants, was nothing but a feverish marsh a hundred and fifty years ago. And there, where no roads naturally lead, the most desolate spot, the most vulnerable and the most remote from any natural center of the Russian Empire, Peter the Great had a whim to found his capital. Twenty thousand workmen a year for ten years were killed by fever, cold, and disease in the building of Petrograd. Nine times the court nobles themselves conspired to wreck the hated city and force the court to return to Moscow; three times they set fire to it, and three times the Tsar hung them at the doors of the palaces he had forced them to build. A powerful section of the Reactionary party has always agitated for the restoration of Moscow as capital, and it is only in the last twenty years that the population of Petrograd has not been artificially kept up.

Great canals of deep, sombre water curve through the city everywhere, and along these move vast wooden barges hundreds of feet long, piled high with birchwood for burning—cut in the gloom of ancient forests with ringing axes, and floated down flat, deserted rivers to the sound of slow minor boat songs under the northern lights. And into the dark water every night obscure and restless, miserable poor throw themselves—multitudes of them. Their bodies go out with the tide, under the frowning interminable barracks, slipping through the caves beneath the streets, and float to sea on the broad Neva along that splendid front of palaces yellow and barbarically red, those fantastic cupolas and pinnacles and gigantic monuments.

In the immense silent squares and wide streets the people are lost; in spite of its two millions or more of human beings Petrograd seems perpetually empty. Only on summer evenings, in the enormous amusement parks, among the open-air theaters, scenic railways, merry-go-rounds, and cafés, hundreds of thousands of people, in great masses and currents of shouting, laughing, singing humanity, move aimlessly to and fro, with a feeling of uncontrollable force like the sea. Or in time of revolution, or during some important religious festival, when the people choke miles of great streets from wall to wall, and the thunder of their untimed feet, the roar of their unorganized singing, the power of their spontaneous will dwarfs even that Imperial City.

On the day of the fiesta of Our Lady of Kazan I was caught at the corner of the Nevski Prospekt and the Morskaia by sudden inundations of great mobs pouring toward the cathedral from every street, hats off, faces exultingly raised, deep voices lifting simple slow hymns. Over their heads swam the jewelled and glittering ikons, upheld by bareheaded, bearded, giant priests in rich vestments all covered with gold. Small choir-boys swung censers. Flanking the holy procession, peasant women walked sideways, hand in hand, with blank exalted faces, guarding the ikons. Men and women crowded in single file to pass under the sacred images, screaming, kicking, and pulling each other; and every few minutes the priests lowered them while a hundred kneeling people flung themselves forward to kiss the pictures with their lips. And all the time the processions moved slowly on in that terrible sea of people, meeting, crossing, wavering over the heads of the crowd, flashing back the sun that burst out between clouds. And for hours a solid mile and a half of people blocked the Nevski Prospekt and all the streets adjoining before the Cathedral of Our Lady of Kazan, praying and crossing themselves with a fluttering motion, and singing.

With Russians religion is extraordinarily alive. On the streets people cross themselves incessantly, especially when passing the churches, and the cab-drivers lift their hats and touch forehead, breast, and shoulders whenever they see an ikon. Little chapels are open all day long, even in the fashionable shopping quarters, and there are continual services for the constantly flowing crowds that stop to kneel and kiss the holy images as they pass. In certain very holy churches and shrines there is always, day and night, a jam of people, kneeling, bowing, muttering before the *ikonostas*. But, as far as I could discover, religion in Russia does not seem to be a temporal power, or a matter of politics, or a moral or ethical rule of life. The priests have often mean, vicious faces, and monks in the great monasteries lead the extravagantly dissolute lives of rich and unrestrained ecclesiastics everywhere; and the church, like all powerful churches, lives fatly and builds its golden altar-screens from the contributions of the poor, by playing on their darkest superstitions. To the simple Russian peasant, however, his religion is a source of spiritual force, both a divine blessing on his undertakings and a mystical communion with God. The thief and the murderer go to kiss the ikons before robbing a house or killing a man. The revolutionists carry the ikons at the head of their ranks, and the mobs that shoot them down also have ikons. In every Russian house an ikon hangs in the corner of the room, and in every hotel and railway-station.

Great religious fervors shake the Russian people, as they did the Jews and the Arabs, splitting them into innumerable mystical sects. Miracles occur frequently; holy men and self-torturing saints wander about the country, healing and preaching strange gospels. Even in Petrograd, the least religious of Russian cities, priests and monks were everywhere, and one of them, Gregory Rasputin, was rumored to be almost the real ruler of the empire.

At night—for it was June—the sun sank slower and slower. At nine o'clock it was as light as late summer evenings at home; at half past ten the sun touched the horizon, and moved slowly around from west to east until half past two in the morning, when it rose again. If you happened to wake up at midnight it was impossible to tell whether it was night or day—especially since the Russians seemed to have no regular hours for going to bed. Outside our window in St. Isaac's Square people would be sitting on the benches reading their newspapers; before the house doors squatted the *dvorniks* huddled in their *shubas*, gossiping; cabs drove past, and people went along the sidewalk, and there were even shops open.

Sometimes we drove. *"Istvosschik!"* I cried, standing in the middle of the street; and immediately there materialized from nowhere twenty or thirty little cabs driven by hairy individuals crowned with glazed, bell-shaped hats with curling brims, and padded under their coats so as to appear monstrously fat. Driving round and round us, they screamed hideously their competitive prices. There was a municipal tariff for cabs, and a copy of it was posted on the back of the driver's seat; but you had to pay at least double the prices on it. And the police always took the cabman's part.

We roamed around the city in the interminable twilight. In front of the barracks dense little crowds surrounded some soldier leaping and kicking on his hams a peasant dance, perhaps from Siberia, to the breathless braying of an accordion. In St. Isaac's Square the new recruits by companies were stamping through their drill, with resounding great boots, and roaring the traditional regimental answers to the greeting of a general.

"Good morning, my children!" cried a high, flat voice.

"Good morning to your Generalship!" bellowed a hundred big men in unison.

"I congratulate you, my children!"

"Happy to have had the opportunity, your Generalship!"

Three or four times a day the bell-ringers in the ponderous cupolas of St. Isaac's Cathedral looped the bell-ropes about their elbows, knees, feet, and hands, and all the great and little bells began to boom and jangle—thirty-five of them—in a wild, dissonant ragtime:

Teeng! Tong! Teeng-ting-a-tang-tong! Boom! Bom-tick-a-ting-tingle-ingle-boom! Tang-tong-tick-a-tangle-tongle-boom-tang-tingle-tick-tick-a-bom!

By hundreds, by thousands the new recruits, still in their peasant clothes, with big numbers chalked on their backs, passed by. There seemed no end to them. Day after day and week after week they poured into Petrograd, and had been pouring in for more than a year, to be roughly whipped into shape, loaded on endless trains, and hurled carelessly westward or south to choke with the slaughter of sheer numbers the terrible German machine. . . . And yet everywhere on the streets, and all over Russia, I saw multitudes of fresh men who had not yet been called to the colors.

Moscow, known affectionately to all Russians as *Matuschka Moskva*, "Little Mother Moscow," is still the Holy City, the intellectual capital, and the last stronghold of the old splendid barbaric Russia. Moscow's streets are narrow, and her cities crowd wall within wall around the sacred citadel which epitomizes all the history of the empire. But the pulse of Russia and the red renewing blood and the flow of change have left Moscow. Her ancient and opulent commerce, however, that made Muscovite merchant princes a legend in Europe in the Middle Ages, is still growing. The number of buildings of modern German architecture strikes one immediately.

That wideness and vastness and lavish disregard of human life so characteristic of Petrograd, of the war, and of Russia as it seemed to me, again appears in the Kremlin, where for a thousand years the hopes and the longings and the faith of the Russian people were centred. The Red Square is as gigantic as any square in the new capital, and immeasurably ancient. Cyclopean red walls, crenellated and topped with fantastic towers, pierced with gates in whose gloom hang great staring ikons, stride down-hill, and along the bank of the river, proudly encircling the most insolently rich capitol in the world. Inside, upon one square, within a hundred yards of each other, stand four cathedrals, each with an altar-screen of solid gold and jewels, glittering up from the long ranks of the tombs of Tsars, into the cloud of blue incense that forever palls a ceiling inlaid with monstrous mosaics. Ivan Veliki leans upward, honeycombed with great bells. Miles of palaces twist and turn, whose rooms are furnished in solid slabs of gold and pillars of semiprecious stones—Imperial throne-room after throne-room, to the gaudy, half-savage apartments where Ivan the Terrible lived, and the treasury that holds the Peacock Throne of Persia, and the Golden Throne of the Tartars, and the Diamond Throne of the Tsars. Monasteries, barracks, ancient arsenals along whose façades are piled the thousands of cannon that Napoleon left on the road from Moscow; the huge bell of Boris Godounov cracked and lying on the ground; the Tsar cannon, too big for any charge—and out through the Spasskya Gate, with the soldiers on guard to see that you remove your hat when you pass under the Ikon of the Redeemer. . . .

On Sunday we took the steamer up the river to the Sparrow Hills, where Napoleon stood to watch Moscow burning. Along the river for miles people were bathing from the bank, groups of men and women, and all over the hills swarmed an immense multitude making holiday. They sprawled on the grass, ran races, moved in big singing droves under the trees; and in little hollows and flat places accordions jiggled, while the wild stamping dances went on. There were drunken people haranguing huge audiences, and senseless men asleep, clutching bottles in their hands, and cripples and idiots followed by laughing throngs, like a mediæval fair. An old woman in rags came hobbling down the hill, her hair streaming about her face, lifted arms with clinched fists over her head, shouting hysterically. A man and a girl pounded each other with their fists, weeping. On a high point of land stood a soberly dressed man with his hands clasped behind his back, evidently making a speech to the restless flowing crowds beneath him. There was in the air a feeling of recklessness and gloom, as if anything might happen. . . .

We sat a long time in the café at the top of the hill, looking out over the plain where the river made a great curve, while the sun sank westward over the innumerable bulbs and cupolas of golden, green, blue, pink, and clashing colors of the four hundred churches of Moscow. And as we sat there, far, faintly, and wild came the galloping clangor of countless bells, beating out the rhythm that has in it all the deep solemnity and mad gayety of Russia.

# PART IV

---

## CONSTANTINOPLE

# Toward the City of Emperors

THE handsome great sleeping-cars bore brass inscriptions in *svelte* Turkish letters and in French, "Orient Express"—that most famous train in the world, which used to run from Paris direct to the Golden Horn in the prehistoric days before the war. A sign in Bulgarian said "Tsarigrad"—literally "City of Emperors"—also the Russian name for the eastern capital that all Slavs consider theirs by right. And a German placard proclaimed pompously, "Berlin-Constantinopel"—an arrogant prophecy in those days, when the Constantinople train went no farther west than Sofia, and the drive on Serbia had not begun.

We were an international company: Three English officers in mufti bound for Dedeagatch; a French engineer on business to Philippopolis; a Bulgar military commission going to discuss the terms of the treaty with Turkey; a Russian school-teacher returning to his home in Burgas; an American tobacco man on a buying tour around the Turkish Black Sea ports; a black eunuch in fez, his frock coat flaring over wide hips and knock knees; a Viennese music-hall dancer and her man headed for the café concerts of Pera; two Hungarian Red Crescent delegates, and assorted Germans to the number of about a hundred. There was a special car full of bullet-headed Krupp workmen for the Turkish munition factories, and two compartments reserved for an *Unterseeboot* crew going down to relieve the men of U-54—boys seventeen or eighteen years old. And in the next compartment to mine a party of seven upper-class Prussians played incessant "bridge": government officials, business men, and intellectuals on their way to Constantinople to take posts in the embassy, the Regie, the Otto-

501

man Debt, and the Turkish universities. Each was a highly efficient cog, trained to fit exactly his place in the marvelous German machine that ground already for the Teutonic Empire of the East.

The biting irony of life in neutral countries went with us. It was curious to watch the ancient habit of cosmopolitan existence take possession of that train-load. Some ticket agent with a sense of humor had paired two Englishmen with a couple of German embassy attachés in the same compartment—they were scrupulously polite to each other. The Frenchman and the other Britisher gravitated naturally to the side of the fair Austrian, where they all laughed and chattered about youthful student days in Vienna. Late at night I caught one of the German diplomats out in the corridor gossiping about Moscow with the Russian teacher. All these men were active on the firing-line, so to speak, except the Russian—and he, of course, was a Slav, and without prejudices. . . .

But in the morning the English, the Frenchman, and the Russian were gone—the breathing-place between borders of hate was past—and we fled through the grim marches of the Turkish Empire.

The shallow, sluggish, yellow Maritza River, bordered by gigantic willows, twisted through an arid valley. Dry, brown hills rolled up, on whose slopes no green thing grew; flat plains baked under scanty scorched grass; straggly corn-fields lay drooping, with roofed platforms on stilts starting up here and there, where black-veiled women squatted with guns across their knees to scare away the crows. Rarely a village—miserable huts of daubed mud, thatched with dirty straw, clustering around the flat dome of a little mosque and its shabby minaret. Westward, a mile away, the ruins of a red-tiled town climbed the hillside, silent and deserted since the Bulgarians bombarded it in 1912, and shot off the tips of the two minarets. The crumbling stumps of minarets stood alone on the desolate flats, marking the spot of some once-living village or town whose very traces had disappeared—so quickly do the ephemeral buildings of the Turks return to the dust; but the minarets stand, for it is forbidden to demolish a mosque that has once been consecrated.

Sometimes we stopped at a little station; a group of huts, a minaret, adobe barracks, and rows of mud-bricks baking in the sun. A dozen gayly painted little *arabas* slung high on their springs waited for passengers; six or seven veiled women would crowd into one, pull the curtains to shield them from the public gaze, and rattle giggling away in a cloud of golden dust. Bare-legged peasant *hanums*, robed all in dull green, shuffled single file along the road, carrying naked babies, with a coquettish lifting of veils for the windows of the train. By the platform were piled shimmering heaps of melons brought from the interior—the luscious green sugar-melon, and the yellow *kavoon*, which smells like flowers and tastes like nothing else in the world. An ancient tree beside the station spread an emerald shade over a tiny café, where the turbaned, slippered old Turks of the country sat gravely at their coffee and *narghilehs*.

Along the railway, aged bent peasants, unfit for the firing-line, stood guard—bare-footed, ragged, armed with rusty hammerlock muskets and belted with soft-nosed bullets of an earlier vintage still. They made a pathetic effort to straighten up in military attitudes as we passed.... But it was at Adrianople that we saw the first regular Turkish soldiers, in their unfitting khaki uniforms, puttees, and those German-designed soft helmets that look like Arab turbans, and come down flat on the forehead, so that a Mohammedan can salaam in prayers without uncovering. A mild-faced, serious, slow-moving people they seemed.

The brisk young Prussian who got on at Adrianople was strikingly different. He wore the uniform of a Bey in the Turkish army, with the tall cap of brown astrakhan ornamented with the gold crescent, and on his breast were the ribbons of the Iron Cross, and the Turkish Order of the Hamidieh. His scarred face was set in a violent scowl, and he strode up and down the corridor, muttering *"Gottverdammte Dummheit!"* from time to time. At the first stop he descended, looked sharply around, and barked something in Turkish to the two tattered old railway guards who were scuffling along the platform.

"*Tchabouk!* Hurry!" he snapped. "Sons of pigs, hurry when I call!"

Startled, they came running at a stiff trot. He looked them up and down with a sneer; then shot a string of vicious words at them. The two old men trotted off and, wheeling, marched stiffly back, trying to achieve the goose-step and salute in Prussian fashion. Again he bawled insultingly in their faces; again, with crest-fallen expression, they repeated the manœuvre. It was ludicrous and pitiable to watch. . . .

"*Gott in Himmel!*" cried the instructor to the world in general, shaking his fists in the air, "were there ever such animals? Again! Again! *Tchabouk!* Run, damn you!"

Meanwhile, the other soldiers and the peasants had withdrawn from range, and stood in clusters at a distance, mildly inspecting this amazing human phenomenon. . . . Of a sudden a little Turk-ish corporal detached himself from the throng, marched up to the Prussian, saluted, and spoke. The other glared, flushed to his hair, the cords stood out on his neck, and he thrust his nose against the little man's nose, and screamed at him.

"Bey *effendi*—" began the corporal. And "Bey *effendi*—" he tried again to explain. But the Bey went brighter scarlet, grew more offensive, and finally drew back in good old Prussian fash-ion and slapped him in the face. The Turk winced and then stood quite still, while the red print of a hand sprang out on his cheek, staring without expression straight into the other's eyes. Undefi-nable, scarcely heard, a faint wind of sound swept over all those watching people. . . .

ALL afternoon we crawled southeast through a blasted land. The low, hot air was heavy, as if with the breath of unnumbered gen-erations of dead; a sluggish haze softened the distance. Thin corn-fields, irregular melon patches, dusty willows around a country well were all the vegetation. Occasionally there was a rus-tic thrashing-floor, where slow oxen drew round and round over the yellow corn a heavy sledge full of laughing, shouting youngsters. Once a caravan of shambling dromedaries, roped together, crossed our vision, rocking along with great dusty bales slung from their humps—the three small boys who were drivers skylarking about them. No living thing for miles and miles, nor any human evidences except the ruins of old cities, abandoned as the ebbing population withdrew into the city or Asia Minor beyond. . . . Yet this land has always been empty and desolate as it is today; even at the height of the Byzantine Empire, it was good policy to keep a barren waste between the City and the countries of the restless barbarians. . . .

Now we began to pass troop-trains. English submarines in the Sea of Marmora had paralyzed water transport to Gallipoli, and the soldiers went by railroad to Kouleli Bourgas, and then marched overland to Bulair. The freight-car doors were crowded with dark, simple faces; there came to us incessant quavering nasal singing to the syncopated accompaniment of shrill pipes and drums. One was full of savage-eyed Arabs from the desert east of Aleppo, dressed still in sweeping gray and brown burnooses, their thin, intense faces more startling for the encircling folds.

Tchataldja was feverishly active; narrow-gauge little trains loaded with guns, steel trench roofs, piles of tools, puffed off along the folds of the hills, and the naked brown slopes swarmed with a multitude of tiny figures working on trenches against the eventuality of Bulgarian invasion. . . .

The sun set behind, warming for an instant with a wash of gold the desolate leagues on leagues of waste. Night came suddenly, a moonless night of overwhelming stars. We moved slower and slower, waiting interminably on switches while the whining, singing troop-trains flashed by. . . . Toward midnight I fell asleep, and woke hours later to find one of the Germans shaking me.

"Constantinople," said he.

I could make out the dim shape of a gigantic wall rushing up as we roared through a jagged breach in it. On the right crumbling half-battlements—the Byzantine sea-wall—fell suddenly away, and showed the sea lapping with tiny waves at the railway embankment; the other side was a rank of tall, unpainted wooden houses leaning crazily against each other, over mouths of gloom which were narrow streets, and piling back up the rising hill of the city in chaotic masses of jumbled roofs. Over these suddenly sprang out against the stars the mighty dome of an imperial mosque, minarets that soared immeasurably into the sky like great lances, broken masses of trees on Seraglio Point, with a glimpse of the steep black wall that had buttressed the Acropolis of the Greeks upon its mountain, the vague forms of kiosks, spiked chimneys of the imperial kitchens in a row, and the wide, flat roof of the Old Seraglio palace—Istamboul, the prize of the world.

# Constantinople Under the Germans

At four hours precisely, Turkish time (or three minutes past nine *à la fraqnue*), on the morning of *chiharshenbi, yigirmi utch* of the month of *Temoos*, year of the Hegira *bin utch yuze otouz utch*, I woke to an immense lazy roar, woven of incredibly varied noises—the indistinct shuffling of a million slippers, shouts, bellows, high, raucous péddler voices, the nasal wail of a *muezzin* strangely calling to prayer at this unusual hour, dogs howling, a donkey braying, and, I suppose, a thousand schools in mosque courtyards droning the Koran. From my balcony I looked down on the roofs of tall Greek apartments which clung timorously to the steep skirts of Pera and broke into a dark foam of myriad Turkish houses that rushed across the valley of Kassim Pasha, swirling around the clean white mosque and two minarets, and the wave of close trees they sprang from. The little houses were all wood—rarely with a roof of old red tiles—unpainted, weathered to a dull violet, clustered where the builder's caprice had set them, threaded with a maze of wriggling streets, and spotted with little windows that caught the sun—golden. Beyond the valley they crowded up the hillside, jumbled at every conceivable angle, like a pile of children's blocks—and all of the windows ablaze. Piale Pasha Mosque started up northward, dazzling, its minaret leaping from the very dome—built to look like the mast of a ship by the great Kaptan Pasha, who broke the sea power of Venice in the sixteenth century. Down this valley Mohammed the Conqueror dragged his ships after hauling them over the high ridge where Pera stands, and launched them in the Golden Horn. Shabby Greek San Dimitri to the right; a dark pageant of cypresses along the crest over Kassim Pasha, that bounds the barren field of the *Ok-Meidan*, whose white stones mark the record shots of great Sultans who were masters of the bow and arrow; the heights of Haskeui, sombre with spacious wooden houses weathered black, where the great Armenian money princes lived in the dangerous days, and where now the Jews spawn in indescribable filth; northward again, over the mighty shoulder of a bald hill, the treeless, thick-clustered field of the Hebrew cemetery, as terrible as a razed city.

Bounding all to the west, the Golden Horn curved, narrowing east, around to north, a sheet of molten brass on which were etched black the Sultan's yacht and the yacht of the Khedive of Egypt—with the blue sphinxes painted on her stern—and the steamer *General*, sleeping quarters of German officers; dismantled second-rate cruisers, the pride of the Turkish navy, long gathering barnacles in the Golden Horn; the little cruiser *Hamedieh*, swarming with tiny dots, which were German sailors in fezzes; and countless swarms of darting *caiks*, like water-beetles.

Up from that bath of gold swept Stamboul from her clustering tangle of shanties on piles, rising in a pattern of huddling little roofs too intricate for any eye to follow, to the jagged crest lifting like music along her seven hills, where the great domes of the imperial mosques soared against the sky and flung aloft their spear-like minarets.

I could see the Stamboul end of the Inner Bridge and a little corner of the Port of Commerce, with the tangled jam of ships which were caught there when the war broke out. Above the bridge lay Phanar, where the Patriarch, who still signs himself "Bishop of New Rome," has his palace, for centuries the powerful fountain of life and death for all the millions of *"Roum-mileti"*; Phanar, refuge of imperial Byzantine families after the fall of the city, home of those merchant princes who astounded Renaissance Europe with their wealth and bad taste; Phanar, for five hundred years center of the Greek race under the Turk. Farther along Balata—the Palatium of the Romans—and Aivan Serai above it, shadowed in the immense sprawling ruins of Byzantine palaces, where the walls of Manuel Commenus stagger up from the water and are lost in the city. Beyond, Eyoub, the sacred village of tombs around that dazzling mosque which no Christian may enter, and the interminable mass of cypresses of that holiest of all cemeteries, climbing the steep hill behind. Greek and Roman walls; the spikes of four hundred minarets; mosques that were built with a king's treasure in a burst of vanity by the old magnificent Sultans, others that were Christian churches under the Empress Irene, whose walls are porphyry and alabaster, and whose mosaics, white-washed over, blaze through in gold and purple splendor; fragments of arches and columns of semiprecious stones, where once the golden statues of emperors stood—and marching splendidly across the sky-line of the city the double-arches of the tree-crowned aqueduct.

THE hotel porter was a clever Italian with a nose for tips. He bent over me deferentially as I breakfasted, rubbing his hands.

"Excellency," he said in French, "the secret police have been here to inquire about your Excellency. Would your Excellency like me to tell them any particular thing . . .?"

Daoud Bey was waiting for me, and together we went out into Tramway Street, where the electric cars clang past, newsboys shout the late editions of the newspapers written in French—and apartment-houses, curiosity-shops, cafés, banks, and embassies look like a shabby quarter in an Italian city. Here every one, men and women, wore European clothes, just a trifle off in fashion, fit, and cloth—like "store clothes" bought on Third Avenue. It was a crowd of no nations and of all bloods, clever, facile, unscrupulous, shallow—Levantine. At the gates of the few open embassies sat the conventional Montenegrin doorkeepers, in savage panoply of wide trousers and little jackets, and enormous sashes stuck full of pistols; *kavases* of consulates and legations slouched around the doors of diplomats, in uniforms covered with gold lace, fezzes with arms blazing on them, and swords. An occasional smart carriage went by, with driver and footmen wearing the barbaric livery of the diplomatic service. Yet turn into any street off the Grand Rue or the Rue des Tramways, and the tall overhanging buildings echoed with appeals of half-naked ladies leaning callously from windows all the way up to the fourth floor. In those narrow, twisting alleys the fakers and the thieves and the vicious and unfit of the Christian Orient crowded and shouted and passed; filth was underfoot, pots of ambiguous liquids rained carelessly down, and the smells were varied and interesting. Miles and miles of such streets, whole quarters given over to a kind of weak debauch; and fronting the cultivated gentlemen and delicate ladies of the European colony only the bold front of the shell of hotels and clubs and embassies.

It was the day after Warsaw fell into German hands. Yesterday the German places had hoisted the German and Turkish flags to celebrate the event. As we walked down the steep street, that with the mercilessness of modern civilization cuts an ancient Turkish cemetery in half so the street-cars may pass, Daoud Bey related interesting details of what followed.

"The Turkish police went around," said he with some gusto, "and ordered the German flags pulled down. We had the devil of a row, for the German embassy made a strong complaint."

"Why did you do that? Aren't you allies?"

He looked at me sideways and smiled mockingly. "No one is more fond than I of our Teutonic brothers (for you know the Germans let our people think they are Mohammedans). According to the German idea, perhaps the taking of Warsaw was also a Turkish victory. But we are getting touchy about the spread of German flags in the city."

I noticed that many shops and hotels had signs newly painted in French, but that on most of them the European languages had been eliminated.

"You will be amused by that," said Daoud Bey. "You see, when the war broke out, the government issued an order that no one in Turkey should use the language of a hostile nation. The French newspapers were suppressed, the French and English signs ordered removed; people were forbidden to speak French, English, or Russian; and letters written in the three languages were simply burned. But they soon found out that the greater part of the population on this side of the Golden Horn speak only French, and no Turkish at all; so they had to let up. As for letters, that was simple. The American consul protested; so just a week ago the papers printed a solemn order of the government that, although French, English, and Russian were still barred, you might write letters in American!"

Daoud Bey was a Turk of wealthy, prominent family—which is extraordinary in Turkey, where families rise and fall in one generation, and there is no family tradition because there is no family name. Daoud, son of Hamid, was all we knew him by; just as I, to the Turkish police, was known as John, son of Charles. In that splendid idle way Turks have, Daoud had been made an admiral in the navy at the age of nineteen. Some years later a British naval commission, by invitation, reorganized the Turkish fleet. Now, it is difficult to pry wealthy young Turks loose from their jobs. The commission therefore asked Daoud Bey very politely if he would like to continue being an admiral. He answered: "I should like to very much, provided I never have to set foot on a ship. I can't bear the sea." So he is no longer in the navy.

I asked him why he was not bleeding and dying with his compatriots in the trenches at Gallipoli.

"Of course," said he, "you Westerners cannot be expected to understand. Here you buy out of military service by paying forty liras. If you don't buy out it amounts to the admission that you haven't forty liras—which is very humiliating. No Turk of any prominence could afford to be seen in the army, unless, of course, he entered the upper official grades as a career. Why, my dear fellow, if I were to serve in this war the disgrace would kill my father. It is quite different from your country. Here the recruiting sergeants beg you to pay your exemption fee—and they jeer at you if you haven't got it!"

At the foot of the hill there is a tangle of meeting streets—Step Street, that used to be the only way to clamber up to Pera; the wriggling narrow alleys that squirm through a Greek quarter of tall, dirty houses to infamous Five-Piastre and Ten-Piastre Streets in the vicious sailor town of Galata; the one street that leads to the cable tunnel, where the cars climb underground to the top of the hill—all opening into the square of Kara-keuy before the *Valideh Sultan Keuprisi*, the far-famed Outer Bridge that leads to Stamboul. White-frocked toll-collectors stood there in rippling rank, closing and parting before the throng, to the rattling chink of ten-para pieces falling into their outstretched hands. And flowing between them like an unending torrent between swaying piles, poured that bubbling ferment of all races and all religions—from Pera to Stamboul, and from Stamboul to Pera. Floating silk Arab head-dresses, helmets, turbans of yellow and red, smart fezzes, fezzes with green turbans around them to mark the relative of the Prophet, fezzes with white turbans around them—priests and teachers—Persian *tarbouches*, French hats, panamas. Veiled women in whose faces no man looked, hurrying along in little groups, robed in *tcharchafs* of black and gray and light brown, wearing extravagantly high-heeled French slippers too big for their feet, and followed by an old black female slave; Arabs from the Syrian desert in floating white cloaks; a saint from the country, bearded to the eyes, with squares of flesh showing through his colored rags, striding along, muttering prayers, with turban all agog, while a little crowd of disciples pressed after to kiss his hand and whine a blessing; bare-legged Armenian porters staggering at a smooth trot, bent under great packing-cases and shouting *"Destour!"* to clear the way; four soldiers on foot with new rifles; helmeted police on horseback; shambling eunuchs in frock coats; a Bulgarian bishop; three Albanians in blue broad-cloth trousers and jackets embroidered with silver; two Catholic Sisters of Charity walking at the head of their little donkey-cart, presented to them by the Mohammedan merchants of the Great Bazaar; a *mevlevi*, or dancing dervish, in tall conical felt hat and gray robes; a bunch of German tourists in Tyrolean hats, equipped with open Baedekers, and led by a plausible Armenian guide; and representatives of five hundred fragments of strange races, left behind by the great invasions of antiquity in the holes and corners of Asia Minor. Pera is European—Greek, Armenian, Italian—anything but Turkish. Where goes this exotic crowd that pours into Pera? You never see them there.

A thousand venders of the most extraordinary merchandise— Angora honey, *helva*, *loukoum* of roses, *kaymak* (made from the milk of buffaloes shut in a dark stable), obscene postal cards, cigarette-holders of German glass, Adrianople melons, safety-pins, carpets manufactured in Newark, New Jersey, celluloid beads—moved among the crowd shouting their wares, bellowing, whining, screaming: "Only a cent, two cents—*On paras, bech paraya.*"

To the right lay the Port of Commerce, crowded with ships, and the Inner Bridge beyond, all up the splendid sweep of Golden Horn. Outside the bridge was a row of pontoons placed there to guard the port from English submarines, and against the barrier the *chirket hariés*—Bosphorus steamboats—backing precipitously out with screaming whistles into the thick flock of *caiks* that scatter like a shoal of fish. Beyond, across the bright-blue dancing water, the coast of Asia rising faintly into mountains, with Scutari dotted white along the shore. Stamboul, plunging from that magnificent point, crowned with palaces and trees, into the sea. . . . From left to right the prodigious sweep of the city, and the great mosques: Agia Sophia, built by the Emperor Justinian a thousand years ago, all clumsy great buttresses of faded red and yellow; the Mosque of Sultan Selim, who conquered Mecca; the Mosque of Sultan Achmet; Yeni Valideh Djami, at the end of the bridge; Sultan Suleyman the Magnificent—he who was a friend of François Premier; Sultan Bayazid. . . .

The floating drawbridge swung slowly open with much confused shouting and the tugging of cables by sputtering launches to allow the passage of a German submarine coming up from the Dardanelles. She was awash, her conning-tower painted a vivid blue with white streaks—the color most disguising in these bright seas; but a momentary cloud passed over the sun, and she stood out startling against the suddenly gray water.

"It takes them about an hour to close the bridge," said Daoud Bey, and drew me into an alley between stone buildings, where little tables and stools hugged the shade of the wall, and a shabby old Turk in flapping slippers and a spotted fez served ices. Outside all roar and clamor, and hot sun beating on the pavement—here cool, quiet peace.

"Daoud Pasha!" said a laughing voice. It was a slender girl in a faded green *feridjé*, with bare brown feet, and a shawl pinned under her chin, in the manner of the very poor, who cannot afford a veil. She could not have been more than fifteen; her skin was golden, and her black eyes flashed mischievously.

"Eli!" cried Daoud, seizing her hand.

"Give me some money!" said Eli imperiously.

"I have no small money."

"All right, then, give me big money."

Daoud laughed and handed her a *medjidieh*—and she gave a scream of pleasure, clapped her hands, and was gone.

"Gypsy," said Daoud, "and the most beautiful girl in all Constantinople. Hamdi, a friend of mine, fell in love with her, and asked her into his harem. So she went to live at Eyoub. But two weeks later I came down here one day, and as I was taking my sherbet I heard a little voice at my elbow: 'Daoud Pasha, some money please.' It was Eli. She said she had tried to be a respectable married lady for fourteen days, because she really loved Hamdi. He was very kind to her—gave her clothes and jewels, and courted her like a lover. But she couldn't stand it any longer; begging on the streets was more fun—she loved the crowd so. So one night she let herself out of the harem door and swam across the Golden Horn!" He laughed and shrugged his shoulders: "You can't tame a *chingani*."

We paid. "May God favor you!" the proprietor said gently, and a Turk sitting at our table bowed and mumbled: "*Afiet-olsoun!* May what you have eaten do you good!"

Outside on the wharf where the *caiks* were ranked, each boatman yelling as loud as he could, a blind old woman in rusty black crouched against the wall and held out her hand. Daoud dropped a copper in it. She raised her sightless eyes to us and said in a sweet voice: "Depart smiling."

"*Kach parava?* How much?" said Daoud. A deafening clamor of voices shouted indistinguishable things.

"Let us take the old man," said my friend, pointing to a figure with a long white beard, burnt-orange skull-cap, red sash, and pink shirt open at the throat to show his hairy old chest. "How much, *effendim*?" He used the term of respect which all Turks use toward each other, no matter what the difference in their ranks.

"Five piastres," said the old man hopefully.

"I pay one piastre and a half," answered Daoud, climbing into the *caik*. Without reply the *caikji* pushed off.

"What is your name, my father?" asked Daoud.

"My name is Abdul, my son," said the old man, rowing and sweating in the sun. "I am born of Mohammed the Short-legged in the city of Trebizond on the sea. For fifty-two years I have been rowing my *caik* across the Stamboul Limani."

I told Daoud to ask him what he thought of the war.

"It is a good war," said Abdul. "All wars against the *giaour* are good, for does not the Koran say that he who dies slaying the infidel will enter paradise?"

"You are learned in the Koran?" exclaimed Daoud. "Perhaps, you are a *sheikh* and lead prayers in the mosque."

"Do I wear the white turban?" said the old man. "I am no priest; but in my youth I was a *muezzin*, and called to prayers from the minaret."

"What should he know of the war?" I said. "It doesn't touch him personally."

Daoud translated.

"I have four sons and two grandsons in the war," said Abdul, with dignity. Then to me: "Are you an *Aleman*—a German—one of our brothers who do not know our language and do not wear the fez? Tell me, of what shape and build are your mosques? Is your Sultan as great as our Sultan?"

I replied evasively that he was very great.

"We shall win this war, *inshallah*—God willing," said Abdul.

"*Mashallah!*" responded Daoud gravely, and I saw that his light European cynicism was a thin veneer over eight centuries of deep religious belief.

# The Heart of Stamboul

O<small>UR</small> *caik* ran into a thick tangle of *caiks* clamorous with shouting, arguing boatmen, Abdul standing upright and screaming: *"Vardah!* Make way, sons of animals! Make way for the passengers! You have no passengers, why do you block the landing-place?" We laid our piastre and a half on the thwart and leaped ashore in Stamboul. Through the narrow, winding street piled high with melons and vegetables and water-casks, and overhung by ragged awnings propped on sticks, we jostled an amazing crowd of porters, *mullahs*, merchants, pilgrims, and peddlers. In the Oriental way, no one moved from our road—we bumped along.

Along a cross street a string of boys and young men—each one carrying a loaf of bread—marched by between double lines of soldiers.

"Recruits," said Daoud Bey. Often we met a non-commissioned officer and two armed men prowling among the crowds, glancing sharply in the faces of the young men; they were looking for possible soldiers who had not yet been called. Shouts and the trampling of feet, angry bellows and screams of pain drew our attention to a side alley, where a hundred men and women of all races swirled against the front of a shop; fez tassels danced in the air, grasping hands leaped out and sank, choking voices yelled, and on the outskirts two policemen beat any back they could reach—thwack! thwack!

"Waiting to buy bread," explained Daoud. "Hundreds of places like that all over Constantinople. There's plenty of grain in Anatolia, but the army needs the freight-cars—so they say."

I said it ought to be an easy matter to feed the city.

"Possibly," he answered with ironical inflection. "Have you heard the rumor that the city officials are holding back the supply so as to get higher prices? Base falsehood, of course—yet such things have happened before. And then our German brothers are more or less responsible. They persuaded our government to take a census of the city—a thing which has never before been possible since the fifteenth century. But trust the Germans to find a way. The government took over the bakeries and closed them for three days, while it was announced that every one must apply for a bread-ticket in order to buy bread. By slow degrees they are getting us all registered—for a man must eat. Last evening, in the back streets of Pera, I came upon a bakery where the last load had just been distributed, with a howling mob outside still unprovided for. First they smashed the windows, in spite of the clubbing of the police, and then they began to tear down the Turkish flags hung out on all the houses to celebrate the fall of Novo-Georgievsk, crying: 'We don't care for victories! Give us bread!' "

WE sat cross-legged in the booth of Youssof Effendi the Hoja, in the *Misr Tcharshee*, or Bazaar of Egypt, where drugs are sold. Dim light filtered through cobweb windows high up in the arched roof that covered in the bazaar—making a cool gloom rich with the smells of perfumes, drugs, herbs, and strange Oriental medicines, of coffee from Aden, of tea from southern Persia. Overhead the whitewashed arch was scrawled with immense black whorls and loops of prayers to Allah, and Esculapian snakes twisted into verses out of the Koran. Above the booth was an intricate cornice of carved wood, covered with spiderwebs, and from this vague twilight depended all sorts of strange objects on chains: dervish beggar-bowls made from the brittle skin of sea animals, ostrich eggs, tortoise-shells, two human skulls, and what was evidently the lower jaw of a horse. On the counter and the shelves behind were crowded glass bottles and earthen pots full of crude amber, lumps of camphor, hashish in powder and in the block, Indian and Chinese opium and the weak opium of Anatolia, bunches of dried herbs to cure the plague, black powder for love philters, crystals of oil for aphrodisiacs, charms to avert the evil eye and to confound your enemies, attar of roses, blocks of sandalwood, and sandal oil. In the dark little room behind the shop were heaped bales and jars, so that when Youssof Effendi lighted his lamp it looked and smelled like the cave of the Forty Thieves.

He stopped us, bowing, with the right hand sweeping down, and fluttering to lips and forehead again and again; a tall, dignified figure in a long caftan of gray silk, and fez with the white turban of a religious teacher wound about it—immaculate. A glossy black beard covered his powerful mouth and dazzling teeth, and he had dark, shrewd, kindly eyes.

"*Salaam aleyboum*, Daoud Bey," said he softly. "Peace be with you."

"*Aleykoum salaam*, Youssof Effendi," answered Daoud, rapidly making the gesture and touching lips and forehead. "Here is my friend from America."

"*Hosh geldin*. You are welcome," said the Hoja courteously to me, with a constant motion of his hands to lips and forehead. He didn't say "*salaam*," which is only used between Mohammedans. The Hoja knew only Turkish.

"Bedri!" he cried and clapped his hands, and a little boy scurried out from somewhere in the bowels of the shop. "Coffee, *haide*! . . ."

We sat sipping the sweet thick liquid, smoking in long wooden *chibouks* cigarettes that we rolled of choice tobacco from Samsoun, in the cool, fragrant gloom.

"Is the *effendim* well?" murmured the Hoja gently, in the ritual of Oriental politeness; each sip we took, each puff at our cigarettes he touched his lips and forehead, and we to him. "May God make it pleasant to your stomachs."

The Hoja was a powerful man in Stamboul. For twenty years he had been *muezzin* in the mosque of Zeirick Kilissi, which was once the church of St. Savior Pantocrator, and in whose shadow still lies the *verde antique* sarcophagus of the Empress Irene; then a leader of prayers on Friday in the great mosques; a popular teacher and charm doctor; and finally sent for by Abdul Hamid to lead private prayers in Yildiz Kiosk, those long years the Sultan shut himself up there in fear of assassination.

"I know many fables about the marvels of America," said Youssof Effendi graciously. "There appear to be palaces taller than those raised by the *djinni* in ancient times, and I have heard there is a demon called Graft"—here his eyes twinkled—"who stalks through your streets and devours people, and is known in no other land. One day I shall go there, for I understand that there opium is worth its weight in gold."

He looked from Daoud Bey to me. "You are different from us, you races of the West," he remarked. "Daoud Bey is handsome, but he is over-refined and thinks too much. He will have nervous jumps some day. He should not smoke tobacco, but eat plenty of eggs and milk. Tell the American *effendi* that I think he does not think too much and is very happy. That is the way I am."

I wanted Daoud to ask how many wives he had. The Hoja understood my ill-mannered curiosity and smiled.

"*Pekki!* How many wives has the *effendi*?" he replied. "Does he think that it is any easier for a Mohammedan to support two wives than a Christian? Allah preserve us! Women are expensive. I know but six friends who have more than one wife. When the Armenian slave dealers come by night to my harem from Scutari with a fair *odalik* to sell, I answer them with a proverb: 'How many bodies can live of one man's meat?' "

"What does Youssof Effendi think of the war?"

"The war?" he answered, and the evasive look on his face showed that I had touched on a subject in which he was deeply involved. "My son is in the trenches at Gallipoli. Allah send what he will! One does not think of whether wars are good or bad. We are a fighting race, we Osmanlis."

"Do the Turks—" I began.

The Hoja interrupted me with a sputtering torrent of language.

"You must not call us 'Turks,' " said Daoud. " 'Turk' means rustic clown—'rube,' as you would say. We are not Turcomans, barbaric, bloodthirsty savages from Central Asia; we are Osman-lis, an ancient and civilized race."

The Hoja talked frankly of the Germans. "I do not like them," he said. "They have no manners. When an Englishman or an American has been one month in Turkey, he comes to my booth with hand to lips, to forehead, and greets me: '*Sabah sherifiniz hair ola.*' Before he buys, he accepts my coffee and my cigarettes, and we talk of indifferent subjects, as is proper. But when the Ger-mans come they salute as they do in their army, and refuse my coffee, and want to buy and be gone, without friendship. I do not sell any more to *Alemanes.*"

Later I observed many of the Germans around the city; there were hundreds of them—officers on leave, tourists, and civil offi-cials. Often they violated the delicate etiquette that governs Mo-hammedan life. They spoke to veiled women on the street; bullied merchants in the Great Bazaar; stamped noisily into mosques during the hour of prayer on Friday, when no European is allowed to enter, and once at a *tekkeh* of the Howling Dervishes I was present in the visitors' gallery, while two German officers read aloud passages from the Koran in German throughout the services—to the furious indignation of the priests. . . .

WE went up with Youssof Effendi through the intricate winding streets of Stamboul, plunging into passages lined with tiny Ar-menian shops, under the walls of the fortress-like *khans* built for the entertainment of strangers by the mothers of bygone Sultans, by secret paths across the quiet courtyards of the great mosques, where children played about delicately carved marble fountains in the shade of enormous ancient trees; down little streets that twisted between the wooden booths of the seal-makers and sellers of *tesbiehs*—bead-chains—where green vines fell like cascades from the roofs; into vast sun-smitten dusty squares, the site of Byzantine forums and of coliseums greater than Rome's; through winding alleys of wooden houses with overhanging *shahnichars*, where there was only an occasional passer-by—a shrill-voiced peddler beating his donkey, a grave-faced *imam*, women hurrying along with averted faces.

When we passed women Daoud began to talk German in a loud voice.

"They think you are a German officer," he said, laughing, "and it makes a terrible hit. All the harems are learning German now, and a lieutenant from Berlin or Hanover is the romantic ideal of most Turkish women!"

Half the people we met saluted the Hoja—saluted him humbly as a person of prominence and power. In the unending maze of covered streets which makes up the Great Bazaar, a double chorus of cries came from both sides: "Youssof Effendi, buy of me! See this beautiful *chibouk*! Honor me with your patronage, Youssof Effendi!" In the Bechistan, that gloomy great square where are the jewels and precious metals, the gold-and-silver-in-laid weapons and ancient carpets, we moved from counter to counter in triumph, followed by the *sheikh* of the Bechistan himself.

"What is the price of this?" asked the Hoja imperiously.

"A Turkish pound, *effendim.*"

"Robber and thief," replied our guide calmly. "I will give you five piastres." He moved on, flinging back over his shoulder: "Dog of a Jew, we go and return no more!"

"Ten piastres! Ten piastres!" screamed the man, while the *sheikh* berated him for his discourtesy to the great Youssof Effendi. . . .

For me he beat down a nervous shouting salesman on an amber *chibouk*, from two and a half pounds to twenty piastres.

"Do not make me shout, Youssof Effendi!" he yelled, his voice breaking, and the sweat standing out on his brow. "You will give me apoplexy!"

"Twenty piastres," said the Hoja calmly, inexorably.

LATE in the morning we sat in the dark cubbyhole behind a little Greek bookshop near the Sublime Porte, looking at hand-illuminated Korans—Daoud Bey, myself, and the clever, pleasant proprietor. Enter a young policeman, in gray coat with red epaulets and a fez of gray astrakhan. He came to where we sat, sighed deeply, and began in a melancholy voice a long story in Turkish. Daoud translated.

"I have eaten offal," said the policeman. "I have been greatly humiliated. Several days ago I observed Ferid Bey and Mahmoud Bey sitting in a café talking to an unveiled girl of the streets, who was a Greek. Ferid Bey came to me and said: 'You must arrest Mahmoud Bey.' 'Why for?' I asked. 'Because he is talking piggishness to a girl.' I was very much surprised. 'I did not know that talking piggishness to a girl was against the law,' I said. 'I am a friend of Bedri Bey, the chief of police,' said Ferid Bey, 'and I demand that you arrest Mahmoud Bey for talking piggishness to that girl.' So I arrested Mahmoud Bey and took him to jail.

"He was in prison for three days, because everybody had forgotten all about him; but at last the keeper of the jail telephoned Bedri Bey, and asked what to do with Mahmoud Bey. Bedri Bey replied that he knew nothing of the man or the matter, so why keep him in prison? Therefore, they let Mahmoud Bey loose, and he telephoned at once to Bedri Bey, and made a complaint about being arrested. 'Talking piggishness,' said he, 'is no offense against the law.' Then Bedri Bey called me before him and applied epithets to me, like 'son of an animal,' and threatened to dismiss me. Together Mahmoud Bey and I went to arrest Ferid Bey. But he was gone, he and the girl together. Then Mahmoud Bey boxed my ears. I am humiliated. I have eaten offal."

WE dined in the restaurant of the Municipal Garden of the Petit Champs at Pera, to the blaring rag-time of the band. The striped awning over the terrace was gay in a flood of yellow light, and electric-lamps hanging high in the full-leaved trees made a dim, checkered shade on the people sitting drinking at iron tables, and the cosmopolitan parade that moved round and round the garden. Vague under the smoky radiance of an immense yellow moon, the Golden Horn glittered, speckled with the red and green lights of ships; beyond lay the dim, obscure mass of Stamboul, like a crouching animal.

The diners were mostly Germans and Austrians—officers on leave, aide-de-camps on duty at the Seraskierat in full-dress

Turkish uniform, civilian officials, and the highly paid workmen of the Krupp factories; many of them with wives and children, in comfortable bourgeois dinner-parties like the restaurants of Berlin. But there were also Frenchmen with smartly dressed wives, English, Italians, and Americans. In the slowly moving throng outside under the trees, were Perote Greeks, Armenians, Levantine Italians, Turks of official rank; German submarine sailors, Germans of the Turkish navy in fezzes, and great rolling ruddy American sailors from the stationnaire *Scorpion*, towering in their white summer uniform head and shoulders above the crowd. It was hard to believe that, just beyond the reach of our ears, the great guns spat and boomed unceasingly day and night across the bitter sands of Gallipoli. . . .

IF I had only space to recount the Homeric battles of those American sailors! The German man-of-war's-men and soldiers were friendly, but the workmen and civilians very quarrelsome. Sometimes an intoxicated or excited Teuton would come over to the American table and begin an argument about munitions of war, or the *Lusitania* case; or a German officer in Turkish uniform would stop them on the street and insist on being saluted. The sailors answered nothing but insults, and then they answered with their fists, Anglo-Saxon fashion. I could write another article simply about the night that Seaman Williams broke the German lieutenant's head with a stone beer-mug, and was transferred back to the United States as being "unfit for diplomatic service." And then there is the wonderful history of the two sailors who laid out seventeen attacking Germans in a café, and were led back to the American Sailors' Club by congratulatory police, while the wounded foe were jailed for three days. . . . Respect and friendship was mutual between the American sailors and the Turkish police. . . .

AFTERWARD we got into a cab and drove down the steep, dark streets to the Inner Bridge; the cabman carefully shrouded his lamps, for lights on the bridges were forbidden on account of possible lurking British submarines. Stamboul was black—they were saving coal. Dim lamps in the interiors of little stores and cafés shed a flickering illumination on mysterious figures shrouded in the voluminous garments of the East, who drifted silently by on slippered feet.

Youssof Effendi was in his favorite café in a street behind the Bayazid mosque. We sat there with him, talking and drinking coffee, and puffing lazily at our *narghilehs*—the gray, cool smoke that makes the sweat stand out on your forehead. . . . Later we walked through the darkness across the city, by ways known to him alone, through arched passages, broken walls, and mosque courtyards. One after the other on mighty minarets, the *muezzins* came out into the heavy night, and cried that quavering singsong which carries so far, and seems the last requiem of an old religion and a worn-out race.

Out of his great courtesy, the Hoja insisted on going with us to Pera; so we invited him to drink a coffee with us at the Petit Champs. On the open-air stage the regular evening vaudeville performance was going on—singing girls, dancing girls, American tramp comedian, Hungarian acrobats, German marionettes—the harsh voices, lascivious gestures, suggestive costumes, ungraceful writhings of the Occident. How vulgar it seemed after the dignified quiet of Stamboul, the exquisite courtesy of Turkish life!

Some Turkish officers from the interior of Asia Minor, who had never before seen women publicly unveiled and showing their legs, sat gaping in the front row, alternately flushing with anger and shame and roaring with laughter at the amazing indecency of the civilized West. . . . The Hoja watched the performance attentively, but his polished politeness gave no sign of embarrassment. Soon it ended, and in spite of many protests on the Hoja's part, we walked down the hill to the bridge with him. He did not speak of the show at all. But I was curious to know his real opinion.

"It was very lovely," replied Youssof Effendi with the most suave courtesy: "I shall take my little granddaughter to see it. . . ."

. . .

DOWN at the dark bridge the draw was open, to let pass a contraband ship full of coal and oil which had crept down the coast from Burgas. Now at night it is forbidden for all but high officers to cross the Golden Horn in *caiks*, so there seemed nothing to do but wait for the interminable closing of the draw. Daoud Bey, however, confidently led the way down to the landing-place. Suddenly, out of the shadow popped a soldier-patrol.

"*Dour!* Stop!" cried the officer. "Where are you going?"

Daoud turned on him rudely. "*Wir sind Deutsche offizieren!*" he bellowed. The man saluted hastily, and fell back into the dark. "The German always does it," chuckled Daoud. . . .

Late at night we climbed once more up Pera Hill. In a dark side-street the crowd was already beginning to gather about the front of a bakery, to stand there until it opened in the morning. We were stopped at Tramway Street by a flock of tooting automobiles rushing up, and street-cars one after another with clanging bells. Through the dark windows we glimpsed white faces staring out, bandaged—another Red Crescent ship had arrived from the front, and they were hurrying the wounded to the hospitals.

# An Interview with a Prince

SUNDAY we took the *chirket-harié* to Kadi-keuy across the Bosphorus, to call upon Achmet Effendi, Prince of the Imperial blood—a son of Abdul Hamid, and seventh in line for the Sultanate. In Turkey the eldest member of the reigning family succeeds; accordingly, it is not very long since each Sultan, on coming to the throne, strangled as a matter of course his cousins, brothers, and uncles, and imprisoned all his sons except the Crown Prince—until the latter himself reached the Caliphate, and released his brothers by poisoned coffee or the cord. In Prince Achmet's time family murder as a royal pastime had gone out, but imprisonment of sons was still in vogue. And for more than twenty years he was immured in a wing of the Palace of Dolmabagcheh on the Bosphorus—shut there with his women and his slaves, no visitors allowed to see him, no newspapers to reach him, no breath of life nor any whisper of the outside world to quicken the sluggish air of the harem. When the revolution of the Young Turks overturned his father, he was set free—a fat, pasty little figure who had hardly learned to read and write, bewildered and lost in the tremendous swirl of modern life.

He lived in the abandoned villa of an Englishman who had fled from Moda at the outbreak of the war. At the ring of the doorbell, a black grinning eunuch in shabby frock coat bowed low to Daoud Bey, and led us into the hideous mid-Victorian parlor; satin-ribbed brown wall-paper, black-walnut furniture upholstered in brilliant blue plush, a horrible watercolor of Dover Cliff on an easel, and flowering ferns in a wooden model of a *caik*. That was funny and pathetic enough—the attempt of that exiled family to make for itself a background of home. But the prince had added his own belongings; cheap wooden taborets inlaid with mother-of-pearl, a rosewood Morris chair of *art nouveau* design with green-velvet cushions, and a number of rugs of slovenly make, of the most screaming cheap German colors. He asked us later to admire these; and confided to Daoud that he had sold the five-century-old Chinese and Persian rugs which had carpeted his palace-prison, and bought these brighter, better ones.

It was a long and elaborate ritual. First the eunuch carried word up-stairs that we wished to see his Highness. Then a sort of butler, with hand fluttering to lips and forehead, salaamed us into chairs. He disappeared, and there were vague sounds of disturbance aloft. Fifteen minutes later the eunuch returned; his Highness would see us. A long wait. The majordomo, a tall, bearded man with an Adam's apple sticking out over his tight Prince Albert, entered smiling, bowing, saluting, with murmurs of "*Salaam aleykoum, salaam effendim—*" He clapped his hands, and coffee and cigarettes appeared on a little tray, the coffee in little cups so hideously daubed with sticky colors that I doubted my eyes.

"Painted by his Highness with colored inks," said the majordomo proudly. "His Highness also does landscape." Whereupon, he led us about the room and exhibited a dozen smears on pieces of isinglass, the kind of picture a very young child makes with his first box of colors. . . .

We stood up, sat down, saluted, rose again, accompanying every sip of coffee with flowery compliments. At the end of this, the cups were removed and the majordomo bowed himself out with hands folded across his stomach. Daoud whispered to me not to cross my legs, as that was the height of Turkish bad manners.

Twenty minutes. A eunuch appeared and summoned us to follow, and we went out into the garden behind the house, to a little nook which the prince had made for himself with potted plants and cane chairs. There the majordomo rejoined us with more bowings and compliments. Fifteen minutes. A distant handclap; out of the shrubbery two eunuchs leaped and stood beside the path; the majordomo jumped as if he had been shot, and hurried down the path to meet his royal master. And Achmet Effendi hove in sight.

He was a dumpy, bloated little man with a pale, mottled face under his fez. A stiff, tiny mustache stood straight out on his upper lip. He wore a gray, cutaway suit, a high, stiff collar, gray-silk Ascot tie with a horseshoe pin of blue glass stuck into it, and his fat feet were crammed into patent-leather shoes with violet-cloth tops, laced with yellow-silk ribbon. His mouth twitched nervously, and as he came up to where we were respectfully standing, he twisted his fingers in each other. He touched lips and forehead rapidly a few times, held out a hand as if to shake mine Western fashion, thought better of it and snatched it back—and sat down gingerly on the edge of a chair. We also sat down; he rose again quickly, making us rise, and tried another chair. Then he glanced at us suspiciously, swiftly, and fixed his glance over our heads.

Daoud gave the customary salutations, to which his Highness responded in what Daoud said was illiterate Turkish.

"I have brought my friend John, son of Charles, an American newspaper correspondent, to pay his humble respects to your Highness," said Daoud.

"I never talk to reporters!" snapped Prince Achmet suddenly; and then realizing he had said an ungracious thing, flushed miserably, and followed it up: "I am greatly honored by his visit and yours. I am very fond of foreigners. Last year I tried to learn English, for I admire the English very much. But I could not make my brain concentrate upon it." He turned suddenly in my direction. *"Peoutefa di!"* said he. I looked at Daoud Bey to translate, but he was making extraordinary signs behind the prince's back. *"Peoutefa di! Peoutefa di! Peoutefa di!"* cried Achmet Effendi in an agonized voice.

"His Highness is saying that it is a 'beautiful day,' in *English*, you fool!" murmured Daoud. The prince colored with anger, Daoud glared, I was prostrated. Ten minutes of strained silence.

"The prince wants to know what New York is like," Daoud interpreted.

I told of subways, elevated railroads, great crowds of people hurrying along narrow straight defiles, where the sun shone only an hour each day, so tall were the great buildings that hemmed them in—twenty stories, thirty stories, forty stories. . . . As I enumerated these, the prince let his eyes travel up into the sky, mouth open, trying to realize my description. He gave it up, shook his head, and smiled. A dearth of conversation prevailed. The prince fidgeted, twisted his fingers.

"You being a correspondent," he said finally, with a kind of nervous sarcasm, "perhaps can tell us some news."

"Your Highness should know," I answered, "that in this war no one knows less news than a correspondent. . . . But your Highness is an Osmanli of high rank in the councils of state. Your Highness should be able to tell *us* some news——"

"What?" he interrupted haughtily, angrily: "You dare ask me that on our first day's acquaintance? You must know me for at least two years before you can put questions to me!" Again he was miserably embarrassed, ashamed of his petty, nervous suspicion. "I know nothing of the war," he added desolately: "I am not in the councils of state." Poor helpless forlorn creature; hating the cruel world that had attacked his country, hating the Turks because they had ruined, deposed, imprisoned, and perhaps murdered his father. . . . Of no importance, with no resources, unable to study mathematics or learn to run an automobile—both of which he had tried—moving vacantly and restlessly around his little universe, and longing for some contact with the world of men—a Prince of the Empire!

I have been to *Selamlik* and seen the white-bearded, weakly-smiling, doddering old Sultan issue from Yildiz to go to prayers, with Enver Pasha, the real ruler of Turkey, by his side—the thirty-three-year-old minister of war who was once a street peddler—while the great dignitaries of the empire ran beside the carriage, and the gorgeous red-coated imperial guards shouted, *"Padish-ah'm tchok yasha!"* I have wandered in the vast grimy corridors of the *Seraskierat*, the war ministry, and furtively inspected the packing-cases still standing in the corridors; three times have the papers and valuables of the ministry been packed for instant flight, when the rumors of English victory at the Dardanelles ran about the city like wild-fire. . . . In unsuspected attics and cellars I have interviewed Armenians who have hidden there for five months or more to escape "deportation"—which means certain death in the deserts of Asia Minor. From the windows of the American Sailors' Club I've hailed the English prisoners as they were marched past—thin, exhausted, sick scarecrows of men, eyes sunken with failure and the sight of too much vain bloodshed. High Turkish officials have told me privately of their smouldering hatred for the Germans, their naïve conviction that after the war the Germans shall withdraw, leaving "Turkey to the Turks. . . ."

"We do not hate the Christians," said Youssof Effendi. "We hate only evil people. There are good Christians and bad Christians, just as there are good Osmanlis and bad Osmanlis; but many bad Christians seem to come to Turkey. In the bazaar today, you asked if a string of beads was real amber; the Armenian merchant said it was, but I knew it was not. A Turk would not lie like that. Armenians and Greeks charge you four times the real price for things, because they see you are a foreigner; a Turk charges the same to foreigners as to Turks, and expects bargaining. The bad women of Pera and Galata are all Christians; there are no Turkish prostitutes.

"Missionaries? The missionaries don't ask us whether we want them to come here, and force Western ideas upon us. We have seen how your people live in Pera, and it doesn't seem much better than our way of living. Your Christ teaches that love and kindness and mercy are better than brute force, and yet all that you have which is better than we have is powerful armies . . . ! Jesus was a great prophet—we pray to him in our mosques. But he was no more the Son of God than Mahomet was the Son of God. We think your religion is blasphemy; but we do not try to change your religion. Yet you try to convert us to a faith that we consider inferior to ours. If Christians would only let us alone, we wouldn't massacre the Armenians. . . ."

A rich Armenian who lived at Buyukdere on the Bosphorus went deeper.

"I agree thoroughly with the Turks," he remarked. "If I were a

Turk I should hate the Christians. Turkey is not, cannot be a political state; it is a theocracy, and the only organic law is the Mohammedan religion. Therefore, all Turkish subjects who are not Moslems are necessarily outside the law, and a source of constant trouble. The Turk is absolutely honest in business dealings—his religion makes him so; but we Christians lie and cheat with a clear conscience. No Moslem can exact interest—the Koran forbids it. So as a natural consequence all trade, banking—in fact economic power of every sort, is in the hands of Christian or Jewish foreigners, with whom the Turks' religion will not allow them to compete. From the Turkish point of view, there is only one solution—all people except Mohammedans must be driven from the empire. . . . I myself would be deported if I didn't mind my own business and play fair with the Turk. I only cheat foreigners.

"And yet they are so simple, so childlike in this mature world of cutthroats and adventurers, that they think they will get rid of the Germans, too, after the war! You and I know better. It is the end of the Turkish Empire—yes, it is the end, whichever side wins. . . ."

# PART V

## THE BURNING BALKANS

# Rumania in Difficulties

$M$Y window, high up in the dazzling neo-French façade of the Athenée Palace Hotel in Bucarest, looks down on a little park smothered in almost tropical luxuriance of trees and flowers, where busts of minor Rumanian celebrities on marble columns stonily ignore each his marble wreath proffered by the languishing Muse kneeling on the pedestal. You've seen millions like them all over France. To the left lies the *Atheneul*, combining the functions of the Louvre, the Pantheon, and the Trocadero, and built to suggest the architecture of the Paris Opera. Its baroque dome bears aloft a frieze of gilt lyres, and the names of the great dead in gilt letters: Shakespeare, Cervantes, Pushkin, Camoens, Beethoven, Racine, etc., and two or three Rumanians unknown to the West. Eastward as far as one can see, red-tile roofs and white-stone copings pile up, broken with vivid masses of trees—palaces and mansions and hotels of the most florid modern French style, with an occasional Oriental dome or the bulb of a Rumanian Greek church. It is like a pleasure city built by Frenchmen in the south, this little "Paris of the Balkans," whose Rumanian name, *Bucureshti*, means literally "City of Joy."

At sunset the town wakes from the baking heat of a cloudless summer day. On the right the principal and smartest street, Calea Victoriei, winds roaring between the High-Life Hotel (pronounced "Hig-Liff") and the Jockey Club building—which might have been bodily transplanted from the Boulevard Haussman. All the world is driving home from the races down on the Chaussee—a combination of the Bois de Boulogne and the Champs Elysées—where it has seen the stable of Mr. Alexandre

535

Marghiloman, chief of the Germanophile branch of the Conservative party, win the Derby as usual—one, two, three. The regular evening parade begins. An endless file of handsome carriages, drawn by superb pairs of horses, trots smartly by in both directions along the twisting, narrow street. The coachmen wear blue-velvet robes to their feet, belted with bright satin ribbons whose ends flutter out behind, so you can guide them right or left by pulling the proper tab. These are public cabs owned communally by their drivers, who are all members of a strange Russian religious sect expelled from their own country; their belief requires that after they have married and had one child, they shall become eunuchs. . . .

Each carriage is the setting for a woman or two women, rouged, enamelled, and dressed more fantastically than the wildest poster girl imagined by French decorators. A dense crowd overflowing from the sidewalks into the street moves slowly from the *Atheneul* up past the King's palace to the boulevards and back again—extravagant women, and youths made up like French decadent poets, and army officers in uniforms of pastel shades, with much gold lace, tassels on their boots, and caps of baby-blue and salmon-pink—color combinations that would make a comic-opera manager sick with envy. They have puffy cheeks and rings under their eyes, these officers, and their cheeks are sometimes painted, and they spend all their time riding up and down the Calea with their mistresses, or eating cream puffs at Capsha's pastry-shop, where all prominent and would-be prominent Bucarestians show themselves every day, and where the vital affairs of the nation are settled. What a contrast between the officers and the rank and file of the army—strong, stocky little peasants who swing by in squads to the blare of bugles, excellently equipped and trained! The numberless cafés and pastry-shops spill tables out on the sidewalk and the streets, crowded with debauched-looking men and women got up like chorus-girls. In the open café-gardens the gypsy orchestras swing into wild rhythms that get to be a a habit like strong drink; a hundred restaurants fill with exotic crowds. Lights flash out. Shop windows gleam with jewels and costly things that men buy for their mistresses. Ten thousand public women parade—for your true Bucarestian boasts that his city supports more prostitutes in proportion than any other four cities in the world combined. . . .

To look at it all you would imagine that Bucarest was as ancient as Sofia or Belgrade. The white stone weathers so swiftly under the hot, dry sun, the oily rich soil bears such a mellowing abundance of vegetation, life is so complex and sophisticated—yet thirty years ago there was nothing here but a wretched village, some old churches, and an older monastery which was the seat of a princely family. Bucarest is a get-rich city, and modern Rumanian civilization is like that—a mushroom growth of thirty years. The fat plain is one of the greatest grain-growing regions in the world, and there are mountains covered with fine timber; but the mainspring of wealth is the oil region. There are oil kings and timber kings and land kings, quickly and fabulously wealthy. It costs more to live in Bucarest than in New York.

There is nothing original about the city, nothing individual. Everything is borrowed. A dinky little German King lives in a dinky little palace that looks like a French Prefecture, surrounded by a pompous little court. The government is modelled on that of Belgium. Although all titles of nobility except in the King's immediate family were abolished years ago, many people call themselves "Prince" and "Count" because their forefathers were Moldavian and Wallachian *boyars;* not to speak of the families who trace their descent from the Emperors of Byzantium! Poets and artists and musicians and doctors and lawyers and politicians have all studied in Paris—and of late Vienna, Berlin, or Munich. Cubism is more cubic and futurism more futuristic in Rumania than at home. Frenchified little policemen bully the market-bound peasants, who dare to drive across the Calea Victoriei and interrupt the procession of kept women. Cabarets and music-halls are like the less amusing places on Montmartre; you can see Revues based on dull French ones, copies of risqué comedies straight from the Theatre Antoine, or the National Theatre—which imitates the Comédie Française, and looks like the Municipal Theatre at Lyons. A surface coating of French frivolity covers everything—without meaning and without charm.

If you want to infuriate a Rumanian, you need only speak of his country as a Balkan state.

"Balkan!" he cries. "Balkan! Rumania is not a Balkan state. How dare you confuse us with half-savage Greeks or Slavs! We are *Latins.*"

One is never allowed to forget that; the newspapers insist every day that Rumanians are Latins—every day there is a reference to "our brothers, the French, or the Spaniards, or the Italians"—but really of purer blood than these "brothers," for the Rumanians are descendants of Roman veterans colonized in Transylvania by the Emperor Trajan. Some local writers complacently insist that Rumania is the inheritor of the Roman Empire; in a square in Bucarest there is a fountain showing Romulus and Remus suckled by the wolf, and some of the public buildings are adorned with the Insignia, the Fasces, the Eagle, and "S. P. Q. R." But those Roman colonists may have been originally drafted into the legions from Tarsus, or the suburbs of Jerusalem, or south Germany. Add to that the blood of the native Dacians, a strong Slavic strain, Magyar, Vlaque, and a great deal of gypsy, and you have the Rumanian. . . . He speaks a Latin language strongly impregnated with Slavic and Asiatic roots—an inflexible tongue to use, and harsh and unmusical to the ear. And he has Latin traits: excitability, candor, wit, and a talent for hysterical argument in critical situations. He is lazy and proud, like a Spaniard, but without a Spaniard's flavor; skeptical and libertine, like a Frenchman, but without a Frenchman's taste; melodramatic and emotional, like an Italian, without Italian charm. One good observer has called Rumanians "bad Frenchmen," and another "Italianized gypsies." Shopkeepers and cabmen and waiters in restaurants are thieving and ungracious; if they can't cheat you they fly into an ugly rage and scream like angry monkeys. How many times have Rumanian friends said to me: "Don't go to so-and-so's shop; he is a Rumanian and will cheat you. Find a German or French place."

It will be said that I have judged Rumanians by the people of Bucarest, and that Bucarest is not all Rumania. But I insist that the metropolis reflects the dominant traits of any nation—that Paris is essentially French, Berlin essentially Prussian, and Buca-

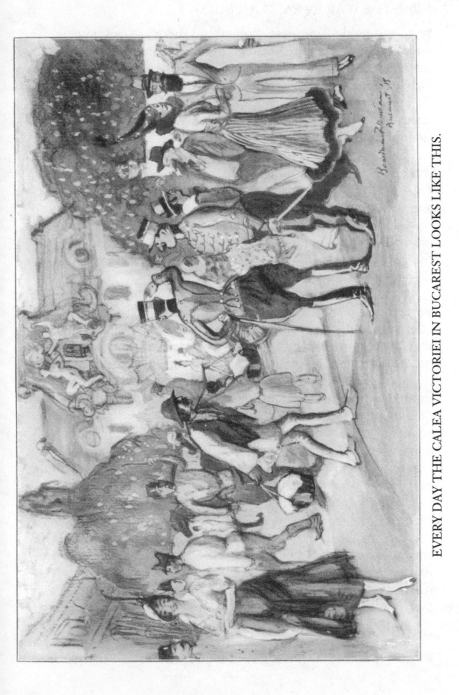

EVERY DAY THE CALEA VICTORIEI IN BUCAREST LOOKS LIKE THIS.

rest thoroughly Rumanian. Sometimes there are peasants on the street; the men in white linen trousers, and shirts that fall to their knees, embroidered in delicate designs of flowers, the women in richly decorated linen skirts and blouses of drawn work exquisitely worked in color, chains of gold coins hanging around their necks. They fit into the comic-opera scheme of things. But one hour by automobile from Bucarest you come upon a village where the people live in burrows in the ground, covered with roofs of dirt and straw. The ground their burrows are dug in is owned by a *boyar*—a landowning noble—who keeps a racing stable in France, and they till his land for him. Two per cent of the population can read and write. There is no school there. Several years ago the proprietor himself built a school for his people, on condition that the government would take it over and support it; for three years now it has been used as a storehouse.

These peasants eat nothing but corn—not because they are vegetarians, but because they are too poor to eat meat. And the church provides frequent fasts, which are the subject of laudatory comments on "frugality and thrift" by satisfied landowners. The peasants are very religious, or superstitious, whichever you want to call it. For instance, they believe that if a man dies without a lighted candle in his hand to guide him through the dark corridors of death, he will not reach heaven. Now many people *do* die suddenly without the lighted candle; and here is where the church comes in. The country priest charges the dead man's family eighty francs to get him into heaven without the candle, and a certain sum yearly to keep him there. The priest also takes advantage of the vampire legend—a superstition, widely believed in Hungary, the Balkans, and south Russia. If a peasant dies and others from his family or village follow in quick succession, the priest suggests that the dead man's spirit is a vampire. To lay this murdering ghost, the body must be exhumed in the dead of night (for it is strictly forbidden by Rumanian criminal law) and the heart torn out by an ordained priest, who drives a wooden peg through it. For this he charges a hundred francs.

Once I went north on a night train which carried the Crown Prince's private car. It was a cold night, with a wind that ate into your bones. Yet all night long we looked from our window upon a line of wretched peasants standing beside the track, one every quarter of a mile, ragged and shivering, holding torches above their heads to do honor to their prince. . . .

Never was a country so ripe for revolution. More than fifty per cent of the arable land is owned by less than ten per cent of the country's landowners—some four and a half thousand big proprietors out of a population of seven and a half millions, seven-eighths of whom are working peasants; and this in spite of the fact that the government has been breaking up the big estates and selling land to the people since 1864. The *boyars* and great landholders seldom live on their estates. Indeed, it is all they can do to keep up their hotels in Paris and Vienna, their houses in Bucarest, their villas at Nice, Constantza, and Sinaia, their winters on the Riviera, art galleries, racing stables, and general blowing of money in the four quarters of the world. One family I met posed as great humanitarians because they provided mud huts for their people, and paid them twenty cents a day—with the cost of living almost what it is in New Jersey. Add to this hopeless condition of affairs the fact that all voters in Rumania are divided into three classes, on the basis of their incomes, so that about one hundred peasants' votes equal one rich man's vote. There have been several revolutions in Rumania, the last one purely agrarian, in 1907; but since the conscript army system exists, it is easy to order peasants in the south to shoot down their northern brothers, and vice versa. You have only to see the Rumanian peasants, gentle, submissive, with almost effeminate dress, manners—even their national songs and dances are pretty and soft—to realize how frightful the pressure that would force them to revolt.

What is the trend of Rumanian public opinion? There is no public opinion in Rumania. The peasants will fight for whatever their masters decide will give them the greatest country to exploit. It is simply another demonstration of how military service delivers a nation bound hand and foot to ambitious politicians. So one must ask the politicians, and they will reply that Rumania will join the side that satisfies "national aspirations"—as they call cupidity in the Balkans.

Now the Rumanians came originally from Transylvania, and settled the flat plain north of the Danube which includes Bessarabia, and stretches eastward to the Black Sea. A race of herders and farmers, they spread far; southern Bucovina is full of Rumanians, and they are found in compact groups throughout Bulgaria, Serbia, the Banat, Macedonia, and Greece. The most civilized section, Transylvania, was early drawn into the Hungarian kingdom; Bucovina was a present from the Turkish Sultan to the Emperor Joseph, and Bessarabia, twice Rumanian, was finally taken by Russia as the price of Rumanian independence after the battle of Plevna. And although many people now alive remember the passing of the Russian armies that freed Rumania from the Turk, they cannot forget the two million Rumanians who fell under the Russian yoke. It was partially to make up for the loss of that great province that Rumania stabbed Bulgaria in the back in 1913, and took away Silistria, where there was no Rumanian population. When there is no other reason for territorial conquest, this kind of "national aspirations" is excused by Balkanians on "strategical grounds."

Bessarabia was forcibly Russianized. The upper classes, of course, easily became Russian, but the prohibition of the Rumanian language in schools and churches had the effect of driving the peasants out of both—of making a brutalized and degraded race, who have lost all connection with or knowledge of their mother country.

In Transylvania, the birthplace of the race, and the Banat beyond, there are some three million Rumanians. But there, in spite of the desperate Hungarian campaign to Magyarize the people as the Russians did in Bessarabia, the racial feeling is strong and growing. The Transylvanians are rich and civilized; when the Rumanian tongue was banned in the higher schools and the churches, they fought a stubborn fight, crossing the mountains into Rumania for education, and spreading the nationalist propaganda at home and abroad so thoroughly that every Rumanian knows and feels for his oppressed brothers on the other side of the Carpathians, and you can travel across Hungary as far as

Buda-Pesth and beyond without speaking any language but Rumanian.

So the "national aspirations" of Rumania, on "ethnographical grounds," include Bessarabia, Bucovina, Transylvania, and the Banat; and I have also seen a map in Bucarest, colored to show that Macedonia should really belong to Rumania, because *the majority of the population are Rumanians!*

All this does not excite the peasant to the verge of war on any side. But there is a mortal wrestling-match going on between pro-Teuton and pro-Ally politicians. How many obscure lawyers are now getting rich in the limelight of political prominence! In the Balkans politics is largely a personal matter; newspapers are the organs of individual men who have jockeyed themselves to be party leaders, in countries where a new party is born every hour over a glass of beer in the nearest café. For instance, *La Politique* is the organ of the millionaire Marghiloman, lately chief of the Conservative party and only partially deposed. He was once so pro-French that it is said he used to send his laundry to Paris—but the Germans got him. His pro-Ally constituents split off under Mr. Filipescu, violently anti-German, whose organ is the *Journal des Balkans*. . . . Then there is the *Independence Roumaine*, property of the family of Mr. Bratianu, the premier—who was pro-German at the beginning of the war, but has become mildly pro-Ally—chief of the Liberal party now in power. And *La Roumanie*, mouthpiece of Mr. Take Ionescu, the leader of the Conservative Democrats, who is the most powerful force in the country on the side of the Entente Powers. The Conservatives are the great proprietors; the Liberals are the capitalists; the Conservative Democrats are about the same as our Progressives, and the peasants' Socialist Agrarian party doesn't count. But all internal programmes were forgotten at the question: On which side shall Rumania enter the war?

Two years ago old King Carol summoned a council of ministers and party leaders at Sinaia, and made a speech advocating immediate entrance on the side of the Central Powers. But when a vote was taken, only one man present was with the King. It was the first time his royal will had ever been thwarted, and a few days later he died without returning to the capital. Ferdinand, the present King, is in the same predicament, and, what is more, he has an English queen. . . . It is a great game being fought over the heads of the King and the people by powerful financial interests, and the ambitions of political jugglers.

Meanwhile, a steady stream of Russian gold has poured into willing pockets, and the methodical Teutons have been creating public sentiment in their own inimitable way. Thousands of Germans and Austrians descended upon Bucarest in holiday attire, their wallets bulging with money. The hotels were full of them. They took the best seats at every play, violently applauding things German and Rumanian, hissing things French and English. They printed pro-German newspapers and distributed them free to the peasants. Restaurants and gambling casinos, dear to the Rumanian heart, were bought by them. German goods at reduced prices flooded the shops. They supported all the girls, bought all the champagne, corrupted all the government functionaries they could reach. . . . A nation-wide agitation was started about "our poor oppressed brothers in Russian Bessarabia"—in order to divert attention from Transylvania and stir up anti-Russian feeling.

To the Rumanian Government, Germany and Austria offered Bessarabia, including even Odessa, and Bucovina would also be ceded if she insisted. The Allies offered Transylvania, the Banat, and the Bucovina plateau north of her frontier. Although there was much talk in the press about "redeeming lost Bessarabia," the Bessarabian question was really not a vital one, while the Transylvanian question was burning and immediate. Moreover, the Rumanians know that Russia is a coming nation, and that forty years from now, even if defeated in this war, she will be there just the same, and stronger; while Austria-Hungary is an old and disintegrating empire, whose drive will be no longer eastward.

Three times since the war began Rumania tentatively agreed with the Allies to enter—and three times she drew back: once in the early spring, when Russia was on the Carpathians, and again when Italy entered. The last time was when I saw Mr. Take

Ionescu at midnight of the day that Bulgaria signed her agreement with Turkey.

"I think Bulgaria has chosen her side," he said very gravely. "We are not such babies as to believe that Turkey would give up any territory for nothing. The Central Powers will drive through Serbia—only we can stop that. And I am in a position to tell you that Serbia can claim our help if she is attacked. The Austrians have closed their frontier to us, and four hundred thousand men are said to be massed ready to march on Bucarest. It is a bluff—a bluff to force the resignation of the Bratianu cabinet, and the calling of Mr. Marghiloman to form a ministry—which would mean a German policy. Even if the Bratianu cabinet fell—which I doubt, for he is not for war—only he and the King working together could pave the way for Marghiloman. And that is impossible."

Three weeks later the German drive on Serbia began; but once more Rumania held aloof.

# Bulgaria Goes to War

---

$B$UT the key to the Balkans is Bulgaria, not Rumania. Leaving Bucarest on a dirty little train, you crawl slowly south over the hot plain, passing wretched little villages made of mud and straw, like the habitations of an inferior tribe in Central Africa. Gentle, submissive-looking peasants in white linen, stand gaping stupidly at the engine. You stop at every tiny station, as if the Rumanian Government were contemptuously indifferent of any one going to Bulgaria, and at Giurgiu there is an unnecessarily rigid examination by petty despotic customs officials, who make it as disagreeable as possible to leave the country.

But across the yellow Danube is another world. While the steamer is yet a hundred yards from the landing-stage somebody hails you with a grin—a big brown policeman who has been in America, and whom you saw once as you passed that way two months ago. Good-natured, clumsy soldiers make a pretense of examining your baggage, and smile you a welcome. As you stand there a well-dressed stranger says in French: "You are a foreigner, aren't you? Can I do anything for you?" He is not a guide; he is just a passenger like yourself, but a Bulgarian and therefore friendly. It is wonderful to see again the simple, flat, frank faces of mountaineers and free men, and to fill your ears with the crackling virility of Slavic speech. Bulgaria is the only country I know where you can speak to any one on the street and get a cordial answer—where if a shopkeeper gives you the wrong change he will follow you to your hotel to return a two-cent piece. Never was sensation more poignant than our relief at being again in a real man's country.

The train labors up through Rustchuk—half Turkish with its minarets, spreading tile roofs, peasants wearing baggy trousers, red sashes, and turbans—into mighty uplands that roll south ever higher toward the mountains. A marriage procession passes; four ox-carts full of uproarious men and girls waving paper streamers, and gay with embroideries of white linen, chains of gold coins, bright-colored blankets, bunches of grapes, and flowers. Ahead a man rides a mule, beating a drum, and a wild squadron of youths on horseback scurry shouting over the plain. . . . Night falls—the cold night of high altitudes—and you wake in the morning hurrying down a winding gorge beside a mountain torrent, between high hills of rocks and scrub, where herdsmen in brown homespun pasture their goats against the sky; past ravines in which little villages are caught, irregular and Turkish, their red roofs smothered in fruit-trees; until finally the mountains break, and you see Sofia crowning her little hill like a toy city of red and yellow, topped by her golden dome and overshadowed by her mountain.

Nothing could be more different from Bucarest than Sofia. A sober little town of practical, ugly buildings, and clean streets paved with brick. Telephone-wires run overhead; many street-cars clang along. Except for an occasional ancient mosque or Byzantine ruin, and a sudden glimpse of shabby squares full of peasants in turbans squatting on their heels, it might be a bustling new city of the Pacific Northwest. There is one hotel where literally everybody goes—the Grand Hotel de Bulgaria; next door is the Grand Café de Bulgaria, where journalists make news, magnates plot and combine, lawyers blackmail, and politicians upset ministries. If you want an interview with the premier or one of the ministers—in one case I know of, with the King—you get a bell-boy of the Grand Hotel to call him up on the telephone. Or if you don't want to do that, simply take a table in the Grand Café—they will all come in some time during the day. . . . Sofia is a little place, friendly and accessible. The unpretentious Royal Palace is right across the street; the National Theatre one block down; the House of Parliament, or *Sobranié*, two blocks in the other direction, near the Foreign Office, and the Cathedral and

Holy Synod just beyond. Every one of any importance lives in a radius of five blocks. . . .

Toward evening the town gets on its best clothes, and strolls out the avenue of the Tsar Liberator to Prince Boris Park. It is a solemn domestic little parade of country people with their wives, daughters, sweethearts, and all the children. The women are comfortably unattractive, and they dress in last year's rural styles. Many officers mingle with the crowd—officers who wear smart, practical uniforms built for campaigning, and look as if they knew how to fight. Squads of burly soldiers in peaked caps and boots tramp stiffly by, roaring slow, hymn-like songs such as you hear in the Russian army. . . .

Darkness brings a chill—for Sofia is a thousand feet up—and sharp on the stroke of eight the crowd scatters home to dinner. There is no restaurant except your hotel, and the food has no subtlety—ham and eggs and spinach being the Bulgarian's favorite dish. Afterward you can sit in the National Casino in the Public Gardens, and drink beer to the strains of a fine military band, or you can listen to interminable Bulgarian dialogues at the Municipal Theatre. There is only one music-hall, called "New America," a dreary place where heavily humorous comedians and unshapely dancers delight the guffawing peasants who have come to town on a jag.

The number of people who speak English is amazing. Almost all the political leaders have been educated at Roberts College, the American missionary school in Constantinople. Roberts College has had such an influence on Bulgaria, that after the consolidation of the country and establishment of the kingdom in 1885, it was hailed as "cradle of Bulgarian liberty." That's why Sofia is so American, and that's why so many American methods are used in Bulgarian politics—even our kind of graft! But there are more powerful influences. Bulgaria was nearest to Constantinople, and longer subject to the Turks than any other Balkan country—the language is full of Turkish words, and the popular life of Turkish customs. Then Russia's freeing her in 1876 turned the entire trend of Bulgarian thought toward her mighty Slav brother. There was also a group of intellectuals, fighting to free Macedonia, who imbibed republican ideals in France. And lastly, Bulgarian army officers, scientists, teachers, journalists, and politicians, for the last fifteen years have studied almost exclusively in Germany.

An hour by automobile from Sofia lies a typical Bulgarian village. The fields around it are owned and farmed communally by the inhabitants, except for the lands belonging to the monastery at the top of the hill. A wild mountain stream tumbling down the ravine turns the wheels of fourteen mills, where the peasants grind their corn; and since the mills all charge the same price, and the highest mill had no trade at all, the peasants and the monks together have agreed to abolish all mills, and build a single large one run by electricity generated by the stream, to be owned in common by the village. Broad, comfortable houses with tile roofs, built of wood or stone or baked clay, straggle along the cobbled streets. Every one seems happy and prosperous, for in Bulgaria each peasant can own five inalienable acres of land, and, as in Serbia, there are no rich men. At the end of the street is a big, fine public school, with room for all the children, and teachers trained in Germany. Telegraph and telephone, train and automobile road connect it with the city. And these evidences of organization and progress are to be seen all over Bulgaria. King Ferdinand and the group of scientific experts with which he has surrounded himself are chiefly responsible for all this. The Bulgars are loyal, honest and easily disciplined, in contrast to the anarchistic Serbs. Centuries of Turkish tyranny have helped to prepare them for the hand of the organizer.

I know three derisive stories told by the peasants of other Balkan peoples about Bulgars for seven hundred years, which illustrate the Bulgarian character better than anything I could say.

A Bulgar who had been mowing late in his fields went home at night with his scythe over his shoulder. Coming to a well, he looked down and saw the moon reflected in it. "Good God!" he cried, "the moon has fallen into the well. I must save it!" So he put his scythe into the water and pulled. But the scythe caught in the rocks of the well. He pulled and pulled and pulled. Suddenly the rock gave way and he fell on his back. Above him in the sky was the moon. "Ha," said he with satisfaction, "I have rescued the moon!"

Four Bulgars walking across the fields came to a pond with a willow-tree bending over it. Wind rustled the leaves and the peasants stopped to look at it. "The tree's talking," said one. "What is it saying?" The others scratched their heads. "It probably says that it wants a drink," replied another. Filled with pity for the poor thirsty tree, the Bulgars climbed out on the branch and weighed it down into the water. It broke and they all drowned.

The Bulgarian army, so goes the story, had been besieging Constantinople for two years without the slightest result. They took counsel together and decided to push down the wall. So the soldiers strung themselves all around the city with their backs to the wall and began to push. They pushed and sweated with all their strength—they pushed so hard that their feet began to sink into the ground. Feeling something give way, the whole army shouted: "Just a little more now! Keep on pushing! She's moving!"

THE Bulgarians were originally a Mongolian race, who invaded the Balkan Peninsula in the seventh century and mingled with the Slavs they found there. Under the legendary Tsar Simeon they erected by conquest an ephemeral "empire," which extended from Adrianople to the mouths of the Danube, northwest so as to include Transylvania and all of Hungary, then south to the Adriatic, taking in Bosnia, Herzegovina, Montenegro, Serbia, Albania, Epirus, and Thessaly—and east to Thrace. Two hundred years later, a Serbian "empire" under the mythical Tsar Dushan had conquered the same territory and subjugated the Bulgars. In the thirteenth century the Bulgars predominated again, and in the fourteenth the Serbs had their turn. Twice during this time Bulgarians laid siege to Byzantium. I mention this to explain Bulgarian "national aspirations" on "historical grounds"—like all Balkan "aspirations," they are practically boundless.

But the Bulgars are really very simple people, without guile.

Why, then, did they enter the war on the side of Germany and Austria? And to go further back, why did they break the Balkan Alliance and provoke the second Balkan War? It is again a question of "aspirations."

The Macedonian question has been the cause of every great European war for the last fifty years, and until that is settled there will be no more peace either in the Balkans or out of them. Macedonia is the most frightful mix-up of races ever imagined. Turks, Albanians, Serbs, Rumanians, Greeks, and Bulgarians live there side by side without mingling—and have so lived since the days of St. Paul. In a space of five square miles you will find six villages of six different nationalities, each with its own customs, language, and traditions. But the vast majority of the population of Macedonia are Bulgars; up to the time of the first Balkan War no intelligent Greek or Serbian or Rumanian ever denied this. Almost all Bulgaria's great men have come from Macedonia. They were the first people, when Macedonia was a Turkish province, to found national schools there, and when the Bulgarian Church revolted from the Greek Patriarch at Constantinople—no other Balkan Church is free—the Turks allowed them to establish bishoprics, because it was so evident that Macedonia was Bulgarian. Ambitious Serbian nationalists followed the Bulgarian example of establishing schools in Macedonia, and sent *comitadjis* there to fight the Bulgarian influence; but Serbian scientists and political leaders recognized for a century that Macedonia was peopled with Bulgarians. The Serbians did not spread south; they came from the north and spread east through Bosnia, Herzegovina, Dalmatia, and beyond Trieste—and that way their logical ambitions lie.

During the last years of Balkan turmoil under the Ottomans, when the Great Powers were bawling for reform in the European *vilayets*, and the end of the Turkish Empire was in sight, Greece also sent *comitadjis* to Macedonia to wage an underground bandit warfare on the Serbs and Bulgars, with the hope of eventually getting a slice. But up to the outbreak of the Balkan War no responsible Greek ever dared to claim Macedonia on any other but "historical" grounds. Constantinople, parts of Thrace, Asia

Minor, and the European littoral of the Ægean and Black Seas were claimed by Greece because Greeks lived there. But that was all.

Even in the treaties of the Balkan Alliance that preceded the war of 1912, Serbia recognized Macedonia as Bulgarian. Mr. Milanovitch, the Serbian premier who helped draw the treaties, said: "There are districts which cannot be disputed between us. Adrianople ought to go to Bulgaria. Old Serbia north of the Char Planina Mountains ought to go to Serbia. Most of Macedonia will be Bulgarian. But a strip of eastern Macedonia ought to be given to Serbia. And the best thing will be to leave the division to the Emperor of Russia as arbitrator." And this was inserted in the treaty. Greece also accepted the principle of Bulgarian dominance.

When the Balkan conflict exploded, Bulgaria, with her superior army, was to leave a strong force in Macedonia, and aid Serbia with more troops if she found things difficult. But, on the contrary, it was Serbia who sent aid to the Bulgars in Thrace; this, Serbia called "the first violation of the agreement." Adrianople fallen, the Bulgars pressed on, amazed at their success. They said they would stop at a line drawn through Midia on the Black Sea to Enos on the Ægean; but the Turks tried so frantically to make peace that they broke the armistice, and drove straight for Constantinople. Only Tchataldja stopped them, and they might finally have stormed that if events in their rear hadn't taken a disquieting turn.

In the meanwhile the Serbians and Greeks, who had occupied all of Macedonia, Epirus, and Thessaly, were jealous of the boundless Bulgar ambition. Nothing in the Balkan Alliance had given Bulgaria the right to seize the capital of the Eastern world. Together Greece and Serbia had conquered the western *vilayets*, and they didn't see why they should give up territory fairly won to any powerful Balkan Empire—no matter what the treaties were. So they made a secret treaty and quietly went to work to Grecianize and Serbianize their new territories. A thousand Greek and Serbian publicists began to fill the world with their shouting about the essentially Greek or Serbian character of the populations of their different spheres. The Serbs gave the unhappy Macedonians twenty-four hours to renounce their nationality and proclaim themselves Serbs, and the Greeks did the same. Refusal meant murder or expulsion. Greek and Serbian colonists were poured into the occupied country and given the property of fleeing Macedonians. Bulgarian school-teachers were shot without mercy, and Bulgarian priests given the choice of death or conversion to the Orthodox religion. The Greek newspapers began to talk about a Macedonia peopled entirely with Greeks—and they explained the fact that no one spoke Greek, by calling the people "Bulgarophone" Greeks or "Vlaquophone" Greeks. The Serbs more diplomatically called them "Macedonian Slavs." The Greek army entered villages where no one spoke their language. "What do you mean by speaking Bulgarian?" cried the officers. "This is Greece and you must speak Greek." Refusal to do so meant death or flight.

Bulgaria concluded a hasty peace with the Turks and turned her attention westward. The Serbs and Greeks were evasive—they declared the Balkan Alliance had been broken by their ally. Bulgaria called upon the Tsar to arbitrate, but Serbia, in possession of far more than she ever had dreamed of gaining, realized that she had powerful friends: Russia, alarmed at the gigantic ambition of her protégé, and Austria, who wanted no powerful state in the Balkans. Finally Tsar Nicholas agreed to settle the question; but just as the two delegates were about to start for St. Petersburg, Bulgaria took a step that justified the fears of the Great Powers, alienated the world's sympathy, and lost her Macedonia. Without warning, her armies suddenly attacked the Serbs and the Greeks and marched on Salonika. The Bulgarian people was not consulted. The news came as a shock to the cabinet, whose policy was one of conciliation and peace. Consternation and fury broke loose in Sofia. Who had given the order? There was only one person who could have done so, and that was King Ferdinand.

King Ferdinand is a regular romantic Balkan King. He perpetually sees himself riding into Constantinople on a white horse—the Tsar of an immense, belligerent empire. And as I write this he has again hurled his people against their will into a war from which they cannot emerge except as losers.

I saw it all. I was in Sofia when the Entente Powers made their offer, and from then off and on until the end. The Allies offered as the price of intervention all of Serbian Macedonia to the Char Planina Mountains, Thrace, and diplomatic support for the recovery of Grecian Macedonia and Silistria. The Central Powers would give Macedonia, part of Serbia, Silistria, free access to Cavalla and Salonika, and a slice of Turkey to be ceded immediately. Germany told Bulgaria that she need only effect a junction with the German forces through Serbian Macedonia, and then she could turn all her attention to occupying these territories; while the Allies wanted her to attack the Turks, and wait for compensation until after the war. The Bulgars clamored for immediate occupation. . . . The Allies replied that they would guarantee her countries for her by occupying the line of the Vardar with Allied troops. But the Bulgarian Government was skeptical of promises to be redeemed "after the war."

The premier, Mr. Radoslavov, said on July 15: "Bulgaria is prepared and ready to enter the war immediately absolute guarantees can be given her that . . . she will attain . . . the realization of her national ideals. The bulk of these aspirations are comprised in Serbian Macedonia, with its Bulgarian population of one and a half millions. It was pledged and assigned to us at the end of the first Balkan War, and it is still ours by right of nationality. When the Powers of the Triple Entente can assure us this territory, and assure us that our minor claims in Grecian Macedonia and elsewhere will be realized, they will find us ready to march with them. But these guarantees must be real and absolute. No mere paper ones can be accepted. Only certainty on this point can induce our people again to pour out their blood."

In that he had the country with him, for there is a very decided public opinion among the Bulgarian peasants. In the first place more than half a million Bulgarians fled from persecution in Macedonia under Turks, Greeks, and Serbs and were scattered throughout the villages of Bulgaria, forever preaching the libera-

A GLIMPSE OF THE SERBIAN RETREAT.
*(October 1915.)*

tion of their country. In the middle of the summer half the population of Sofia was composed of Macedonian refugees, and you could visit a camp in the outskirts of the city where sixteen thousand of them lived under tents, at great expense and annoyance to the government. While I was in Sofia in September, there arrived five thousand Bulgarians who had been taken prisoners by the Austrians after being forced to serve in the Serbian army—returned with the compliments of the Emperor Franz Joseph. Every day the press was full of bitter tales brought by the refugees, and expressions of hatred against the Serbians; the Serbian press responded as bitterly, accusing the Bulgarians of raiding across the frontier, burning and slaughtering. Both were true. To offset this hatred there was the traditional love and gratefulness—very strong among the peasants—to Russia the Liberator, and the memory of the generation who had seen her armies rout the Turks.

Bulgarian statesmen are just as they are in Rumania; they play the game of personal ambition and personal profits—with the important difference that in Bulgaria they must wheedle the people, and are subject to an unscrupulous and irresponsible monarch who has real royal power. All Bulgarians were agreed on the program of regaining Macedonia; they only differed on the question of which group of Powers could give it to them. As Mr. Joseph Herbst said to me: "If Zululand would give us Macedonia we would march with Zululand!" A bitter and exhausting struggle went on between the two parties—between hatred of the Serbs and love for Russia. The Radoslavov government showed itself benevolent toward the Central Powers in a hundred ways—for instance, by allowing the military censorship to suppress six pro-Ally newspapers on the ground that they were "bought with Russian gold."

By an agreement of all political parties at the outbreak of the European war, power to act was left in the hands of the government, and the *Sobranié* adjourned indefinitely. But as the government's attitude became defined, the growing opposition demanded the calling of Parliament to consider the country's position. This the King absolutely refused to do, for he knew that the majority of the country was still pro-Ally. In its desperation the Liberal government was forced to a trick. The provinces of New Bulgaria were electing their first deputies, and they were so gerrymandered that all the twenty deputies were Liberals. How the voters felt about it was made plain when a confidential man journeyed south to find out what side the peasants would like to fight on. "You give us guns first," they replied threateningly, "and we'll show you which side we'll fight on!" In spite of the twenty, however, there was still a majority against the Germans when Bulgaria went to war.

As I passed through Sofia in the middle of August the pro-Ally sympathizers were jubilant. Mr. Guenadiev, leader of the Stamboulovist party, seemed to think Bulgaria would accept the last offer of the Entente Powers, to which Serbia had conditionally agreed. Mr. Guechov, chief of the Nationalists, talked of a coming demonstration in force by the opposition, to compel the summoning of the *Sobranié*. And Mr. Malinov of the Democratic party believed that his country knew how fatal to Bulgarian predominance would be the German drive eastward.

But when I returned two weeks later all was changed. The Duke of Mecklenburg had twice visited the King, the Turco-Bulgarian secret treaty had been signed, the first gold instalment of an immense German loan had arrived, and Mr. Guechov told me that the Central Powers were now urging Bulgaria to attack Rumania, in case attempted negotiations between Austria and Serbia came off. "If the Germans come through Serbia to our frontier," said Mr. Guenadiev, "what can our small army do against them? We do not want to be another Belgium." A politician who had once told me with glowing approval how the peasants loved Russia, now seemed lukewarm. "The peasants are very simple folk," said he; "they remember Russia the Liberator, but they are not intelligent enough to realize that freeing Bulgaria was merely a step in the Russian march toward Constantinople. You and I know better; we understand that the peasants will do what they are told, and that a people needs thoughtful leaders." And he hurried away with an important, furtive air.

In the first week in September the *Opoltchenié*, or Macedonian

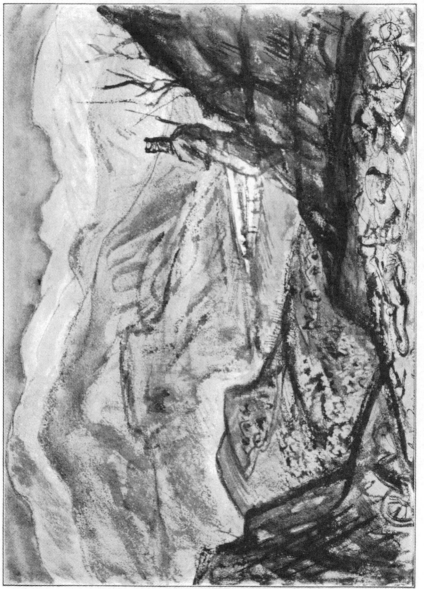

THE PIROT COUNTRY—WHERE THE SERBIANS DESPERATELY RESISTED
THE BULGARIAN ADVANCE ON NISH.

Legion, composed of refugees, was called to the colors "for forty-five days' training." No one was fooled. The government press breathed double hate against the Serbs, and cried: "Macedonians! The hour is at hand to free your country from the oppressor!" Sixteen thousand Macedonians were summoned—sixty thousand responded, and with them some fifteen thousand Albanians, and ten thousand Armenians who had been given asylum from Turkish persecution. A grand demonstration was arranged with true Bulgarian thoroughness; the new volunteers, all slow, exalted faces, and rough, brown homespun, surged through the streets cheering and singing behind their war-worn flag. They knew that they were to head a Bulgarian invasion of Macedonia. In twenty speeches delivered from the balcony of the Military Club, from the steps of the *Sobranié*, and from the Tsar Liberator monument, they were told so.

Next Sunday, September 6, was the national holiday, celebrating the thirtieth anniversary of the union of the Bulgarian kingdom. The printed programme of the parade announced that the *Opoltchenié* and the troops of the garrison of Sofia would participate; but on Saturday night a Bulgarian wood merchant told me that he had received an order from the government to unload twelve railroad cars full of timber in four hours, and turn them over to the government. Late in the evening most of the cab horses in the city were seized by government quartermasters. That very night the Macedonians mysteriously disappeared; and when the parade began in the morning the garrison of Sofia—horse, foot, and artillery—had also vanished, except for two companies. In the afternoon there was a grand patriotic demonstration by civilians, punctuated with bellicose speeches; in the evening a torchlight procession of students singing Macedonian songs. My, how full of politicians and journalists was the Grand Café de Bulgaria that night! But, in spite of the national holiday and the critical situation of events, there was no excitement whatever. There never is in Sofia—the Bulgars are an unemotional people. Even the demonstrations were methodical, organized, and directed like flocks of sheep. The party chiefs and politicians refused to be interviewed—and when that occurs in

Bulgaria, things are serious indeed. Too late the Opposition leaders were scurrying around for support to stop the resistless march
of events.

The last act of the *coup d'état* was brief and dramatic. On Friday, September 18, the Opposition leaders, representing six out
of the eleven Bulgarian parties, had a conference with the King.
Tsanov, representing the two Radical parties, Danev the Progressive Liberals, Stamboliisky the Agrarians, Guechov the Nationalists, and Malinov the Democrats, were received by his majesty in
the presence of his secretary, Doctor Dobrovitch, and the Crown
Prince Boris. Malinov, in his speech, said that the military situation in Europe and the political situation in the country made it
extremely dangerous for Bulgaria to enter the war on either side
at present. He believed firmly in continued neutrality; but if the
government thought that entrance in the war would help realize
the national ideals, his constituents desired that it should be on
the side of the Entente Powers. Stamboliisky then presented a
memorandum signed by himself and his colleagues, which respectfully demanded:

*First.* That the government should take no action without
calling the *Sobranié* and consulting the wishes of the country.

*Second.* That before any action was taken a coalition cabinet
should be formed (after the model of the English and French war
governments), with an enlarged number of ministers to represent
the eleven political parties.

*Third.* That the Crown should present to the government in
power the demands of the Opposition, with the indorsement of
the Crown.

Guechov took the floor, pointing out by means of figures and
calculations the inevitable final victory of the Entente Powers.
"The moment for our entrance into the war is unripe," he said.
Tsanov followed with a speech along the same general lines; and
after a discussion precising the details of the memorandum, the
King, Prince Boris, and Doctor Dobrovitch withdrew for a private discussion.

When they returned it became apparent from what Doctor
Dobrovitch said that the government had made up its mind to a

course of action, on the basis of information which could not be made public.

"What most concerns the people of this country," burst out Stamboliisky, "must remain a secret then?"

"I had no idea that you represented the people of this country, Mr. Stamboliisky," said the King. "Why is it that you have never come to see me before?"

"Because the democratic principles of my party forbid it," said Stamboliisky; "but I waive principles when the country is in danger. And let me remind your Majesty that dynasties which thwart the popular will do not last long!"

"My head is old," replied the King, "and not of much value. But you had better take care of your own!"

In vain Malinov and Guechov tried to quiet things. By this time Tsanov had lost his temper and joined Stamboliisky, and "for a while," said an imaginative observer, "they all kicked each other's shins."

Finally the King rose and said very sternly: "Gentlemen, I shall present your demands to the government. I can tell you that we have decided on a policy which will be thoroughly carried out at any cost. Mr. Stamboliisky, I am happy at last to have made your acquaintance!"

Two days later we left Sofia for Nish, and three days after that the Bulgarian mobilization was announced.

# Serbia Revisited, and Greece

FIFTEEN minutes out from Sofia the train plunges again into mounting defiles between ever more towering hills, through tunnel after tunnel. Stony peaks colored wonderfully in reds and browns and subtle grays seem animals crouching, so living is their texture. Southward the crinkled Balkans march across the sky, blue with distance. It is a breeding-place of hard men and fighters. Two hours, and we are over the divide, screaming down beside a stream that leaps in cascades. A dry, hot, little valley opens out, ringed around with arid mountains; there lies Tsaribrod, the last Bulgarian station, piled high with heaps of army supplies and buzzing with troops. A neat little town with substantial houses and public buildings, two factories, good roads running east and north, schools, electric lights, and a sewer system. A neat little station paved with concrete, where the ticket-agent who was so cordial when we stopped there four months ago, leans from his window to shake hands. The train roars through a tunnel, and twists between precipitous hills. Where they open out a little, arid and quivering with heat, lies Pirot, the first town in Serbia.

What a contrast even between these two first cousins—Bulgars and Serbs! The town straggled out, an overgrown village, all deep, wide houses roofed with Turkish tiles; no school visible. On the dirt platform before the ramshackle wooden station, a customs officer, the station-master in gold-lace uniform with a sword, a policeman in blue with red facings, and a sword, too, and two army officers, were having an animated discussion, entirely oblivious of the train. The rapid, flexible eloquence of the Serbian language struck on our ears like a jet of fresh water. Around them in easy familiarity crowded peasant soldiers in shabby gray uniforms, sandals, and the distinctive crushed-in cap of the Serbian army, listening and joining in the argument.

"Mr. Pachitch!" cried the station-master vehemently: "Mr. Pachitch is no true Serbian! His father was a Bulgarian and his mother was a Turk! Who couldn't make a better prime minister than any Young Radical?" He pounded himself on the chest. "Why, I myself——"

The customs officer slapped the major on the shoulder, and burst into a shout of laughter. All the soldiers laughed, too. Down at the end of the station fence, reservists of the last call were coming through a gate, one by one, while a sergeant called their names on the roster and ticked them off. Old men and young boys they were, in every variety of improvised uniform, tattered sandals on their feet—but all with the military cap and all equipped with new rifles. A boy who could not have been more than sixteen, so drunk that he could hardly stagger, reeled through with his peasant mother holding him upright. The tears streamed down her face; she wiped his sweating face with a handkerchief and straightened his lapels, and patted him twice on the chest. Growling, he made for the sleeping-car. A policeman grabbed him by the arm. "Forward!" he yelled; "get forward into the box car!" Without a word the boy threw his arms around the policeman and they fell to the ground, a waving mass of arms and legs. Everybody laughed. An incredibly aged man with one arm came hobbling up on a stick and touched a gray-haired giant who bore a rifle. He turned and they kissed each other on the mouth. Tears ran down the old man's face. "Do not let the Bulgars through!" he shrilled. . . .

The customs officer came into our apartment. He simply glanced at our passports and never touched the baggage.

"You came from Sofia?" he said eagerly, sitting down and offering cigarettes. "What is the news? We've been hearing exciting rumors here. Is Bulgaria going to war? She'd better not—we'll march to Sofia in two days!"

"But if Austria and Germany attack you?"

"Pooh, they tried it once! Let them all come! Serbia can whip the world! . . ."

Ahead of us, as the train rattled along, rose a great chorus from five box cars full of soldiers. They were singing a new ballad about the Bulgarians, which began:

"King Ferdinand, the Bulgar, got up one day in his palace in
   Sofia and looked out the window,
And he said to his son, the Crown Prince Boris: 'My son and
   heir, it is a fine day and the Serbian army is very busy,
So I think if we attack their women and children we may
   not be defeated. . . .' "

One's first impression on crossing the Greek frontier is of a mob of money-changers, bootblacks, venders of chocolates and fruit and last week's papers—shrewd, brown little traders of harsh, quick speech and keen eyes. Three years ago there were no Greeks whatever in this arid mountain valley of southern Macedonia; now it is all Greek. That is what happens in every new Greek country; all but the lowest peasants tilling the soil are forced out by the most bitter economic competition—and even they are working for Greeks. The Rumanians are gay and graceful; the Bulgars honest and friendly; the Serbs witty, brave, and charming; after these the Greeks seem a stunted, unfriendly people without any flavor.

I think I must have asked a hundred Greek soldiers what they thought of the war. Now the salient characteristic of Balkan peoples is bitter hatred of the nearest aliens. The Greeks hated the Serbians normally, but when they spoke of the Bulgars it was in terms of torture and burning alive. Venezelos they idolized almost to a man; but I found that they would even vote against him, for they thought he meant to force them into war—and the Greeks did not want to fight. But Greeks are very sentimental; you only have to wave a flag and shout "glory" to them, and they will go to war for a good cause or a bad one. Greek ambitions are limitless. They consider themselves the heirs of Periclean Athens,

THE SERB.

of the Byzantine Empire, the conquests of Alexander the Great, and the far-flung colonies of the ancient Greek city-states. An editorial paragraph from a Greek newspaper displays their ordinary frame of mind:

"Greece, which has a history five thousand years old, and is the mother of Western civilization, should not let itself be surpassed by nations who have managed to assemble their children under their hegemony, as Piedmont dominated Italy, as Prussia dominated Germany. The Hellenic nation should not show itself incompetent, powerless, and inferior to certain new states, such as Austria-Hungary, Bulgaria, and Turkey, which are so many mosaics constituted in Europe by barbarians coming from Central Asia."

And this in face of the fact that the new Greek provinces are inefficiently and corruptly governed, and that Athens itself is a hotbed of lies and bribery. A typical example is the Greek railroad official who was bribed by Germans to hinder the mobilization of the Greek army. And remember, that the first time the *casus federis* of the Greco-Serbian treaty was ever invoked Greece refused to fulfill her obligations. . . .

The last day I was at Salonika a great cloud of black smoke appeared at the foot of the gulf; a little destroyer steamed full speed for the city and anchored off the *quai*. Three boats were landed, containing English officers in campaign uniform, with the red tabs that mark Staff officials, twenty-five boxes and trunks, and a couple of British marines carrying rifles with fixed bayonets. The baggage was piled in the street and the officers went into the Hotel de Rome. In fifteen minutes the rumor was all over the town that Sir Ian Hamilton was in Salonika. Wild excitement seized the Greek officials. Around the two sentries guarding the baggage prowled a solemn, uneasy circle of policemen; a dense mass of townspeople stood silently watching. Hot wires clamored the news to Athens; frightened officials cried: "What does it mean? What shall we do?"

In the meantime we had run into the King of England's Messenger on his way home through Italy with despatches from the

Balkans. He was pretty reasonably mellow with much Scotch and soda, as we went to lunch in the Hotel de Rome.

Five tables away from us sat the general himself—a tall, bronzed, solid Englishman with a gray mustache—and all his Staff. He and the King's Messenger bowed to one another. A few minutes afterward a waiter came to our table.

"General Hamilton would like to speak with the King's Messenger." Our friend rose, reeling slightly, and went over. Pretty soon he came back, holding on to chairs and piloting himself with difficulty. He sat down at the table and grinned.

"It is too, too funny," he said weakly. "The old duffer wants me to go immediately to Athens and ask the British ambassador for instructions.

" 'Damme,' he said to me, 'what the devil have they sent us here for? Here I am—and not a word of instructions. What the devil do they want me to do?' "

That night we took ship for the Piræus and home. Next morning, steaming down between far islands that lay like clouds on the sea, we met twelve transports full of British troops on their way to Salonika.

# Ten Days That Shook the World

# Contents

# Introduction

W ITH the greatest interest and with never-slackening attention I read John Reed's book, *Ten Days That Shook the World.* Unreservedly do I recommend it to the workers of the world. Here is a book which I should like to see published in millions of copies and translated into all languages. It gives a truthful and most vivid exposition of the events so significant to the comprehension of what really is the Proletarian Revolution and the Dictatorship of the Proletariat. These problems are widely discussed, but before one can accept or reject these ideas one must understand the full significance of such a decision. John Reed's book will undoubtedly help to clear this question, which is the fundamental problem of the universal workers' movement.

NIKOLAI LENIN
(Vladimir Ilyich Ulyanov)

# Preface

T HIS book is a slice of intensified history—history as I saw it. It does not pretend to be anything but a detailed account of the November Revolution, when the Bolsheviki, at the head of the workers and soldiers, seized the state power of Russia and placed it in the hands of the Soviets.

Naturally, most of it deals with "Red Petrograd," the capital and heart of the insurrection. But the reader must realize that what took place in Petrograd was almost exactly duplicated, with greater or lesser intensity, at different intervals of time, all over Russia.

In this book, the first of several which I am writing, I must confine myself to a chronicle of those events which I myself observed and experienced, and those supported by reliable evidence; preceded by two chapters briefly outlining the background and causes of the November Revolution. I am aware that these two chapters make difficult reading, but they are essential to an understanding of what follows.

Many questions will suggest themselves to the mind of the reader. What is Bolshevism? What kind of a government structure did the Bolsheviki set up? If the Bolsheviki championed the Constituent Assembly before the November Revolution, why did they disgorge it by force of arms afterwards? And if the bourgeoisie opposed the Constituent Assembly until the danger of Bolshevism became apparent, why did they champion it afterward?

These and many other questions cannot be answered here. In another volume, *Kornilov to Brest-Litovsk*, I trace the course of the

Revolution up to and including the German peace. There I explain the origin and functions of the Revolutionary organizations, the evolution of popular sentiment, the dissolution of the Constituent Assembly, the structure of the Soviet state, and the course and outcome of the Brest-Litovsk negotiations. . . .

In considering the rise of the Bolsheviki, it is necessary to understand that Russian economic life and the Russian army were the logical result of a process which began as far back as 1915. The corrupt reactionaries in control of the Czar's Court deliberately undertook to wreck Russia in order to make a separate peace with Germany. The lack of arms on the front, which had caused the great retreat of the summer of 1915, the lack of food in the army and in the great cities, the breakdown of manufactures and transportation in 1916—all these we know now were part of a gigantic campaign of sabotage. This was halted in time by the March Revolution.

For the first few months of the new régime, in spite of the confusion incident upon a great Revolution, when one hundred and sixty millions of the world's most oppressed peoples suddenly achieved liberty, both the internal situation and the combative power of the army actually improved.

But the "honeymoon" was short. The propertied classes wanted merely a political revolution, which would take the power from the Czar and give it to them. They wanted Russia to be a constitutional republic, like France or the United States; or a constitutional monarchy, like England. On the other hand, the masses of the people wanted real industrial and agrarian democracy.

William English Walling, in his book, *Russia's Message*, an account of the Revolution of 1905, describes very well the state of mind of the Russian workers, who were later to support Bolshevism almost unanimously:

> They [the working people] saw it was possible that even under a free Government, if it fell into the hands of other social classes, they might still continue to starve. . . .
> The Russian workman is revolutionary, but he is neither violent,

dogmatic, nor unintelligent. He is ready for barricades, but he has studied them, and alone of the workers of the world he has learned about them from actual experience. He is ready and willing to fight his oppressor, the capitalist class, to a finish. But he does not ignore the existence of other classes. He merely asks that the other classes take one side or the other in the bitter conflict that draws near. . . .

They [the workers] were all agreed that our [American] political institutions were preferable to their own, but they were not very anxious to exchange one despot for another (i.e., the capitalist class). . . .

The working men of Russia did not have themselves shot down, executed by hundreds in Moscow, Riga, and Odessa, imprisoned by thousands in every Russian jail, and exiled to the deserts and the Arctic regions, in exchange for the doubtful privileges of the working men of Goldfields and Cripple Creek. . . .

And so developed in Russia, in the midst of a foreign war, the social revolution on top of the political revolution, culminating in the triumph of Bolshevism.

Mr. A. J. Sack, director in this country of the Russian Information Bureau, which opposes the Soviet Government, has this to say in his book *The Birth of the Russian Democracy:*

> The Bolsheviki organized their own cabinet, with Nicholas Lenin as Premier and Leon Trotsky Minister of Foreign Affairs. The inevitability of their coming into power became evident almost immediately after the March Revolution. The history of the Bolsheviki, after the Revolution, is a history of their steady growth. . . .

Foreigners, and Americans especially, frequently emphasize the "ignorance" of the Russian workers. It is true they lacked the political experience of the peoples of the West, but they were very well trained in voluntary organization. In 1917 there were more than twelve million members of the Russian Consumers' Cooperative Societies; and the Soviets themselves are a wonderful demonstration of their organizing genius. Moreover, there is probably not a people in the world so well educated in Socialist theory and its practical application.

William English Walling thus characterizes them·

The Russian working people are for the most part able to read and write. For many years the country has been in such a disturbed condition that they have had the advantage of leadership not only of intelligent individuals in their midst, but of a large part of the equally revolutionary educated class, who have turned to the working people with their ideas for the political and social regeneration of Russia. . . .

Many writers explain their hostility to the Soviet Government by arguing that the last phase of the Russian Revolution was simply a struggle of the "respectable" elements against the brutal attacks of Bolshevism. However, it was the propertied classes, who, when they realized the growth in power of the popular revolutionary organizations, undertook to destroy them and to halt the Revolution. To this end the propertied classes finally resorted to desperate measures. In order to wreck the Kerensky Ministry and the Soviets, transportation was disorganized and internal troubles provoked; to crush the Factory-Shop Committees, plants were shut down, and fuel and raw materials diverted; to break the Army Committees at the front, capital punishment was restored and military defeat connived at.

This was all excellent fuel for the Bolshevik fire. The Bolsheviki retorted by preaching the class war, and by asserting the supremacy of the Soviets.

Between these two extremes, with the other factions which whole-heartedly or half-heartedly supported them, were the so-called "moderate" Socialists, the Mensheviki and Socialist Revolutionaries, and several smaller parties. These groups were also attacked by the propertied classes, but their power of resistance was crippled by their theories.

Roughly, the Mensheviki and Socialist Revolutionaries believed that Russia was not economically ripe for a social revolution—that only a *political* revolution was possible. According to their interpretation, the Russian masses were not educated enough to take over the power; any attempt to do so would inevitably bring on a reaction, by means of which some ruthless opportunist might restore the old régime. And so it followed that when the "moderate" Socialists were forced to assume the power, they were afraid to use it.

They believed that Russia must pass through the stages of political and economic development known to Western Europe, and emerge at last, with the rest of the world, into full-fledged Socialism. Naturally, therefore, they agreed with the propertied classes that Russia must first be a parliamentary State—though with some improvements on the Western democracies. As a consequence, they insisted upon the collaboration of the propertied classes in the Government.

From this it was an easy step to supporting them. The "moderate" Socialists needed the bourgeoisie. But the bourgeoisie did not need the "moderate" Socialists. So it resulted in the Socialist Ministers being obliged to give way, little by little, on their entire program, while the propertied classes grew more and more insistent.

And at the end, when the Bolsheviki upset the whole hollow compromise, the Mensheviki and Socialist Revolutionaries found themselves fighting on the side of the propertied classes. . . . In almost every country in the world today the same phenomenon is visible.

Instead of being a destructive force, it seems to me that the Bolsheviki were the only party in Russia with a constructive program and the power to impose it on the country. If they had not succeeded to the Government when they did, there is little doubt in my mind that the armies of imperial Germany would have been in Petrograd and Moscow in December, and Russia would again be ridden by a Czar. . . .

It is still fashionable, after a whole year of the Soviet Government, to speak of the Bolshevik insurrection as an "adventure." Adventure it was, and one of the most marvelous mankind ever embarked upon, sweeping into history at the head of the toiling masses, and staking everything on their vast and simple desires. Already the machinery had been set up by which the land of the great estates could be distributed among the peasants. The Factory-Shop Committees and the trade unions were there to put into operation workers' control of industry. In every village, town, city, district, and province there were Soviets of Workers', Soldiers', and Peasants' Deputies, prepared to assume the task of local administration.

No matter what one thinks of Bolshevism, it is undeniable that the Russian Revolution is one of the great events of human history, and the rise of the Bolsheviki a phenomenon of world-wide importance. Just as historians search the records for the minutest details of the story of the Paris Commune, so they will want to know what happened in Petrograd in November 1917, the spirit which animated the people, and how the leaders looked, talked, and acted. It is with this in view that I have written this book.

In the struggle my sympathies were not neutral. But in telling the story of those great days I have tried to see events with the eye of a conscientious reporter, interested in setting down the truth.

J. R.

New York,
1 January 1919

# Notes and Explanations

To the average reader the multiplicity of Russian organizations—political groups, Committee and Central Committees, Soviets, Dumas, and Unions—will prove extremely confusing. For this reason I am giving here a few brief definitions and explanations.

## Political Parties

In the elections to the Constituent Assembly, there were seventeen tickets in Petrograd, and in some of the provincial towns as many as forty; but the following summary of the aims and composition of political parties is limited to the groups and factions mentioned in this book. Only the essence of their programs and the general character of their constituencies can be noticed. . . .

1. *Monarchists* of various shades, *Octobrists*, etc. These once-powerful factions no longer existed openly; they either worked underground, or their members joined the *Cadets*, as the *Cadets* came by degrees to stand for their political program. Representatives in this book, Rodzianko, Shulgin.

2. *Cadets.* So-called from the initials of its name, Constitutional Democrats. Its official name is "Party of the People's Freedom." Under the Czar composed of Liberals from the propertied classes, the *Cadets* were the great party of *political* reform, roughly corresponding to the Progressive Party in America. When the revolution broke out in March 1917 the *Cadets* formed the first Provisional Government. The *Cadet* Ministry was overthrown in

April because it declared itself in favor of Allied imperialistic aims, including the imperialistic aims of the Czar's Government. As the revolution became more and more a *social economic* revolution, the *Cadets* grew more and more conservative. Its representatives in this book are: Milyukov, Vinaver, Shatsky.

(a) *Group of Public Men.* After the *Cadets* had become unpopular through their relations with the Kornilov counter-revolution, the *Group of Public Men* was formed in Moscow. Delegates from the *Group of Public Men* were given portfolios in the last Kerensky Cabinet. The *Group* declared itself non-partisan, although its intellectual leaders were men like Rodzianko and Shulgin. It was composed of the more "modern" bankers, merchants, and manufacturers, who were intelligent enough to realize that the Soviets must be fought by their own weapon—economic organization. Typical of the *Group:* Lianozov, Konovalov.

3. *Populist Socialists,* or *Trudoviki* (Labor Group). Numerically a small party, composed of cautious intellectuals, the leaders of the cooperative societies, and conservative peasants. Professing to be Socialists, the *Populists* really supported the interests of the petty bourgeoisie—clerks, shopkeepers, etc. By direct descent, inheritors of the compromising tradition of the Labor Group in the Fourth Imperial Duma, which was composed largely of peasant representatives. Kerensky was the leader of the *Trudoviki* in the Imperial Duma when the Revolution of March 1917 broke out. The *Populist Socialists* are a nationalistic party. Their representatives in this book are: Peshekhanov, Chaikovsky.

4. *Russian Social Democratic Labor Party.* Originally Marxian Socialists. At a party congress held in 1903 the party split, on the question of tactics, into two factions—the Majority (Bolshinstvo), and the Minority (Menshinstvo). From this sprang the names "Bolsheviki" and "Mensheviki"—"members of the majority" and "members of the minority." These two wings became two separate parties, both calling themselves "Russian Social Democratic Labor Party," and both professing to be Marxians. Since the revolution of 1905 the Bolsheviki were really the minority, becoming again the majority in September 1917.

(a) *Mensheviki.* This party includes all shades of Socialists who believe that society must progress by natural evolution toward Socialism, and that the working class must conquer political power first. Also a nationalistic party. This was the party of the Socialist intellectuals, which means: all the means of education having been in the hands of the propertied classes, the intellectuals instinctively reacted to their training, and took the side of the propertied classes. Among their representatives in this book are: Dan, Lieber, Tseretelly.

(b) *Mensheviki Internationalists.* The radical wing of the *Mensheviki*, internationalists, and opposed to all coalition with the propertied classes yet unwilling to break loose from the conservative Mensheviki, and opposed to the dictatorship of the working class advocated by the Bolsheviki. Trotsky was long a member of this group. Among their leaders: Martov, Martinov.

(c) *Bolsheviki.* Now call themselves the *Communist Party*, in order to emphasize their complete separation from the tradition of "moderate" or "parliamentary" Socialism, which dominates the Mensheviki and the so-called Majority Socialists in all countries. The *Bolsheviki* proposed immediate proletarian insurrection, and seizure of the reins of Government, in order to hasten the coming of Socialism by forcibly taking over industry, land, natural resources, and financial institutions. This party expresses the desires chiefly of the factory workers, but also of a large section of the poor peasants.

The name "Bolshevik" can *not* be translated by "Maximalist." The Maximalists are a separate group. (See paragraph 5b.) Among the leaders: Lenin, Trotsky, Lunacharsky.

(d) *United Social Democrats Internationalists.* Also called the *Novaya Zhizn* (New Life) group, from the name of the very influential newspaper which was its organ. A little group of intellectuals with a very small following among the working class, except the personal following of Maxim Gorky, its leader. Intellectuals, with almost the same program as the *Mensheviki Internationalists,* except that the *Novaya Zhizn* group refused to be tied to either of the two great factions. Opposed the Bolshevik tactics, but remained in the Soviet Government. Other representatives in this book: Avilov, Kramarov.

(e) *Yedinstvo*. A very small and dwindling group, composed almost entirely of the personal following of Plekhanov, one of the pioneers of the Russian Social Democratic movement in the 80s, and its greatest theoretician; now an old man, Plekhanov was extremely patriotic, too conservative even for the Mensheviki. After the Bolshevik *coup d'état*, *Yedinstvo* disappeared.

5. *Socialist Revolutionary Party*. Called *Essaires* from the initials of their name. Originally the revolutionary party of the peasants, the party of the Fighting Organizations—the Terrorists. After the March Revolution, it was joined by many who had never been Socialists. At that time it stood for the abolition of private property in land only, the owners to be compensated in some fashion. Finally the increasing revolutionary feeling of peasants compelled the *Essaires* to abandon the "compensation" clause, and led to the younger and more fiery intellectuals breaking off from the main party in the fall of 1917 and forming a new party, the *Left Socialist Revolutionary Party*. The *Essaires*, who were afterwards always called by the radical groups *"Right Social Revolutionaries,"* adopted the political attitude of the Mensheviki, and worked together with them. They finally came to represent the wealthier peasants, the intellectuals, and the politically uneducated populations of remote rural districts. Among them there was, however, a wider difference of shades of political and economic opinion than among the Mensheviki. Among their leaders mentioned in these pages: Avksentiev, Gotz, Kerensky, Chernov, "Babushka" Breshkovskaya.

(a) *Left Socialist Revolutionaries*. Although theoretically sharing the Bolshevik program of dictatorship of the working class, at first were reluctant to follow the ruthless Bolshevik tactics. However, the *Left Socialist Revolutionaries* remained in the Soviet Government, sharing the Cabinet portfolios, especially that of Agriculture. They withdrew from the Government several times, but always returned. As the peasants left the ranks of the *Essaires* in increasing numbers they joined the *Left Socialist Revolutionary Party*, which became the great peasant party supporting the Soviet Government, standing for confiscation without compensation of the great landed estates, and their disposition by the peasants themselves. Among the leaders: Spiridonova, Karelin, Kamkov, Kalagayev.

(b) *Maximalists.* An offshoot of the *Socialist Revolutionary Party* in the revolution of 1905, when it was a powerful peasant movement, demanding the immediate application of the maximum socialist program. Now an insignificant group of peasant anarchists.

## Parliamentary Procedure

Russian meetings and conventions are organized after the Continental model rather than our own. The first action is usually the election of officers and the *presidium.*

The *presidium* is a presiding committee, composed of representatives of the groups and political factions represented in the assembly, in proportion to their numbers. The *presidium* arranges the Order of Business, and its members can be called upon by the president to take the chair *pro tem.*

Each question *(vopros)* is stated in a general way and then debated, and at the close of the debate resolutions are submitted by the different factions, and each one voted on separately. The Order of Business can be, and usually is, smashed to pieces in the first half hour. On the plea of "emergency," which the crowd almost always grants, anybody from the floor can get up and say anything on any subject. The crowd controls the meeting, practically the only functions of the Speaker being to keep order by ringing a little bell, and to recognize speakers. Almost all the real work of the session is done in caucuses of the different groups and political factions, which almost always cast their votes in a body and are represented by floor-leaders. The result is, however, that at every important new point, or vote, the session takes a recess to enable the different groups and political factions to hold a caucus.

The crowd is extremely noisy, cheering or heckling speakers, overriding the plans of the *presidium.* Among the customary cries are: *"Prosim!* Please! Go on!" *"Pravilno!"* or *"Eto vierno!* That's true! Right!" *"Do volno!* Enough!" *"Doloi!* Down with him!" *"Posor!* Shame!" and *"Teeshe!* Silence! Not so noisy!"

**Popular Organizations**

1. *Soviet.* The word *soviet* means "council." Under the Czar the Imperial Council of State was called *Gosudarstvennyi Soviet.* Since the Revolution, however, the term *Soviet* has come to be associated with a certain type of parliament elected by members of working-class economic organizations—the Soviet of Workers', of Soldiers', or of Peasants' Deputies. I have therefore limited the word to these bodies, and wherever else it occurs I have translated it "Council."

Besides the local *Soviets,* elected in every city, town, and village of Russia—and in large cities, also Ward *(Raionny) Soviets*—there are also the *oblastny* or *gubiernsky* (district or provincial) *Soviets,* and the Central Executive Committee of the All-Russian *Soviets* in the capital, called from its initials *Tsay-ee-kah.* (See below, "Central Committees.")

Almost everywhere the *Soviets* of Workers' and of Soldiers' Deputies combined very soon after the March Revolution. In special matters concerning their peculiar interests, however, the Workers' and the Soldiers' Sections continued to meet separated. The *Soviets* of Peasants' Deputies did not join the other two until after the Bolshevik *coup d'état.* They, too, were organized like the workers and soldiers, with an Executive Committee of the All-Russian Peasants' *Soviets* in the capital.

2. *Trade Unions.* Although mostly industrial in form, the Russian labor unions were still called Trade Unions, and at the time of the Bolshevik Revolution had from three to four million members. These Unions were also organized in an All-Russian body, a sort of Russian Federation of Labor, which had its Central Executive Committee in the capital.

3. *Factory-Shop Committees.* These were spontaneous organizations created in the factories by the workers in their attempt to control industry, taking advantage of the administrative breakdown incident upon the Revolution. Their function was by revolutionary action to take over and run the factories. The *Factory-Shop Committees* also had their All-Russian organization,

with a Central Committee at Petrograd, which cooperated with the trade unions.

4. *Dumas.* The word *duma* means roughly "deliberative body." The old Imperial Duma, which persisted six months after the revolution, in a democratized form, died a natural death in September 1917. The *City Duma* referred to in this book was the reorganized Municipal Council, often called "Municipal Self-Government." It was elected by direct and secret ballot, and its only reason for failure to hold the masses during the Bolshevik Revolution was the general decline in influence of all purely *political* representation in the face of the growing power of organizations based on *economic* groups.

5. *Zemstvos.* May be roughly translated "county councils." Under the Tsar semi-political, semi-social bodies with very little administrative power, developed and controlled largely by intellectual Liberals among the landowning classes. Their most important function was education and social service among the peasants. During the War the *Zemstvos* gradually took over the entire feeding and clothing of the Russian army, as well as the buying from foreign countries, and work among the soldiers generally corresponding to the work of the American Y.M.C.A. at the front. After the March Revolution the *Zemstvos* were democratized, with a view to making them the organs of local government in the rural districts. But like the *City Dumas*, they could not compete with the *Soviets*.

6. *Cooperatives.* These were the workers' and peasants' Consumers' Cooperative Societies, which had several million members all over Russia before the Revolution. Founded by Liberals and "moderate" socialists, the cooperative movement was not supported by the revolutionary Socialist groups, because it was a substitute for the complete transference of means of production and distribution into the hands of the workers. After the March Revolution the *Cooperatives* spread rapidly, and were dominated by Populist Socialists, Mensheviki, and Socialist Revolutionaries, and acted as a conservative political force until the Bolshevik Rev-

olution. However, it was the *Cooperatives* which fed Russia when the old structure of commerce and transportation collapsed.

7. *Army Committees.* The *Army Committees* were formed by the soldiers at the front to combat the reactionary influence of the old régime officers. Every company, regiment, brigade, division, and corps had its committee, over all of which was elected the *Army Committee.* The *Central Army Committee* cooperated with the General Staff. The administrative breakdown in the army incident upon the Revolution threw upon the shoulders of the *Army Committees* most of the work of the Quartermaster's Department, and in some cases even the command of troops.

8. *Fleet Committees.* The corresponding organizations in the navy.

## Central Committees

In the spring and summer of 1917, All-Russian conventions of every sort of organization were held at Petrograd. There were national congresses of Workers', Soldiers', and Peasants' Soviets, Trade Unions, Factory-Shop Committees, Army and Fleet Committees—besides every branch of the military and naval service, cooperatives, nationalities, etc. Each of these conventions elected a Central Committee, or a Central Executive Committee, to guard its particular interests at the seat of Government. As the Provisional Government grew weaker, these Central Committees were forced to assume more and more administrative powers.

The most important Central Committees mentioned in this book are:

*Union of Unions.* During the revolution of 1905, Professor Milyukov and other Liberals established unions of professional men—doctors, lawyers, physicians, etc. These were united under one central organization, the *Union of Unions.* In 1905 the *Union of Unions* acted with the revolutionary democracy; in 1917, however, the *Union of Unions* opposed the Bolshevik uprising, and united the Government employees who went on strike against the authority of the Soviets.

*Tsay-ee-kah.* All-Russian Central Executive Committee of the

Soviets of Workers' and Soldiers' Deputies. So called from the initials of its name.

*Tsentroflot.* "Center-Fleet"—the Central Fleet Committee.

*Vikzhel.* All-Russian Central Committee of the Railway Workers' Union. So called from the initials of its name.

**Other Organizations**

*Red Guards.* The armed factory workers of Russia. The *Red Guards* were first formed during the Revolution of 1905, and sprang into existence again in the days of March 1917, when a force was needed to keep order in the city. At that time they were armed, and all efforts of the Provisional Government to disarm them were more or less unsuccessful. At every great crisis in the Revolution the *Red Guards* appeared on the streets, untrained and undisciplined, but full of revolutionary zeal.

*White Guards.* Bourgeois volunteers, who emerged in the last stages of the Revolution, to defend private property from the Bolshevik attempt to abolish it. A great many of them were university students.

*Tekhintsi.* The so-called "Savage Division" in the army, made up of Mohammedan tribesmen from Central Asia, and personally devoted to General Kornilov. The *Tekhintsi* were noted for their blind obedience and their savage cruelty in warfare.

*Death Battalions.* Or *Shock Battalions.* The Women's Battalion is known to the world as the *Death Battalion*, but there were many *Death Battalions* composed of men. These were formed in the summer of 1917 by Kerensky, for the purpose of strengthening the discipline and combative fire of the army by heroic example. The *Death Battalions* were composed mostly of intense young patriots. These came for the most part from among the sons of the propertied classes.

*Union of Officers.* An organization formed among the reactionary officers in the army to combat politically the growing power of the Army Committees.

*Knights of St. George.* The Cross of St. George was awarded for distinguished action in battle. Its holder automatically became a

*Knight of St. George.* The predominant influence in the organization was that of the supporters of the military idea.

*Peasants' Union.* In 1905 the *Peasants' Union* was a revolutionary peasants' organization. In 1917, however, it had become a political expression of the more prosperous peasants, to fight the growing power and revolutionary aims of the Soviets of Peasants' Deputies.

## Chronology and Spelling

I have adopted in this book our calendar throughout, instead of the former Russian calendar, which was thirteen days earlier.

In the spelling of Russian names and words, I have made no attempt to follow any scientific rules for transliteration, but have tried to give the spelling which would lead the English-speaking reader to the simplest approximation of their pronunciation.

## Sources

Much of the material in this book is from my own notes. I have also relied, however, upon a heterogeneous file of several hundred assorted Russian newspapers, covering almost every day of the time described, of files of the English paper, the *Russian Daily News*, and of the two French papers, *Journal de Russie* and *Entente*. But far more valuable than these is the *Bulletin de la Presse* issued daily by the French Information Bureau in Petrograd, which reports all important happenings, speeches, and the comment of the Russian press. Of this I have an almost complete file from the spring of 1917 to the end of January 1918.

Besides the foregoing, I have in my possession almost every proclamation, decree and announcement posted on the walls of Petrograd from the middle of September 1917 to the end of January 1918. Also the official publication of all Government decrees and orders, and the official Government publication of the secret treaties and other documents discovered in the Ministry of Foreign Affairs when the Bolsheviki took it over.

# 1

# Background

Toward the end of September 1917, an alien professor of sociology visiting Russia came to see me in Petrograd. He had been informed by business men and intellectuals that the Revolution was slowing down. The professor wrote an article about it and then traveled around the country, visiting factory towns and peasant communities—where, to his astonishment, the Revolution seemed to be speeding up. Among the wage-earners and the land-working people it was common to hear talk of "all land to the peasants, all factories to the workers." If the professor had visited the front, he would have heard the whole Army talking Peace. . . .

The professor was puzzled, but he need not have been; both observations were correct. The property-owning classes were becoming more conservative, the masses of the people more radical.

There was a feeling among business men and the *intelligentsia* generally that the Revolution had gone quite far enough, and lasted too long; that things should settle down. This sentiment was shared by the dominant "moderate" Socialist groups, the *oborontsi*[1] Mensheviki and Socialist Revolutionaries, who supported the Provisional Government of Kerensky.

On 14 October the official organ of the "moderate" Socialists said:

The drama of the Revolution has two acts; the destruction of the old régime and the creation of the new one. The first act has lasted

1. References numbered in this manner refer to the Appendix, p. 853.

591

long enough. Now it is time to go on to the second, and to play it as rapidly as possible. As a great revolutionist put it, "Let us hasten, friends, to terminate the Revolution. He who makes it last too long will not gather the fruits. . . ."

Among the worker, soldier, and peasant masses, however, there was a stubborn feeling that the "first act" was not yet played out. On the front the Army Committees were always running foul of officers who could not get used to treating their men like human beings; in the rear the Land Committees elected by the peasants were being jailed for trying to carry out Government regulations concerning the land; and the workmen[2] in the factories were fighting blacklists and lock-outs. Nay, furthermore, returning political exiles were being excluded from the country as "undesirable" citizens; and in some cases men who returned from abroad to their villages were prosecuted and imprisoned for revolutionary acts committed in 1905.

To the multiform discontent of the people the "moderate" Socialists had one answer: Wait for the Constituent Assembly, which is to meet in December. But the masses were not satisfied with that. The Constituent Assembly was all well and good; but there were certain definite things for which the Russian Revolution had been made and for which the revolutionary martyrs rotted in their stark Brotherhood Grave on Mars Field, that must be achieved, Constituent Assembly or no Constituent Assembly: Peace, Land, and Workers' Control of Industry. The Constituent Assembly had been postponed and postponed— would probably be postponed again, until the people were calm enough—perhaps to modify their demands! At any rate here were eight months of the Revolution gone, and little enough to show for it. . . .

Meanwhile the soldiers began to solve the peace question by simply deserting, the peasants burned manor-houses and took over the great estates, the workers sabotaged and struck. . . . Of course, as was natural, the manufacturers, landowners, and army officers exerted all their influence against any democratic compromise. . . .

The policy of the Provisional Government alternated between ineffective reforms and stern repressive measures. An edict from the Socialist Minister of Labor ordered all the Workers' Committees henceforth to meet only after working hours. Among the troops at the front, "agitators" of opposition political parties were arrested, radical newspapers closed down, and capital punishment applied—to revolutionary propagandists. Attempts were made to disarm the Red Guard. Cossacks were sent to keep order in the provinces. . . .

These measures were supported by the "moderate" Socialists and their leaders in the Ministry, who considered it necessary to cooperate with the propertied classes. The people rapidly deserted them, and went over to the Bolsheviki, who stood for Peace, Land, and Workers' Control of Industry, and a Government of the working class. In September 1917, matters reached a crisis. Against the overwhelming sentiment of the country, Kerensky and the "moderate" Socialists succeeded in establishing a Government of Coalition with the propertied classes; and as a result, the Mensheviki and Socialist Revolutionaries lost the confidence of the people for ever.

An article in *Rabochi Put* (Workers' Way) about the middle of October, entitled "The Socialist Ministers," expressing the feeling of the masses of the people against the "moderate" Socialists:

> Here is a list of their services.[3]
> Tseretelly: disarmed the workmen with the assistance of General Polovtsev, checkmated the revolutionary soldiers, and approved of capital punishment in the army.
> Skobeliev: commenced by trying to tax the capitalists 100 percent of their profits, and finished—and finished by an attempt to dissolve the Workers' Committees in the shops and factories.
> Avksentiev: put several hundred peasants in prison, members of the Land Committees, and suppressed dozens of workers' and soldiers' newspapers.
> Chernov: signed the "Imperial" manifesto, ordering the dissolution of the Finnish Diet.
> Savinkov: concluded an open alliance with General Kornilov. If this savior of the country was not able to betray Petrograd, it was due to reasons over which he had no control.

Zarudny: with the sanction of Alexinsky and Kerensky, put some of the best workers of the Revolution, soldiers and sailors, in prison.

Nikitin: acted as a vulgar policeman against the railway workers.

Kerensky: it is better not to say anything about him. The list of his services is too long. . . .

A Congress of delegates of the Baltic Fleet, at Helsingfors, passed a resolution which began as follows:

We demand the immediate removal from the ranks of the Provisional Government of the "Socialist," the political adventurer—Kerensky, as one who is scandalizing and ruining the great Revolution, and with it the revolutionary masses, by his shameless political blackmail on behalf of the bourgeoisie. . . .

The direct result of all this was the rise of the Bolsheviki. . . .

Since March 1917, when the roaring torrents of workmen and soldiers beating upon the Tauride Palace compelled the reluctant Imperial Duma to assume the supreme power in Russia, it was the masses of the people, workers, soldiers, and peasants which forced every change in the course of the Revolution. They hurled the Miliukov Ministry down; it was their Soviet which proclaimed to the world the Russian peace terms—"No annexations, no indemnities, and the right of self-determination of peoples"; and again, in July, it was the spontaneous rising of the unorganized proletariat which once more stormed the Tauride Palace, to demand that the Soviets take over the Government of Russia.

The Bolsheviki, then a small political sect, put themselves at the head of the movement. As a result of the disastrous failure of the rising, public opinion turned against them, and their leaderless hordes slunk back into the Viborg Quarter, which is Petrograd's St. Antoine. Then followed a savage hunt of the Bolsheviki; hundreds were imprisoned, among them Trotsky, Madame Kollontai, and Kameniev; Lenin and Zinoviev went into hiding, fugitives from justice; the Bolshevik papers were suppressed. Provocators and reactionaries raised the cry that the Bolsheviki were German agents, until people all over the world believed it.

But the Provisional Government found itself unable to substantiate its accusations; the documents proving pro-German conspiracy were discovered to be forgeries\*; and one by one the Bolsheviki were released from prison without trial, on nominal or no bail—until only six remained. The impotence and indecision of the ever-changing Provisional Government was an argument nobody could refute. The Bolsheviki raised again the slogan so dear to the masses, "All Power to the Soviets!"—and they were not merely self-seeking, for at that time the majority of the Soviets was "moderate" Socialist, their bitter enemy.

But more potent still, they took the crude, simple desires of the workers, soldiers, and peasants, and from them built their immediate program. And so, while the *oborontsi* Mensheviki and Socialist Revolutionaries involved themselves in compromise with the bourgeoisie, the Bolsheviki rapidly captured the Russian masses. In July they were hunted and despised; by September the metropolitan workmen, the sailors of the Baltic Fleet, and the soldiers had been won almost entirely to their cause. The September municipal elections in the large cities[4] were significant; only 18 percent of the returns were Menshevik and Socialist Revolutionary, against more than 70 percent in June. . . .

There remains a phenomenon which puzzled foreign observers; the fact that the Central Executive Committees of the Soviets, the Central Army and Fleet Committees,† and the Central Committees of some of the Unions—notably, the Post and Telegraph Workers and the Railway Workers—opposed the Bolsheviki with the utmost violence. These Central Committees had all been elected in the middle of the summer, or even before, when the Mensheviki and Socialist Revolutionaries had an enormous following; and they delayed or prevented any new elections. Thus, according to the constitution of the Soviets of Workers' and Soldiers' Deputies, the All-Russian Congress *should have been called in September*; but the Tsay-ee-kah† would not call the meeting, on the ground that the Constituent Assembly was only two months away, at which time, they hinted, the Soviets would abdi-

\*Part of the famous "Sisson Documents."
†See Notes and Explanations.

cate. Meanwhile, one by one, the Bolsheviki were winning in the local Soviets all over the country, in the Union branches and the ranks of all the soldiers and sailors. The Peasants' Soviets remained still conservative, because in the sluggish rural districts political consciousness developed slowly, and the Socialist Revolutionary party had been for a generation the party which had agitated among the peasants. . . . But even among the peasants a revolutionary wing was forming. It showed itself clearly in October, when the left wing of the Socialist Revolutionaries split off, and formed a new political faction, the Left Socialist Revolutionaries.

At the same time there were signs everywhere that the forces of reaction were gaining confidence.[5] At the Troitsky Farce Theater in Petrograd, for example, a burlesque called *Sins of the Czar* was interrupted by a group of monarchists, who threatened to lynch the actors for "insulting the Emperor." Certain newspapers began to sigh for a "Russian Napoleon." It was the usual thing among bourgeois *intelligentsia* to refer to the Soviets of Workers' Deputies (Rabochikh Deputatov) as *Sabachikh* Deputatove— Dogs' Deputies.

On 15 October I had a conversation with a great Russian Capitalist, Stepan Georgevich Lianozov, known as the "Russian Rockefeller"—a Cadet by political faith.

"Revolution," he said "is a sickness. Sooner or later the foreign powers must intervene here—as one would intervene to cure a sick child, and teach it how to walk. Of course, it would be more or less improper, but the nations must realize the danger of Bolshevism in their own countries—such contagious ideas as 'proletarian dictatorship,' and 'world social revolution.' . . . There is a chance that this intervention may not be necessary. Transportation is demoralized, the factories are closing down, and the Germans are advancing. Starvation and defeat may bring the Russian people to their senses."

Mr. Lianozov was emphatic in his opinion that whatever happened, it would be impossible for merchants and manufacturers to permit the existence of the workers' Shop Committees, or to allow the workers any share in the management of industry.

"As for the Bolsheviki, they will be done away with by one of two methods. The Government can evacuate Petrograd, then a state of siege declared, and the military commander of the district can deal with these gentlemen without legal formalities.... *Or if, for example, the Constituent Assembly manifests any Utopian tendencies, it can be dispersed by force of arms....*"

Winter was coming on—the terrible Russian winter. I heard business men speak of it so: "Winter was always Russia's best friend. Perhaps now it will rid us of Revolution." On the freezing front miserable armies continued to starve and die without enthusiasm. The railways were breaking down, food lessening, factories closing. The desperate masses cried out that the bourgeoisie was sabotaging the life of the people, causing defeat on the front. Riga had been surrendered just after General Kornilov said publicly, "Must we pay with Riga the price of bringing the country to a sense of its duty?"*

To Americans it is incredible that the class war should develop to such a pitch. But I have personally met officers on the Northern Front who frankly preferred military disaster to cooperation with the Soldiers' Committees. The secretary of the Petrograd branch of the Cadet party told me that the breakdown of the country's economic life was part of a campaign to discredit the Revolution. An Allied diplomat, whose name I promised not to mention, confirmed this from his own knowledge. I know of certain coal mines near Kharkov which were fired and flooded by their owners, of textile factories at Moscow whose engineers put the machinery out of order when they left, of railroad officials caught by the workers in the act of crippling locomotives....

A large section of the propertied classes preferred the Germans to the Revolution—even to the Provisional Government—and didn't hesitate to say so. In the Russian household where I lived, the subject of conversation at the dinner-table was almost invariably the coming of the Germans, bringing "law and order."...

One evening I spent at the house of a Moscow merchant; during tea we asked the eleven people at the table whether they preferred

*See *Kornilov to Brest-Litovsk*, by John Reed, Boni and Liveright, N.Y., 1919.

"Wilhelm or the Bolsheviki." The vote was ten to one for Wilhelm. . . .

The speculators took advantage of the universal disorganization to pile up fortunes, and to spend them in fantastic revelry or the corruption of Government officials. Foodstuffs and fuel were hoarded, or secretly sent out of the country to Sweden. In the first four months of the Revolution, for example, the reserve food supplies were almost openly looted from the great Municipal warehouses of Petrograd, until the two years' provision of grain had fallen to less than enough to feed the city for one month. . . . According to the official report of the last Minister of Supplies in the Provisional Government, coffee was bought wholesale in Vladivostok for two roubles a pound, and the consumer in Petrograd paid thirteen. In all the stores of the large cities were tons of food and clothing; but only the rich could buy them.

In a provincial town I knew a merchant family turned speculator—*maradior* (bandit, ghoul) the Russians call it. The three sons had bribed their way out of military service. One gambled in foodstuffs. Another sold illegal gold from the Lena mines to mysterious parties in Finland. The third owned a controlling interest in a chocolate factory, which supplied the local Cooperative societies—on condition that the Cooperatives furnished him everything he needed. And so, while the masses of the people got a quarter pound of black bread on their bread cards, he had an abundance of white bread, sugar, tea, candy, cake, and butter. . . . Yet, when the soldiers at the front could no longer fight from cold, hunger, and exhaustion, how indignantly did this family scream "Cowards!"—how "ashamed" they were "to be Russians." . . . When finally the Bolsheviki found and requisitioned vast hoarded stores of provisions, what "Robbers" they were.

Beneath all this external rottenness moved the old-time Dark Forces, unchanged since the fall of Nicholas the Second, secret still and very active. The agents of the notorious Okhrana still functioned, for and against the Czar, for and against Kerensky—whoever would pay. . . . In the darkness, underground organizations of all sorts, such as the Black Hundreds, were busy attempting to restore reaction in some form or other.

In this atmosphere of corruption, of monstrous half-truths, one clear note sounded day after day, the deepening chorus of the Bolsheviki, "All Power to the Soviets! All Power to the direct representatives of millions on millions of common workers, soldiers, peasants. Land, bread, an end to the senseless war, an end to secret diplomacy, speculation, treachery. . . . The Revolution is in danger and with it the cause of the people all over the world!"

The struggle between the proletariat and the middle class, between the Soviets and the Government, which had begun in the first March days, was about to culminate. Having at one bound leaped from the Middle Ages into the twentieth century, Russia showed the startled world two systems of Revolution—the political and the social—in mortal combat.

What a revelation of the vitality of the Russian Revolution, after all these months of starvation and disillusionment! The bourgeoisie should have better known its Russia. Not for a long time in Russia will the "sickness" of Revolution have run its course. . . .

Looking back, Russia before the November insurrection seems of another age, almost incredibly conservative. So quickly did we adapt ourselves to the new, swifter life; just as Russian politics swung bodily to the Left—until the Cadets were outlawed as "enemies of the people," Kerensky became a "counter-revolutionist," the "middle" Socialist leaders, Tseretelly, Dan, Lieber, Gotz, and Avksentiev, were too reactionary for their following, and men like Victor Chernov, and even Maxim Gorky, belonged to the Right Wing. . . .

About the middle of December 1917, a group of Socialist Revolutionary leaders paid a private visit to Sir George Buchanan, the British Ambassador, and implored him not to mention the fact that they had been there because they were "considered too far Right."

"And to think," said Sir George, "one year ago my Government instructed me not to receive Milyukov, because he was so dangerously Left!"

September and October are the worst months of the Russian year—especially the Petrograd year. Under dull gray skies, in the shortening days, the rain fell drenching, incessant. The mud underfoot was deep, slippery, and clinging, tracked everywhere by heavy boots, and worse than usual because of the complete breakdown of the Municipal administration. Bitter damp winds rushed in from the Gulf of Finland, and the chill fog rolled through the streets. At night, for motives of economy as well as fear of Zeppelins, the street-lights were few and far between; in private dwellings and apartment houses the electricity was turned on from six o'clock until midnight, with candles forty cents apiece and little kerosene to be had. It was dark from three in the afternoon to ten in the morning. Robberies and house-breaking increased. In apartment houses the men took turns at all-night guard duty, armed with loaded rifles. This was under the Provisional Government.

Week by week food became scarcer. The daily allowance of bread fell from a pound and a half to a pound, then three-quarters, half, and a quarter-pound. Toward the end there was a week without any bread at all. Sugar one was entitled to at the rate of two pounds a month—if one could get it at all, which was seldom. A bar of chocolate or a pound of tasteless candy cost anywhere from seven to ten roubles—at least a dollar. There was milk for about half the babies in the city; most hotels and private houses never saw it for months. In the fruit season apples and pears sold for a little less than a rouble apiece on the street corner. . . .

For milk and bread and sugar and tobacco one had to stand in queue long hours in the chill rain. Coming home from an all-night meeting I have seen the *kvost* (tail) beginning to form before dawn, mostly women, some with babies in their arms. . . . Carlyle, in his *French Revolution*, has described the French people as distinguished above all others by their faculty of standing in queue. Russia had accustomed herself to the practice, begun in the reign of Nicholas the Blessed as long ago as 1915, and from then continued intermittently until the summer of 1917, when it settled down as the regular order of things. Think of the poorly clad people standing on the iron-white streets of Petrograd whole days in the Russian winter! I have listened in the bread-lines, hearing the bitter, acrid note of discontent which from time to time burst up through the miraculous good nature of the Russian crowd. . . .

Of course all the theaters were going every night, including Sundays. Karsavina appeared in a new Ballet at the Marinsky, all dance-loving Russia coming to see her. Chaliapin was singing. At the Alexandrinsky they were reviving Meyerhold's production of Tolstoy's *Death of Ivan the Terrible*; and at that performance I remember noticing a student of the Imperial School of Pages, in his dress uniform, who stood up correctly between the acts and faced the empty Imperial box, with its eagles all erased. . . . The Krivoye Zerkalo staged a sumptuous version of Schnitzler's *Reigen.*

Although the Hermitage and other picture galleries had been evacuated to Moscow, there were weekly exhibitions of paintings. Hordes of the female *intelligentsia* went to hear lectures on Art, Literature, and the Easy Philosophies. It was a particularly active season for Theosophists. And the Salvation Army, admitted to Russia for the first time in history, plastered the walls with announcements of gospel meetings, which amused and astounded Russian audiences. . . .

As in all such times, the petty conventional life of the city went on, ignoring the Revolution as much as possible. The poets made verses—but not about the Revolution. The realistic painters painted scenes from medieval Russian history—anything but the Revolution. Young ladies from the provinces came up to the capital to learn French and cultivate their voices, and the gay young beautiful officers wore their gold-trimmed crimson *bashliki* and their elaborate Caucasian swords around the hotel lobbies. The ladies of the minor bureaucratic set took tea with each other in the afternoon, carrying each her little gold or silver or jeweled sugar-box, and half a loaf of bread in her muff, and wished that the Czar were back, or that the Germans would come, or anything that would solve the servant problem. . . . The daughter of a friend of mine came home one afternoon in hysterics because the woman street-car conductor had called her "Comrade!"

All around them great Russia was in travail, bearing a new world. The servants one used to treat like animals and pay next to nothing were getting independent. A pair of shoes cost more than a hundred roubles, and as wages averaged about thirty-five roubles a month the servants refused to stand in queue and wear out their shoes. But more than that. In the new Russia every man and woman could vote; there were working-class newspapers, saying new and startling things; there were the Soviets; and there were the Unions. The *izvozchiki* (cab-drivers) had a Union; they were also represented in the Petrograd Soviet. The waiters and hotel servants were organized, and refused tips. On the walls of restaurants they put up signs which read, "No tips taken here—" or, "Just because a man has to make his living waiting on table is no reason to insult him by offering him a tip!"

At the front the soldiers fought their fight with the officers and learned self-government through their committees. In the factories, those unique Russian organizations, the Factory-Shop Committees,* gained experience and strength and a realization of their historical mission by combat with the old order. All Russia was learning to read, and *reading*—politics, economics, history—because the people wanted to *know*. . . . In every city, in most towns, along the front, each political faction had its newspaper—sometimes several. Hundreds of thousands of pamphlets were distributed by thousands of organizations, and poured into the armies, the villages, the factories, the streets. The thirst for education, so long thwarted, burst with the Revolution into a frenzy of expression. From Smolny Institute alone, the first six months, went out every day tons, car-loads, train-loads of literature, saturating the land. Russia absorbed reading matter like hot sand drinks water, insatiable. And it was not fables, falsified history, diluted religion, and the cheap fiction that corrupts—but social and economic theories, philosophy, the works of Tolstoy, Gogol, and Gorky. . . .

Then the Talk, beside which Carlyle's "flood of French speech" was a mere trickle. Lectures, debates, speeches—in theaters, circuses, school-houses, clubs, Soviet meeting-rooms, Union headquarters, barracks. . . . Meetings in the trenches at the

*See Notes and Explanations.

front, in village squares, factories. . . . What a marvelous sight to see Putilovsky Zavod (the Putilov factory) pour out its forty thousand to listen to Social Democrats, Socialist Revolutionaries, Anarchists, anybody, whatever they had to say, as long as they would talk! For months in Petrograd, and all over Russia, every street-corner was a public tribune. In railway trains, street-cars, always the spurting up of impromptu debate, everywhere. . . .

And the All-Russian Conferences and Congresses, drawing together the men of two continents—conventions of Soviets, of Cooperatives, Zemstvos,* nationalities, priests, peasants, political parties; the Democratic Conference, the Moscow Conference, the Council of the Russian Republic. There were always three or four conventions going on in Petrograd. At every meeting, attempts to limit the time of speakers voted down, and every man free to express the thought that was in him. . . .

We came down to the front of the Twelfth Army, back of Riga, where gaunt and bootless men sickened in the mud of desperate trenches; and when they saw us they started up, with their pinched faces and the flesh showing blue through their torn clothing, demanding eagerly, "Did you bring anything to *read?*"

What though the outward and visible signs of change were many, what though the statue of Catherine the Great before the Alexandrinsky Theater bore a little red flag in its hand, and others—somewhat faded—floated from all public buildings; and the Imperial monograms and eagles were either torn down or covered up; and in place of the fierce *gorodovoye* (city police) a mild-mannered and unarmed citizen militia patroled the streets—still, there were many quaint anachronisms.

For example, Peter the Great's *Tabel o Rangov*—Table of Ranks—which he riveted upon Russia with an iron hand, still held sway. Almost everybody from the schoolboy up wore his prescribed uniform, with the insignia of the Emperor on button and shoulder-strap. Along about five o'clock in the afternoon the streets were full of subdued old gentlemen in uniform, with portfolios, going home from work in the huge, barrack-like Ministries

*See Notes and Explanations.

or Government institutions, calculating perhaps how great a mortality among their superiors would advance them to the coveted *chin* (rank) of Collegiate Assessor, or Privy Councillor, with the prospect of retirement on a comfortable pension, and possibly the Cross of St. Anne. . . .

There is the story of Senator Sokolov, who in full tide of Revolution came to a meeting of the Senate one day in civilian clothes, and was not admitted because he did not wear the prescribed livery of the Czar's service!

It was against this background of a whole nation in ferment and disintegration that the pageant of the Rising of the Russian Masses unrolled. . . .

# 2

# The Coming Storm

In September General Kornilov marched on Petrograd to make himself military dictator of Russia. Behind him was suddenly revealed the mailed fist of the bourgeoisie, boldly attempting to crush the Revolution. Some of the Socialist Ministers were implicated; even Kerensky was under suspicion.[6] Savinkov, summoned to explain to the Central Committee of his party, the Socialist Revolutionaries, refused and was expelled. Kornilov was arrested by the Soldiers' Committees. Generals were dismissed, Ministers suspended from their functions, and the Cabinet fell.

Kerensky tried to form a new Government, including the Cadets, party of the bourgeoisie. His party, the Socialist Revolutionaries, ordered him to exclude the Cadets. Kerensky declined to obey, and threatened to resign from the Cabinet if the Socialists insisted. However, popular feeling ran so high that for the moment he did not dare oppose it, and a temporary Directorate of Five of the old Ministers, with Kerensky at the head, assumed the power until the question should be settled.

The Kornilov affair drew together all the Socialist groups—"moderates" as well as revolutionists—in a passionate impulse of self-defense. There must be no more Kornilovs. A new Government must be created, responsible to the elements supporting the Revolution. So the Tsay-ee-kah invited the popular organizations to send delegates to a Democratic Conference, which should meet at Petrograd in September.

In the Tsay-ee-kah three factions immediately appeared. The Bolsheviki demanded that the All-Russian Congress of Soviets be summoned, and that they take over the power. The "center" Socialist Revolutionaries, led by Chernov, joined with the Left Socialist Revolutionaries, led by Kamkov and Spiridonova, the Mensheviki Internationalists under Martov, and the "center" Mensheviki,* represented by Bogdanov and Skobeliev, in demanding a purely Socialist Government. Tseretelly, Dan, and Lieber, at the head of the right-wing Mensheviki, and the Right Socialist Revolutionaries under Avksentiev and Gotz, insisted that the propertied classes must be represented in the new Government.

Almost immediately the Bolsheviki won a majority in the Petrograd Soviet, and the Soviets of Moscow, Kiev, Odessa, and other cities followed suit.

Alarmed, the Mensheviki and Socialist Revolutionaries in control of the Tsay-ee-kah decided that after all they feared the danger of Kornilov less than the danger of Lenin. They revised the plan of representation in the Democratic Conference,[7] admitting more delegates from the Cooperative Societies and other conservative bodies. Even this packed assembly at first voted for a *Coalition Government without the Cadets.* Only Kerensky's open threat of resignation, and the alarming cries of the "moderate" Socialists that "the Republic is in danger" persuaded the Conference, by a small majority, to declare in favor of the principle of coalition with the bourgeoisie, and to sanction the establishment of a sort of consultative Parliament, without any legislative power, called the Provisional Council of the Russian Republic. In the new Ministry the propertied class practically controlled, and in the Council of the Russian Republic they occupied, a disproportionate number of seats.

The fact is that the Tsay-ee-kah no longer represented the rank and file of the Soviets, and had illegally refused to call another All-Russian Congress of Soviets, due in September. It had no intention of calling this Congress or of allowing it to be called. Its official organ, *Izvestia* (News), began to hint that the function of the Soviets was nearly at an end,[8] and that they might soon be dissolved. . . . At this time, too, the new Government announced

*See Notes and Explanations.

as part of its policy the liquidation of "irresponsible organizations"—i.e., the Soviets.

The Bolsheviki responded by summoning the All-Russian Soviets to meet at Petrograd on 2 November and take over the Government of Russia. At the same time they withdrew from the Council of the Russian Republic, stating that they would not participate in a "Government of Treason to the People."⁹

The withdrawal of the Bolsheviki, however, did not bring tranquility to the ill-fated Council. The propertied classes, now in a position of power, became arrogant. The Cadets declared that the Government had no legal right to declare Russia a republic. They demanded stern measures in the Army and Navy to destroy the Soldiers' and Sailors' Committees, and denounced the Soviets. On the other side of the chamber the Mensheviki Internationalists and the Left Socialist Revolutionaries advocated immediate peace, land to the peasants, and workers' control of industry—practically the Bolshevik program.

I heard Martov's speech in answer to the Cadets. Stooped over the desk of the tribune like the mortally sick man he was, and speaking in a voice so hoarse it could hardly be heard, he shook his finger toward the right benches:

"You call us defeatists, but the real defeatists are those who wait for a more propitious moment to conclude peace, insist upon postponing peace until later, until nothing is left of the Russian army, until Russia becomes the subject of bargaining between the different imperialist groups. . . . You are trying to impose upon the Russian people a policy dictated by the interests of the bourgeoisie. The question of peace should be raised without delay. . . . You will see then that not in vain has been the work of those whom you call German agents, of those Zimmerwaldists* who in all the lands have prepared the awakening of the conscience of the democratic masses. . . ."

Between these two groups the Mensheviki and Socialist Revolutionaries wavered, irresistibly forced to the left by the pressure

---

*Members of the revolutionary international wing of the Socialists of Europe, so called because of their participation in the International Conference held at Zimmerwald, Switzerland, in 1915.

of the rising dissatisfaction of the masses. Deep hostility divided the chamber into irreconcilable groups.

This was the situation when the long-awaited announcement of the Allied Conference in Paris brought up the burning question of foreign policy. . . .

Theoretically all Socialist parties in Russia were in favor of the earliest possible peace on democratic terms. As long ago as May 1917 the Petrograd Soviet, then under control of the Mensheviki and Socialist Revolutionaries, had proclaimed the famous Russian peace-conditions. They had demanded that the Allies hold a conference to discuss war aims. This conference had been promised for August; then postponed until September; then until October; and now it was fixed for 10 November.

The Provisional Government suggested two representatives—General Alexeyev, reactionary military man, and Tereshchenko, Minister of Foreign Affairs. The Soviets chose Skobeliev to speak for them and drew up a manifesto, the famous *nakaz*[10]—instructions. The Provisional Government objected to Skobeliev and his *nakaz*; the Allied ambassadors protested and finally Bonar Law in the British House of Commons, in answer to a question, responded coldly, "As far as I know the Paris Conference will not discuss the aims of the war at all, but only the methods of conducting it. . . ."

At this the conservative Russian press was jubilant, and the Bolsheviki cried, "See where the compromising tactics of the Mensheviki and Socialist Revolutionaries have led them!"

Along a thousand miles of front the millions of men in Russia's armies stirred like the sea rising, pouring into the capital their hundreds upon hundreds of delegations, crying, "Peace! Peace!"

I went across the river to the Cirque Moderne, to one of the great popular meetings which occurred all over the city, more numerous night after night. The bare, gloomy amphitheater, lit by five tiny lights hanging from a thin wire, was packed from the ring up the steep sweep of grimy benches to the very roof—soldiers, sailors, workmen, women, all listening as if their lives depended upon it. A soldier was speaking—from the Five Hundred and Forty-Eighth Division, wherever and whatever that was:

"Comrades," he cried, and there was real anguish in his drawn face and despairing gestures. "The people at the top are always calling upon us to sacrifice more, sacrifice more, while those who have everything are left unmolested.

"We are at war with Germany. Would we invite German generals to serve on our Staff? Well, we're at war with the capitalists too, and yet we invite them into our Government. . . .

"The soldier says, 'Show me what I am fighting for. Is it Constantinople, or is it free Russia? Is it the democracy, or is it the capitalist plunderers? If you can prove to me that I am defending the Revolution then I'll go out and fight without capital punishment to force me.'

"When the land belongs to the peasants, and the factories to the workers, and the power to the Soviets, then we'll know we have something to fight for, and we'll fight for it!"

In the barracks, the factories, on the street corners, endless soldier speakers, all clamoring for an end to the war, declaring that if the Government did not make an energetic effort to get peace, the army would leave the trenches and go home.

The spokesman for the Eighth Army:

"We are weak, we have only a few men left in each company. They must give us food and boots and reinforcements, or soon there will be left only empty trenches. Peace or supplies . . . either let the Government end the war or support the Army. . . ."

For the Forty-Sixth Siberian Artillery:

"The officers will not work with our Committees, they betray us to the enemy, they apply the death penalty to our agitators, and the counter-revolutionary Government supports them. We thought that the Revolution would bring peace. But now the Government forbids us even to talk of such things, and at the same time doesn't give us enough food to live on, or enough ammunition to fight with. . . ."

From Europe came rumors of peace at the expense of Russia. . . .[11]

News of the treatment of Russian troops in France added to the discontent. The First Brigade had tried to replace its officers with Soldiers' Committees, like their comrades at home, and had refused an order to go to Salonika, demanding to be sent to Russia. They had been surrounded and starved, and then fired on by artillery, and many killed. . . .[12]

On 29 October I went to the white marble and crimson hall of the Marinsky Palace, where the Council of the Republic sat, to hear Tereshchenko's declaration of the Government's foreign policy, awaited with such terrible anxiety by all the peace-thirsty and exhausted land.

A tall, impeccably dressed young man with a smooth face and high cheek-bones, suavely reading his careful non-committal speech.[13] Nothing. . . . Only the same platitudes about crushing German militarism with the help of the Allies—about the "State interests" of Russia, about the "embarrassment" caused by Skobeliev's *nakaz*. He ended with the keynote:

"Russia is a great power. Russia will remain a great power, whatever happens. We must all defend her, we must show that we are defenders of a great ideal, and children of a great power."

Nobody was satisfied. The reactionaries wanted a "strong" imperialist policy; the democratic parties wanted an assurance that the Government would press for peace. . . . I reproduce an editorial in *Rabochi i Soldat* (Worker and Soldier), organ of the bolshevik Petrograd Soviet:

THE GOVERNMENT'S ANSWER TO THE TRENCHES

The most taciturn of our Ministers, Mr. Tereshchenko, has actually told the trenches the following:

1. We are closely united with our Allies. (Not with the peoples, but with the Governments.)

2. There is no use for the democracy to discuss the possibility or impossibility of a winter campaign. That will be decided by the Governments of our Allies.

3. The 1 July offensive was beneficial and a very happy affair. (He did not mention the consequences.)

4. It is not true that our Allies do not care about us. The Minister had in his possession very important declarations. (Declarations? What about deeds? What about the behavior of the British fleet?[14] The parleying of the British king with exiled counter-revolutionary General Gurko? The Minister did not mention all this.)

5. The *nakaz* to Skobeliev is bad; the Allies don't like it and the Russian diplomats don't like it. In the Allied Conference we must all "speak one language."

And is that all? That is all. What is the way out? The solution is, faith in the Allies and in Tereshchenko. When will peace come? When the Allies permit.

That is how the Government replied to the trenches about peace!

Now in the background of Russian politics began to form the vague outlines of a sinister power—the Cossacks. *Novaya Zhizn* (New Life), Gorky's paper, called attention to their activities:

> At the beginning of the Revolution the Cossacks refused to shoot down the people. When Kornilov marched on Petrograd they refused to follow him. From passive loyalty to the Revolution the Cossacks have passed to an active political offensive (against it). From the background of the Revolution they have suddenly advanced to the front of the stage. . . .

Kaledin, *ataman* of the Don Cossacks, had been dismissed by the Provisional Government for his complicity in the Kornilov affair. He flat refused to resign, and surrounded by three immense Cossack armies lay at Novocherkask, plotting and menacing. So great was his power that the Government was forced to ignore his insubordination. More than that, it was compelled formally to recognize the Council of the Union of Cossack Armies, and to declare illegal the newly formed Cossack Section of the Soviets. . . .

In the first part of October a Cossack delegation called upon Kerensky, arrogantly insisting that the charges against Kaledin be dropped, and reproaching the Minister-President for yielding to the Soviets. Kerensky agreed to let Kaledin alone, and then is reported to have said, "In the eyes of the Soviet leaders I am a despot and a tyrant. . . . As for the Provisional Government, not only does it not depend upon the Soviets, but it considers it regrettable that they exist at all."

At the same time another Cossack mission called upon the British ambassador, treating with him boldly as representatives of "the free Cossack people."

In the Don something very like a Cossack Republic had been established. The Kuban declared itself an independent Cossack State. The Soviets of Rostov on Don and Yekaterinburg were dispersed by armed Cossacks, and the headquarters of the Coal Miners' Union at Kharkov raided. In all its manifestations the Cossack movement was anti-Socialist and militaristic. Its leaders were nobles and great landowners, like Kaledin, Kornilov, Generals Dutov, Karaulov, and Bardizhe, and it was backed by the powerful merchants and bankers of Moscow. . . .

Old Russia was rapidly breaking up. In the Ukraine, in Finland, Poland, White Russia, the nationalist movements gathered strength and became bolder. The local Governments, controlled by the propertied classes, claimed autonomy, refusing to obey orders from Petrograd. At Helsingfors the Finnish Senate declined to loan money to the Provisional Government, declared Finland autonomous, and demanded the withdrawal of Russian troops. The bourgeois Rada at Kiev extended the boundaries of the Ukraine until they included all the richest agricultural lands of South Russia, as far east as the Urals, and began the formation of a national army. Premier Vinnichenko hinted at a separate peace with Germany—and the Provisional Government was helpless. Siberia, the Caucasus, demanded separate constituent Assemblies. And in all these countries there was the beginning of a bitter struggle between the authorities and the local Soviets of Workers' and Soldiers' Deputies. . . .

Conditions were daily more chaotic. Hundreds of thousands of soldiers were deserting the front and beginning to move in vast, aimless tides over the face of the land. The peasants of Tambov and Tver Governments, tired of waiting for the land, exasperated by the repressive measures of the Government, were burning manor-houses and massacring landowners. Immense strikes and lock-outs convulsed Moscow, Odessa, and the coal-mines of the Don. Transport was paralyzed; the army was starving, and in the big cities there was no bread.

The Government, torn between the democratic and reactionary factions, could do nothing; when forced to act it always supported the interests of the propertied classes. Cossacks were sent to restore order among the peasants, to break the strikes. In Tashkent Government authorities suppressed the Soviet. In Petrograd the Economic Council, established to rebuild the shattered economic life of the country, came to a deadlock between the opposing forces of capital and labor, and was dissolved by Kerensky. The old régime military men, backed by Cadets, demanded that harsh measures be adopted to restore discipline in the Army and Navy. In vain Admiral Verderevsky, the venerable Minister of Marine, and General Verkhovsky, Minister of War, insisted that only a new, voluntary, democratic discipline, based on cooperation with the Soldiers' and Sailors' Committees, could save the Army and Navy. Their recommendations were ignored.

The reactionaries seemed determined to provoke popular anger. The trial of Kornilov was coming on. More and more openly the bourgeois press defended him, speaking of him as "the great Russian patriot." Burtzev's paper, *Obshchee Dielo* (Common Cause), called for a dictatorship of Kornilov, Kaledin, and Kerensky!

I had a talk with Burtzev one day in the press gallery of the Council of the Republic. A small, stooped figure with a wrinkled face, eyes near-sighted behind thick glasses, untidy hair and beard streaked with gray.

"Mark my words, young man! What Russia needs is a Strong Man. We should get our minds off the Revolution now and concentrate on the Germans. Bunglers, bunglers, to defeat Kornilov; and back of the bunglers are the German agents. Kornilov should have won. . . ."

On the extreme right the organs of the scarcely veiled Monarchists, Purishkevich's *Narodny Tribun* (People's Tribune), *Novaya Rus* (New Russia), and *Zhivoye Slovo* (Living Word), openly advocated the extermination of the revolutionary democracy. . . .

On 23 October occurred the naval battle with a German squadron in the Gulf of Riga. On the pretext that Petrograd was in danger, the Provisional Government drew up plans for evacuating the capital. First the great munitions works were to go, distributed widely throughout Russia; and then the Government itself was to move to Moscow. Instantly the Bolsheviki began to cry out that the Government was abandoning the Red Capital in order to weaken the Revolution. Riga had been sold to the Germans; now Petrograd was being betrayed!

The bourgeois press was joyful. "At Moscow," said the Cadet paper *Ryech* (Speech), "the Government can pursue its work in a tranquil atmosphere, without being interfered with by anarchists." Rodzianko, leader of the right wing of the Cadet party, declared in *Utro Rossii* (The Morning of Russia) that the taking of Petrograd by the Germans would be a blessing, because it would destroy the Soviets and get rid of the revolutionary Baltic Fleet:

> Petrograd is in danger [he wrote]. I say to myself, "Let God take care of Petrograd." They fear that if Petrograd is lost the central revolutionary organizations will be destroyed. To that I answer that I rejoice if all these organizations are destroyed; for they will bring nothing but disaster upon Russia. . . .
> With the taking of Petrograd the Baltic Fleet will also be destroyed. . . . But there will be nothing to regret; most of the battleships are completely demoralized. . . .

In the face of a storm of popular disapproval the plan of evacuation was repudiated.

Meanwhile the Congress of Soviets loomed over Russia like a thundercloud, shot through with lightnings. It was opposed, not only by the Government, but by all the "moderate" Socialists. The Central Army and Fleet Committees, the Central Committees of some of the Trade Unions, the Peasants' Soviets, but most of all the Tsay-ee-kah itself, spared no pains to prevent the meeting. *Izvestia* and *Golos Soldata* (Voice of the Soldier), newspapers founded by the Petrograd Soviet but now in the hands of the Tsay-ee-kah, fiercely assailed it, as did the entire artillery of the Socialist Revolutionary party press, *Dielo Naroda* (People's Cause) and *Volia Naroda* (People's Will).

Delegates were sent through the country, messages flashed by wire to committees in charge of local Soviets, to Army Committees, instructing them to halt or delay elections to the Congress. Solemn public resolutions against the Congress, declarations that the democracy was opposed to the meeting so near the date of the

Constituent Assembly, representatives from the front, from the Union of Zemstvos, the Peasants' Union, Union of Cossack Armies, Union of Officers, Knights of St. George, Death Battalions,* protesting. . . . The Council of the Russian Republic was one chorus of disapproval. The entire machinery set up by the Russian Revolution of March functioned to block the Congress of Soviets. . . .

On the other hand was the shapeless will of the proletariat—the workmen, common soldiers, and poor peasants. Many local Soviets were already Bolshevik; then there were the organizations of the industrial workers, the *Fabrichno-Zavodskiye Comitieti*—Factory-Shop Committees; and the insurgent Army and Fleet organizations. In some places the people, prevented from electing their regular Soviet delegates, held rump meetings, and chose one of their number to go to Petrograd. In others they smashed the old obstructionist committees and formed new ones. A groundswell of revolt heaved and cracked the crust which had been slowly hardening on the surface of revolutionary fires dormant all those months. Only a spontaneous mass movement could bring about the All-Russian Congress of Soviets. . . .

Day after day the Bolshevik orators toured the barracks and factories, violently denouncing "this Government of civil war." One Sunday we went, on a top-heavy steam tram that lumbered through oceans of mud, between stark factories and immense churches, to Obukhovsky Zavod, a Government munitions plant out on the Schlüsselburg Prospekt.

The meeting took place between the gaunt brick walls of a huge unfinished building, ten thousand black-clothed men and women packed around a scaffolding draped in red, people heaped on piles of lumber and bricks, perched high up on shadowy girders, intent and thunder-voiced. Through the dull, heavy sky now and again burst the sun, flooding reddish light through the skeleton windows upon the mass of simple faces upturned to us.

Lunacharsky, a slight, student-like figure with the sensitive face of an artist, was telling why the power must be taken by the

*See Notes and Explanations.

Soviets. Nothing else could guarantee the Revolution against its enemies, who were deliberately ruining the country, ruining the army, creating opportunities for a new Kornilov.

A soldier from the Rumanian front, thin, tragical, and fierce, cried, "Comrades! We are starving at the front, we are stiff with cold. We are dying for no reason. I ask the American comrades to carry word to America that the Russians will never give up their Revolution until they die. We will hold the fort with all our strength until the peoples of the world rise and help us! Tell the American workers to rise and fight for the Social Revolution!"

Then came Petrovsky, slight, slow-voiced, implacable:

"Now is the time for deeds, not words. The economic situation is bad, but we must get used to it. They are trying to starve us and freeze us. They are trying to provoke us. But let them know that they can go too far—that if they dare to lay their hands upon the organizations of the proletariat we will sweep them away like scum from the face of the earth!"

The Bolshevik press suddenly expanded. Besides the two party papers, *Rabochi Put* and *Soldat* (Soldier), there appeared a new paper for the peasants, *Derevenskaya Byednota* (Village Poorest), poured out in a daily half-million edition; and on 17 October, *Rabochi i Soldat*. It's leading article summed up the Bolshevik point of view:

> The fourth year's campaign will mean the annihilation of the army and the country. . . . There is a danger for the safety of Petrograd. . . . Counter-revolutionists rejoice in the people's misfortunes. . . . The peasants brought to desperation come out in open rebellion; the landlords and Government authorities massacre them with punitive expeditions; factories and mine are closing down, workmen are threatened with starvation. . . . The bourgeoisie and its generals want to restore a blind discipline in the army. . . . Supported by the bourgeoisie, the Kornilovtsi are openly getting ready to break up the meeting of the Constituent Assembly. . . .
>
> The Kerensky Government is against the people. He will destroy the country. . . . This paper stands for the people and by the people—the poor classes, workers, soldiers, and peasants. The people can only be saved by the completion of the Revolution . . . and for this purpose the full power must be in the hands of the Soviets. . . .

This paper advocates the following:

All power to the Soviets—both in the capital and in the provinces.
Immediate truce on all fronts. An honest peace between peoples.
Landlord estates—without compensation—to the peasants.
Workers' control over industrial production.
A faithfully and honestly elected Constituent Assembly.

It is interesting to reproduce here a passage from that same paper—the organ of those Bolsheviki so well known to the world as German agents:

The German kaiser, covered with the blood of millions of dead people, wants to push his army against Petrograd. Let us call to the German workmen, soldiers, and peasants, who want peace not less than we do, to . . . stand up against this damned war!

This can be done only by a revolutionary Government, which would speak really for the workmen, soldiers, and peasants of Russia, and would appeal over the heads of the diplomats directly to the German troops, fill the German trenches with proclamations in the German language. . . . Our airmen would spread these proclamations all over Germany. . . .

In the Council of the Republic the gulf between the two sides of the chamber deepened day by day.

"The propertied classes," cried Karelin, for the Left Socialist Revolutionaries, "want to exploit the revolutionary machine of the State to bind Russia to the war-chariot of the Allies! The revolutionary parties are absolutely against this policy. . . ."

Old Nicholas Chaikovsky, representing the Populist Socialists, spoke against giving the land to the peasants, and took the side of the Cadets:

"We must have immediately strong discipline in the army. . . . Since the beginning of the war I have not ceased to insist that it is a crime to undertake social and economic reforms in war-time. We are committing that crime, and yet I am not the enemy of these reforms, because I am a Socialist."

Cries from the Left, "We don't believe you!" Mighty applause from the Right. . . .

Adzhemov, for the Cadets, declared that there was no necessity to tell the army what it was fighting for, since every soldier ought to realize that the first task was to drive the enemy from Russian territory.

Kerensky himself came twice, to plead passionately for national unity, once bursting into tears at the end. The assembly heard him coldly, interrupting with ironical remarks.

SMOLNY Institute, headquarters of the Tsay-ee-kah and of the Petrograd Soviet, lay miles out on the edge of the city, beside the wide Neva. I went there on a streetcar, moving snail-like with a groaning noise through the cobbled, muddy streets, and jammed with people. At the end of the line rose the graceful smoke-blue cupolas of Smolny Convent outlined in dull gold, beautiful, and beside it the great barracks-like façade of Smolny Institute, two hundred yards long and three lofty stories high, the Imperial arms carved hugely in stone still insolent over the entrance. . . .

Under the old régime a famous convent school for the daughters of the Russian nobility, patronized by the Czarina herself, the Institute had been taken over by revolutionary organizations of workers and soldiers. Within were more than a hundred huge rooms, white and bare, on their doors enameled plaques still informing the passer-by that within was "Ladies' Class-room Number 4" or "Teachers' Bureau"; but over these hung crudely-lettered signs, evidence of the vitality of the new order: "Central Committee of the Petrograd Soviet" and "Tsay-ee-kah" and "Bureau of Foreign Affairs"; "Union of Socialist Soldiers," "Central Committee of the All-Russian Trade Unions," "Factory-Shop Committees," "Central Army Committee"; and the central offices and caucus-rooms of the political parties. . . .

The long, vaulted corridors, lit by rare electric lights, were thronged with hurrying shapes of soldiers and workmen, some bent under the weight of huge bundles of newspapers, proclamations, printed propaganda of all sorts. The sound of their heavy boots made a deep and incessant thunder on the wooden floor. . . . Signs were posted up everywhere: "Comrades: For the sake of your health, preserve cleanliness!" Long tables stood at the head of the stairs on every floor, and on the landings, heaped with pamphlets and the literature of the different political parties for sale. . . .

The spacious, low-ceilinged refectory downstairs was still a dining-room. For two roubles I bought a ticket entitling me to dinner, and stood in line with a thousand others, waiting to get to the long serving-tables, where twenty men and women were ladling from immense cauldrons cabbage soup, hunks of meat and piles of *kasha*, slabs of black bread. Five kopeks paid for tea in a tin cup. From a basket one grabbed a greasy wooden spoon. . . . The benches along the wooden tables were packed with hungry proletarians, wolfing their food, plotting, shouting rough jokes across the room. . . .

Upstairs was another eating-place, reserved for the Tsay-ee-kah—though everyone went there. Here could be had bread thickly buttered and endless glasses of tea. . . .

In the south wing on the second floor was the great hall of meetings, the former ballroom of the Institute. A lofty white room lighted by glazed white chandeliers holding hundreds of ornate electric bulbs, and divided by two rows of massive columns; at one end a dais, flanked with two tall many-branched light standards, and a gold frame behind, from which the Imperial portrait had been cut. Here on festal occasions had been banked brilliant military and ecclesiastical uniforms, a setting for Grand Duchesses. . . .

Just across the hall outside was the office of the Credentials Committee for the Congress of Soviets. I stood there watching the new delegates come in—burly, bearded soldiers, workmen in black blouses, a few long-haired peasants. The girl in charge—a member of Plekhanov's Yedinstvo* group—smiled contemptuously. "These are very different people from the delegates to the first *Siezd* (Congress)," she remarked. "See how rough and ignorant they look! The Dark People. . . ." It was true; the depths of Russia had been stirred, and it was the bottom which came uppermost now. The Credentials Committee, appointed by the old

*See Notes and Explanations.

Tsay-ee-kah, was challenging delegate after delegate, on the ground that they had been illegally elected. Karakhan, member of the Bolshevik Central Committee, simply grinned. "Never mind," he said, "when the time comes we'll see that you get your seats. . . ."

*Rabochi i Soldat* said:

> The attention of delegates to the new All-Russian Congress is called to attempts of certain members of the Organizing Committee to break up the Congress, by asserting that it will not take place, and that delegates had better leave Petrograd. . . . Pay no attention to these lies. . . . Great days are coming. . . .

It was evident that a quorum would not come together by 2 November, so the opening of the Congress was postponed to the seventh. But the whole country was not aroused; and the Mensheviki and Socialist Revolutionaries, realizing that they were defeated, suddenly changed their tactics and began to wire frantically to their provisional organizations to elect as many "moderate" Socialist delegates as possible. At the same time the Executive Committee of the Peasants' Soviets issued an emergency call for a Peasants' Congress, to meet 13 December and offset whatever action the workers and soldiers might take. . . .

What would the Bolsheviki do? Rumors ran through the city that there would be an armed "demonstration," a *vystuplenie*— "coming out" of the workers and soldiers. The bourgeois and reactionary press prophesied insurrection, and urged the Government to arrest the Petrograd Soviet, or at least to prevent the meeting of the Congress. Such sheets as *Novaya Rus* advocated a general Bolshevik massacre.

Gorky's paper, *Novaya Zhizn*, agreed with the Bolsheviki that the reactionaries were attempting to destroy the Revolution, and that if necessary they must be resisted by force of arms; but all the parties of the revolutionary democracy must present a united front.

> As long as the democracy has not organized its principal forces, so long as the resistance to its influence is still strong, there is no advan-

tage in passing to the attack. But if the hostile elements appeal to force, then the revolutionary democracy should enter the battle to seize the power, and it will be sustained by the most profound strata of the people. . . .

Gorky pointed out that both reactionary and Government newspapers were inciting the Bolsheviki to violence. An insurrection, however, would prepare the way for a new Kornilov. He urged the Bolsheviki to deny the rumors. Potressov, in the Menshevik *Dien* (Day), published a sensational story, accompanied by a map, which professed to reveal the secret Bolshevik plan of campaign.

As if by magic the walls were covered with warnings,[15] proclamations, appeals, from the Central Committees of the "moderate" and conservative factions and the Tsay-ee-kah, denouncing any "demonstrations," imploring the workers and soldiers not to listen to agitators. For instance, this from the Military Section of the Socialist Revolutionary party:

> Again rumors are spreading around the town of an intended *vystuplenie*. What is the source of these rumors? What organization authorizes these agitators who preach insurrection? The Bolsheviki, to a question addressed to them in the Tsay-ee-kah, denied that they have anything to do with it. . . . But these rumors themselves carry with them a great danger. It may easily happen that, not taking into consideration the state of mind of the majority of the workers, soldiers, and peasants, individual hot-heads will call out part of the workers and soldiers on the streets, inciting them to an uprising. . . . In this fearful time through which revolutionary Russia is passing, any insurrection can easily turn into civil war, and there can result from it the destruction of all organizations of the proletariat, built up with so much labor. . . . The counter-revolutionary plotters are planning to take advantage of this insurrection to destroy the Revolution, open the front to Wilhelm, and wreck the Constituent Assembly. . . . Stick stubbornly to your posts! Do not come out!

On 28 October, in the corridors of Smolny, I spoke with Kameniev, a little man with a reddish pointed beard and Gallic gestures. He was not at all sure that enough delegates would come. "If there *is* a Congress," he said, "it will represent the overwhelming sentiment of the people. If the majority is Bolshevik, as I think it will be, we shall demand that the power be given to the Soviets, and the Provisional Government must resign. . . ."

Volodarsky, a tall, pale youth with glasses and a bad complexion, was more definite. "The 'Lieber-Dans' and the other compromisers are sabotaging the Congress. If they succeed in preventing its meeting—well, then we are realists enough not to depend on *that*!"

Under date of 29 October I find entered in my notebook the following items culled from the newspapers of the day:

> Moghilev (General Staff Headquarters). Concentration here of loyal Guard Regiments, the Savage Division, Cossacks, and Death Battalions.
> The *yunkers* of the Officers' Schools of Pavlovsk, Tsarskoye Selo Peterhof ordered by the Government to be ready to come to Petrograd. Oranienbaum *yunkers* arrive in the city.
> Part of the Armored Car Division of the Petrograd garrison stationed in the Winter Palace.
> Upon orders signed by Trotsky, several thousand rifles delivered by the Government Arms Factory at Sestroretzk to delegates of the Petrograd workmen.
> At a meeting of the City Militia of the Lower Liteiny Quarter, a resolution demanding that all power be given to the Soviets.

This is just a sample of the confused events of those feverish days when everybody knew that something was going to happen, but nobody knew just what.

At a meeting of the Petrograd Soviet in Smolny, the night of 30 October, Trotsky branded the assertions of the bourgeois press that the Soviet contemplated armed insurrection as "an attempt of the reactionaries to discredit and wreck the Congress of Soviets. . . . The Petrograd Soviet," he declared, "had not ordered any *vystuplenie*. If it is necessary we shall do so, and we will be supported by the Petrograd garrison. . . . They [the Government] are preparing a counter-revolution; and we shall answer with an offensive which will be merciless and decisive."

It is true that the Petrograd Soviet had not ordered a demonstration, but the Central Committee of the Bolshevik party was considering the question of insurrection. All night long the twenty-third they met. There were present all the party intellectuals, the leaders—and delegates of the Petrograd workers and garrison.* Alone of the intellectuals Lenin and Trotsky stood for insurrection. Even the military men opposed it. A vote was taken. Insurrection was defeated!

Then arose a rough workman, his face convulsed with rage. "I speak for the Petrograd proletariat," he said harshly. "We are in favor of insurrection. Have it your own way, but I tell you now that if you allow the Soviets to be destroyed, *we're through with you!*" Some soldiers joined him. . . . And after that they voted again—insurrection won. . . .

However, the right wing of the Bolsheviki, led by Riazanov, Kameniev, and Zinoviev, continued to campaign against an armed rising. On the morning of 31 October appeared in *Rabochi Put* the first instalment of Lenin's "Letter to the Comrades,"[16] one of the most audacious pieces of political propaganda the world has ever seen. In it Lenin seriously presented the arguments in favor of insurrection, taking as text the objections of Kameniev and Riazanov.

"Either we must abandon our slogan, 'All Power to the Soviets,'" he wrote, "or else we must make an insurrection. There is no middle course. . . ."

That same afternoon Paul Milyukov, leader of the Cadets, made a brilliant, bitter speech[17] in the Council of the Republic, branding the Skobeliev *nakaz* as pro-German, declaring that the "revolutionary democracy" was destroying Russia, sneering at Tereshchenko, and openly declaring that he preferred German diplomacy to Russian. . . . The Left benches were one roaring tumult all through. . . .

On its part the Government could not ignore the significance of the success of the Bolshevik propaganda. On the twenty-ninth

---

*John Reed's facts are not quite accurate here. The Central Committee decided in principle on an insurrection by a large majority (10–2), without any such intervention of outside delegates.—Ed.

a joint commission of the Government and the Council of the Republic hastily drew up two laws, one for giving the land temporarily to the peasants, and the other for pushing an energetic foreign policy of peace. The next day Kerensky suspended capital punishment in the army. That same afternoon was opened with great ceremony the first session of the new "Commission for Strengthening the Republican Régime and Fighting Against Anarchy and Counter-Revolution"—of which history shows not the slightest further trace. . . . The following morning with two other correspondents I interviewed Kerensky[18]—the last time he received journalists.

"The Russian people," he said bitterly, "are suffering from economic fatigue—and from disillusionment with the Allies! The world thinks that the Russian Revolution is at an end. Do not be mistaken. The Russian Revolution is just beginning. . . ." Words more prophetic, perhaps, than he knew.

Stormy was the all-night meeting of the Petrograd Soviet the thirtieth of October, at which I was present. The "moderate" Socialist intellectuals, officers, members of Army Committees, the Tsay-ee-kah, were there in force. Against them rose up workmen, peasants, and common soldiers, passionate and simple.

A peasant told of the disorders in Tver, which he said were caused by the arrest of the Land Committees. "This Kerensky is nothing but a shield to the *pomieshchiki* (landowners)," he cried. "They know that at the Constituent Assembly we will take the land anyway, so they are trying to destroy the Constituent Assembly!"

A machinist from the Putilov works described how the superintendents were closing down the departments one by one on the pretext that there was no fuel or raw materials. The Factory-Shop Committee, he declared, had discovered huge hidden supplies.

"It is a *provocatzia*," said he. "They want to starve us—or drive us to violence!"

Among the soldiers one began, "Comrades! I bring you greetings from the place where men are digging their graves and call them trenches!"

Then arose a tall, gaunt young soldier, with flashing eyes, met with a roar of welcome. It was Chudnovsky, reported killed in the July fighting, and now risen from the dead.

"The soldier masses no longer trust their officers. Even the Army Committees, who refused to call a meeting of our Soviet, betrayed us. . . . The masses of the soldiers want the Constituent Assembly to be held exactly when it was called for, and those who dare to postpone it will be cursed—and not only platonic curses either, for the Army has guns too. . . ."

He told of the electoral campaign for the Constituent Assembly now raging in the Fifth Army. "The officers, and especially the Mensheviki and the Socialist Revolutionaries, are trying deliberately to cripple the Bolsheviki. Our papers are not allowed to circulate in the trenches. Our speakers are arrested—"

"Why don't you speak about the lack of bread?" shouted another soldier.

"Man shall not live by bread alone," answered Chudnovsky, sternly. . . .

Followed him an officer, delegate from the Vitebsk Soviet, a Menshevik *oboronets*. "It isn't the question of who has the power. The trouble is not with the Government, but with the war . . . and the war must be won before any change—" At this hoots and ironical cheers. "These Bolshevik agitators are demagogues!" The hall rocked with laughter. "Let us for a moment forget the class struggle—" But he got no farther. A voice yelled, "Don't you wish we would!"

PETROGRAD presented a curious spectacle in those days. In the factories the committee-rooms were filled with stacks of rifles, couriers came and went, the Red Guard* drilled. . . . In all the barracks meetings every night, and all day long interminable hot arguments. On the streets the crowds thickened toward gloomy evening, pouring in slow voluble tides up and down the Nevsky, fighting for the newspapers. . . . Hold-ups increased to such an extent that it was dangerous to walk down side streets. . . . On the Sadovaya one afternoon I saw a crowd of several hundred people

*See Notes and Explanations.

beat and trample to death a soldier caught stealing. . . . Mysterious individuals circulated around the shivering women who waited in queue long cold hours for bread and milk, whispering that the Jews had cornered the food supply—and that while the people starved, the Soviet members lived luxuriously. . . .

At Smolny there were strict guards at the door and the outer gates, demanding everybody's pass. The committee-rooms buzzed and hummed all day and all night, hundreds of soldiers and workmen slept on the floor, wherever they could find room. Upstairs in the great hall a thousand people crowded to the uproarious sessions of the Petrograd Soviet. . . .

Gambling clubs functioned hectically from dusk to dawn, with champagne flowing and stakes of twenty thousand roubles. In the center of the city at night prostitutes in jewels and expensive furs walked up and down, crowded the cafés. . . .

Monarchist plots, German spies, smugglers hatching schemes. . . .

And in the rain, the bitter chill, the great throbbing city under gray skies rushing faster and faster toward—what?

# 3

# On the Eve

In the relations of a weak Government and a rebellious people there comes a time when every act of the authorities exasperates the masses, and every refusal to act excites their contempt. . . .

The proposal to abandon Petrograd raised a hurricane; Kerensky's public denial that the Government had any such intentions was met with hoots of derision.

> Pinned to the wall by the pressure of the Revolution [cried *Rabochi Put*], the Government of "provisional" bourgeois tried to get free by giving out lying assurances that it never thought of fleeing from Petrograd, and that it didn't wish to surrender the capital. . . .

In Kharkov thirty thousand coal miners organized, adopting the preamble of the I.W.W. constitution: "The working class and the employing class have nothing in common." Dispersed by Cossacks, some were locked out by the mine-owners, and the rest declared a general strike. Minister of Commerce and Industry Konovalov appointed his assistant, Orlov, with plenary powers, to settle the trouble. Orlov was hated by the miners. But the Tsay-ee-kah not only supported his appointment, but refused to demand that the Cossacks be recalled from the Don Basin. . . .

This was followed by the dispersal of the Soviet at Kaluga. The Bolsheviki, having secured a majority in the Soviet, set free some political prisoners. With the sanction of the Government Commissar the Municipal Duma called in troops from Minsk, and bombarded the Soviet headquarters with artillery. The Bolsheviki yielded, but as they left the building Cossacks attacked them, crying, "This is what we'll do to all the other Bolshevik Soviets, including those of Moscow and Petrograd!" This incident sent a wave of panic rage throughout Russia. . . .

In Petrograd was ending a regional Congress of Soviets of the North, presided over by the Bolshevik Krylenko. By an immense majority it resolved that all power should be assumed by the All-Russian Congress; and concluded by greeting the Bolsheviki in prison, bidding them rejoice, for the hour of their liberation was at hand. At the same time the first All-Russian Conference of Factory-Shop Committees[19] declared emphatically for the Soviets, and continued significantly:

> After liberating themselves politically from Czardom, the working class wants to see the democratic régime triumphant in the sphere of its productive activity. This is best expressed by Workers' Control over industrial production, which naturally arose in the atmosphere of economic decomposition created by the criminal policy of the dominating classes. . . .

The Union of Railwaymen was demanding the resignation of Liverovsky, Minister of Ways and Communications. . . .

In the name of the Tsay-ee-kah, Skobeliev insisted that the *nakaz* be presented at the Allied Conference, and formally protested against the sending of Tereshchenko to Paris. Tereshchenko offered to resign. . . .

General Verkhovsky, unable to accomplish his reorganization of the army, only came to Cabinet meetings at long intervals. . . .

On 3 November Burtzev's *Obshchee Dielo* came out with great headlines:

> Citizens! Save the fatherland!
> I have just learned that yesterday, at a meeting of the Commission for National Defense, Minister of War, General Verkhovsky, one of the principal persons responsible for the fall of Kornilov, proposed to sign a separate peace, independently of the Allies.
> That is treason to Russia!
> Tereshchenko declared that the Provisional Government had not even examined Verkhovsky's proposition.

"You might think," said Tereshchenko, "that we were in a madhouse!"

The members of the Commission were astounded at the General's words.

General Alexeyev wept.

No! It is not madness! It is worse. It is direct treason to Russia! Kerensky, Tereshchenko, and Nekrassov must immediately answer us concerning the words of Verkhovsky.

Citizens, arise!

Russia is being sold!

Save her!

What Verkhovsky really said was that the Allies must be pressed to offer peace, because the Russian army could fight no longer. . . .

Both in Russia and abroad the sensation was tremendous. Verkhovsky was given "indefinite leave of absence for ill-health," and left the Government. *Obshchee Dielo* was suppressed. . . .

Sunday, 4 November, was designated as the day of the Petrograd Soviet, with immense meetings planned all over the city, ostensibly to raise money for the organization and the press; really, to make a demonstration of strength. Suddenly it was announced that on the same day the Cossacks would hold a *Krestni Khod*— Procession of the Cross—in honor of the Ikon of 1612, through whose miraculous intervention Napoleon had been driven from Moscow. The atmosphere was electric; a spark might kindle civil war. The Petrograd Soviet issued a manifesto, headed "Brothers—Cossacks!"

> You, Cossacks, are being incited against us, workers and soldiers. This plan of Cain is being put into operation by our common enemies the oppressors, the privileged classes—generals, bankers, landlords, former officials, former servants of the Czar. . . . We are hated by all grafters, rich men, princes, nobles, generals, including your Cossack generals. They are ready at any moment to destroy the Petrograd Soviet and crush the Revolution. . . .
>
> On the fourth of November somebody is organizing a Cossack religious procession. It is a question of the free consciousness of every individual whether he will or will not take part in this procession. We do not interfere in this matter, nor do we obstruct anybody. . . . How-

ever, we warn you, Cossacks! Look out and see to it that under the pretext of a *Krestni Khod*, your Kaledins do not instigate you against workmen, against soldiers. . . .

The procession was hastily called off. . . .

In the barracks and the working-class quarters of the town the Bolsheviki were preaching, "All Power to the Soviets!" and agents of the Dark Forces were urging the people to rise and slaughter the Jews, shopkeepers, Socialist leaders. . . .

On one side the Monarchist press, inciting to bloody repression—on the other Lenin's great voice roaring, "Insurrection! . . . We cannot wait any longer!"

Even the bourgeois press was uneasy.[20] *Birzhevya Viedomosti* (Exchange Gazette) called the Bolshevik propaganda an attack on "the most elementary principles of society—personal security, and the respect for private property."

But it was the "moderate" Socialist journals which were the most hostile.[21] "The Bolsheviki are the most dangerous enemies of the Revolution," declared *Dielo Naroda*. Said the Menshevik *Dien*, "The Government ought to defend itself and defend us." Plekhanov's paper, *Yedinstvo* (Unity),[22] called the attention of the Government to the fact that the Petrograd workers were being armed, and demanded stern measures against the Bolsheviki.

Daily the Government seemed to become more helpless. Even the Municipal administration broke down. The columns of the morning papers were filled with accounts of the most audacious robberies and murders, and the criminals were unmolested.

On the other hand, armed workers patroled the streets at night, doing battle with marauders and requisitioning arms wherever they found them.

On the first of November Colonel Polkovnikov, Military Commander of Petrograd, issued a proclamation:

> Despite the difficult days through which the country is passing, irresponsible appeals to armed demonstrations and massacres are still being spread around Petrograd, and from day to day robbery and disorder increase.
>
> This state of things is disorganizing the life of the citizens, and

hinders the systematic work of the Government and the Municipal Institutions.

In full consciousness of my responsibility and my duty before my country, I command:

1. Every military unit, in accordance with special instructions and within the territory of its garrison, to afford every assistance to the Municipality, to the Commissars, and to the militia, in the guarding of Government institutions.

2. The organization of patrols, in cooperation with the District Commander and the representatives of the city militia, and the taking of measures for the arrest of criminals and deserters.

3. The arrest of all persons entering barracks and inciting to armed demonstrations and massacres, and their delivery to the headquarters of the Second Commander of the city.

4. To suppress any armed demonstration or riot at its start, with all armed forces at hand.

5. To afford assistance to the Commissars in preventing unwarranted searches in houses and unwarranted arrests.

6. To report immediately all that happens in the district under charge of the Staff of the Petrograd Military District.

I call upon all Army Committees and organizations to afford their help to the commanders in fulfillment of the duties with which they are charged.

In the Council of the Republic Kerensky declared that the Government was fully aware of the Bolshevik preparations, and had sufficient force to cope with any demonstration.[23] He accused *Novaya Rus* and *Rabochi Put* of both doing the same kind of subversive work. "But owing to the absolute freedom of the press," he added, "the Government is not in a position to combat printed lies. . . ."* Declaring that these were two aspects of the same propaganda, which had for its objects the counter-revolution, so ardently desired by the Dark Forces, he went on:

"I am a doomed man, it doesn't matter what happens to me, and I have the audacity to say that the other enigmatic part is that of the unbelievable provocation created in the city by the Bolsheviki!"

On 2 November, only fifteen delegates to the Congress of

---

*This was not quite candid. The Provisional Government had suppressed Bolshevik papers before, in July, and was planning to do so again.

Soviets had arrived. Next day there were a hundred, and the morning after that a hundred and seventy-five, of whom one hundred and three were Bolsheviki. . . . Four hundred constituted a quorum, and the Congress was only three days off. . . .

I spent a great deal of time at Smolny. It was no longer easy to get in. Double rows of sentries guarded the outer gates, and once inside the front door there was a long line of people waiting to be let in, four at a time, to be questioned as to their identity and their business. Passes were given out, and the pass system was changed every few hours; for spies continually sneaked through. . . .

One day as I came up to the outer gate I saw Trotsky and his wife just ahead of me. They were halted by a soldier. Trotsky searched through his pockets, but could find no pass.

"Never mind," he said finally. "You know me. My name is Trotsky."

"You haven't got a pass," answered the soldier stubbornly. "You cannot go in. Names don't mean anything to me."

"But I am the president of the Petrograd Soviet."

"Well," replied the soldier, "if you're as important a fellow as that you must at least have one little paper."

Trotsky was very patient. "Let me see the Commandant," he said. The soldier hesitated, grumbling something about not wanting to disturb the Commandant for every devil that came along. He beckoned finally to the soldier in command of the guard. Trotsky explained matters to him. "My name is Trotsky," he repeated.

"Trotsky?" The other soldier scratched his head. "I've heard the name somewhere," he said at length. "I guess it's all right. You can go on in, comrade. . . ."

In the corridor I met Karakhan, member of the Bolshevik Central Committee, who explained to me what the new Government would be like.

"A loose organization, sensitive to the popular will as expressed through the Soviets, allowing local forces full play. At present the Provisional Government obstructs the action of the local democratic will, just as the Czar's Government did. The initiative of the new society shall come from below. . . . The form of the Gov-

ernment will be modeled on the Constitution of the Russian Social Democratic Labor Party. The new Tsay-ee-kah, responsible
to frequent meetings of the All-Russian Congress of Soviets, will
be the parliament; the various Ministries will be headed by *col-
legia*—committees—instead of by Ministers, and will be directly
responsible to the Soviets. . . ."

On 30 October, by appointment, I went up to a small bare
room in the attic of Smolny, to talk with Trotsky. In the middle of
the room he sat on a rough chair at a bare table. Few questions
from me were necessary; he talked rapidly for more than an hour.
The substance of his talk, in his own words, I give here:

"The Provisional Government is absolutely powerless. The
bourgeoisie is in control, but this control is masked by a fictitious
coalition with the *oborontsi* parties. Now, during the Revolution,
one sees revolts of peasants who are tired of waiting for their
promised land; and all over the country, in all the toiling classes,
the same disgust is evident. This domination by the bourgeoisie is
only possible by means of civil war. The Kornilov method is the
only way by which the bourgeoisie can control. But it is force
which the bourgeoisie lacks. . . . The Army is with us. The conciliators and pacifists, Socialist Revolutionaries, and Mensheviki,
have lost all authority—because the struggle between the peasants and the landlords, between the workers and the employers,
between the soldiers and the officers, has become more bitter,
more irreconcilable than ever. Only by the concerted action of
the popular mass, only by the victory of proletarian dictatorship,
can the Revolution be achieved and the people saved. . . .

"The Soviets are the most perfect representatives of the people—perfect in their revolutionary experience, in their ideas and
objects. Based directly upon the army in the trenches, the workers
in the factories, and the peasants in the fields, they are the back-
bone of the Revolution.

"There has been an attempt to create a power without the
Soviets—and only powerlessness has been created. Counter-revolutionary schemes of all sorts are now being hatched in the corridors of the Council of the Russian Republic. The Cadet party
represents the counter-revolution militant. On the other side, the

Soviets represent the cause of the people. Between the two camps there are no groups of serious importance. . . . It is the *lutte finale.* The bourgeois counter-revolution organizes all its forces and waits for the moment to attack us. Our answer will be decisive. We will complete the work scarcely begun in March, and advanced during the Kornilov affair. . . ."

He went on to speak of the new Government's foreign policy:

"Our first act will be to call for an immediate armistice on all fronts, and a conference of peoples to discuss democratic peace terms. The quantity of democracy we get in the peace settlement depends on the quantity of revolutionary response there is in Europe. If we create here a Government of the Soviets, that will be a powerful factor for immediate peace in Europe; for this Government will address itself directly and immediately to all peoples, over the heads of their Governments, proposing an armistice. At the moment of the conclusion of peace the pressure of the Russian Revolution will be in the direction of 'no annexations, no indemnities, the right of self-determination of peoples,' and a *Federated Republic of Europe.* . . .

"At the end of this war I see Europe re-created, not by the diplomats, but by the proletariat. The Federated Republic of Europe—the United States of Europe—that is what must be. National autonomy no longer suffices. Economic evolution demands the abolition of national frontiers. If Europe is to remain split into national groups, then Imperialism will recommence its work. Only a Federated Republic of Europe can give peace to the world." He smiled—that fine, faintly ironical smile of his. "But without the action of the European masses, these ends cannot be realized—now. . . ."

Now while everybody was waiting for the Bolsheviki to appear suddenly on the streets one morning and begin to shoot down people with white collars on, the real insurrection took its way quite naturally and openly.

The Provisional Government planned to send the Petrograd garrison to the front.

The Petrograd garrison numbered about sixty thousand men,

who had taken a prominent part in the Revolution. It was they who had turned the tide in the great days of March, created the Soviets of Soldiers' Deputies, and hurled back Kornilov from the gates of Petrograd.

Now a large part of them were Bolsheviki. When the Provisional Government talked of evacuating the city, it was the Petrograd garrison which answered, "If you are not capable of defending the capital, conclude peace; if you cannot conclude peace, go away and make room for a People's Government which can do both. . . ."

It was evident that any attempt at insurrection depended upon the attitude of the Petrograd garrison. The Government's plan was to replace the garrison regiments with "dependable" troops—Cossacks, Death Battalions. The Army Committee, the "moderate" Socialists and the Tsay-ee-kah supported the Government. A widespread agitation was carried on at the front and in Petrograd, emphasizing the fact that for eight months the Petrograd garrison had been leading an easy life in the barracks of the capital, while their exhausted comrades in the trenches starved and died.

Naturally there was some truth in the accusation that the garrison regiments were reluctant to exchange their comparative comfort for the hardships of a winter campaign. But there were other reasons why they refused to go. The Petrograd Soviet feared the Government's intentions, and from the front came hundreds of delegates, chosen by the common soldiers, crying, "It is true we need reinforcements, but more important, we must know that Petrograd and the Revolution are well guarded. . . . Do you hold the rear, comrades, and we will hold the front!"

On 25 October, behind closed doors, the Central Committee of the Petrograd Soviet discussed the formation of a special Military Committee to decide the whole question. The next day a meeting of the Soldiers' Section of the Petrograd Soviet elected a Committee, which immediately proclaimed a boycott of the bourgeois newspapers, and condemned the Tsay-ee-kah for opposing the Congress of Soviets. On the twenty-ninth, in open session of the Petrograd Soviet, Trotsky proposed that the Soviet formally sanction the Military Revolutionary Committee. "We ought," he said, "to create our special organization to march to battle, and if necessary to die. . . ." It was decided to send to the front two delegations, one from the Soviet and one from the garrison, to confer with the Soldiers' Committees and the General Staff.

At Pskov, the Soviet delegates were met by General Cheremissov, commander of the Northern Front, with the curt declaration that he had ordered the Petrograd garrison to the trenches, and that was all. The garrison committee was not allowed to leave Petrograd. . . .

A delegation of the Soldiers' Section of the Petrograd Soviet asked that a representative be admitted to the Staff of the Petrograd District. Refused. The Petrograd Soviet demanded that no orders be issued without the approval of the Soldiers' Section. Refused. The delegates were roughly told, "We only recognize the Tsay-ee-kah. We do not recognize you; if you break any laws we shall arrest you."

On the thirtieth a meeting of representatives of all the Petrograd regiments passed a resolution: *"The Petrograd garrison no longer recognizes the Provisional Government. The Petrograd Soviet is our Government. We will obey only the orders of the Petrograd Soviet, through the Military Revolutionary Committee."* The local military units were ordered to wait for instructions from the Soldiers' Section of the Petrograd Soviet.

Next day the Tsay-ee-kah summoned its own meeting, composed largely of officers, formed a Committee to cooperate with the Staff, and detailed Commissars in all quarters of the city.

A great soldier meeting at Smolny on the third resolved:

> Saluting the creation of the Military Revolutionary Committee, the Petrograd garrison promises it complete support in all its actions, to unite more closely the front and the rear in the interests of the Revolution.
>
> The garrison, moreover, declares that with the revolutionary proletariat it assures the maintenance of revolutionary order in Petrograd. Every attempt at provocation on the part of the Kornilovtsi or the bourgeoisie will be met with merciless resistance.

Now conscious of its power, the Military Revolutionary Committee peremptorily summoned the Petrograd Staff to submit to its control. To all printing plants it gave orders not to publish any appeals or proclamations without the Committee's authorization. Armed Commissars visited the Kronversk arsenal and seized great quantities of arms and ammunition, halting a shipment of ten thousand bayonets which was being sent to Novocherkask, headquarters of Kaledin. . . .

Suddenly awake to the danger, the Government offered immunity if the Committee would disband. Too late. At midnight, 5 November, Kerensky himself sent Malevsky to offer the Petrograd Soviet representation on the Staff. The Military Revolutionary Committee accepted. An hour later General Manikovsky, acting Minister of War, countermanded the offer. . . .

Tuesday morning, 6 November, the city was thrown into excitement by the appearance of a placard signed, "Military Revolutionary Committee attached to the Petrograd Soviet of Workers' and Soldiers' Deputies."

> To the Population of Petrograd. Citizens!
> Counter-revolution has raised its criminal head. The Kornilovtsi are mobilizing their forces in order to crush the All-Russian Congress of Soviets and break the Constituent Assembly. At the same time the *pogromists* may attempt to call upon the people of Petrograd for trouble and bloodshed. The Petrograd Soviet of Workers' and Soldiers' Deputies takes upon itself the guarding of revolutionary order in the city against counter-revolutionary and *pogrom* attempts.
> The Petrograd garrison will not allow any violence or disorders. The population is invited to arrest hooligans and Black Hundred agitators and take them to the Soviet Commissars at the nearest barracks. At the first attempt of the Dark Forces to make trouble on the streets of Petrograd, whether robbery or fighting, the criminals will be wiped off the face of the earth!
> Citizens! We call upon you to maintain complete quiet and self-possession. The cause of order and Revolution is in strong hands.
> Lists of regiments where there are Commissars of the Military Revolutionary Committee. . . .

On the third the leaders of the Bolsheviki had another historic meeting behind closed doors. Notified by Zalkind, I waited in the corridor outside the door; and Volodarsky as he came out told me what was going on.

Lenin spoke: "November sixth will be too early. We must have an all-Russian basis for the rising; and on the sixth all the delegates to the Congress will not have arrived. . . . On the other hand, November eighth will be too late. By that time the Congress will be organized, and it is difficult for a large organized body of people to take swift, decisive action. We must act on the seventh, the day the Congress meets, so that we may say to it, 'Here is the power! What are you going to do with it?' "

In a certain upstairs room sat a thin-faced, long-haired individual, once an officer in the armies of the Czar, then revolutionist and exile, a certain Avseenko, called Antonov, mathematician and chess-player; he was drawing careful plans for the seizure of the capital.

On its side the Government was preparing. Inconspicuously, certain of the most loyal regiments, from widely separated divisions, were ordered to Petrograd. The *yunker* artillery was drawn into the Winter Palace. Patrols of Cossacks made their appearance in the streets for the first time since the July days. Polkovnikov issued order after order, threatening to repress all insubordination with the "utmost energy." Kishkin, Minister of Public Instruction, the worst-hated member of the Cabinet, was appointed Special Commissar to keep order in Petrograd; he named as assistants two men no less unpopular, Rutenburg and Palchinsky. Petrograd, Kronstadt, and Finland were declared in a state of siege—upon which the bourgeois *Novoye Vremya* (New Times) remarked ironically:

> Why the state of siege? The Government is no longer a power. It has no moral authority and it does not possess the necessary apparatus to use force. . . . In the most favorable circumstances it can only negotiate with anyone who consents to parley. Its authority goes no farther. . . .

Monday morning, the fifth, I dropped in at the Marinsky Palace, to see what was happening in the Council of the Russian Republic. Bitter debate on Tereshchenko's foreign policy. Echoes of the Burtzev-Verkhovsky affair. All the diplomats present except the Italian ambassador, who everybody said was prostrated by the Carso disaster. . . .

As I came in the Left Socialist Revolutionary Karelin was reading aloud an editorial from the London *Times*, which said, "The remedy for Bolshevism is bullets!" Turning to the Cadets he cried, "That's what *you* think, too!"

Voices from the Right, "Yes! Yes!"

"Yes, I know you think so," answered Karelin, hotly. "But you haven't the courage to try it!"

Then Skobeliev, looking like a matinée idol with his soft blond beard and wavy yellow hair, rather apologetically defended the Soviet *nakaz*. Tereshchenko followed, assailed from the Left by cries of "Resignation! Resignation!" He insisted that the delegates of the Government and of the Tsay-ee-kah to Paris should have a common point of view—his own. A few words about the restoration of discipline in the army, about war to victory. . . . Tumult, and over the stubborn opposition of the truculent Left, the Council of the Republic passed to the simple order of the day.

There stretched the rows of Bolshevik seats—empty since that first day when they left the Council, carrying with them so much life. As I went down the stairs it seemed to me that in spite of the bitter wrangling, no real voice from the rough world outside could penetrate this high, cold hall, and that the Provisional Government was wrecked—on the same rock of War and Peace that had wrecked the Miliukov Ministry. . . . The doorman grumbled as he put on my coat, "I don't know what is becoming of poor Russia. All these Mensheviki and Bolsheviki and Trudoviki. . . . This Ukraine and this Finland and the German imperialists and the English imperialists. I am forty-five years old, and in all my life I never heard so many words as in this place. . . ."

In the corridor I met Professor Shatsky, a rat-faced individual in a dapper frock-coat, very influential in the councils of the Cadet party. I asked him what he thought of the much-talked-of Bolshevik *vystuplenie*. He shrugged, sneering.

"They are cattle—*canaille*," he answered. "They will not dare, or if they dare they will soon be sent flying. From our point of view it will not be bad, for then they will ruin themselves and have no power in the Constituent Assembly. . . .

"But, my dear sir, allow me to outline to you my plan for a form of Government to be submitted to the Constituent Assembly. You see, I am chairman of a commission appointed from this body, in conjunction with the Provisional Government, to work out a constitutional project. . . . We will have a legislative assembly of two chambers, such as you have in the United States. In the lower chamber will be territorial representatives; in the upper, representatives of the liberal professions, zemstvos, Cooperatives—and Trade Unions. . . ."

Outside a chill, damp wind came from the west, and the cold mud underfoot soaked through my shoes. Two companies of *yunkers* passed swinging up the Morskaya, tramping stiffly in their long coats and singing an old-time crashing chorus, such as soldiers used to sing under the Czar. . . . At the first cross-street I noticed that the City Militiamen were mounted, and armed with revolvers in bright new holsters; a little group of people stood silently staring at them. At the corner of the Nevsky I bought a pamphlet by Lenin, *Will the Bolsheviki be Able to Hold the Power?* paying for it with one of the stamps which did duty for small change. The usual streetcars crawled past, citizens and soldiers clinging to the outside in a way to make Theodore P. Shonts green with envy. . . . Along the sidewalk a row of deserters in uniform sold cigarettes and sunflower seeds. . . .

Up the Nevsky in the sour twilight crowds were battling for the latest papers, and knots of people were trying to make out the multitudes of appeal[24] and proclamations pasted in every flat place; from the Tsay-ee-kah, the Peasants' Soviets, the "moderate" Socialist parties, the Army Committees—threatening, cursing, beseeching the workers and soldiers to stay home, to support the Government. . . .

An armored automobile went slowly up and down, siren screaming. On every corner, in every open space, thick groups were clustered; arguing soldiers and students. Night came swiftly down, the wide-spaced street-lights flickered on, the tides of people flowed endlessly. . . . It is always like that in Petrograd just before trouble. . . .

The city was nervous, starting at every sharp sound. But still no sign from the Bolsheviki; the soldiers stayed in the barracks, the workmen in the factories. . . . We went to a moving picture show near the Kazan Cathedral—a bloody Italian film of passion and intrigue. Down front were some soldiers and sailors, staring at the screen in child-like wonder, totally unable to comprehend why there should be so much violent running about, and so much homicide. . . .

From there I hurried to Smolny. In room 10 on the top floor, the Military Revolutionary Committee sat in continuous session, under the chairmanship of a tow-headed, eighteen-year-old boy named Lazimir. He stopped, as he passed, to shake hands rather bashfully.

"Peter-Paul Fortress has just come over to us," said he, with a pleased grin. "A minute ago we got word from a regiment that was ordered by the Government to come to Petrograd. The men were suspicious, so they stopped the train at Gatchina and sent a delegation to us. 'What's the matter?' they asked. 'What have you got to say? We have just passed a resolution, "All Power to the Soviets." ' . . . The Military Revolutionary Committee sent back word. 'Brothers! We greet you in the name of the Revolution. Stay where you are until further instructions!' "

All telephones, he said, were cut off: but communication with the factories and barracks was established by means of military telephonograph apparatus. . . .

A steady stream of couriers and Commissars came and went. Outside the door waited a dozen volunteers, ready to carry word to the farthest quarters of the city. One of them, a gypsy-faced man in the uniform of a lieutenant, said in French, "Everything is ready to move at the push of a button. . . ."

There passed Podvoisky, the thin, bearded civilian whose brain conceived the strategy of insurrection; Antonov, unshaven, his collar filthy, drunk with loss of sleep; Krylenko, the squat, wide-faced soldier, always smiling, with his violent gestures and tumbling speech; and Dybenko, the giant bearded sailor with the placid face. These were the men of the hour—and of other hours to come.

Downstairs in the office of the Factory-Shop Committees sat Seratov, signing orders on the Government Arsenal for arms—one hundred and fifty rifles for each factory. . . . Delegates waited in line, forty of them. . . .

In the hall I ran into some of the minor Bolshevik leaders. One showed me a revolver. "The game is on," he said, and his face was pale. "Whether we move or not, the other side knows it must finish us or be finished. . . ."

The Petrograd Soviet was meeting day and night. As I came into the great hall Trotsky was just finishing.

"We are asked," he said, "if we intend to have a *vystuplenie*. I can give a clear answer to that question. The Petrograd Soviet feels that at last the moment has arrived when the power must fall into the hands of the Soviets. This transfer of government will be accomplished by the All-Russian Congress. Whether an armed demonstration is necessary will depend on . . . those who wish to interfere with the All-Russian Congress. . . .

"We feel that our Government, entrusted to the personnel of the Provisional Cabinet, is a pitiful and helpless Government, which only awaits the sweep of the broom of History to give way to a really popular Government. But we are trying to avoid a conflict, even now, today. We hope that the All-Russian Congress will take . . . into its hands that power and authority which rests upon the organized freedom of the people. If, however, the Government wants to utilize the short period it is expected to live—twenty-four, forty-eight, or seventy-two hours—to attack us, then we shall answer with counter-attacks, blow for blow, steel for iron!"

Amid cheers he announced that the Left Socialist Revolutionaries had agreed to send representatives into the Military Revolutionary Committee. . . .

As I left Smolny, at three o'clock in the morning, I noticed that two rapid-firing guns had been mounted, one on each side of the door, and that strong patrols of soldiers guarded the gates and the near-by street corners. Bill Shatov* came bounding up the steps. "Well," he cried, "we're off. Kerensky sent the *yunkers* to close down our papers, *Soldat* and *Rabochi Put*. But our troops went down and smashed the Government seals, and now we're sending detachments to seize the bourgeois newspaper offices!" Exultantly he slapped me on the shoulder, and ran in. . . .

On the morning of the sixth I had business with the censor, whose office was in the Ministry of Foreign Affairs. Everywhere, on all the walls, hysterical appeals to the people to remain "calm." Polkovnikov emitted *prikaz* after *prikaz:*

> I order all military units and detachments to remain in their barracks until further orders from the Staff of the Military District. . . . All officers who act without orders from their superiors will be court-martialled for mutiny. I forbid absolutely any execution by soldiers of instructions from other organizations. . . .

The morning paper announced that the Government had suppressed the papers *Novaya Rus, Zhivoye Slovo, Rabochi Put,* and *Soldat,* and decreed the arrest of the leaders of the Petrograd Soviet and the members of the Military Revolutionary Committee. . . .

As I crossed the Palace Square several batteries of *yunker* artillery came through the Red Arch at a jingling trot, and drew up before the Palace. The great red building of the General Staff was unusually animated, several armored automobiles ranked before the door, and motors full of officers were coming and going. . . . The censor was very much excited, like a small boy at a circus. Kerensky, he said, had just gone to the Council of the Republic to offer his resignation. I hurried down to the Marinsky Palace, arriving at the end of that passionate and almost incoherent speech of Kerensky's, full of self-justification and bitter denunciation of his enemies.

"I will cite here the most characteristic passage from a whole series of articles published in *Rabochi Put* by Ulyanov-Lenin, a state criminal who is in hiding and whom we are trying to find. . . . This state criminal has invited the proletariat and the

*Well known in the American labor movement.

Petrograd garrison to repeat the experience of 16–18 July, and insists upon the immediate necessity for an armed rising. . . . Moreover, other Bolshevik leaders have taken the floor in a series of meetings, and also made an appeal to immediate insurrection. Particularly should be noticed the activity of the present president of the Petrograd Soviet, Bronstein-Trotsky. . . .

"I ought to bring to your notice . . . that the expressions and the style of a whole series of articles in *Rabochi Put* and *Soldat* resemble absolutely those of *Novaya Rus.* . . . We have to do not so much with the movement of such and such political party, as with the exploitation of the political ignorance and criminal instincts of a part of the population, a sort of organization whose object it is to provoke in Russia, cost what it may, an inconscient movement of destruction and pillage; for, given the state of mind of the masses, any movement at Petrograd will be followed by the most terrible massacres, which will cover with eternal shame the name of free Russia. . . .

". . . By the admission of Ulyanov-Lenin himself, the situation of the extreme left wing of the Social-Democrats in Russia is very favorable."

Here Kerensky read the following quotation from Lenin's article:

> Think of it! . . . The German comrades have only one Liebknecht, without newspapers, without freedom of meeting, without a Soviet. . . . They are opposed by the incredible hostility of all classes of society—and yet the German comrades try to act; while we, having dozens of newspapers, freedom of meeting, the majority of the Soviets, we, the best-placed international proletarians of the entire world, can we refuse to support the German revolutionists and insurrectionary organizations? . . .

Kerensky then continued:

"The organizers of rebellion recognize thus implicitly that the most perfect conditions for the free action of a political party obtain now in Russia, administered by a Provisional Government, at the head of which is, in the eyes of this party, 'a usurper and a man who has sold himself to the bourgeoisie, the Minister-President Kerensky....'

"... The organizers of the insurrection do not come to the aid of the German proletariat, but of the German governing classes, and they open the Russian front to the iron fists of Wilhelm and his friends.... Little matter to the Provisional Government the motives of these people, little matter if they act consciously or unconsciously; but in any case, from this tribune, in full consciousness of my responsibility I qualify such acts of a Russian political party as acts of treason to Russia!

"... I place myself at the point of view of the Right, and I propose immediately to proceed to an investigation and make the necessary arrests." (Uproar from the Left.) "Listen to me!" he cried in a powerful voice. "At the moment when the state is in danger, because of conscious or unconscious treason, the Provisional Government, and myself among others, prefer to be killed rather than betray the life, the honor, and the independence of Russia...."

At this moment a paper was handed to Kerensky.

"I have just received the proclamation which they are distributing to the regiments. Here is the contents." Reading:

" 'The Petrograd Soviet of Workers' and Soldiers' Deputies is menaced. We order immediately the regiments to mobilize on a war footing and to await new orders. All delay or non-execution of this order will be considered as an act of treason to the Revolution. The Military Revolutionary Committee. For the President, Podvoisky. The Secretary, Antonov.'

"In reality this is an attempt to raise the populace against the existing order of things, to break the Constituent and to open the front to the regiments of the iron fist of Wilhelm....

"I say 'populace' intentionally, because the conscious democracy and its Tsay-ee-kah, all the Army organizations, all that free Russia glorifies, the good sense, the honor and the conscience of the great Russian democracy, protests against these things....

"I have not come here with a prayer, but to state my firm conviction that the Provisional Government, which defends at this moment our new liberty—that the new Russian state, destined to a brilliant future, will find unanimous support except among those who have never dared to face the truth. . . .

". . . The Provisional Government has never violated the liberty of all citizens of the State to use their political rights. . . . But now the Provisional Government . . . declares: in this moment those elements of the Russian nation, those groups and parties who have dared to lift their hands against the free will of the Russian people, at the same time threatening to open the front to Germany, must be liquidated with decision! . . .

"Let the population of Petrograd understand that it will encounter a firm power, and perhaps at the last moment good sense, conscience, and honor will triumph in the hearts of those who still possess them. . . ."

All through this speech the hall rang with deafening clamor. When the Minister-President had stepped down, pale-faced and wet with perspiration, and strode out with his suite of officers, speaker after speaker from the Left and Center attacked the Right, all one angry roaring. Even the Socialist Revolutionaries, through Gotz:

"The policy of the Bolsheviki is demagogic and criminal, in their exploitation of the popular discontent. But there is a whole series of popular demands which have received no satisfaction up to now. . . . The questions of peace, land, and the democratization of the army ought to be stated in such a fashion that no soldier, peasant, or worker would have the least doubt that our Government is attempting, firmly and infallibly, to solve them. . . .

"We Mensheviki do not wish to provoke a Cabinet crisis, and we are ready to defend the Provisional Government with all our energy, to the last drop of our blood—if only the Provisional Government, on all these burning questions, will speak the clear and precise words awaited by the people with such impatience. . . ."

Then Martov, furious:

"The words of the Minister-President, who allowed himself to speak of 'populace' when it is question of the movement of important sections of the proletariat and the army—although led in

the wrong direction—are nothing but an incitement to civil war."
The order of the day proposed by the Left was voted. It
amounted practically to a vote of lack of confidence:

1. The armed demonstration which has been preparing for some
days past has for its object a *coup d'état*, threatens to provoke civil war,
creates conditions favorable to *pogroms* and counter-revolution, the
mobilization of counter-revolutionary forces, such as the Black Hundreds, which will inevitably bring about the impossibility of convok-
ing the Constituent, will cause a military catastrophe, the death of the
Revolution, paralyze the economic life of the country and destroy
Russia;
2. The conditions favorable to this agitation have been created by
delay in passing urgent measures, as well as objective conditions
caused by the war and the general disorder. It is necessary before everything to promulgate at once a decree transmitting the land to the
peasants' Land Committees, and to adopt an energetic course of action abroad in proposing to the Allies to proclaim their peace terms
and to begin peace parleys;
3. To cope with Monarchist manifestations and *pogromist* movements it is indispensable to take immediate measures to suppress
these movements, and for this purpose to create at Petrograd a Committee of Public Safety, composed of representatives of the Municipality and the organs of the revolutionary democracy, acting in
contact with the Provisional Government. . . .

It is interesting to note that the Mensheviki and Socialist Revolutionaries all rallied to this resolution. . . . When Kerensky saw
it, however, he summoned Avksentiev to the Winter Palace to
explain. If it expressed a lack of confidence in the Provisional
Government, he begged Avksentiev to form a new Cabinet. Dan,
Gotz, and Avksentiev, the leaders of the "compromisers," performed their last compromise. . . . They explained to Kerensky
that it was not meant as a criticism of the Government!

At the corner of the Morskaya and the Nevsky, squads of soldiers with fixed bayonets were stopping all private automobiles,
turning out the occupants, and ordering them toward the Winter
Palace. A large crowd had gathered to watch them. Nobody knew
whether the soldiers belonged to the Government or the Military
Revolutionary Committee. Up in front of the Kazan Cathedral

the same thing was happening, machines being directed back up the Nevsky. Five or six sailors with rifles came along, laughing excitedly, and fell into conversation with two of the soldiers. On the sailors' hat bands were *Avrora* and *Zaria Svobody*—the names of the leading Bolshevik cruisers of the Baltic Fleet. One of them said, "Kronstadt is coming!" . . . It was as if, in 1792, on the streets of Paris, someone had said "The Marseillais are coming!" For at Kronstadt were twenty-five thousand sailors, convinced Bolsheviki and not afraid to die.

*Rabochi i Soldat* was just out, all its front page one huge proclamation:

### SOLDIERS! WORKERS! CITIZENS!

The enemies of the people passed last night to the offensive. The Kornilovists of the Staff are trying to draw in from the suburbs *yunkers* and volunteer battalions. The Oranienbaum *yunkers* and the Tsarskoye Selo volunteers refused to come out. A stroke of high treason is being contemplated against the Petrograd Soviet. . . . The campaign of the counter-revolutionists is being directed against the All-Russian Congress of Soviets on the eve of its opening, against the Constituent Assembly, against the people. The Petrograd Soviet is guarding the Revolution. The Military Revolutionary Committee is directing the repulse of the conspirators' attack. The entire garrison and proletariat of Petrograd are ready to deal the enemy of the people a crushing blow.

The Military Revolutionary Committee decrees:

1. All regimental, division, and battleship Committees, together with the Soviet Commissars, and all revolutionary organizations, shall meet in continuous session, concentrating in their hands all information about the plans of the conspirators.

2. Not one soldier shall leave his division without permission of the Committee.

3. To send to Smolny at once two delegates from each military unit and five from each Ward Soviet.

4. All members of the Petrograd Soviet and all delegates to the All-Russian Congress are invited immediately to Smolny for an extraordinary meeting.

Counter-revolution has raised its criminal head.

A great danger threatens all the conquests and hopes of the soldiers and workers.

But the forces of the Revolution by far exceed those of its enemies. The cause of the People is in strong hands. The conspirators will be crushed.

No hesitation or doubts! Firmness, steadfastness, discipline, determination!

Long live the Revolution!

*The Military Revolutionary Committee*

The Petrograd Soviet was meeting continuously at Smolny, a center of storm, delegates falling down asleep on the floor and rising again to take part in the debate, Trotsky, Kameniev, Volodarsky speaking six, eight, twelve hours a day. . . .

I went down to room 18 on the first floor where the Bolshevik delegates were holding caucus, a harsh voice steadily booming, the speaker hidden by the crowd: "The compromisers say that we are isolated. Pay no attention to them. Once it begins they must be dragged along with us, or else lose their following. . . ."

Here he held up a piece of paper. "We are dragging them! A message has just come from the Mensheviki and Socialist Revolutionaries! They say that they condemn our action, but that if the Government attacks us they will not oppose the cause of the proletariat!" Exultant shouting. . . .

As night fell the great hall filled with soldiers and workmen, a monstrous dun mass, deep-humming in a blue haze of smoke. The old Tsay-ee-kah had finally decided to welcome the delegates to that new Congress which would mean its own ruin—and perhaps the ruin of the revolutionary order it had built. At this meeting, however, only members of the Tsay-ee-kah could vote. . . .

It was after midnight when Gotz took the chair and Dan rose to speak, in a tense silence, which seemed to me almost menacing.

"The hours in which we live appear in the most tragic colors," he said. "The enemy is at the gates of Petrograd, the forces of the democracy are trying to organize to resist him, and yet we await bloodshed in the streets of the capital, and famine threatens to destroy, not only our homogeneous Government but the Revolution itself. . . .

"The masses are sick and exhausted. They have no interest in the Revolution. If the Bolsheviki start anything, that will be the end of the Revolution. . . ." (Cries, "That's a lie!") "The counter-revolutionists are waiting with the Bolsheviki to begin riots and massacres. . . . If there is any *vystuplenie*, there will be no Constituent Assembly. . . ." (Cries, "Lie! Shame!")

"It is inadmissible that in the zone of military operations the Petrograd garrison shall not submit to the orders of the Staff. . . . You must obey the orders of the Staff and of the Tsay-ee-kah elected by you. All Power to the Soviets—that means death! Robbers and thieves are waiting for the moment to loot and burn. . . . When you have such slogans put before you, 'Enter the houses, take away the shoes and clothes from the bourgeoisie—' " (Tumult. Cries, "No such slogan! A lie! A lie!") "Well, it may start differently, but it will end that way!

"The Tsay-ee-kah has full power to act, and must be obeyed. . . . We are not afraid of bayonets. . . . The Tsay-ee-kah will defend the Revolution with its body. . . ." (Cries, "It was a dead body long ago!")

Immense continued uproar, in which his voice could be heard screaming, as he pounded the desk, "Those who are urging this are committing a crime!"

Voice: "You committed a crime long ago, when you captured the power and turned it over to the bourgeoisie!"

Gotz, ringing the chairman's bell: "Silence, or I'll have you put out!"

Voice: "Try it!" (Cheers and whistling.)

"Now concerning our policy about peace." (Laughter.) "Unfortunately Russia can no longer support the continuation of the war. There is going to be peace, but not permanent peace—not a democratic peace. . . . Today, at the Council of the Republic, in order to avoid bloodshed, we passed an order of the day demanding the surrender of the land to the Land Committees and immediate peace negotiations. . . ." (Laughter, and cries, "Too late!")

Then for the Bolsheviki, Trotsky mounted the tribune, borne on a wave of roaring applause that burst into cheers and a rising

house, thunderous. His thin, pointed face was positively Mephis-
tophelian in its expression of malicious irony.

"Dan's tactics prove that the masses—the great, dull, indifferent masses—are absolutely with him!" (Titanic mirth.) He turned
toward the chairman, dramatically. "When we spoke of giving
the land to the peasants you were against it. We told the peasants,
'If they don't give it to you, take it yourselves!' and the peasants
followed our advice. And now you advocate what we did six
months ago. . . .

"I don't think Kerensky's order to suspend the death penalty
in the army was dictated by his ideals. I think Kerensky was
persuaded by the Petrograd garrison, which refused to obey
him. . . .

"Today Dan is accused of having made a speech in the Council
of the Republic which proves him to be a secret Bolshevik. . . .
The time may come when Dan will say that the flower of the Revolution participated in the rising of 16 and 18 July. . . . In Dan's
resolution today at the Council of the Republic there was no
mention of enforcing discipline in the army, although that is
urged into the propaganda of his party. . . .

"No. The history of the last seven months shows that the
masses have left the Mensheviki. The Mensheviki and the Socialist Revolutionaries conquered the Cadets, and then when they
got the power they gave it to the Cadets. . . .

"Dan tells you that you have no right to make an insurrection.
Insurrection is the right of all revolutionists! When the down-
trodden masses revolt it is their right. . . ."

Then the long-faced, cruel-tongued Lieber, greeted with
groans and laughter.

"Engels and Marx said that the proletariat had no right to take
power until it was ready for it. In a bourgeois revolution like this
. . . the seizure of power by the masses means the tragic end of the
Revolution. . . . Trotsky, as a Social-Democratic theorist, is himself opposed to what he is now advocating. . . ." (Cries, "Enough!
Down with him!")

Martov constantly interrupted: "The Internationalists are not opposed to the transmission of power to the democracy, but they disapprove of the methods of the Bolsheviki. This is not the moment to seize the power. . . ."

Again Dan took the floor, violently protesting against the action of the Military Revolutionary Committee, which had sent a Commissar to seize the office of *Izvestia* and censor the paper. The wildest uproar followed. Martov tried to speak, but could not be heard. Delegates of the Army and the Baltic Fleet stood up all over the hall, shouting that the Soviet was *their* Government. . . .

Amid the wildest confusion Ehrlich offered a resolution, appealing to the workers and soldiers to remain calm and not to respond to provocations to demonstrate, recognizing the necessity of immediately creating a Committee at once to pass decrees transferring the land to the peasants and beginning peace negotiations. . . .

Then up leaped Volodarsky, shouting harshly that the Tsay-ee-kah, on the eve of the Congress, had no right to assume the functions of the Congress. The Tsay-ee-kah was practically dead, he said, and the resolution was simply a trick to bolster up its waning power. . . .

"As for us, Bolsheviki, we will not vote on this resolution!" Whereupon all the Bolsheviki left the hall and the resolution was passed. . . .

Toward four in the morning I met Zorin in the outer hall, a rifle slung from his shoulder.

"We're moving!"[25] said he, calmly, but with satisfaction. "We pinched the Assistant Minister of Justice and the Minister of Religions. They're down cellar now. One regiment is on the march to capture the Telephone Exchange, another the Telegraph Agency, another the State Bank. The Red Guard is out. . . ."

On the steps of Smolny, in the chill dark, we first saw the Red Guard—a huddled group of boys in workmen's clothes, carrying guns with bayonets, talking nervously together.

Far over the still roofs westward came the sound of scattered rifle fire, where the *yunkers* were trying to open the bridges over the Neva, to prevent the factory workers and soldiers of the Viborg quarter from joining the Soviet forces in the center of the city; and the Kronstadt sailors were closing them again. . . .

Behind us great Smolny, bright with lights, hummed like a gigantic hive. . . .

# 4

# The Fall of the Provisional Government

W EDNESDAY, 7 November, I rose very late. The noon cannon boomed from Peter-Paul as I went down the Nevsky. It was a raw, chill day. In front of the State Bank some soldiers with fixed bayonets were standing at the closed gates.

"What side do you belong to?" I asked. "The Government?"

"No more Government," one answered with a grin. "*Slava Bogu!* Glory to God!" That was all I could get out of him. . . .

The street-cars were running on the Nevsky, men, women, and small boys hanging on every projection. Shops were open, and there seemed even less uneasiness among the street crowds than there had been the day before. A whole crop of new appeals against insurrection had blossomed out on the walls during the night—to the peasants, to the soldiers at the front, to the workmen of Petrograd. One read:

FROM THE PETROGRAD MUNICIPAL DUMA

The Municipal Duma informs the citizens that in the extraordinary meeting of 6 November the Duma formed a Committee of Public Safety, composed of members of the Central and Ward Dumas, and representatives of the following revolutionary democratic organizations: The Tsay-ee-kah, the All-Russian Executive Committee of Peasant Deputies, the Army organizations, the Tsentroflot, the Petrograd Soviet Workers' and Soldiers' Deputies (!), the Council of Trade Unions, and others.

Members of the Committee of Public Safety will be on duty in the building of the Municipal Duma. Telephones No. 15–40, 223–7, 138–36.

7 November 1917

654

Though I didn't realize it then, this was the Duma's declaration of war against the Bolsheviki.

I bought a copy of *Rabochi Put*, the only newspaper which seemed on sale, and a little later paid a soldier fifty kopeks for a second-hand copy of *Dien*. The Bolshevik paper, printed on large-sized sheets in the conquered office of the *Russkaya Volia*, had huge headlines: "ALL POWER—TO THE SOVIETS OF WORKERS, SOLDIERS, AND PEASANTS! PEACE! BREAD! LAND!" The leading article was signed "Zinoviev"—Lenin's companion in hiding. It began:

> Every soldier, every worker, every real Socialist, every honest democrat, realizes that there are only two alternatives to the present situation.
>
> Either—the power will remain in the hands of the bourgeois-landlord crew, and this will mean every kind of repression for the workers, soldiers, and peasants, continuation of the war, inevitable hunger and death. . . .
>
> Or—the power will be transferred to the hands of the revolutionary workers, soldiers, and peasants; in that case it will mean a complete abolition of landlord tyranny, immediate check of the capitalists, immediate proposal of a just peace. Then the land is assured to the peasants, then control of industry is assured to the workers, then bread is assured to the hungry, then the end of this nonsensical war! . . .

*Dien* contained fragmentary news of the agitated night. Bolsheviki capture of the Telephone Exchange, the Baltic station, the Telegraph Agency; the Peterhof *yunkers* unable to reach Petrograd; the Cossacks undecided; arrest of some of the Ministers; shooting of Chief of the City Militia Meyer; arrests, counter-arrests, skirmishes between clashing patrols of soldiers, *yunkers*, and Red Guards.[26]

On the corner of the Morskaya I ran into Captain Comberg, Menshevik *oboronets*, secretary of the Military Section of his party. When I asked him if the insurrection had really happened he shrugged his shoulders in a tired manner and replied, *"Chort znayet!* The devil knows! Well, perhaps the Bolsheviki can seize the power, but they won't be able to hold it more than three days.

They haven't the men to run a government. Perhaps it's a good thing to let them try—that will finish them. . . ."

The Military Hotel at the corner of St. Isaac's Square was picketed by armed sailors. In the lobby were many of the smart young officers, walking up and down or muttering together; the sailors wouldn't let them leave. . . .

Suddenly came the sharp crack of a rifle outside, followed by a scattered burst of firing. I ran out. Something unusual was going on around the Marinsky Palace, where the Council of the Russian Republic met. Diagonally across the wide square was drawn a line of sailors, rifles ready, staring at the hotel roof.

"*Provocatzia!* Shot at us!" snapped one, while another went running toward the door.

At the western corner of the Palace lay a big armored car with a red flag flying from it, newly lettered in red paint: "S.R.S.D." *(Soviet Rabochikh Soldatskikh Deputatov);* all the guns trained toward St. Isaac's. A barricade had been heaped up across the mouth of Novaya Ulitsa—boxes, barrels, an old bed-spring, a wagon. A pile of lumber barred the end of the Moika quay. Short logs from a neighboring wood-pile were being built up along the front of the building to form breastworks. . . .

"Is there going to be any fighting?" I asked.

"Soon, soon," answered a soldier, nervously. "Go away, comrade, you'll get hurt. They will come from that direction," pointing toward the Admiralty.

"Who will?"

"That I couldn't tell you, brother," he answered, and spat.

Before the door of the Palace was a crowd of soldiers and sailors. A sailor was telling of the end of the Council of the Russian Republic. "We walked in there," he said, "and filled all the doors with comrades. I went up to the counter-revolutionist Kornilovits who sat in the president's chair. 'No more Council,' I says. 'Run along home now!' "

There was laughter. By waving assorted papers I managed to get around to the door of the press gallery. There an enormous smiling sailor stopped me, and when I showed my pass, just said, "If you were Saint Michael himself, comrade, you couldn't pass here!" Through the glass of the door I made out the distorted face and gesticulating arms of a French correspondent, locked in. . . .

Around in front stood a little, gray-moustached man in the uniform of a general, the center of a knot of soldiers. He was very red in the face.

"I am General Alexeyev," he cried. "As your superior officer and as a member of the Council of the Republic I demand to be allowed to pass!" The guard scratched his head, looking uneasily out of the corner of his eye, he beckoned to an approaching officer, who grew very agitated when he saw who it was and saluted before he realized what he was doing.

"*Vashe Vuisokoprevoskhoditelstvo*—your High Excellency—" he stammered in the manner of the old régime. "Access to the Palace is strictly forbidden—I have no right—"

An automobile came by, and I saw Gotz sitting inside, laughing apparently with great amusement. A few minutes later another, with armed soldiers on the front seat, full of arrested members of the Provisional Government. Peters, Lettish member of the Military Revolutionary Committee, came hurrying across the Square.

"I thought you bagged all those gentlemen last night," said I, pointing to them.

"Oh," he answered, with the expression of a disappointed schoolboy. "The damn fools let most of them go again before we made up our minds. . . ."

Down the Voskressensky Prospect a great mass of sailors were drawn up, and behind them came marching soldiers, as far as the eye could reach.

We went toward the Winter Palace by way of the Admiralteisky. All the entrances to the Palace Square were closed by sentries, and a cordon of troops stretched clear across the western end, besieged by an uneasy throng of citizens. Except for far-away soldiers who seemed to be carrying wood out of the Palace courtyard and piling it in front of the main gateway, everything was quiet.

We couldn't make out whether the sentries were pro-Government or pro-Soviet. Our papers from Smolny had no effect, however, so we approached another part of the line with an important air and showed our American passports, saying, "Official business!" and shouldered through. At the door of the Palace the same old *shveitzari*, in their brass-buttoned blue uniforms with the red-and-gold collars, politely took our coats and hats, and we went upstairs. In the dark, gloomy corridor, stripped of its tapestries, a few old attendants were lounging about, and in front of Kerensky's door a young officer paced up and down, gnawing his moustache. We asked if we could interview the Minister-President. He bowed and clicked his heels.

"No, I am sorry," he replied in French. "Alexander Feodorovich is extremely occupied just now. . . ." He looked at us for a moment. "In fact, he is not here. . . ."

"Where is he?"

"He has gone to the front.[27] And do you know, there wasn't enough gasoline for his automobile. We had to send to the English Hospital and borrow some."

"Are the Ministers here?"

"They are meeting in some room—I don't know where."

"Are the Bolsheviki coming?"

"Of course. Certainly they are coming. I expect a telephone call every minute to say that they are coming. But we are ready. We have *yunkers* in the front of the Palace. Through that door there."

"Can we go in there?"

"No. Certainly not. It is not permitted." Abruptly he shook hands all round and walked away. We turned to the forbidden door, set in a temporary partition dividing the hall and locked on the outside. On the other side were voices, and somebody laughing. Except for that the vast spaces of the old Palace were as silent as the grave. An old *shveitzar* ran up. "No, *barin*, you must not go in there."

"Why is the door locked?"

"To keep the soldiers in," he answered. After a few minutes he said something about having a glass of tea and went back up the hall. We unlocked the door.

Just inside a couple of soldiers stood on guard, but they said nothing. At the end of the corridor was a large, ornate room with gilded cornices and enormous crystal lusters, and beyond it several smaller ones, wainscoted with dark wood. On both sides of the parqueted floor lay rows of dirty mattresses and blankets, upon which occasional soldiers were stretched out; everywhere was a litter of cigarette butts, bits of bread, cloth, and empty bottles with expensive French labels. More and more soldiers with the red shoulder-straps of the *yunker* schools, moved about in a stale atmosphere of tobacco-smoke and unwashed humanity. One had a bottle of white Burgundy, evidently filched from the cellars of the Palace. They looked at us with astonishment as we marched past, through room after room, until at last we came out into a series of great state-salons, fronting their long and dirty windows on the Square. The walls were covered with huge canvases in massive gilt frames—historical battle scenes. . . . "12 October 1812" and "6 November 1812" and "16/28 August 1813". . . . One had a gash across the upper right-hand corner.

The place was all a huge barrack, and evidently had been for weeks, from the look of the floor and walls. Machine-guns were mounted on window-sills, rifles stacked between the mattresses.

As we were looking at the pictures an alcoholic breath assailed me from the region of my left ear, and a voice said in thick but fluent French, "I see, by the way you admire the paintings, that you are foreigners." He was a short, puffy man with a baldish head as he removed his cap.

"Americans? Enchanted. I am Stabs-Captain Vladimir Artzibashev, absolutely at your service." It did not seem to occur to him that there was anything unusual in four strangers, one a woman, wandering through the defenses of an army awaiting attack. He began to complain of the state of Russia.

"Not only these Bolsheviki," he said, "but the fine traditions of the Russian army are broken down. Look around you. These are all students in the officers' training schools. But are they gentlemen? Kerensky opened the officers' schools to the ranks, to any soldier who could pass an examination. Naturally there are many, many who are contaminated by the Revolution. . . ."

Without consequence he changed the subject. "I am very anxious to get away from Russia. I have made up my mind to join the American army. Will you please go to your Consul and make arrangements? I will give you my address." In spite of our protestations he wrote it on a piece of paper, and seemed to feel better at once. I have it still—"Oranienbaumskaya Shkola Praporshchikov 2nd, Staraya Peterhof."

"We had a review this morning early," he went on, as he guided us through the rooms and explained everything. "The Women's Battalion decided to remain loyal to the Government."

"Are the women soldiers in the Palace?"

"Yes, they are in the back rooms, where they won't be hurt if any trouble comes." He sighed. "It is a great responsibility," said he.

For a while we stood at the window, looking down on the Square before the Palace, where three companies of long-coated *yunkers* were drawn up under arms, being harangued by a tall, energetic-looking officer I recognized as Stankievich, chief Military Commissar of the Provisional Government. After a few minutes two of the companies shouldered arms with a clash, barked three sharp shouts, and went swinging off across the Square, disappearing through the Red Arch into the quiet city.

"They are going to capture the Telephone Exchange," said someone. Three cadets stood by us, and we fell into conversation. They said they had entered the schools from the ranks, and gave their names—Robert Olev, Alexei Vasilienko, and Erni Sachs, an Estonian. But now they didn't want to be officers any more, because officers were very unpopular. They didn't seem to know what to do, as a matter of fact, and it was plain that they were not happy.

But soon they began to boast. "If the Bolsheviki come we shall show them how to fight. They do not dare to fight, they are cowards. But if we should be overpowered, well, every man keeps one bullet for himself. . . ."

At this point there was a burst of rifle-fire not far off. Out on the Square all the people began to run, falling flat on their faces, and the *izvozchiki* standing on the corners galloped in every direction. Inside all was uproar, soldiers running here and there, grabbing up guns, rifle-belts and shouting, "Here they come! Here they come! . . . But in a few minutes it quieted down again. The *izvozchiki* came back, the people lying down stood up. Through the Red Arch appeared the *yunkers*, marching a little out of step, one of them supported by two comrades.

It was getting late when we left the Palace. The sentries in the Square had all disappeared. The great semi-circle of Government buildings seemed deserted. We went into the Hotel France for dinner, and right in the middle of soup the waiter, very pale in the face, came up and insisted that we move to the main dining-room at the back of the house, because they were going to put out the lights in the café. "There will be much shooting," he said.

When we came out on the Morskaya again it was quite dark, except for one flickering street-light on the corner of the Nevsky. Under this stood a big armored automobile, with racing engine and oil-smoke pouring out of it. A small boy had climbed up the side of the thing and was looking down the barrel of a machine-gun. Soldiers and sailors stood around, evidently waiting for something. We walked back up to the Red Arch, where a knot of soldiers was gathered staring at the brightly lighted Winter Palace and talking in loud tones.

"No, comrades," one was saying. "How can we shoot at them? The Women's Battalion is in there—they will say we have fired on Russian women."

As we reached the Nevsky again another armored car came around the corner, and a man poked his head out of the turret-top.

"Come on!" he yelled. "Let's go on through and attack!"

The driver of the other car came over, and shouted so as to be heard above the roaring engine. "The Committee says to wait. They have got artillery behind the wood-piles in there. . . ."

Here the streetcars had stopped running, few people passed, and there were no lights; but a few blocks away we could see the trams, the crowds, the lighted shop-windows and the electric signs of the moving-picture shows—life going on as usual. We had tickets to the Ballet at the Marinsky Theater—all the theaters were open—but it was too exciting out of doors. . . .

In the darkness we stumbled over lumber-piles barricading the Police Bridge, and before the Stroganov Palace made out some soldiers wheeling into position a three-inch field-gun. Men in various uniforms were coming and going in an aimless way, and doing a great deal of talking. . . .

Up the Nevsky the whole city seemed to be out promenading. On every corner immense crowds were massed around a core of hot discussion. Pickets of a dozen soldiers with fixed bayonets lounged at the street crossings, red-faced old men in rich fur coats shook their fists at them, smartly-dressed women screamed epithets; the soldiers argued feebly, with embarrassed grins. . . . Armored cars went up and down the street, named after the first Czars—Oleg, Rurik, Svietoslav—and daubed with huge red letters, "R.S.D.R.P." *(Rossiskaya Sotsial-Democrateecheskaya Rabochaya Partia).** At the Mikhailovsky a man appeared with an armful of newspapers, and was immediately stormed by frantic people, offering a rouble, five roubles, ten roubles, tearing at each other like animals. It was *Rabochi i Soldat*, announcing the victory of the Proletarian Revolution, the liberation of the Bolsheviki still in prison, calling upon the Army front and rear for support . . . a feverish little sheet of four pages, running to enormous type, containing no news. . . .

On the corner of the Sadovaya about two thousand citizens had gathered, staring up at the roof of a tall building, where a tiny red spark glowed and waned.

"See!" said a tall peasant, pointing to it. "It is a provocator. Presently he will fire on the people. . . ." Apparently no one thought of going to investigate.

THE massive façade of Smolny blazed with lights as we drove up, and from every street converged upon it streams of hurrying shapes dim in the gloom. Automobiles and motor-cycles came and went; an enormous elephant-colored armored automobile, with two red flags flying from the turret, lumbered out with screaming siren. It was cold, and at the outer gate the Red Guards

*Russian Social-Democratic Labor Party.

had built themselves a bonfire. At the inner gate, too, there was a blaze, by the light of which sentries slowly spelled out our passes and looked us up and down. The canvas covers had been taken off the four rapid-fire guns on each side of the doorway, and the ammunition-belts hung snake-like from their breeches. A dun herd of armored cars stood under the trees in the courtyard, engines going. The long, bare, dimly illuminated halls roared with the thunder of feet, calling, shouting. . . . There was an atmosphere of recklessness. A crowd came pouring down the staircase, workers in black blouses and round black fur hats, many of them with guns slung over their shoulders, soldiers in rough dirt-colored coats and gray fur *shapki* pinched flat, a leader or so—Lunacharsky, Kameniev—hurrying along in the center of a group all talking at once, with harassed anxious faces, and bulging portfolios under their arms. The extraordinary meeting of the Petrograd Soviet was over. I stopped Kameniev—a quick-moving little man, with a wide, vivacious face set close to his shoulders. Without preface he read in rapid French a copy of the resolution just passed:

The Petrograd Soviet of Workers' and Soldiers' Deputies, saluting the victorious Revolution of the Petrograd proletariat and garrison, particularly emphasizes the unity, organization, discipline, and complete cooperation shown by the masses in this rising; rarely has less blood been spilled, and rarely has an insurrection succeeded so well.

The Soviet expresses its firm conviction that the Workers' and Peasants' Government which, as the government of the Soviets, will be created by the Revolution, and which will assure the industrial proletariat of the support of the entire mass of poor peasants, will march firmly toward Socialism, the only means by which the country can be spared the miseries and unheard-of horrors of war.

The new Workers' and Peasants' Government will propose immediately a just and democratic peace to all the belligerent countries.

It will suppress immediately the great landed property, and transfer the land to the peasants. It will establish workmen's control over production and distribution of manufactured products, and will set up a general control over the banks, which it will transform into a state monopoly.

The Petrograd Soviet of Workers' and Soldiers' Deputies calls upon the workers and peasants of Russia to support with all their energy and all their devotion the Proletarian Revolution. The Soviet expresses its conviction that the city workers, allies of the poor peasants, will assure complete revolutionary order, indispensable to the victory of Socialism. The Soviet is convinced that the proletariat of the countries of Western Europe will aid us in conducting the cause of Socialism to a real and lasting victory.

"You consider it won then?"

He lifted his shoulders. "There is much to do. Horribly much. It is just beginning. . . ."

On the landing I met Riazanov, vice-president of the Trade Unions, looking black and biting his gray beard. "It's insane! Insane!" he shouted. "The European working class won't move! All Russia—" He waved his hand distractedly and ran off. Riazanov and Kameniev had both opposed the insurrection, and felt the lash of Lenin's terrible tongue. . . .

It had been a momentous session. In the name of the Military Revolutionary Committee Trotsky had declared that the Provisional Government no longer existed.

"The characteristic of bourgeois governments," he said, "is to deceive the people. We, the Soviets of Workers', Soldiers', and Peasants' Deputies, are going to try an experiment unique in history; we are going to found a power which will have no other aim but to satisfy the needs of the soldiers, workers, and peasants."

Lenin had appeared, welcomed with a mighty ovation, prophesying world-wide Social Revolution. . . . And Zinoviev, crying, "This day we have paid our debt to the international proletariat, and struck a terrible blow at the war, a terrible body-blow at all the imperialists, and particularly at Wilhelm the Executioner. . . ."

Then Trotsky, that telegrams had been sent to the front announcing the victorious insurrection, but no reply had come. Troops were said to be marching against Petrograd—a delegation must be sent to tell them the truth.

Cries, "You are anticipating the will of the All-Russian Congress of Soviets!"

Trotsky, coldly, "The will of the All-Russian Congress of Soviets has been anticipated by the rising of the Petrograd workers and soldiers!"

So we came into the great meeting-hall, pushing through the clamorous mob at the door. In the rows of seats, under the white chandeliers, packed immovably in the aisles and on the sides, perched on every window-sill, and even the edge of the platform, the representatives of the workers and soldiers of all Russia waited in anxious silence or wild exultation the ringing of the chairman's bell. There was no heat in the hall but the stifling heat of unwashed human bodies. A foul blue cloud of cigarette smoke rose from the mass and hung in the thick air. Occasionally someone in authority mounted the tribune and asked the comrades not to smoke; then everybody, smokers and all, took up the cry, "Don't smoke, comrades!" and went on smoking. Petrovsky, Anarchist delegate from the Obukhov factory, made a seat for me beside him. Unshaven and filthy, he was reeling from three nights' sleepless work on the Military Revolutionary Committee.

On the platform sat the leaders of the old Tsay-ee-kah—for the last time dominating the turbulent Soviets, which they had ruled from the first days, and which were now risen against them. It was the end of the first period of the Russian revolution, which these men had attempted to guide in careful ways. . . . The three greatest of them were not there: Kerensky, flying to the front through country towns all doubtfully heaving up; Chkheidze, the old eagle, who had contemptuously retired to his own Georgian mountains, there to sicken with consumption; and the high-souled Tseretelly, also mortally stricken, who, nevertheless, would return and pour out his beautiful eloquence for the lost cause. Gotz sat there, Dan, Lieber, Bogdanov, Broido, Fillipovsky—white-faced, hollow-eyed and indignant. Below them the second *siezed* of the All-Russian Soviets boiled and swirled, and over their heads the Military Revolutionary Committee functioned white-hot, holding in its hands the threads of insurrection and striking with a long arm. . . . It was 10:40 P.M.

Dan, a mild-faced, baldish figure in a shapeless military surgeon's uniform, was ringing the bell. Silence fell sharply, intense, broken by the scuffling and disputing of the people at the door. . . .

"We have the power in our hands," he began sadly, stopped for a moment, and then went on in a low voice. "Comrades! The Congress of Soviets is meeting in such unusual circumstances and in such an extraordinary moment that you will understand why the Tsay-ee-kah considers it unnecessary to address you with a political speech. This will become much clearer to you if you will recollect that I am a member of the Tsay-ee-kah, and that at this moment our Party comrades are in the Winter Palace under bombardment, sacrificing themselves to execute the duty put on them by the Tsay-ee-kah." (Confused uproar.)

"I declare the first session of the Second Congress of Soviets of Workers' and Soldiers' Deputies open!"

The election of the presidium took place amid stir and moving about. Avanessov announced that by agreement of the Bolsheviki, Left Socialist Revolutionaries, and Mensheviki Internationalists, it was decided to base the presidium upon proportionality. Several Mensheviki leaped to their feet protesting. A bearded soldier shouted at them, "Remember what you did to us Bolsheviki when *we* were in the minority!" Result—14 Bolsheviki, 7 Socialist Revolutionaries, 3 Mensheviki, and 1 Internationalist (Gorky's group). Hendelmann, for the right and center Socialist Revolutionaries, said that they refused to take part in the presidium, the same from Khinchuk, for the Mensheviki; and from the Mensheviki Internationalists, that until the verification of certain circumstances, they too could not enter the presidium. Scattering applause and hoots. One voice, "Renegades, you call yourselves Socialists!" A representative of the Ukrainian delegates demanded, and received, a place. Then the old Tsay-ee-kah stepped down, and in their places appeared Trotsky, Kameniev, Lunacharsky, Madame Kollontai, Nogin. . . . The hall rose, thundering. How far they had soared, these Bolsheviki, from a despised and hunted sect less than four months ago, to this supreme place, the helm of great Russia in full tide of insurrection!

The order of the day, said Kameniev, was first Organization of

Power; second, War and Peace; and third, the Constitutional Assembly. Lozovsky, rising, announced that upon agreement of the bureaux of all factions, it was proposed to hear and discuss the report of the Petrograd Soviet, then to give the floor to members of the Tsay-ee-kah and the different parties, and finally to pass to the order of the day.

But suddenly a new sound made itself heard, deeper than the tumult of the crowd, persistent, disquieting—the dull shock of guns. People looked anxiously toward the clouded windows, and a sort of fever came over them. Martov, demanding the floor, croaked hoarsely, "The civil war is beginning, comrades! The first question must be a peaceful settlement of the crisis. On principle and from a political standpoint we must urgently discuss a means of averting civil war. Our brothers are being shot down in the streets! At this moment, when before the opening of the Congress of Soviets the question of Power is being settled by means of a military plot organized by one of the revolutionary parties—" for a moment he could not make himself heard above the noise, "All of the revolutionary parties must face the fact! The first *vopros* (question) before the Congress is the question of power, and this question is already being settled by force of arms in the streets! . . . We must create a power which will be recognized by the whole democracy. If the Congress wishes to be the voice of the revolutionary democracy it must not sit with folded hands before the developing civil war, the result of which may be a dangerous outburst of counter-revolution. . . . The possibility of a peaceful outcome lies in the formation of a united democratic authority. . . . We must elect a delegation to negotiate with the other Socialist parties and organizations. . . ."

Always the methodical muffled boom of cannon through the windows, and the delegates, screaming at each other. . . . So, with the crash of artillery, in the dark, with hatred, and fear, and reckless daring, new Russia was being born.

The Left Socialist Revolutionaries and the United Social Democrats supported Martov's proposition. It was accepted. A soldier announced that the All-Russian Peasants' Soviets had refused to send delegates to the Congress; he proposed that a committee be sent with a formal invitation. "Some delegates are present," he said. "I move that they be given votes." Accepted.

Kharash, wearing the epaulettes of a captain, passionately demanded the floor. "The political hypocrites who control this Congress," he shouted, "told us we were to settle the question of Power—and it is being settled behind our backs, before the Congress opens! Blows are being struck against the Winter Palace, and it is by such blows that the nails are being driven into the coffin of the political party which has risked such an adventure!" Uproar. Followed him Gharra: "While we are here discussing propositions of peace, there is a battle on in the streets. . . . The Socialist Revolutionaries and Mensheviki refuse to be involved in what is happening, and call upon all public forces to resist the attempt to capture the power. . . ." Kuchin, delegate of the 12th Army and representative of the Trudoviki: "I was sent here only for information, and I am returning at once to the front, where all the Army Committees consider that the taking of power by the Soviets, only three weeks before the Constituent Assembly, is a stab in the back of the Army and a crime against the people—!" Shouts of "Lie! You lie!" . . . When he could be heard again, "Let's make an end of this adventure in Petrograd! I call upon all the delegates to leave this hall in order to save the country and the revolution!" As he went down the aisle in the midst of a deafening noise, people surged upon him, threatening. . . . Then an officer with a long brown goatee, speaking suavely and persuasively: "I speak for the delegates from the front. The Army is imperfectly represented in this Congress, and furthermore, the Army does not consider the Congress of Soviets necessary at this time, only three weeks before the opening of the Constituent—" shouts and stamping, always growing more violent. "The Army does not consider that the Congress of the Soviets has the necessary authority—" Soldiers began to stand up all over the hall.

"Who are you speaking for? What do you represent?" they cried.

"The Central Executive Committee of the Soviet of the Fifth

Army, the Second F——Regiment, the First N——Regiment, the Third S——Rifles. . . ."

"When were you elected? You represent the officers, not the soldiers! What do the soldiers say about it?" Jeers and hoots.

"We, the front group, disclaim all responsibility for what has happened and is happening, and we consider it necessary to mobilize all self-conscious revolutionary forces for the salvation of the Revolution! The front group will leave the Congress. . . . The place to fight is out on the streets!"

Immense bawling outcry. "You speak for the Staff—not for the Army!"

"I appeal to all reasonable soldiers to leave this Congress!"

"Kornilovist! Counter-revolutionist! Provocator!" were hurled at him.

On behalf of the Mensheviki, Khinchuk then announced that the only possibility of a peaceful solution was to begin negotiations with the Provisional Government for the formation of a new Cabinet, which would find support in all strata of society. He could not proceed for several minutes. Raising his voice to a shout he read the Menshevik declaration:

"Because the Bolsheviki have made a military conspiracy with the aid of the Petrograd Soviet, without consulting the other factions and parties, we find it impossible to remain in the Congress, and therefore withdraw, inviting the other groups to follow us and to meet for discussion of the situation!"

"Deserter!" At intervals in the almost continuous disturbance Hendelmann, for the Socialist Revolutionaries, could be heard protesting against the bombardment of the Winter Palace. . . . "We are opposed to this kind of anarchy. . . ."

Scarcely had he stepped down when a young, lean-faced soldier, with flashing eyes, leaped to the platform, and dramatically lifted his hand:

"Comrades!" he cried, and there was a hush. "My *familia* (name) is Peterson—I speak for the Second Lettish Rifles. You have heard the statements of two representatives of the Army committees; these statements would have some value *if their au-*

*thors had been representatives of the Army*—" Wild applause. *"But they do not represent the soldiers!"* Shaking his fist. "The Twelfth Army has been insisting for a long time upon the re-election of the Great Soviet and the Army Committee, but just as your own Tsay-ee-kah, our Committee refused to call a meeting of the representatives of the masses until the end of September, so that the reactionaries could elect their own false delegates to this Congress. I tell you now, the Lettish soldiers have many times said, 'No more resolutions! No more talk! We want deeds—the Power must be in our hands!' Let these impostor delegates leave the Congress! The Army is not with them!"

The hall rocked with cheering. In the first moments of the session, stunned by the rapidity of events, startled by the sound of cannon, the delegates had hesitated. For an hour hammer-blow after hammer-blow had fallen from that tribune, welding them together but beating them down. Did they stand then alone? Was Russia rising against them? Was it true that the Army was marching on Petrograd? Then this clear-eyed young soldier had spoken, and in a flash they knew it for the truth.... *This* was the voice of the soldiers—the stirring millions of uniformed workers and peasants were men like them, and their thoughts and feelings were the same....

More soldiers.... Gzhelshakh; for the Front delegates, announcing that they had only decided to leave the Congress by a small majority, and that *the Bolshevik members had not even taken part in the vote*, as they stood for division according to political parties, and not groups. "Hundreds of delegates from the front," he said, "are being elected without the participation of the soldiers because the Army Committees are no longer the real representatives of the rank and file...." Lukianov, crying that officers like Kharash and Khinchuk could not represent the Army in this Congress—but only the high command. "The real inhabitants of the trenches want with all their hearts the transfer of Power into the hands of the Soviets, and they expect very much from it!" ... The tide was turning.

Then came Abramovich, for the *Bund*, the organ of the Jewish

Social-Democrats—his eyes snapping behind thick glasses, trembling with rage.

"What is taking place now in Petrograd is a monstrous calamity! The *Bund* group joins with the declaration of the Mensheviki and Socialist Revolutionaries and will leave the Congress!" He raised his voice and hand. "Our duty to the Russian proletariat doesn't permit us to remain here and be responsible for these crimes. Because the firing on the Winter Palace doesn't cease, the Municipal Duma together with the Mensheviki and Socialist Revolutionaries, and the Executive Committee of the Peasants' Soviet, has decided to perish with the Provisional Government, and we are going with them! Unarmed we will expose our breasts to the machine-guns of the Terrorists. . . . We invite all delegates to this Congress—" The rest was lost in a storm of hoots, menaces, and curses which rose to a hellish pitch as fifty delegates got up and pushed their way out. . . .

Kameniev jangled the bell, shouting, "Keep your seats and we'll go on with our business!" And Trotsky, standing up with a pale, cruel face, letting out his rich voice in cool contempt, "All these so-called Socialist compromisers, these frightened Mensheviki, Socialist Revolutionaries, *Bund*—let them go! They are just so much refuse which will be swept away into the garbage-heap of history!"

Riazanov, for the Bolsheviki, stated that at the request of the City Duma the Military Revolutionary Committee had sent a delegation to offer negotiations to the Winter Palace. "In this way we have done everything possible to avoid bloodshed. . . ."

We hurried from the place, stopping for a moment at the room where the Military Revolutionary Committee worked at furious speed, engulfing and spitting out panting couriers, dispatching Commissars armed with power of life and death to all corners of the city, amid the buzz of the telephonographs. The door opened, a blast of stale air and cigarette-smoke rushed out, we caught a glimpse of disheveled men bending over a map under the glare of a shaded electric-light. . . . Comrade Josephov-Dukhvinski, a smiling youth with a mop of pale yellow hair, made out passes for us.

When we came into the chill night, all the front of Smolny was one huge park of arriving and departing automobiles, above the sound of which could be heard the far-off slow beat of the cannon. A great motor-truck stood there, shaking to the roar of its engine. Men were tossing bundles into it, and others receiving them, with guns beside them.

"Where are you going?" I shouted.

"Down-town—all over—everywhere!" answered a little workman, grinning, with a large exultant gesture.

We showed our passes. "Come along!" they invited. "But there'll probably be shooting—" We climbed in: the clutch slid home with a raking jar, the great car jerked forward, we all toppled backward on top of those who were climbing in; past the huge fire by the gate, and then the fire by the outer gate, glowing red on the faces of the workmen with rifles who squatted around it, and went bumping at top speed down the Suvorovsky Prospect, swaying from side to side. . . . One man tore the wrapping from a bundle and began to hurl handfuls of papers into the air. We imitated him, plunging down through the dark street with a tail of white papers floating and eddying out behind. The late passer-by stooped to pick them up; the patrols around bonfires on the corners ran out with uplifted arms to catch them. Sometimes armed men loomed up ahead, crying *"Stoi!"* and raising their guns, but our chauffeur only yelled something unintelligible and we hurtled on. . . .

I picked up a copy of the paper, and under a fleeting street-light read:

TO THE CITIZENS OF RUSSIA!

The Provisional Government is deposed. The State Power has passed into the hands of the organ of the Petrograd Soviet of Workers' and Soldiers' Deputies, the Military Revolutionary Committee, which stands at the head of the Petrograd proletariat and garrison.

The cause for which the people were fighting: immediate proposal of a democratic peace, abolition of landlord property-rights over the land, labor control over production, creation of a Soviet Government—that cause is securely achieved.

LONG LIVE THE REVOLUTION OF WORKMEN, SOLDIERS, AND PEASANTS!
*Military Revolutionary Committee*
*Petrograd Soviet of Workers' and Soldiers' Deputies*

A slant-eyed, Mongolian-faced man who sat beside me, dressed in a goatskin Caucasian cape, snapped, "Look out! Here the provocators always shoot from the windows!" We turned into Znamensky Square, dark and almost deserted, careened around Trubetskoy's brutal statue and swung down the wide Nevsky, three men standing up with rifles ready, peering at the windows. Behind us the street was alive with people running and stooping. We could no longer hear the cannon, and the nearer we drew to the Winter Palace end of the city the quieter and more deserted were the streets. The City Duma was all brightly lighted. Beyond that we made out a dark mass of people, and a line of sailors, who yelled furiously at us to stop. The machine slowed down, and we climbed out.

It was an astonishing scene. Just at the corner of the Ekaterina Canal, under an arc-light, a cordon of armed sailors was drawn across the Nevsky, blocking the way to a crowd of people in column of fours. There were about three or four hundred of them, men in frock coats, well-dressed women, officers—all sorts and conditions of people. Among them we recognized many of the delegates from the Congress, leaders of the Mensheviki and Socialist Revolutionaries; Avksentiev, the lean, red-bearded president of the Peasants' Soviets, Sarokin, Kerensky's spokesman, Khinchuk, Abramovich; and at the head white-bearded old Schreider, Mayor of Petrograd, and Prokopovich, Minister of Supplies in the Provisional Government, arrested that morning and released. I caught sight of Malkin, reporter for the *Russian Daily News*. "Going to die in the Winter Palace," he shouted cheerfully. The procession stood still, but from the front of it came loud argument. Schreider and Prokopovich were bellowing at the big sailor who seemed in command.

"We demand to pass!" they cried. "See, these comrades come from the Congress of Soviets! Look at their tickets! We are going to the Winter Palace!"

The sailor was plainly puzzled. He scratched his head with an enormous hand, frowning. "I have orders from the Committee not to let anybody go to the Winter Palace," he grumbled. "But I will send a comrade to telephone to Smolny. . . ."

"We insist upon passing! We are unarmed! We will march on whether you permit us or not!" cried old Schreider, very much excited.

"I have orders—" repeated the sailor sullenly.

"Shoot us if you want to! We will pass! Forward!" came from all sides. "We are ready to die, if you have the heart to fire on Russians and comrades! We bare our breasts to your guns!"

"No," said the sailor, looking stubborn, "I can't allow you to pass."

"What will you do if we go forward? Will you shoot?"

"No, I'm not going to shoot people who haven't any guns. We won't shoot unarmed Russian people. . . ."

"We will go forward! What can you do?"

"We will do something!" replied the sailor, evidently at a loss. "We can't let you pass. We will do something."

"What will you do? What will you do?"

Another sailor came up, very much irritated. "We will spank you!" he cried energetically. "And if necessary we will shoot you too. Go home now, and leave us in peace!"

At this there was a great clamor of anger and resentment. Prokopovich had mounted some sort of box, and waving his umbrella, he made a speech:

"Comrades and citizens!" he said. "Force is being used against us! We cannot have our innocent blood upon the hands of these ignorant men! It is beneath our dignity to be shot down here in the streets by switchmen—" (What he meant by "switchmen" I never discovered.) "Let us return to the Duma and discuss the best means of saving the country and the Revolution!"

Whereupon, in dignified silence, the procession marched around and back up the Nevsky, always in column of fours. And taking advantage of the diversion we slipped past the guards and set off in the direction of the Winter Palace.

Here it was absolutely dark, and nothing moved but pickets of soldiers and Red Guards grimly intent. In front of the Kazan Cathedral a three-inch field-gun lay in the middle of the street, slewed sideways from the recoil of its last shot over the roofs. Soldiers were standing in every doorway talking in loud tones and peering down toward the Police Bridge. I heard one voice saying: "It is possible that we have done wrong. . . ." At the corners patrols stopped all passers-by—and the composition of these patrols was interesting, for in command of the regular troops was invariably a Red Guard. . . . The shooting had ceased.

Just as we came to the Morskaya somebody was shouting: "The *yunkers* have sent word that they want us to go and get them out!" Voices began to give commands, and in the thick gloom we made out a dark mass moving forward, silent but for the shuffle of feet and the clinking of arms. We fell in with the first ranks.

Like a black river, filling all the street, without song or cheer we poured through the Red Arch, where the man just ahead of me said in a low voice: "Look out, comrades! Don't trust them. They will fire, surely!" In the open we began to run, stooping low and bunching together, and jammed up suddenly behind the pedestal of the Alexander Column.

"How many of you did they kill?" I asked.

"I don't know. About ten. . . ."

After a few minutes huddling there, some hundreds of men, the Army seemed reassured and without any orders suddenly began again to flow forward. By this time, in the light that streamed out of all the Winter Palace windows, I could see that the first two or three hundred men were Red Guards, with only a few scattered soldiers. Over the barricade of fire-wood we clambered, and leaping down inside gave a triumphant shout as we stumbled on a heap of rifles thrown down by the *yunkers* who had stood there. On both sides of the main gateway the doors stood wide open, light streamed out, and from the huge pile came not the slightest sound.

Carried along by the eager wave of men we were swept into the right-hand entrance, opening into a great bare vaulted room, the cellar of the east wing, from which issued a maze of corridors and staircases. A number of huge packing cases stood about, and upon these the Red Guards and soldiers fell furiously, battering them open with the butts of their rifles, and pulling out carpets, curtains, linen, porcelain, plates, glass-ware. . . . One man went strutting around with a bronze clock perched on his shoulder; another found a plume of ostrich feathers, which he stuck in his hat. The looting was just beginning when somebody cried, "Comrades! Don't take anything. This is the property of the People!" Immediately twenty voices were crying, "Stop! Put everything back! Don't take anything! Property of the People!" Many hands dragged the spoilers down. Damask and tapestry were snatched from the arms of those who had them; two men took away the bronze clock. Roughly and hastily the things were crammed back in their cases, and self-appointed sentinels stood guard. It was all utterly spontaneous. Through corridors and up staircases the cry could be heard growing fainter and fainter in the distance. "Revolutionary discipline! Property of the People. . . ."

We crossed back over to the left entrance, in the west wing. There order was also being established. "Clear the Palace!" bawled a Red Guard, sticking his head through an inner door. "Come, comrades, let's show that we're not thieves and bandits. Everybody out of the Palace except the Commissars, until we get sentries posted."

Two Red Guards, a soldier and an officer, stood with revolvers in their hands. Another soldier sat at a table behind them, with pen and paper. Shouts of "All out! All out!" were heard far and near within, and the Army began to pour through the door, jostling, expostulating, arguing. As each man appeared he was seized by the self-appointed committee, who went through his pockets and looked under his coat. Everything that was plainly not his property was taken away, the man at the table noted it on his paper, and it was carried into a little room. The most amazing assortment of objects were thus confiscated; statuettes, bottles of ink, bed-spreads worked with the Imperial monogram, candles, a small oil-painting, desk blotters, gold-handled swords, cakes of soap, clothes of every description, blankets. One Red Guard carried three rifles, two of which he had taken away from *yunkers;* another had four portfolios bulging with written documents. The culprits either sullenly surrendered or pleaded like children. All talking at once the committee explained that stealing was not worthy of the people's champions; often those who had been caught turned around and began to help go through the rest of the comrades.[28]

*Yunkers* came out in bunches of three or four. The committee seized upon them with an excess of zeal, accompanying the search with remarks like, "Ah, Provocators! Kornilovists! Counter-revolutionists! Murderers of the People!" But there was no violence done, although the *yunkers* were terrified. They too had their pockets full of small plunder. It was carefully noted down by the scribe, and piled in the little room. . . . The *yunkers* were disarmed. "Now, will you take up arms against the People any more?" demanded clamoring voices.

"No," answered the *yunkers,* one by one. Whereupon they were allowed to go free.

We asked if we might go inside. The committee was doubtful, but the big Red Guard answered firmly that it was forbidden. "Who are you anyway?" he asked. "How do I know that you are not all Kerenskys?" (There were five of us, two women.)

*"Pazhal'st', tovarishchi!* Way, Comrades!" A soldier and a Red Guard appeared in the door, waving the crowd aside, and other guards with fixed bayonets. After them followed single file half a dozen men in civilian dress—the members of the Provisional Government. First came Kishkin, his face drawn and pale, then Rutenberg, looking sullenly at the floor; Tereshchenko was next, glancing sharply around; he stared at us with cold fixity. . . . They passed in silence; the victorious insurrectionists crowded to see, but there were only a few angry mutterings. It was only later that we learned how the people in the street wanted to lynch them, and shots were fired—but the sailors brought them safely to Peter-Paul. . . .

In the meanwhile unrebuked we walked into the Palace. There was still a great deal of coming and going, of exploring newfound apartments in the vast edifice, of searching for hidden garrisons of *yunkers* which did not exist. We went upstairs and wandered through room after room. This part of the Palace had been entered also by other detachments from the side of the Neva. The paintings, statues, tapestries, and rugs of the great state apartments were unharmed; in the offices, however, every desk and cabinet had been ransacked, the papers scattered over the floor, and in the living-rooms beds had been stripped of their coverings and wardrobes wrenched open. The most highly prized loot was clothing, which the working people needed. In a room where furniture was stored we came upon two soldiers ripping the elaborate Spanish leather upholstery from chairs. They explained it was to make boots with. . . .

The old Palace servants in their blue and red and gold uniforms stood nervously about, from force of habit repeating, "You can't go in there, *barin*! It is forbidden—" We penetrated at length to the gold and malachite chamber with crimson brocade hangings where the Ministers had been in session all that day and night, and where the *shveitzari* had betrayed them to the Red Guards. The long table covered with green baize was just as they had left it, under arrest. Before each empty seat was pen, ink, and paper; the papers were scribbled over with beginnings of plans of action, rough drafts of proclamations and manifestoes. Most of these were scratched out, as their futility became evident, and the rest of the sheet covered with absent-minded geometrical designs, as the writers sat despondently listening while Minister after Minister proposed chimerical schemes. I took one of these scribbled pages, in the handwriting of Konovalov, which read, "The Provisional Government appeals to all classes to support the Provisional Government—"

All this time, it must be remembered, although the Winter Palace was surrounded, the Government was in constant communication with the front and with provincial Russia. The Bolsheviki had captured the Ministry of War early in the morning, but they did not know of the military telegraph office in the attic, nor of the private telephone line connecting it with the Winter Palace. In that attic a young officer sat all day, pouring out over the country a flood of appeals and proclamations; and when he heard the Palace had fallen, put on his hat and walked calmly out of the building. . . .

Interested as we were, for a considerable time we didn't notice a change in the attitude of the soldiers and Red Guards around us. As we strolled from room to room a small group followed us, until by the time we reached the great picture-gallery where we had spent the afternoon with the *yunkers*, about a hundred men surged in upon us. One giant of a soldier stood in our path, his face dark with sullen suspicion.

"Who are you?" he growled. "What are you doing here?" The others massed slowly around, staring and beginning to mutter. "*Provocatori!*" I heard somebody say, "Looters!" I produced our passes from the Military Revolutionary Committee. The soldier took them gingerly, turned them upside down and looked at them without comprehension. Evidently he could not read. He handed them back and spat on the floor. "*Bumagi!* Papers!" said he with contempt. The mass slowly began to close in, like wild cattle around a cow-puncher on foot. Over their heads I caught sight of an officer, looking helpless, and shouted to him. He made for us, shouldering his way through.

"I'm the Commissar," he said to me. "Who are you? What is it?" The others held back, waiting. I produced the papers.

"You are foreigners?" he rapidly asked in French. "It is very dangerous. . . ." Then he turned to the mob, holding up our documents. "Comrades!" he cried, "These people are foreign comrades—from America. They have come here to be able to tell their countrymen about the bravery and the revolutionary discipline of the proletarian army!"

"How do you know that?" replied the big soldier. "I tell you they are provocators! They say they came here to observe the revolutionary discipline of the proletarian army, but they have been wandering freely through the Palace, and how do we know they haven't their pockets full of loot?"

"*Pravilno!*" snarled the others, pressing forward.

"Comrades! Comrades!" appealed the officer, sweat standing out on his forehead. "I am Commissar of the Military Revolutionary Committee. Do you trust me? Well, I tell you that these passes are signed with the same names that are signed to my pass!"

He led us down through the Palace and out through a door opening on to the Neva quay, before which stood the usual committee going through pockets. . . . "You have narrowly escaped," he kept muttering, wiping his face.

"What happened to the Women's Battalion?" we asked.

"Oh—the women!" He laughed. "They were all huddled up in a back room. We had a terrible time deciding what to do with them—many were in hysterics, and so on. So finally we marched them up to the Finland Station and put them on a train to Levashovo, where they have a camp. . . ."[29]

We came out into the cold, nervous night, murmurous with obscure armies on the move, electric with patrols. From across the river, where loomed the darker mass of Peter-Paul came a hoarse shout. . . . Underfoot the sidewalk was littered with broken stucco, from the cornice of the Palace where two shells from the battleship *Avrora* had struck; that was the only damage done by the bombardment.

It was now after three in the morning. On the Nevsky all the street-lights were again shining, the cannon gone, and the only signs of war were Red Guards and soldiers squatting around fires. The city was quiet—probably never so quiet in its history; on that night not a single hold-up occurred, not a single robbery.

But the City Duma Building was all illuminated. We mounted to the galleried Alexander Hall, hung with its great gold-framed, red-shrouded Imperial portraits. About a hundred people were grouped around the platform, where Skobeliev was speaking. He urged that the Committee of Public Safety be expanded, so as to unite all the anti-Bolshevik elements in one huge organization, to be called the Committee for Salvation of Country and Revolution. And as we looked on, the Committee for Salvation was formed—that Committee which was to develop into the most powerful enemy of the Bolsheviki, appearing, in the next week, sometimes under its own partisan name, and sometimes as the strictly non-partisan Committee of Public Safety. . . .

Dan, Gotz, Avksentiev were there, some of the insurgent Soviet delegates, members of the Executive Committee of the Peasants' Soviets, old Prokopovich, and even members of the Council of the Republic—among whom Vinaver and other Cadets. Lieber cried that the convention of the Soviets was not a legal convention, that the old Tsay-ee-kah was still in office. . . . An appeal to the country was drafted.

We hailed a cab. "Where to?" But when we said "Smolny," the *izvozchik* shook his head. "*Niet!*" said he, "there are devils. . . ." It was only after weary wandering that we found a driver willing to take us—and he wanted thirty roubles, and stopped two blocks away.

The windows of Smolny were still ablaze, motors came and went, and around the still-leaping fires the sentries huddled close, eagerly asking everybody the latest news. The corridors were full of hurrying men, hollow-eyed and dirty. In some of the committee-rooms people lay sleeping on the floor, their guns beside them. In spite of the seceding delegates, the hall of meetings was crowded with people roaring like the sea. As we came in, Kameniev was reading the list of arrested Ministers. The name of Tereshchenko was greeted with thunderous applause, shouts of satisfaction, laughter; Rutenberg came in for less; and at the mention of Palchinsky, a storm of hoots, angry cries, cheers burst forth. . . . It was announced that Chudnovsky had been appointed Commissar of the Winter Palace.

Now occurred a dramatic interruption. A big peasant, his bearded face convulsed with rage, mounted the platform and pounded with his fist on the presidium table.

"We, Socialist Revolutionaries, insist on the immediate release of the Socialist Ministers arrested in the Winter Palace! Comrades! Do you know that four comrades who risked their lives and their freedom fighting against tyranny of the Czar, have been flung into Peter-Paul prison—the historical tomb of Liberty?" In the uproar he pounded and yelled. Another delegate climbed up beside him and pointed at the presidium.

"Are the representatives of the revolutionary masses going to sit here quietly while the Okhrana of the Bolsheviki tortures their leaders?"

Trotsky was gesturing for silence. "These 'comrades' who are now caught plotting the crushing of the Soviets with the adventurer Kerensky—is there any reason to handle them with gloves? After 16 and 18 July they didn't use much ceremony with us!" With a triumphant ring in his voice he cried, "Now that the *oborontsi* and the faint-hearted have gone, and the whole task of defending and saving the Revolution rests on our shoulders, it is particularly necessary to work—work—work! We have decided to die rather than give up!"

Followed him a Commissar from Tsarkoye Selo, panting and covered with the mud of his ride. "The garrison of Tsarskoye Selo is on guard at the gates of Petrograd, ready to defend the Soviets and the Military Revolutionary Committee!" Wild cheers. "The Cycle Corps sent from the front has arrived at Tsarskoye, and the soldiers are now with us; they recognize the power of the Soviets, the necessity of immediate transfer of land to the peasants and industrial control to the workers. The Fifth Battalion of Cyclists, stationed at Tsarskoye, is ours. . . ."

Then the delegate of the Third Cycle Battalion. In the midst of delirious enthusiasm he told how the cycle corps had been ordered *three days before* from the South-west front to the "defense of Petrograd." They suspected, however, the meaning of the order; and at the station of Peredolsk were met by representatives of the Fifth Battalion from Tsarkoye. A joint meeting was held, and it was discovered that "among the cyclists not a single man was found willing to shed the blood of his fathers, or to support a Government of bourgeois and landowners!"

Kapelinsky, for the Mensheviki Internationalists, proposed to elect a special committee to find a peaceful solution to the civil war. "There isn't any peaceful solution!" bellowed the crowd. "Victory is the only solution!" The vote was overwhelmingly against, and the Mensheviki Internationalists left the Congress in a whirlwind of jocular insults. There was no longer any panic fear. . . . Kameniev from the platform shouted after them, "The Mensheviki Internationalists claimed 'emergency' for the question of 'peaceful solution,' but they always voted for suspension of the order of the day in favor of declarations of factions which wanted to leave the Congress. It is evident," finished Kameniev, "that the withdrawal of all these renegades was decided upon beforehand!"

The assembly decided to ignore the withdrawal of the factions, and proceed to the appeal to the workers, soldiers, and peasants of all Russia.

## TO WORKERS, SOLDIERS, AND PEASANTS

The Second All-Russian Congress of Soviets of Workers' and Soldiers' Deputies has opened. It represents the great majority of the Soviets. There are also a number of Peasant deputies. Based upon the will of the great majority of the workers, soldiers, and peasants, based upon the triumphant uprising of the Petrograd workmen and soldiers, the Congress assumes power.

The Provisional Government is deposed. Most of the members of the Provisional Government are already arrested.

The Soviet authority will at once propose an immediate democratic peace to all nations, and an immediate truce on all fronts. It will assure the free transfer of landlord, crown, and monastery lands to the Land Committees, defend the soldiers' rights, enforcing a complete democratization of the Army, establish workers' control over production, ensure the convocation of the Constitutent Assembly at the proper date, take means to supply bread to the cities and articles of first necessity to the villages, and secure to all nationalities living in Russia a real right to independent existence.

The Congress resolves: that all local power shall be transferred to the Soviets of Workers', Soldiers', and Peasants' Deputies, which must enforce revolutionary order.

The Congress calls upon the soldiers in the trenches to be watchful and steadfast. The Congress of Soviets is sure that the revolutionary Army will know how to defend the Revolution against all attacks of Imperialism, until the new Government shall have brought about the conclusion of the democratic peace which it will directly propose to all nations. The new Government will take all necessary steps to secure everything needful to the revolutionary Army, by means of a determined policy of requisition and taxation of the propertied classes, and also to improve the situation of the soldiers' families.

The Kornilovtsi—Kerensky, Kaledin, and others, are endeavoring to lead troops against Petrograd. Several regiments, deceived by Kerensky, have sided with the insurgent People.

Soldiers! Make active resistance to the Kornilovets—Kerensky! Be on guard!

Railway men! Stop all troop-trains being sent by Kerensky against Petrograd!

Soldiers, Workers, Clerical employees! The destiny of the Revolution and democratic peace is in your hands!

Long live the Revolution!

*The All-Russian Congress of Soviets of Workers' and Soldiers' Deputies Delegates from the Peasants' Soviets*

It was exactly 5:17 A.M. when Krylenko, staggering with fatigue, climbed to the tribune with a telegram in his hand.

"Comrades! From the Northern Front. The Twelfth Army sends greetings to the Congress of Soviets, announcing the formation of a Military Revolutionary Committee which has taken over the command of the Northern Front!" Pandemonium, men weeping, embracing each other. "General Chermissov has recognized the Committee—Commissar of the Provisional Government Voitinsky has resigned!"

So. Lenin and the Petrograd workers had decided on insurrection, the Petrograd Soviet had overthrown the Provisional Government, and thrust the *coup d'état* upon the Congress of Soviets. Now there was all great Russia to win—and then the world! Would Russia follow and rise? And the world—what of it? Would the peoples answer and rise, a red world-tide?

Although it was six in the morning, night was yet heavy and chill. There was only a faint unearthly pallor stealing over the silent streets, dimming the watch-fires, the shadow of a terrible dawn gray-rising over Russia. . . .

# 5

---

# Plunging Ahead

Thursday, 8 November. Day broke on a city in the wildest excitement and confusion, a whole nation heaving up in long hissing swells of storm. Superficially all was quiet; hundreds of thousands of people retired at a prudent hour, got up early and went to work. In Petrograd the streetcars were running, the stores and restaurants open, theaters going, an exhibition of paintings advertised. . . . All the complex routine of common life—humdrum even in war-time—proceeded as usual. Nothing is so astounding as the vitality of the social organism—how it persists, feeding itself, clothing itself, amusing itself, in the face of the worst calamities. . . .

The air was full of rumors about Kerensky, who was said to have raised the front, and to be leading a great army against the capital. *Volia Naroda* published a *prikaz* launched by him at Pskov:

> The disorders caused by the insane attempt of the Bolsheviki place the country on the verge of a precipice, and demand the effort of our entire will, our courage and the devotion of every one of us, to win through the terrible trial which the fatherland is undergoing. . . .
>
> Until the declaration of the composition of the new Government—if one is formed—everyone ought to remain at his post and fulfill his duty toward bleeding Russia. It must be remembered that the least interference with existing Army organizations can bring on irreparable misfortunes by opening the front to the enemy. Therefore it is indispensable to preserve at any price the morale of the troops, by assuring complete order and the preservation of the Army from new shocks, and by maintaining absolute confidence between officers and their subordinates. I order all the chiefs and Commissars, in the name of the safety of the country, to stay at their posts as I

myself retain the post of Supreme Commander, until the Provisional Government of the Republic declare its will. . . .

In answer, this placard on all the walls:

FROM THE ALL-RUSSIAN CONGRESS OF SOVIETS

The ex-Ministers Konovalov, Kishkin, Tereshchenko, Maliantovich, Nikitin, and others have been arrested by the Military Revolutionary Committee. Kerensky has fled. All Army organizations are ordered to take every measure for the immediate arrest of Kerensky and his conveyance to Petrograd.

All assistance given to Kerensky will be punished as a serious crime against the State.

With brakes released the Military Revolutionary Committee whirled, throwing off orders, appeals, decrees, like sparks. . . .[30] Kornilov was ordered to be brought into Petrograd. Members of the Peasant Land Committees imprisoned by the Provisional Government were declared free. Capital punishment in the army was abolished. Government employees were ordered to continue their work, and threatened with severe penalties if they refused. All pillage, plunder, and speculation were forbidden under pain of death. Temporary Commissars were appointed in the various Ministries: Foreign Affairs, Uritsky and Trotsky; Interior and Justice, Rykov; Labor, Shliapnikov; Finance, Menzhinsky; Public Welfare, Madame Kollontai; Commerce, Ways, and Communications, Riazanov; Navy, the sailor Korbir; Posts and Telegraphs, Spiro; Theaters, Muraviov; State Printing Office, Gherbychev; for the City of Petrograd, Lieutenant Nesterov; for the Northern Front, Pozern. . . .

To the Army, appeal to set up Military Revolutionary Committees. To the railway workers, to maintain order, especially not to delay the transport of food to the cities and the front. . . . In return, they were promised representation in the Ministry of Ways and Communications.

Cossack brothers! [said one proclamation]. You are being led against Petrograd. They want to force you into battle with the revolutionary workers and soldiers of the capital. Do not believe a word that is said by our common enemies, the landowners and the capitalists.

At our Congress are represented all the conscious organizations of workers, soldiers, and peasants of Russia. The Congress also wishes to welcome into its midst the worker-Cossacks. The Generals of the Black Band, henchmen of the landowners, of Nikolai the Cruel, are our enemies.

They tell you the Soviets wish to confiscate the land of the Cossacks. This is a lie. It is only from the great Cossack landlords that the Revolution will confiscate the land to give it to the people.

Organize Soviets of Cossacks' Deputies! Join with the Soviets of Workers' and Soldiers' Deputies!

Show the Black Band that you are not traitors to the People, and that you do not wish to be cursed by the whole of revolutionary Russia. . . .

Cossack brothers, execute no orders of the enemies of the people. Send your delegates to Petrograd to talk it over with us. . . . The Cossacks of the Petrograd garrison, to their honor, have not justified the hope of the People's enemies. . . .

Cossack brothers! The All-Russian Congress of Soviets extends to you a fraternal hand. Long live the brotherhood of the Cossacks with the soldiers, workers, and peasants of all Russia!

On the other side, what a storm of proclamations posted up, handbills scattered everywhere, newspapers—screaming and cursing and prophesying evil. Now raged the battle of the printing-press—all other weapons being in the hands of the Soviets.

First, the appeal of the Committee for Salvation of Country and Revolution, flung broadcast over Russia and Europe;

TO THE CITIZENS OF THE RUSSIAN REPUBLIC

Contrary to the will of the revolutionary masses, on 7 November the Bolsheviki of Petrograd criminally arrested part of the Provisional Government, dispersed the Council of the Republic, and proclaimed an illegal power. Such violence committed against the Government of revolutionary Russia at the moment of its greatest external danger is an indescribable crime against the fatherland.

The insurrection of the Bolsheviki deals a mortal blow to the cause of national defense, and postpones immeasurably the moment of peace so greatly desired.

Civil war, begun by the Bolsheviki, threatens to deliver the country to the horrors of anarchy and counter-revolution, and cause the failure of the Constituent Assembly, which must affirm the republican régime and transmit to the People for ever their right to the land.

Preserving the continuity of the only legal Governmental power, the Committee for Salvation of Country and Revolution, established on the night of 7 November, takes the initiative in forming a new Provisional Government; which, basing itself on the forces of democracy, will conduct the country to the Constituent Assembly and save it from anarchy and counter-revolution. The Committee for Salvation summons you, citizens, to refuse to recognize the power of violence. Do not obey its orders!

Rise for the defense of the country and the Revolution!

Support the Committee for Salvation!

Signed by the Council of the Russian Republic, the Municipal Duma of Petrograd, the Tsay-ee-kah *(First Congress)*, the Executive Committee of the Peasants' Soviets, and from the Congress itself the Front group, the factions of Socialist Revolutionaries, Mensheviki, Populist Socialists, United Social Democrats, and the group "Yedinstvo."

Then posters from the Socialist Revolutionary party, the Mensheviki *oborontsi*, Peasants' Soviets again; from the Central Army Committee, the Tsentroflot. . . .

. . . Famine will crush Petrograd! (they cried). The German armies will trample on our liberty. Black Hundred *pogroms* will spread over Russia, if we all—conscious workers, soldiers, citizens—do not unite. . . .

Do not trust the promises of the Bolsheviki! The promise of immediate peace—is a lie! The promise of bread—a hoax! The promise of land—a fairy tale. . . .

They were all in this manner.

Comrades! You have been basely and cruelly deceived! The seizure of power has been accomplished by the Bolsheviki alone. . . . They concealed their plots from the other Socialist parties composing the Soviet. . . .

You have been promised land and freedom, but the counter-revolution will profit by the anarchy called forth by the Bolsheviki, and will deprive you of land and freedom. . . .

The newspapers were as violent.

> Our duty (said the *Dielo Naroda*) is to unmask these traitors to the working-class. Our duty is to mobilize all our forces and mount guard over the cause of the Revolution! . . .

*Izvestia*, for the last time, speaking in the name of the old Tsay-ee-kah, threatened awful retribution:

"As for the Congress of Soviets, we affirm that there has been no Congress of Soviets! We affirm that it was merely a private conference of the Bolshevik faction! And in that case, they have no right to cancel the powers of the Tsay-ee-kah. . . ."

*Novaya Zhizn*, while pleading for a new Government that should unite all the Socialist parties, criticized severely the action of the Socialist Revolutionaries and the Mensheviki in quitting the Congress, and pointed out that the Bolshevik insurrection meant one thing very clearly: that all illusions about coalition with the bourgeoisie were henceforth demonstrated vain. . . .

*Rabochi Put* blossomed out as *Pravda*, Lenin's newspaper which had been suppressed in July. It crowed, bristling:

> Workers, soldiers, peasants! In March you struck down the tyranny of the clique of nobles. Yesterday you struck down the tyranny of the bourgeois gang. . . .
>
> The first task is to guard the approaches to Petrograd.
>
> The second is definitely to disarm the counter-revolutionary elements of Petrograd.
>
> The third is definitely to organize the revolutionary power and assure the realization of the popular program. . . .

What few Cadet organs appeared, and the bourgeoisie, generally, adopted a detached, ironical attitude toward the whole business, a sort of contemptuous "I told you so" to the other parties. Influential Cadets were to be seen hovering around the Municipal Duma, and on the outskirts of the Committee for Salvation. Other than that, the bourgeoisie lay low, abiding its hour—which could not be far off. That the Bolsheviki would remain in power longer than three days never occurred to anybody—except perhaps to Lenin, Trotsky, the Petrograd workers, and the simpler soldiers. . . .

In the high, amphitheatrical Nikolai Hall that afternoon I saw the Duma sitting in *permanence*, tempestuous, grouping around it all the forces of opposition. The old Mayor, Schreider, majestic with his white hair and beard, was describing his visit to Smolny the night before, to protest in the name of the Municipal Self-Government. "The Duma, being the only existing legal Government in the city, elected by equal, direct and secret suffrage, would not recognize the new power," he had told Trotsky. And Trotsky had answered, "There is a constitutional remedy for that. The Duma can be dissolved and re-elected. . . ." At this report there was a furious outcry.

"If one recognizes a Government by bayonet," continued the old man, addressing the Duma, "well, we have one; but I consider legitimate only a Government recognized by the people, by a majority, and not one created by the usurpation of a minority!" Wild applause on all benches except those of the Bolsheviki. Amid renewed tumult the Mayor announced that the Bolsheviki were violating Municipal autonomy by appointing Commissars in many departments.

The Bolshevik speaker shouted, trying to make himself heard, that the decision of the Congress of Soviets meant that all Russia backed up the action of the Bolsheviki.

"You!" he cried. "You are not the real representative of the people of Petrograd!" Shrieks of "Insult! Insult!" The old Mayor, with dignity, reminded him that the Duma was elected by the freest possible popular vote. "Yes," he answered, "but that was a long time ago—like the Tsay-ee-kah—like the Army Committee."

"There has been no new Congress of Soviets!" they yelled at him.

"The Bolshevik faction refuses to remain any longer in this nest of counter-revolution—" Uproar. "—and we demand a re-election of the Duma. . . ." Whereupon the Bolsheviki left the chamber, followed by cries of "German agents! Down with the traitors!"

Shingariov, Cadet, then demanded that all Municipal functionaries who had consented to be Commissars of the Military Revolutionary Committee be discharged from their position and indicted. Schreider was on his feet, putting a motion to the effect that the Duma protested against the menace of the Bolsheviki to dissolve it, and as the legal representative of the population, it would refuse to leave its post.

Outside, the Alexander Hall was crowded for the meeting of the Committee for Salvation, and Skobeliev was again speaking. "Never yet," he said, "was the fate of the Revolution so acute, never yet did the question of the existence of the Russian State excite so much anxiety, never yet did history put so harshly and categorically the question—is Russia to be or not to be! The great hour for the salvation of the Revolution has arrived, and in consciousness thereof we observe the close union of the live forces of the revolutionary democracy, by whose organized will a center for the salvation of the country and the Revolution has already been created. . . ." And much of the same sort. "We shall die sooner than surrender our post!"

Amid violent applause it was announced that the Union of Railway Workers had joined the Committee for Salvation. A few moments later the Post and Telegraph Employees came in; then some Mensheviki Internationalists entered the hall, to cheers. The Railway men said they did not recognize the Bolsheviki and had taken the entire railroad apparatus into their own hands, refusing to entrust it to any usurpatory power. The Telegraphers' delegate declared that the operators had flatly refused to work their instruments as long as the Bolshevik Commissar was in the office. The Postmen would not deliver or accept mail at Smolny. . . . All the Smolny telephones were cut off. With great glee it was reported how Uritsky had gone to the Ministry of Foreign Affairs to demand the secret treaties and how Neratov had put him out. The Government employees were all stopping work. . . .

It was war—war deliberately planned, Russian fashion: war by strike and sabotage. As we sat there the chairman read a list of names and assignments; so-and-so was to make the round of the Ministries; and another was to visit the banks; some ten or twelve were to work the barracks and persuade the soldiers to remain neutral—"Russian soldiers, do not shed the blood of your brothers!"; a committee was to go and confer with Kerensky; still others were dispatched to provincial cities, to form branches of the Committee for Salvation, and link together the anti-Bolshevik elements.

The crowd was in high spirits. "These Bolsheviki *will* try to dictate to the *intelligentsia*? We'll show them!" . . . Nothing could be more striking than the contrast between this assemblage and the Congress of Soviets. There, great masses of shabby soldiers, grimy workmen, peasants—poor men, bent and scarred in the brute struggle for existence; here the Menshevik and Socialist Revolutionary leaders—Avksentievs, Dans, Liebers—the former Socialist Ministers—Skobelievs, Chernovs—rubbed shoulders with Cadets like oily Shatsky, sleek Vinaver; with journalists, students, intellectuals of almost all camps. This Duma crowd was well fed, well dressed; I did not see more than three proletarians among them all. . . .

News came. Kornilov's faithful Tekhintsi* had slaughtered his guards at Bykhov, and he had escaped. Kaledin was marching north. . . . The Soviet of Moscow had set up a Military Revolutionary Committee, and was negotiating with the commandant of the city for possession of the arsenal, so that the workers might be armed.

With these facts was mixed an astounding jumble of rumors, distortions, and plain lies. For instance, an intelligent young Cadet, formerly private secretary to Milyukov and then to Tereshchenko, drew us aside and told us all about the taking of the Winter Palace.

"The Bolsheviki were led by German and Austrian officers," he affirmed.

*See Notes and Explanations.

"Is that so?" we replied, politely. "How do you know?"

"A friend of mine was there and saw them."

"How could he tell they were German officers?"

"Oh, because they wore German uniforms!"

There were hundreds of such absurd tales, and they were not only solemnly published by the anti-Bolshevik press, but believed by the most unlikely persons—Socialist Revolutionaries and Mensheviki who had always been distinguished by their sober devotion to facts. . . .

But more serious were the stories of Bolshevik violence and terrorism. For example, it was said and printed that the Red Guards had not only thoroughly looted the Winter Palace, but that they had massacred the *yunkers* after disarming them, had killed some of the Ministers in cold blood; and as for the women soldiers, most of them had been violated, and many had committed suicide because of the tortures they had gone through. . . . All these stories were swallowed whole by the crowd in the Duma. But worse still, the mothers and fathers of the students and the women read these frightful details (often accompanied by lists of names), and toward nightfall the Duma began to be besieged by frantic citizens. . . .

A typical case is that of Prince Tumanov, whose body it was announced in many newspapers had been found floating in the Moika Canal. A few hours later this was denied by the Prince's family, who added that the Prince was under arrest, so the press identified the dead man as General Denissov. The General having also come to life, we investigated, and could find no trace of any body having been found whatever. . . .

As we left the Duma building two boy scouts were distributing handbills[31] to the enormous crowd which blocked the Nevsky in front of the door—a crowd composed almost entirely of business men, shopkeepers, *chinovniki*, clerks. One read:

#### FROM THE MUNICIPAL DUMA

The Municipal Duma in its meeting of 26 October, in view of the events of the day, decrees: To announce the inviolability of private dwellings. Through the House of Committees it calls upon the population of the town of Petrograd to meet with decisive repulse all attempts to enter by force private apartments, not stopping at the use of arms, in the interests of the self-defense of citizens.

Up on the corner of the Liteiny, five or six Red Guards and a couple of sailors had surrounded a newsdealer and were demanding that he hand over his copies of the Menshevik *Rabochaya Gazeta* (Workers' Gazette). Angrily he shouted at them, shaking his fist, as one of the sailors tore the papers from his stand. An ugly crowd had gathered around, abusing the patrol. One little workman kept explaining doggedly to the people and the newsdealer, over and over again, "It has Kerensky's proclamation in it. It says we killed Russian people. It will make bloodshed. . . ."

Smolny was tenser than ever, if that were possible. The same running men in the dark corridors, squads of workers with rifles, leaders with bulging portfolios arguing, explaining, giving orders as they hurried anxiously along, surrounded by friends and lieutenants. Men literally out of themselves, living prodigies of sleeplessness and work—men unshaven, filthy, with burning eyes who drove upon their fixed purpose full speed on engines of exaltation. So much they had to do, so much! Take over the Government, organize the City, keep the garrison loyal, fight the Duma and the Committee for Salvation, keep out the Germans, prepare to do battle with Kerensky, inform the provinces what had happened, propagandize from Archangel to Vladivostok. . . . Government and Municipal Employees refusing to obey their Commissars, post and telegraph refusing them communication, railroads stonily ignoring their appeals for trains, Kerensky coming, the garrison not altogether to be trusted, the Cossacks waiting to come out. . . . Against them not only the organized bourgeoisie, but all the other Socialist parties except the Left Socialist Revolutionaries, a few Mensheviki Internationalists, and the Social Democrat Internationalists, and even they undecided whether to stand by or not. With them, it is true, the workers and the soldier-masses—the peasants an unknown quantity—but after all the Bolsheviki were a political faction not rich in trained and educated men. . . .

Riazanov was coming up the front steps, explaining in a sort of humorous panic that he, Commissar of Commerce, knew nothing whatever of business. In the upstairs café sat a man all by himself in the corner, in a goatskin cape and clothes which had been—I was going to say "slept in," but of course he hadn't slept—and a three days' growth of beard. He was anxiously figuring on a dirty envelope, and biting his pencil meanwhile. This was Menzhinsky, Commissar of Finance, whose qualifications were that he had once been a clerk in a French bank. . . . And these four half-running down the hall from the office of the Military Revolutionary Committee, and scribbling on bits of paper as they run—these were Commissars dispatched to the four corners of Russia to carry the news, argue, or fight—with whatever arguments or weapons came to hand. . . .

The Congress was to meet at one o'clock, and long since the great meeting-hall had filled, but by seven there was yet no sign of the presidium. . . . The Bolshevik and Left Social Revolutionary factions were in session in their own rooms. All the live-long afternoon Lenin and Trotsky had fought against compromise. A considerable part of the Bolsheviki were in favor of giving way so far as to create a joint all-Socialist government. "We can't hold on!" they cried. "Too much is against us. We haven't got the men. We will be isolated, and the whole thing will fall." So Kameniev, Riazanov, and others.

But Lenin, with Trotsky beside him, stood firm as a rock.* "Let the compromisers accept our program and they can come in! We won't give way an inch. If there are comrades here who haven't the courage and the will to dare what we dare, let them leave with the rest of the cowards and conciliators! Backed by the workers and the soldiers we shall go on."

At five minutes past seven came word from the left Socialist

---

*Lenin was not against an All-Socialist Government, provided it was responsible to the Soviets and accepted the Bolshevik minimum program. See *The Errors of Trotskyism*.

Revolutionaries to say that they would remain in the Military Revolutionary Committee.

"See!" said Lenin. "They are following!"

A little later, as we sat at the press table in the big hall, an Anarchist who was writing for the bourgeois papers proposed to me that we go and find out what had become of the presidium. There was nobody in the Tsay-ee-kah office, nor in the bureau of the Petrograd Soviet. From room to room we wandered, through vast Smolny. Nobody seemed to have the slightest idea where to find the governing body of the Congress. As we went my companion described the ancient revolutionary activities, his long and pleasant exile in France. . . . As for the Bolsheviki, he confided to me that they were common, rude, ignorant persons, without aesthetic sensibilities. He was a real specimen of the Russian *intelligentsia*. . . . So we came at last to room 17, office of the Military Revolutionary Committee, and stood there in the midst of all the furious coming and going. The door opened and out shot a squat, flat-faced man in a uniform without insignia, who seemed to be smiling—which smile, after a minute, one saw to be the fixed grin of extreme fatigue. It was Krylenko.

My friend, who was a dapper, civilized-looking young man gave a cry of pleasure and stepped forward.

"Nikolai Vasilievich!" he said, holding out his hand. "Don't you remember me, comrade? We were in prison together."

Krylenko made an effort and concentrated his mind and sight. "Why, yes," he answered finally, looking the other up and down with an expression of great friendliness. "You are S—. *Zdra'-stvuitye!*" They kissed. "What are you doing in all this?" He waved his arm around.

"Oh, I'm just looking on. . . . You seem very successful."

"Yes," replied Krylenko, with a sort of doggedness, "the proletarian Revolution is a great success." He laughed. "Perhaps—perhaps, however, we'll meet in prison again!"

When we got out into the corridor again my friend went on with his explanations. "You see, I'm a follower of Kropotkin. To us the Revolution is a great failure; it has not aroused the patriotism of the masses. Of course that only proves that the people are not ready for Revolution. . . ."

It was just 8:40 when a thundering wave of cheers announced the entrance of the presidium, with Lenin—great Lenin—among them. A short, stocky figure, with a big head set down on his shoulders, bald and bulging. Little eyes, a snubbish nose, wide generous mouth, and heavy chin; clean-shaven now but already beginning to bristle with the well-known beard of his past and future. Dressed in shabby clothes, his trousers much too long for him. Unimpressive, to be the idol of a mob, loved and revered as perhaps few leaders in history have been. A strange popular leader—a leader purely by virtue of intellect; colorless, humorless, uncompromising and detached, without picturesque idiosyncrasies—but with the power of explaining profound ideas in simple terms, of analyzing a concrete situation. And combined with shrewdness, the greatest intellectual audacity.

Kameniev was reading the report of the actions of the Military Revolutionary Committee; abolition of capital punishment in the Army, restoration of the free right of propaganda, release of officers and soldiers arrested for political crimes, orders to arrest Kerensky and confiscation of food supplies in private storehouses. . . . Tremendous applause.

Again the representative of the *Bund*. The uncompromising attitude of the Bolsheviki would mean the crushing of the Revolution; therefore, the *Bund* delegates must refuse any longer to sit in the Congress. Cries from the audience, "We thought you walked out last night! How many more times are you going to walk out?"

Then the representative of the Mensheviki Internationalists. Shouts "What! You here still?" The speaker explained that only part of the Mensheviki Internationalists left the Congress; the rest were going to stay—

"We consider it dangerous and perhaps even mortal for the Revolution to transfer the power to the Soviets"—interruptions—"but we feel it our duty to remain in the Congress and vote against the transfer here!"

Other speakers followed, apparently without any order. A delegate of the coal-miners of the Don Basin called upon the Congress to take measures against Kaledin, who might cut off coal and food from the capital. Several soldiers just arrived from the front brought the enthusiastic greetings of their regiments. . . . Now Lenin, gripping the edge of the reading stand, letting his little winking eyes travel over the crowd as he stood there waiting, apparently oblivious to the long-rolling ovation, which lasted several minutes. When it finished, he said simply, "We shall now proceed to construct the Socialist order!" Again that overwhelming human roar.

"The first thing is the adoption of practical measures to realize peace. . . . We shall offer peace to the peoples of all the belligerent countries upon the basis of the Soviet terms—no annexations, no indemnities, and the right of self-determination of peoples. At the same time, according to our promise, we shall publish and repudiate the secret treaties. . . . The question of War and Peace is so clear that I think that I may, without preamble, read the project of a Proclamation to the Peoples of All the Belligerent Countries. . . ."

His great mouth, seeming to smile, opened wide as he spoke; his voice was hoarse—not unpleasantly so, but as if it had hardened that way after years and years of speaking—and went on monotonously, with the effect of being able to go on for ever. . . . For emphasis he bent forward slightly. No gestures. And before him, a thousand simple faces looking up in intent adoration.

### PROCLAMATION TO THE PEOPLES AND GOVERNMENTS OF ALL THE BELLIGERENT NATIONS

The Workers' and Peasants' Government, created by the revolution of 6 and 7 November and based on the Soviet of Workers', Soldiers', and Peasants' Deputies, proposes to all the belligerent peoples and to their Governments to begin immediately negotiations for a just and democratic peace.

The Government means by a just and democratic peace, which is desired by the majority of the workers and the laboring classes, exhausted and depleted by the war—that peace which the Russian workers and peasants, after having struck down the Czarist monarchy, have not ceased to demand categorically—immediate peace without annexations (that is to say without conquest of foreign territory, without forcible annexation of other nationalities), and without indemnities.

The Government of Russia proposes to all the belligerent peoples immediately to conclude such a peace, by showing themselves willing to enter upon decisive steps of negotiations aiming at such a peace, at once, without the slightest delay, before the definitive ratification of all the conditions of such a peace by the authorized assemblies of the peoples of all countries and of all nationalities.

By annexation or conquest of foreign territory the Government means—conformably to the conception of democratic rights in general, and the rights of the working class in particular—all union to a great and strong State of a small or weak nationality, without the voluntary, clear, and precise expression of its consent and desire; whatever be the moment when such an annexation by force was accomplished, whatever be the degree of civilization of the nation annexed by force or maintained outside the frontiers of another State, no matter if that nation be in Europe or in the far countries across the sea.

If any nation is retained by force within the limits of another State; if, in spite of the desire expressed by it (it matters little if that desire be expressed by the press, by popular meetings, decisions of political parties, or by disorders and riots against national oppression), that nation is not given the right of deciding by free vote—without the slightest constraint, after the complete departure of the armed forces of the nation which has annexed it or wishes to annex it or is stronger in general—the form of its national and political organization, such a union constitutes an annexation—that is to say, conquest and an act of violence.

To continue their war in order to permit the strong and rich nations to divide among themselves the weak and conquered nationalities is considered by the Government the greatest possible crime against humanity, and the Government solemnly proclaims its decision to sign a treaty of peace which will put an end to this war upon the above conditions, equally fair for all nationalities without exception.

The Government abolishes secret diplomacy, expressing before the whole country its firm decision to conduct all the negotiations in the light of day before the people, and will proceed immediately to the full publication of all secret treaties confirmed or concluded by the Government of the landowners and capitalists from March until

7 November 1917. All the clauses of the secret treaties which, as occur in the majority of cases, have for their object to procure advantages and privileges for Russian imperialists, are denounced by the Government immediately and without discussion.

In proposing to all Governments and all peoples to engage in public negotiations for peace, the Government declares itself ready to carry on these negotiations by telegraph, by post, or by pourparlers between the different countries, or at a conference of these representatives. To facilitate these pourparlers, the Government appoints its authorized representatives in the neutral countries.

The Government proposes to all the governments and to all the peoples of all the belligerent countries to conclude an immediate armistice, at the same time suggesting that the armistice ought to last three months, during which time it is perfectly possible, not only to hold the necessary pourparlers between the representatives of all the nations and nationalities without exception drawn into the war or forced to take part in it, but also to convoke authorized assemblies of representatives of the people of all countries, for the purpose of the definite acceptance of the conditions of peace.

In addressing this offer of peace to the Governments and to the peoples of all the belligerent countries, the Provisional Workers' and Peasants' Government of Russia addresses equally and in particular the conscious workers of the three nations most devoted to humanity and the three most important nations among those taking part in the present war—England, France, and Germany. The workers of these countries have rendered the greatest services to the cause of progress and Socialism. The splendid examples of the Chartist movement in England, the series of revolutions, of world-wide historical significance, accomplished by the French proletariat—and finally, in Germany, the historic struggle against the Laws of Exception, an example for the workers of the whole world of prolonged and stubborn action, and the creation of formidable organizations of German proletarians—all these models of proletarian heroism, these monuments of history, are for us a sure guarantee that the workers of these countries will understand the duty imposed upon them to liberate humanity from the horrors and consequences of war; and that these workers, by decisive, energetic, and continued action, will help us to bring to a successful conclusion the cause of peace—and at the same time, the cause of the liberation of the exploited working masses from all slavery and all exploitation.

When the grave thunder of applause had died away, Lenin spoke again:

"We propose to the Congress to ratify this declaration. We address ourselves to the Governments as well as to the peoples, for a declaration which would be addressed only to the peoples of the belligerent countries might delay the conclusion of peace. The conditions of peace, drawn up during the armistice, will be ratified by the Constituent Assembly. In fixing the duration of the armistice at three months, we desire to give to the peoples as long a rest as possible after this bloody extermination, and ample time for them to elect their representatives. This proposal of peace will meet with resistance on the part of the imperialist governments— we don't fool ourselves on that score. But we hope that revolution will soon break out in all the belligerent countries; that is why we address ourselves to the workers of France, England, and Germany. . . .

"The revolution of 6 and 7 November," he ended, "has opened the era of the Social Revolution. . . . The labor movement, in the name of peace and Socialism, shall win, and fulfill its destiny. . . ."

There was something quiet and powerful in all this, which stirred the souls of men. It was understandable why people believed when Lenin spoke. . . .

By crowd vote it was quickly decided that only representatives of political factions should be allowed to speak on the motion and that speakers should be limited to fifteen minutes.

First Karelin for the Left Socialist Revolutionaries. "Our faction had no opportunity to propose amendments to the text of the proclamation; it is a private document of the Bolsheviki. But we will vote for it because we agree with its spirit. . . ."

For the Social Democrat Internationalists Kramarov, long, stoop-shouldered, and near-sighted—destined to achieve some notoriety as the Clown of the Opposition. Only a Government composed of all the Socialist parties, he said, could possess the authority to take such important action. If a Socialist coalition was formed, his faction would support the entire program; if not, only part of it. As for the proclamation, the Internationalists were in thorough accord with its main points. . . .

Then one after another, amid rising enthusiasm; Ukrainian Social Democracy, support; Lithuanian Social Democracy, support; Populist Socialists, support; Polish Social Democracy, support; Polish Socialists, support—but would prefer a Socialist coalition; Lettish Social Democracy, support. . . . Something was kindled in these men. One spoke of the "coming World-Revolution, of which we are the advance-guard"; another of "the new age of brotherhood, when all the peoples will become one great family. . . ." An individual member claimed the floor. "There is contradiction here," he said. "First you offer peace without annexations and indemnities, and then you say you will consider all peace offers. To consider means to accept. . . ."

Lenin was on his feet. "We want a just peace, but we are not afraid of a revolutionary war. . . . Probably the imperialist Governments will not answer our appeal—but we shall not issue an ultimatum to which it will be easy to say no. . . . If the German proletariat realizes that we are ready to consider all offers of peace, that will perhaps be the last drop which overflows the bowl—revolution will break out in Germany. . . .

"We consent to examine all conditions of peace, but that doesn't mean that we shall accept them. . . . For some of our terms we shall fight to the end—but possibly for others will find it impossible to continue the war. . . . Above all, we want to finish the war. . . ."

It was exactly 10:35 when Kameniev asked all in favor of the proclamation to hold up their cards. One delegate dared to raise his hand against, but the sudden outburst around him brought it swiftly down. . . . Unanimous.

Suddenly, by common impulse, we found ourselves on our feet, mumbling together into the smooth lifting unison of the *Internationale*. A grizzled old soldier was sobbing like a child. Alexandra Kollontai rapidly winked the tears back. The immense sound rolled through the hall, burst windows and doors and soared into the quiet sky. "The war is ended! The war is ended!" said a young workman near me, his face shining. And when it was over, as we stood there in a kind of awkward hush, someone in the back of the room shouted, "Comrades! Let us remember those who have died for liberty!" So we began to sing the Funeral March, that slow, melancholy, and yet triumphant chant, so Russian and so moving. The *Internationale* is an alien air, after all. The Funeral March seemed the very soul of those dark masses whose delegates sat in this hall, building from their obscure visions a new Russia—and perhaps more.

You fell in the fatal fight
For the liberty of the people, for the honor of the people.
You gave up your lives and everything dear to you,
You suffered in horrible prisons,
You went to exile in chains. . . .
Without a word you carried your chains because you could not ignore
 your suffering brothers,
Because you believed that justice is stronger than the sword. . . .
The time will come when your surrendered life will count.
That time is near; when tyranny falls the people will rise, great and
 free!
Farewell, brothers, you chose a noble path,
At your grave we swear to fight, to work for freedom and the people's
 happiness. . . .

For this did they lie there, the martyrs of March, in their cold Brotherhood Grave on Mars Field; for this thousands and tens of thousands had died in the prisons, in exile, in Siberian mines. It had not come as they expected it would come, nor as the *intelligentsia* desired it; but it had come—rough, strong, impatient of formulas, contemptuous of sentimentalism; *real*. . . .

Lenin was reading the Decree on Land:

(1) All private ownership of land is abolished immediately without compensation.

(2) All landowners' estates and all lands belonging to the Crown, to monasteries, church lands with all their live stock and inventoried property, buildings and all appurtenances, are transferred to the disposition of the township Land Committees and the district Soviets of Peasants' Deputies until the Constituent Assembly meets.

(3) Any damage whatever done to the confiscated property which from now on belongs to the whole People, is regarded as a serious crime, punishable by the revolutionary tribunals. The district Soviets of Peasants' Deputies shall take all necessary measures for the observ-

ance of the strictest order during the taking over of the landowners' estates, for the determination of the dimensions of the plots of land and which of them are subject to confiscation, for the drawing up of an inventory of the entire confiscated property, and for the strictest revolutionary protection of all the farming property on the land, with all buildings, improvements, cattle, supplies of products, etc., passing into the hands of the people.

(4) For guidance during the realization of the great land reforms until their final resolution by the Constituent Assembly, shall serve the following peasant *nakaz* (instructions),[32] drawn up on the basis of 242 local peasants *nakazi* by the editorial board of the *"Izvestia* of the All-Russian Soviet of Peasants' Deputies," and published in No. 88 of said *"Izvestia"* (Petrograd, No. 88, 29 August 1917).

The lands of peasants and of Cossacks serving in the Army shall not be confiscated.

"This is not," explained Lenin, "the project of former Minister Chernov, who spoke of 'erecting a framework' and tried to realize reforms from above. From below, on the spot will be decided the questions of division of the land. The amount of land received by each peasant will vary according to the locality. . . .

"Under the Provisional Government, the *pomieshchiki* flatly refused to obey the orders of the Land Committees—those Land Committees projected by Lvov, brought into existence by Shingariov, and administered by Kerensky!"

Before the debates could begin a man forced his way violently through the crowd in the aisle and climbed upon the platform. It was Pianikh, member of the Executive Committee of the Peasants' Soviets, and he was mad clean through.

"The Executive Committee of the All-Russian Soviets of Peasants' Deputies protests against the arrest of our comrades, the Ministers Salazkin and Mazlov!" he flung harshly in the faces of the crowd. "We demand their instant release! They are now in Peter-Paul fortress. We must have immediate action! There is not a moment to lose!"

Another followed him, a soldier with a disordered beard and flaming eyes. "You sit here and talk about giving the land to the peasants, and you commit an act of tyrants and usurpers against the peasants' chosen representatives! I tell you"—he raised his fist—"if one hair of their heads is harmed you'll have a revolt on your hands!" The crowd stirred confusedly.

Then up rose Trotsky, calm and venomous, conscious of power, greeted with a roar. "Yesterday the Military Revolutionary Committee decided to release the Socialist Revolutionary and Menshevik Ministers, Mazlov, Salazkin, Gvozdov, and Maliantovich—on principle. That they are still in Peter-Paul is only because we have had so much to do. . . . They will, however, be detained at their homes under arrest until we have investigated their complicity in the treacherous acts of Kerensky during the Kornilov affair!"

"Never," shouted Pianikh, "in any revolution have such things been seen as go on here!"

"You are mistaken," responded Trotsky. "Such things have been seen even in this revolution. Hundreds of our comrades were arrested in the July days. . . . When Comrade Kollontai was released from prison by the doctor's orders, Avksentiev placed at her door two former agents of the Czar's secret police!" The peasants withdrew, muttering, followed by ironical hoots.

The representative of the Left Socialist Revolutionaries spoke on the Land Decree. While agreeing in principle, his faction could not vote on the question until after discussion. The Peasants' Soviets should be consulted. . . .

The Mensheviki Internationalists, too, insisted on a party caucus.

Then the leader of the Maximalists, the Anarchist wing of the peasants: "We must do honor to a political party which puts such an act into effect the first day, without jawing about it!"

A typical peasant was in the tribune, long hair, boots and sheepskin coat, bowing to all corners of the hall. "I wish you well, comrades and citizens," he said. "There are some Cadets walking around outside. You arrested our Socialist peasants—why not arrest them?"

This was the signal for a debate of excited peasants. It was precisely like the debate of soldiers of the night before. Here were the real proletarians of the land. . . .

"Those members of our Executive Committee, Avksentiev and

the rest, whom we thought were the peasants' protectors—they are only Cadets too! Arrest them! Arrest them!"

Another, "Who are these Pianikhs, these Avksentievs? They are not peasants at all! They only wag their tails!"

How the crowd rose to them, recognizing brothers!

The Left Socialist Revolutionaries proposed a half-hour intermission. As delegates streamed out, Lenin stood up in his place.

"We must not lose time, comrades! News all-important to Russia must be on the press tomorrow morning. No delay!"

And above the hot discussion, argument, shuffling of feet could be heard the voice of an emissary of the Military Revolutionary Committee, crying, "Fifteen agitators wanted in room 17 at once! To go to the front! . . ."

It was almost two hours and a half later that the delegates came straggling back, the presidium mounted the platform, and the session commenced by the reading of telegrams from regiment after regiment, announcing their adhesion to the Military Revolutionary Committee.

In leisurely manner the meeting gathered momentum. A delegate from the Russian troops on the Macedonian front spoke bitterly of their situation. "We suffer there more from the friendship of our 'Allies' than from the enemy," he said. Representatives of the Tenth and Twelfth Armies, just arrived in hot haste, reported, "We support you with all our strength!" A peasant soldier protested against the release of "the traitor Socialists Mazlov and Salazkin"; as for the Executive Committee of the Peasants' Soviets, it should be arrested *en masse*! Here was real revolutionary talk. . . . A deputy from the Russian Army in Persia declared he was instructed to demand all power to the Soviets. . . . A Ukrainian officer, speaking in his native tongue: "There is no nationalism in this crisis. . . . *Da zdravstvuyet* the proletarian dictatorship of all lands!" Such a deluge of high and hot thoughts that surely Russia would never again be dumb!

Kameniev remarked that the anti-Bolshevik forces were trying to stir up disorders everywhere, and read an appeal of the Congress to all the Soviets of Russia:

The All-Russian Congress of Soviets of Workers' and Soldiers' Deputies, including some Peasants' Deputies, calls upon the local Soviets to take immediate energetic measures to oppose all counter-revolutionary anti-Jewish action and all *pogroms* whatever they may be. The honor of the Workers', Peasants', and Soldiers' Revolution demands that no *pogrom* be tolerated.

The Red Guard of Petrograd, the revolutionary garrison and the sailors have maintained complete order in the capital.

Workers, soldiers, and peasants, you should follow everywhere the example of the workers and soldiers of Petrograd.

Comrade soldiers and Cossacks, on us falls the duty of assuring real revolutionary order.

All revolutionary Russia and the entire world have their eyes on us. . . .

At two o'clock the Land Decree was put to the vote, with only one against and the peasant delegates wild with joy. . . . So plunged the Bolsheviki ahead, irresistible, overriding hesitation and opposition—the only people in Russia who had a definite program of action while the others talked for eight long months.

Now arose a soldier, gaunt, ragged and eloquent, to protest against the clause of the *nakaz* tending to deprive military deserters from a share in village land allotments. Bawled at and hissed at first, his simple, moving speech finally made silence. "Forced against his will into the butchery of the trenches," he cried, "which you yourselves, in the Peace decree, have voted senseless as well as horrible, he greeted the Revolution with hope of peace and freedom. Peace? The Government of Kerensky forced him again to go forward into Galicia to slaughter and be slaughtered; to his pleas for peace, Tereshchenko simply laughed. . . . Freedom? Under Kerensky he found his Committees suppressed, his newspapers cut off, his party speakers put in prison. . . . At home in his village, the landlords were defying his Land Committees, jailing his comrades. . . . In Petrograd the bourgeoisie, in alliance with the Germans, were sabotaging the food and ammunition for the Army. . . . He was without boots or clothes. . . . Who forced him to desert? The Government of Kerensky, which you have overthrown!" At the end there was applause.

But another soldier hotly denounced it: "The Government of Kerensky is not a screen behind which can be hidden dirty work like desertion! Deserters are scoundrels, who run away home and leave their comrades to die in the trenches alone! Every deserter is a traitor and should be punished. . . ." Uproar, shouts of *"Do volno! Teeshe!"* Kameniev hastily proposed to leave the matter to the Government for decision.[33]

At 2:30 A.M. fell a tense hush. Kameniev was reading the decree of the Constitution of Power:

> Until the meeting of the Constituent Assembly, a provisional Workers' and Peasants' Government is formed, which shall be named the Council of People's Commissars.[34]
>
> The administration of the different branches of state activity shall be entrusted to commissions, whose composition shall be regulated to ensure the carrying out of the program of the Congress, in close union with the mass organizations of working-men, working-women, sailors, soldiers, peasants, and clerical employees. The governmental power is vested in a *collegium* made up of the chairmen of these commissions, that is to say, the Council of the People's Commissars.
>
> Control over the activities of the People's Commissars, and the right to replace them, shall belong to the All-Russian Congress of Soviets of Workers', Peasants', and Soldiers' Deputies, and its Central Committee.

Still silence; as he read the list of Commissars, bursts of applause after each name, Lenin's and Trotsky's especially.

> *President of the Council:* Vladimir Ulyanov (*Lenin*).
> *Interior:* A. I. Rykov.
> *Agriculture:* V. P. Milyutin.
> *Labor:* A. G. Shliapnikov.
> *Military and Naval Affairs:* A committee composed of V. A. Avseenko (*Antonov*), N. V. Krylenko, and F. M. Dybenko.
> *Commerce and Industry:* V. P. Nogin.
> *Popular Education:* A. V. Lunacharsky.
> *Finance:* I. I. Skvortsov (*Stepanov*).
> *Foreign Affairs:* L. D. Bronstein (*Trotsky*).
> *Justice:* G. E. Oppokov (*Lomov*).

*Supplies:* E. A. Teodorovich.
*Post and Telegraph:* N. P. Avilov (*Gliebov*).
*Chairman for Nationalities:* I. V. Djugashvili (*Stalin*).
*Railroads:* To be filled later.

There were bayonets at the edges of the room, bayonets pricking up among the delegates; the Military Revolutionary Committee was arming everybody, Bolshevism was arming for the decisive battle with Kerensky, the sound of whose trumpets came up the southwest wind. . . . In the meanwhile nobody went home; on the contrary, hundreds of newcomers filtered in, filling the great room solid with stern-faced soldiers and workmen who stood for hours and hours, indefatigably intent. The air was thick with cigarette smoke, and human breathing, and the smell of coarse clothes and sweat.

Avilov of the staff of *Novaya Zhizn* was speaking in the name of the Social Democratic Internationalists and the remnant of the Mensheviki Internationalists; Avilov, with his young, intelligent face, looking out of place in his smart frock-coat.

"We must ask ourselves where we are going. . . . The ease with which the Coalition Government was upset cannot be explained by the strength of the left wing of the democracy, but only by the incapacity of the Government to give the people peace and bread. And the left wing cannot maintain itself in power unless it can solve these questions. . . .

"Can it give bread to the people? Grain is scarce. The majority of the peasants will not be with you, for you cannot give them the machinery they need. Fuel and other primary necessities are almost impossible to procure. . . .

"As for peace, that will be even more difficult. The Allies refused to talk with Skobeliev. They will never accept the proposition of a peace conference from *you*. You will not be recognized either in London and Paris or in Berlin. . . .

"You cannot count on the effective help of the proletariat of the Allied countries because in most countries it is very far from the revolutionary struggle; remember, the Allied democracy was unable to convoke the Stockholm Conference. Concerning the

German Social Democrats, I have just talked with Comrade Goldenberg, one of our delegates to Stockholm; he was told by the representatives of the Extreme Left that revolution in Germany was impossible during the war. . . ." Here interruptions began to come thick and fast, but Avilov kept on.

"The isolation of Russia will fatally result either in the defeat of the Russian Army by the Germans, and the patching up of a peace between the Austro-German coalition and the Franco-British coalition *at the expense of Russia*—or in a separate peace with Germany.

"I have just learned that the Allied ambassadors are preparing to leave, and that Committees for Salvation of Country and Revolution are forming in all the cities of Russia. . . .

"No one party can conquer these enormous difficulties. The majority of the people, supporting a government of Socialist coalition, can alone accomplish the Revolution. . . ."

He then read the resolution of the two factions:

> Recognizing that for the salvation of the conquests of the Revolution it is indispensable immediately to constitute a government based on the Soviet of Workers', Soldiers', and Peasants' Deputies, recognizing, moreover, that the task of this government is the quickest possible attainment of peace, the transfer of the land into the hands of the agrarian committees, the organization of control over industrial production, and the convocation of the Constituent Assembly on the date decided, the Congress appoints an executive committee to constitute such a government after an agreement with the groups of the democracy which are taking part in the Congress.

In spite of the revolutionary exaltation of the triumphant crowd, Avilov's cool, tolerant reasoning had shaken them. Toward the end the cries and hisses died away, and when he finished there was even some clapping.

Karelin followed him—also young, fearless, whose sincerity no one doubted—for the Left Socialist Revolutionaries, the party of Marie Spiridonova, the party which almost alone followed the Bolsheviki, and which represented the revolutionary peasants.

"Our party has refused to enter the Council of People's Com-

missars because we do not wish for ever to separate ourselves
from the part of the revolutionary army which left the Congress,
a separation which would make it impossible for us to serve as
intermediaries between the Bolsheviki and the other groups of
the democracy. . . . And that is our principal duty at this moment.
We cannot sustain any government except a government of Socialist coalition. . . .

"We protest, moreover, against the tyrannical conduct of the
Bolsheviki. Our Commissars have been driven from their posts.
Our only organ, *Znamia Truda* (Banner of Labor), was forbidden
to appear yesterday. . . .

"The Central Duma is forming a powerful Committee for Salvation of Country and Revolution to fight you. Already you are
isolated, and your Government is without the support of a single
other democratic group. . . ."

And now Trotsky stood upon the raised tribune, confident and
dominating, with that sarcastic expression about his mouth which
was almost a sneer. He spoke in a ringing voice, and the great
crowd rose to him.

"These considerations on the danger of isolation of our party
are not new. On the eve of insurrection our fatal defeat was also
predicted. Everybody was against us; only a faction of the Socialist Revolutionaries of the Left was with us in the Military Revolutionary Committee. How is it that we were able to overturn the
Government almost without bloodshed? . . . That fact is the most
striking proof that we *were not isolated.* In reality the Provisional
Government was isolated; the democratic parties which march
against us were isolated, are isolated, and for ever cut off from the
proletariat!

"They speak of the necessity for a coalition. There is only one
coalition possible—the coalition of the workers, soldiers, and
poorest peasants; and it is our party's honor to have realized that
coalition. . . . What sort of coalition did Avilov mean? A coalition
with those who supported the Government of Treason to the
People? Coalition doesn't always add to strength. For example,
could we have organized the insurrection with Dan and Avksentiev in our ranks?" Roars of laughter.

"Avksentiev gave little bread. Will a coalition with the *oborontsi* furnish more? Between the peasants and Avksentiev, who ordered the arrest of the Land Committees, we choose the peasants! Our Revolution will remain the classic revolution of history. . . .

"They accuse us of repelling an agreement with the other democratic parties. But is it we who are to blame? Or must we, as Karelin put it, blame it on a 'misunderstanding'? No, comrades. When a party in full tide of revolution, still wreathed in powder-smoke, comes to say, 'Here is the Power—take it!'—and when those to whom it is offered go over to the enemy, that is not a misunderstanding . . . that is a declaration of pitiless war. And it isn't we who have declared war. . . .

"Avilov menaces us with failure of our peace efforts—if we remain 'isolated.' I repeat, I don't see how a coalition with Skobeliev, or even Tereshchenko, can help us to get peace! Avilov tries to frighten us by the threat of a peace at our expense. And I answer that in any case, if Europe continues to be ruled by the imperialist bourgeoisie, revolutionary Russia will inevitably be lost. . . .

"There are only two alternatives; either the Russian Revolution will create a revolutionary movement in Europe, or the European powers will destroy the Russian Revolution!"

They greeted him with an immense crusading acclaim, kindling to the daring of it, with the thought of championing mankind. And from that moment there was something conscious and decided about the insurrectionary masses in all their actions, which never left them.

But on the other side, too, battle was taking form. Kameniev recognized a delegate from the Union of Railway Workers, a hard-faced, stocky man with an attitude of implacable hostility. He threw a bombshell.

"In the name of the strongest organization in Russia I demand the right to speak, and I say to you: the Vikzhel charges me to make known the decision of the Union concerning the constitution of Power. The Central Committee refuses absolutely to support the Bolsheviki if they persist in isolating themselves from the whole democracy of Russia!" Immense tumult all over the hall.

"In 1905, and in the Kornilov days, the Railway Workers were the best defenders of the Revolution. But you did not invite us to your Congress—" Cries, "It was the old Tsay-ee-kah which did not invite you!" The orator paid no attention. "We do not recognize the legality of this Congress; since the departure of the Mensheviki and Socialist Revolutionaries there is not a legal quorum. . . . The Union supports the old Tsay-ee-kah, and declares that the Congress has no right to elect a new Committee. . . .

"The Power should be a Socialist and revolutionary Power, responsible before the authorized organs of the entire revolutionary democracy. Until the constitution of such a power, the Union of Railway Workers, which refuses to transport counter-revolutionary troops to Petrograd, at the same time forbids the execution of any order whatever without the consent of the Vikzhel. The Vikzhel also takes into its hands the entire administration of the railroads of Russia."

At the end he could hardly be heard for the furious storm of abuse which beat upon him. But it was a heavy blow—that could be seen in the concern on the faces of the presidium. Kameniev, however, merely answered that there could be no doubt of the legality of the Congress, as even the quorum established by the old Tsay-ee-kah was exceeded—in spite of the secession of the Mensheviki and Socialist Revolutionaries. . . .

Then came the vote on the Constitution of Power, which carried the Council of People's Commissars into office by an enormous majority. . . .

The election of the new Tsay-ee-kah, the new parliament of the Russian Republic, took barely fifteen minutes. Trotsky announced its composition: 100 members, of which 70 Bolsheviki. . . . As for the peasants, and the seceding factions, places were to be reserved for them. "We welcome into the Government all parties and groups which will adopt our program," ended Trotsky.

And thereupon the Second All-Russian Congress of Soviets was dissolved, so that the members might hurry to their homes in the four corners of Russia and tell of the great happenings. . . .

It was almost seven when we woke the sleeping conductors and motor-men of the streetcars which the Street-Railway Workers'

Union always kept waiting at Smolny to take the Soviet delegates to their homes. In the crowded car there was less happy hilarity than the night before, I thought. Many looked anxious; perhaps they were saying to themselves, "Now we are masters, how can we do our will?"

At our apartment-house we were held up in the dark by an armed patrol of citizens and carefully examined. The Duma's proclamation was doing its work. . . .

The landlady heard us come in, and stumbled out in a pink silk wrapper.

"The House Committee has again asked that you take your turn on guard duty with the rest of the men," she said.

"What's the reason for this guard duty?"

"To protect the house and the women and children."

"Who from?"

"Robbers and murderers."

"But suppose there came a Commissar from the Military Revolutionary Committee to search for arms?"

"Oh, that's what they'll say they are. . . . And besides, what's the difference?"

I solemnly affirmed that the Consul had forbidden all American citizens to carry arms—especially in the neighborhood of the Russian *intelligentsia*. . . .

# 6

# The Committee for Salvation

F~RIDAY~, 9 November. . . .

Novocherkask, 8 November.

In view of the revolt of the Bolsheviki, and their attempt to depose the Provisional Government and to seize the power in Petrograd. . . . The Cossack Government declares that it considers these acts criminal and absolutely inadmissable. In consequence, the Cossacks will lend all their support to the Provisional Government, which is a government of coalition. Because of these circumstances, and until the return of the Provisional Government to power, and the restoration of order in Russia, I take upon myself, beginning 7 November, all power in that which concerns the region of the Don.

Signed: ATAMAN KALEDIN
*President of the Government of
Cossack Troops*

*Prikaz* of the Minister-President Kerensky, dated at Gatchina:

I, Minister-President of the Provisional Government, and Supreme Commander of all the armed forces of the Russian Republic, declare that I am at the head of regiments from the Front who have remained faithful to the fatherland.

I order all the troops of the military District of Petrograd, who through mistake or folly have answered the appeal of the traitors to the country and the Revolution, to return to their duty without delay.

This order will be read in all regiments, battalions, and squadrons.

Signed: *Minister-President of the Provisional
Government and Supreme Commander*
A. F. KERENSKY

Telegram from Kerensky to the General in Command of the Northern Front:

> The town of Gatchina has been taken by the loyal regiments without bloodshed. Detachments of Kronstadt sailors, and of the Semionovsky and Ismailovsky regiments gave up their arms without resistance and joined the Government troops.
> I order all the designated units to advance as quickly as possible. The Military Revolutionary Committee has ordered its troops to retreat. . . .

Gatchina, about thirty kilometers southwest, had fallen during the night. Detachments of the two regiments mentioned—not the sailors—while wandering captainless in the neighborhood, had indeed been surrounded by Cossacks and given up their arms; but it was not true that they had joined the Government troops. At this very moment crowds of them, bewildered and ashamed, were up at Smolny trying to explain. They did not think the Cossacks were so near. . . . They had tried to argue with the Cossacks. . . .

Apparently the greatest confusion prevailed along the revolutionary front. The garrisons of all the little towns southward had split hopelessly, bitterly into two factions—or three: the high command being on the side of Kerensky, in default of anything stronger, the majority of the rank and file with the Soviets, and the rest unhappily wavering.

Hastily the Military Revolutionary Committee appointed to command the defense of Petrograd an ambitious regular Army captain, Muraviov; the same Muraviov who had organized the Death Battalions during the summer, and had once been heard to advise the Government that "it was too lenient with the Bolsheviki; they must be wiped out." A man of military mind, who admired power and audacity, perhaps sincerely. . . .

Beside my door when I came down in the morning were posted two new orders of the Military Revolutionary Committee, directing that all shops and stores should open as usual, and that all empty rooms and apartments should be put at the disposal of the Committee. . . .

· · ·

FOR thirty-six hours now the Bolsheviki had been cut off from provincial Russia and the outside world. The railwaymen and telegraphers had refused to transmit their dispatches, the postmen would not handle their mail. Only the Government wireless at Tsarskoye Selo launched half-hourly bulletins and manifestoes to the four corners of heaven; the Commissars of Smolny raced the Commissars of the City Duma on speeding trains half across the earth; and two airplanes, laden with propaganda, fled high up toward the front. . . .

But the eddies of insurrection were spreading through Russia with a swiftness surpassing any human agency. Helsingfors Soviet passed resolutions of support; Kiev Bolsheviki captured the arsenal and the telegraph station, only to be driven out by delegates of the Congress of Cossacks, which happened to be meeting there; in Kazan, a Military Revolutionary Committee arrested the local garrison staff and the Commissar of the Provisional Government; from far Krasnoyarsk, in Siberia, came news that the Soviets were in control of the Municipal institutions; at Moscow, where the situation was aggravated by a great strike of leather workers on one side and a threat of a general lock-out on the other, the Soviets had voted overwhelmingly to support the action of the Bolsheviki in Petrograd. . . . Already a Military Revolutionary Committee was functioning.

Everywhere the same thing happened. The common soldiers and the industrial workers supported the Soviets by a vast majority; the officers, *yunkers*, and middle class generally were on the side of the Government—as were the bourgeois Cadets and the "moderate" Socialist parties. In all these towns sprang up Committees for Salvation of Country and Revolution, arming for civil war. . . .

Vast Russia was in a state of solution. As long ago as 1905 the process had begun; the March Revolution had merely hastened it, and giving birth to a sort of forecast of the new order, had ended by merely perpetuating the hollow structure of the old régime. Now, however, the Bolsheviki, in one night, had dissipated it, as one blows away smoke. Old Russia was no more; human society flowed molten in primal heat, and from the tossing sea of flame was emerging the class struggle, stark and pitiless—and the fragile, slowly cooling crust of new planets. . . .

In Petrograd sixteen Ministries were on strike, led by the Ministries of Labor and of Supplies—the only two created by the All-Socialist Government of August.

If ever men stood alone, the "handful of Bolsheviki" apparently stood alone that gray, chill morning, with all storms towering over them.[35] Back against the wall, the Military Revolutionary Committee struck—for its life. *"De l'audace, encore de l'audace, et toujours de l'audace. . . ."* At five in the morning the Red Guards entered the printing office of the City Government, confiscated thousands of copies of the Appeal-Protest of the Duma, and suppressed the official Municipal organ—the *Viestnik Gorodskovo Samoupravleniya* (Bulletin of the Municipal Self-Government). All the bourgeois newspapers were torn from the presses, even the *Golos Soldata*, journal of the old Tsay-ee-kah—which, however, changing its name to *Soldatski Golos*, appeared in an edition of a hundred thousand copies, bellowing rage and defiance:

> The men who began their stroke of treachery in the night, who have suppressed the newspapers, will not keep the country in ignorance long. The country will know the truth! It will appreciate you, Messrs. the Bolsheviki! We shall see! . . .

As we came down the Nevsky a little after midday the whole street before the Duma building was crowded with people. Here and there stood Red Guards and sailors, with bayoneted rifles, each one surrounded by about a hundred men and women—clerks, students, shopkeepers, *chinovniki*—shaking their fists and bawling insults and menaces. On the steps stood boy scouts and officers distributing copies of the *Soldatski Golos*. A workman with a red band around his arm and a revolver in hand was trembling with rage and nervousness in the middle of a hostile throng at the foot of the stairs, demanding the surrender of the papers. . . . Nothing like this, I imagine, ever occurred in history. On one side a handful of workmen and common soldiers, with arms in their hands, representing a victorious insurrection—and perfectly miserable; on the other side a frantic mob made up of the kind of people that crowd the sidewalks of Fifth Avenue at noontime, sneering, abusing, shouting, "Traitors! Provocators! *Oprichniki!*"*

The doors were guarded by students and officers with white arm-bands lettered in red, "Militia of the Committee of Public Safety," and a half-dozen boy scouts came and went. Upstairs the place was all commotion. Captain Gomberg was coming down the stairs. "They're going to dissolve the Duma," he said. "The Bolshevik Commissar is with the Mayor now." As we reached the top Riazanov came hurrying out. He had been to demand that the Duma recognize the Council of People's Commissars, and the Mayor had given him a flat refusal.

In the offices a great babbling crowd, hurrying, shouting, gesticulating—Government officials, intellectuals, journalists, foreign correspondents, French and British officers. . . . The City Engineer pointed to them triumphantly. "The Embassies recognize the Duma as the only power now," he explained. "For these Bolshevik murderers and robbers it is only a question of hours. All Russia is rallying to us. . . ."

In the Alexander Hall a monster meeting of the Committee for Salvation. Fillipovsky in the chair and Skobeliev again in the tribune, reporting, to immense applause, new adhesions to the Committee; Executive Committee of Peasants' Soviets, old Tsay-ee-kah, Central Army Committee, Tsentroflot, Menshevik, Socialist Revolutionary and Front group delegates from the Congress of Soviets, Central Committees of the Mensheviki, Socialist Revolutionary, Populist Socialist parties, Yedinstvo group, Peasants' Union, Cooperatives, Zemstvos, Municipalities, Post and Telegraph Unions, Vikzhel, Council of the Russian Republic, Union of Unions,† Merchants' and Manufacturers' Association. . . .

". . . The power of the Soviets is not a democratic power, but a

---

*Savage bodyguards of Ivan the Terrible, seventeenth century.
†See Notes and Explanations.

dictatorship—and not the dictatorship of the proletariat, but *against* the proletariat. All those who have felt or know how to feel revolutionary enthusiasm must join now for the defense of the Revolution. . . .

"The problem of the day is not only to render harmless irresponsible demagogues, but to fight against the counter-revolution. . . . If rumors are true that certain generals in the provinces are attempting to profit by events in order to march on Petrograd with other designs, it is only the more proof that we must establish a solid base of democratic government. Otherwise troubles with the Right will follow troubles from the Left. . . .

"The garrison of Petrograd cannot remain indifferent when citizens buying the *Golos Soldata* and newsboys selling the *Rabochaya Gazeta* are arrested in the streets. . . .

"The hour of resolutions has passed. . . . Let those who have no longer faith in the Revolution retire. . . . To establish a united power we must again restore the prestige of the Revolution. . . .

"Let us swear that either the Revolution shall be saved—or we shall perish!"

The hall rose, cheering, with kindling eyes. There was not a single proletarian anywhere in sight. . . .

Then Weinstein:

"We must remain calm, and not act until public opinion is firmly grouped in support of the Committee for Salvation—then we can pass from the defensive to action!"

The Vikzhel representative announced that his organization was taking the initiative in forming the new Government, and its delegates were now discussing the matter with Smolny. . . . Followed a hot discussion, were the Bolsheviki to be admitted to the new Government? Martov pleaded for their admission; after all, he said, they represented an important political party. Opinions were very much divided upon this, the right wing Mensheviki and Socialist Revolutionaries, as well as the Populist Socialists, the Cooperatives, and the bourgeois elements being bitterly against. . . .

"They have betrayed Russia," one speaker said. "They have

started civil war and opened the front to the Germans. The Bolsheviki must be mercilessly crushed. . . ."

Skobeliev was in favor of excluding both the Bolsheviki and the Cadets.

We got into conversation with a young Socialist Revolutionary, who had walked out of the Democratic Conference together with the Bolsheviki that night when Tseretelly and the "compromisers" forced Coalition upon the democracy of Russia.

"You here?" I asked him.

His eyes flashed fire. "Yes!" he cried. "I left the Congress with my party Wednesday night. I have not risked my life for twenty years and more to submit now to the tyranny of the Dark People. Their methods are intolerable. But they have not counted on the peasants. . . . When the peasants begin to act then it is a question of minutes before they are done for."

"But the peasants—will they act? Doesn't the Land decree settle the peasants? What more do they want?"

"Ah, the Land decree! It is our decree—it is the Socialist Revolutionary program intact! My party framed that policy, after the most careful compilation of the wishes of the peasants themselves. It is an outrage. . . ."

"But if it is your own policy, why do you object? If it is the peasants' wishes, why will the people oppose it?"

"You don't understand! Don't you see that the peasants will immediately realize that it is all a trick—that these usurpers have stolen the Socialist Revolutionary program?"

I asked if it were true that Kaledin was marching north.

He nodded and rubbed his hands with a sort of bitter satisfaction. "Yes. Now you see what these Bolsheviki have done. They have raised the counter-revolution against us. The Revolution is lost. The Revolution is lost."

"But won't you defend the Revolution?"

"Of course we will defend it—to the last drop of our blood. But we won't cooperate with the Bolsheviki in any way. . . ."

"But if Kaledin comes to Petrograd, and the Bolsheviki defend the city. Won't you join with them?"

"Of course not. We will defend the city also, but we won't support the Bolsheviki. Kaledin is the enemy of the Revolution, but the Bolsheviki are equally enemies of the Revolution."

"Which do you prefer—Kaledin or the Bolsheviki?"

"It is not a question to be discussed!" he burst out impatiently. "I tell you the Revolution is lost. And it is the Bolsheviki who are to blame. But listen—why should we talk of such things? Kerensky is coming. . . . Day after tomorrow we shall pass to the offensive. . . . Already Smolny has sent delegates inviting us to form a new Government. But we have them now—they are absolutely impotent. . . . We shall not cooperate. . . ."

Outside there was a shot. We ran to the windows. A Red Guard, finally exasperated by the taunts of the crowd, had shot into it, wounding a young girl in the arm. We could see her being lifted into a cab, surrounded by an excited throng, the clamor of whose voices floated up to us. As we looked, suddenly an armored automobile appeared around the corner of the Mikhailovsky, its guns slung this way and that. Immediately the crowd began to run, as Petrograd crowds do, falling down and lying still in the street, piled in the gutters, heaped up behind telephone-poles. The car lumbered up to the steps of the Duma and a man stuck his head out of the turret, demanding the surrender of the *Soldatski Golos*. The boy scouts jeered and scuttled into the building. After a moment the automobile wheeled undecidedly around and went off up the Nevsky, while some hundreds of men and women picked themselves up and began to dust their clothes. . . .

Inside was a prodigious running about of people with armfuls of *Soldatski Golos*, looking for places to hide them. . . .

A journalist came running into the room, waving a paper.

"Here's a proclamation from Krasnov!" he cried. Everybody crowded around. "Get it printed—get it printed quick, and around to the barracks!"

By order of the Supreme Commander I am appointed commandant of the troops concentrated under Petrograd.

Citizens, soldiers, valorous Cossacks of the Don, of the Kuban, and of the Transbaikal, of the Amur, of the Yenissei, to all you who have remained faithful to your oath I appeal; to you who have sworn to guard inviolate your oath of Cossack—I call upon you to save Petrograd from anarchy, from famine, from tyranny, and to save Russia from the indelible shame to which a handful of ignorant men, bought by the gold of Wilhelm, are trying to submit her.

The Provisional Government, to which you swore fidelity in the great days of March, is not overthrown, but by violence expelled from the edifice in which it held its meetings. However, the Government, with the help of the Front armies, faithful to their duty, with the help of the Council of Cossacks, which has united under its command all the Cossacks, and which, strong with the morale which reigns in its ranks, and acting in accordance with the will of the Russian people, has sworn to serve the country as its ancestors served it in the Troublous Times of 1612, when the Cossacks of the Don delivered Moscow, menaced by the Swedes, the Poles, and the Lithuanians. Your Government still exists. . . .

The active army considers these criminals with horror and contempt. Their acts of vandalism and pillage, their crimes, the German mentality with which they regard Russia—stricken down but not yet surrendered—have alienated them from the entire people.

Citizens, soldiers, valorous Cossacks of the Garrison of Petrograd; send me your delegates so that I may know who are the traitors to their country and who are not, that there may be avoided an effusion of innocent blood.

Almost the same moment word ran from group to group that the building was surrounded by Red Guards. An officer strode in, a red band around his arm, demanding the Mayor. A few minutes later he left and old Schreider came out of his office, red and pale by turns.

"A special meeting of the Duma!" he cried. "Immediately!"

In the big hall proceedings were halted. "All members of the Duma for a special meeting!"

"What's the matter?"

"I don't know—going to arrest us—going to dissolve the Duma—arresting the members at the door—" so ran the excited comments.

In the Nikolai Hall there was barely room to stand. The Mayor announced that troops were stationed at all the doors, prohibiting all exit and entrance, and that a Commissar had threatened arrest and the dispersal of the Municipal Duma. A flood of impassioned speeches from members, and even from the galleries, responded. The freely elected City Government could not be dissolved by *any* power; the Mayor's person and that of all the members were inviolable; the tyrants, the provocators, the German agents should never be recognized; as for these threats to dissolve us, let them try—only over our dead bodies shall they seize this chamber, where like the Roman senators of old we wait with dignity the coming of the Goths. . . .

Resolution, to inform the Dumas and Zemstvos of all Russia by telegraph. Resolution, that it was impossible for the Mayor or the Chairman of the Duma to enter into any relations whatever with representatives of the Military Revolutionary Committee or with the so-called Council of People's Commissars. Resolution, to address another appeal to the population of Petrograd to stand up for the defense of their elected town government. Resolution, to remain in permanent session. . . .

In the meanwhile one member arrived with the information that he had telephoned to Smolny, and that the Military Revolutionary Committee said that no orders had been given to surround the Duma, that the troops would be withdrawn. . . .

As we went downstairs Riazanov burst in through the front door, very agitated.

"Are you going to dissolve the Duma?" I asked.

"My God, no!" he answered. "It is all a mistake. I told the Mayor this morning that the Duma would be left alone. . . ."

Out on the Nevsky, in the deepening dusk, a long double file of cyclists came riding, guns slung on their shoulders. They halted, and the crowd pressed in and deluged them with questions.

"Who are you? Where do you come from?" asked a fat old man with a cigar in his mouth.

"Twelfth Army. From the Front. We came to support the Soviets against the damn bourgeoisie!"

"Ah!" were furious cries. "Bolshevik gendarmes! Bolshevik Cossacks!"

A little officer in a leather coat came running down the steps. "The garrison is turning!" he muttered in my ear. "It's the begin-

ning of the end of the Bolsheviki. Do you want to see the turn of
the tide? Come on!" He started at a half-trot up the Mikhailovsky, and we followed.

"What regiment is it?"

"The Bronneviki. . . ." Here was indeed serious trouble. The
Bronneviki were the Armored Car troops, the key to the situation; whoever controlled the Bronneviki controlled the city.
"The Commissars of the Committee for Salvation and the Duma
have been talking to them. There's a meeting on to decide. . . ."

"Decide what? Which side they'll fight on?"

"Oh, no. That's not the way to do it. They'll never fight against
the Bolsheviki. They will vote to remain neutral—and then the
*yunkers* and Cossacks—"

THE door of the great Mikhailovsky Riding-School yawned
blackly. Two sentinels tried to stop us, but we brushed by hurriedly, deaf to their indignant expostulations. Inside only a single
arc lamp burned dimly, high up near the roof of the enormous
hall, whose forty pilasters and rows of windows vanished in the
gloom. Around dimly squatted the monstrous shapes of the armored cars. One stood alone in the center of the place, under the
light, and round it were gathered some two thousand dun-
colored soldiers, almost lost in the immensity of that imperial
building. A dozen men, officers, chairmen of the Soldiers' Committees and speakers, were perched on top of the car, and from
the central turret a soldier was speaking. This was Khanjunov,
who had been president of last summer's all-Russian Congress of
Bronneviki. A lithe, handsome figure in his leather coat with lieutenant's shoulder-straps, he stood, pleading eloquently for neutrality.

"It is an awful thing," he said, "for Russians to kill their Russian brothers. There must not be civil war between soldiers who
stood shoulder to shoulder against the Czar, and conquered the
foreign enemy in battles which will go down in history! What
have we, soldiers, got to do with these squabbles of political parties? I will not say to you that the Provisional Government was a
democratic Government; we want no coalition with the bour-

geoisie—no. But we must have a Government of the united democracy, or Russia is lost! With such a Government there will be no need for civil war, and the killing of brother by brother!"

This sounded reasonable—the great hall echoed to the crash of hands and voices.

A soldier climbed up, his face white and strained. "Comrades!" he cried, "I come from the Rumanian front, to urgently tell you all: there must be peace! Peace at once! Whoever can give us peace, whether it be the Bolsheviki or this new Government, we will follow. Peace! We at the front cannot fight any longer. We cannot fight either Germans or Russians—" With that he leaped down, and a sort of confused agonized sound rose up from all that surging mass, which burst into something like anger when the next speaker, a Menshevik *oboronets*, tried to say that the war must go on until the Allies were victorious.

"You talk like Kerensky!" shouted a rough voice.

A Duma delegate, pleading for neutrality. Him they listened to, muttering uneasily, feeling him not one of them. Never have I seen men trying so hard to understand, to decide. They never moved, stood staring with a sort of terrible intentness at the speaker, their brows wrinkled with the effort of thought, sweat standing out on their foreheads; great giants of men with the innocent clear eyes of children and the faces of epic warriors. . . .

Now a Bolshevik was speaking, one of their own men, violently, full of hate. They liked him no more than the other. It was not their mood. For the moment they were lifted out of the ordinary run of common thoughts, thinking in terms of Russia, of Socialism, the world, as if it depended on them whether the Revolution were to live or die. . . .

Speaker succeeded speaker, debating amid tense silence, roars of approval, or anger: should we come out or not? Khanjunov returned, persuasive and sympathetic. But wasn't he an officer, and an *oboronets*, however much he talked of peace? Then a workman from Vasili Ostrov, but him they greeted with, "And are *you* going to give us peace, working-man?" Near us some men, many of them officers, formed a sort of claque to cheer the advocates of neutrality. They kept shouting, "Khanjunov! Khanjunov!" and whistled insultingly when the Bolsheviki tried to speak.

Suddenly the committee men and officers on top of the automobile began to discuss something with great heat and much gesticulation. The audience shouted to know what was the matter, and all the great mass tossed and stirred. A soldier, held back by one of the officers, wrenched himself loose and held up his hand.

"Comrades!" he cried, "Comrade Krylenko is here and wants to speak to us." An outburst of cheers, whistlings, yells of *"Prosim! Prosim! Doloi!* Go ahead! Go ahead! Down with him!" in the midst of which the People's Commissar for Military Affairs clambered up the side of the car, helped by hands before and behind, pushed and pulled from below and above. Rising he stood for a moment, and then walked out on the radiator, put his hands on his hips and looked around smiling, a squat, short-legged figure, bareheaded, without insignia on his uniform.

The claque near me kept up a fearful shouting. "Khanjunov! We want Khanjunov! Down with him! Shut up! Down with the traitor!" The whole place seethed and roared. Then it began to move like an avalanche bearing down upon us, great blackbrowed men forcing their way through.

"Who is breaking up our meeting?" they shouted. "Who is whistling here?" The claque, rudely burst asunder, went flying—nor did they gather again. . . .

"Comrade soldiers!" began Krylenko, in a voice husky with fatigue. "I cannot speak well to you; I am sorry; but I have not had any sleep for four nights. . . .

"I don't need to tell you that I am a soldier. I don't need to tell you that I want peace. What I must say is that the Bolshevik Party, successful in the Workers' and Soldiers' Revolution, by the help of you and of all the rest of the brave comrades who have hurled down for ever the power of the bloodthirsty bourgeoisie, promised to offer peace to all the peoples, and that has already been done—today!" Tumultuous applause.

"You are asked to remain neutral—to remain neutral while the *yunkers* and the Death Battalions, who are *never* neutral, shoot us down in the streets and bring back to Petrograd Kerensky—or perhaps some other of the gang. Kaledin is marching from the Don. Kerensky is coming from the front. Kornilov is raising the Tekhintsi to repeat his attempt of August. All these Mensheviki and Socialist Revolutionaries who call upon you now to prevent civil war—how have they retained the power except by civil war, that civil war which has endured ever since July, and in which they constantly stood on the side of the bourgeoisie, as they do now?

"How can I persuade you, if you have made up your minds? The question is very plain. On one side are Kerensky, Kaledin, Kornilov, the Mensheviki, Socialist Revolutionaries, Cadets, Dumas, officers. . . . They tell us that their objects are good. On the other side are the workers, the soldiers and sailors, the poorest peasants. The Government is in your hands. You are the masters. Great Russia belongs to you. Will you give it back?"

While he spoke he kept himself up by sheer evident effort of will, and as he went on the deep sincere feeling back of his words broke through the tired voice. At the end he tottered, almost falling; a hundred hands reached up to help him down, and the great dim spaces of the hall gave back the surf of sound that beat upon him.

Khanjunov tried to speak again, but "Vote! Vote! Vote!" they cried. At length, giving in, he read the resolution: that the Bronneviki withdraw their representative from the Military Revolutionary Committee, and declare their neutrality in the present civil war. All those in favor should go to the right; those opposed, to the left. There was a moment of hesitation, a still expectancy, and then the crowd began to surge faster and faster, stumbling over one another, to the left, hundreds of big soldiers in a solid mass rushing across the dirt floor in the faint light. . . . Near us about fifty men were left stranded, stubbornly in favor, and even as the high roof shook under the shock of victorious roaring, they turned and rapidly walked out of the building—and, some of them, out of the Revolution. . . .

Up at Smolny the new Council of People's Commissars was not idle. Already the first decree was on the presses, to be circulated in thousands through the city streets that night, and shipped in bales by every train southward and east:

> In the name of the Government of the Russian Republic, chosen by the All-Russian Congress of Soviets of Workers' and Soldiers' Deputies with participation of peasant deputies, the Council of People's Commissars decrees:
> 1. That the elections of the Constituent Assembly shall take place at the date determined upon—12 November.
> 2. All electoral commissions, organs of self-government, Soviets of Workers', Soldiers', and Peasants' Deputies and soldiers' organizations on the front should make every effort to assure free and regular elections at the date determined upon.
> In the name of the Government of the Russian Republic.
> *President of the Council of People's Commissars,*
> VLADIMIR ULYANOV—LENIN

In the Municipal building the Duma was in full blast. A member of the Council of the Republic was talking as we came in. The Council, he said, did not consider itself dissolved at all, but merely unable to continue its labors until it secured a new meeting-place. In the meanwhile, its Committee of Elders had determined to enter *en masse* the Committee for Salvation. . . . This, I may remark parenthetically, is the last time history mentions the Council of the Russian Republic. . . .

Then followed the customary string of delegates from the Ministries, the Vikzhel, the Union of Posts and Telegraphs, for the hundredth time reiterating their determination not to work for the Bolshevik usurpers. A *yunker* who had been in the Winter Palace told a highly colored tale of the heroism of himself and his comrades, and disgraceful conduct of the Red Guards—all of which was devoutly believed. Somebody read aloud an account in the Socialist Revolutionary paper *Narod*, which stated that five hundred million roubles' worth of damage had been done in the Winter Palace, and describing in great detail the loot and breakage.

From time to time couriers came from the telephone with news. The four Socialist Ministers had been released from prison.

Krylenko had gone to Peter-Paul to tell Admiral Verderevsky that the Ministry of Marine was deserted, and to beg him, for the sake of Russia, to take charge under the authority of the Council of People's Commissars; and the old seaman had consented. . . . Kerensky was advancing north from Gatchina, the Bolshevik garrisons falling back before him. Smolny had issued another decree, enlarging the powers of the City Duma to deal with food supplies.

This last piece of insolence caused an outburst of fury. He, Lenin, the usurper, the tyrant, whose Commissars had seized the Municipal garage, entered the Municipal warehouses, were interfering with the Supply Committees and the distribution of food—he presumed to define the limits of power of the free, independent, autonomous City Government! One member, shaking his fist, moved to cut off the food of the city if the Bolsheviki dared to interfere with the Supply Committees. . . . Another, representative of the Special Supply Committee, reported that the food situation was very grave, and asked that emissaries be sent out to hasten food trains.

Diedonenko announced dramatically that the garrison was wavering. The Semionovsky regiment had already decided to submit to the orders of the Socialist Revolutionary party; the crews of the torpedo-boats on the Neva were shaky. Seven members were at once appointed to continue the propaganda. . . .

Then the old mayor stepped into the tribune: "Comrades and citizens! I have just learned that the prisoners in Peter-Paul are in danger. Fourteen *yunkers* of the Pavlovsk school have been stripped and tortured by the Bolshevik guards. One has gone mad. They are threatening to lynch the Ministers!" There was a whirlwind of indignation and horror, which only grew more violent when a stocky little woman dressed in gray demanded the floor, and lifted up her hard metallic voice. This was Vera Slutskaya, veteran revolutionist and Bolshevik member of the Duma.

"That is a lie and a provocation!" she said, unmoved at the torrent of abuse. "The Workers' and Peasants' Government, which has abolished the death penalty, cannot permit such deeds. We demand that this story be investigated, at once; if there is any truth in it, the Government will take energetic measures!"

A commission composed of members of all parties was immediately appointed, and, with the Mayor, sent to Peter-Paul to investigate. As we followed them out, the Duma was appointing another commission to meet Kerensky—to try and avoid bloodshed when he entered the capital. . . .

It was midnight when we bluffed our way past the guards at the gates of the fortress, and went forward under the faint glimmer of rare electric lights along the side of the church where lie the tombs of the Czars, beneath the slender golden spire and chimes, which, for months, continued to play *Bozhe Czaria Khrani** every day at noon. . . . The place was deserted; in most of the windows there were not even lights. Occasionally we bumped into a burly figure stumbling along in the dark, who answered questions with the usual, *"Ya nié znayu."*

On the left loomed the dark outline of Trubetskoi Bastion, that living grave in which so many martyrs of liberty had lost their lives or their reason in the days of the Czar, where the Provisional Government had in turn shut up the Ministers of the Czar, and now the Bolsheviki had shut up the Ministers of the Provisional Government.

A friendly sailor led us to the office of the commandant, in a little house near the Mint. Half a dozen Red Guards, sailors, and soldiers were sitting around a hot room full of smoke, in which a samovar steamed cheerfully. They welcomed us with great cordiality, offering tea. The commandant was not in; he was escorting a commission of *"sabotazhniki"* (sabotageurs) from the City Duma, who insisted that the *yunkers* were all being murdered. This seemed to amuse them very much. At one side of the room sat a bald-headed, dissipated-looking little man in a frock-coat and a rich fur coat, biting his moustache and staring around him like a cornered rat. He had just been arrested. Somebody said, glancing carelessly at him, that he was a Minister or some-

*"God save the Czar."

thing. . . . The little man didn't seem to hear it; he was evidently terrified, although the occupants of the room showed no animosity whatever toward him.

I went across and spoke to him in French. "Count Tolstoy," he answered, bowing stiffly. "I do not understand why I was arrested. I was crossing the Troitsky Bridge on my way home when two of these—of these—persons held me up. I was a Commissar of the Provisional Government attached to the General Staff, but in no sense a member of the Government. . . ."

"Let him go," said a sailor. "He's harmless. . . ."

"No," responded the soldier who had brought the prisoner. "We must ask the commandant."

"Oh, the commandant!" sneered the sailor. "What did you make a revolution for? To go on obeying officers?"

A *praporshchik* of the Pavlovsky regiment was telling us how the insurrection started. "The *polk* (regiment) was on duty at the General Staff the night of the sixth. Some of my comrades and I were standing guard; Ivan Pavlovich and another man—I don't remember his name—well, they hid behind the window-curtains in the room where the Staff was having a meeting, and they heard a great many things. For example, they heard orders to bring the Gatchina *yunkers* to Petrograd by night, and an order for the Cossacks to be ready to march in the morning. . . . The principal points in the city were to be occupied before dawn. Then there was the business of opening the bridges. But when they began to talk about surrounding Smolny, then Ivan Pavlovich couldn't stand it any longer. That minute there was a good deal of coming and going, so he slipped out and came down to the guardroom, leaving the other comrade to pick up what he could.

"I was already suspicious that something was going on. Automobiles full of officers kept coming, and all the Ministers were there. Ivan Pavlovich told me what he had heard. It was half past two in the morning. The secretary of the regimental Committee was there, so we told him and asked what to do.

" 'Arrest everybody coming and going!' he says. So we began to do it. In an hour we had some officers and a couple of Ministers, whom we sent up to Smolny right away. But the Military Revolutionary Committee wasn't ready; they didn't know what to do; and pretty soon came back the order to let everybody go and not arrest anybody else. Well, we ran all the way to Smolny, and I guessed we talked for an hour before they finally saw that it was war. It was five o'clock when we got back to the Staff, and by that time most of them were gone. But we got a few, and the garrison was all on the march. . . ."

A Red Guard from Vasili Ostrov described in great detail what had happened in his district on the great day of the rising. "We didn't have any machine-guns over there," he said, laughing, "and we couldn't get any from Smolny. Comrade Zalkind, who was a member of the Uprava (Central Bureau) of the Ward Duma, remembered all at once that there was lying in the meeting-room of the Uprava a machine-gun which had been captured from the Germans. So he and I and another comrade went there. The Mensheviki and Socialist Revolutionaries were having a meeting. Well, we opened the door and walked right in on them, as they sat around the table—twelve or fifteen of them, three of us. When they saw us they stopped talking and just stared. We walked right across the room, uncoupled the machine-gun, Comrade Zalkind picked up one part, I the other, we put them on our shoulders and walked out—and not a single man said a word!"

"Do you know how the Winter Palace was captured?" asked a third man, a sailor. "Along about eleven o'clock we found out there weren't any more *yunkers* on the Neva side. So we broke in the doors and filtered up different stairways one by one or in little bunches. When we got to the top of the stairs the *yunkers* held us up and took away our guns. Still our fellows kept coming up, little by little until we had a majority. Then we turned around and took away the *yunkers'* guns. . . ."

Just then the commandant entered—a merry-looking young non-commissioned officer with his arm in a sling, and deep circles of sleeplessness under his eyes. His eye first fell on the prisoner, who at once began to explain.

"Oh, yes," interrupted the other. "You were one of the committee who refused to surrender the Staff Wednesday afternoon. However, we don't want you, citizen. Apologies—" He opened the door and waved his arm for Count Tolstoy to leave. Several of the others, especially the Red Guards, grumbled protests, and the sailor remarked triumphantly, *"Vot!* There! Didn't I say so?"

Two soldiers now engaged his attention. They had been elected a committee of the fortress garrison to protest. The prisoners, they said, were getting the same food as the guards, when there wasn't even enough to keep a man from being hungry. "Why should the counter-revolutionaries be treated so well?"

"We are revolutionaries, comrades, not bandits," answered the commandant. He turned to us. We explained that rumors were going about that the *yunkers* were being tortured, and the lives of the Ministers threatened. "Could we perhaps see the prisoners, so as to be able to tell the world—?"

"No," said the young soldier irritably. "I am not going to disturb the prisoners again. I have just been compelled to wake them up—they were sure we were going to massacre them. . . . Most of the *yunkers* have been released, anyway, and the rest will go out tomorrow." He turned abruptly away.

"Could we talk to the Duma commission, then?"

The commandant, who was pouring himself a glass of tea, nodded. "They are still in the hall," he said carelessly.

Indeed they stood there just outside the door, in the feeble light of an oil lamp, grouped around the Mayor and talking excitedly.

"Mr. Mayor," I said, "we are American correspondents. Will you please tell us officially the result of your investigations?"

He turned to us his face of venerable dignity.

"There is no truth in the reports," he said slowly. "Except for the incidents which occurred as the Ministers were being brought here, they have been treated with every consideration. As for the *yunkers*, not one has received the slightest injury. . . ."

Up the Nevsky, in the empty, after-midnight gloom, an interminable column of soldiers shuffled in silence—to battle Kerensky. In dim back streets automobiles without lights flitted to and fro, and there was a furtive activity in Fontanka 6, headquarters of the Peasants' Soviet, in a certain apartment of a huge building on the Nevsky, and in the Inzhenierny Zamok (School of Engineers); the Duma was illuminated. . . .

In Smolny Institute the Military Revolutionary Committee flashed baleful fire, pounding like an overloaded dynamo. . . .

# The Revolutionary Front

Saturday, 10 November. . . .

> Citizens!
> The Military Revolutionary Committee declares that it will not tolerate any violation of revolutionary order.
> Theft, brigandage, assault, and attempts at massacre will be severely punished. . . .
> Following the example of the Paris Commune, the Committee will destroy without mercy any looter or instigator of disorder. . . .

Quiet lay the city. Not a hold-up, not a robbery, not even a drunken fight. By night armed patrols went through the silent street, and on the corners, soldiers and Red Guards squatted around little fires, laughing and singing. In the day-time great crowds gathered on the sidewalks listening to interminable hot debates between students and soldiers, business men and workmen.

Citizens stopped each other in the street.

"The Cossacks are coming?"

"No. . . ."

"What's the latest?"

"I don't know anything. Where's Kerensky?"

"They say only eight versts from Petrograd. . . . Is it true that the Bolsheviki have fled to the battleship *Avrora*?"

"They say so. . . ."

Only the walls screamed, and the few newspapers; denunciation, appeal, decree. . . .

An enormous poster carried the hysterical manifesto of the Executive Committee of the Peasants' Soviets:

> ... They (the Bolsheviki) dare to say that they are supported by the Soviets of Peasants' Deputies, and that they are speaking on behalf of the peasants' Deputies. ...
>
> Let all the working-class Russia know that this is a LIE AND THAT ALL THE WORKING PEASANTS—in the person of the EXECUTIVE COMMITTEE OF THE ALL-RUSSIAN SOVIETS OF PEASANTS' DEPUTIES—refute with indignation all participation of the organized peasantry in this criminal violation of the will of the working class. ...

From the Soldier Section of the Socialist Revolutionary party:

> The insane attempt of the Bolsheviki is on the eve of collapse. The garrison is divided. ... The Ministries are on strike and bread is getting scarcer. All factions except the few Bolsheviki have left the Congress. The Bolsheviki are alone. ...
>
> We call upon all sane elements to group themselves around the Committee for Salvation of Country and Revolution, and to prepare themselves to be ready at the first call of the Central Committee. ...

In a handbill the Council of the Republic recited its wrongs:

> Ceding to the force of bayonets, the Council of the Republic has been obliged to separate, and temporarily to interrupt its meetings.
>
> The usurpers, with the words "Liberty and Socialism" on their lips, have set up a rule of arbitrary violence. They have arrested the members of the Provisional Government, closed the newspapers, seized the printing shops. ... This power must be considered the enemy of the people and the Revolution; it is necessary to do battle with it, and to pull it down. ...
>
> The Council of the Republic, until the resumption of its labors, invites the citizens of the Russian Republic to group themselves around the ... local Committees for Salvation of Country and Revolution, which are organizing the overthrow of the Bolsheviki and the creation of a Government capable of leading the country to the Constituent Assembly.

*Dielo Naroda* said:

A revolution is a rising of all the people. . . . But here what have we? Nothing but a handful of poor fools deceived by Lenin and Trotsky. . . . Their decrees and their appeals will simply add to the museum of historical curiosities. . . .

And *Narodnoye Slovo* (People's Word—Populist Socialist):

"Workers' and Peasants' Government?" That is only a pipe-dream; nobody, either in Russia or in the countries of our Allies, will recognize this "Government"—or even in the enemy countries. . . .

The bourgeois press had temporarily disappeared. . . .

*Pravda* had an account of the first meeting of the new Tsay-ee-kah, now the parliament of the Russian Soviet Republic. Milyu-tin, Commissar of Agriculture, remarked that the Peasants' Executive Committee had called an All-Russian Peasant Congress for 13 December.

"But we cannot wait," he said. "We must have the backing of the peasants. I propose that we call the Congress of Peasants, and do it immediately. . . ." The Left Socialist Revolutionaries agreed. An appeal to the Peasants of Russia was hastily drafted, and a committee of five elected to carry out the project.

The question of detailed plans for distributing the land, and the question of the Workers' Control of Industry, were post-poned until the experts working on them should submit a report.

Three decrees[36] were read and approved: first, Lenin's "General Rules for the Press," ordering the suppression of all news-papers inciting to resistance and disobedience to the new Government, inciting to criminal acts, or deliberately perverting the news; the Decree of Moratorium for House-rents; and the Decree Establishing a Workers' Militia. Also orders, one giving the Municipal Duma power to requisition empty apartments and houses, the other directing the unloading of freight-cars in the railroad terminals, to hasten the distribution of necessities and to free the badly needed rolling-stock. . . .

Two hours later the Executive Committee of the Peasants' Soviets were sending broadcast over Russia the following telegram:

> The arbitrary organization of the Bolsheviki, which is called "Bureau of Organization for the National Congress of Peasants," is inviting all the Peasants' Soviets to send delegates to the Congress at Petrograd. . . .
>
> The Executive Committee of the Soviets of Peasants' Deputies declares that it considers, now as well as before, that it would be dangerous to take away from the provinces at this moment the forces necessary to prepare for elections to the Constituent Assembly, which is the only salvation of the working class and the country. We confirm the date of the Congress of Peasants, *13 December.*

At the Duma all was excitement, officers coming and going, the Mayor in conference with the leaders of the Committee for Salvation. A Councillor ran in with a copy of Kerensky's proclamation, dropped by hundreds from an airplane low-flying down the Nevsky, which threatened terrible vengeance on all who did not submit, and ordered soldiers to lay down their arms and assemble immediately in Mars Field.

The Minister-President had taken Tsarskoye Selo, we were told, and was already in the Petrograd campagna, five miles away. He would enter the city tomorrow—in a few hours. The Soviet troops in contact with his Cossacks were said to be going over to the Provisional Government. Chernov was somewhere in between, trying to organize the "neutral" troops into a force to halt the civil war.

In the city the garrison regiments were leaving the Bolsheviki, they said. Smolny was already abandoned. . . . All the Governmental machinery had stopped functioning. The employees of the State Bank had refused to work under Commissars from Smolny, refused to pay out money to them. All the private banks were closed. The Ministries were on strike. Even now a committee from the Duma was making the rounds of the business houses, collecting a fund[37] to pay the salaries of the strikers. . . .

Trotsky had gone to the Ministry of Foreign Affairs and ordered the clerks to translate the Decree of Peace into foreign languages, six hundred functionaries had hurled their resignations in his face. . . . Shliapnikov, Commissar of Labor, had commanded all the employees of the Ministry to return to their places within twenty-four hours, or lose their places and their pension rights, only the door-servants had responded. . . . Some of the branches of the Special Food Supply Committee had suspended work rather than submit to the Bolsheviki. . . . In spite of lavish promises of high wages and better conditions, the operators at the Telephone Exchange would not connect Soviet headquarters. . . .

The Socialist Revolutionary Party had voted to expel all members who had remained in the Congress of Soviets, and all who were taking part in the insurrection. . . .

News from the provinces. Moghilev had declared against the Bolsheviki. At Kiev the Cossacks had overthrown the Soviets and arrested all the insurrectionary leaders. The Soviet and garrison at Luga, thirty thousand strong, affirmed its loyalty to the Provisional Government, and appealed to all Russia to rally around it. Kaledin had dispersed all Soviets and Unions in the Don Basin, and his forces were moving north. . . .

Said a representative of the Railway Workers: "Yesterday we sent a telegram all over Russia demanding that war between the political parties must cease, and insisting on the formation of a coalition Socialist Government. Otherwise we shall call a strike tomorrow night. . . . In the morning there will be a meeting of all factions to consider the question. The Bolsheviki seem anxious for an agreement. . . ."

"If they last that long!" laughed the City Engineer, a stout, ruddy man. . . .

As we came up to Smolny—not abandoned, but busier than ever, throngs of workers and soldiers running in and out, and doubled guards everywhere—we met the reporters for the bourgeois and "moderate" Socialist papers.

"Threw us out!" cried one, from *Volia Naroda*. "Bonch-Bruevich came down to the Press Bureau and told us to leave! Said we were spies!" They all began to talk at once. "Insult! Outrage! Freedom of the press!"

In the lobby were great tables heaped with stacks of appeals, proclamations and orders of the Military Revolutionary Committee. Workmen and soldiers staggered past, carrying them to waiting automobiles.

One began:

### TO THE PILLORY!

In this tragic moment through which the Russian masses are living, the Mensheviki and their followers and the Right Socialist Revolutionaries have betrayed the working class. They have enlisted on the side of Kornilov, Kerensky, and Savinkov. . . .

They are printing orders of the traitor Kerensky and creating a panic in the city, spreading the most ridiculous rumors of mythical victories by that renegade. . . .

Citizens! Don't believe these false rumors. No power can defeat the People's Revolution. . . . Premier Kerensky and his followers await speedy and well-deserved punishment. . . .

We are putting them in the Pillory. We are abandoning them to the enmity of the workers, soldiers, sailors, and peasants, on whom they are trying to rivet the ancient chains. They will never be able to wash from their bodies the stain of the people's hatred and contempt. . . .

Shame and curses to the traitors of the People. . . .

The Military Revolutionary Committee had moved into larger quarters, room 17 on the top floor. Red Guards were at the door. Inside, the narrow space in front of the railing was crowded with well-dressed persons, outwardly respectful but inwardly full of murder—bourgeois who want permits for their automobiles, or passports to leave the city, among them many foreigners. . . . Bill Shatov and Peters were on duty. They suspended all other business to read us the latest bulletins.

The One Hundred and Seventy-Ninth Reserve Regiment offers its unanimous support. Five thousand stevedores at the Putilov wharves greet the new Government. Central Committee of the Trade Unions—enthusiastic support. The garrison and squadron at Reval elect Military Committees to cooperate, and dispatch troops. Military Revolutionary Committees control in

Pskov and Minsk. Greetings from Soviets of Tsaritzin, Rovno on Don, Chernigovsk, Sevastopol. . . . The Finland Division, the new Committees of the Fifth and Twelfth Armies, offer allegiance. . . .

From Moscow the news is uncertain. Troops of the Military Revolutionary Committee occupy the strategic points of the city; two companies on duty in the Kremlin have gone over to the Soviets, but the Arsenal is in the hands of Colonel Diabtsev and his *yunkers*. The Military Revolutionary Committee demanded arms for the workers, and Diabtsev parleyed with them until this morning, when suddenly he sent an ultimatum to the Committee, ordering Soviet troops to surrender and the Committee to disband. Fighting has begun. . . .

In Petrograd the Staff submitted to Smolny's Commissars at once. The Tsentroflot, refusing, was stormed by Dybenko and a company of Kronstadt sailors, and a new Tsentroflot set up, supported by the Baltic and the Black Sea battleships. . . .

But beneath all the breezy assurances there was a chill premonition, a feeling of uneasiness in the air. Kerensky's Cossacks were coming fast; they had artillery. Skripnik, Secretary of the Factory-Shop Committees, his face drawn and yellow, assured me that there was a whole army corps of them, but he added fiercely, "They'll never take us alive!" Petrovsky laughed weariedly. "Tomorrow maybe we'll get a sleep—a long one. . . ." Lozovsky, with his emaciated, red-bearded face, said, "What chance have we? All alone. . . . A mob against trained soldiers!"

South and southwest the Soviets had fled before Kerensky, and the garrisons of Gatchina, Pavlovsk, Tsarskoye Selo were divided—half voting to remain neutral, the rest, without officers, falling back on the capital in the wildest disorder.

In the halls they were posting up bulletins:

FROM KRASNOYE SELO, 10 NOVEMBER, 8 A.M.

*To be communicated to all Commanders of Staffs, Commanders-in-Chief, Commanders, everywhere and to all, all, all.*
The ex-Minister Kerensky has sent a deliberately false telegram to

everyone everywhere to the effect that the troops of revolutionary Petrograd have voluntarily surrendered their arms and joined the armies of the former Government, the Government of Treason, and that the soldiers have been ordered by the Military Revolutionary Committee to retreat. The troops of a free people do not retreat nor do they surrender.

Our troops have left Gatchina in order to avoid bloodshed between ourselves and their mistaken brother-Cossacks, and in order to take a more convenient position, which is at present so strong that if Kerensky and his companions in arms should even increase their forces ten times, still there would be no cause for anxiety. The spirit of our troops is excellent.

In Petrograd all is quiet.

> *Chief of the Defense of Petrograd and the Petrograd District,*
> Lieutenant-Colonel MURAVIOV

As we left the Military Revolutionary Committee Antonov entered, a paper in his hand, looking like a corpse.

"Send this," said he.

TO ALL DISTRICT SOVIETS OF WORKERS' DEPUTIES AND
FACTORY-SHOP COMMITTEES
*Order*

The Kornilovist bands of Kerensky are threatening the approaches to the capital. All the necessary orders have been given to crush mercilessly the counter-revolutionary attempt against the people and its conquests.

The Army and the Red Guard of the Revolution are in need of the immediate support of the workers.

WE ORDER THE WARD SOVIETS AND FACTORY-SHOP
COMMITTEES:

1. To move out the greatest possible number of workers for the digging of trenches, the erection of barricades and reinforcing of wire entanglements.

2. Wherever it shall be necessary for this purpose to stop work at the factories this shall be done immediately.

3. All common and barbed wire available must be assembled, and also all implements for the digging of trenches and the erection of barricades.

4. All available arms must be taken.

5. THE STRICTEST DISCIPLINE IS TO BE OBSERVED, AND EVERYONE MUST BE READY TO SUPPORT THE ARMY OF THE REVOLUTION BY ALL MEANS.

*Chairman of the Petrograd Soviet of Workers' and Soldiers' Deputies,* People's Commissar LEON TROTSKY
*Chairman of the Military Revolutionary Committee,* Commander-in-Chief PODVOISKY

As we came out into the dark and gloomy day all around the gray horizon factory whistles were blowing, a hoarse and nervous sound, full of foreboding. By tens of thousands the working-people poured out, men and women; by tens of thousands the humming slums belched out their dun and miserable hordes. Red Petrograd was in danger! Cossacks! South and southwest they poured through the shabby streets toward the Moskovsky Gate, men, women, and children, with rifles, picks, spades, rolls of wire, cartridge-belts over their working clothes. . . . Such an immense, spontaneous outpouring of a city was never seen! They rolled along torrent-like, companies of soldiers borne with them, guns, motor-trucks, wagons—the revolutionary proletariat defending with its breast the capital of the Workers' and Peasants' Republic!

Before the door of Smolny was an automobile. A slight man with thick glasses magnifying his red-rimmed eyes, his speech a painful effort, stood leaning against a mud-guard with his hands in the pockets of a shabby raglan. A great bearded sailor, with the clear eyes of youth, prowled restlessly about, absently toying with an enormous blue-steel revolver, which never left his hand. These were Antonov and Dybenko.

Some soldiers were trying to fasten two military bicycles on the running-board. The chauffeur violently protested; the enamel would get scratched, he said. True, he was a Bolshevik, and the automobile was commandeered from a bourgeois; true, the bicycles were for the use of orderlies. But the chauffeur's professional pride was revolted. . . . So the bicycles were abandoned. . . .

The People's Commissars for War and Marine were going to inspect the revolutionary front—wherever that was. Could we go with them? Certainly not. The automobile only held five—the two Commissars, two orderlies, and the chauffeur. However, a Russian acquaintance of mine, whom I will call Trusishka, calmly got in and sat down, nor could any argument dislodge him. . . .

I see no reason to doubt Trusishka's story of the journey. As they went down the Suvorovsky Prospect someone mentioned food. They might be out for three or four days, in a country indifferently well provisioned. They stopped the car. Money? The Commissar of War looked through his pockets. He hadn't a kopek. The Commissar of Marine was broke. So was the chauffeur. Trusishka bought the provisions. . . .

Just as they turned into the Nevsky a tire blew out.

"What shall we do?" asked Antonov.

"Commandeer another machine!" suggested Dybenko, waving his revolver. Antonov stood in the middle of the street and signaled a passing machine, driven by a soldier.

"I want that machine," said Antonov.

"You won't get it," responded the soldier.

"Do you know who I am?" Antonov produced a paper upon which was written that he had been appointed Commander-in-Chief of all the armies of the Russian Republic, and that everyone should obey him without question.

"I don't care if you're the devil himself," said the soldier, hotly. "This machine belongs to the First Machine-Gun Regiment, and we're carrying ammunition in it, and you can't have it. . . ."

The difficulty, however, was solved by the appearance of an old battered taxi-cab, flying the Italian flag. (In time of trouble private cars were registered in the name of foreign consulates, so as to be safe from requisition.) From the interior of this was dislodged a fat citizen in an expensive fur coat, and the party continued on its way.

Arrived at Narvskaya Zastava, about ten miles out, Antonov called for the commandant of the Red Guard. He was led to the edge of the town, where some few hundred workmen had dug trenches and were waiting for the Cossacks.

"Everything all right here, comrade?" asked Antonov.

"Everything perfect, comrade," answered the commandant. "The troops are in excellent spirits. . . . Only one thing—we have no ammunition. . . ."

"In Smolny there are two billion rounds," Antonov told him. "I will give you an order." He felt in his pockets. "Has anyone a piece of paper?"

Dybenko had none—nor the couriers. Trusishka had to offer his note-book. . . .

"Devil! I have no pencil!" cried Antonov. "Who's got a pencil?" Needless to say, Trusishka had the only pencil in the crowd. . . .

We who were left behind made for the Tsarskoye Selo station. Up the Nevsky, as we passed, Red Guards were marching, all armed, some with bayonets, some without. The early twilight of winter was falling. Heads up they tramped in the chill mud, irregular lines of four, without music, without drums. A red flag crudely lettered in gold, "Peace! Land!" floated over them. They were very young. The expression on their faces was that of men who know they are going to die. . . . Half-fearful, half-contemptuous, the crowds on the sidewalk watched them pass, in hateful silence. . . .

At the railroad station nobody knew just where Kerensky was, or where the front lay. Trains went no further, however, than Tsarskoye.

Our car was full of commuters and country people going home, laden with bundles and evening papers. The talk was all of the Bolshevik rising. Outside of them, however, one would never have realized that civil war was rending mighty Russia in two, and that the train was headed into the zone of battle. Through the window we could see, in the swiftly deepening darkness, masses of soldiers going along the muddy road toward the city, flinging out their arms in argument. A freight-train, swarming with troops and lit up by huge bonfires, was halted on a siding. That was all. Back along the flat horizon the glow of the city's lights faded down the night. A streetcar crawled distantly along a far-flung suburb. . . .

Tsarskoye Selo station was quiet, but knots of soldiers stood here and there talking in low tones and looking uneasily down the empty track in the direction of Gatchina. I asked some of them which side they were on. "Well," said one, "we don't exactly know the rights of the matter. . . . There is no doubt that Kerensky is a provocator, but we do not consider it right for Russian men to be shooting Russian men."

In the station commandant's office was a big, jovial, bearded common soldier, wearing the red arm-band of a regimental committee. Our credentials from Smolny commanded immediate respect. He was plainly for the Soviets, but bewildered.

"The Red Guards were here two hours ago, but they went away again. A Commissar came this morning, but he returned to Petrograd when the Cossacks arrived."

"The Cossacks are here, then?"

He nodded gloomily. "There has been a battle. The Cossacks came early in the morning. They captured two or three hundred of our men, and killed about twenty-five."

"Where are the Cossacks?"

"Well, they didn't go this far. I don't know just where they are. Off that way. . . ." He waved his arm vaguely westward.

We had dinner—an excellent dinner, better and cheaper than could be got in Petrograd—in the station restaurant. Near by sat a French officer who had just come on foot from Gatchina. All was quiet there, he said. Kerensky held the town. "Ah, these Russians," he went on. "They are original! What a civil war! Everything except the fighting!"

We sallied out into the town. Just at the door of the station stood two soldiers with rifles and bayonets fixed. They were surrounded by about a hundred business men, Government officials and students, who attacked them with passionate argument and epithet. The soldiers were uncomfortable and hurt, like children unjustly scolded.

A tall young man with a supercilious expression, dressed in the uniform of a student, was leading the attack.

"You realize, I presume," he said insolently, "that by taking up arms against your brothers you are making yourselves the tools of murderers and traitors?"

"Now, brother," answered the soldier earnestly, "you don't understand. There are two classes, don't you see, the proletariat and the bourgeoisie. We—"

"Oh, I know that silly talk!" broke in the student rudely. "A bunch of ignorant peasants like you hear somebody bawling a few catch-words. You don't understand what they mean. You just catch them like a lot of parrots." The crowd laughed. "I'm a Marxian student. And I tell you that this isn't Socialism you are fighting for. It's just plain pro-German anarchy!"

"Oh, yes, I know," answered the soldier, with sweat dripping from his brow. "You are an educated man, that is easy to see, and I am a simple man. But it seems to me—"

"I suppose," interrupted the other contemptuously, "that you believe Lenin is a real friend of the proletariat?"

"Yes, I do," answered the soldier, suffering.

"Well, my friend, do you know that Lenin was sent through Germany in a closed car? Do you know that Lenin took money from the Germans?"

"Well, I don't know much about that," answered the soldier stubbornly, "but it seems to me that what he says is what I want to hear, and all the simple men like me. Now there are two classes, the bourgeoisie and the proletariat—"

"You are a fool! Why, my friend, I spent two years in Schlüsselburg for revolutionary activity, when you were still shooting down revolutionists and singing, 'God Save the Czar!' My name is Vasili Georgevich Panyin. Didn't you ever hear of me?"

"I'm sorry to say I never did," answered the soldier with humility. "But then, I am not an educated man. You are probably a great hero."

"I am," said the student with conviction. "And I am opposed to the Bolsheviki, who are destroying our Russia, our free Revolution. Now how do you account for that?"

The soldier scratched his head. "I can't account for it at all," he said, grimacing with the pain of his intellectual processes. "To me it seems perfectly simple—but then, I'm not well educated. It seems like there are only two classes, the proletariat and the bourgeoisie—"

"There you go again with your silly formula!" cried the student.

"—only two classes," went on the soldier, doggedly. "And whoever isn't on one side is on the other. . . ."

We wandered on up the street, where the lights were few and far between, and where people rarely passed. A threatening silence hung over the place—as of a sort of purgatory between heaven and hell, a political no-man's-land. Only the barber shops were all brilliantly lighted and crowded, and a line formed at the doors of the public bath; for it was Saturday night, when all Russia bathes and perfumes itself. I haven't the slightest doubt that Soviet troops and Cossacks mingled in the places where these ceremonies were performed.

The nearer we came to the Imperial Park, the more deserted were the streets. A frightened priest pointed out the headquarters of the Soviet, and hurried on. It was in the wing of one of the Grand Ducal palaces, fronting the Park. The windows were dark, the door locked. A soldier, lounging about with his hands in the top of his trousers, looked us up and down with gloomy suspicion. "The Soviet went away two days ago," said he. "Where?" A shrug. *"Nié znayu.* I don't know."

A little further along was a large building, brightly illuminated. From within came a sound of hammering. While we were hesitating, a soldier and a sailor came down the street, hand in hand. I showed them my pass from Smolny. "Are you for the Soviets?" I asked. They did not answer, but looked at each other in a frightened way.

"What is going on there?" asked the sailor, pointing to the building.

"I don't know."

Timidly the soldier put out his hand and opened the door a crack. Inside a great hall hung with bunting and evergreens, rows of chairs, a stage being built.

A stout woman with a hammer in her hand and her mouth full of tacks came out. "What do you want?" she asked.

"Is there a performance tonight?" said the sailor, nervously.

"There will be private theatricals Sunday night," she answered severely. "Go away."

We tried to engage the soldier and sailor in conversation, but they seemed frightened and unhappy, and drew off into the darkness.

We strolled toward the Imperial Palaces, along the edge of the vast, dark gardens, their fantastic pavilions and ornamental bridges looming uncertainly in the night, and soft water splashing from the fountains. At one place, where a ridiculous iron swan spat unceasingly from an artificial grotto, we were suddenly aware of observation, and looked up to encounter the sullen, suspicious gaze of half a dozen gigantic armed soldiers, who stared moodily down from a grassy terrace. I climbed up to them. "Who are you?" I asked.

"We are the guard," answered one. They all looked very depressed, as undoubtedly they were, from weeks and weeks of all-day, all-night argument and debate.

"Are you Kerensky's troops or the Soviets'?"

There was a silence for a moment, as they looked uneasily at each other. Then, "We are neutral," said he.

We went through the arch of the huge Ekaterina Palace, into the Palace enclosure itself, asking for headquarters. A sentry outside a door in a curving white wing of the Palace said that the commandant was inside.

In a graceful, white Georgian room, divided into unequal parts by a two-sided fire-place, a group of officers stood anxiously talking. They were pale and distracted, and evidently hadn't slept. To one, an oldish man with a white beard, his uniform studded with decorations, who was pointed out as the Colonel, we showed our Bolshevik papers.

He seemed surprised. "How did you get here without being killed?" he asked politely. "It is very dangerous in the streets just now. Political passion is running very high in Tsarskoye Selo. There was a battle this morning, and there will be another tomorrow morning. Kerensky is to enter the town at eight o'clock."

"Where are the Cossacks?"

"About a mile over that way." He waved his arm.

"And you will defend the city against them?"

"Oh, dear, no!" He smiled. "We are holding the city for Kerensky." Our hearts sank, for our passes stated that we were revolutionary to the core. The Colonel cleared his throat. "About those passes of yours," he went on. "Your lives will be in danger if you are captured. Therefore, if you want to see the battle, I will give you an order for rooms in the officers' hotel, and if you will come back here at seven o'clock in the morning, I will give you new passes."

"So you are for Kerensky?"

"Well, not exactly *for* Kerensky." The Colonel hesitated. "You see, most of the soldiers in the garrison are Bolsheviki, and today, after the battle, they all went away in the direction of Petrograd, taking the artillery with them. You might say that none of the *soldiers* are for Kerensky; but some of them just don't want to fight at all. The *officers* have almost all gone over to Kerensky's forces, or simply gone away. We are—ahem—in a most difficult position, as you see...."

He did not believe that there would be any battle....

The Colonel courteously sent his orderly to escort us to the railway station. He was from the south, born of French immigrant parents in Bessarabia. "Ah," he kept saying, "it is not the danger or the hardship that I mind, but being so long, three years, away from my mother...."

Looking out of the window of the train as we sped through the cold dark toward Petrograd, I caught glimpses of clumps of soldiers gesticulating in the light of fires, and of clusters of armored cars halted together at cross-roads, the chauffeurs hanging out of the turrets and shouting at each other....

All the troubled night over the bleak flats leaderless bands of soldiers and Red Guards wandered, clashing and confused, and the Commissars of the Military Revolutionary Committee hurried from one group to another, trying to organize a defense....

Back in town excited throngs were moving in tides up and down the Nevsky. Something was in the air. From the Warsaw Railway station could be heard far-off cannonade. In the *yunker* schools there was feverish activity. Duma members went from barracks to barracks, arguing and pleading, narrating fearful stories of Bolshevik violence—massacre of the *yunkers* in the Winter Palace, rape of the women soldiers, the shooting of the girl before the Duma, the murder of Prince Tumanov. . . . In the Alexander Hall of the Duma building the Committee for Salvation was in special session; Commissars came and went, running. . . . All the journalists expelled from Smolny were there in high spirits. They did not believe our report of conditions in Tsarskoye. Why, everybody knew that Tsarskoye was in Kerensky's hands, and that the Cossacks were now at Pulkovo. A committee was being elected to meet Kerensky at the railway station in the morning. . . .

One confided to me, in the strictest secrecy, that the counter-revolution would begin at midnight. He showed me two proclamations, one signed by Gotz and Polkovnikov, ordering the *yunker* schools, soldier convalescents in the hospitals, and the Knights of St. George to mobilize on a war footing and wait for orders from the Committee for Salvation; the other from the Committee for Salvation itself, which read as follows:

> To the Population of Petrograd!
> Comrades, workers, soldiers, and citizens of revolutionary Petrograd!
> The Bolsheviki, while appealing for peace at the front, are inciting to civil war in the rear.
> Do not listen to their provocatory appeals!
> Do not dig trenches!
> Down with the traitorous barricades!
> Lay down your arms!
> Soldiers, return to your barracks!
> The war begun in Petrograd—is the death of the Revolution!
> In the name of liberty, land, and peace, unite all around the Committee for Salvation of Country and Revolution!

As we left the Duma a company of Red Guards, stern-faced and desperate, came marching down the dark, deserted street with a dozen prisoners—members of the local branch of the Council of

Cossacks, caught red-handed plotting counter-revolution in their headquarters. . . .

A soldier, accompanied by a small boy with a pail of paste, was sticking up great flaring notices:

> By virtue of the present, the city of Petrograd and its suburbs are declared in a state of siege. All assemblies or meetings in the streets, and generally in the open air, are forbidden until further orders.
>
> N. PODVOISKY, President of the Military Revolutionary Committee

As we went home the air was full of confused sound—automobile horns, shouts, distant shots. The city stirred uneasily, wakeful.

In the small hours of the morning a company of *yunkers*, disguised as soldiers of the Semionovsky Regiment, presented themselves at the Telephone Exchange just before the hour of changing guard. They had the Bolshevik password, and took charge without arousing suspicion. A few minutes later Antonov appeared making a round of inspection. Him they captured and locked in a small room. When the relief came it was met with a blast of rifle-fire, several being killed.

Counter-revolution had begun. . . .

# Counter-Revolution

N EXT morning, Sunday the eleventh, the Cossacks entered Tsarskoye Selo, Kerensky[38] himself riding a white horse and all the church-bells clamoring. From the top of a little hill outside the town could be seen the golden spires and many-colored cupolas, the sprawling gray immensity of the capital spread along the dreary plain, and beyond, the steely Gulf of Finland.

There was no battle. But Kerensky made a fatal blunder. At seven in the morning he sent word to the Second Tsarskoye Selo Rifles to lay down their arms. The soldiers replied that they would remain neutral, but would not disarm. Kerensky gave them ten minutes in which to obey. This angered the soldiers; for eight months they had been governing themselves by committee, and this smacked of the old régime. . . . A few minutes later Cossack artillery opened fire on the barracks, killing eight men. From that moment there were no more "neutral" soldiers in Tsarskoye. . . .

Petrograd woke to bursts of rifle-fire, and the tramping thunder of men marching. Under the high dark sky a cold wind smelled of snow. At dawn the Military Hotel and the Telegraph Agency had been taken by large forces of *yunkers*, and bloodily recaptured. The telephone station was besieged by sailors, who lay behind barricades of barrels, boxes, and tin sheets in the middle of the Morskaya, or sheltered themselves at the corner of the Gorokhovaya, and of St. Isaac's Square, shooting at anything that moved. Occasionally an automobile passed in and out, flying the Red Cross flag. The sailors let it pass. . . .

Albert Rhys Williams was in the Telephone Exchange. He

went out with the Red Cross automobile which was ostensibly full of wounded. After circulating about the city, the car went by devious ways to the Mikhailovsky *yunker* school, headquarters of the counter-revolution. A French officer, in the courtyard, seemed to be in command. . . . By this means ammunition and supplies were conveyed to the Telephone Exchange. Scores of these pretended ambulances acted as couriers and ammunition trains for the *yunkers*.

Five or six armored cars, belonging to the disbanded British Armored Car Division, were in their hands. As Louise Bryant was going along St. Isaac's Square one came rolling up from the Admiralty, on its way to the Telephone Exchange. At the corner of Ulitsa Gogolia, right in front of her, the engine stalled. Some sailors ambushed behind wood-piles began shooting. The machine-gun in the turret of the thing slewed around and spat a hail of bullets indiscriminately into the wood-piles and the crowd. In the archway where Miss Bryant stood seven people were shot dead, among them two little boys. Suddenly, with a shout, the sailors leaped up and rushed into the flaming open; closing around the monster, they thrust their bayonets into the loopholes again and again, yelling. . . . The chauffeur pretended to be wounded, and they let him go free—to run to the Duma and swell the tale of Bolshevik atrocities. . . . Among the dead was a British officer. . . .

Later the newspapers told of another French officer, captured in a *yunker* armored car and sent to Peter-Paul. The French Embassy promptly denied this, but one of the City Councillors told me that he himself had procured the officer's release from prison. . . .

Whatever the official attitude of the Allied Embassies, individual French and British officers were active these days, even to the extent of giving advice at executive sessions of the Committee for Salvation.

All day long in every quarter of the city there were skirmishes between *yunkers* and Red Guards, battles between armored cars. . . . Volleys, single shots, and the shrill chatter of machine-guns could be heard, far and near. The iron shutters of the shops were drawn, but business still went on. Even the moving-picture shows, all outside lights dark, played to crowded houses. The streetcars ran. The telephones were all working; when you called Central, shooting could be plainly heard over the wire. . . . Smolny was cut off, but the Duma and the Committee for Salvation were in constant communication with all the *yunker* schools and with Kerensky at Tsarskoye.

At seven in the morning the Vladimir *yunker* school was visited by a patrol of soldiers, sailors, and Red Guards, who gave the *yunkers* twenty minutes to lay down their arms. The ultimatum was rejected. An hour later the *yunkers* got ready to march, but were driven back by a violent fusillade from the corner of the Grebetskaya and the Bolshoy Prospekt. Soviet troops surrounded the building and opened fire, two armored cars cruising back and forth with machine-guns raking it. The *yunkers* telephoned for help. The Cossacks replied that they dare not come, because a large body of sailors with two cannon commanded their barracks. The Pavlovsk school was surrounded. Most of the Mikhailov *yunkers* were fighting in the streets. . . .

At half past seven three field-pieces arrived. Another demand to surrender was met by the *yunkers* shooting down two of the Soviet delegates under the white flag. Now began a real bombardment. Great holes were torn in the walls of the school. The *yunkers* defended themselves desperately; shouting waves of Red Guards, assaulting, crumpled under the withering blast. . . . Kerensky telephoned from Tsarskoye to refuse all parley with the Military Revolutionary Committee.

Frenzied by defeat and their heaps of dead, the Soviet troops opened a tornado of steel and flame against the battered building. Their own officers could not stop the terrible bombardment. A Commissar from Smolny named Kirilov tried to halt it; he was threatened with lynching. The Red Guards' blood was up.

At half past two the *yunkers* hoisted a white flag; they would surrender if they were guaranteed protection. This was promised. With a rush and a shout thousands of soldiers and Red Guards poured through windows, doors, and holes in the wall. Before it could be stopped five *yunkers* were beaten and stabbed to death. The rest, about two hundred, were taken to Peter-Paul under escort, in small groups so as to avoid notice. On the way a mob set upon the party, killing eight more *yunkers*. . . . More than a hundred Red Guards and soldiers had fallen. . . .

Two hours later the Duma got a telephone message that the victors were marching toward the Inzhenierny Zamok—the Engineers' school. A dozen members immediately set out to distribute among them armfuls of the latest proclamations of the Committee for Salvation. Several did not come back. . . . All the other schools surrendered without a resistance, and the *yunkers* were sent unharmed to Peter-Paul and Kronstadt. . . .

The Telephone Exchange held out until afternoon, when a Bolshevik armored car appeared, and the sailors stormed the place. Shrieking, the frightened telephone girls ran to and fro; the *yunkers* tore from their uniforms all distinguishing marks, and one offered Williams *anything* for the loan of his overcoat, as a disguise. . . . "They will massacre us! They will massacre us!" they cried, for many of them had given their word at the Winter Palace not to take up arms against the People. Williams offered to mediate if Antonov were released. This was immediately done; Antonov and Williams made speeches to the victorious sailors, inflamed by their many dead—and once more the *yunkers* went free. . . . All but a few, who in their panic tried to flee over the roofs, or to hide in the attic, and were found and hurled into the street.

Tired, bloody, triumphant, the sailors and workers swarmed into the switchboard room, and finding so many pretty girls, fell back in an embarrassed way and fumbled with awkward feet. Not a girl was injured, not one insulted. Frightened, they huddled in the corners, and then, finding themselves safe, gave vent to their spite. "Ugh! The dirty, ignorant people! The fools!" . . . The sailors and Red Guards were embarrassed. "Brutes! Pigs!" shrilled the girls indignantly, putting on their coats and hats. Romantic had been their experience passing up cartridges and dressing the wounds of their dashing young defenders, the *yunkers*, many of them members of noble families, fighting to restore their beloved Czar! These were just common workmen, peasants, "Dark People". . . .

The Commissar of the Military Revolutionary Committee, little Vishniak, tried to persuade the girls to remain. He was effusively polite. "You have been badly treated," he said. "The telephone system is controlled by the Municipal Duma. You are paid sixty roubles a month, and have to work ten hours and more. . . . From now on all that will be changed. The Government intends to put the telephones under control of the Ministry of Posts and Telegraphs. Your wages will be immediately raised to one hundred and fifty roubles, and your working hours reduced. As members of the working class you should be happy—"

Members of the *working class* indeed! Did he mean to infer that there was anything in common between these—these animals—and *us*? Remain? Not if they offered a thousand roubles! . . . Haughty and spiteful, the girls left the place. . . .

The employees of the building, the line-men and laborers—they stayed. But the switchboards must be operated—the telephone was vital. . . . Only half a dozen trained operators were available. Volunteers were called for; a hundred responded, sailors, soldiers, workers. The six girls scurried backwards and forwards, instructing, helping, scolding. . . . So, crippled, halting, but *going*, the wires began to hum. The first thing was to connect Smolny with the barracks and the factories; the second, to cut off the Duma and the *yunker* schools. . . . Late in the afternoon word of it spread through the city, and hundreds of bourgeois called up to scream, "Fools! Devils! How long do you think you will last? Wait till the Cossacks come!"

Dusk was already falling. On the almost deserted Nevsky, swept by a bitter wind, a crowd had gathered before the Kazan Cathedral, continuing the endless debate; a few workmen, some soldiers and the rest shopkeepers, clerks, and the like.

"But Lenin won't get Germany to make peace!" cried one.

A violent young soldier replied, "And whose fault is it? Your damn Kerensky, dirty bourgeois! To hell with Kerensky! We don't want him. We want Lenin. . . ."

Outside the Duma an officer with a white arm-band was tearing down posters from the wall, swearing loudly. One read:

To the Population of Petrograd!

At this dangerous hour, when the Municipal Duma ought to use every means to calm the population, to assure it bread and other necessities, the Right Socialist Revolutionaries and the Cadets, forgetting their duty, have turned the Duma into a counter-revolutionary meeting, trying to raise part of the population against the rest, so as to facilitate the victory of Kornilov-Kerensky. Instead of doing their duty, the Right Socialist Revolutionaries and the Cadets have transformed the Duma into an arena of political attack upon the Soviets of Workers', Soldiers', and Peasants' Deputies, against the revolutionary Government of peace, bread, and liberty.

Citizens of Petrograd, we, the Bolshevik Municipal Councillors, elected by you—we want you to know that the Right Socialist Revolutionaries and the Cadets are engaged in a counter-revolutionary action, have forgotten their duty, and are leading the population to famine, to civil war. We, elected by 183,000 votes, consider it our duty to bring the attention of our constituents to what is going on in the Duma, and declare that we disclaim all responsibility for the terrible but inevitable consequences. . . .

Far away still sounded occasional shots, but the city lay quiet, cold, as if exhausted by the violent spasms which had torn it.

In the Nikolai Hall the Duma session was coming to an end. Even the truculent Duma seemed a little stunned. One after another the Commissars reported capture of the Telephone Exchange, street-fighting, the taking of the Vladimir school. . . .

"The Duma," said Trupp, "is on the side of the democracy in its struggle against arbitrary violence; but in any case, whichever side wins, the Duma will always be against lynchings and torture. . . ."

Konovsky, Cadet, a tall old man with a cruel face: "When the troops of the legal Government arrive in Petrograd, they will shoot down these insurgents, and that will not be lynching!" Protests all over the hall, even from his own party.

Here there was doubt and depression. The counter-revolution was being put down. The Central Committee of the Socialist Revolutionary party had voted lack of confidence in its officers;

the left wing was in control; Avksentiev had resigned. A courier reported that the Committee of Welcome sent to meet Kerensky at the railway station had been arrested. In the streets could be heard the dull rumble of distant cannonading, south and south-west. Still Kerensky did not come. . . .

Only three newspapers were out—*Pravda, Dielo Naroda,* and *Novaya Zhizn.* All of them devoted much space to the new "coalition" Government. The Socialist Revolutionary paper demanded a Cabinet without either Cadets or Bolsheviki. Gorky was hopeful; Smolny had made concessions. A purely Socialist Government was taking shape—all elements except the bourgeoisie. As for *Pravda,* it sneered:

> We ridicule these coalitions with political parties whose most prominent members are petty journalists of doubtful reputation; our "coalition" is that of the proletariat and the revolutionary Army with the poor peasants. . . .

On the walls a vainglorious announcement of the Vikzhel, threatening to strike if both sides did not compromise:

> The conquerors of these riots, the saviors of the wreck of our country, these will be neither the Bolsheviki, nor the Committee for Salvation, nor the troops of Kerensky—but we, the Union of Railwaymen. . . .

Red Guards are incapable of handling a complicated business like the railways; as for the Provisional Government, it has shown itself incapable of holding the power. . . .

> We refuse to lend our services to any party which does not act by authority of . . . a Government based on the confidence of all the democracy. . . .

Smolny thrilled with the boundless vitality of inexhaustible humanity in action.

In trade union headquarters Lozovsky introduced me to a delegate of the Railway Workers of the Nikolai line, who said that the men were holding huge mass meetings, condemning the action of their leaders.

"All power to the Soviets!" he cried, pounding on the table. "The *oborontsi* in the Central Committee are playing Kornilov's game. They tried to send a mission to the Stavka, but we arrested them at Minsk. . . . Our branch has demanded an All-Russian Convention, and they refuse to call it. . . ."

The same situation as in the Soviets, the Army Committees. One after another the various democratic organizations all over Russia were cracking and changing. The Cooperatives were torn by internal struggles; the meetings of the Peasants' Executive broke up in stormy wrangling; even among the Cossacks there was trouble. . . .

On the top floor the Military Revolutionary Committee was in full blast, striking and slacking not. Men went in, fresh and vigorous; night and day and night and day they threw themselves into the terrible machine; and came out limp, blind with fatigue, hoarse and filthy, to fall on the floor and sleep. . . . The Committee for Salvation had been outlawed. Great piles of new proclamations[39] littered the floor:

> . . . The conspirators, who have no support among the garrison or the working class above all counted on the suddenness of their attack. Their plan was discovered in time by Sub-Lieutenant Blagonravov, thanks to the revolutionary vigilance of a soldier of the Red Guard, whose name shall be made public. At the center of the plot was the Committee for Salvation. Colonel Polkovnikov was in command of their forces, and the orders were signed by Gotz, former member of the Provisional Government, allowed at liberty on his word of honor. . . .
>
> Bringing these facts to the attention of the Petrograd population, the Military Revolutionary Committee orders the arrest of all concerned in the conspiracy, who shall be tried before the Revolutionary Tribunal. . . .

From Moscow, word that the *yunkers* and Cossacks had surrounded the Kremlin and ordered the Soviet troops to lay down their arms. The Soviet forces complied, and as they were leaving the Kremlin, were set upon and shot down. Small forces of Bolsheviki had been driven from the Telephone and Telegraph offices; the *yunkers* now held the center of the city. . . . But all around them the Soviet troops were mustering. Street fighting was slowly gathering way; all attempts at compromise had failed. . . . On the side of the Soviet ten thousand garrison soldiers and a few Red Guards; on the side of the Government, six thousand *yunkers*, twenty-five hundred Cossacks and two thousand White Guards.

The Petrograd Soviet was meeting, and next door the new Tsay-ee-kah, acting on the decrees and orders[40] which came down in a steady stream from the Council of People's Commissars in session upstairs; on the Order in Which Laws Are to be Ratified and Published, Establishing an Eight-hour Day for Workers, and Lunacharsky's "Basis for a System of Popular Education." Only a few hundred people were present at the two meetings, most of them armed. Smolny was almost deserted, except for the guards, who were busy at the hall windows, setting up machine-guns to command the flanks of the building.

In the Tsay-ee-kah a delegate of the Vikzhel was speaking:

"We refuse to transport the troops of either party. . . . We have sent a committee to Kerensky to say that if he continues to march on Petrograd we will break his lines of communication. . . ."

He made the usual plea for a conference of all the Socialist parties to form a new Government. . . .

Kameniev answered discreetly. The Bolsheviki would be very glad to attend a conference. The center of gravity, however, lay not in composition of such a Government, but in its acceptance of the program of the Congress of Soviets. . . . The Tsay-ee-kah had deliberated on the declaration made by the Left Socialist Revolutionaries and the Social Democrat Internationalists, and had accepted the proposition of proportional representation at the conference, even including delegates from the Army Committees and the Peasants' Soviets. . . .

In the great hall, Trotsky recounted the events of the day.

"We offered the Vladimir *yunkers* a chance to surrender," he said. "We wanted to settle matters without bloodshed. But now that blood has been spilled there is only one way—pitiless struggle. It would be childish to think we can win by any other means. . . . The moment is decisive. Everybody must cooperate with the Military Revolutionary Committee, report where there are stores of barbed wire, benzine, guns. . . . We've won the power; now we must keep it!"

The Menshevik Yoffe tried to read his party's declaration, but Trotsky refused to allow "a debate about principle."

"Our debates are now in the streets," he cried. "The decisive step has been taken. We all, and I in particular, take the responsibility for what is happening. . . ."

Soldiers from the front, from Gatchina, told their stories. One from the Death Battalion, Four Hundred Eighty-First Artillery: "When the trenches hear of this they will cry, 'This is *our* Government!' " A *yunker* from Peterhof said that he and two others had refused to march against the Soviets; and when his comrades had returned from the defense of the Winter Palace they appointed him their Commissar, to go to Smolny and offer their services to the *real* Revolution. . . .

Then Trotsky again, fiery, indefatigable, giving orders, answering questions.

"The petty bourgeoisie, in order to defeat the workers, soldiers, and peasants, would combine with the devil himself!" he said once. Many cases of drunkenness had been remarked the last two days. "No drinking, comrades! No one must be on the streets after eight in the evening, except the regular guards. All places suspected of having stores of liquor should be searched, and the liquor destroyed.[41] No mercy to the sellers of liquor. . . ."

The Military Revolutionary Committee sent for the delegation from the Viborg section; then for the members from Putilov. They clumped out hurriedly.

"For each revolutionist killed," said Trotsky, "we shall kill five counter-revolutionists!"

DOWN-TOWN again. The Duma brilliantly illuminated and great crowds pouring in. In the lower hall wailing and cries of grief; the throng surged back and forth before the bulletin-board, where was posted a list of *yunkers* killed in the day's fighting—or supposed to be killed, for most of the dead afterwards turned up safe and sound. . . . Up in the Alexander Hall the Committee for Salvation held forth. The gold-and-red epaulettes of officers were conspicuous, the familiar faces of the Menshevik and Socialist Revolutionary intellectuals, the hard eyes and bulky magnificence of bankers and diplomats, officials of the old régime, and well-dressed women. . . .

The telephone girls were testifying. Girl after girl came to the tribune—over-dressed, fashion-aping little girls, with pinched faces and leaky shoes. Girl after girl, flushing with pleasure at the applause of the "nice" people of Petrograd, of the officers, the rich, the great names of politics—girl after girl, to narrate her sufferings at the hands of the proletariat, and proclaim her loyalty to all that was old-established and powerful. . . .

The Duma was again in session in the Nikolai Hall. The Mayor said hopefully that the Petrograd regiments were ashamed of their actions; propaganda was making headway.

. . . Emissaries came and went, reporting horrible deeds of the Bolsheviki, interceding to save the *yunkers*, busily investigating. . . .

"The Bolsheviki," said Trupp, "will be conquered by moral force, and not by bayonets. . . ."

Meanwhile all was not well on the revolutionary front. The enemy had brought up armored trains, mounted with cannon. The Soviet forces, mostly raw Red Guards, were without officers and without a definite plan. Only five thousand regular soldiers had joined them; the rest of the garrison was either busy suppressing the *yunker* revolt, guarding the city, or undecided what to do. At ten in the evening, Lenin addressed a meeting of delegates from the city regiments, who voted overwhelmingly to fight. A Committee of five soldiers was elected to serve as General Staff, and in the small hours of the morning the regiments left their barracks in full battle-array. Going home I saw them pass, swinging along with the regular tread of veterans, bayonets in perfect alignment, through the deserted streets of the conquered city. . . .

At the same time, in the headquarters of the Vikzhel down on the Sadovaya, the conference of all the Socialist parties to form a new Government was under way. Abramovich, for the center Mensheviki, said that there should be neither conquerors nor conquered—that bygones should be bygones. . . . In this were agreed all the left-wing parties. Dan, speaking in the name of the right Mensheviki, proposed to the Bolsheviki the following conditions of a truce; the Red Guard to be disarmed, and the Petrograd garrison to be placed at the orders of the Duma; the troops of Kerensky not to fire a single shot or arrest a single man; a Ministry of all the Socialist parties *except the Bolsheviki.* For Smolny Riazanov and Kameniev declared that a coalition ministry of all parties was acceptable, but protested at Dan's proposals. The Socialist Revolutionaries were divided; but the Executive Committee of the Peasants' Soviet and the Populist Socialists flatly refused to admit the Bolsheviki. . . . After bitter quarrelling a commission was elected to draw up a workable plan. . . .

All that night the commission wrangled, and all the next day and the next night. Once before, on the ninth of November, there had been a similar effort at conciliation, led by Martov and Gorky; but at the approach of Kerensky and the activity of the Committee for Salvation, the right wing of the Mensheviki, Socialist Revolutionaries, and Populist Socialists suddenly withdrew. Now they were awed by the crushing of the *yunker* rebellion. . . .

Monday the twelfth was a day of suspense. The eyes of all Russia were fixed on the gray plain beyond the gates of Petrograd, where all the available strength of the old order faced the unorganized power of the new, the unknown. In Moscow a truce had been declared; both sides parleyed, awaiting the result in the capital. Now the delegates to the Congress of Soviets, hurrying on speeding trains to the farthest ends of Asia, were coming to their homes, carrying the fiery cross. In wide-spreading ripples news of the miracle spread over the face of the land, and in its wake towns, cities, and far villages stirred and broke, Soviets and Military Revolutionary Committees against Dumas, Zemstvos, and Government Commissars—Red Guards against White—street fighting and passionate speech. . . . The result waited on the word from Petrograd. . . .

Smolny was almost empty, but the Duma was thronged and noisy. The old Mayor, in his dignified way, was protesting against the Appeal of the Bolshevik Councillors.

"The Duma is not a center of counter-revolution," he said, warmly. "The Duma takes no part in the present struggle between the parties. But at a time when there is no legal power in the land, the only center of order is the Municipal Self-Government. The peaceful population recognizes this fact; the foreign Embassies recognize only such documents as are signed by the Mayor of the town. The mind of a European does not admit of any other situation, as the Municipal Self-Government is the only organ which is capable of protecting the interests of the citizens. The City is bound to show hospitality to all organizations which desire to profit by such hospitality, and therefore the Duma cannot prevent the distribution of any newspapers whatever within the Duma building. The sphere of our work is increasing, and we must be given full liberty of action, and our rights must be respected by both parties. . . .

"We are perfectly neutral. When the Telephone Exchange was occupied by the *yunkers* Colonel Polkovnikov ordered the telephones to Smolny disconnected, but I protested, and the telephones were kept going. . . ."

At this there was ironic laughter from the Bolshevik benches and imprecations from the right.

"And yet," went on Schreider, "they look upon us as counter-revolutionaries and report us to the population. They deprive us of our means of transport by taking away our last motor-cars. It will not be our fault if there is famine in the town. Protests are of no use. . . ."

Kobozev, Bolshevik member of the Town Board, was doubtful whether the Military Revolutionary Committee had requisitioned the municipal automobiles. Even granting the fact, it was probably done by some unauthorized individual in the emergency.

"The Mayor," he continued, "tells us we must not make political meetings out of the Duma. But every Menshevik and Socialist here talks nothing but party propaganda, and at the door they distribute their illegal newspapers, *Iskri* (Sparks), *Soldatski Golos*, and *Rabochaya Gazeta*, inciting to insurrection. What if we Bolsheviki should also begin to distribute our papers here? But this shall not be, for we respect the Duma. We have not attacked the Municipal Self-Government, and we shall not do so. But you have addressed an Appeal to the population, and we are entitled to do so. . . ."

Followed him Shingariov, Cadet, who said that there could be no common language with those who were liable to be brought before the Attorney-General for indictment, and who must be tried on the charge of treason. . . . He proposed again that all Bolshevik members should be expelled from the Duma. This was tabled, however, for there were no personal charges against the members, and they were active in the Municipal administration.

Then two Mensheviki Internationalists, declaring that the Appeal of the Bolshevik Councillors was a direct incitement to massacre. "If everything that is against the Bolsheviki is counter-revolutionary," said Pinkevich, "then I do not know the difference between revolution and anarchy. . . . The Bolsheviki are depending upon the passions of the unbridled masses; we have nothing but moral force. We will protest against massacres and violence from both sides, as our task is to find a peaceful issue."

"The notice posted in the streets under the heading 'To the Pillory,' which calls upon the people to destroy the Mensheviki and Socialist Revolutionaries," said Nazariev, "is a crime which you, Bolsheviki, will not be able to wash away. Yesterday's horrors are but a preface to what you are preparing by such a proclamation. . . . I have always tried to reconcile you with other parties, but at present I feel for you nothing but contempt!"

The Bolshevik Councillors were on their feet, shouting angrily, assailed by hoarse, hateful voices and waving arms. . . .

Outside the hall I ran into the City Engineer, the Menshevik Gomberg, and three or four reporters. They were all in high spirits.

"See!" they said. "The cowards are afraid of us. They don't dare arrest the Duma! Their Military Revolutionary Committee doesn't care to send a Commissar into this building. Why, on the corner of the Sadovaya today I saw a Red Guard try to stop a boy selling *Soldatski Golos*. . . . The boy just laughed at him, and a crowd of people wanted to lynch the bandit. It's only a few hours more now. Even if Kerensky wouldn't come they haven't the men to run a Government. Absurd! I understand they're even fighting among themselves at Smolny!"

A Socialist Revolutionary friend of mine drew me aside. "I know where the Committee for Salvation is hiding," he said. "Do you want to go and talk with them?"

By this time it was dusk. The city had again settled down to normal—shop-shutters up, lights shining, and on the streets great crowds of people slowly moving up and down and arguing. . . .

At Number 86 Nevsky we went through a passage into a courtyard, surrounded by tall apartment buildings. At the door of apartment 229 my friend knocked in a peculiar way. There was a sound of scuffling; an inside door slammed; then the front door opened a crack and a woman's face appeared. After a minute's observation she led us in—a placid-looking, middle-aged lady who at once cried, "Kyril, it's all right!" In the dining-room, where a samovar steamed on the table and there were plates full of bread and raw fish, a man in uniform emerged from behind the window curtains, and another, dressed like a workman, from a closet. They were delighted to meet an American reporter. With a certain amount of gusto both said that they would certainly be shot if the Bolsheviki caught them. They would not give me their names, but both were Socialist Revolutionaries. . . .

"Why," I asked, "do you publish such lies in your newspapers?"

Without taking offense the officer replied, "Yes, I know; but what can we do?" He shrugged. "You must admit that it is necessary for us to create a certain frame of mind in the people. . . ."

The other interrupted. "This is merely an adventure on the part of the Bolsheviki. They have no intellectuals. . . . The Ministries won't work. . . . Russia is not a city, but a whole country. . . . Realizing that they can only last a few days, we have decided to come to the aid of the strongest force opposed to them—Kerensky—and help to restore order."

"That is all very well," I said. "But why do you combine with the Cadets?"

The pseudo-workman smiled frankly. "To tell you the truth, at this moment the masses of the people are following the Bolsheviki. We have no following—now. We can't mobilize a handful of soldiers. There are no arms available. . . . The Bolsheviki are right to a certain extent; there are at this moment in Russia only two parties with any force—the Bolsheviki and the reactionaries, who are all hiding under the coat-tails of the Cadets. When we smash the Bolsheviki we shall turn against the Cadets. . . ."

"Will the Bolsheviki be admitted into the new Government?"

He scratched his head. "That's a problem," he admitted. "Of course if they are not admitted, they'll probably do this all over again. At any rate, they will have a chance to hold the balance of power in the Constituent—that is, if there *is* a Constituent."

"And then, too," said the officer, "that brings up the question of admitting the Cadets into the new Government—and for the same reasons. You know the Cadets do not really want the Constituent Assembly—not if the Bolsheviki can be destroyed now." He shook his head. "It is not easy for us Russians, politics. You Americans are born politicians; you have had politics all your lives. But for us—"

"What do you think of Kerensky?" I asked.

"Oh, Kerensky is guilty of the sins of the Provisional Government," answered the other man. "Kerensky himself forced us to accept coalition with the bourgeoisie. If he had resigned, as he threatened, it would have meant a new Cabinet crisis only sixteen weeks before the Constituent Assembly, and that we wanted to avoid."

"But didn't it amount to that, anyway?"

"Yes, but how were we to know? They tricked us—the Kerenskys and Avksentievs. Gotz is a little more radical. I stand with Chernov, who is a real revolutionist. . . . Why, only today Lenin sent word that he would not object to Chernov entering the Government.

"We wanted to get rid of the Kerensky Government too, but we thought it better to wait for the Constituent. . . . At the beginning of this affair I was with the Bolsheviki, but the Central Committee of my party voted unanimously against it—and what could I do? It was a matter of party discipline. . . .

"In a week the Bolshevik Government will go to pieces; if the Socialist Revolutionaries could only stand aside and wait, the Government would fall into their hands. But if we wait a week the country will be so disorganized that the German imperialists will be victorious. That is why we began our revolt with only two regiments of soldiers promising to support us—and they turned against us. . . . That left only the *yunkers*. . . ."

"How about the Cossacks?"

The officer sighed. "They did not move. At first they said they would come out if they had infantry support. They said, moreover, that they had their men with Kerensky, and that they were doing their part. . . . Then, too, they said that the Cossacks were always accused of being the hereditary enemies of democracy. . . . And finally, 'The Bolsheviki promise that they will not take away our land. There is no danger to us. We remain neutral.' "

During this talk people were constantly entering and leaving—most of them officers, their shoulder-straps torn off. We could see them in the hall, and hear their low, vehement voices. Occasionally, through the half-drawn portières, we caught a glimpse of a door opening into a bathroom, where a heavily built officer in a colonel's uniform sat on the toilet, writing something on a pad held in his lap. I recognized Colonel Polkovnikov, former commandant of Petrograd, for whose arrest the Military Revolutionary Committee would have paid a fortune.

"Our program?" said the officer. "That is it. Land to be turned over to the Land Committees. Workmen to have full representation in the control of industry. An energetic peace program, but not an ultimatum to the world such as the Bolsheviki issued. The Bolsheviki cannot keep their promises to the masses, even in the country itself. We won't let them. . . . They stole our land program in order to get the support of the peasants. That is dishonest. If they had waited for the Constituent Assembly—"

"It doesn't matter about the Constituent Assembly!" broke in the other. "If the Bolsheviki want to establish a Socialist state here, we cannot work with them in any event! Kerensky made the great mistake. He let the Bolsheviki know what he was going to do by announcing in the Council of the Republic that he had ordered their arrest. . . ."

"But what," I said, "do you intend to do now?"

The two men looked at one another. "You will see in a few days. If there are enough troops from the front on our side we shall not compromise with the Bolsheviki. If not, perhaps we shall be forced to. . . ."

Out again on the Nevsky we swung on the step of a streetcar bulging with people, its platform bent down from the weight and scraping along the ground, which crawled with agonizing slowness the long miles to Smolny.

Meshkovsky, a neat, frail little man, was coming down the hall, looking worried. The strikes in the Ministries, he told us, were having their effect. For instance, the Council of People's Commissars had promised to publish the secret treaties; but Neratov, the functionary in charge, had disappeared, taking the documents with him. They were supposed to be hidden in the British Embassy. . . .

Worst of all, however, was the strike in the banks. "Without money," said Menzhinsky, "we are helpless. The wages of the railroad men, and of the telegraph employees, must be paid. . . . The banks are closed; and the key to the situation, the State Bank, is also shut. All the bank-clerks in Russia have been bribed to stop work. . . .

"But Lenin has issued an order to dynamite the State Bank

vaults, and there is a Decree just out, ordering the private banks to open tomorrow, or we will open them ourselves!"

The Petrograd Soviet was in full swing, thronged with armed men, Trotsky reporting:

"The Cossacks are falling back from Krasnoye Selo." (Sharp, exultant cheering.) "But the battle is only beginning. At Pulkovo heavy fighting is going on. All available forces must be hurried there. . . .

"From Moscow, bad news. The Kremlin is in the hands of the *yunkers,* and the workers have only a few arms. The result depends upon Petrograd.

"At the front, the decrees on Peace and Land are provoking great enthusiasm. Kerensky is flooding the trenches with tales of Petrograd burning and bloody, of women and children massacred by the Bolsheviki. But no one believes him. . . .

"The cruisers *Oleg, Avrora,* and *Respublika* are anchored in the Neva, their guns trained on the approaches to the city. . . ."

"Why aren't you out there with the Red Guards?" shouted a rough voice.

"I'm going now!" answered Trotsky, and left the platform. His face a little paler than usual, he passed down the side of the room, surrounded by eager friends, and hurried out to the waiting automobile.

Kameniev now spoke, describing the proceedings of the reconciliation conference. The armistice conditions proposed by the Mensheviki, he said, had been contemptuously rejected. Even the branches of the Railwaymen's Union had voted against such a proposition. . . .

"Now that we've won the power and are sweeping all Russia," he declared, "all they ask of us are three things: 1. To surrender the power. 2. To make the soldiers continue the war. 3. To make the peasants forget about the land. . . ."

Lenin appeared for a moment to answer the accusations of the Socialist Revolutionaries:

"They charge us with stealing their land program. . . . If that was so we bow to them. It is good enough for us. . . ."

So the meeting roared on, leader after leader explaining, exhorting, arguing, soldier after soldier, workman after workman, standing up to speak his mind and his heart. . . . The audience flowed, changing and renewed continually. From time to time men came in, yelling for the members of such and such a detachment, to go to the front; others, relieved, wounded, or coming to Smolny for arms and equipment, poured in. . . .

It was almost three o'clock in the morning when, as we left the hall, Holtzman, of the Military Revolutionary Committee, came running down the hall with a transfigured face.

"It's all right!" he shouted, grabbing my hands. "Telegram from the front. Kerensky is smashed. Look at this!"

He held out the sheet of paper, scribbled hurriedly in pencil, and then, seeing we couldn't read it, he declaimed aloud:

Pulkovo. Staff. 2:10 A.M.

The night of 30 to 31 October* will go down in history. The attempt of Kerensky to move counter-revolutionary troops against the capital of the Revolution has been decisively repulsed. Kerensky is retreating, we are advancing. The soldiers, sailors, and workers of Petrograd have shown that they can and will with arms in their hands enforce the will and authority of the democracy. The bourgeoisie tried to isolate the revolutionary army. Kerensky attempted to break it by the force of the Cossacks. Both plans met a pitiful defeat.

The grand idea of the domination of the worker and peasant democracy closed the ranks of the army and hardened its will. All the country from now on will be convinced that the power of the Soviets is no ephemeral thing, but an invincible fact. . . . The repulse of Kerensky is the repulse of the landowners, the bourgeoisie, and the Kornilovists in general. The repulse of Kerensky is the confirmation of the right of the people to a peaceful free life, to land, to bread, and power. The Pulkovo detachment by its valorous blow has strengthened the cause of the Workers' and Peasants' Revolution. There is no return to the past. Before us are struggles, obstacles, and sacrifices. But the road is clear and victory is certain.

Revolutionary Russia and the Soviet Power can be proud of their

---

*These dates are given according to the Old Calendar, thirteen days behind the Western Calendar, which was only introduced later. The date according to our calendar was 12–13 November. Lower down, as we see, an Order of the Day was dated in the new style.

Pulkovo detachment, acting under the command of Colonel Walden. Eternal memory to those who fell! Glory to the warriors of the Revolution, the soldiers and the officers who were faithful to the People!

Long live revolutionary, popular, Socialist Russia!

In the name of the Council,

L. TROTSKY, People's Commissar . . .

Driving home across Znambensky Square, we made out an unusual crowd in front of the Nikolai Railway Station. Several thousand sailors were massed there, bristling with rifles.

Standing on the steps a member of the Vikzhel was pleading with them.

"Comrades, we cannot carry you to Moscow. We are neutral. We do not carry troops for either side. We cannot take you to Moscow, where already there is terrible civil war. . . ."

All the seething square roared at him; the sailors began to surge forward. Suddenly another door was flung wide; in it stood two or three brakemen, a fireman or so.

"This way, comrades!" cried one. "We will take you to Moscow—or Vladivostok, if you like. Long live the Revolution!"

# Victory

*Order Number 1*
*To the Troops of the Pulkovo Detachment*

13 November 1917. 38 minutes past 9 A.M.
After a cruel fight the troops of the Pulkovo detachment completely routed the counter-revolutionary forces, who retreated from their positions in disorder, and under cover of Tsarskoye Selo fell back toward Pavlovsk II and Gatchina.

Our advanced units occupied the north-eastern extremity of Tsarskoye Selo and the station Alexandrovskaya. The Colpinno detachment was on our left, the Krasnoye Selo detachment to our right.

I ordered the Pulkovo forces to occupy Tsarskoye Selo, to fortify its approaches, especially on the side of Gatchina.

Also to pass and occupy Pavlovskoye, fortifying its southern side, and to take up the railroad as far as Dno.

The troops must take all measures to strengthen the positions occupied by them, arranging trenches and other defensive works.

They must enter into close liaison with the detachments of Colpinno and Krasnoye Selo, and also with the Staff of the Commander-in-Chief for the Defense of Petrograd.

Signed,
*Commander-in-Chief over all Forces acting against*
*the Counter-revolutionary Troops of Kerensky,*
Lieutenant-Colonel MURAVIOV

Tuesday morning. But how is this? Only two days ago the Petrograd campagna was full of leaderless bands, wandering aimlessly; without food, without artillery, without a plan. What had fused that disorganized mass of undisciplined Red Guards, and soldiers without officers, into an army obedient to its own elected high command, tempered to meet and break the assault of cannon and Cossack cavalry?[42]

People in revolt have a way of defying military precedent. The ragged armies of the French Revolution are not forgotten—Valmy and the Lines of Weissembourg. Massed against the Soviet forces were *yunkers*, Cossacks, landowners, nobility, Black Hundreds—the Czar come again, Okhrana and Siberian chains; and the vast and terrible menace of the Germans. . . . Victory, in the words of Carlyle, meant "Apotheosis and Milennium without end!"

Sunday night, the Commissars of the Military Revolutionary Committee returning desperately from the field, the garrison of Petrograd elected its Committee of Five, its Battle Staff, three soldiers and two officers, all certified free from counter-revolutionary taint. Colonel Muraviov, ex-patriot, was in command—an efficient man, but to be carefully watched. At Colpinno, at Obukhovo, at Pulkovo and Krasnoye Selo were formed provisional detachments, increased in size as the stragglers came in from the surrounding country—mixed soldiers, sailors, and Red Guards, parts of regiments, infantry, cavalry, and artillery all together, and a few armored cars.

Day broke, and the pickets of Kerensky's Cossacks came in touch. Scattered rifle-fire, summons to surrender. Over the bleak plain on the cold quiet air spread the sound of battle, falling upon the ears of roving bands as they gathered about their little fires, waiting. . . . So it was beginning! They made toward the battle; and the worker hordes pouring out along the straight roads quickened their pace. . . . Thus upon all the points of attack automatically converged angry human swarms, to be met by Commissars and assigned positions, or work to do. This was *their* battle, for *their* world; the officers in command were elected by *them*. For the moment that incoherent multiple will was one will. . . .

Those who participated in the fighting described to me how the sailors fought until they ran out of cartridges, and then stormed; how the untrained workmen rushed the charging Cossacks and tore them from their horses; how the anonymous hordes of the people, gathering in the darkness around the battle, rose like a tide and poured over the enemy. . . . Before midnight of Monday the Cossacks broke and were fleeing, leaving their artillery behind them, and the army of the proletariat, on a long ragged front, moved forward and rolled into Tsarskoye, before the enemy had a chance to destroy the great Government wireless station, from which now the Commissars of Smolny were hurling out to the world paeans of triumph. . . .

TO ALL SOVIETS OF WORKERS' AND SOLDIERS' DEPUTIES

The twelfth of November, in a bloody combat near Tsarskoye Selo, the revolutionary army defeated the counter-revolutionary troops of Kerensky and Kornilov. In the name of the Revolutionary Government I order all regiments to take the offensive against the enemies of the revolutionary democracy, and to take all measures to arrest Kerensky, and also to oppose the adventure which might menace the conquests of the Revolution and the victory of the proletariat.

Long live the Revolutionary Army!

MURAVIOV

News from the provinces. . . .

At Sevastopol the local Soviet had assumed the power; a huge meeting of the sailors on the battleships in the harbor had forced their officers to line up and swear allegiance to the new Government. At Nizhni Novgorod the Soviet was in control. From Kazan came reports of a battle in the streets, *yunkers* and a brigade of artillery against the Bolshevik garrison. . . .

Desperate fighting had broken out again in Moscow. The *yunkers* and White Guards held the Kremlin and the center of the town, beaten upon from all sides by the troops of the Military Revolutionary Committee. The Soviet artillery was stationed in Skobeliev Square, bombarding the City Duma building, the Prefecture, and the Hotel Metropole. The cobble-stones of the Tverskaya and Nikitskaya had been torn up for trenches and barricades. A hail of machine-gun fire swept the quarters of the great banks and commercial houses. There were no lights, no telephones; the bourgeois population lived in the cellars. . . . The last bulletin said that the Military Revolutionary Committee had delivered an ultimatum to the Committee of Public Safety, demanding the immediate surrender of the Kremlin, or bombardment would follow.

"Bombard the Kremlin?" cried the ordinary citizen. "They dare not!"

From Vologda to Chita in far Siberia, from Pskov to Sevastopol on the Black Sea, in great cities and little villages, civil war burst into flame. From thousands of factories, peasant communes, regiments, and armies, ships on the wide sea, greetings poured into Petrograd—greetings to the Government of the People.

The Cossack Government of Novocherkask telegraphed to Kerensky, *"The Government of the Cossack troops invites the Provisional Government and the members of the Council of the Republic to come, if possible, to Novocherkask, where we can organize in common the struggle against the Bolsheviki."*

In Finland, also, things were stirring. The Soviet of Helsingfors and the Tsentrobalt (Central Committee of the Baltic Fleet), jointly proclaimed a state of siege, and declared that all attempts to interfere with the Bolshevik forces, and all armed resistance to its orders, would be severely repressed. At the same time the Finnish Railway Union called a country-wide general strike, to put into operation the laws passed by the Socialist Diet of June 1917, dissolved by Kerensky....

Early in the morning I went out to Smolny. Going up the long wooden sidewalk from the outer gate I saw the first thin, hesitating snowflakes fluttering down from the gray, windless sky. "Snow!" cried the soldier at the door, grinning with delight. "Good for the health!" Inside, the long, gloomy halls and bleak rooms seemed deserted. No one moved in all the enormous pile. A deep, uneasy sound came to my ears, and looking around, I noticed that everywhere on the floor, along the walls, men were sleeping. Rough, dirty men, workers and soldiers, spattered and caked with mud, sprawled alone or in heaps, in the careless attitudes of death. Some wore ragged bandages marked with blood. Guns and cartridge-belts were scattered about.... The victorious proletarian army!

In the upstairs buffet so thick they lay that one could hardly walk. The air was foul. Through the clouded windows a pale light streamed. A battered samovar, cold, stood on the counter, and many glasses holding dregs of tea. Beside them lay a copy of the Military Revolutionary Committee's last bulletin, upside down, scrawled with painful handwriting. It was a memorial written by some soldier to his comrades fallen in the fight against Kerensky, just as he had set it down before falling on the floor to sleep. The writing was blurred with what looked like tears. . . .

| | |
|---|---|
| Alexei Vinogradov | S. Stolbikov |
| D. Maskvin | D. Preobrazhensky |
| A. Voskressensky | V. Laidansky |
| D. Leonsky | M. Berchikov |

These men were drafted into the Army on 15 November 1916. Only three are left of the above.
Mikhail Berchikov.
Alexei Voskressensky.
Dmitri Leonsky.

*Sleep, warrior eagles, sleep with peaceful soul.*
*You have deserved, our own ones, happiness and*
*Eternal peace. Under the earth of the grave*
*You have straitly closed your ranks. Sleep, Citizens!*

Only the Military Revolutionary Committee still functioned, unsleeping. Skripnik, emerging from the inner room, said that Gotz had been arrested, but had flatly denied signing the proclamation of the Committee of Salvation, as had Avksentiev; and the Committee for Salvation itself had repudiated the Appeal to the garrison. There was still disaffection among the city regiments, Skripnik reported; the Volhynsky Regiment had refused to fight against Kerensky.

Several detachments of "neutral" troops, with Chernov at their head, were at Gatchina, trying to persuade Kerensky to halt his attack on Petrograd.

Skripnik laughed. "There can be no 'neutrals' now," he said.

"We've won!" His sharp, bearded face glowed with an almost religious exaltation. "More than sixty delegates have arrived from the front, with assurances of support by all the armies except the troops on the Rumanian front, who have not been heard from. The Army Committees have suppressed the news from Petrograd, but we now have a regular system of couriers. . . ."

Down in the front hall Kameniev was just entering, worn out by the all-night session of the Conference to Form a New Government, but happy. "Already the Socialist Revolutionaries are inclined to admit us into the new Government," he told me. "The right-wing groups are frightened by the Revolutionary Tribunals; they demand, in a sort of panic, that we dissolve them before going any further. . . . We have accepted the proposition of the Vikzhel to form a homogeneous Socialist Ministry, and they're working on that now. You see, it all springs from our victory. When we were down, they wouldn't have us at any price; now everybody's in favor of some agreement with the Soviets. . . . What we need is a really decisive victory. Kerensky wants an armistice, but he'll have to surrender. . . ."[43]

That was the temper of the Bolshevik leaders. To a foreign journalist who asked Trotsky what statement he had to make to the world, Trotsky replied: "At this moment the only statement possible is the one we are making through the mouths of our cannon!"

But there was an undercurrent of real anxiety in the tide of victory: the question of finances. Instead of opening the banks, as had been ordered by the Military Revolutionary Committee, the Union of Bank Employees had held a meeting and declared a formal strike. Smolny had demanded some thirty-five million roubles from the State Bank, and the cashier had locked the vaults, only paying out money to the representatives of the Provisional Government. The reactionaries were using the State Bank as a political weapon; for instance, when the Vikzhel demanded money to pay the salaries of the employees of the Government railroads, it was told to apply to Smolny. . . .

I went to the State Bank to see the new Commissar, a red-haired Ukrainian Bolshevik named Petrovich. He was trying to bring order out of the chaos in which affairs had been left by the striking clerks. In all the offices of the huge place perspiring volunteer workers, soldiers and sailors, their tongues sticking out of their mouths in the intensity of their effort, were poring over the great ledgers with a bewildered air. . . .

The Duma building was crowded. There were still isolated cases of defiance toward the new Government, but they were rare. The Central Land Committee had appealed to the Peasants, ordering them not to recognize the Land Decree passed by the Congress of the Soviets, because it would cause confusion and civil war. Mayor Schreider announced that because of the Bolshevik insurrection, the election to the Constituent Assembly would have to be indefinitely postponed.

Two questions seemed to be uppermost in all minds, shocked by the ferocity of the civil war; first, a truce to the bloodshed[44]— second, the creation of a new Government. There was no longer any talk of "destroying the Bolsheviki"—and very little about excluding them from the Government, except from the Populist Socialists and the Peasants' Soviets. Even the Central Army Committee at the Stavka, the most determined enemy of Smolny, telephoned from Moghilev: "If, to constitute the new Ministry, it is necessary to come to an understanding with the Bolsheviki, we agree to admit them *in a minority* to the Cabinet."

*Pravda,* ironically calling attention to Kerensky's "humanitarian sentiments," published his dispatch to the Committee for Salvation:

> In accord with the proposals of the Committee for Salvation and all the democratic organizations united around it, I have halted all military action against the rebels. A delegate of the Committee has been sent to enter into negotiations. Take all measures to stop the useless shedding of blood.

The Vikzhel sent a telegram to all Russia:

> The Conference of the Union of Railway Workers with the representatives of both the belligerent parties, who admit the necessity of

an agreement, protest energetically against the use of political terrorism in the civil war, especially when it is carried on between different
factions of the revolutionary democracy, and declare that political
terrorism, in whatever form, is in contradiction to the very idea of the
negotiations for a new Government. . . .

Delegations from the Conference were sent to the front, to
Gatchina. In the Conference itself everything seemed on the
point of final settlement. It had even been decided to elect a Provisional People's Council, composed of about four hundred
members—seventy-five representing Smolny, seventy-five the
old Tsay-ee-kah, and the rest split up among the Town Dumas,
the Trade Unions, Land Committees, and political parties. Chernov was mentioned as the new Premier. Lenin and Trotsky,
rumor said, were to be excluded. . . .

About noon I was again in front of Smolny, talking with the
driver of an ambulance bound for the revolutionary front. Could
I go with him? Certainly! He was a volunteer, a University student, and as we rolled down the street shouted over his shoulder
to me phrases of execrable German: "*Also, gut! Wir mach die Kas-
ernen zu essen gehen!*" I made out that there would be lunch at
some barracks.

On the Kirochnaya we turned into an immense courtyard surrounded by military buildings, and mounted a dark stairway to a
low room lit by one window. At a long wooden table were seated
some twenty soldiers, eating *shchi* (cabbage soup) from a great tin
wash-tub with wooden spoons, and talking loudly with much
laughter.

"Welcome to the Battalion Committee of the Sixth Reserve
Engineers' Battalion!" cried my friend, and introduced me as an
American Socialist. Whereat everyone rose to shake my hand,
and one old soldier put his arms around me and gave me a hearty
kiss. A wooden spoon was produced and I took my place at the
table. Another tub, full of *kasha*, was brought in, a huge loaf of
black bread, and of course the inevitable teapots. At once everyone began asking me questions about America: Was it true that
people in a free country sold their votes for *money*? If so, how did

they get what they wanted? How about this "Tammany"? Was it true that in a free country a little group of people could control a whole city, and exploited it for their personal benefit? Why did the people stand it? Even under the Czar such things could not happen in Russia; true, here there was always graft, but to buy and sell a whole city full of people! And in a free country! Had the people no revolutionary feeling? I tried to explain that in my country people tried to change things by law.

"Of course," nodded a young sergeant, named Baklanov, who spoke French. "But you have a highly developed capitalist class? Then the capitalist class must control the legislatures and the courts. How then can the people change things? I am open to conviction, for I do not know your country, but to me it is incredible. . . ."

I said that I was going to Tsarskoye Selo. "I, too," said Baklanov suddenly. "And I—and I—" The whole roomful decided on the spot to go to Tsarskoye Selo.

Just then came a knock on the door. It opened, and in it stood the figure of the Colonel. No one rose, but all shouted a greeting. "May I come in?" asked the Colonel. "*Prosim! Prosim!*" they answered heartily. He entered, smiling, a tall, distinguished figure in a goatskin cape embroidered with gold. "I think I heard you say that you were going to Tsarskoye Selo, comrades," he said. "Could I go with you?"

Baklanov considered. "I do not think there is anything to be done here today," he answered. "Yes, comrade, we shall be very glad to have you." The Colonel thanked him and sat down, filling a glass of tea.

In a low voice, for fear of wounding the Colonel's pride, Baklanov explained to me. "You see, I am the chairman of the Committee. We control the Battalion absolutely, except in action, when the Colonel is delegated by us to command. In action his orders must be obeyed, but he is strictly responsible to us. In barracks he must ask our permission before taking any action. . . . You might call him our Executive Officer. . . ."

Arms were distributed to us, revolvers and rifles—"we might meet some Cossacks, you know"—and we all piled into the ambulance, together with three great bundles of newspapers for the front. Straight down the Liteiny we rattled, and along the Zagorodny Prospect. Next to me sat a youth with the shoulder-straps of a lieutenant, who seemed to speak all European languages with equal fluency. He was a member of the Battalion Committee.

"I am not a Bolshevik," he assured me emphatically. "My family is a very ancient and noble one. I, myself, am, you might say, a Cadet. . . ."

"But how—?" I began, bewildered.

"Oh, yes, I am a member of the Committee. I make no secret of my political opinions, but the others do not mind, because they know I do not believe in opposing the will of the majority. . . . I have refused to take any action in the present civil war, however, for I do not believe in taking up arms against my brother Russians. . . ."

"Provocator! Kornilovist!" the others cried at him gaily, slapping him on the shoulder. . . .

Passing under the huge gray stone archway of the Moskovsky Gate, covered with golden hieroglyphics, ponderous Imperial eagles and the names of Czars, we sped out on the wide, straight highway, gray with the first light fall of snow. It was thronged with Red Guards, stumbling along on foot toward the revolutionary front, shouting and singing; and others, gray-faced and muddy, coming back. Most of them seemed to be mere boys. Women with spades, some with rifles and bandoliers, others wearing the Red Cross on their arm-bands—the bowed, toil-worn women of the slums. Squads of soldiers marching out of step, with an affectionate jeer for the Red Guards; sailors, grim-looking; children with bundles of food for their fathers and mothers; all these, coming and going, trudged through the whitened mud that covered the cobbles of the highway inches deep. We passed cannon, jingling southward with their caissons; trucks bound both ways, bristling with armed men; ambulances full of wounded from the direction of the battle, and once a peasant cart, creaking slowly along, in which sat a white-faced boy bent over his shattered stomach and screaming monotonously. In the fields on either side women and old men were digging trenches and stringing barbed wire entanglements.

Back northward the clouds rolled away dramatically, and the pale sun came out. Across the flat, marshy plain Petrograd glittered. To the right, white and gilded and colored bulbs and pinnacles; to the left, tall chimneys, some pouring out black smoke; and beyond, a lowering sky over Finland. On each side of us were churches, monasteries. . . . Occasionally a monk was visible, silently watching the pulse of the proletarian army throbbing on the road.

At Pulkovo the road divided, and there we halted in the midst of a great crowd, where the human streams poured from three directions, friends meeting, excited and congratulatory, describing the battle to one another. A row of houses facing the crossroads was marked with bullets, and the earth was trampled into mud half a mile around. The fighting had been furious here. . . . In the near distance riderless Cossack horses circled hungrily, for the grass of the plain had died long ago. Right in front of us an awkward Red Guard was trying to ride one, falling off again and again, to the childlike delight of a thousand rough men.

The left road, along which the remnants of the Cossacks had retreated, led up a little hill to a hamlet, where there was a glorious view of the immense plain, gray as a windless sea, tumultuous clouds towering over, and the imperial city disgorging its thousands along all the roads. Far over to the left lay the little hill of Krasnoye Selo, the parade-ground of the Imperial Guards' summer camp, and the Imperial Dairy. In the middle distance nothing broke the flat monotony but a few walled monasteries and convents, some isolated factories, and several large buildings with unkempt grounds that were asylums and orphanages. . . .

"Here," said the driver, as we went on over a barren hill, "here was where Vera Slutskaya died. Yes, the Bolshevik member of the Duma. It happened early this morning. She was in an automobile, with Zalkind and another man. There was a truce, and they started for the front trenches. They were talking and laughing, when all of a sudden, from the armored train in which Kerensky himself was riding, somebody saw the automobile and fired a cannon. The shell struck Vera Slutskaya and killed her. . . ."

And so we came into Tsarskoye, all bustling with the swaggering heroes of the proletarian horde. Now the palace where the Soviet had met was a busy place. Red Guards and sailors filled the courtyard, sentries stood at the doors, and a stream of couriers and Commissars pushed in and out. In the Soviet room a samovar had been set up, and fifty or more workers, soldiers, sailors, and officers stood around, drinking tea and talking at the top of their voices. In one corner two clumsy-handed working men were trying to make a multigraphing machine go. At the center table, the huge Dybenko bent over a map, marking out positions for the troops with red and blue pencils. In his free hand he carried, as always, the enormous blue-steel revolver. Anon he sat himself down at a typewriter and pounded away with one finger; every little while he would pause, pick up the revolver, and lovingly spin the chamber.

A couch lay along the wall, and on this was stretched a young workman. Two Red Guards were bending over him, the rest of the company did not pay any attention. In his breast was a hole; through his clothes fresh blood came welling up with every heartbeat. His eyes were closed, and his young, bearded face was greenish-white. Faintly and slowly he still breathed, with every breath sighing, *"Mir boudit! Mir boudit!* (Peace is coming! Peace is coming!)"

Dybenko looked up as we came in. "Ah," he said to Baklanov. "Comrade, will you go up to the Commandant's headquarters and take charge? Wait; I will write you credentials." He went to the typewriter and slowly picked out the letters.

The new Commandant of Tsarskoye Selo and I went toward the Ekaterina Palace, Baklanov very excited and important. In the same ornate, white room some Red Guards were rummaging curiously around, while my old friend, the Colonel, stood by the window biting his moustache. He greeted me like a long-lost brother. At a table near the door sat the French Bessarabian. The Bolsheviki had ordered him to remain, and continue his work. "What could I do?" he muttered. "People like myself cannot fight on either side in such a war as this, no matter how much we may instinctively dislike the dictatorship of the mob. . . . I only regret that I am so far from my mother in Bessarabia!"

Baklanov was formally taking over office from the Commandant. "Here," said the Colonel nervously, "are the keys to the desk."

A Red Guard interrupted. "Where's the money?" he asked rudely. The Colonel seemed surprised. "Money? Money? Ah, you mean the chest. There it is," said the Colonel, "just as I found it when I took possession three days ago. Keys?" The Colonel shrugged. "I have no keys."

The Red Guard sneered knowingly. "Very convenient," he said.

"Let us open the chest," said Baklanov. "Bring an axe. Here is an American comrade. Let him smash the chest open, and write down what he finds there."

I swung the axe. The wooden chest was empty.

"Let's arrest him," said the Red Guard, venomously. "He is Kerensky's man. He has stolen the money and given it to Kerensky."

Baklanov did not want to. "Oh, no," he said. "It was the Kornilovist before him. He is not to blame."

"The devil!" said the Red Guard. "He is Kerensky's man, I tell you. If you won't arrest him then we will, and we'll take him to Petrograd and put him in Peter-Paul, where he belongs!" At this the other Red Guards growled assent. With a piteous glance at us the Colonel was led away. . . .

Down in front of the Soviet palace an auto-truck was going to the front. Half a dozen Red Guards, some sailors, and a soldier or two, under command of a huge workman, clambered in, and shouted to me to come along. Red Guards issued from headquarters, each of them staggering under an arm-load of small, corrugated-iron bombs, filled with *grubit*—which, they say, is ten times as strong, and five times as sensitive as dynamite; these they threw into the truck. A three-inch cannon was loaded and then tied on to the tail of the truck with bits of rope and wire.

We started with a shout, at top speed, of course; the heavy

truck swaying from side to side. The cannon leaped from one wheel to the other, and the *grubit* bombs went rolling back and forth over our feet, fetching up against the sides of the car with a crash.

The big Red Guard, whose name was Vladimir Nikolayevich, plied me with questions about America. "Why did America come into the war? Are the American workers ready to throw over the capitalists? What is the situation in the Mooney case now? Will they extradite Berkman to San Francisco?" and others, very difficult to answer, all delivered in a shout above the roaring of the truck, while we held on to each other and danced amid the caroming bombs.

Occasionally a patrol tried to stop us. Soldiers ran out into the road before us, shouted "*Stoi!*" and threw up their guns.

We paid no attention. "The devil take you!" cried the Red Guards. "We don't stop for anybody! We're Red Guards!" And we thundered imperiously on, while Vladimir Nikolayevich bellowed to me about the internationalization of the Panama Canal and such matters. . . .

"Where's the front, brothers?"

The foremost sailor halted and scratched his head. "This morning," he said, "it was about half a kilometer down the road. But the damn thing isn't anywhere now. We walked and walked and walked, but we couldn't find it."

They climbed into the truck, and we proceeded. It must have been about a mile further that Vladimir Nikolayevich cocked his ear and shouted to the chauffeur to stop.

"Firing!" he said. "Do you hear it?" For a moment dead silence, and then, a little ahead and to the left, three shots in rapid succession. Along here the side of the road was heavily wooded. Very much excited now, we crept along, speaking in whispers, until the truck was nearly opposite the place where the firing had come from. Descending, we spread out, and every man carrying his rifle, went stealthily into the forest.

Two comrades, meanwhile, detached the cannon and slewed it around until it aimed as nearly as possible at our backs.

It was silent in the woods. The leaves were gone, and the tree-trunks were a pale wan color in the low, sickly autumn sun. Not a thing moved, except the ice of little woodland pools shivering under our feet. Was it an ambush?

We went uneventfully forward until the trees began to thin, and paused. Beyond, in a little clearing, three soldiers sat around a small fire, perfectly oblivious.

Vladimir Nikolayevich stepped forward. "*Zra'zvuitye*, comrades!" he greeted, while behind him one cannon, twenty rifles, and a truck-load of *grubit* bombs hung by a hair. The soldiers scrambled to their feet.

"What was the shooting going on around here?"

One of the soldiers answered, looking relieved, "Why, we were just shooting a rabbit or two, comrade. . . ."

The truck hurtled on toward Romanov, through the bright, empty day. At the first cross-roads two soldiers ran out in front of us, waving their rifles. We slowed down, and stopped.

"Passes, comrades!"

The Red Guards raised a great clamor. "We are Red Guards. We don't need any passes. . . . Go on, never mind them!"

But a sailor objected. "This is wrong, comrades. We must have revolutionary discipline. Suppose some counter-revolutionaries came along in a truck and said: 'We don't need any passes'? The comrades don't know you."

At this there was a debate. One by one, however, the sailors and soldiers joined with the first. Grumbling, each Red Guard produced his dirty *bumaga* (paper). All were alike except mine, which had been issued by the Revolutionary Staff at Smolny. The sentries declared that I must go with them. The Red Guards objected strenuously, but the sailor who had spoken first insisted. "This comrade we know to be a true comrade," he said. "But there are orders of the Committee, and these orders must be obeyed. That is revolutionary discipline. . . ."

In order not to make any trouble, I got down from the truck and watched it disappear careening down the road, all the company waving farewell. The soldiers consulted in low tones for a moment, and then led me to a wall, against which they placed me. It flashed upon me suddenly; they were going to shoot me!

In all three directions not a human being was in sight. The only sign of life was smoke from the chimney of a *dacha*, a rambling wooden house a quarter of a mile up the side road. The two soldiers were walking out in the road. Desperately I ran after them.

"But, comrades! See! Here is the seal of the Military Revolutionary Committee!"

They stared stupidly at my pass, then at each other.

"It is different from the others," said one, sullenly. "We cannot read, brother."

I took him by the arm, "Come!" I said. "Let's go to that house. Someone there can surely read." They hesitated. "No," said one. The other looked me over. "Why not?" he muttered. "After all, it is a serious crime to kill an innocent man."

We walked up to the front door of the house and knocked. A short, stout woman opened it, and shrank back in alarm, babbling, "I don't know anything about them! I don't know anything about them!" One of my guards held out the pass. She screamed. "Just to read it, comrade." Hesitatingly she took the paper and read aloud, swiftly:

> The bearer of this pass, John Reed, is a representative of the American Social-Democracy, an internationalist. . . .

Out on the road again the two soldiers held another consulsultation. "We must take you to the Regimental Committee," they said. In the fast-developing twilight we trudged along the muddy road. Occasionally we met squads of soldiers, who stopped and surrounded me with looks of menace, handing my pass around and arguing violently as to whether or not I should be killed. . . .

It was dark when we came to the barracks of the Second Tsarskoye Selo Rifles, low, sprawling buildings huddled along the post-road. A number of soldiers slouching at the entrance asked eager questions. A spy? A provocator? We mounted a winding stair and emerged into a great, bare room with a huge stove in the center, and rows of cots on the floor, where about a thousand soldiers were playing cards, talking, singing, and asleep. In the roof was a jagged hole made by Kerensky's cannon. . . .

I stood in the doorway, and a sudden silence ran among the groups, who turned and stared at me. Of a sudden they began to move, slowly and then with a rush, thundering, with faces full of hate. "Comrades! Comrades!" yelled one of my guards. "Committee! Committee!" The throng halted, banked around me, muttering. Out of them shouldered a lean youth, wearing a red arm-band.

"Who is this?" he asked roughly. The guards explained. "Give me the paper!" He read it carefully, glancing at me with keen eyes. Then he smiled and handed me the pass. "Comrades, this is an American comrade. I am chairman of the committee, and I welcome you to the regiment. . . ." A sudden general buzz grew into a roar of greeting, and they pressed forward to shake my hand.

"You have not dined? Here we have had our dinner. You shall go the Officers' Club, where there are some who speak your language. . . ."

He led me across the courtyard to the door of another building. An aristocratic-looking youth, with the shoulder-straps of a lieutenant, was entering. The Chairman presented me, and shaking hands, went back.

"I am Stepan Georgevich Morovsky, at your service," said the lieutenant in perfect French. From the ornate entrance-hall a ceremonial staircase led upward, lighted by glittering lusters. On the second floor billiard-rooms, card-rooms, a library opened from the hall. We entered the dining room, at a long table in the center of which sat about twenty officers in full uniform, wearing their gold and silver handled swords, the ribbons and crosses of Imperial decorations. All rose politely as I entered, and made a place for me beside the colonel, a large, impressive man with a grizzled beard. Orderlies were deftly serving dinner. The atmosphere was that of any officers' mess in Europe. Where was the Revolution?

"You are not Bolsheviki?" I asked Morovsky.

A smile went around the table, but I caught one or two glancing furtively at the orderly.

"No," answered my friend. "There is only one Bolshevik officer in this regiment. He is in Petrograd tonight. The colonel is a Menshevik. Captain Kherlov there is a Cadet. I myself am a Socialist-Revolutionary of the Right wing. . . . I should say that most of the officers in the Army are not Bolsheviki, but like me they believe in democracy; they believe that they must follow the soldier-masses. . . ."

Dinner over, maps were brought, and the colonel spread them out on the table. The rest crowded around to see.

"Here," said the colonel, pointing to pencil marks, "were our positions this morning. Vladimir Kyrilovich, where is your company?"

Captain Kherlov pointed. "According to orders, we occupied the position along this road. Karsavin relieved me at five o'clock."

Just then the door of the room opened, and there stood the chairman of the regimental committee, with another soldier. They joined the group behind the colonel, peering at the map.

"Good," said the colonel. "Now the Cossacks have fallen back ten kilometers in our sector. I do not think it is necessary to take up advanced positions. Gentlemen, for tonight you will hold the present line, strengthening the positions by—"

"If you please," interrupted the chairman of the regimental committee. "The orders are to advance with all speed, and prepare to engage the Cossacks north of Gatchina in the morning. A crushing defeat is necessary. Kindly make the proper dispositions."

There was a short silence. The colonel again turned to the map. "Very well," he said, in a different voice. "Stepan Georgevich, you will please—" Rapidly tracing lines with a blue pencil, he gave his orders, while a sergeant made shorthand notes. The sergeant then withdrew, and ten minutes later returned with the orders typewritten, and one carbon copy. The chairman of the committee studied the map with a copy of the orders before him.

"All right," he said, rising. Folding the carbon copy, he put it in his pocket. Then he signed the other, stamped it with a round seal taken from his pocket, and presented it to the colonel. . . .

Here was the Revolution!

I returned to the Soviet palace in Tsarskoye in the regimental staff automobile. Still the crowds of workers, soldiers, and sailors pouring in and out, still the choking press of trucks, armored cars, cannon before the door, and the shouting, the laughter of unwonted victory. Half a dozen Red Guards forced their way through, a priest in the middle. This was Father Ivan, they said, who had blessed the Cossacks when they entered the town. I heard afterwards that he was shot. . . .[45]

Dybenko was just coming out, giving rapid orders right and left. In his hand he carried the big revolver. An automobile stood with racing engine at the curb. Alone he climbed in the rear seat, and was off—off to Gatchina, to conquer Kerensky.

Toward nightfall he arrived at the outskirts of the town, and went on afoot. What Dybenko told the Cossacks nobody knows, but the fact is that General Krasnov and his staff and several thousand Cossacks surrendered and advised Kerensky to do the same.[46]

As for Kerensky—I reprint here the deposition made by General Krasnov on the morning of 14 November:

"Gatchina, 14 November 1917. Today, about three o'clock (A.M.), I was summoned by the Supreme Commander (Kerensky). He was very agitated, and very nervous.

" 'General,' he said to me, 'you have betrayed me. Your Cossacks declare categorically that they will arrest me and deliver me to the sailors.'

" 'Yes,' I answered, 'there is talk of it, and I know that you have no sympathy anywhere.'

" 'But the officers say the same thing.'

" 'Yes, most of all it is the officers who are discontented with you.'

" 'What shall I do? I ought to commit suicide!'

" 'If you are an honorable man you will go immediately to Petrograd with a white flag, you will present yourself to the Military Revolutionary Committee, and enter into negotiations as Chief of the Provisional Government.'

" 'All right. I will do that, general.'

" 'I will give you a guard and ask that a sailor go with you.'

" 'No, no, not a sailor. Do you know whether it is true that Dybenko is here?'

" 'I don't know who Dybenko is.'

" 'He is my enemy.'

" 'There is nothing to do. If you play for high stakes you must know how to take a chance.'

" 'Yes. I'll leave tonight!'

" 'That would be a flight. Leave calmly and openly, so that everyone can see that you are not running away.'

" 'Very well. But you must give me a guard on which I can count.'

" 'Good.'

"I went out and called the Cossack Russkov, of the Tenth Regiment of the Don, and ordered him to pick out ten Cossacks to accompany the Supreme Commander. Half an hour later the Cossacks came to tell me that Kerensky was not in his quarters, that he had run away.

"I gave the alarm and ordered that he be searched for, supposing that he could not leave Gatchina, but he could not be found. . . ."

And so Kerensky fled alone, "disguised in the uniform of a sailor," and by that act lost whatever popularity he had retained among the Russian masses. . . .

I went back to Petrograd riding on the front seat of an autotruck, driven by a workman and filled with Red Guards. We had no kerosene, so our lights were not burning. The road was crowded with the proletarian army going home, and new reserves pouring out to take their places. Immense trucks like ours, columns of artillery, wagons, loomed up in the night, without lights as we were. We hurtled furiously on, wrenched right and left to avoid collisions that seemed inevitable, scraping wheels, followed by the epithets of pedestrians.

Across the horizon spread the glittering lights of the capital, immeasurably more splendid by night than by day, like a dike of jewels on the barren plain.

The old workman who drove held the wheel in one hand, while with the other he swept the far-gleaming capital in an exultant gesture.

"Mine!" he cried, his face all alight. "All mine now! My Petrograd!"

# Moscow

T HE Military Revolutionary Committee, with a fierce intensity, followed up its victory:

14 November.

To all Army corps, divisional and regimental Committees, to all Soviets of Workers', Soldiers', and Peasants' Deputies, to all, all, all.

Conforming to the agreement between the Cossacks, *yunkers*, soldiers, sailors, and workers, it has been decided to arraign Alexander Feodorovich Kerensky before a tribunal of the people. We demand that Kerensky be arrested, and that he be ordered, in the name of the organization hereinafter mentioned, to come immediately to Petrograd and present himself to the tribunal.

> Signed,
> *The Cossacks of the First Division of Ussur*
> *Cavalry; the Committee of Yunkers of the*
> *Petrograd detachment of Franc-Tireurs; the*
> *delegate of the Fifth Army*
> *People's Commissar,* DYBENKO

The Committee for Salvation, the Duma, the Central Committee of the Socialist Revolutionary Party—proudly claiming Kerensky as a member—all passionately protested that he could only be held responsible to the Constituent Assembly.

On the evening of 16 November I watched two thousand Red Guards swing down the Zagorodny Prospekt behind a military band playing the *Marseillaise*—and how appropriate it sounded— with blood-red flags over the dark ranks of workmen, to welcome home again their brothers who had defended "Red Petrograd." In the bitter dusk they tramped, men and women, their tall bayonets swaying; through streets faintly lighted and slippery with mud, between silent crowds of bourgeois, contemptuous but fearful. . . .

All were against them—business men, speculators, investors, landowners, army officers, politicians, teachers, students, professional men, shopkeepers, clerks, agents. The other Socialist parties hated the Bolsheviki with an implacable hatred. On the side of the Soviets were the rank and file of the workers, the sailors, all the undemoralized soldiers, the landless peasants and a few—a very few—intellectuals.

From the farthest corners of great Russia, whereupon desperate street fighting burst like a wave, news of Kerensky's defeat came echoing back the immense roar of proletarian victory. Kazan, Saratov, Novgorod, Vinnitza—where the streets had run with blood; Moscow, where the Bolsheviki had turned their artillery against the last stronghold of the bourgeoisie—the Kremlin.

"They are bombarding the Kremlin!" The news passed from mouth to mouth in the streets of Petrograd, almost with a sense of terror. Travelers from "white and shining little mother Moscow" told fearful tales. Thousands killed; the Tverskaya and the Kuznetsky Most in flames; the church of Vasili Blazhenny a smoking ruin; Usspensky Cathedral crumbling down; the Spasskaya Gate of the Kremlin tottering; the Duma burned to the ground.[47]

Nothing that the Bolsheviki had done could compare with this fearful blasphemy in the heart of Holy Russia. To the ears of the devout sounded the shock of guns crashing in the face of the Holy Orthodox Church, and pounding to dust the sanctuary of the Russian nation. . . .

On 15 November Lunacharsky, Commissar of Education, broke into tears at the session of the Council of People's Commissars, and rushed from the room, crying, "I cannot stand it! I cannot bear the monstrous destruction of beauty and tradition. . . ."

That afternoon his letter of resignation was published in the newspapers:

I have just been informed, by people arriving from Moscow, what has happened there.

The Cathedral of St. Basil the Blessed, the Cathedral of the Assumption, are being bombarded. The Kremlin, where are now gathered the most important art treasures of Petrograd and of Moscow, is under artillery fire. There are thousands of victims.

The fearful struggle there has reached a pitch of bestial ferocity. What is left? What more can happen?

I cannot bear this. My cup is full. I am unable to endure these horrors. It is impossible to work under the pressure of thoughts which drive me mad!

That is why I am leaving the Council of People's Commissars.

I fully realize the gravity of this decision. But I can bear no more. . . .[48]

That same day the White Guards and *yunkers* in the Kremlin surrendered, and were allowed to march out unharmed. The treaty of peace follows:

1. The Committee of Public Safety ceases to exist.

2. The White Guard gives up its arms and dissolves. The officers retain their swords and regulation side-arms. In the Military Schools are retained only the arms necessary for instruction; all others are surrendered by the *yunkers*. The Military Revolutionary Committee guarantees the liberty and inviolability of the person.

3. To settle the question of disarmament, as set forth in section 2, a special commission is appointed, consisting of representatives from all organizations which took part in the peace negotiations.

4. From the moment of the signature of this peace treaty, both parties shall immediately give order to cease firing and halt all military operation, taking measures to ensure punctual obedience to this order.

5. At the signature of the treaty, all prisoners made by the two parties shall be released. . . .

For two days now the Bolsheviki had been in control of the city. The frightened citizens were creeping out of their cellars to see their dead; the barricades in the streets were being removed. Instead of diminishing, however, the stories of destruction in Moscow continued to grow. . . . And it was under the influence of these fearful reports that we decided to go there.

Petrograd, after all, in spite of being for a century the seat of Government, is still an artificial city. Moscow is real Russia, Russia as it was and will be; in Moscow we would get the true feeling of the Russian people about the Revolution. Life was more intense there.

For the past week the Petrograd Military Revolutionary Committee, aided by the rank and file of the Railway Workers, had seized control of the Nikolai Railroad, and hurled trainload after trainload of sailors and Red Guards southwest. . . . We were provided with passes from Smolny, without which no one could leave the capital. . . . When the train backed into the station, a mob of shabby soldiers, all carrying huge sacks of eatables, stormed the doors, smashed the windows and poured into all the compartments, filling up the aisles and even climbing on to the roof. Three of us managed to wedge our way into a compartment, but almost immediately about twenty soldiers entered. . . . There was room for only four people; we argued, expostulated, and the conductor joined us—but the soldiers merely laughed. Were they to bother about the comfort of a lot of *boorzhui* (bourgeois)? We produced the passes from Smolny; instantly the soldiers changed their attitude.

"Come, comrades," cried one, "these are American *tovarishchi*. They have come thirty thousand versts to see our revolution, and they are naturally tired. . . ."

With polite and friendly apologies the soldiers began to leave. Shortly afterwards we heard them breaking into a compartment occupied by two stout, well-dressed Russians, who had bribed the conductor and locked their door. . . .

About seven o'clock in the evening we drew out of the station, an immense long train drawn by a weak little locomotive burning wood, and stumbled along slowly, with many stops. The soldiers on the roof kicked their heels and sang whining peasant songs; and in the corridor, so jammed that it was impossible to pass, violent political debates raged all night long. Occasionally the conductor came through, as a matter of habit, looking for tickets. He found very few except ours, and after a half-hour of futile wrangling, lifted his arms despairingly and withdrew. The atmosphere was stifling, full of smoke and foul odors; if it hadn't been for the broken windows we would doubtless have smothered during the night.

In the morning, hours late, we looked out upon a snowy world. It was bitter cold. About noon a peasant woman got on with a basket full of bread-chunks and a great can of luke-warm coffee-substitute. From then on until dark there was nothing but the packed train, jolting and stopping, and occasional stations where a ravenous mob swooped down on the scantily furnished buffet and swept it clean. . . . At one of these halts I ran into Nogin and Rykov, the seceding Commissars, who were returning to Moscow to put their grievances before their own Soviet;* and further along was Bukharin, a short red-bearded man with the eyes of a fanatic—"more Left than Lenin," they said of him. . . .

Then the three strokes of the bell and we made a rush for the train, worming our way through the packed and noisy aisle. . . . A good-natured crowd, bearing the discomfort with humorous patience, interminably arguing about everything from the situation in Petrograd to the British trade-union system, and disputing loudly with the few *boorzhui* who were on board. Before we reached Moscow almost every car had organized a committee to secure and distribute food, and these committees became divided into political factions, who wrangled over fundamental principles. . . .

The station at Moscow was deserted. We went to the office of the Commissar, in order to arrange for our return tickets. He was a sullen youth with the shoulder-straps of a lieutenant; when we showed him our papers from Smolny he lost his temper and declared that he was no Bolshevik, that he represented the Committee of Public Safety.. . . . It was characteristic—in the general turmoil attending the conquest of the city, the chief railway station had been forgotten by the victors. . . .

Not a cab in sight. A few blocks down the street, however, we woke up a grotesquely padded *izvozchik* asleep upright on the box of his little sleigh. "How much to the center of the town?"

*See Chapter 11.

He scratched his head. "The *barini* won't be able to find a room in any hotel," he said. "But I'll take you around for a hundred roubles. . . ." Before the Revolution it cost *two*! We objected, but he simply shrugged his shoulders. "It takes a good deal of courage to drive a sleigh nowadays," he went on. We could not beat him down below fifty. . . . As we sped along the silent, snowy, half-lighted streets he recounted his adventures during the six days' fighting. "Driving along, or waiting for a fare on the corner," he said, "all of a sudden *pooff!* a cannon ball exploding here, *pooff!* a cannon ball there, *ratt-tatt!* a machine-gun. . . . I gallop, the devils shooting all around. I get to a nice quiet street and stop, doze a little, *pooff!* another cannon ball, *ratt-tatt.* . . . Devils! Devils! Devils! B-r-r-r!"

In the center of the town the snow-piled streets were quiet with the stillness of convalescence. Only a few arc-lights were burning, only a few pedestrians hurried along the sidewalks. An icy wind blew from the great plain, cutting to the bone. At the first hotel we entered an office illuminated by two candles.

"Yes, we have some very comfortable rooms, but all the windows are shot out. If the *gospodin* does not mind a little fresh air. . . ."

Down the Tverskaya the shop-windows were broken, and there were shell holes and torn-up paving-stones in the street. Hotel after hotel, all full, or the proprietors still so frightened that all they could say was, "No, no, there is no room! There is no room!" On the main streets, where the great banking houses and mercantile houses lay, the Bolshevik artillery had been indiscriminately effective. As one Soviet official told me, "Whenever we didn't know just where the *yunkers* and White Guards were, we bombarded their pocket-books. . . ."

At the big Hotel National they finally took us in; for we were foreigners, and the Military Revolutionary Committee had promised to protect the dwellings of foreigners. . . . On the top floor the manager showed us where shrapnel had shattered several windows. "The animals!" said he, shaking his fist at imaginary Bolsheviki. "But wait! Their time will come; in just a few days now their ridiculous Government will fall, and then we shall make them suffer!"

We dined at a vegetarian restaurant with the enticing name, I Eat Nobody, and Tolstoy's picture prominent on the walls, and then sallied out into the streets.

The headquarters of the Moscow Soviet was in the palace of the former Governor-General, an imposing white building fronting Skobeliev Square. Red Guards stood sentry at the door. At the head of the wide, formal stairway, whose walls were plastered with announcements of committee meetings and addresses of political parties, we passed through a series of lofty ante-rooms, hung with red-shrouded pictures in gold frames, to the splendid state salon, with its magnificent crystal lusters and gilded cornices. A low-voiced hum of talk underlaid with the whirring bass of a score of sewing machines, filled the place. Huge bolts of red and black cotton cloth were unrolled, serpentining across the parqueted floor and over tables, at which sat half a hundred women, cutting and sewing streamers and banners for the Funeral of the Revolutionary Dead. The faces of these women were roughened and scarred with life at its most difficult; they worked now sternly, many of them with eyes red from weeping. . . . The losses of the Red Army had been heavy.

At a desk in one corner was Rogov, an intelligent, bearded man with glasses, wearing the black blouse of a worker. He invited us to march with the Central Executive Committee in the funeral procession next morning. . . .

"It is impossible to teach the Socialist Revolutionaries and the Mensheviki anything!" he exclaimed. "They compromise from sheer habit. Imagine! They proposed that we hold a joint funeral with the *yunkers.*"

Across the hall came a man in a ragged soldier-coat and *shapka*, whose face was familiar; I recognized Melnichansky, whom I had known as the watchmaker George Melcher in Bayonne, New Jersey, during the great Standard Oil strike. Now, he told me, he was secretary of the Moscow Metal-Workers' Union, and a Commissar of the Military Revolutionary Committee during the fighting. . . .

"You see me!" he cried, showing his decrepit clothing. "I was with the boys in the Kremlin when the *yunkers* came the first time. They shut me up in the cellar and swiped my overcoat, my money, watch, and even the ring on my finger. This is all I've got to wear!"

From him I learned many details of the bloody six-day battle which had rent Moscow in two. Unlike Petrograd, in Moscow the City Duma had taken command of the *yunkers* and White Guards. Rudnev, the mayor, and Minor, president of the Duma, had directed the activities of the Committee of Public Safety and the troops. Riabtsev, commandant of the city, a man of democratic instincts, had hesitated about opposing the Military Revolutionary Committee; but the Duma had forced him. . . . It was the Mayor who had urged the occupation of the Kremlin: "They will never dare fire on you there," he said. . . .

One garrison regiment, badly demoralized by long inactivity, had been approached by both sides. The regiment held a meeting to decide what action to take. Resolved, that the regiment remain neutral, and continue its present activities—which consisted in peddling rubbers and sunflower seeds!

"But worst of all," said Melnichansky, "we had to organize while we were fighting. The other side knew just what it wanted; but here the soldiers had their Soviet and the workers theirs. . . . There was a fearful wrangle over who should be commander-in-chief; some regiments talked for days before they decided what to do; and when the officers suddenly deserted us, we had no battle-staff to give orders. . . ."

Vivid little pictures he gave me. On a cold, gray day he had stood at a corner of the Nikitskaya, which was swept by blasts of machine-gun fire. A throng of little boys were gathered there—street waifs who used to be newsboys. Shrill, excited as if with a new game, they waited until the firing slackened, and then tried to run across the street. . . . Many were killed, but the rest dashed backward and forward, laughing, daring each other. . . .

Late in the evening I went to the Dvorianskoye Sobranie—the Nobles' Club—where the Moscow Bolsheviki were to meet and consider the report of Nogin, Rykov, and the others who had left the Council of People's Commissars.

The meeting-place was a theater, in which, under the old régime, to audiences of officers and glittering ladies, amateur presentations of the latest French comedy had once taken place.

At first the place filled with the intellectuals—those who lived near the center of the town. Nogin spoke, and most of his listeners were plainly with him. It was very late before the workers arrived; the working-class quarters were on the outskirts of the town, and no streetcars were running. But about midnight they began to clump up the stairs, in groups of ten or twenty—big, rough men, in coarse clothes, fresh from the battle-line, where they had fought like devils for a week, seeing their comrades fall all about them.

Scarcely had the meeting formally opened before Nogin was assailed with a tempest of jeers and angry shouts. In vain he tried to argue, to explain; they would not listen. He had left the Council of People's Commissars; he had deserted his post while the battle was raging. As for the bourgeois press, here in Moscow there was no more bourgeois press; even the City Duma had been dissolved.[49] Bukharin stood up, savage, logical, with a voice which plunged and struck, plunged and struck. . . . Him they listened to with shining eyes. Resolution, to support the action of the Council of People's Commissars, passed by overwhelming majority. So spoke Moscow. . . .

Late in the night we went through the empty streets and under the Iberian Gate to the great Red Square in front of the Kremlin. The church of Vasili Blazhenny loomed fantastic, its bright-colored, convoluted, and blazoned cupolas vague in the darkness. There was no sign of any damage. . . . Along one side of the square the dark towers and walls of the Kremlin stood up. On the high walls flickered redly the light of hidden flames; voices reached us across the immense place, and the sound of picks and shovels. We crossed over.

Mountains of dirt and rock were piled high near the base of the wall. Climbing these we looked down into two massive pits, ten or fifteen feet deep and fifty yards long, where hundreds of soldiers and workers were digging in the light of huge fires.

A young soldier spoke to us in German. "The Brotherhood Grave," he explained. "Tomorrow we shall bury here five hundred proletarians who died for the Revolution."

He took us down into the pit. In frantic haste swung the picks and shovels, and the earth-mountains grew. No one spoke. Overhead the night was thick with stars, and the ancient Imperial Kremlin wall towered up immeasurably.

"Here in this holy place," said the student, "holiest of all Russia, we shall bury our most holy. Here where are the tombs of the Czars, our Czar—the People—shall sleep. . . ." His arm was in a sling, from a bullet wound gained in the fighting. He looked at it. "You foreigners look down on us Russians because so long we tolerated a medieval monarchy," said he. "But we saw that the Czar was not the only tyrant in the world; capitalism was worse, and in all the countries of the world capitalism was Emperor. . . . Russian revolutionary tactics are best. . . ."

As we left, the workers in the pit, exhausted and running with sweat in spite of the cold, began to climb wearily out. Across the Red Square a dark knot of men came hurrying. They swarmed into the pits, picked up the tools and began digging, digging, without a word. . . .

So, all the long night volunteers of the People relieved each other, never halting in their driving speed, and the cold light of the dawn laid bare the great square, white with snow, and the yawning brown pits of the Brotherhood Grave, quite finished.

We rose before sunrise, and hurried through the dark streets to Skobeliev Square. In all the great city not a human being could be seen; but there was a faint sound of stirring, far and near, like a deep wind coming. In the pale half-light a little group of men and women were gathered before the Soviet headquarters, with a sheaf of gold-lettered red banners—the Central Executive Committee of the Moscow Soviets. It grew light. From afar the vague stirring sound deepened and became louder, a steady and tremendous bass. The city was rising. We set out down the Tverskaya, the banners flapping overhead. The little street chapels along our way were locked and dark, as was the Chapel of the Iberian Virgin, which each new Czar used to visit before he went to the Kremlin to crown himself, and which, day or night, was always open and crowded, and brilliant with the candles of the devout gleaming on the gold and silver and jewels of the ikons. Now, for the first time since Napoleon was in Moscow, they say, the candles were out.

The Holy Orthodox Church had withdrawn the light of its countenance from Moscow, the nest of irreverent vipers who had bombarded the Kremlin. Dark and silent and cold were the churches; the priests had disappeared. There were no popes to officiate at the Red Burial, there had been no sacrament for the dead, nor were any prayers to be said over the grave of the blasphemers. Tikhon, Metropolitan of Moscow, was soon to excommunicate the Soviets. . . .

Also the shops were closed, and the propertied classes stayed at home—but for other reasons. This was the Day of the People, the rumor of whose coming was thunderous as surf. . . .

Already through the Iberian Gate a human river was flowing, and the vast Red Square was spotted with people, thousands of them. I remarked that as the throng passed the Iberian Chapel, where always before the passer-by had crossed himself, they did not seem to notice it. . . .

We forced our way through the dense mass packed near the Kremlin wall, and stood upon one of the dirt-mountains. Already several men were there, among them Muranov, the soldier who had been elected commandant of Moscow—a tall, simple-looking, bearded man with a gentle face.

Through all the streets to the Red Square, the torrents of people poured, thousands upon thousands of them, all with the look of the poor and the toiling. A military band came marching up playing the *Internationale*, and spontaneously the song caught and spread like wind-ripples on a sea, slow and solemn. From the top of the Kremlin wall gigantic banners unrolled to the ground red, with great letters in gold and in white, saying, "Martyrs of the

Beginning of World Social Revolution," and "Long Live the Brotherhood of Workers of the World."

A bitter wind swept the square, lifting the banners. Now from the far quarters of the city the workers of the different factories were arriving, with their dead. They could be seen coming through the Gate, the blare of their banners, and the dull red—like blood—of the coffins they carried. These were rude boxes, made of unplaned wood and daubed with crimson, borne high on the shoulders of rough men who marched with tears streaming down their faces, and followed by women who sobbed and screamed, or walked stiffly, with white, dead faces. Some of the coffins were open, the lid carried behind them; others were covered with gilded or silvered cloth, or had a soldier's hat nailed on the top. There were many wreaths of hideous artificial flowers.

Through an irregular lane that opened and closed again the procession slowly moved toward us. Now through the gate was flowing an endless stream of banners, all shades of red and silver and gold lettering, knots of crepe hanging from the top—and some anarchist flags, black with white letters. The band was playing the Revolutionary Funeral March, and against the immense singing of the mass of people, standing uncovered, the paraders sang hoarsely, choked with sobs. . . .

Between the factory workers came companies of soldiers with their coffins, too, and squadrons of cavalry, riding at salute, and artillery batteries, the cannon wound with red and black—for ever, it seemed. Their banners said, "Long live the Third International!" or "We Want an Honest, General, Democratic Peace!"

Slowly the marchers came with their coffins to the entrance of the grave, and the bearers clambered up with their burdens and went down into the pit. Many of them were women—squat, strong proletarian women. Behind the dead came other women—women young and broken, or old, wrinkled women making noises like hurt animals, who tried to follow their sons and husbands into the Brotherhood Grave, and shrieked when compassionate hands restrained them. The poor love each other so!

All the long day the funeral procession passed, coming in by the Iberian Gate and leaving the square by way of the Nikolskaya, a river of red banners, bearing words of hope and brotherhood and stupendous prophecies, against a background of fifty thousand people—under the eyes of the world's workers and their descendants for ever. . . .

One by one the five hundred coffins were laid in the pits. Dusk fell, and still the banners came drooping and fluttering, the band played the Funeral March, and the huge assemblage chanted. In the leafless branches of the trees above the grave the wreaths were hung, like strange, multi-colored blossoms. Two hundred men began to shovel in the dirt. It rained dully down upon the coffins with a thudding sound, audible beneath the singing. . . .

The lights came out. The last banners passed, and the last moaning women, looking back with awful intensity as they went. Slowly from the Red Square ebbed the proletarian tide. . . .

I suddenly realized that the devout Russian people no longer needed priests to pray them into heaven. On earth they were building a kingdom more bright than any heaven had to offer, and for which it was a glory to die. . . .

# 11

---

# The Conquest of Power[50]

DECLARATION OF THE RIGHTS OF THE PEOPLES OF RUSSIA[51]

. . . The first Congress of Soviets, in June of this year, proclaimed the rights of the peoples of Russia to self-determination.

The second Congress of Soviets, in November last, confirmed this inalienable right of the peoples of Russia more decisively and definitely.

Executing the will of these Congresses, the Council of People's Commissars has resolved to establish as a basis for its activity in the question of Nationalities, the following principles:

(1) The equality and sovereignty of the peoples of Russia.

(2) The right of the peoples of Russia to free self-determination, even to the point of separation and the formation of an independent state.

(3) The abolition of any and all national and national-religious privileges and disabilities.

(4) The free development of national minorities and ethnographic groups inhabiting the territory of Russia.

Decrees will be prepared immediately upon the formation of a Commission on Nationalities.

> In the name of the Russian Republic,
> People's Commissar for Nationalities,
> DJUGASHVILI-STALIN
> President of the Council of People's Commissars,
> V. ULYANOV (LENIN)

The Central Rada at Kiev immediately declared Ukraine an independent republic, as did the Government of Finland, through the Senate at Helsingfors. Independent "Governments" sprang up in Siberia and the Caucasus. The Polish Chief Military

Committee swiftly gathered together the Polish troops in the Russian Army, abolished their committees and established an iron discipline. . . .

All these "Governments" and "movements" had two characteristics in common; they were controlled by the propertied classes, and they feared and detested Bolshevism. . . .

Steadily, amid the chaos of shocking change, the Council of People's Commissars hammered at the scaffolding of the Socialist order. Decree on Social Insurance, on Workers' Control, Regulations for Volost Land Committees, Abolition of Ranks and Titles, Abolition of Courts and the Creation of People's Tribunals. . . .[52]

Army after army, fleet after fleet, sent deputations, "joyfully to greet the new Government of the People."

In front of Smolny, one day, I saw a ragged regiment just come from the trenches. The soldiers were drawn up before the great gates, thin and gray-faced, looking up at the building as if God were in it. Some pointed out the Imperial eagles over the door, laughing. . . . Red Guards came to mount guard. All the soldiers turned to look, curiously, as if they had heard of them but never seen them. They laughed good-naturedly and pressed out of line to slap the Red Guards on the back, with half-joking, half-admiring remarks. . . .

The Provisional Government was no more. On 15 November, in all the churches of the capital, the priests stopped praying for it. But as Lenin himself told the Tsay-ee-kah, that was "only the beginning of the conquest of power." Deprived of arms, the opposition, which still controlled the economic life of the country, settled down to organize disorganization, with all the Russian genius for cooperative action—to obstruct, cripple, and discredit the Soviets.

The strike of Government employees was well organized, financed by the banks and commercial establishments. Every move of the Bolsheviki to take over the Government apparatus was resisted.

Trotsky went to the Ministry of Foreign Affairs; the functionaries refused to recognize him, locked themselves in, and when the doors were forced resigned. He demanded the keys of the archives; only when he brought workmen to force the locks were they given up. Then it was discovered that Neratov, former assistant Foreign Minister, had disappeared with the Secret Treaties. . . .

Shliapnikov tried to take possession of the Ministry of Labor. It was bitterly cold, and there was no one to light the fires. Of all the hundreds of employees, not one would show him where the office of the Minister was. . . .

Alexandra Kollontai, appointed the thirteenth of November Commissar of Public Welfare—the department of charities and public institutions—was welcomed with a strike of all but forty of the functionaries in the Ministry. Immediately the poor of the great cities, the inmates of institutions, were plunged in miserable want; delegations of starving cripples, of orphans, with blue pinched faces, besieged the building. With tears streaming down her face, Kollontai arrested the strikers until they should deliver the keys of the office and the safe; when she got the keys, however, it was discovered that the former Minister, Countess Panina, had gone off with all the funds, which she refused to surrender except on the order of the Constituent Assembly.[53]

In the Ministry of Agriculture, the Ministry of Supplies, the Ministry of Finance, similar incidents occurred. And the employees, summoned to return or forfeit their positions and their pensions, either stayed away or returned to sabotage. . . . Almost all the *intelligentsia* being anti-Bolshevik, there was nowhere for the Soviet Government to recruit new staffs. . . .

The private banks remained stubbornly closed, with a back door open for speculators. When Bolshevik Commissars entered, the clerks left, secreting the books and removing the funds. All the employees of the State Bank struck except the clerks in charge of the vaults and the manufacture of money, who refused all demands from Smolny and privately paid out huge sums to the Committee for Salvation and the City Duma.

Twice a Commissar, with a company of Red Guards, came formally to insist upon the delivery of large sums for Government expenses. The first time, the City Duma members and the Men-

shevik and Socialist Revolutionary leaders were present in imposing numbers, and spoke so gravely of the consequences that the
Commissar was frightened. The second time he arrived with a
warrant, which he proceeded to read aloud in due form; but
someone called his attention to the fact that it had no date and no
seal, and the traditional Russian respect for "documents" forced
him again to withdraw. . . .

The officials of the Credit Chancery destroyed their books, so
that all record of the financial relations of Russia with foreign
countries was lost.

The Supply Committees, the administrations of the municipal-
owned public utilities, either did not work at all, or sabotaged.
And when the Bolsheviki, compelled by the desperate needs of
the city population, attempted to help or to control the public
service, all the employees went on strike immediately, and the
Duma flooded Russia with telegrams about Bolshevik "violation
of municipal autonomy."

At military headquarters, and in the offices of the Ministries of
War and Marine, where the old officials had consented to work,
the Army Committees and the high command blocked the Soviets in every way possible, even to the extent of neglecting the
troops at the front. The Vikzhel was hostile, refusing to transport
Soviet troops; every troop train that left Petrograd was taken out
by force, and railway officials had to be arrested each time—
whereupon the Vikzhel threatened an immediate general strike
unless they were released. . . .

Smolny was plainly powerless. The newspapers said that all the
factories of Petrograd must shut down for lack of fuel in three
weeks; the Vikzhel announced that trains must cease running by 1
December, there was food for three days only in Petrograd, and
no more coming in; and the Army on the front was starving. . . .
The Committee for Salvation, the various Central Committees,
sent word all over the country, exhorting the population to ignore
the Government decrees. And the Allied Embassies were either
coldly indifferent or openly hostile. . . .

The opposition newspapers, suppressed one day and reappear-
ing next morning under new names, heaped bitter sarcasm on the

new régime.[54] Even *Novaya Zhizn* characterized it as "a combination of demagoguery and impotence."

> From day to day (it said) the Government of the People's Commissars sinks deeper and deeper into the mire of superficial haste. Having easily conquered the power . . . the Bolsheviki cannot make use of it.
> Powerless to direct the existing mechanism of Government, they are unable at the same time to create a new one which might work easily and freely according to the theories of social experimenters.
> Just a little while ago the Bolsheviki hadn't enough men to run their growing party—a work above all of speakers and writers; where then are they going to find trained men to execute the diverse and complicated functions of government?
> The new Government acts and threatens, it sprays the country with decrees, each one more radical and more "socialist" than the last. But in this exhibition of Socialism on Paper—more likely designed for the stupefaction of our descendants—there appears neither the desire nor the capacity to solve the immediate problems of the day!

Meanwhile the Vikzhel's Conference to Form a New Government continued to meet night and day. Both sides had already agreed in principle to the basis of the Government; the composition of the People's Council was being discussed; the Cabinet was tentatively chosen, with Chernov as Premier; the Bolsheviki were admitted in a large minority, but Lenin and Trotsky were barred. The Central Committees of the Menshevik and Socialist Revolutionary parties, the Executive Committee of the Peasants' Soviets, resolved that, although unalterably opposed to the "criminal politics" of the Bolsheviki, they would "in order to halt the fratricidal bloodshed," not oppose their entrance into the People's Council.

The flight of Kerensky, however, and the astounding success of the Soviets everywhere altered the situation. On the sixteenth, in a meeting of the Tsay-ee-kah, the Left Socialist Revolutionaries insisted that the Bolsheviki should form a coalition Government with the other Socialist parties; otherwise they would withdraw from the Military Revolutionary Committee and the Tsay-ee-kah. Malkin said: "The news from Moscow, where our comrades are dying on both sides of the barricades, determines us to bring up once more the question of organization of power, and it is not only our right to do so but our duty. . . . We have won the right to sit with the Bolsheviki here within the walls of Smolny Institute, and to speak from this tribune. After the bitter internal party struggle we shall be obliged, if you refuse to compromise, to pass to open battle outside. . . . We must propose to the democracy terms of an acceptable compromise. . . ."

After a recess to consider this ultimatum the Bolsheviki returned with a resolution, read by Kameniev:

The Tsay-ee-kah considers it necessary that there enter into the Government representatives of *all the Socialist parties comprising the Soviets of Workers', Soldiers', and Peasants' Deputies who recognize the conquests of the Revolution of 7 November—that is to say, the establishment of a Government of Soviets, the decrees on peace, land, workers' control over industry, and the arming of the working-class.* The Tsay-ee-kah therefore resolves to propose negotiations concerning the constitution of the Government to all parties *of the Soviet,* and insists upon the following conditions as a basis:

The Government is responsible to the Tsay-ee-kah. The Tsay-ee-kah shall be enlarged to 150 members. To these 150 delegates of the Soviets of Workers' and Soldiers' Deputies shall be added 75 delegates of the *Provincial* Soviets of Peasants' Deputies, 80 from the front organizations of the Army and Navy, 40 from the Trade Unions (25 from the various All-Russian Unions, in proportion to their importance, 10 from the Vikzhel, and 5 from the Post and Telegraph Workers), and 50 delegates from the Socialist groups in the Petrograd City Duma. In the Ministry itself, at least one half the portfolios must be reserved for the Bolsheviki. The Ministries of Labor, Interior, and Foreign Affairs must be given to the Bolsheviki. The command of the garrisons of Petrograd and Moscow must remain in the hands of delegates of the Moscow and Petrograd Soviets.

The Government undertakes the systematic arming of the workers of all Russia.

It is resolved to insist upon the candidature of comrades Lenin and Trotsky.

Kameniev explained. "The so-called 'People's Council,'" he said, "proposed by the Conference, would consist of about 420 members, of which about 150 would be Bolsheviki. Besides, there would be delegates from the counter-revolutionary old Tsay-ee-kah, 100 members chosen by the Municipal Dumas—Kornilovtsi all; 100 delegates from the Peasants' Soviets—appointed by Avksentiev, and 80 from the old Army Committees, who no longer represent the soldier masses.

"We refuse to admit the old Tsay-ee-kah, and also the representatives of the Municipal Dumas. The delegates from the Peasants' Soviets shall be elected by the Congress of Peasants, which we have called, and which will at the same time elect a new Executive Committee. The proposal to exclude Lenin and Trotsky is a proposal to decapitate our party, and we do not accept it. And finally, we see no necessity for a 'People's Council' anyway: the Soviets are open to all Socialist parties, and the Tsay-ee-kah represents them in their real proportions among the masses. . . ."

Karelin, for the Left Socialist Revolutionaries, declared that his party would vote for the Bolshevik resolution, reserving the right to modify certain details, such as the representation of the peasants, and demanding that the Ministry of Agriculture be reserved for the Left Socialist Revolutionaries. This was agreed to. . . .

Later, at a meeting of the Petrograd Soviet, Trotsky answered a question about the formation of the new Government: "I don't know anything about that. I am not taking part in the negotiations. . . . However, I don't think that they are of great importance. . . ."

That night there was great uneasiness in the Conference. The delegates of the City Duma withdrew. . . .

But at Smolny itself, in the ranks of the Bolshevik party, a formidable opposition to Lenin's policy was growing. On the night of 17 November the great hall was packed and ominous for the meeting of the Tsay-ee-kah.

Larin, Bolshevik, declared that the moment of elections to the Constituent Assembly approached, and it was time to do away with "political terrorism."

"The measures taken against the freedom of the press should be modified. They had their reason during the struggle, but now they have no further excuse. The press should be free, except for appeals to riot and insurrection...."

In a storm of hisses and hoots from his own party, Larin offered the following resolution:

> The decree of the Council of People's Commissars concerning the press is herewith repealed.
>
> Measures of political repression can only be employed subject to decision of a special tribunal, elected by the Tsay-ee-kah proportionately to the strength of the different parties represented; and this tribunal shall have the right also to reconsider measures of repression already taken.

This was met by a thunder of applause, not only from the Left Socialist Revolutionaries, but also from a part of the Bolsheviki.

Avanessov, for the Leninites, hastily proposed that the question of the press be postponed until after some compromise between the Socialist parties had been reached. Overwhelmingly voted down.

"The revolution which is now being accomplished," went on Avanessov, "has not hesitated to attack private property; and it is as private property that we must examine the question of the press...."

Thereupon he read the official Bolshevik resolution:

> The suppression of the bourgeois press was dictated not only by purely military needs in the course of the insurrection, and for the checking of counter-revolutionary action, but it is also necessary as a measure of transition toward the establishment of a new régime with regard to the press—a régime under which the capitalist owners of printing-presses and of paper cannot be the all-powerful and exclusive manufacturers of public opinion.
>
> We must further proceed to the confiscation of private printing plants and supplies of paper, which should become the property of the Soviets, both in the capital and in the provinces, so that the political parties and groups can make use of the facilities of printing in proportion to the actual strength of the ideas they represent—in other words, proportionally to the number of their constituents.
>
> The reestablishment of the so-called "freedom of the press," the simple return of printing presses and paper to the capitalists—poi-

soners of the mind of the people—this would be an inadmissible surrender to the will of capital, a giving up of one of the most important
conquests of the Revolution; in other words, it would be a measure of
unquestionably counter-revolutionary character.

Proceeding from the above, the Tsay-ee-kah categorically rejects
all propositions aiming at the reestablishment of the old régime in
the domain of the press, and unequivocally supports the point of view
of the Council of People's Commissars on this question against pre-
tensions and ultimatums dictated by petty bourgeois prejudices, or by
evident surrender to the interests of the counter-revolutionary bourgeoisie.

The reading of this resolution was interrupted by ironical
shouts from the Left Socialist Revolutionaries, and bursts of indignation from the insurgent Bolsheviki. Karelin was on his feet,
protesting. "Three weeks ago the Bolsheviki were the most ardent defenders of the freedom of the press. . . . The arguments in
this resolution suggest singularly the point of view of the old
Black Hundreds and the censors of the Czarist régime—for they
also talked of 'poisoners of the mind of the people.' "

Trotsky spoke at length in favor of the resolution. He distinguished between the press during the civil war, and the press after
the victory. "During civil war the right to use violence belongs
only to the oppressed. . . ." (Cries of "Who's the oppressed now?
Cannibal!")

"The victory over our adversaries is not yet achieved, and the
newspapers are arms in their hands. In these conditions, the closing of the newspapers is a legitimate measure of defense. . . ."
Then passing to the question of the press after the victory,
Trotsky continued:

"The attitude of Socialists on the question of freedom of the
press should be the same as their attitude toward the freedom of
business. . . . The rule of the democracy which is being established in Russia demands that the domination of the press by private property must be abolished, just as the domination of
industry by private property. . . . The power of the Soviets should
confiscate all printing plants." (Cries, "Confiscate the printing
shop of *Pravda!*")

"The monopoly of the press by the bourgeoisie must be abolished. Otherwise it isn't worth while for us to take the power. Each group of citizens should have access to print-shops and paper. . . . The ownership of print-type and of paper belongs first to the workers and peasants, and only afterwards to the bourgeois parties, which are in a minority. . . . The passing of the power into the hands of the Soviets will bring about a radical transformation of the essential conditions of existence, and this transformation will necessarily be evident in the press. . . . If we are going to nationalize the banks, can we then tolerate the financial journals? The old régime must die: that must be understood once and for all. . . ." Applause and angry cries.

Karelin declared that the Tsay-ee-kah had no right to pass upon this important question, which should be left to a special committee. Again, passionately, he demanded that the press be free.

Then Lenin, calm, unemotional, his forehead wrinkled, as he spoke slowly, choosing his words; each sentence falling like a hammer-blow. "The civil war is not yet finished; the enemy is still with us; consequently it is impossible to abolish the measures of repression against the press.

"We Bolsheviki have always said that when we reached a position of power we would close the bourgeois press. To tolerate the bourgeois newspapers would mean to cease being a Socialist. When one makes a Revolution, one cannot mark time; one must always go forward—or go back. He who now talks about the 'freedom of the press' goes backward, and halts our headlong course toward Socialism.

"We have thrown off the yoke of capitalism, just as the first revolution threw off the yoke of Czarism. *If the first revolution had the right to suppress the monarchist newspapers,* then we have the right to suppress the bourgeois press. It is impossible to separate the question of the freedom of the press from the other questions of the class struggle. We have promised to close these newspapers, and we shall do it. The immense majority of the people is with us!

"Now that the insurrection is over we have absolutely no desire to suppress the papers of the other Socialist parties, except inasmuch as they appeal to armed insurrection, or to disobedience to the Soviet Government. However, we shall not permit them, under the pretense of freedom of the Socialist press, to obtain through the secret support of the bourgeoisie, a monopoly of printing-presses, ink, and paper. . . . These essentials must become the property of the Soviet Government, and be apportioned, first of all to the Socialist parties in strict proportion to their voting strength. . . ."

Then the vote. The resolution of Larin and the Left Socialist Revolutionaries was defeated by 31 to 22; the Lenin motion was carried by 34 to 24. Among the minority were the Bolsheviki Riazanov and Lozovsky, who declared that it was impossible for them to vote for any restriction on the freedom of the press.

Upon this the Left Socialist Revolutionaries declared they could no longer be responsible for what was being done, and withdrew from the Military Revolutionary Committee and all other positions of executive responsibility.

Five members—Nogin, Rykov, Milyutin, Teodorovich and Shliapnikov—resigned from the Council of People's Commissars, declaring:

> We are in favor of a Socialist Government composed of all the parties in the Soviets. We consider that only the creation of such a Government can possibly guarantee the results of the heroic struggle of the working-class and the revolutionary army. Outside of that, there remains only one way: the constitution of a purely Bolshevik Government by means of political terrorism. This last is the road taken by the Council of People's Commissars. We cannot and will not follow it. We see that this leads directly to the elimination from political life of many proletarian organizations, to the establishment of an irresponsible régime, and to the destruction of the Revolution and the country. We cannot take the responsibility for such a policy, and we renounce before the Tsay-ee-kah our function as People's Commissars.

Other Commissars, without resigning their positions, signed the declaration—Riazanov, Derbychev of the Press Department,

Arbuzov of the Government Printing-plant, Yureniev of the Red Guard, Feodorov of the Commissariat of Labor, and Larin, secretary of the Section of Elaboration of Decrees.

At the same time Kameniev, Rykov, Milyutin, Zinoviev, and Nogin resigned from the Central Committee of the Bolshevik Party, making public their reasons:

> ... The constitution of such a Government (composed of all the parties of the Soviet) is indispensable to prevent a new flow of blood, the coming of famine, the destruction of the Revolution by the Kaledinists, to assure the convocation of the Constituent Assembly at the proper time, and to apply effectively the program adopted by the Congress of Soviets. . . .
>
> We cannot accept the responsibility for the disastrous policy of the Central Committee, carried on against the will of an enormous majority of the proletariat and the soldiers, who are eager to see the rapid end of the bloodshed between the different political parties of the democracy. . . . We renounce our title as members of the Central Committee, in order to be able to say openly our opinion to the masses of workers and soldiers. . . .
>
> We leave the Central Committee at the moment of victory; we cannot calmly look on while the policy of the chiefs of the Central Committee leads toward the loss of the fruits of victory and the crushing of the proletariat. . . .

The masses of the workers, the soldiers of the garrison, stirred restlessly, sending their delegations to Smolny, to the Conference for Formation of the New Government, where the break in the ranks of the Bolsheviki caused the liveliest joy.

But the answer of the Leninites was swift and ruthless. Shliapnikov and Teodorovich submitted to party discipline and returned to their posts. Kameniev was stripped of his powers as president of the Tsay-ee-kah, and Sverdlov elected in his place. Zinoviev was deposed as president of the Petrograd Soviet. On the morning of the fifteenth *Pravda* contained a ferocious proclamation to the people of Russia, written by Lenin, which was printed in hundreds of thousands of copies, posted on the walls everywhere, and distributed over the face of Russia.

The second All-Russian Congress of Soviets gave the majority to the Bolshevik party. Only a Government formed by this party can therefore be a Soviet Government. And it is known to all that the Central Committee of the Bolshevik party, a few hours before the formation of the new Government and before proposing the list of its members to the All-Russian Congress of Soviets, invited to its meeting three of the most eminent members of the Left Socialist Revolutionary group, comrades Kamkov, Spiro, and Karelin, and ASKED THEM to participate in the new Government. We regret infinitely that the invited comrades refused; we consider their refusal inadmissible for revolutionists and champions of the working-class; we are willing at any time to include the Left Socialist Revolutionaries in the Government, but we believe that, as the party of the majority at the second All-Russian Congress of Soviets, we are entitled and BOUND before the people to form a Government. . . .

. . . Comrades! Several members of the Central Committee of our party and the Council of People's Commissars, Kamenev, Zinoviev, Nogin, Rykov, Milyutin, and a few others left yesterday, 17 November, the Central Committee of our party, and the last three the Council of People's Commissars. . . .

The comrades who left us acted like deserters, because they not only abandoned the posts entrusted to them, but also disobeyed the direct instructions of the Central Committee of our party, to the effect that they should wait the decisions of the Petrograd and Moscow party organizations before retiring. We blame decisively such desertion. We are firmly convinced that all conscious workers, soldiers, and peasants, belonging to our party or sympathizing with it, will also disapprove of the behavior of the deserters. . . .

Remember, comrades, that two of these deserters, Kamenev and Zinoviev, even before the uprising in Petrograd, appeared as deserters and strike-breakers, by voting at the decisive meeting of the Central Committee, 23 October 1917, against the insurrection; and even AFTER the resolution passed by the Central Committee, they continued their campaign at a meeting of the party workers. . . . But the great impulse of the masses, the great heroism of millions of workers, soldiers, and peasants, in Moscow, Petrograd, at the front, in the trenches, in the villages, pushed aside the deserters as a railway train scatters sawdust. . . .

Shame upon those who are of little faith, who hesitate, who doubt, who allow themselves to be frightened by the bourgeoisie, or who succumb before the cries of the latter's direct or indirect accomplices.

There is NOT A SHADOW of hesitation in the MASSES of Petrograd, Moscow, and the rest of Russia. . . .

. . . We shall not submit to any ultimatums from small groups of intellectuals which are not followed by the masses, which are PRACTICALLY only supported by Kornilovists, Savinkovists, *yunkers*, and so forth. . . .

The response from the whole country was like a blast of hot storm. The insurgents never got a chance to "say openly their opinion to the masses of workers and soldiers." Upon the Tsayee-kah rolled in like breakers the fierce popular condemnation of the "deserters." For days Smolny was thronged with angry delegations and committees, from the front, from the Volga, from the Petrograd factories. "Why did they dare leave the Government? Were they paid by the bourgeoisie to destroy the Revolution? They must return and submit to the decisions of the Central Committee!"

Only in the Petrograd garrison was there still uncertainty.[55] A great soldier meeting was held on 24 November, addressed by representatives of all the political parties. By a vast majority Lenin's policy was sustained, and the Left Socialist Revolutionaries were told that they must enter the government. . . .*

The Mensheviki delivered a final ultimatum, demanding that all Ministers and *yunkers* be released, that all newspapers be allowed full freedom, that the Red Guard be disarmed and the garrison put under command of the Duma. To this Smolny answered that all the Socialist Ministers and also that all but a very few *yunkers* had been already set free, that all newspapers were free except the bourgeois press, and that the Soviet would remain in command of the armed forces. . . . On the nineteenth the Conference to Form a New Government disbanded, and the opposition one by one slipped away to Moghilev, where, under the wing of the General Staff, they continued to form Government after Government, until the end. . . .

Meanwhile the Bolsheviki had been undermining the power of the Vikzhel. An appeal of the Petrograd Soviet to all railway

*See page 920.

workers called upon them to force the Vikzhel to surrender its power. On the fifteenth the Tsay-ee-kah, following its procedure toward the peasants, called an All-Russian Congress of Railway Workers for 1 December; the Vikzhel immediately called its own Congress for two weeks later. On 16 November, the Vikzhel members took their seats in the Tsay-ee-kah. On the night of 2 December, at the opening session of the All-Russian Congress of Railway Workers, the Tsay-ee-kah formally offered the post of Commissar of Ways and Communications to the Vikzhel—which accepted. . . .

Having settled the question of power, the Bolsheviki turned their attention to problems of practical administration. First of all the city, the country, the Army must be fed. Bands of sailors and Red Guards scoured the warehouses, the railway terminals, even the barges in the canals, unearthing and confiscating thousands of *poods** of food held by private speculators. Emissaries were sent to the provinces, where with the assistance of the Land Committees they seized the storehouses of the great grain dealers. Expeditions of sailors, heavily armed, were sent out in groups of five thousand to the South, to Siberia, with roving commissions to capture cities still held by the White Guards, establish order and *get food*. Passenger traffic on the Trans-Siberian Railroad was suspended for two weeks, while thirteen trains, loaded with bolts of cloth and bars of iron assembled by the Factory-Shop Committees, were sent out eastward, each in charge of a Commissar, to barter with the Siberian peasants for grain and potatoes. . . .

Kaledin being in possession of the coal mines of the Don, the fuel question became urgent. Smolny shut off all electric lights in theaters, shops, and restaurants, cut down the number of street-cars, and confiscated the private stores of firewood held by the fuel dealers. . . . And when the factories of Petrograd were about to close down for lack of coal, the sailors of the Baltic Fleet turned over to the workers two hundred thousand *poods* from the bunkers of battleships. . . .

Toward the end of November occurred the "wine-pogrom"[56]

*A *pood* is thirty-six pounds.

—looting of the wine cellars—beginning with the plundering of the Winter Palace vaults. For days there were drunken soldiers on the streets. . . . In all this was evident the hand of the counter-revolutionists, who distributed among the regiments plans showing the location of the stores of liquor. The Commissars of Smolny began by pleading and arguing, which did not stop the growing disorder, followed by pitched battles between soldiers and Red Guards. . . . Finally the Military Revolutionary Committee sent out companies of sailors with machine-guns, who fired mercilessly upon the rioters, killing many; and by executive order the wine-cellars were invaded by Committees with hatchets, who smashed the bottles—or blew them up with dynamite. . . .[57]

Companies of Red Guards, disciplined and well-paid, were on duty at the headquarters of the Ward Soviets day and night, replacing the old Militia. In all quarters of the city small elective Revolutionary Tribunals were set up by the workers and soldiers to deal with petty crime. . . .

The great hotels, where the speculators still did a thriving business, were surrounded by Red Guards, and the speculators thrown into jail. . . .[58]

Alert and suspicious, the working class of the city constituted itself a vast spy system, through the servants prying into bourgeois households, and reporting all information to the Military Revolutionary Committee, which struck with an iron hand, unceasing. In this way was discovered the Monarchist plot led by a former Duma-member Purishkevich and a group of nobles and officers, who had planned an officers' uprising, and had written a letter inviting Kaledin to Petrograd. . . .[59] In this way was unearthed the conspiracy of the Petrograd Cadets, who were sending money and recruits to Kaledin. . . .

Neratov, frightened at the outburst of popular fury provoked by his flight, returned and surrendered the Secret Treaties to Trotsky, who began their publication in *Pravda*, scandalizing the world. . . .

The restrictions on the press were increased by a decree[60] making advertisements a monopoly of the official Government newspaper. At this all the other papers suspended publication as a protest, or disobeyed the law and were closed. . . . Only three weeks later did they finally submit.

Still the strike of the Ministries went on, still the sabotage of the old officials, the stoppage of normal economic life. Behind Smolny was only the will of the vast, unorganized popular masses; and with them the Council of People's Commissars dealt, directing revolutionary mass action against its enemies. In eloquent proclamations,[61] couched in simple words and spread over Russia, Lenin explained the Revolution, urged the people to take the power into their own hands, by force to break down the resistance of the propertied classes, by force to take over the institutions of Government. Revolutionary order. Revolutionary discipline! Strict accounting and control! No strikes! No loafing![62]

On the twentieth of November the Military Revolutionary Committee issued a warning:

> The rich classes oppose the power of the Soviets—the Government of workers, soldiers, and peasants. Their sympathizers halt the work of the employees of the Government and the Duma, incite strikes in the banks, try to interrupt communication by the railways, the post, and the telegraph. . . .
>
> We warn them that they are playing with fire. The country and the Army are threatened with famine. To fight against it the regular functioning of all services is indispensable. The Workers' and Peasants' Government is taking every measure to assure the country and the Army all that is necessary. Opposition to these measures is a crime too against the People. We warn the rich classes and their sympathizers that if they do not cease their sabotage and their provocation in halting the transportation of food they will be the first to suffer. They will be deprived of the right of receiving food. All reserves which they possess will be requisitioned. The property of the principal criminals will be confiscated.
>
> We have done our duty in warning those who play with fire.
>
> We are convinced that in case decisive measures become necessary we shall be solidly supported by all workers, soldiers, and peasants.

On the twenty-second of November the walls of the city were placarded with a sheet headed "EXTRAORDINARY COMMUNICATION":

The Council of People's Commissars has received an urgent telegram from the Staff of the Northern Front. . . .

"There must be no further delay; do not let the Army die of hunger; the armies of the Northern Front have not received a crust of bread for several days now, and in two or three days they will not have any more biscuits—which are being doled out to them from reserve supplies until now never touched. . . . Already delegates from all parts of the front are talking of a necessary removal of part of the Army to the rear, foreseeing that in a few days there will be headlong flight of the soldiers, dying from hunger, ravaged by the three years' war in the trenches, sick, insufficiently clothed, bare-footed, driven mad by superhuman misery."

The Military Revolutionary Committee brings this to the notice of the Petrograd garrison and the workers of Petrograd. The situation at the front demands the most urgent and decisive measures. . . . Meanwhile the higher functionaries of the Government institutions, banks, railroads, post, and telegraph are on strike and impeding the work of the Government in supplying the front with provisions. . . . Each hour of delay may cost the life of thousands of soldiers. The counter-revolutionary functionaries are most dishonest criminals toward their hungry and dying brethren on the front. . . .

THE MILITARY REVOLUTIONARY COMMITTEE GIVES THESE CRIMINALS A LAST WARNING. In the event of the least resistance or opposition on their part the harshness of the measures which will be adopted against them will correspond to the seriousness of their crime. . . .

The masses of workers and soldiers responded by a savage tremor of rage, which swept all Russia. In the capital the Government and bank employees got out hundreds of proclamations and appeals,[63] protesting, defending themselves, such as this one:

### TO THE ATTENTION OF ALL CITIZENS
#### THE STATE BANK IS CLOSED!
##### WHY?

Because the violence exercised by the Bolsheviki against the State Bank has made it impossible for us to work. The first act of the People's Commissars was to DEMAND TEN MILLION ROUBLES, and on 27 November THEY DEMANDED TWENTY-FIVE MILLIONS, without any indication as to where the money was to go.

. . . We functionaries cannot take part in plundering the people's property. We stopped work.

CITIZENS! The money in the State Bank is yours, the people's money acquired by your labor, your sweat, your blood. CITIZENS! Save the people's property from robbery, and us from violence, and we shall immediately resume work.

EMPLOYEES OF THE STATE BANK

From the Ministry of Supplies, the Ministry of Finance, from the Special Supply Committee, declarations that the Military Revolutionary Committee made it impossible for the employees to work, appeals to the population to support them against Smolny. . . . But the dominant worker and soldier did not believe them; it was firmly fixed in the popular mind that the employees were sabotaging, starving the Army, starving the people. . . . In the long bread lines, which as formerly stood in the iron winter streets, it was not the *Government* which was blamed, as it had been under Kerensky, but the *chinovniki*, the sabotageurs; for the Government was *their* Government, *their* Soviets—and the functionaries of the Ministries were against it. . . .

At the center of all this opposition was the Duma, and its militant organ, the Committee for Salvation, protesting against all the decrees of the Council of People's Commissars, voting again and again not to recognize the Soviet Government, openly cooperating with the new counter-revolutionary "Governments" set up at Moghilev. . . . On the seventeenth of November, for example, the Committee for Salvation addressed "all Municipal Governments, Zemstvos, and all democratic and revolutionary organizations of peasants, workers, soldiers, and other citizens," in these words:

> Do not recognize the Government of the Bolsheviki, and struggle against it.
> Form local Committees for Salvation of Country and Revolution, who will unite all democratic forces, so as to aid the All-Russian Committee for Salvation in the tasks it has set itself. . . .

Meanwhile the elections for the Constituent Assembly in Petrograd[64] gave an enormous plurality to the Bolsheviki; so that even the Mensheviki Internationalists pointed out that the Duma ought to be re-elected, as it no longer represented the political composition of the Petrograd population. . . . At the same time floods of resolutions from workers' organizations, from military units, even from the peasants in the surrounding country, poured in upon the Duma, calling it "counter-revolutionary, Kornilovist," and demanding that it resign. The last days of the Duma were stormy with the bitter demands of the Municipal workers for decent living wages, and the threat of strikes. . . .

On the twenty-third a formal decree of the Military Revolutionary Committee dissolved the Committee for Salvation. On the twenty-ninth, the Council of People's Commissars ordered the dissolution and re-election of the Petrograd City Duma:

> In view of the fact that the Central Duma of Petrograd, elected 2 September . . . has definitely lost the right to represent the population of Petrograd, being in complete discaccord with its state of mind and its aspirations . . . and in view of the fact that the personnel of the Duma majority, although having lost all political following, continues to make use of its prerogatives to resist in a counter-revolutionary manner the will of the workers, soldiers, and peasants, to sabotage and obstruct the normal work of the Government—the Council of People's Commissars considers it its duty to invite the population of the capital to pronounce judgment on the policy of the organ of Municipal autonomy.
>
> To this end the Council of People's Commissars resolves:
>
> (1) To dissolve the Municipal Duma: The dissolution to take effect 30 November 1917.
>
> (2) All functionaries elected or appointed by the present Duma shall remain at their posts and fulfill the duties confided to them, until their places shall be filled by representatives of the new Duma.
>
> (3) All Municipal employees shall continue to fulfill their duties; those who leave the service of their own accord shall be considered discharged.
>
> (4) The new elections for the Municipal Duma of Petrograd are fixed for 9 December 1917. . . .
>
> (5) The Municipal Duma of Petrograd shall meet 11 December, at two o'clock.
>
> (6) Those who disobey this decree, as well as those who intentionally harm or destroy the property of the Municipality, shall be immediately arrested and brought before the Revolutionary Tribunals. . . .

The Duma met defiantly, passing resolutions to the effect that it would "defend its position to the last drop of its blood," and appealing desperately to the population to save their "own elected City Government." But the population remained indifferent or hostile. On the thirty-first, Mayor Schreider and several members were arrested, interrogated and released. That day and the next the Duma continued to meet, interrupted frequently by Red Guards and sailors, who politely requested the assembly to disperse. At the meeting of 2 December, an officer and some sailors entered the Nikolai Hall while a member was speaking, and ordered the members to leave or force would be used. They did so, protesting to the last, but finally "ceding to violence."

The new Duma, which was elected ten days later, and for which the "Moderate" Socialists refused to vote, was almost entirely Bolshevik. . . .[65]

There remained several centers of dangerous opposition, such as the "republics" of Ukraine and Finland, which were showing definitely anti-Soviet tendencies. Both at Helsingfors and at Kiev the Governments were gathering troops which could be depended upon, and entering upon campaigns of crushing Bolshevism, and of disarming and expelling Russian troops. The Ukrainian Rada had taken command of all southern Russia, and was furnishing Kaledin reinforcements and supplies. Both Finland and Ukraine were beginning secret negotiations with the Germans, and were promptly recognized by the Allied Governments, which loaned them huge sums of money, joining with the propertied classes to create counter-revolutionary centers of attack upon Soviet Russia. In the end, when Bolshevism had conquered in both these countries, the defeated bourgeoisie called in the Germans to restore them to power. . . .

But the most formidable menace to the Soviet Government was internal and two-headed—the Kaledin movement, and the Staff at Moghilev, where General Dukhonin had assumed command.

The ubiquitous Muraviov was appointed commander of the war against the Cossacks, and a Red Army was recruited from among the factory workers. Hundreds of propagandists were sent to the Don. The Council of People's Commissars issued a proclamation to the Cossacks,[66] explaining what the Soviet Government was, how the propertied classes, the *chinovniki,* landlords, bankers, and their allies, the Cossack princes, landowners, and generals, were trying to destroy the Revolution, and prevent the confiscation of their wealth by the people.

On 27 November a committee of Cossacks came to Smolny to see Trotsky and Lenin. They demanded if it were true that the Soviet Government did not intend to divide the Cossack lands among the peasants of Great Russia? "No," answered Trotsky. The Cossacks deliberated for a while. "Well," they asked, "does the Soviet Government intend to confiscate the estates of our great Cossack landowners and divide them among the Cossacks?" To this Lenin replied. "That," he said, "is for you to do. We shall support the working Cossacks in all their actions. . . . The best way to begin is to form Cossack Soviets; you will be given representation in the Tsay-ee-kah, and then it will be *your* Government, too. . . ."

The Cossacks departed, thinking hard. Two weeks later General Kaledin received a deputation from his troops. "Will you," they asked, "promise to divide the great estates of the Cossack landlords among the working Cossacks?"

"Only over my dead body," responded Kaledin. A month later, seeing his army melt away before his eyes, Kaledin blew out his brains. And the Cossack movement was no more. . . .

Meanwhile at Moghilev were gathered the old Tsay-ee-kah, the "moderate" Socialist leaders—from Avksentiev to Chernov— the active chiefs of the old Army Committees, and the reactionary officers. The Staff steadily refused to recognize the Council of People's Commissars. It had united about it the Death Battalions, the Knights of St. George, and the Cossacks of the front, and was in close and secret touch with the Allied military attachés, and with the Kaledin movement and the Ukrainian Rada. . . .

The Allied Governments had made no reply to the Peace decree of 8 November, in which the Congress of Soviets had asked for a general armistice.

On 20 November Trotsky addressed a note to the Allied Ambassadors:[67]

> I have the honor to inform you, Mr. Ambassador, that the All-Russian Congress of Soviets . . . on 8 November constituted a new Government of the Russian Republic, in the form of the Council of People's Commissars. The President of the Government is Vladimir Ilyich Lenin. The direction of foreign affairs has been entrusted to me, as People's Commissar for Foreign Affairs. . . .
>
> In drawing your attention to the text approved by the All-Russian Congress, of the proposition of an armistice and a democratic peace without annexations or indemnities, based on the right of self-determination of peoples, I have the honor to request you to consider that document as a formal proposal of an immediate armistice on all fronts, and the opening of immediate peace negotiations; a proposal which the authorized Government of the Russian Republic addresses at the same time to all the belligerent peoples and their Governments.
>
> Please accept, Mr. Ambassador, the profound assurance of the esteem of the Soviet Government toward your people, who cannot but wish for peace, like all the other peoples exhausted and drained by this unexampled butchery. . . .

The same night the Council of People's Commissars telegraphed to General Dukhonin:

> . . . The Council of People's Commissars considers it indispensable without delay to make a formal proposal of armistice to all the powers both enemy and Allied. A declaration conforming to this decision has been sent by the Commissar for Foreign Affairs to the representatives of the Allied powers in Petrograd.
>
> The Council of People's Commissars orders you, Citizen Commander, . . . to propose to the enemy military authorities immediately to cease hostilities, and enter into negotiations for peace. In charging you with the conduct of these preliminary pourparlers, the Council of People's Commissars orders you:
>
> 1. To inform the Council by direct wire immediately of any and all steps in the pourparlers with the representatives of the enemy armies.
>
> 2. Not to sign the act of armistice until it has been passed upon by the Council of People's Commissars.

The Allied Ambassadors received Trotsky's note with contemptuous silence, accompanied by anonymous interviews in the newspapers, full of spite and ridicule. The order to Dukhonin was characterized openly as an act of treason. . . .

As for Dukhonin, he gave no sign. On the night of 22 November he was communicated with by telephone, and asked if he intended to obey the order. Dukhonin answered that he could not, unless it emanated from "a Government sustained by the Army and the country."

By telegraph he was immediately dismissed from the post of Supreme Commander, and Krylenko appointed in his place. Following his tactics of appealing to the masses, Lenin sent a radiogram to all regimental, divisional, and corps Committees, to all soldiers and sailors of the Army and the Fleet, acquainting them with Dukhonin's refusal, and ordering that "the regiments on the front shall elect delegates to begin negotiations with the enemy detachments opposite their positions. . . ."

On the twenty-third the military attachés of the Allied nations, acting on instructions from their Governments, presented a note to Dukhonin, in which he was solemnly warned not to "violate the conditions of the treaties concluded between the Powers of the Entente." The note went on to say that if a separate armistice with Germany were concluded, that act "would result in the most serious consequences" to Russia. This communication Dukhonin at once sent out to all the soldiers' Committees. . . .

Next morning Trotsky made another appeal to the troops, characterizing the note of the Allied representatives as a flagrant interference in the internal affairs of Russia, and a bald attempt "to force by threats the Russian Army and the Russian people to continue the war in execution of the treaties concluded by the Czar. . . ."

From Smolny poured out proclamation after proclamation,[68] denouncing Dukhonin and the counter-revolutionary officers about him, denouncing the reactionary politicians gathered at Moghilev, rousing, from one end of the thousand-mile front to the other, millions of angry, suspicious soldiers. And at the same time Krylenko, accompanied by three detachments of fanatical sailors, set out for the Stavka, breathing threats of vengeance,[69] and received by the soldiers everywhere with tremendous ovations—a triumphal progress. The Central Army Committee issued a declaration in favor of Dukhonin; and at once ten thousand troops moved upon Moghilev. . . .

On 2 December the garrison of Moghilev rose and seized the city, arresting Dukhonin and the Army Committee, and going out with victorious red banners to meet the new Supreme Commander. Krylenko entered Moghilev next morning, to find a howling mob gathered about the railway-car in which Dukhonin had been imprisoned. Krylenko made a speech in which he implored the soldiers not to harm Dukhonin, as he was to be taken to Petrograd and judged by the Revolutionary Tribunal. When he had finished, suddenly Dukhonin himself appeared at the window, as if to address the throng. But with a savage roar the people rushed the car, and falling upon the old general, dragged him out and beat him to death on the platform. . . .

So ended the revolt of the Stavka. . . .

Immensely strengthened by the collapse of the last important stronghold of hostile military power in Russia the Soviet Government began with confidence the organization of the State. Many of the old functionaries flocked to its banner, and many members of other parties entered the Government service. The financially ambitious, however, were checked by the decree on Salaries of Government Employees, fixing the salaries of the People's Commissars—the highest—at five hundred rouble (about fifty dollars) a month. . . . The strike of Government employees, led by the Union of Unions, collapsed, deserted by the financial and commercial interests which had been backing it. The bank clerks returned to their jobs. . . .

With the decree on the Nationalization of Banks, the formation of the Supreme Council of People's Economy, the putting into practical operation of the Land Decree in the villages, the democratic reorganization of the Army, and the sweeping changes in all branches of the Government and of life—with all these, effective only by the will of the masses of workers, soldiers, and peasants, slowly began, with many mistakes and hitches, the molding of proletarian Russia.

Not by compromise with the propertied classes, or with the other political leaders; not by conciliating the old Government mechanism, did the Bolsheviki conquer the power. Nor by the organized violence of a small clique. If the masses all over Russia had not been ready for insurrection it must have failed. The only reason for Bolshevik success lay in their accomplishing the vast and simple desires of the most profound strata of the people, calling them to the work of tearing down and destroying the old, and afterwards, in the smoke of falling ruins, cooperating with them to erect the framework of the new. . . .

# The Peasants' Congress

It was on 18 November that the snow came. In the morning we woke to window-ledges heaped white, and snowflakes falling so whirling thick that it was impossible to see ten feet ahead. The mud was gone; in a twinkling the gloomy city became white, dazzling. The *droshki* with their padded coachmen turned into sleighs, bounding along the uneven street at headlong speed, their drivers' beards stiff and frozen.... In spite of Revolution, all Russia plunging dizzily into the unknown and terrible future, joy swept the city with the coming of the snow. Everybody was smiling; people ran into the streets, holding out their arms to the soft, falling flakes, laughing. Hidden was all the grayness; only the gold and colored spires and cupolas, with heightened barbaric splendor, gleamed through the white snow.

Even the sun came out, pale and watery, at noon. The colds and rheumatism of the rainy months vanished. The life of the city grew gay, and the very Revolution ran swifter....

I sat one evening in a *traktir*—a kind of lower-class inn—across the street from the gates of Smolny; a low-ceilinged, loud place called "Uncle Tom's Cabin," much frequented by Red Guards. They crowded it now, packed close around the little tables with their dirty table-cloths and enormous china teapots, filling the place with foul cigarette smoke, while the harassed waiters ran about crying "*Seichass! Seichass!* In a minute! Right away!"

In one corner sat a man in the uniform of a captain, addressing the assembly, which interrupted him at every few words.

"You are no better than murderers!" he cried. "Shooting down your Russian brothers on the streets!"

"When did we do that?" asked a worker.

"Last Sunday you did it, when the *yunkers*—"

"Well, didn't they shoot us?" One man exhibited his arm in a sling. "Haven't I got something to remember them by, the devils?"

The captain shouted at the top of his voice. "You should remain neutral! You should remain neutral! Who are you to destroy the legal Government? Who is Lenin? A German—"

"Who are you? A counter-revolutionist! A provocator!" they bellowed at him.

When he could make himself heard the captain stood up. "All right!" said he. "You call yourselves the people of Russia. But you're not the people of Russia. The peasants are the people of Russia. Wait until the peasants—"

"Yes," they cried, "wait until the peasants speak. We know what the peasants will say. . . . Aren't they working-men like ourselves?"

In the long run everything depended upon the peasants. While the peasants had been politically backward, still they had their own peculiar ideas, and they constituted more than eighty percent of the people of Russia. The Bolsheviki had a comparatively small following among the peasants; and a permanent dictatorship of Russia by the industrial workers was impossible. . . . The traditional peasant party was the Socialist Revolutionary Party; of all the parties now supporting the Soviet Government, the Left Socialist Revolutionaries were the logical inheritors of peasant leadership—and the Left Socialist Revolutionaries, who were at the mercy of the organized city proletariat, desperately needed the backing of the peasants. . . .

Meanwhile Smolny had not neglected the peasants. After the Land Decree, one of the first actions of the Tsay-ee-kah had been to call a Congress of Peasants, over the head of the Executive Committee of the Peasants' Soviets. A few days later was issued detailed Regulations for the Volost (Township) Land Committees, followed by Lenin's *Instruction to Peasants*,[70] which explained the Bolshevik revolution and the new Government in simple terms; and on 16 November Lenin and Milyutin published the

*Instructions to Provisional Emissaries*, of whom thousands were sent by the Soviet Government into the villages.

1. Upon his arrival in the province to which he is accredited the emissary should call a joint meeting of the Central Executive Committees of the Soviets of Workers', Soldiers', and Peasants' Deputies, to whom he should make a report on the agrarian laws, and then demand that a joint plenary session of the Soviets be summoned. . . .

2. He must study the aspects of the agrarian problem in the province.

    (a) Has the landowners' property been taken over, and if so, in what districts?

    (b) Who administers the confiscated land—the former proprietors or the Land Committees?

    (c) What has been done with the agricultural machinery and with the farm animals?

3. Has the ground cultivated by the peasants been augmented?

4. How much and in what respect does the amount of land now under cultivation differ from the amount fixed by the Government as an average minimum?

5. The emissary must insist that, after the peasants have received the land, it is imperative that they increase the amount of cultivated land as quickly as possible, and that they hasten the sending of grain to the cities, as the only means of avoiding famine.

6. What are the measures projected or put into effect for the transfer of land from the landowners to the Land Committees and similar bodies appointed by the Soviets?

7. It is desirable that agricultural properties well appointed and well organized should be administered by Soviets composed of the regular employees of those properties, under the direction of competent agricultural scientists.

All through the villages a ferment of change was going on, caused not only by the electrifying action of the Land Decree, but also by thousands of revolutionary-minded peasant-soldiers returning from the front. . . . These men, especially, welcomed the call to a Congress of Peasants.

Like the old Tsay-ee-kah in the matter of the second Congress of Workers' and Soldiers' Soviets, the Executive Committee tried to prevent the Peasant Congress summoned by Smolny. And like the old Tsay-ee-kah, finding its resistance futile, the Executive Committee sent frantic telegrams ordering the election of Conservative delegates. Word was even spread among the peasants that the Congress would meet at Moghilev, and some delegates went there; but by 23 November about four hundred had gathered in Petrograd, and the party caucuses had begun.

The first session took place in the Alexander Hall of the Duma building, and the first vote showed that more than half of all the delegates were Left Socialist Revolutionaries, while the Bolsheviki controlled a bare fifth, the conservative Socialist Revolutionaries a quarter, and all the rest were united only in their opposition to the old Executive Committee, dominated by Avksentiev, Chaikovsky, and Peshekhonov. . . .

The great hall was jammed with people and shaken with continual clamor; deep, stubborn bitterness divided the delegates into angry groups. To the right was a sprinkling of officers' epaulettes and the patriarchal, bearded faces of the older, more substantial peasants; in the center were a few peasants, noncommissioned officers, and some soldiers; and on the left almost all the delegates wore the uniforms of common soldiers. These last were the young generation, who had been serving in the army . . . The galleries were thronged with workers—who, in Russia, still remember their peasant origin. . . .

Unlike the old Tsay-ee-kah, the Executive Committee, in opening the session, did not recognize the Congress as official; the official Congress was called for 13 December; amid a hurricane of applause and angry cries, the speaker declared that this gathering was merely "Extraordinary Conference." . . . But the "Extraordinary Conference" soon showed its attitude toward the Executive Committee by electing as presiding officer Maria Spiridonova, leader of the Left Socialist Revolutionaries.

Most of the first day was taken up by a violent debate as to whether the representatives of Volost Soviets should be seated, or only delegates from the provincial bodies; and just as in the Workers' and Soldiers' Congress, an overwhelming majority declared in favor of the widest possible representation. Whereupon the old Executive Committee left the hall. . . .

Almost immediately it was evident that most of the delegates were hostile to the Government of the People's Commissars. Zinoviev, attempting to speak for the Bolsheviki, was hooted down, and as he left the platform, amid laughter, there were cries, "There's how a People's Commissar sits in a mud-puddle!"

"We Left Socialist Revolutionaries refuse," cried Nazariev, a delegate from the Provinces, "to recognize this so-called Workers' and Peasants' Government until the peasants are represented in it. At present it is nothing but a dictatorship of the workers. . . . We insist upon the formation of a new Government which will represent the entire democracy!"

The reactionary delegates shrewdly fostered this feeling, declaring, in the face of protests from the Bolshevik benches, that the Council of People's Commissars intended either to control the Congress or dissolve it by force of arms—an announcement which was received by the peasants with bursts of fury. . . .

On the third day Lenin suddenly mounted the tribune; for ten minutes the room went mad. "Down with him!" they shrieked. "We will not listen to any of your People's Commissars! We don't recognize your Government!"

Lenin stood there quite calmly, gripping the desk with both hands, his little eyes thoughtfully surveying the tumult beneath. Finally, except for the right side of the hall, the demonstration wore itself out somewhat.

"I do not come here as a member of the Council of People's Commissars," said Lenin, and waited again for the noise to subside, "but as a member of the Bolshevik faction, duly elected to this Congress." And he held his credentials up so that all might see them.

"However," he went on in an unmoved voice, "nobody will deny that the present Government of Russia has been formed by the Bolshevik Party"—he had to wait a moment—"so that for all purposes it is the same thing. . . ." Here the right benches broke into deafening clamor, but the center and left were curious, and compelled silence.

Lenin's argument was simple. "Tell me frankly, you peasants, to whom we have given the lands of the *pomieshchiki*; do you want to prevent the workers from getting control of industry? This is class war. The *pomieshchiki* of course oppose the peasants, and the manufacturers oppose the workers. Are you going to allow the ranks of the proletariat to be divided? Which side will you be on?

"We, the Bolsheviki, are the party of the proletariat—of the peasant proletariat as well as the industrial proletariat. We, the Bolsheviki, are the protectors of the Soviets—of the Peasants' Soviets as well as those of the Workers' and Soldiers'. The present Government is a Government of Soviets; we have not only invited the Peasants' Soviets to join that Government, but we have also invited representatives of the Left Socialist Revolutionaries to enter the Council of People's Commissars. . . .

"The Soviets are the most perfect representatives of the people—of the workers in the factories and mines, of the workers in the fields. Anybody who attempts to destroy the Soviets is guilty of an anti-democratic and counter-revolutionary act. And I serve notice here on you, comrades Right Socialist Revolutionaries—and on you, Messrs. Cadets—that if the Constituent Assembly attempts to destroy the Soviets we shall not permit the Constituent Assembly to do this thing!"

On the afternoon of 25 November Chernov arrived in hot haste from Moghilev, summoned by the Executive Committee. Only two months before considered an extreme revolutionist, and very popular with the peasants, he was now called to check the dangerous drift of the Congress toward the Left. Upon his arrival Chernov was arrested and taken to Smolny, where, after a short conversation, he was released.

His first act was bitterly to rebuke the Executive Committee for leaving the Congress. They agreed to return, and Chernov entered the hall, welcomed with great applause by the majority, and the hoots and jeers of the Bolsheviki.

"Comrades! I have been away. I participated in the Conference of the Twelfth Army on the question of calling a Congress of all the Peasant delegates of the armies of the Western Front, and I know very little about the insurrection which occurred here—"

Zinoviev rose in his seat, and shouted, "Yes, you were away—

for a few minutes!" Fearful tumult. Cries, "Down with the Bolsheviki!"

Chernov continued. "The accusation that I helped lead an army on Petrograd has no foundation, and is entirely false. Where does such an accusation come from? Show me the source!"

Zinoviev: "*Izvestia* and *Dielo Naroda*—your own paper—that's where it comes from!"

Chernov's wide face, with the small eyes, waving hair and grayish beard, became red with wrath, but he controlled himself and went on. "I repeat, I know practically nothing about what has happened here, and I did not lead any army except this army (he pointed to the peasant delegates), which I am largely responsible for bringing here!" Laughter and shouts of "Bravo!"

"Upon my return I visited Smolny. No such accusation was made against me there. . . . After a brief conversation I left—and that's all! Let anyone present make such an accusation!"

An uproar followed, in which the Bolsheviki and some of the Left Socialist Revolutionaries were on their feet all at once, shaking their fists and yelling, and the rest of the assembly tried to yell them down.

"This is an outrage, not a session!" cried Chernov, and he left the hall; the meeting was adjourned because of the noise and disorder. . . .

Meanwhile the question of the status of the Executive Committee was agitating all minds. By declaring the assembly "Extraordinary Conference" it had been planned to block the re-election of the Executive Committee. But this worked both ways: the Left Socialist Revolutionists decided that if the Congress had no power over the Executive Committee, then the Executive Committee had no power over the Congress. On 25 November the assembly resolved that the powers of the Executive Committee be assumed by the Extraordinary Conference, in which only members of the Executive who had been elected as delegates might vote. . . .

The next day, in spite of the bitter opposition of the Bolsheviki, the resolution was amended to give all the members of the Executive Committee, whether elected as delegates or not, voice and vote in the assembly.

On the twenty-seventh occurred the debate on the land question, which revealed the differences between the agrarian program of the Bolsheviki, and the Left Socialist Revolutionaries.

Kolchinsky, for the Left Socialist Revolutionaries, outlined the history of the land question during the Revolution. The first Congress of Peasants' Soviets, he said, had voted a precise and formal resolution in favor of putting the landed estates immediately into the hands of the Land Committees. But the directors of the Revolution, and the bourgeois in the Government, had insisted that the question could not be solved until the Constituent Assembly met. . . . The second period of the Revolution, the period of "compromise," was signaled by the entrance of Chernov into the Cabinet. The peasants were convinced that now the practical solution of the land question would begin; but in spite of the imperative decision of the first Peasant Congress the reactionaries and conciliators in the Executive Committee had prevented any action. This policy provoked a series of agrarian disorders, which appeared as the natural expression of impatience and thwarted energy on the part of the peasants. The peasants understood the exact meaning of the Revolution—they tried to turn words into action. . . .

"The recent events," said the orator, "do not indicate a simple riot, or a 'Bolshevik adventure,' but, on the contrary, a real popular rising, which has been greeted with sympathy by the whole country. . . .

"The Bolsheviki in general took the correct attitude toward the land question; but in recommending that the peasants seize the land by force they committed a profound error. . . . From the first days the Bolsheviki declared that the peasants should take over the land 'by revolutionary mass action.' This is nothing but anarchy; the land can be taken over in an organized manner. . . . For the Bolsheviki it was important that the problems of the Revolution should be solved in the quickest possible manner—but the Bolsheviki were not interested in how these questions were to be solved. . . .

"The land decree of the Congress of Soviets is identical in its fundamentals with the decisions of the first Peasants' Congress. Why then did not the new Government follow the tactics outlined by that Congress? Because the Council of People's Commissars wanted to hasten the settlement of the land question, so that the Constituent Assembly would have nothing to do. . . .

"But also the Government saw that it was necessary to adopt practical measures, so without further reflection it adopted the Regulations for Land Committees, thus creating a strange situation; for the Council of People's Commissars abolished private property in land, but the Regulations drawn up by the Land Committees are based on private property. . . . However, no harm has been done by that; for the Land Committees are paying no attention to the Soviet decrees, but are putting into operation their own practical decisions—decisions based on the will of the vast majority of the peasants. . . .

"These Land Committees are not attempting the legislative solution of the land question, which belongs to the Constituent Assembly alone. . . . But will the Constituent Assembly desire to do the will of the Russian peasants? Of that we cannot be sure. . . . All we can be sure of is that the revolutionary determination of the peasants is now aroused, and that the Constituent will be forced to settle the land question the way the peasants want it settled. . . . The Constituent Assembly will not dare to break with the will of the people. . . ."

Followed him Lenin, listened to now with absorbing intensity. "At this moment we are not only trying to solve the land question, but the question of Social Revolution—not only here in Russia, but all over the world. The land question cannot be solved independently of the other problems of the Social Revolution. . . . For example, the confiscation of the landed estates will provoke the resistance not only of Russian landowners, but also of foreign capital—with whom the great landed properties are connected through the intermediary of the banks. . . .

"The ownership of the land in Russia is the basis for immense oppression, and the confiscation of the land by the peasants is the most important step of our Revolution. But it cannot be separated from the other steps, as is clearly manifested by the stages through which the Revolution has had to pass. The first stage was the crushing of autocracy and the crushing of the power of the industrial capitalists and landowners, whose interests are closely related. The second stage was the strengthening of the Soviets and the political compromise with the bourgeoisie. The mistake of the Left Socialist Revolutionaries lies in the fact that at that time they did not oppose the policy of compromise, because they held the theory that the consciousness of the masses was not yet fully developed. . . .

"*If Socialism can only be realized when the intellectual development of all the people permits it, then we shall not see Socialism for at least five hundred years.* . . . The Socialist political party—this is the vanguard of the working class; it must not allow itself to be halted by the lack of education of the mass average, but it must lead the masses, using the Soviets as organs of revolutionary initiative. . . . But in order to lead the wavering, the comrades Left Socialist Revolutionaries themselves must stop hesitating. . . .

"In July last a series of open breaks began between the popular masses and the 'compromisers'; but now, in November, the Left Socialist Revolutionaries are still holding out their hand to Avksentiev, who is pulling the people with his little finger. . . . If compromise continues the Revolution disappears. No compromise with the bourgeoisie is possible; its power must be absolutely crushed. . . .

"We Bolsheviki have not changed our land program; we have not given up the abolition of private property in the land, and we do not intend to do so. We adopted the Regulations for Land Committees—which are *not* based on private property at all—because we want to accomplish the popular will in the way the people have themselves decided to do it, so as to draw closer the coalition of all the elements who are fighting for the Social Revolution.

"We invite the Left Socialist Revolutionaries to enter that coalition, insisting, however, that they cease looking backward, and that they break with the 'conciliators' of their party. . . .

"As far as the Constituent Assembly is concerned, it is true, as the preceding speaker has said, that the work of the Constituent Assembly will depend on the revolutionary determination of the masses. I say: Count on the revolutionary determination, but don't forget your gun!"

Lenin then read the Bolshevik resolution:

The Peasants' Congress, fully supporting the Land decree of 8 November . . . approves of the Provisional Workers' and Peasants' Government of the Russian Republic, established by the second All-Russian Congress of Soviets of Workers' and Soldiers' Deputies.

The Peasants' Congress . . . invites all peasants unanimously to sustain that law, and to apply it immediately to themselves; and at the same time invites the peasants to appoint to posts and positions of responsibility only persons who have proved, not by words but by acts, their entire devotion to the interests of the exploited peasant-workers, their desire and their ability to defend these interests against all resistance on the part of the great landowners, the capitalists, their partisans and accomplices.

The Peasants' Congress, at the same time, expresses its conviction that the complete realization of all the measures which make up the Land decree can only be successful through the triumph of the Workers' Social Revolution, which began 7 November 1917; for only the Social Revolution can accomplish the definite transfer, without possibility of return, of the land to the peasant-workers, the confiscation of model farms, and their surrender to the peasant communes, the confiscation of agricultural machinery belonging to the great landowners, the safeguarding of the interests of the agricultural workers by the complete abolition of wage-slavery, the regular and methodical distribution among all regions of Russia of the products of agriculture and industry, and the seizure of the banks (without which the possession of land by the whole people would be impossible, after the abolition of private property), and all sorts of assistance by the State to the workers. . . .

For these reasons the Peasants' Congress sustains entirely the Revolution of 7 November . . . as a social revolution, and expresses its unalterable will to put into operation, with whatever modifications are necessary, but without hesitation, the social transformation of the Russian Republic.

The indispensable conditions of the victory of the Socialist Revolution, which alone will secure the lasting success and the complete realization of the land decree, is the close union of the peasant-workers with the industrial working-class, with the proletariat of all advanced countries. From now on, in the Russian Republic, all the organization and administration of the State, from top to bottom, must rest on that union. That union, crushing all attempts, direct or indirect, open or dissimulated, to return to the policy of conciliation with the bourgeoisie—conciliation, damned by experience, with the chiefs of bourgeois politics—can alone ensure the victory of Socialism throughout the world.

The reactionaries of the Executive Committee no longer dared openly to appear. Chernov, however, spoke several times, with a modest and winning impartiality. He was invited to sit on the platform.... On the second night of the Congress an anonymous note was handed up to the chairman, requesting that Chernov be made honorary President. Ustinov read the note aloud, and immediately Zinoviev was on his feet, screaming that this was a trick of the old Executive Committee to capture the convention; in a moment the hall was one bellowing mass of waving arms and angry faces, on both sides.... Nevertheless, Chernov remained very popular.

In the stormy debates on the land question and the Lenin resolution, the Bolsheviki were twice on the point of quitting the assembly, both times restrained by their leaders.... It seemed to me as if the Congress were hopelessly deadlocked.

But none of us knew that a series of secret conferences was already going on between the Left Socialist Revolutionaries and the Bolsheviki at Smolny. At first the Left Socialist Revolutionaries had demanded that there be a Government composed of all the Socialist parties in and out of the Soviets, to be responsible to a People's Council, composed of an equal number of delegates from the Workers' and Soldiers' organization, and that of the Peasants, and completed by representatives of the City Dumas and the Zemstvos; Lenin and Trotsky were to be eliminated, and the Military Revolutionary Committee and other repressive organs dissolved.

Wednesday morning, 28 November, after a terrible all-night struggle, an agreement was reached. The Tsay-ee-kah composed of 108 members, was to be augmented by 108 members elected proportionately from the Peasants' Congress; by 100 delegates elected directly from the Army and the Fleet; and by 50 representatives of the Trade Unions (35 from the general unions, 10 Railway Workers, and 5 from the Post and Telegraph Workers). The Dumas and Zemstvos were dropped. Lenin and Trotsky remained in the Government, and the Military Revolutionary Committee continued to function.

The sessions of the Congress had now been removed to the Imperial Law School building, Fontanka 6, headquarters of the Peasants' Soviets. There in the great meeting-hall the delegates gathered on Wednesday afternoon. The old Executive Committee had withdrawn, and was holding a rump convention of its own in another room of the same building, made up of bolting delegates and representatives of the Army Committees.

Chernov went from one meeting to the other, keeping a watchful eye on the proceedings. He knew that an agreement with the Bolsheviki was being discussed, but he did not know that it had been concluded.

He spoke to the rump convention. "At present, when everybody is in favor of forming an all-Socialist Government, many people forget the first Ministry, which was not a coalition Government, and in which there was only one Socialist—Kerensky; a Government which, in its time, was very popular. Now people accuse Kerensky; they forget that he was raised to power, not only by the Soviets, but also by the popular masses. . . .

"Why did public opinion change toward Kerensky? The savages set up gods to which they pray, and which they punish if one of their prayers is not answered. . . . That is what is happening at this moment. . . . Yesterday Kerensky; today Lenin and Trotsky; another tomorrow. . . .

"We have proposed to both Kerensky and the Bolsheviki to retire from the power. Kerensky has accepted—today he announced from his hiding-place that he has resigned as Premier;

but the Bolsheviki wish to retain the power, and they do not know how to use it. . . .

"If the Bolsheviki succeed, or if they fail, the fate of Russia will not be changed. The Russian villages understand perfectly what they want, and they are now carrying out their own measures. . . . The villages will save us in the end. . . ."

In the meanwhile, in the great hall Ustinov had announced the agreement between the Peasants' Congress and Smolny, received by the delegates with the wildest joy. Suddenly Chernov appeared and demanded the floor.

"I understand," he began, "that an agreement is being concluded between the Peasants' Congress and Smolny. Such an agreement would be illegal, seeing that the true Congress of Peasants' Soviets does not meet until next week. . . .

"Moreover, I want to warn you now that the Bolsheviki will never accept your demands. . . ."

He was interrupted by a great burst of laughter; and realizing the situation, he left the platform and the room, taking his popularity with him. . . .

Late in the afternoon of Thursday, 29 November, the Congress met in extraordinary session. There was a holiday feeling in the air; on every face was a smile. . . . The remainder of the business before the assembly was hurried through, and then old Nathanson, the white-bearded dean of the left wing of the Socialist Revolutionaries, his voice trembling and tears in his eyes, read the report of the "wedding" of the Peasants' Soviets with the Workers' and Soldiers' Soviets. At every mention of the word "union" there was ecstatic applause. . . . At the end Ustinov announced the arrival of a delegation from Smolny, accompanied by representatives of the Red Army, greeted with a rising ovation. One after another a workman, a soldier, and a sailor took the floor, hailing them.

Then Boris Reinstein, delegate of the American Socialist Labor Party: "The day of the union of the Congress of Peasants and the Soviets of Workers' and Soldiers' Deputies is one of the great days of the Revolution. The sound of it will ring with resounding echoes throughout the whole world—in Paris, in London, and across the ocean—in New York. This union will fill with happiness the hearts of all toilers.

"A great idea has triumphed. The West and America expected from Russia, from the Russian proletariat, something tremendous. . . . The proletariat of the world is waiting for the Russian Revolution, waiting for the great things that it is accomplishing. . . ."

Sverdlov, president of the Tsay-ee-kah, greeted them. And with the shout, "Long live the end of civil war! Long live the United Democracy!" the peasants poured out of the building.

It was already dark, and on the ice-covered snow glittered the pale light of moon and star. Along the bank of the canal were drawn up in full marching order the soldiers of the Pavlovsky Regiment, with their band, which broke into the *Marseillaise*. Amid the crashing full-throated shouts of the soldiers, the peasants formed in line, unfurling the great red banner of the Executive Committee of the All-Russian Peasants' Soviets, embroidered newly in gold, "Long live the union of the revolutionary and toiling masses!" Following were other banners; of the District Soviets—of Putilov Factory, which read, "We bow to this flag in order to create the brotherhood of all peoples!"

From somewhere torches appeared, blazing orange in the night, a thousand times reflected in the facets of the ice, streaming smokily over the throng as it moved down the bank of the Fontanka singing, between crowds that stood in astonished silence.

"Long live the Revolutionary Army! Long live the Red Guard! Long live the Peasants!"

So the great procession wound through the city, growing and unfurling ever new red banners lettered in gold. Two old peasants, bowed with toil, were walking hand in hand, their faces illumined with child-like bliss.

"Well," said one, "I'd like to see them take away our land again, *now!*"

Near Smolny the Red Guard was lined up on both sides of the street, wild with delight. The other old peasant spoke to his comrade, "I am not tired," he said. "I walked on air all the way!"

On the steps of Smolny about a hundred Workers' and Soldiers' Deputies were massed, with their banner, dark against the blaze of light streaming out between the arches. Like a wave they rushed down, clasping the peasants in their arms and kissing them; and the procession poured in through the great door and up the stairs, with a noise like thunder. . . .

In the immense white meeting-room the Tsay-ee-kah was waiting, with the whole Petrograd Soviet and a thousand spectators beside, with that solemnity which attends great conscious moments in history.

Zinoviev announced the agreement with the Peasants' Congress, to a shaking roar which rose and burst into storm as the sound of music blared down the corridor, and the head of the procession came in. On the platform the presidium rose and made place for the Peasants' presidium, the two embracing; behind them the two banners were intertwined against the white wall, over the empty frame from which the Czar's picture had been torn. . . .

Then opened the "triumphal session." After a few words of welcome from Sverdlov, Maria Spiridonova, slight, pale, with spectacles, and hair drawn flatly down, and the air of a New England school-teacher, took the tribune—the most loved and the most powerful woman in all Russia.

". . . Before the workers of Russia open new horizons which history has never known. . . . All workers' movements in the past have been defeated. But the present movement is international, and that is why it is invincible. There is no force in the world which can put out the fire of the Revolution! The old world crumbles down, the new world begins. . . ."

Then Trotsky, full of fire: "I wish you welcome, comrades peasants! You come here not as guests, but as masters of this house, which holds the heart of the Russian Revolution. The will of millions of workers is now concentrated in this hall. . . . There is now only one master of the Russian land: the union of the workers, soldiers, and peasants. . . ."

With biting sarcasm he went on to speak of the Allied diplomats, till then contemptuous of Russia's invitation to an armistice, which had been accepted by the Central Powers.

"A new humanity will be born of this war. . . . In this hall we swear to workers of all lands to remain at our revolutionary post. If we are broken, then it will be in defending our flag. . . ."

Krylenko followed him, explained the situation at the front, where Dukhonin was preparing to resist the Council of People's Commissars. "Let Dukhonin and those with him understand well that we shall not deal gently with those who bar the road to peace!"

Dybenko saluted the assembly in the name of the Fleet, and Krushinsky, member of the Vikzhel, said, "From this moment, when the union of all true Socialists is raised, the whole army of railway workers places itself absolutely at the disposition of the revolutionary democracy!" And Lunacharsky, almost weeping, and Proshian, for the Left Socialist Revolutionaries, and finally Saharashvili, for the United Social Democrats Internationalists, composed of members of Martov's and of Gorky's groups, who declared:

"We left the Tsay-ee-kah because of the uncompromising policy of the Bolsheviki, and to force them to make concessions in order to realize the union of all the revolutionary democracy. Now that that union is brought about, we consider it a sacred duty to take our places once more in the Tsay-ee-kah. . . . We declare that all those who have withdrawn from the Tsay-ee-kah should now return."

Stachkov, a dignified old peasant of the presidium of the Peasants' Congress, bowed to the four corners of the room. "I greet you with the christening of a new Russian life and freedom!"

Gronsky, in the name of the Polish Social Democracy; Skripnik, for the Factory-Shop Committees; Tifonov, for the Russian soldiers at Salonika; and others, interminably, speaking out of full hearts, with the happy eloquence of hopes fulfilled. . . .

It was late in the night when the following resolution was put and passed unanimously:

"The Tsay-ee-kah, united in extraordinary session with the

Petrograd Soviet and the Peasants' Congress, confirms the Land and Peace decrees adopted by the Second Congress of Soviets of Workers' and Soldiers' Deputies, and also the decree on Workers' Control adopted by the Tsay-ee-kah.

"The joint session of the Tsay-ee-kah and the Peasants' Congress expresses its firm conviction that the union of workers, soldiers, and peasants, this fraternal union of all the workers and all the exploited, will consolidate the power conquered by them, that it will take all revolutionary measures to hasten the passing of the power into the hands of the working class in other countries, and that it will assure in this manner the lasting accomplishment of a just peace and the victory of Socialism."[71]

# Appendix

## Chapter 1

1 (p. 591).

*Oborontsi*—"Defenders." All the "moderate" Socialist groups adopted or were given this name, because they consented to the continuation of the war under Allied leadership, on the ground that it was a war of National Defense. The Bolsheviki, the Left Socialist Revolutionaries, the Mensheviki Internationalists (Martov's faction), and the Social Democrats Internationalists (Gorky's group) were in favor of forcing the Allies to declare democratic war-aims, and to offer peace to Germany on those terms.

2 (p. 592). WAGES AND COST OF LIVING BEFORE AND DURING THE REVOLUTION

The following table of wages and costs were compiled, in October 1917, by a joint Committee from the Moscow Chamber of Commerce and the Moscow section of the Ministry of Labor, and published in *Novaya Zhizn*, 26 October 1917:

WAGES PER DAY (ROUBLES AND KOPEKS)

| Trade | *July 1914* | *July 1916* | *August 1917* |
|---|---|---|---|
| Carpenter, cabinet-maker | 1.60–2.0 | 4.0 –6.0 | 8.50 |
| Terrassier | 1.30–1.50 | 3.0 –3.50 | — |
| Mason, plasterer | 1.70–2.35 | 4.0 –6.0 | 8.0 |

| | | | |
|---|---|---|---|
| Painter, upholsterer | 1.80–2.20 | 3.0 –5.50 | 8.0 |
| Blacksmith | 1.0 –2.25 | 4.0 –5.0 | 8.50 |
| Chimney-sweep | 1.50–2.0 | 4.0 –5.50 | 7.50 |
| Locksmith | 0.90–2.0 | 3.50–6.0 | 9.0 |
| Helper | 1.0 –1.50 | 2.50–4.50 | 8.0 |

In spite of numerous stories of gigantic advances in wages, immediately following the Revolution of March 1917, these figures, which were published by the Ministry of Labor as characteristic of conditions all over Russia, show that wages did not rise immediately after the Revolution, but little by little. On an average wages increased slightly more than 500 percent. . . .

But at the same time, the value of the rouble fell to less than one third its former purchasing power, and the cost of necessities of life increased enormously.

The following table was compiled by the Municipal Duma of Moscow, where food was cheaper and more plentiful than in Petrograd:

Cost of Food (roubles and kopeks)

| | | August 1914 | August 1917 | Percent Increase |
|---|---|---|---|---|
| Black bread | (Funt) | 0.02 | 0.12 | 330 |
| White bread | (Funt) | 0.05 | 0.20 | 300 |
| Beef | (Funt) | 0.22 | 1.10 | 400 |
| Veal | (Funt) | 0.26 | 2.15 | 727 |
| Pork | (Funt) | 0.23 | 2.0 | 770 |
| Herring | (Funt) | 0.06 | 0.52 | 767 |
| Cheese | (Funt) | 0.40 | 3.50 | 754 |
| Butter | (Funt) | 0.48 | 3.20 | 557 |
| Eggs | (Doz.) | 0.30 | 1.60 | 443 |
| Milk | (Krushka) | 0.07 | 0.40 | 471 |

On an average, food increased in price 556 percent, or 51 percent more than wages.

As for the other necessities, the price of these increased tremendously.

The following table was compiled by the Economic section of the Moscow Soviet of Workers' Deputies, and accepted as correct by the Ministry of Supplies of the Provisional Government.

Cost of Other Necessities (roubles and kopecks)

| | | August 1914 | August 1917 | Percent Increase |
|---|---|---|---|---|
| Calico | (Arshin) | 0.11 | 1.40 | 1,173 |
| Cotton cloth | (Arshin) | 0.15 | 2.0 | 1,233 |
| Dress goods | (Arshin) | 2.0 | 40.0 | 1,900 |
| Castor cloth | (Arshin) | 6.0 | 80.0 | 1,233 |
| Men's shoes | (Pair) | 12.0 | 144.0 | 1,097 |
| Rubbers | (Pair) | 2.50 | 15.0 | 500 |
| Men's clothing | (Suit) | 40.0 | 400–455 | 900–1,109 |
| Tea | (Funt) | 4.50 | 18.0 | 300 |
| Sole leather | | 20.0 | 400.0 | 1,900 |
| Matches | (Cartons) | 0.10 | 0.50 | 400 |
| Soap | (Pood) | 4.50 | 40.0 | 780 |
| Gasoline | (Vedro) | 1.70 | 11.0 | 547 |
| Candles | (Pood) | 8.50 | 100.0 | 1,076 |
| Caramel | (Funt) | 0.30 | 4.50 | 1,406 |
| Firewood | (Load) | 10.0 | 120.0 | 1,100 |
| Charcoal | | 0.80 | 13.0 | 1,523 |
| Sundry metal ware | | 1.0 | 20.0 | 1,900 |

On an average the above categories of necessities increased about 1,109 percent in price, more than twice the increase of salaries. The difference, of course, went into the pockets of speculators and merchants.

In September 1917, when I arrived in Petrograd, the average daily wage of a skilled industrial worker—for example, a steelworker, in the Putilov factory—was about 8 roubles. At the same time, profits were enormous. . . . I was told by one of the owners of the Thornton Woollen Mills, an English concern on the outskirts of Petrograd, that while wages had increased about 300 percent in his factory, his profits had gone up 900 percent.

3 (p. 593). The Socialist Ministers

The history of the efforts of the Socialists in the Provisional Government of July to realize their program in coalition with the bourgeois Ministers is an illuminating example of class struggle in politics. Says Lenin, in explanation of this phenomenon:

The capitalists . . . seeing that the position of the Government was untenable, resorted to a method which since 1848 has been for decades practiced by the capitalists in order to befog, divide, and finally overpower the working-class. This method is the so-called "Coalition Ministry," composed of bourgeois and of renegades from the Socialist camp.

In those countries where political freedom and democracy have existed side by side with the revolutionary movement of the workers—for example, in England and France—the capitalists make use of this subterfuge, and very successfully too. The "Socialist" leaders, upon entering the Ministries, invariably prove mere figure-heads, puppets, simply a shield for the capitalists, a tool with which to defraud the workers. The "democratic" and "republican" capitalists in Russia set in motion this very same scheme. The Socialist Revolutionaries and Mensheviki fell victim to it, and on 1 June a "Coalition" Ministry, with the participation of Chernov, Tseretelly, Skobeliev, Avksentiev, Savinkov, Zarudny, and Nikitin became an accomplished fact. . . ."
—*Problems of the Revolution*


4 (p. 595). SEPTEMBER MUNICIPAL ELECTIONS IN MOSCOW

In the first week of October 1917, *Novaya Zhizn* published the following comparative table of election results, pointing out that this meant the bankruptcy of the policy of Coalition with the propertied classes. "If civil war can yet be avoided, it can only be done by a united front of all the revolutionary democracy. . . ."

ELECTIONS FOR THE MOSCOW CENTRAL AND WARD DUMAS (NUMBERS OF MEMBERS)

|  | June 1917 | September 1917 |
|---|---|---|
| Socialist Revolutionaries | 58 | 14 |
| Cadets | 17 | 30 |
| Mensheviki | 12 | 4 |
| Bolsheviki | 11 | 47 |


5 (p. 596). GROWING ARROGANCE OF THE REACTIONARIES

18 September. The Cadet Shulgin, writing in a Kiev newspaper, said that the Provisional Government's declaration that Russia was a Republic constituted a gross abuse of its powers. "We can-

not admit either a Republic or the present Republican Government. . . . And we are not sure that we want a Republic in Russia. . . ."

23 October. At a meeting of the Cadet party held at Riazan, M. Dukhonin declared, "On 1 March we established a Constitutional Monarchy. We must not reject the legitimate heir to the throne, Mikhail Alexandrovich. . . ."

27 October. Resolution passed by the Conference of Business Men at Moscow:

> The Conference . . . insists that the Provisional Government take the following immediate measures in the Army:
> 1. Forbidding of all political propaganda; the Army must be out of politics.
> 2. Propaganda of anti-national and international ideas and theories deny the necessity for armies, and hurt discipline; it should be forbidden, and all propagandists punished. . . .
> 3. The function of the Army Committees must be limited to economic questions exclusively. All their decisions should be confirmed by their superior officers, who have the right to dissolve the Committees at any time. . . .
> 4. The salute to be reestablished and made obligatory. Full establishment of disciplinary power in the hands of officers, with right of review of sentence. . . .
> 5. Expulsion from the Corps of Officers of those who dishonor it by participating in the movement of the soldier-masses, which teaches them disobedience. . . . Reestablishment for this purpose of the Courts of Honor. . . .
> 6. The Provisional Government should take the necessary measures to make possible the return to the army of generals and other officers unjustly discharged under the influence of Committees, and other irresponsible organizations. . . .

**Chapter 2**

6 (p. 605).

The Kornilov revolt is treated in detail in my forthcoming volume, *Kornilov to Brest-Litovsk*. The responsibility of Kerensky for the situation which gave rise to Kornilov's attempt is now pretty clearly established. Many apologists for Kerensky say that he knew of Kornilov's plans, and by a trick drew him out prematurely, and then crushed him. Even Mr. A. J. Sack, in his book, *The Birth of the Russian Democracy*, says:

> Several things . . . are almost certain. The first is that Kerensky knew about the movement of several detachments from the front toward Petrograd, and it is possible that as Prime Minister and Minister of War, realizing the growing Bolshevist danger, he called for them. . . .

The only flaw in that argument is that there was no "Bolshevist danger" at the time, the Bolsheviki still being a powerless minority in the Soviets, and their leaders in jail or hiding.

7 (p. 606). DEMOCRATIC CONFERENCE

When the Democratic Conference was first proposed to Kerensky he suggested an assembly of all the elements of the nation—"the live forces," as he called them—including bankers, manufacturers, landowners, and representatives of the Cadet party. The Soviet refused, and drew up the following table of representation (numbers of delegates), which Kerensky agreed to:

100 All-Russian Soviets Workers' and Soldiers' Deputies
100 All-Russian Soviets Peasants' Deputies
 50 Provincial Soviets Workers' and Soldiers' Deputies
 50 Peasants' District Land Committees
100 Trade Unions
 84 Army Committees at the Front
150 Workers' and Peasants' Cooperative Societies
 20 Railway Workers' Union
 10 Post and Telegraph Workers' Union
 20 Commercial Clerks
 15 Liberal Professions—Doctors, Lawyers, Journalists, etc.
 50 Provincial Zemstvos
 50 Nationalist Organizations—Poles, Ukrainians, etc.

This proportion was altered twice or three times. The final disposition of delegates was:

| | |
|---|---|
| 300 All-Russian Workers', Soldiers', and Peasants' Deputies | 150 Provincial Zemstvos |
| | 200 Trade Unions |
| | 100 Nationalist organizations |
| 300 Cooperative Societies | 200 Several small groups |
| 300 Municipalities | |
| 150 Army Committees at the Front | |

8 (p. 606). THE FUNCTION OF THE SOVIETS IS ENDED

On 28 September 1917, *Izvestia*, organ of the Tsay-ee-kah, published an article which said, speaking of the last Provisional Ministry:

> At last a truly democratic government born of the will of all classes of the Russian people, the first rough form of the future liberal parliamentary régime has been formed. Ahead of us is the Constituent Assembly, which will solve all questions of fundamental law and whose composition will be essentially democratic. The function of the Soviets is at an end, and the time is approaching when they must retire, with the rest of the revolutionary machinery, from the stage of a free and victorious people, whose weapons shall hereafter be the peaceful ones of political action.

The leading article of *Izvestia* for 23 October was called "The Crisis in the Soviet Organizations." It began by saying that travelers reported a lessening activity of local Soviets everywhere.

> This is natural [said the writer]. For the people are becoming interested in the more permanent legislative organs—the Municipal Dumas and the Zemstvos.
> In the important centers of Petrograd and Moscow, where the Soviets were best organized, they did not take in all the democratic elements. . . . The majority of the intellectuals did not participate, and many workers also; some of the workers because they were politically backward, others because the center of gravity for them was in their unions. . . . We cannot deny that these organizations are firmly united with the masses, whose everyday needs are better served by them. . . .
> That the local democratic administrations are being energetically organized is highly important. The City Dumas are elected by uni-

versal suffrage, and in purely local matters have more authority than the Soviets. Not a single democrat will see anything wrong in this. . . .

. . . Elections to the Municipalities are being conducted in a better and more democratic way than the elections of the Soviets. . . . All classes are represented in the Municipalities. . . . And as soon as the local Self-Governments begin to organize life in the Municipalities, the role of the local Soviets naturally ends. . . .

. . . There are two factors in the falling off of interest in the Soviets. The first we may attribute to the lowering of political interest in the masses; the second, to the growing effort of provincial and local governing bodies to organize the building of new Russia. . . . The more the tendency lies in this latter direction, the sooner disappears the significance of the Soviets. . . .

We ourselves are being called the "undertakers" of our organization. In reality we ourselves are the hardest workers in constructing the new Russia. . . .

When autocracy and the whole bureaucratic régime fell we set up the Soviets as a barracks in which all the democracy could find temporary shelter. Now, instead of barracks, we are building the permanent edifice of a new system, and naturally the people will gradually leave the barracks for more comfortable quarters.

9 (p. 607). TROTSKY'S SPEECH AT THE COUNCIL OF THE RUSSIAN REPUBLIC

The purpose of the Democratic Conference, which was called by the Tsay-ee-kah, was to do away with the irresponsible personal government which produced Kornilov, and to establish a responsible government which would be capable of finishing the war, and ensure the calling of the Constituent Assembly at the given time. In the meanwhile, behind the back of the Democratic Conference, by trickery, by deals between Citizen Kerensky, the Cadets, and the leaders of the Menshevik and Socialist Revolutionary parties, we received the opposite result from the officially announced purpose. A power was created around which and in which we have open and secret Kornilovs playing leading parts. The irresponsibility of the Government is officially proclaimed, when it is announced that the Council of the Russian Republic is to be a *consultative* and not a *legislative* body. In the eighth month of the Revolution, the irresponsible Government creates a cover for itself in this new edition of Bulygin's Duma.

The propertied classes have entered this Provisional Council in a proportion which clearly shows, from elections all over the country, that many of them have no right here whatever. In spite of that the Cadet party which until yesterday wanted the Provisional Government to be responsible to the State Duma—this same Cadet party secured the independence of the Government from the Council of the Republic. In the Constituent Assembly the propertied classes will no doubt have a less favorable position than they have in this Council, and they will not be able to be irresponsible to the Constituent Assembly.

If the propertied classes were really getting ready for the Constituent Assembly six weeks from now, there could be no reason for establishing the irresponsibility of the Government at this time. The whole truth is that the bourgeoisie, which directs the politics of the Provisional Government, has for its aim to break the Constituent Assembly. At present this is the main purpose of the propertied classes, which control our entire national policy—external and internal. In the industrial, agrarian, and supply departments the politics of the propertied classes, acting with the Government, increases the natural disorganization caused by the war. The classes which are provoking civil war, and openly hold their course on the bony hand of hunger, with which they intend to overthrow the Revolution and finish with the Constituent Assembly!

No less criminal also is the international policy of the bourgeoisie and its Government. After forty months of war the capital is threatened with mortal danger. In reply to this arises a plan to move the Government to Moscow. The idea of abandoning the capital does not stir the indignation of the bourgeoisie. Just the opposite. It is accepted as a natural part of the general policy designed to promote counter-revolutionary conspiracy. . . . Instead of recognizing that the salvation of the country lies in concluding peace, instead of throwing openly the idea of immediate peace to all the war-worn peoples, over the heads of diplomats and imperialists, and making the continuation of the war impossible—the Provisional Government, by order of the Cadets, the Counter-Revolutionists, and the Allied Imperialists, without sense, without purpose and without a plan, continues to drag on the murderous war, sentencing to useless death new hundreds of thousands of soldiers and sailors, and preparing to give up Petrograd, and to wreck the Revolution. At a time when Bolshevik soldiers and sailors are dying with other soldiers and sailors as a result of the mistakes and crimes of others, the so-called Supreme Commander (Kerensky) continues to suppress the Bolshevik press. The leading parties of the Council are acting as a voluntary cover for these policies.

We, the faction of Social Democrats Bolsheviki, announce that with this Government of Treason to the People we have nothing in common. We have nothing in common with the work of these Murderers of the People which goes on behind official curtains. We refuse either directly or indirectly to cover up one day of this work. While Wilhelm's troops are threatening Petrograd, the Government of Kerensky and Kornilov is preparing to run away from Petrograd and turn Moscow into a base of counter-revolution!

We warn the Moscow workers and soldiers to be on their guard. Leaving this Council, we appeal to the manhood and wisdom of the workers, peasants, and soldiers of all Russia. Petrograd is in danger! The Revolution is in danger! The Government has increased the danger—the ruling classes intensify it. Only the people themselves can save themselves and the country.

We appeal to the people. Long live immediate, honest, democratic peace! All power to the Soviets! All land to the people! Long live the Constituent Assembly!

## 10 (p. 608). THE "NAKAZ" TO SKOBELIEV *(Resumé)*

Passed by the Tsay-ee-kah and given to Skobeliev as an instruction for the representative of the Russian Revolutionary democracy at the Paris Conference.

The peace treaty must be based on the principle, "No annexations, no indemnities, the right of self-determination of peoples."

### *Territorial Problems*

(1) Evacuation of German troops from invaded Russia. Full right of self-determination to Poland, Lithuania, and Livonia.

(2) For Turkish Armenia autonomy, and later complete self-determination, as soon as local Governments are established.

(3) The question of Alsace-Lorraine to be solved by a plebiscite, after the withdrawal of all foreign troops.

(4) Belgium to be restored. Compensation for damages from an international fund.

(5) Serbia and Montenegro to be restored, and aided by an international relief fund. Serbia to have an outlet on the Adriatic. Bosnia and Herzegovina to be autonomous.

(6) The disputed provinces in the Balkans to have provisional autonomy, followed by a plebiscite.

(7) Rumania is to be restored, but forced to give complete self-determination to the Dobrudja. . . . Rumania must be forced to execute the clauses of the Berlin Treaty concerning the Jews, and recognize them as Rumanian citizens.

(8) In Italia Irridenta a provisional autonomy, followed by a plebiscite to determine state dependence.

(9) The German colonies to be returned.

(10) Greece and Persia to be restored.

### Freedom of the Seas

All straits opening into inland seas, as well as the Suez and Panama Canals, are to be neutralized. Commercial shipping to be free. The right of privateering to be abolished. The torpedoing of commercial ships to be forbidden.

### Indemnities

All combatants to renounce demands for any indemnities, either direct or indirect—as, for instance, charges for the maintenance of prisoners. Indemnities and contributions collected during the war must be refunded.

### Economic Terms

Commercial treaties are not to be part of the peace terms. Every country must be independent in its commercial relations, and must not be obliged to, or prevented from, concluding an economic treaty, by the Treaty of Peace. Nevertheless, all nations should bind themselves, by the Peace Treaty, not to practice an economic blockade after the war, nor to form separate tariff agreements. The right of most favored nation must be given to all countries without distinction.

### Guarantees of Peace

Peace is to be concluded at the Peace Conference by delegates elected by the national representative institution of each country. The peace terms are to be confirmed by these parliaments.

Secret diplomacy is to be abolished; all parties are to bind themselves not to conclude any secret treaties. Such treaties are declared in contradiction of international law, and void. All treaties, until confirmed by the parliaments of the different nations, are to be considered void.

Gradual disarmament both on land and sea, and the establishment of a militia system. The "League of Nations" advanced by President Wilson may become a valuable aid to international law, provided that (a) all nations are to be obliged to participate in it with equal rights, and (b) international politics are to be democratized.

*Ways to Peace*

The Allies are to announce immediately that they are willing to open peace negotiations as soon as the enemy powers declare their consent to the renunciation of all forcible annexations.

The Allies must bind themselves not to begin any peace negotiations, nor to conclude peace, except in a general Peace Conference with the participation of delegates from all the neutral countries.

All obstacles to the Stockholm Conference are to be removed, and passports are to be given immediately to all delegates of parties and organizations who wish to participate.

The Executive Committee of the Peasants' Soviets also issued a *nakaz*, which differs little from the above.

11 (p. 609). PEACE AT RUSSIA'S EXPENSE

The Ribot revelations of Austria's peace-offer to France; the so-called "Peace Conference" at Berne, Switzerland, during the summer of 1917, in which delegates participated from all the belligerent countries, representing large financial interests in all these countries; and the attempted negotiations of an English agent with a Bulgarian church dignitary; all pointed to the fact that there were strong currents, on both sides, favorable to patching up a peace at the expense of Russia. In my next book, *Kornilov to Brest-Litovsk*, I intend to treat this matter at some length, publishing several secret documents discovered in the Ministry of Foreign Affairs at Petrograd.

12 (p. 610). RUSSIAN SOLDIERS IN FRANCE

*Official Report of the Provisional Government*

From the time the news of the Russian Revolution reached Paris, Russian newspapers of extreme tendencies immediately began to appear; and these newspapers, as well as individuals, freely circulated among the soldier masses and began a Bolshevik propaganda, often spreading false news which appeared in the French journals. In the absence of all official news, and of precise details, this campaign provoked discontent among the soldiers. The result was a desire to return to Russia, and a hatred toward the officers.

Finally it all turned into rebellion. In one of their meetings the soldiers issued an appeal to refuse to drill, since they had decided to fight no more. It was decided to isolate the rebels, and General Zankievich ordered all soldiers loyal to the Provisional Government to leave the camp of Courtine, and to carry with them all ammunition. On 25 June the order was executed; there remained at the camp only the soldiers who said they would submit "conditionally" to the Provisional Government. The soldiers at the camp of Courtine received several times the visit of the Commander-in-Chief of the Russian Armies abroad, of Rapp, the Commissar of the Ministry of War, and of several distinguished former exiles who wished to influence them, but these attempts were unsuccessful, and finally Commissar Rapp insisted that the rebels lay down their arms, and, in sign of submission, march in good order to a place called Clairvaux. The order was only partially obeyed; first 500 men went out, of whom 22 were arrested; 24 hours later about 6,000 followed. . . . About 2,000 remained. . . .

It was decided to increase the pressure; their rations were diminished, their pay was cut off, and the roads toward the village of Courtine were guarded by French soldiers. General Zankievich, having discovered that a Russian artillery brigade was passing through France, decided to form a mixed detachment of infantry and artillery to reduce the rebels. A deputation was sent to the rebels; the deputation returned several hours later, convinced of the futility of the negotiations. On 1 September General Zankievich sent an ultimatum to the rebels demanding that they lay down their arms, and menacing in case of refusal to open fire with artillery if the order was not obeyed by 3 September at 10 o'clock.

The order not being executed, a light fire of artillery was opened on the place at the hour agreed upon. Eighteen shells were fired, and the rebels were warned that the bombardment would become more intense. In the night of 3 September 160 men surrendered. On 4 September the artillery bombardment recommenced and at 11 o'clock, after 36 shells had been fired, the rebels raised two white flags and began to leave the camp without arms. By evening 8,300 men had surrendered; 150 men who remained in the camp opened fire with machine-guns that night. The fifth of September, to make an end of the affair, a heavy barrage was laid on the camp, and our soldiers occupied it little by little. The rebels kept up a heavy fire with their machine-guns. On 6 September, at 9 o'clock, the camp was entirely occupied. . . . After the disarmament of the rebels, 81 arrests were made. . . .

Thus the report. From secret documents discovered in the Ministry of Foreign Affairs, however, we knew that the account is not strictly accurate. The first trouble arose when the soldiers tried to form a Committee, as their comrades in Russia were doing. They demanded to be sent back to Russia, which was refused; and then, being considered a dangerous influence in France, they were ordered to Salonika. They refused to go, and the battle followed. . . . It was discovered that they had been left in camp without officers for about two months, and badly treated, before they became rebellious. All attempts to find out the name of the "Russian artillery brigade" which had fired on them were futile; the telegrams discovered in the Ministry left it to be inferred that French artillery was used. . . .

After their surrender more than two hundred of the mutineers were shot in cold blood.

## 13 (p. 610). Tereshchenko's Speech (Resumé)

. . . The questions of foreign policy are closely related to those of national defense. . . . And so, if in questions of national defense you think it is necessary to hold session in secret, also in our foreign policy we are sometimes forced to observe the same secrecy. . . .

German diplomacy attempts to influence public opinion. . . . Therefore the declarations of directors of great democratic organizations who talk loudly of a revolutionary Congress, and the impossibility of another winter campaign, are dangerous. . . . All these declarations cost human lives. . . .

I wish to speak merely of governmental logic, without touching the questions of the honor and dignity of the State. From the point of view of logic, the foreign policy of Russia ought to be based on a real comprehension of the *interests* of Russia. . . . These interests mean that it is impossible that our country remain alone, and that the present alignment of forces with us (the Allies) is satisfactory. . . . All humanity longs for peace, but in Russia no one will permit a humiliating peace which would violate the State interests of our fatherland!

The orator pointed out that such a peace would for long years, if not for centuries, retard the triumph of democratic principles in the world, and would inevitably cause new wars.

All remember the days of May, when the fraternization on our Front threatened to end the war by a simple cessation of military operations, and lead the country to a shameful separate peace . . . and what efforts it was necessary to use to make the soldier masses at the front understand that it was not by this method that the Russian State must end the war and guarantee its interest.

He spoke of the miraculous effect of the July offensive, what strength it gave to the words of the Russian ambassadors abroad, and the despair in Germany caused by the Russian victories. And also, the disillusionment in Allied countries which followed the Russian defeat. . . .

As to the Russian Government, it adhered strictly to the formula of May, "No annexations and no punitive indemnities." We consider it essential not only to proclaim the self-determination of peoples, but also to renounce imperialistic aims. . . .

Germany is continually trying to make peace. The only talk in Germany is of peace; she knows she cannot win.

I reject the reproaches aimed at the Government which allege that Russian foreign policy does not speak clearly enough about the aims of the war. . . .
If the question arises as to what ends the Allies are pursuing, it is indispensable first to demand what aims the Central Powers have agreed upon. . . .
The desire is often heard that we publish the details of the treaties

which bind the Allies, but people forget that, up to now, we do not know the treaties which bind the Central Powers. . . .

Germany, he said, evidently wants to separate Russia from the West by a series of weak buffer-states.

This tendency to strike at the vital interests of Russia must be checked. . . .

And will the Russian democracy, which has inscribed on its banner the rights of nations to dispose of themselves, allow calmly the continuation of oppression upon the most civilized peoples (in Austria-Hungary)?

Those who fear that the Allies will try to profit by our difficult situation, to make us support more than our share of the burden of war, and to solve the questions of peace at our expense, are entirely mistaken. . . . Our enemy looks upon Russia as a market for its products. The end of the war will leave us in a feeble condition, and with our frontier open the flood of German products can easily hold back for years our industrial development. Measures must be taken to guard against this. . . .

I say frankly and openly: the combination of forces which unites us to the Allies is *favourable to the interests of Russia*. . . . It is therefore important that our views on the question of war and peace shall be in accord with the views of the Allies as clearly and precisely as possible. . . . To avoid all misunderstanding, I must say frankly that Russia must present to the Paris Conference *one point of view*. . . .

He did not want to comment on the *nakaz* to Skobeliev, but he referred to the Manifesto of the Dutch-Scandinavian Committee, just published in Stockholm. This Manifesto declared for the autonomy of Lithuania and Livonia; "but it is clearly impossible," said Tereshchenko, "for Russia must have free ports on the Baltic all the year round. . . ."

In this question the problems of foreign policy are also closely related to interior politics, for if there existed a strong sentiment of unity of all great Russia, one would not witness the repeated manifestations, everywhere, of a desire of people to separate from the Central Government. . . . Such separations are contrary to the interests of Russia, and the Russian delegates cannot raise the issue. . . .

14 (p. 610). The British Fleet (etc.)

At the time of the naval battle of the Gulf of Riga, not only the Bolsheviki, but also the Ministers of the Provisional Government, considered that the British Fleet had deliberately abandoned the Baltic, as one indication of the attitude so often expressed publicly by the British press, and semi-publicly by British representatives in Russia, "Russia's finished! No use bothering about Russia!"

See interview with Kerensky (Appendix 18).

GENERAL GURKO was a former Chief of Staff of the Russian armies under the Czar. He was a prominent figure in the corrupt Imperial court. After the Revolution he was one of the very few persons exiled for his political and personal record. The Russian naval defeat in the Gulf of Riga coincided with the public reception, by King George in London, of General Gurko, a man whom the Russian Provisional Government considered dangerously pro-German as well as reactionary!

15 (p. 621). Appeals Against Insurrection

### To the Workers and Soldiers

"Comrades! The Dark Forces are increasingly trying to call forth in Petrograd and other towns DISORDERS AND *Pogroms*. Disorder is necessary to the Dark Forces, for disorder will give them an opportunity for crushing the revolutionary movement in blood. Under the pretext of establishing order, and of protecting the inhabitants, they hope to establish the domination of Kornilov, which the revolutionary people succeeded in suppressing not long ago. Woe to the people if these hopes are realized! The triumphant counter-revolution will destroy the Soviets and the Army Committees, will disperse the Constituent Assembly, will stop the transfer of the land to the Land Committees, will put an end to all the hopes of the people for a speedy peace, and will fill all the prisons with revolutionary soldiers and workers.

In their calculations, the counter-revolutionists and Black Hundred leaders are counting on the serious discontent of the unenlightened part of the people with the disorganization of the food supply, the continuation of the war, and the general difficulties of life. They hope to transform every demonstration of soldiers and workers into a *pogrom*, which will frighten the peaceful population and throw it into the arms of the Restorers of Law and Order.

Under such conditions every attempt to organize a demonstration in these days, although for the most laudable object, would be a crime. All conscious workers and soldiers who are displeased with the policy of the Government will only bring injury to themselves and to the Revolution if they indulge in demonstrations.

THEREFORE THE TSAY-EE-KAH ASKS ALL WORKERS NOT TO OBEY ANY CALLS TO DEMONSTRATE.

WORKERS AND SOLDIERS! DO NOT YIELD TO PROVOCATION! REMEMBER YOUR DUTY TO YOUR COUNTRY AND THE REVOLUTION! DO NOT BREAK THE UNITY OF THE REVOLUTIONARY FRONT BY DEMONSTRATIONS WHICH ARE BOUND TO BE UNSUCCESSFUL!

*The Central Committee of the Soviets of Workers' and Soldiers' Deputies (Tsay-ee-kah)*

*Russian Social Democratic Labor Party*
THE DANGER IS NEAR!
To All Workers and Soldiers
*(Read and Hand to Others)*

*Comrades Workers and Soldiers!*

Our country is in danger. On account of this danger our freedom and our Revolution are passing through difficult days. The enemy is at the gates of Petrograd. The disorganization is growing with every hour. It becomes more and more difficult to obtain bread for Petrograd. All, all from the smallest to the greatest, must redouble their efforts, must endeavor to arrange things properly. . . . We must save our country, save freedom. . . . More arms and provisions for the Army! Bread—for the great cities. Order and organization in the country.

And in these terrible critical days rumors creep about that SOMEWHERE a demonstration is being prepared, that SOMEONE is calling on the soldiers and workers to destroy revolutionary peace and order. . . . *Rabochi Put*, the newspaper of the Bolsheviki, is pouring oil on the flames: it is flattering, trying to please the unenlightened people, tempting the workers and soldiers, urging them against the Government, promising them mountains of good things. . . . The confiding, ignorant men believe, they do not reason. . . . And from the other side come also rumors—rumors that the Dark Forces, the friends of the Czar, the German spies, are rubbing their hands with glee. They are ready to join the Bolsheviki, and with them fan the disorders into civil war.

The Bolsheviki and the ignorant soldiers and workers seduced by them cry senselessly: "Down with the Government! All power to the Soviets!" And the Dark servants of the Czar and the spies of Wilhelm will egg them on: "Beat the Jews, beat the shopkeepers, rob the markets, devastate the shops, pillage the wine stores! Slay, burn, rob!"

And then will come a terrible confusion, a war between one part of the people and the other. All will become still more disorganized, and perhaps once more blood will be shed on the streets of the capital. And then—what then?

Then the road to Petrograd will be open to Wilhelm. Then, no bread will come to Petrograd, the children will die of hunger. Then, the Army at the front will remain without support, our brothers in the trenches will be delivered to the fire of the enemy. Then, Russia will lose all prestige in other countries, our money will lose its value; everything will be so dear as to make life impossible. Then the long awaited Constituent Assembly will be postponed—it will be impossible to convene it in time. And then—Death to the Revolution, Death to our Liberty. . . .

Is it this that you want, workers and soldiers? No! If you do not, then go, go to the ignorant people seduced by the betrayers, and tell them the whole truth, which we have told you!

Let all know that EVERY MAN WHO IN THESE TERRIBLE DAYS CALLS ON YOU TO COME OUT IN THE STREETS AGAINST THE GOVERNMENT, IS EITHER A SECRET SERVANT OF THE CZAR, A PROVOCATOR, OR AN UNWISE ASSISTANT OF THE ENEMIES OF THE PEOPLE, OR A PAID SPY OF WILHELM!

Every conscious worker revolutionist, every conscious peasant, every revolutionary soldier, all who understand what harm a demonstration or a revolt against the Government might cause to the people, must join together and not allow the enemies of the people to destroy our freedom.

*The Petrograd Electoral Committee of the Mensheviki-oborontsi*

## 16 (p. 623). LENIN'S "LETTER TO THE COMRADES"

This series of articles appeared in *Rabochi Put* several days running, at the end of October and beginning of November 1917. I give here only extracts from two instalments:

1. Kameniev and Riazanov say that we have not a majority among the people, and that without a majority insurrection is hopeless.

Answer: People capable of speaking such things are falsifiers, pedants, or simply don't want to look the real situation in the face. In the last elections we received in all the country more than fifty percent of all the votes. . . .

The most important thing in Russia today is the peasants' revolution. In Tambov Government there has been a real agrarian uprising with wonderful political results. . . . Even *Dielo Naroda* has been scared into yelling that the land must be turned over to the peasants, and not only the Socialist Revolutionaries in the Council of the Republic, but also the Government itself, have been similarly affected. Another valuable result was the bringing of bread which had been hoarded by the *pomieshchiki* to the railroad stations in that province. The *Russkaya Volia* had to admit that the stations were filled with bread after the peasants' uprising. . . .

2. We are not sufficiently strong to take over the Government, and the bourgeoisie is not sufficiently strong to prevent the Constituent Assembly.

Answer: This is nothing but timidity, expressed by pessimism as regards workers and soldiers, and optimism as regards the failure of the bourgeoisie. If *yunkers* and Cossacks say they will fight, you believe them; if workmen and soldiers say so, you doubt it. What is the distinction between such doubts and siding politically with the bourgeoisie?

Kornilov proved that the Soviets were really a power. To believe Kerensky and the Council of the Republic, if the bourgeoisie is not strong enough to break the Soviets, it is not strong enough to break the Constituent. But that is wrong. The bourgeoisie will break the Constituent by sabotage, by lock-outs, by giving up Petrograd, by opening the front to the Germans. This has already been done in the case of Riga. . . .

3. The Soviets must remain a revolver at the head of the Government to force the calling of the Constituent Assembly, and to suppress any further Kornilov attempts.

Answer: Refusal of insurrection is refusal of "All Power to the Soviets." Since September the Bolshevik party has been discussing the question of insurrection. Refusing to rise means to trust our hopes in the faith of the good bourgeoisie, who have "promised" to call the Constituent Assembly. When the Soviets have all the power, the calling of the Constituent is guaranteed, and its success assured.

Refusal of insurrection means surrender to the "Lieber-Dans." Either we must drop "All Power to the Soviets" or make an insurrection; there is no middle course.

4. The bourgeoisie cannot give up Petrograd, although the Rod-

ziankos want it, because it is not the bourgeoisie who are fighting, but our heroic soldiers and sailors.

Answer: This did not prevent two Admirals from running away at the Moonsund battle. The Staff has not changed; it is composed of Kornilovtsi. If the Staff, with Kerensky at its head, wants to give up Petrograd, it can do it doubly or trebly. It can make arrangements with the Germans or the British; open the fronts. It can sabotage the Army's food supply. At all these doors has it knocked.

We have no right to wait until the bourgeoisie chokes the Revolution. Rodzianko is a man of action, who has faithfully and truthfully served the bourgeoisie for years. . . . Half the Lieber-Dans are cowardly compromisers; half of them simple fatalists. . . .

5. We are getting stronger every day. We shall be able to enter the Constituent Assembly as a stronger opposition. Then why should we play everything on one card?

Answer: This is the argument of a sophomore with no practical experience, who reads that the Constituent Assembly is being called and trustfully accepts the legal and constitutional way. Even the voting of the Constituent Assembly will not do away with hunger or beat Wilhelm. . . . The issue of hunger and of surrendering Petrograd cannot be decided by waiting for the Constituent Assembly. Hunger is not waiting. The peasants' Revolution is not waiting. The Admirals who ran away did not wait.

Blind people are surprised that hungry people, betrayed by Admirals and Generals, do not take an interest in voting.

6. If the Kornilovtsi make an attempt, we will show them our strength. But why should we risk everything by making an attempt ourselves?

Answer: History doesn't repeat. "Perhaps Kornilov will some day make an attempt!" What a serious base for proletarian action! But suppose Kornilov waits for starvation, for the opening of the fronts, what then? This attitude means to build the tactics of a revolutionary party on one of the bourgeoisie's former mistakes.

Let us forget everything except that there is no way out but by the dictatorship of the proletariat—either that or the dictatorship of Kornilov.

Let us wait, comrades, for—a miracle!

## 17 (p. 623). MILYUKOV'S SPEECH (Resumé)

Everyone admits, it seems, that the defense of the country is our principal task, and that, to assure it, we must have discipline in the Army and order in the rear. To achieve this there must be a power capable of daring, not only by persuasion but also by force. . . . The germ of all our evils comes from the point of view, original, truly Russian, concerning foreign policy, which passes for the International point of view.

The noble Lenin only imitates the noble Keroyevsky when he holds that from Russia will come the New World which shall resuscitate the aged West, and which will replace the old banner of doctrinary Socialism by the new direct action of starving masses—and that will push humanity forward and force it to break in the doors of the social paradise. . . .

These men sincerely believed that the decomposition of Russia would bring about the decomposition of the whole capitalist régime. Starting from that point of view, they were able to commit the unconscious treason, in wartime, of calmly telling the soldiers to abandon the trenches, and instead of fighting the external enemy, creating internal civil war and attacking the proprietors and capitalists. . . .

Here Milyukov was interrupted by furious cries from the Left, demanding what Socialist had ever advised such action. . . .

Martov says that only the revolutionary pressure of the proletariat can condemn and conquer the evil will of imperialist cliques and break down the dictatorship of these cliques. . . . Not by an accord between Governments for a limitation of armaments, but by the disarming of these Governments and the radical democratization of the military system. . . .

He attacked Martov viciously, and then turned on the Mensheviki and Socialist Revolutionaries, whom he accused of entering the Government as Ministers with the avowed purpose of carrying on the class struggle!

The Socialists of Germany and of the Allied countries contemplated these gentlemen with ill-concealed contempt, but they decided that it was for Russia, and sent us some apostles of the Universal Conflagration. . . .

The formula of our democracy is very simple; no foreign policy, no art of diplomacy, an immediate democratic peace, a declaration to the Allies, "We want nothing, we haven't anything to fight with!" And then our adversaries will make the same declaration, and the brotherhood of peoples will be accomplished!

Milyukov took a fling at the Zimmerwald Manifesto, and declared that even Kerensky has not been able to escape the influence of "that unhappy document which will for ever be your indictment." He then attacked Skobeliev, whose position in foreign assemblies, where he would appear as a Russian delegate, yet opposed to the foreign policy of his Government, would be so strange that people would say, "What's that gentleman carrying, and what shall we talk to him about?" As for the *nakaz*, Milyukov said that he himself was a pacifist; that he believed in the creation of an International Arbitration Board, and the necessity for a limitation of armaments, and parliamentary control over secret diplomacy, which did not mean the abolition of secret diplomacy.

As for the Socialist ideas in the *nakaz*, which he called "Stockholm ideas"—peace without victory, the right of self-determination of peoples, and renunciation of the economic war—

> The German successes are directly proportionate to the successes of those who call themselves the revolutionary democracy. I do not wish to say, "to the successes of the Revolution," because I believe that the defeats of the revolutionary democracy are victories for the Revolution. . . .
> The influence of the Soviet leaders abroad is not unimportant. One had only to listen to the speech of the Minister of Foreign Affairs to be convinced that, in this hall, the influence of the revolutionary democracy on foreign policy is so strong that the Minister does not dare to speak face to face with it about the honor and dignity of Russia!
> We can see, in the *nakaz* of the Soviets, that the ideas of the Stockholm Manifesto have been elaborated in two directions—that of Utopianism and that of German interests. . . .

Interrupted by the angry cries of the Left, and rebuked by the President, Milyukov insisted that the proposition of peace concluded by popular assemblies, not by diplomats, and the proposal to undertake peace negotiations as soon as the enemy had renounced annexations, were pro-German. Recently Kuhlman said that a personal declaration bound only him who made it. . . . "Anyway, we will imitate the Germans before we will imitate the Soviet of Workers' and Soldiers' Deputies. . . ."

The sections treating of the independence of Lithuania and Livonia were symptoms of nationalist agitation in different parts of Russia, supported, said Milyukov, by German money. . . . Amid bedlam from the Left, he contrasted the clauses of the *nakaz* concerning Alsace-Lorraine, Rumania, and Serbia with those treating of the nationalities in Germany and Austria. The *nakaz* embraced the German and Austrian point of view, said Milyukov, being afraid to speak the thought in his mind, and even afraid to think in terms of the greatness of Russia. The Dardanelles must belong to Russia. . . .

> You are continually saying that the soldier does not know why he is fighting, and that when he does know he'll fight. . . . It is true that the soldier doesn't know why he is fighting, but now you have told him that there is no reason for him to fight, that we have no national interests, and that we are fighting for alien ends. . . .

Paying tribute to the Allies, who, he said, with the assistance of America, "will yet save the cause of humanity," he ended:

> Long live the light of humanity, the advanced democracies of the West, who for a long time have been traveling the way we now only begin to enter, with ill-assured and hesitating steps! Long live our brave Allies!

18 (p. 624). Interview with Kerensky

The Associated Press man tried his hand. "Mr. Kerensky," he began, "in England and France people are disappointed with the Revolution—"

"Yes, I know," interrupted Kerensky, quizzically. "Abroad the Revolution is no longer fashionable!"

"What is your explanation of why the Russians have stopped fighting?"

"That is a foolish question to ask." Kerensky was annoyed. "Russia of all the Allies entered the war first and for a long time she bore the whole brunt of it. Her losses have been inconceivably greater than those of all the other nations put together. Russia has now the right to demand of the Allies that they bring greater force of arms to bear." He stopped for a moment and stared at his interlocutor. "You are asking why the Russians have stopped fighting, and the Russians are asking where is the British fleet—with German battleships in the Gulf of Riga?" Again he ceased suddenly, and as suddenly burst out. "The Russian Revolution hasn't failed and the revolutionary Army hasn't failed. It is not the Revolution which caused disorganization in the Army—that disorganization was accomplished years ago by the old régime. Why aren't the Russians fighting? I will tell you. Because the masses of the people are economically exhausted—and because they are disillusioned with the Allies!"

The interview of which this is an excerpt was cabled to the United States, and in a few days sent back by the American State Department, with a demand that it be "altered." This Kerensky refused to do; but it was done by his secretary, Dr. David Soskice—and, thus purged of all offensive references to the Allies, was given to the press of the world. . . .

## Chapter 3

19 (p. 628). RESOLUTION OF THE FACTORY-SHOP COMMITTEES

### Workers' Control

1. (See page 628.)
2. The organization of Workers' Control is a manifestation of the same healthy activity in the sphere of industrial production as are party organizations in the sphere of politics, trade unions in employment, cooperatives in the domain of consumption, and literary clubs in the sphere of culture.
3. The working-class has much more interest in the proper and uninterrupted operation of factories . . . than the capitalist class. Workers' Control is a better security in this respect for the interests of modern society, of the whole people, than the arbitrary will of the owners, who are guided only by their selfish desire for material profits or political privileges. Therefore Workers' Control is demanded by the proletariat not only in their own interest, but in the interests of the whole country, and should be supported by the revolutionary peasantry as well as the revolutionary Army.

4. Considering the hostile attitude of the majority of the capitalist class toward the Revolution, experience shows that proper distribution of raw materials and fuel, as well as the most efficient management of factories, is impossible without Workers' Control.

5. Only Workers' Control over capitalist enterprises, cultivating the workers' conscious attitude toward work, and making clear its social meaning, can create conditions favorable to the development of a firm self-discipline in labor, and the development of all labor's possible productivity.

6. The impending transformation of industry from a war to a peace basis, and the redistribution of labor all over the country, as well as among the different factories, can be accomplished without great disturbances only by means of the democratic self-government of the workers themselves.... Therefore the realization of Workers' Control is an indispensable preliminary to the demobilization of industry.

7. In accordance with the slogan proclaimed by the Russian Social Democratic Labor Party (Bolsheviki), Workers' Control on a national scale, in order to bring results, must extend to all capitalist concerns, and not be organized accidentally, without system; it must be well planned, and not separated from the industrial life of the country as a whole.

8. The economic life of the country—agriculture, industry, commerce, and transport—must be subjected to one unified plan, constructed so as to satisfy the individual and social requirements of the wide masses of the people; it must be approved by their elected representatives, and carried out under the direction of these representatives by means of national and local organizations.

9. That part of the plan which deals with land-labor must be carried out under supervision of the peasants' and land-workers' organizations; that relating to industry, trade, and transport operated by wage-earners, by means of Workers' Control; the natural organs of Workers' Control inside the industrial plant will be the Factory-Shop and similar Committees; and in the labor market, the Trade Unions.

10. The collective wage agreements arranged by the Trade Unions for the majority of workers in any branch of labor, must be binding on all the owners of plants employing this kind of labor in the given district.

11. Employment bureaux must be placed under the control and management of the Trade Unions, as class organizations acting within the limits of the whole industrial plan, and in accordance with it.

12. Trade Unions must have the right, upon their own initiative, to begin legal action against all employers who violate labor contracts or labor legislation, and also on behalf of any individual worker in any branch of labor.

13. On all questions relating to Workers' Control over production, distribution, and employment the Trade Unions must confer with the workers of individual establishments through their Factory-Shop Committees.

14. Matters of employment and discharge, vacations, wage scales, refusal of work, degree of productivity and skill, reasons for abrogating agreements, disputes with the administration, and similar problems of the internal life of the factory, must be settled exclusively according to the findings of the Factory-Shop Committee, which has the right to exclude from participation in the discussion any members of the factory administration.

15. The Factory-Shop Committee forms a commission to control the supplying of the factory with raw materials, fuel, orders, labor power, and technical staff (including equipment), and all other supplies and arrangements, and also to assure the factory's adherence to the general industrial plan. The factory administration is obliged to surrender to the organs of Workers' Control, for their aid and information, all data concerning the business; to make it possible to verify this data, and to produce the books of the company upon demand of the Factory-Shop Committee.

16. Any illegal acts on the part of the administration discovered by the Factory-Shop Committees, or any suspicion of any such illegal acts, which cannot be investigated or remedied by the workers alone, shall be referred to the district central organization of Factory-Shop Committees charged with the particular branch of labor involved, which shall discuss the matter with the institutions charged with the execution of the general industrial plan, and find means to deal with the matter, even to the extent of confiscating the factory.

17. The union of the Factory-Shop Committees of different concerns must be accomplished on the basis of the different trades, in order to facilitate control over the whole branch of industry, so as to come within the general industrial plan; and so as to create an effective plan of distribution among the different factories, of orders, raw materials, fuel, technical and labor power, and also to facilitate cooperation with the Trade Unions, which are organized by trades.

18. The central councils of Trade Unions and Factory-Shop Committees represent the proletariat in the corresponding provincial and local institutions formed to elaborate and carry out the general industrial plan, and to organize economic relations between the

towns and the villages (workers and peasants). They also possess final authority for the management of Factory-Shop Committees and Trade Unions, so far as Workers' Control in their district is concerned, and they shall issue obligatory regulations concerning workers' discipline in the routine of production—which regulations, however, must be approved by vote of the workers themselves.

## 20 (p. 630). THE BOURGEOIS PRESS ON THE BOLSHEVIKI

*Russkaya Volia*, 28 October:

The decisive moment approaches. . . . It is decisive for the Bolsheviki. Either they will give us . . . a second edition of the events of 16–18 July or they will have to admit that with their plans and intentions, with their impertinent policy of wishing to separate themselves from everything consciously national, they have been definitely defeated. . . .
What are the chances of Bolshevik success?
It is difficult to answer that question, for their principal support is the . . . ignorance of the popular masses. They speculate on it, they work upon it by a demagogy which nothing can stop. . . .
The Government must play its part in this affair. Supporting itself morally by the Council of the Republic, the Government must take a clearly defined attitude toward the Bolsheviki. . . .
And if the Bolsheviki provoke an insurrection against the legal power, and thus facilitate the German invasion, they must be treated as mutineers and traitors. . . .

*Birzhevya Viedomosti*, 28 October:

Now that the Bolsheviki have separated themselves from the rest of the democracy, the struggle against them is very much simpler—and it is not reasonable, in order to fight against Bolshevism, to wait until they make a manifestation. The Government should not even allow the manifestation. . . .
The appeals of the Bolsheviki to insurrection and anarchy are acts punishable by the criminal courts, and in the freest countries their authors would receive severe sentences. For what the Bolsheviki are carrying on is not a political struggle against the Government, or even for the power; it is propaganda for anarchy, massacres, and civil war. This propaganda must be extirpated at its roots; it would be

strange to wait, in order to begin an action against an agitation for *pogroms*, until the *pogroms* actually occurred. . . .

*Novoye Vremya*, 1 November:

. . . Why is the Government excited only about 2 November (date of calling of the Congress of Soviets), and not about 12 September, or 3 October?

This is not the first time that Russia burns and falls in ruins, and that the smoke of the terrible conflagration makes the eyes of our Allies smart. . . .

Since it came to power has there been a single order issued by the Government for the purpose of halting anarchy, or has anyone attempted to put out the Russian conflagration?

There were other things to do. . . .

The Government turned its attention to a more immediate problem. It crushed an insurrection (the Kornilov attempt) concerning which everyone is now asking, "Did it ever exist?"

## 21 (p. 630). MODERATE SOCIALIST PRESS ON THE BOLSHEVIKI

*Dielo Naroda*, 28 October (Socialist Revolutionary):

The most frightful crime of the Bolsheviki against the Revolution is that they impute exclusively to the bad intentions of the revolutionary Government all the calamities which the masses are so cruelly suffering; when as a matter of fact these calamities spring from objective causes.

They make golden promises to the masses, knowing in advance that they can fulfill none of them; they lead the masses on a false trail, deceiving them as to the source of all their troubles. . . .

The Bolsheviki are the most dangerous enemies of the Revolution. . . .

*Dien*, 30 October (Menshevik):

Is this really "the freedom of the press"? Every day *Novaya Rus* and *Rabochi Put* openly incite to insurrection. Every day these papers commit in their columns actual crimes. Every day they urge *pogroms*. . . . Is that "the freedom of the press"? . . .

The Government ought to defend itself and defend us. We have the right to insist that the Government machinery does not remain passive while the threat of bloody riots endangers the lives of its citizens. . . .

## 22 (p. 630). "YEDINSTVO"

Plekhanov's paper, *Yedinstvo*, suspended publication a few weeks after the Bolsheviki seized the power. Contrary to popular report, *Yedinstvo* was not suppressed by the Bolshevik Government; an announcement in the last number admitted that it was unable to continue *because there were too few subscribers.* . . .

## 23 (p. 631). WERE THE BOLSHEVIKI CONSPIRATORS?

The French newspaper *Entente* of Petrograd, on 15 November, published an article of which the following is a part:

> The Government of Kerensky discusses and hesitates. The Government of Lenin and Trotsky attacks and acts.
> This last is called a Government of Conspirators, but that is wrong. Government of usurpers, yes, like all revolutionary Governments which triumph over their adversaries. Conspirators—no!
> No! They did not conspire. On the contrary, openly, audaciously, without mincing words, without dissimulating their intentions, they multiplied their agitation, intensified their propaganda in the factories, the barracks, at the front, in the country, everywhere, even fixing in advance the date of their taking up arms, the date of their seizure of the power. . . .
> *They*—conspirators? Never. . . .

## 24 (p. 640). APPEAL AGAINST INSURRECTION

*From the Central Army Committee*
> . . . Above everything we insist upon the inflexible execution of the organized will of the majority of the people, expressed by the Provisional Government in accord with the Council of the Republic and the Tsay-ee-kah as organ of the popular power. . . .
> Any demonstration to dispose this power by violence, at a moment when a Government crisis will infallibly create disorganization, the ruin of the country, and civil war, will be considered by the Army as a counter-revolutionary act, and repressed by force of arms. . . .

The interests of private groups and classes should be submitted to a single interest—that of augmenting industrial production, and distributing the necessities of life with fairness. . . .

All who are capable of sabotage, disorganization, or disorder, all deserters, all slackers, all looters, should be forced to do auxiliary service in the rear of the Army. . . .

We invite the Provisional Government to form, out of these violators of the people's will, these enemies of the Revolution, labor detachments to work in the rear, on the front, in the trenches under enemy fire. . . .

## 25 (p. 652). EVENTS OF THE NIGHT, 6 NOVEMBER

Toward evening bands of Red Guards began to occupy the printing-shops of the bourgeois press, where they printed *Rabochi Put*, *Soldat*, and various proclamations by the hundred thousand. The City Militia was ordered to clear these places, but found the offices barricaded, and armed men defending them. Soldiers who were ordered to attack the print-shops refused.

About midnight a colonel with a company of *yunkers* arrived at the club "Free Mind," with a warrant to arrest the editor of *Rabochi Put*. Immediately an enormous mob gathered in the street outside and threatened to lynch the *yunkers*. The Colonel thereupon begged that he and the *yunkers* be arrested and taken to Peter-Paul prison for safety. This request was granted.

At 1 A.M. a detachment of soldiers and sailors from Smolny occupied the Telegraph Agency. At 1:35 the Post Office was occupied. Toward morning the Military Hotel was taken, and at 5 o'clock the Telephone Exchange. At dawn the State Bank was surrounded. And at 10 A.M. a cordon of troops was drawn about the Winter Palace.

## Chapter 4

## 26 (p. 655). EVENTS OF 7 NOVEMBER

From 4 A.M. until dawn Kerensky remained at the Petrograd Staff Headquarters, sending orders to the Cossacks and to the *yunkers* in the Officers' Schools in and around Petrograd—all of whom answered that they were unable to move.

Colonel Polkovnikov, Commandant of the City, hurried between the Staff and the Winter Palace, evidently without any plan. Kerensky gave an order to open the bridges; three hours passed without any action, and then an officer and five men went out on their own initiative, and putting to flight a picket of Red Guards, opened the Nikolai Bridge. Immediately after they left, however, some sailors closed it again.

Kerensky ordered the print-shops of *Rabochi Put* to be occupied. The officer detailed to the work was promised a squad of soldiers; two hours later he was promised some *yunkers;* then the order was forgotten.

An attempt was made to recapture the Post Office and the Telegraph Agency; a few shots were fired, and the Government troops announced that they would no longer oppose the Soviets.

To a delegation of *yunkers* Kerensky said, "As chief of the Provisional Government and as Supreme Commander, I know nothing. I cannot advise you; but as a veteran revolutionist I appeal to you, young revolutionists, to remain at your post and defend the conquests of the Revolution."

*

Orders of Kishkin, 7 November:

> By decree of the Provisional Government. . . . I am invested with extraordinary powers for the reestablishment of order in Petrograd, in complete command of all civil and military authorities. . . .
>
> In accordance with the powers conferred upon me by the Provisional Government, I herewith relieve from his functions as Commandant of the Petrograd Military District Colonel George Polkovnikov. . . .

*

*Appeal to the Population* signed by Vice-Premier Konovalov, 7 November:

> Citizens! Save the fatherland, the republic, and your freedom. Maniacs have raised a revolt against the only government power chosen by the people, the Provisional Government. . . .

The members of the Provisional Government fulfill their duty, remain at their post, and continue to work for the good of the fatherland, the reestablishment of order, and the convocation of the Constituent Assembly, future sovereign of Russia and of all the Russian peoples. . . .

Citizens, you must support the Provisional Government. You must strengthen its authority. You must oppose these maniacs, with whom are joined all the enemies of liberty and order, and the followers of the Czarist régime, in order to wreck the Constituent Assembly, destroy the conquests of the Revolution, and the future of our dear fatherland. . . .

Citizens! Organize around the Provisional Government for the defense of its temporary authority, in the name of order and the happiness of all peoples. . . .

*

*Proclamation of the Provisional Government*

The Petrograd Soviet . . . has declared the Provisional Government overthrown and has demanded that the Governmental power be turned over to it, under threat of bombarding the Winter Palace with the cannon of Peter-Paul Fortress, and of the cruiser *Avrora*, anchored in the Neva.

The Government can surrender its authority only to the Constituent Assembly; for that reason it has decided not to submit, and to demand aid from the population and the Army. A telegram has been sent to the Stavka; and an answer received says that a strong detachment of troops is being sent. . . .

Let the Army and the People reject the irresponsible attempts of the Bolsheviki to create a revolt in the rear. . . .

About 9 A.M. Kerensky left for the front.

Toward evening two soldiers on bicycles presented themselves at the Staff Headquarters, as delegates of the garrison of Peter-Paul Fortress. Entering the meeting-room of the Staff, where Kishkin, Rutenburg, Palchinsky, General Bagratouni, Colonel Paradielov and Count Tolstoy were gathered, they demanded the immediate surrender of the Staff; threatening, in case of refusal, to bombard headquarters. . . . After two panicky conferences the Staff retreated to the Winter Palace, and the headquarters were occupied by Red Guards. . . .

Late in the afternoon several Bolshevik armored cars cruised around the Palace Square, and Soviet soldiers tried unsuccessfully to parley with the *yunkers*. . . .

Firing on the Palace began about 7 o'clock in the evening. . . .

At 10 P.M. began an artillery bombardment from three sides, in which most of the shells were blanks, only three small shrapnels striking the façade of the Palace. . . .

27 (p. 658). KERENSKY IN FLIGHT

Leaving Petrograd in the morning of 7 November, Kerensky arrived by automobile at Gatchina, where he demanded a special train. Toward evening he was in Ostrov, Province of Pskov. The next morning, extraordinary session of the local Soviet of Workers' and Soldiers' Deputies, with participation of Cossack delegates—there being 6,000 Cossacks at Ostrov.

Kerensky spoke to the assembly, appealing for aid against the Bolsheviki, and addressed himself almost exclusively to the Cossacks. The soldier delegates protested.

"Why did you come here?" shouted voices. Kerensky answered, "To ask the Cossacks' assistance in crushing the Bolshevik insurrection!" At this there were violent protestations, which increased when he continued, "I broke the Kornilov attempt, and I will break the Bolsheviki!" The noise became so great that he had to leave the platform. . . .

The soldier deputies and the Ussuri Cossacks decided to arrest Kerensky, but the Don Cossacks prevented them, and got him away by train. . . . A Military Revolutionary Committee, set up during the day, tried to inform the garrison of Pskov, but the telephone and telegraph wires were cut. . . .

Kerensky did not arrive at Pskov. Revolutionary soldiers had cut the railway line, to prevent troops being sent against the capital. On the night of 8 November he arrived by automobile at Luga, where he was well received by the Death Battalions stationed there.

Next day he took train for the Southwest Front, and visited the Army Committee at headquarters. The Fifth Army, however, was wild with enthusiasm over the news of the Bolshevik success, and the Army Committee was unable to promise Kerensky any support.

From there he went to the Stavka, at Moghilev, where he ordered ten regiments from different parts of the front to move against Petrograd. The soldiers almost unanimously refused; and those regiments which did start halted on the way. About five thousand Cossacks finally followed him. . . .

28 (p. 677). LOOTING OF THE WINTER PALACE

I do not mean to maintain that there was no looting in the Winter Palace. Both after and *before* the Winter Palace fell there was considerable pilfering. The statement of the Socialist Revolutionary paper *Narod*, and of members of the City Duma, to the effect that precious objects to the value of 500,000,000 roubles had been stolen, was, however, a gross exaggeration.

The most important art treasures of the Palace—paintings, statues, tapestries, rare porcelains, and armories—had been transferred to Moscow during the month of September; and they were still in good order in the basement of the Imperial Palace there, ten days after the capture of the Kremlin by Bolshevik troops. I can personally testify to this. . . .

Individuals, however, especially the general public, which was allowed to circulate freely through the Winter Palace for several days after its capture, made away with table silver, clocks, bedding, mirrors, and some odd vases of valuable porcelain and semiprecious stones, to the value of about 50,000 dollars.

The Soviet Government immediately created a special commission, composed of artists and archaeologists, to recover the stolen objects. On 1 November two proclamations were issued:

CITIZENS OF PETROGRAD!

We urgently ask all citizens to exert every effort to find whatever possible of the objects stolen from the Winter Palace on the night of 7–8 November, and to forward them to the Commandant of the Winter Palace.

Receivers of stolen goods, antiquarians, and all who are proved to be hiding such objects will be held legally responsible and punished with all severity.

*Commissars for the Protection of Museums
and Artistic Collections,*

G. YATMANOV, B. MANDELBAUM

\*

To REGIMENTAL AND FLEET COMMITTEES

In the night of 7–8 November, in the Winter Palace, which is the inalienable property of the Russian people, valuable objects of art were stolen.

We urgently appeal to all to exert every effort, so that the stolen objects are returned to the Winter Palace.

*Commissars,*

G. YATMANOV, B. MANDELBAUM

About half the loot was recovered, some of it in the baggage of foreigners leaving Russia.

A conference of artists and archaeologists, held at the suggestion of Smolny, appointed a commission to make an inventory of the Winter Palace treasures, which was given complete charge of the Palace and of all artistic collections and State museums in Petrograd. On 16 November the Winter Palace was closed to the public while the inventory was being made. . . .

During the last week of November a decree was issued by the Council of People's Commissars, changing the name of the Winter Palace to "People's Museum," entrusting it to the complete charge of the artistic-archaeological commissions, and declaring that henceforth all Government activities within its walls were prohibited. . . .

29 (p. 680). RAPE OF THE WOMEN'S BATTALION

Immediately following the taking of the Winter Palace all sorts of sensational stories were published in the anti-Bolshevik press, and told in the City Duma, about the fate of the Women's Battalion defending the Palace. It was said that some of the girl-soldiers had been thrown from the windows into the street, most of the rest had been violated, and many had committed suicide as a result of the horrors they had gone through.

The City Duma appointed a commission to investigate the matter. On 16 November the commission returned from Levashovo, headquarters of the Women's Battalion. Madame Tyrkova reported that the girls had been at first taken to the barracks of the Pavlovsky Regiment, and that there some of them had been badly treated; but that at present most of them were at Levashovo, and the rest scattered about the city in private houses. Dr. Mandelbaum, another of the commission, testified dryly that *none* of the women had been thrown out of the windows of the Winter Palace, that *none* were wounded, that three had been violated, and that one had committed suicide, leaving a note which said that she had been "disappointed in her ideals."

On 21 November the Military Revolutionary Committee officially dissolved the Women's Battalion, at the request of the girls themselves, who returned to civilian clothes.

In Louise Bryant's book, *Six Red Months in Russia*, there is an interesting description of the girl-soldiers during this time.

## Chapter 5

30 (p. 686). APPEALS AND PROCLAMATIONS
*From the Military Revolutionary Committee, 8 November*

To All Army Committees and All Soviets of Soldiers' Deputies

The Petrograd garrison has overturned the Government of Kerensky, which had risen against the Revolution and the People. . . . In sending this news to the front and the country, the Military Revolutionary Committee requests all soldiers to keep vigilant watch on the conduct of officers. Officers who do not frankly and openly declare for the Revolution should be immediately arrested as enemies.

The Petrograd Soviet interprets the program of the new Government as: immediate proposals of a general democratic peace, the immediate transfer of the Constituent Assembly. The people's revolutionary Army must not permit troops of doubtful morale to be sent to Petrograd. Act by means of arguments, by means of moral suasion—but if that fails halt the movement of troops by implacable force.

The present order must be immediately read to all military units of every branch of the service. Whoever keeps the knowledge of this order from the soldier-masses . . . commits a serious crime against the Revolution, and will be punished with all the rigor of revolutionary law.

Soldiers! For peace, bread, land, and popular government!

*

To All Front and Rear Army, Corps, Divisional, Regimental, and Company Committees, and All Soviets of Workers', Soldiers', and Peasants' Deputies.

Soldiers and Revolutionary officers!

The Military Revolutionary Committee, by agreement with the majority of the workers, soldiers, and peasants, has decreed that General Kornilov and all the accomplices of his conspiracy shall be brought immediately to Petrograd for incarceration in Peter-Paul Fortress and arraignment before a military revolutionary court-martial. . . .

All who resist the execution of this decree are declared by the Committee to be traitors to the Revolution, and their orders are herewith declared null and void.

*The Military Revolutionary Committee Attached to the Petrograd Soviet of Workers' and Soldiers' Deputies*

*

To all Provincial and District Soviets of Workers', Soldiers', and Peasants' Deputies.

By resolution of the All-Russian Congress of Soviets, all arrested members of Land Committees are immediately set free. The Commissars who arrested them are to be arrested.

From this moment all power belongs to the Soviets. The Commissars of the Provisional Government are removed. The presidents of the various local Soviets are invited to enter into direct relations with the revolutionary Government.

*Military Revolutionary Committee*

## 31 (p. 693). PROTEST OF THE MUNICIPAL DUMA

The Central City Duma, elected on the most democratic principles, has undertaken the burden of managing Municipal affairs and food supplies at the time of the greatest disorganization. At the present moment the Bolshevik party, three weeks before the elections to the Constituent Assembly, and in spite of the menace of the external enemy, having removed by armed force the only legal revolutionary authority, is making an attempt against the rights and independence of the Municipal Self-Government, demanding submission to its Commissars and its illegal authority.

In this terrible and tragic moment the Petrograd City Duma, in the face of its constituents, and of all Russia, declares loudly that it will not submit to any encroachments on its rights and its independence, and will remain at the post of responsibility to which it has been called by the will of the population of the capital.

The Central City Duma of Petrograd appeals to all Dumas and Zemstvos of the Russian Republic to rally to the defense of one of the greatest conquests of the Russian Revolution—the independence and inviolability of popular self-government.

## 32 (p. 704). Land Decree—Peasants' "Nakaz"

The land question can only be permanently settled by the general Constituent Assembly.

The most equitable solution of the land question should be as follows:

1. The right of private ownership of land abolished for ever; land cannot be sold, nor leased, nor mortgaged, nor alienated in any way. All dominical lands, lands attached to titles, lands belonging to the Emperor's cabinet, to monasteries, churches, possession lands, entailed lands, private estates, communal lands, peasant freeholds, and others, are confiscated without compensation, and become national property, and are placed at the disposition of the workers who cultivate them.

Those who are damaged because of this social transformation of the rights of property are entitled to public aid during the time necessary for them to adapt themselves to the new conditions of existence.

2. All the riches beneath the earth—ores, oil, coal, salt, etc.—as well as forest and waters having a national importance, become the exclusive property of the State. All minor streams, lakes, and forests are placed in the hands of the communities, on condition of being managed by the local organs of government.

3. All plots of land scientifically cultivated—gardens, plantations, nurseries, seed-plots, green-houses, and others—shall not be divided, but transformed into model farms, and pass into the hands of the State or of the community, according to their size and importance.

Buildings, communal lands, and villages with their private gardens and their orchards remain in the hands of their present owners; the dimensions of these plots and the rates of taxes for their use shall be fixed by law.

4. All studs, governmental and private cattle-breeding and bird-breeding establishments, and others, are confiscated and become national property, and are transferred either to the State or to the community, according to their size and importance.

All questions of compensation for the above are within the competence of the Constituent Assembly.

5. All inventoried agricultural property of the confiscated lands, machinery, and livestock are transferred without compensation to the State or the community, according to their quality and importance.

The confiscation of such machinery or livestock shall not apply to the small properties of peasants.

6. The right to use the land is granted to all citizens, without distinction of sex, who wish to work the land themselves, with the help of their families, or in partnership, and only so long as they are able to work. No hired labor is permitted.

In the event of the incapacity for work of a member of the commune for a period of two years, the commune shall be bound to render him assistance during this time by working the land in common.

Farmers who through old age or sickness have permanently lost the capacity to work the land themselves, shall surrender their land and receive instead a Government pension.

7. The use of the land shall be equalized—that is to say, the land shall be divided among the workers according to local conditions, the unit of labor, and the needs of the individual.

The way in which land is to be used may be individually determined upon: as homesteads, as farms, by communes, by partnerships, as will be decided by the villages and settlements.

8. All land upon its confiscation is pooled in the general People's Land Fund. Its distribution among the workers is carried out by the local and central organs of administration, beginning with the village democratic organizations and ending with the central provincial institutions—with the exception of urban and rural societies.

The Land Fund is subject to periodical redistribution according to the increase of population and the development of productivity and rural economy.

In case of modification of the boundaries of allotments, the original center of the allotment remains intact.

The lands of persons retiring from the community return to the Land Fund; providing that near relations of the persons retiring, or friends designated by them, shall have preference in the redistribution of those lands.

When lands are returned to the Land Fund the money expended

for manuring or improving the land, which has not been exhausted, shall be reimbursed.

If in some localities the Land Fund is insufficient to satisfy the local population, the surplus population should emigrate.

The organization of the emigration, also the costs thereof, and the providing of emigrants with the necessary machinery and livestock, shall be the business of the State.

The emigration shall be carried out in the following order: first, the peasants without land who express their wish to emigrate, then the undesirable members of the community, deserters, etc., and finally by drawing lots on agreement.

All which is contained in this *nakaz*, being the expression of the indisputable will of the great majority of conscious peasants of Russia, is declared to be a temporary law, and until the convocation of the Constituent Assembly, becomes effective immediately so far as is possible, and in some parts of it gradually, as will be determined by the District Soviets of Peasants' Deputies.


33 (p. 708). THE LAND AND THE DESERTERS

The Government was not forced to make any decision concerning the rights of deserters to the land. The end of the war and the demobilization of the army automatically removed the deserter problem. . . .


34 (p. 708). THE COUNCIL OF PEOPLE'S COMMISSARS

The Council of People's Commissars was at first composed entirely of Bolsheviki. This was not entirely the fault of the Bolsheviki, however. On 8 November they offered portfolios to members of the Left Socialist Revolutionaries, who declined.


**Chapter 6**


35 (p. 718). APPEALS AND DENUNCIATIONS

Appeal to all Citizens and to the Military Organizations of the Socialist Revolutionary Party.

The senseless attempt of the Bolsheviki is on the eve of complete failure. The garrison is disaffected. . . . The Ministries are idle, bread is lacking. All factions except a handful of Bolsheviki have left the Congress of Soviets. The Bolsheviki are alone! Abuses of all sorts, acts of vandalism and pillage, the bombardment of the Winter Palace, arbitrary arrests—all these crimes committed by the Bolsheviki have aroused against them the resentment of the majority of the sailors and soldiers. The Tsentroflot refuses to submit to the orders of the Bolsheviki. . . .

We call upon all sane elements to gather around the Committee for Salvation of Country and Revolution; to take serious measures to be ready, at the first call of the Central Committee of the Party, to act against the counter-revolutionists, who will doubtless attempt to profit by these troubles provoked by the Bolshevik adventure, and to watch closely the external enemy, who also would like to take advantage of this opportune moment when the front is weakened. . . .

> *The Military Section of the Central Committee*
> *of the Socialist Revolutionary Party*

*

From *Pravda:*

What is Kerensky?

A usurper, whose place is in Peter-Paul prison, with Kornilov and Kishkin.

A criminal and a traitor to the workers, soldiers, and peasants, who believed in him.

Kerensky? A murderer of soldiers!

Kerensky? A public executioner of peasants!

Kerensky? A strangler of workers!

Such is the second Kornilov who now wants to butcher liberty!

## Chapter 7

36 (p. 738). Two Decrees

*On the Press*

In the serious decisive hour of the Revolution and the days immediately following it, the Provisional Revolutionary Committee is compelled to adopt a series of measures against the counter-revolutionary press of all shades.

Immediately on all sides are cries that the new Socialist authority is in this violating the essential principles of its own program by an attempt against the freedom of the press.

The Workers' and Peasants' Government calls the attention of the population to the fact that in our country, behind this liberal shield, is hidden the opportunity of the wealthier classes to seize the lion's share of the whole press, and by this means to poison the popular mind and bring confusion into the consciousness of the masses.

Everyone knows that the bourgeois press is one of the most powerful weapons of the bourgeoisie. Especially in this critical moment, when the new authority of the workers and peasants is in process of consolidation, it is impossible to leave it in the hands of the enemy, at a time when it is not less dangerous than bombs and machine-guns. This is why temporary and extraordinary measures have been adopted for the purpose of stopping the flow of filth and calumny in which the yellow and green press would be glad to drown the young victory of the people.

As soon as the new order is consolidated, all administrative measures against the press will be suspended; full liberty will be given it within the limits of responsibility before the law, in accordance with the broadest and most progressive regulations. . . .

Bearing in mind, however, the fact that any restrictions of the freedom of the press, even in critical moments, are admissible only within the bounds of necessity, the Council of People's Commissars decrees as follows:

1. The following classes of newspaper shall be subject to closure: (a) Those inciting to open resistance or disobedience to the Workers' and Peasants' Government; (b) those creating confusion by obviously and deliberately perverting the news; (c) those inciting to acts of a criminal character punishable by the laws.

2. The temporary or permanent closing of any organ of the press shall be carried out by virtue of a resolution of the Council of People's Commissars.

3. The present decree is of a temporary nature and will be revoked by a special *ukaz* when normal conditions of public life are reestablished.

> *President of the Council of People's Commissars*
> VLADIMIR ULYANOV (LENIN)

*

*On Workers' Militia*

1. All Soviets of Workers' and Soldiers' Deputies shall form a Workers' Militia.

2. This Workers' Militia shall be entirely at the orders of the Soviets of Workers' and Soldiers' Deputies.

3. Military and Civil authorities must render every assistance in arming the workers and in supplying them with technical equipment, even to the extent of requisitioning arms belonging to the War Department of the Government.

4. This decree shall be promulgated by telegraph.

Petrograd, 10 November 1917.

*People's Commissar of the Interior,*
A. I. RYKOV

*

This decree encouraged the formation of companies of Red Guards all over Russia, which became the most valuable arm of the Soviet Government in the ensuing civil war.

37 (p. 739). THE STRIKE FUND

The fund for the striking Government employees and bank clerks was subscribed by banks and business houses of Petrograd and other cities, and also by foreign corporations doing business in Russia. All who consented to strike against the Bolsheviki were paid full wages, and in some cases their pay was increased. It was the realization of the strike fund contributors that the Bolsheviki were firmly in power, followed by their refusal to pay strike benefits, which finally broke the strike.

**Chapter 8**

38 (p. 754). KERENSKY'S ADVANCE

On 9 November Kerensky and his Cossacks arrived at Gatchina, where the garrison, hopelessly split into two factions, immediately surrendered. The members of the Gatchina Soviet were arrested, and at first threatened with death; later they were released on good behavior.

The Cossack advance-guards, practically unopposed, occupied Pavlovsk, Alexandrovsk, and other stations, and reached the outskirts of Tsarskoye Selo next morning—10 November. At once the garrison divided into three groups—the officers, loyal to Kerensky; part of the soldiers and non-commissioned officers, who declared themselves "neutral"; and most of the rank and file, who were for the Bolsheviki. The Bolshevik soldiers, who were without leaders or organization, fell back toward the capital. The local Soviet also withdrew to the village of Pulkovo.

From Pulkovo six members of the Tsarskoye Selo Soviet went with an automobile load of proclamations to Gatchina, to propagandize the Cossacks. They spent most of the day going around Gatchina from one Cossack barracks to another, pleading, arguing, and explaining. Toward evening some officers discovered their presence and they were arrested and brought before General Krasnov, who said, "You fought against Kornilov, now you are opposing Kerensky. I'll have you all shot!"

After reading aloud to them the order appointing him commander-in-chief of the Petrograd District, Krasnov asked if they were Bolsheviki. They replied in the affirmative, upon which Krasnov went away; a short time later an officer came and set them free, saying it was by order of General Krasnov. . . .

In the meantime delegations continued to arrive from Petrograd; from the Duma, the Committee for Salvation, and, last of all, from the Vikzhel. The Union of Railway Workers insisted that some agreement be reached to halt the civil war, and demanded that Kerensky treat with the Bolsheviki, and that he stop the advance on Petrograd. In case of refusal the Vikzhel threatened a general strike at midnight of 11 November.

Kerensky asked to be allowed to discuss the matter with the Socialist Ministers and with the Committee for Salvation. He was plainly undecided.

On the eleventh Cossack outposts reached Krasnoye Selo, from which the local Soviet and the heterogeneous forces of the Military Revolutionary Committee precipitately retired, some of them surrendering. . . . That night they also touched Pulkovo, where the first real resistance was encountered. . . .

Cossack deserters began to dribble into Petrograd, declaring that Kerensky had lied to them, that he had spread broadcast over the front proclamations which said that Petrograd was burning, that the Bolsheviki had invited the Germans to come in, and that they were murdering women and children and looting indiscriminately. . . .

39 (p. 761). PROCLAMATIONS OF THE MILITARY REVOLUTIONARY COMMITTEE

To All Soviets of Workers', Soldiers', and Peasants' Deputies.

The All-Russian Congress of Soviets of Workers', Soldiers', and Peasants' Deputies charges the local Soviets immediately to take the most energetic measures to oppose all counter-revolutionary anti-Semitic disturbances, and all *pogroms* of whatever nature. The honor of the workers', peasants', and soldiers' Revolution cannot tolerate any disorders. . . .

The Red Guard of Petrograd, the revolutionary garrison, and the sailors have maintained complete order in the capital.

Workers, soldiers, and Cossacks, on us falls the duty of keeping real revolutionary order.

All revolutionary Russia and the whole world have their eyes on you. . . .

\*

The All-Russian Congress of Soviets decrees:

To abolish capital punishment at the front, which was reintroduced by Kerensky.

Complete freedom of propaganda is to be reestablished in the country. All soldiers and revolutionary officers now under arrest for so-called political "crimes" are at once to be set free.

\*

The ex-Premier Kerensky, overthrown by the people, refuses to submit to the Congress of Soviets and attempts to struggle against the legal Government elected by the All-Russian Congress—the Council of People's Commissars. The front has refused to aid Kerensky. Moscow has rallied to the new Government. In many cities (Minsk, Moghilev, Kharkov) the power is in the hands of the Soviets. No infantry detachment consents to march against the Workers' and Peasants' Government, which, in accord with the firm will of the Army and the people, has begun peace negotiations and has given the land to the peasants. . . .

We give public warning that if the Cossacks do not halt Kerensky, who has deceived them and is leading them against Petrograd, the revolutionary forces will rise with all their might for the defense of the precious conquests of the Revolution—Peace and Land.

Citizens of Petrograd! Kerensky fled from the city, abandoning the authority to Kishkin, who wanted to surrender the capital to the Germans; Rutenburg, of the Black Band, who sabotaged the Municipal Food Supply; and Palchinsky, hated by the whole democracy. Kerensky has fled, abandoning you to the Germans, to famine, to bloody massacres. The revolting people have arrested Kerensky's Ministers, and you have seen how the order and supplying of Petrograd at once improved. Kerensky, at the demand of the aristocrat proprietors, the capitalists, speculators, marches against you for the purpose of giving back the land to the landowners, and continuing the hated and ruinous war.

Citizens of Petrograd! We know that the great majority of you are in favor of the peoples' revolutionary authority, against the Kornilovtsi led by Kerensky. Do not be deceived by the lying declarations of the impotent bourgeois conspirators, who will be pitilessly crushed.

Workers, soldiers, peasants! We call upon you for revolutionary devotion and discipline.

Millions of peasants and soldiers are with us.

The victory of the people's Revolution is assured!

## 40 (p. 762). ACTS OF THE COUNCIL OF PEOPLE'S COMMISSARS

In this book I am giving only such decrees as are in my opinion pertinent to the Bolshevik conquest of power. The rest belong to a detailed account of the structure of the Soviet State, for which I have no place in this work. This will be dealt with very fully in the second volume, now in preparation, *Kornilov to Brest-Litovsk*.

### Concerning Dwelling-Places

1. The independent Municipal Self-Governments have the right to sequestrate all unoccupied or uninhabited dwelling-places.

2. The Municipalities may, according to laws and arrangements established by them, install in all available lodgings citizens who have no place to live, or who live in congested or unhealthy lodgings.

3. The Municipalities may establish a service of inspection of dwelling-places, organize it, and define its powers.

4. The Municipalities may issue orders on the institution of House Committees, define their organization, their powers, and give them juridicial authority.

5. The Municipalities may create Housing Tribunals, define their powers and their authority.

6. This decree is promulgated by telegraph.

*People's Commissar of the Interior,*
A. I. RYKOV

*

## On Social Insurance

The Russian proletariat has inscribed on its banners the promise of complete Social Insurance of wage-workers, as well as of the town and village poor. The Government of the Czar, the proprietors and the capitalists, as well as the Government of coalition and conciliation, failed to realize the desires of the workers with regard to Social Insurance.

The Workers' and Peasants' Government, relying upon the support of the Soviets of Workers', Soldiers', and Peasants' Deputies, announces to the working class of Russia and to the town and village poor, that it will immediately prepare laws on Social Insurance based on the formulas proposed by the Labor organizations:

1. Insurances for all wage-earners without exception, as well as for all urban and rural poor.

2. Insurance to cover all categories of loss of working capacity, such as illness, infirmities, old age, child-birth, widowhood, orphanage, and unemployment.

3. All the costs of insurance to be charged to employers.

4. Compensation of at least full wages in all loss of working capacity and unemployment.

5. Complete workers' self-government of all Insurance institutions.

In the name of the Government of the Russian Republic.

*The People's Commissar of Labor,*
ALEXANDER SHLIAPNIKOV

*

## On Popular Education

Citizens of Russia!

With the insurrection of 7 November the working masses have won for the first time the real power.

The All-Russian Congress of Soviets has temporarily transferred this power both to its Executive Committee and the Council of People's Commissars.

By the will of the revolutionary people, I have been appointed People's Commissar of Education.

The work of guiding in general the people's education, inasmuch as it remains with the central government, is, until the Constituent Assembly meets, entrusted to a Commission on the People's Education, whose chairman and executive is the People's Commissar.

Upon what fundamental proposition will rest this State Commission? How is its sphere of competence determined?

*The General Line of Educational Activity:* Every genuinely democratic power must, in the domain of education, in a country where illiteracy and ignorance reign supreme, make its first aim in the struggle against this darkness. It must acquire in the shortest time *universal literacy,* by organizing a network of schools answering to the demands of modern pedagogics; it must introduce universal, obligatory, and free tuition for all, and establish at the same time a series of such teachers' institutes and seminaries as will in the shortest time furnish a powerful army of people's teachers so necessary for the universal instruction of the population of our boundless Russia.

*Decentralization:* The State Commission on People's Education is by no means a central power governing the institutions of instruction and education. On the contrary, the entire school work ought to be transferred to the organs of local self-government. The independent work of the workers, soldiers, and peasants, establishing on their own initiative cultural educational organizations, must be given full autonomy, both by the State center and the Municipal centers.

The work of the State Commission serves as a link and helpmate to organize resources of material and moral support to the Municipal and private institutions, particularly to those with a class-character established by the workers.

*The State Committee on People's Education:* A whole series of invaluable law projects was elaborated from the beginning of the Revolution by the State Committee for People's Education, a tolerably democratic body as to its composition, and rich in experts. The State Commission sincerely desires the collaboration of this Committee.

It has addressed itself to the bureau of the Committee, with the request at once to convoke an extraordinary session of the Committee for the fulfillment of the following program.

1. The revision of rules of representation in the Committee, in the sense of greater democratization.

2. The revision of the Committee's rights in the sense of widening them, and of converting the Committee into a fundamental State institute for the elaboration of law projects calculated to recognize public instruction and education in Russia upon democratic principles.

3. The revision, jointly with the new State Commission, of the

laws already created by the Committee, a revision required by the fact that in editing them the Committee had to take into account the bourgeois spirit of previous Ministries, which obstructed it even in this its narrowed form.

After this revision these laws will be put into effect without any bureaucratic red tape, in the revolutionary order.

*The Pedagogues and the Societists:* The State Commission welcomes the pedagogues to the bright and honorable work of educating the people—the masters of the country.

No one measure in the domain of the people's education ought to be adopted by any power without the attentive deliberation of those who represent the pedagogues.

On the other hand, a decision cannot by any means be reached exclusively through the cooperation of specialists. This refers as well to reforms of the institutes of general education.

The cooperation of the pedagogues with the social forces: this is how the Commission will work both in its own constitution, in the State Committee, and in all its activities.

As its first task the Commission considers the improvement of the teachers' status, and first of all of those very poor though almost most important contributors to the work of culture—the elementary school-teachers. Their just demands ought to be satisfied at once and at any cost. The proletariat of the schools has in vain demanded an increase of salary to one hundred roubles per month. It would be a disgrace any longer to keep in poverty the teachers of the overwhelming majority of the Russian people.

But a real democracy cannot stop at mere literacy, at universal elementary instruction. It must endeavor to organize a uniform secular school of several grades. The ideal is, equal and if possible higher education for all citizens. So long as this idea has not been realized for all, the natural transition through all the schooling grades up to the university—a transition to a higher stage—must depend entirely upon the pupil's aptitude, and not upon the resources of his family.

The problem of a genuinely democratic organization of instruction is particularly difficult in a country impoverished by a long, criminal, imperialistic war; but the workers who have taken the power must remember that education will serve them as the greatest instrument in their struggle for a better lot and for a spiritual growth. However needful it may be to curtail other articles of the people's budget, the expenses on education must stand high. A large educational budget is the pride and glory of a nation. The free and enfranchised peoples of Russia will not forget this.

The fight against illiteracy and ignorance cannot be confined to a thorough establishment of school education for children and youths. Adults, too, will be anxious to save themselves from the debasing position of a man who cannot read and write. The school for adults must occupy a conspicuous place in the general plan of popular instruction.

*Instruction and Education:* One must emphasize the difference between instruction and education.

Instruction is the transmission of ready knowledge by the teacher to his pupil. Education is a creative process. The personality of the individual is being "educated" throughout life, is being formed, grows richer in content, stronger and more perfect.

The toiling masses of the people—workmen, the peasants, the soldiers—are thirsting for elementary and advanced instruction. But they are also thirsting for education. Neither the government nor the intellectuals nor any other power outside of themselves can give it to them. The school, the book, the theater, the museum, etc., may here be only aids. They have their own ideas, formed by their social position, so different from the position of those ruling classes and intellectuals who have hitherto created culture. They have their own ideas, their own emotions, their own ways of approaching the problems of personality and society. The city laborer, according to his own fashion, the rural toiler according to his, will each build his clear world-conception permeated with the class-idea of the workers. There is no more superb or beautiful phenomenon than the one of which our nearest descendants will be both witnesses and participants: the building by collective Labor of its own general, rich, and free soul.

Instruction will surely be an important but not a decisive element. What is more important here is the criticism, the creativeness of the masses themselves; for science and art have only in some of their parts a general human importance. They suffer radical changes with every far-reaching class upheaval.

Throughout Russia, particularly among the city laborers, but also among the peasants, a powerful wave of cultural educational movement has arisen; workers' and soldiers' organizations of this kind are multiplying rapidly. To meet them, to lend them support, to clear the road before them, is the first task of a revolutionary and popular government in the domain of democratic education.

*The Constituent Assembly* will doubtless soon begin its work. It alone can permanently establish the order of national and social life in our country, and at the same time the general character of the organization of popular education.

Now, however, with the passage of power to the Soviets, the really democratic character of the Constituent Assembly is assured. The line which the State Commission, relying upon the State Committee, will follow, will hardly suffer any modification under the influence of the Constituent Assembly. Without predetermining it, the new People's Government considers itself within its rights in enacting in this domain a series of measures which aim at encircling and enlightening as soon as possible the spiritual life of the country.

*The Ministry:* The present work must in the interim proceed through the Ministry of the People's Education. Of all the necessary alterations in its composition and construction the State Commission will have charge, elected by the Executive Committee of the Soviets and the State Committee. Of course the order of State authority in the domain of the people's education will be established by the Constituent Assembly. Until then the Ministry must play the part of the executive apparatus for both the State Committee and the State Commission for People's Education.

The pledge of the country's effort of the working people and of the honest enlightened intellectuals will lead the country out of its painful crisis, and through complete democracy to the reign of Socialism and the brotherhood of nations.

*People's Commissar on Education,*
A. V. LUNACHARSKY

*

*On the Order in Which the Laws are to be Ratified and Published*

1. Until the convocation of the Constituent Assembly, the enacting and publishing of laws shall be carried out in the order decreed by the present Provisional Workmen's and Peasants' Government, elected by the All-Russian Congress of Workers', Peasants', and Soldiers' Deputies.

2. Every Bill is presented for consideration of the Government by the respective Ministry, signed by the duly authorized People's Commissar; or it is presented by the legislative section attached to the Government, signed by the chief of the section.

3. After its ratification by the Government the decree in its final edition, in the name of the Russian Republic, is signed by the president of the Council of People's Commissars, or for him by the People's Commissar who presented it for the consideration of the Government, and is then published.

4. The date of publishing it in the official *Gazette of the Provisional Workmen's and Peasants' Government* is the date of its becoming law.

5. In the decree there may be appointed a date, other than the date

of publication, on which it shall become law, or it may be promulgated by telegraph; in which case it is to be regarded in every locality as becoming law upon the publication of the telegram.

6. The promulgation of legislative Acts of the Government of the State Senate is abolished. The Legislative Section attached to the Council of People's Commissars issues periodically a collection of regulations and orders of the Governments which possess the force of law.

7. The Central Executive Committee of the Soviets of Workers', Peasants', and Soldiers' Deputies (Tsay-ee-kah) has at all times the right to cancel, alter, or annul any of the Government decrees.

*In the name of the Russian Republic, the President of the Council of People's Commissars,*

V. ULYANOV–LENIN

## 41 (p. 763). The Liquor Problem

*Order Issued by the Military Revolutionary Committee*

1. Until further order the production of alcohol and alcoholic drinks is prohibited.

2. It is ordered to all producers of alcohol and alcoholic drinks to inform not later than on the twenty-seventh inst. of the exact site of their stores.

3. All culprits against this order will be tried by a Military Revolutionary Court.

THE MILITARY REVOLUTIONARY COMMITTEE

*

## Order No. 2

*From the Committee of the Finland Guard Reserve Regiment to all House Committees and to the citizens of Vasili Ostrov.*

The bourgeoisie has chosen a very sinister method of fighting against the proletariat; it has established in various parts of the city huge wine depots, and distributes liquor among the soldiers, in this manner attempting to sow dissatisfaction in the ranks of the Revolutionary army.

It is herewith ordered to all house committees that at 3 o'clock, the time set for posting this order, they shall in person and secretly notify the President of the Committee of the Finland Guard Regiment, concerning the amount of wine in their premises.

Those who violate this order will be arrested and given trial before a merciless court, and their property will be confiscated, and the stock of wine discovered will be

**BLOWN UP WITH DYNAMITE**

*two hours after this warning*

because more lenient measures, as experience has shown, do not bring the desired results.

**REMEMBER, THERE WILL BE NO OTHER WARNING BEFORE THE EXPLOSIONS**

*Regimental Committee of the Finland Guard Regiment*

## Chapter 9

42 (p. 776). MILITARY REVOLUTIONARY COMMITTEE. BULLETIN No. 2

November the twelfth, in the evening, Kerensky sent a proposition to the revolutionary troops—"to lay down their arms." Kerensky's men opened artillery fire. Our artillery answered and compelled the enemy to be silent. The Cossacks assumed the offensive. The deadly fire of the sailors, the Red Guards, and the soldiers forced the Cossacks to retreat. Our armored cars rushed in among the ranks of the enemy. The enemy is fleeing. Our troops are in pursuit. The order has been given to arrest Kerensky. Tsarskoye Selo has been taken by the revolutionary troops.

*The Lettish Riflemen:* The Military Revolutionary Committee has received precise information that the valiant Lettish Riflemen have arrived from the front and taken up a position in the rear of Kerensky's bands.

*From the Staff of the Military Revolutionary Committee*

The seizure of Gatchina and Tsarskoye Selo by Kerensky's detachments is to be explained by the complete absence of artillery and machine-guns in these places, whereas Kerensky's cavalry was provided with artillery from the beginning. The last two days were days of enforced work for our Staff, to provide the necessary quantity of guns, machine-guns, field telephones, etc., for the revolutionary troops. When this work—with the energetic assistance of the District Soviets and the factories (the Putilov Works, Obukhov and others)—was accomplished, the issue of the expected encounter left no place for doubt; on the side of the revolutionary troops there was not only a surplus in quantity and such a powerful material base as Petrograd, but also an enormous moral advantage. All the Petrograd regiments moved out to the positions with tremendous enthusiasm. The Garrison Conference elected a Control Commission of five soldiers, thus securing a complete unity between the commander-in-chief and the garrison. At the Garrison Conference it was unanimously decided to begin decisive action.

The artillery fire on the twelfth of November developed with extraordinary force by 3 P.M. The Cossacks were completely demoralized. A parlementaire came from them to the staff of the detachment at Krasnoye Selo, and proposed to stop the firing, threatening otherwise to take "decisive" measures. He was answered that the firing would cease when Kerensky laid down his arms.

In the developing encounter all sections of the troops—the sailors, soldiers, and the Red Guard—showed unlimited courage. The sailors continued to advance until they had fired their last cartridges. The number of casualties has not been established yet, but it is larger on the part of the counter-revolutionary troops, who experienced great losses through one of our armored cars.

Kerensky's staff, fearing that they would be surrounded, gave the order to retreat, which retreat speedily assumed a disorderly character. By 11–12 P.M. Tsarskoye Selo, including the wireless station, was entirely occupied by the troops of the Soviets. The Cossacks retreated toward Gatchina and Colpinno.

The morale of the troops is beyond all praise. The order has been given to pursue the retreating Cossacks. From the Tsarskoye Selo station a radio-telegram was sent immediately to the front and to all local Soviets throughout Russia. Further details will be communicated. . . .

## 43 (p. 780). Events of the Thirteenth in Petrograd

Three regiments of the Petrograd garrison refused to take any part in the battle against Kerensky. On the morning of the thirteenth they summoned to a joint conference sixty delegates from the front, in order to find some way to stop the civil war. This conference appointed a committee to go and persuade Kerensky's troops to lay down their arms. They proposed to ask the Government soldiers the following questions: Will the soldiers and Cossacks of Kerensky recognize the Tsay-ee-kah as the repository of Government power, responsible to the Congress of Soviets? Will the soldiers and Cossacks accept the Land and Peace decrees? Will they agree to cease hostilities and return to their units? Will they consent to the arrest of Kerensky, Krasnov, and Savinkov?

At the meeting of the Petrograd Soviet, Zinoviev said,

> It would be foolish to think that this committee could finish the affair. The enemy can only be broken by force. However, it would be a crime for us not to try every peaceful means to bring the Cossacks over to us. . . . What we need is a military victory. . . . The news of an armistice is premature. Our Staff will be ready to conclude an armistice when the enemy can no longer do any harm. . . .
>
> At present the influence of our victory is creating new political conditions. . . . Today the Socialist Revolutionaries are inclined to admit the Bolsheviki into the new Government. . . . A decisive victory is indispensable, so that those who hesitate will have no further hesitation. . . .

At the City Duma all attention was concentrated on the formation of the new Government. In many factories and barracks already Revolutionary Tribunals were operating, and the Bolsheviki were threatening to set up more of these, and try Gotz and Avksentiev before them. Dan proposed that an ultimatum be sent demanding the abolition of these Revolutionary Tribunals, or the other members of the Conference would immediately break off all negotiations with the Bolsheviki.

Shingariov, Cadet, declared that the Municipality ought not to take part in any agreement with the Bolsheviki. . . .

> Any agreement with the maniacs is impossible until they lay down their arms and recognize the authority of independent courts of law. . . .

Yartsev, for the Yedinstvo group, declared that any agreement with the Bolsheviki would be equivalent to a Bolshevik victory. . . .

Mayor Schreider, for the Socialist Revolutionaries, stated that he was opposed to all agreement with the Bolsheviki. . . .

As for a Government, that ought to spring from the popular will; and since the popular will has been expressed in the municipal elections, the popular will which can create a Government is actually concentrated in the Duma. . . .

After other speakers, of which only the representative of the Mensheviki Internationalists was in favor of considering the admission of the Bolsheviki in the new Government, the Duma voted to continue its representatives in the Vikzhel's conference, but to insist upon the restoration of the Provisional Government before everything, and to exclude the Bolsheviki from the new power. . . .

## 44 (p. 781). TRUCE. KRASNOV'S ANSWER TO THE COMMITTEE FOR SALVATION

In answer to your telegram proposing an immediate armistice, the Supreme Commander, not wishing further futile bloodshed, consents to enter into negotiations and to establish relations between the armies of the Government and the insurrectionists. He proposes to the General Staff of the insurrectionists to recall its regiments to Petrograd, to declare the line Ligovno-Pulkovo-Colpinno neutral, and to allow the advance-guards of the Government cavalry to enter Tsarskoye Selo, for the purpose of establishing order. The answer to this proposal must be placed in the hands of our envoys before eight o'clock tomorrow morning.

KRASNOV

## 45 (p. 793). EVENTS AT TSARSKOYE SELO

On the evening that Kerensky's troops retreated from Tsarskoye Selo, some priests organized a religious procession through the streets of the town, making speeches to the citizens, in which they asked the people to support the rightful authority, the Provisional Government. When the Cossacks had retreated, and the first Red Guards entered the town, witnesses reported that the priests had incited the people against the Soviets, and had said prayers at the grave of Rasputin, which lies behind the Imperial Palace. One of the priests, Father Ivan Kuchurov, was arrested and shot by the infuriated Red Guards. . . .

Just as the Red Guards entered the town the electric lights were shut off, plunging the streets in complete darkness. The director of the electric light plant, Lubovich, was arrested by the Soviet troops and asked why he had shut off the lights. He was found some time later in the room where he had been imprisoned with a revolver in his hand and a bullet hole in his temple.

The Petrograd anti-Bolshevik papers came out next day with headlines, "Plekhanov's temperature 39 degrees!" Plekhanov lived at Tsarskoye Selo, where he was lying ill in bed. Red Guards arrived at the house and searched it for arms, questioning the old man.

"What class of society do you belong to?" they asked him.

"I am a revolutionist," answered Plekhanov, "who for forty years has devoted his life to the struggle for liberty!"

"Anyway," said a workman, "you have now sold yourself to the bourgeoisie!"

The workers no longer knew Plekhanov, pioneer of the Russian Social Democracy!

## 46 (p. 793). APPEAL OF THE SOVIET GOVERNMENT

The detachments at Gatchina, deceived by Kerensky, have laid down their arms and decided to arrest Kerensky. The chief of the counter-revolutionary campaign has fled. The Army, by an enormous majority, has pronounced in favor of the second All-Russian Congress of Soviets, and of the Government which it has created. Scores of delegates from the front have hastened to Petrograd to assure the Soviet Government of the Army's fidelity. No twisting of the facts, no calumny against the revolutionary workers, soldiers, and peasants have been able to defeat the People. The Workers' and Soldiers' Revolution is victorious. . . .

The Tsay-ee-kah appeals to the troops which march under the flag of the counter-revolution, and invites them immediately to lay down their arms—to shed no longer the blood of their brothers in the interests of a handful of landowners and capitalists. The Workers', Soldiers', and Peasants' Revolution curses those who remain even for a moment under the flag of the People's enemies. . . .

Cossacks! Come over to the rank of the victorious People! Railwaymen, postmen, telegraphers—all, all support the new Government of the People!

**Chapter 10**

47 (p. 797). Damage to the Kremlin

I myself verified the damage to the Kremlin, which I visited immediately after the bombardment. The Little Nikolai Palace, a building of no particular importance, which was occupied occasionally by receptions of one of the Grand Duchesses, had served as barracks for the *yunkers*. It was not only bombarded, but pretty well sacked; fortunately there was nothing in it of particular historical value.

Usspensky Cathedral had a shell-hole in one of the cupolas, but except for a few feet of mosaic in the ceiling was undamaged. The frescoes on the porch of Blagoveshchensky Cathedral were badly damaged by a shell. Another shell hit the corner of Ivan Veliki. Chudovsky Monastery was hit about thirty times, but only one shell went through a window into the interior, the others breaking the brick window-molding and the roof-cornices.

The clock over the Spasskaya Gate was smashed. Troitsky Gate was battered, but easily reparable. One of the lower towers had lost its brick spire.

The church of St. Basil was untouched, as was the great Imperial Palace, with all the treasures of Moscow and Petrograd in its cellar, and the crown jewels in the Treasury. These places were not even entered.

48 (p. 798). Lunacharsky's Declaration

Comrades! You are the young masters of the country, and although now you have much to do and think about, you must know how to defend your artistic and scientific treasures.

Comrades! That which is happening in Moscow is a horrible, irreparable misfortune.... The People in its struggle for the power has mutilated our glorious capital.

It is particularly terrible in these days of violent struggle, of destructive warfare, to be Commissar of Public Education. Only the hope of the victory of Socialism, the source of a new and superior culture, brings me comfort. On me weighs the responsibility of protecting the artistic wealth of the people.... Not being able to remain at my post, where I had no influence, I resigned. My comrades, the other Commissars considered this resignation inadmissible. I shall therefore remain at my post.... And, moreover, I understand that the damage done to the Kremlin is not as serious as has been reported....

But I beg you, comrades, to give me your support.... Preserve for yourselves and your descendants the beauty of our land; be the guardians of the property of the People.

Soon, very soon, even the most ignorant, who have been held in ignorance so long, will awake and understand what a source of joy, strength, and wisdom is art....

## 49 (p. 804). REVOLUTIONARY FINANCIAL MEASURE

### Order

In virtue of the powers vested in me by the Military Revolutionary Committee attached to the Moscow Soviet of Workers' and Soldiers' Deputies, I decree:

1. All banks with branches, the Central State Savings Bank with branches, and the savings banks at the Post and Telegraph offices are to be opened beginning 22 November, from 11 A.M. to 1 P.M., until further order.

2. On current accounts and on the books of the savings banks, payments will be made by the above-mentioned institutions of not more than 150 roubles during the course of the next week.

3. Payments of amounts exceeding 150 roubles a week on current accounts and savings bank books, also payments on other accounts of all kinds will be allowed during the next three days, 22, 23, and 24 November, only in the following cases:

(a) On the accounts of military organizations for the satisfaction of their needs;

(b) For the payment of salaries of employees and the earnings of workers according to the tables and lists certified by the Factory Committees or Soviets of Employees, and attested by the signatures of the Commissars, or the representatives of the Military Revolutionary Committee, and the district Military Revolutionary Committee.

4. Not more than 150 roubles are to be paid against drafts; the remaining sums are to be entered on current account, payments on which are to be made in the order established by the present decree.

5. All other banking operations are prohibited during these three days.

6. The receipt of money on all accounts is allowed for any amount.

7. The representatives of the Finance Council for the certification of the authorization indicated in Clause 3 will hold their office in the building of the Stock Exchange, Ilyinka Street, from 10 A.M. to 2 P.M.

8. The Banks and Savings Banks shall send the totals of daily cash operations by 5 P.M. to the headquarters of the Soviet, Skobeliev Square, to the Military Revolutionary Committee, for the Finance Council.

9. All employees and managers of credit institutions of all kinds who refuse to comply with this decree shall be responsible as enemies of the Revolution, and of the mass of the population, before the Revolutionary Tribunals. Their names shall be published for general information.

10. For the control of the operations of Branches of the Savings Banks and Banks within the limits of this decree, the district Military Revolutionary Committees shall elect three representatives and appoint their place of business.

*Fully Authorized Commissar of the Military Revolutionary Committee,*
S. SHEVERDIN-MAKSIMENKO

## Chapter 11

### 50 (p. 809). LIMITATIONS TO THIS CHAPTER

This chapter extends over a period of two months, more or less. It covers the time of negotiations with the Allies, the negotiations and armistice with the Germans, and the beginning of the Peace negotiations at Brest-Litovsk, as well as the period in which were laid the foundations of the Soviet State.

However, it is no part of my purpose in this book to describe and interpret these very important historical events, which require more space. They are therefore reserved for another volume, *Kornilov to Brest-Litovsk.*

In this chapter, then, I have confined myself to the Soviet Government's attempts to consolidate its political power at home, and sketched its successive conquests of hostile domestic elements—which process was temporarily interrupted by the disastrous Peace of Brest-Litovsk.

51 (p. 809). Preamble—Declaration of the Rights of the Peoples of Russia

The October Revolution of the workers and peasants began under the common banner of Emancipation.

The peasants are being emancipated from the power of the land-owners, for there is no longer the landowners' property right in the land—it has been abolished. The soldiers and sailors are being emancipated from the power of autocratic generals, for generals will henceforth be elective and subject to recall. The working men are being emancipated from the whims and arbitrary will of the capitalists, for henceforth there will be established the control of the workers over mills and factories. Everything living and capable of life is being emancipated from the hateful shackles.

There remain only the peoples of Russia, who have suffered and are suffering oppression and arbitrariness, and whose emancipation must immediately begin, whose liberation must be effected resolutely and definitely.

During the period of Czarism the peoples of Russia were systematically incited one against another. The results of such a policy are known; massacres and *pogroms* on the one hand, slavery of peoples on the other.

There can be and there must be no return to this disgraceful policy. Henceforth the policy of a voluntary and honest union of the peoples of Russia must be substituted.

In the period of imperialism, after the March revolution, when the power was transferred into the hands of the Cadet bourgeoisie, the naked policy of provocation gave way to one of cowardly distrust of the peoples of Russia, to a policy of fault-finding, of meaningless "freedom," and "equality" of peoples. The results of such a policy are known; the growth of national enmity, the impairment of mutual confidence.

An end must be put to this unworthy policy of falsehood and distrust, of fault-finding and provocation. Henceforth it must be replaced by an open and honest policy leading to the complete mutual confidence of the peoples of Russia. Only as the result of such a trust can there be found an honest and lasting union of the peoples of Russia. Only as the result of such a union can the workers and peasants of the peoples of Russia be cemented into one revolutionary force able to resist all attempts on the part of the imperialist-annexationist bourgeoisie.

## 52 (p. 810). DECREES

### On the Nationalization of the Banks

In the interest of the regular organization of the national economy, of the thorough eradication of bank speculation and the complete emancipation of the workers, peasants, and the whole laboring population from the exploitation of banking capital, and with a view to the establishment of a single national bank of the Russian Republic which shall serve the real interests of the people and the poorer classes, the Central Executive Committee (Tsay-ee-kah) resolves:

1. The banking business is declared a State monopoly.
2. All existing private joint-stock banks and banking offices are merged in the State Bank.
3. The assets and liabilities of the liquidated establishments are taken over by the State Bank.
4. The order of the merger of private banks in the State Bank is to be determined by a special decree.
5. The temporary administration of the affairs of the private banks is entrusted to the board of the State Bank.
6. The interests of the small depositors will be safeguarded.

\*

### On the Equality of Rank of All Military Men

In realization of the will of the revolutionary people regarding the prompt and decisive abolition of all remnants of former inequality in the Army, the Council of People's Commissars decrees:

1. All ranks and grades in the Army, beginning with the rank of Corporal and ending with the rank of General, are abolished. The Army of the Russian Republic consists now of free and equal citizens, bearing the honorable title of Soldiers of the Revolutionary Army.
2. All privileges connected with the former ranks and grades, also all outward marks of distinction, are abolished.
3. All addressing by titles is abolished.
4. All decorations, orders, and other marks of distinction are abolished.

5. With the abolition of the rank of officer all separate officers' organizations are abolished.

Note.—Orderlies are left only for headquarters, chanceries, Committees, and other Army organizations.

*President of the Council of People's Commissars,*
VL. ULYANOV (LENIN)
*People's Commissar for Military and Naval Affairs,*
N. KRYLENKO
*People's Commissar for Military Affairs,*
N. PODVOISKY
*Secretary of the Council,*
N. GORBUNOV

*

*On the Elective Principle and the Organization of Authority in the Army*

1. The army serving the will of the toiling people is subject to its supreme representative—the Council of People's Commissars.

2. Full authority within the limits of military units and combinations is vested in the respective Soldiers' Committees of Soviets.

3. Those phases of life and activity of the troops which are already under the jurisdiction of the Committees are now formally placed in their direct control. Over such branches of activity which the Committees cannot assume, the control of the Soldiers' Soviets is established.

4. The election of commanding Staff and officers is introduced. All commanders up to the commanders of regiments, inclusive, are elected by general suffrage of squads, platoons, companies, squadrons, batteries, divisions (artillery, 2–3 batteries), and regiments. All commanders higher than the commander of a regiment, and up to the Supreme Commander, inclusive, are elected by congresses or conferences of Committees.

Note.—By the term "conference" must be understood a meeting of the respective Committees together with delegates of committees one degree lower in rank. [Such as a "conference" of Regimental Committees with delegates from Company Committees.—Author.]

5. The elected commanders above the rank of commander of regiment must be confirmed by the nearest Supreme Committee.

Note.—In the event of a refusal by a Supreme Committee to confirm an elected commander, with a statement of reasons for such refusal, a commander elected by the lower Committee a second time must be confirmed.

6. The commanders of Armies are elected by Army congresses.

Commanders of Fronts are elected by congresses of the respective Fronts.

7. To posts of a technical character, demanding special knowledge or other practical preparation, namely: doctors, engineers, technicians, telegraph and wireless operators, aviators, automobilists, etc., only such persons as possess the required special knowledge may be elected, by the Committees of the units of the respective services.

8. Chiefs of Staff must be chosen from among persons with special military training for that post.

9. All other members of the Staff are appointed by the Chief of Staff, and confirmed by the respective congresses.

Note.—All persons with special training must be listed in a special list.

10. The right is reserved to retire from the service all commanders on active service who are not elected by the soldiers to any post, and who consequently are ranked as privates.

11. All other functions besides these pertaining to the command, with the exception of posts in the economic departments, are filled by the appointment of the respective elected commanders.

12. Detailed instructions regarding the election of the commanding Staff will be published separately.

*President of the Council of People's Commissars,*
VL. ULYANOV (LENIN)
*People's Commissar for Military and Naval Affairs,*
N. KRYLENKO
*People's Commissar for Military Affairs,*
N. PODVOISKY
*Secretary of the Council,*
N. GORBUNOV

\*

*On the Abolition of Classes and Titles*

1. All classes and class divisions, all class privileges and delimitations, all class organizations and institutions and all civil ranks are abolished.

2. All classes of society (nobles, merchants, petty bourgeois, etc.), and all titles (Prince, Count, and others), and all denominations of civil rank (Privy State Councillors and others), are abolished, and there is established the general denomination of Citizen of the Russian Republic.

3. The property and institutions of the classes of nobility are transferred to the corresponding autonomous Zemstvos.

4. The property of merchant and bourgeois organizations is transferred immediately to the Municipal Self-Government.

5. All class institutions of any sort, with their property, their rules of procedure, and their archives, are transferred to the administration of the Municipalities and Zemstvos.

6. All articles of existing laws applying to these matters are herewith repealed.

7. The present decree becomes effective on the day it is published and applied by the Soviets of Workers', Soldiers', and Peasants' Deputies.

The present decree has been confirmed by the Tsay-ee-kah at the meeting of 23 November 1917, and signed by:

> *President of the Tsay-ee-kah,*
> SVERDLOV
> *President of the Council of People's Commissars,*
> VL. ULYANOV (LENIN)
> *Executive of the Council of People's Commissars,*
> V. BONCH-BRUEVICH
> *Secretary of the Council,*
> N. GORBUNOV

On 3 December the Council of People's Commissars resolved "to reduce the salaries of functionaries and employees in all Governmental institutions and establishments, general or special, without exception."

To begin with, the Council fixed the salary of a People's Commissar at 500 roubles per month, with 100 roubles additional for each grown member of the family incapable of work....

This was the highest salary paid to any Government official....

53 (p. 811).

Countess Panina was arrested and brought to trial before the first Supreme Revolutionary Tribunal. The trial is described in the chapter on "Revolutionary Justice" in my forthcoming volume, *Kornilov to Brest-Litovsk*. The prisoner was sentenced to "return the money, and then be liberated to the public contempt." In other words, she was set free!

## 54 (p. 813). RIDICULE OF THE NEW RÉGIME

From *Drug Naroda* (Menshevik), 18 November:

The story of the "immediate peace" of the Bolsheviki reminds us of a joyous moving-picture film. . . . Neratov runs—Trotsky pursues; Neratov climbs a wall, Trotsky too; Neratov dives into the water—Trotsky follows; Neratov climbs on to the roof—Trotsky right behind him; Neratov hides under the bed—and Trotsky has him! He has him! Naturally peace is immediately signed. . . .

All is empty and silent at the Ministry of Foreign Affairs. The couriers are respectful, but their faces wear a caustic expression. . . .

How about arresting an ambassador and signing an armistice or a Peace Treaty with him? But they are strange folk, these ambassadors. They keep silent as if they had heard nothing. Hola, hola, England, France, Germany! We have signed an armistice with you! Is it possible that you know nothing about it? Nevertheless, it has been published in all the papers and posted on the walls. On a Bolshevik's word of honor, Peace has been signed. We're not asking much of you; you just have to write two words. . . .

The ambassadors remain silent. The Powers remain silent. All is empty and silent in the office of the Minister of Foreign Affairs.

"Listen," says Robespierre-Trotsky to his assistant Marat-Uritsky, "run over to the British Ambassador's, tell him we're proposing peace."

"Go yourself," says Marat-Uritsky. "He's not receiving."

"Telephone him, then."

"I've tried. The receiver's off the hook."

"Send him a telegram."

"I did."

"Well, with what result?"

Marat-Uritsky sighs and does not answer. Robespierre-Trotsky spits furiously into the corner. . . .

"Listen, Marat," recommences Trotsky, after a moment. "We must absolutely show that we're conducting an active foreign policy. How can we do that?"

"Launch another decree about arresting Neratov," answers Uritsky, with a profound air.

"Marat, you're a blockhead!" cries Trotsky. All of a sudden he arises, terrible and majestic, looking at this moment like Robespierre. "Write, Uritsky!" he says with severity. "Write a letter to the British ambassador, a registered letter with receipt demanded. Write! I also will write! The peoples of the world await an immediate peace!"

In the enormous and empty Ministry of Foreign Affairs are to be heard only the sound of two typewriters. With his own hands Trotsky is conducting an active foreign policy. . . .

## 55 (p. 822). On the Question of an Agreement

[Announcement, posted on the walls of Petrograd, of the result of a meeting of representatives of the garrison regiments, called to consider the question of forming a new Government.]

To the attention of All Workers and All Soldiers.

November eleventh, in the club of the Preobrazhensky Regiment, was held an extraordinary meeting of representatives of all the units of the Petrograd garrison.

The meeting was called upon the initiative of the Preobrazhensky and Semionovsky Regiments, for the discussion of the question as to which Socialist parties are for the power of the Soviets, which are against, which are for the people, which against, and if an agreement between them is possible.

The representatives of the Tsay-ee-kah, of the Municipal Duma, of the Avksentiev Peasants' Soviets, and of all the political parties from the Bolsheviki to the Populist Socialists, were invited to the meeting.

After long deliberation, having heard the declarations of all parties and organizations, the meeting by a tremendous majority of votes agreed that only the Bolsheviki and the Left Socialist Revolutionaries are for the people, and that all the other parties are only attempting under cover of seeking an agreement, to deprive the people of the conquests won in the days of the great Workers' and Peasants' Revolution of November.

Here is the text of the resolution carried at this meeting of the Petrograd garrison, by 61 votes against 11, and 12 not voting:

"The garrison conference, summoned at the initiative of the Semionovsky and Preobrazhensky Regiments, on hearing the representatives of all the Socialist parties and popular organizations on the question of an agreement between the different political parties finds that:

"1. The representatives of the Tsay-ee-kah, the representatives of the Bolshevik party and the Left Socialist Revolutionaries, declared definitely that they stand for a Government of the Soviets, for the decrees on Land, Peace, and Workers' Control of Industry, and that upon this platform they are willing to agree with all the Socialist parties.

"2. At the same time the representatives of the other parties (Mensheviki, Socialist Revolutionaries) either gave no answer at all, or declared simply that they were opposed to the power of the Soviets and against the decrees on Land, Peace, and Workers' Control.

"In view of this the meeting resolves:

" '1. To express censure of all parties which, under cover of an agreement, wish practically to annul the popular conquests of the Revolution of November.

" '2. To express full confidence in the Tsay-ee-kah and the Council of People's Commissars, and to promise them complete support.'

"At the same time the meeting deems it necessary that the comrades Left Socialist Revolutionaries should enter the People's Government."

## 56 (p. 823). WINE "POGROMS"

It was afterward discovered that there was a regular organization, maintained by the Cadets, for provoking rioting among the soldiers. There would be telephone messages to the different barracks, announcing that wine was being given away at such and such an address, and when the soldiers arrived at the spot an individual would point out the location of the cellar. . . .

The Council of People's Commissars appointed a Commissar for the Fight Against Drunkenness, who, besides mercilessly putting down the wine riots, destroyed hundreds of thousands of bottles of liquor. The Winter Palace cellars, containing rare vintages valued at more than five million dollars, were at first flooded, and then the liquor was removed to Kronstadt and destroyed.

In this work the Kronstadt sailors, "flower and pride of the revolutionary forces," as Trotsky called them, acquitted themselves with iron self-discipline. . . .

57 (p. 824). OBLIGATORY ORDINANCE

1. The city of Petrograd is declared to be in a state of siege.
2. All assemblies, meetings, and congregations on the streets and squares are prohibited.
3. Attempts to loot wine-cellars, warehouses, factories, stores, business premises, private dwellings, etc., etc., *will be stopped by machine-gun fire without warning.*
4. House Committees, doormen, janitors, and Militiamen are charged with the duty of keeping strict order in all houses, courtyards, and in the streets, and house-doors and carriage entrances must be locked at 9 o'clock in the evening, and opened at 7 o'clock in the morning. After 9 o'clock in the evening only tenants may leave the house, under strict control of the House Committees.
5. Those guilty of the distribution, sale, or purchase of any kind of alcoholic liquor, and also those guilty of the violation of sections 2 and 4 will be immediately arrested and subjected to the most severe punishment.

Petrograd, 6 December, 3 o'clock in the night.

*Committee to Fight Against Pogroms, attached to the Executive Committee of the Soviet of Workers' and Soldiers' Deputies*

58 (p. 824). SPECULATORS

Two orders concerning them:

*Council of People's Commissars*
*To the Military Revolutionary Committee*

The disorganization of the food supply created by the war, and the lack of system, is becoming to the last degree acute, thanks to the speculators, marauders, and their followers on the railways, in the steamship offices, forwarding offices, etc.

Taking advantage of the nation's greatest misfortune, these criminal spoliators are playing with the health and life of millions of soldiers and workers, for their own benefit.

Such a situation cannot be borne a single day longer.

The Council of People's Commissars proposes to the Military Revolutionary Committee to take the most decisive measures toward the uprooting of speculation, sabotage, hiding of supplies, fraudulent detention of cargoes, etc.

All persons guilty of such actions shall be subject, by special orders of the Military Revolutionary Committee, to immediate arrest, and Confinement in the prisons of Kronstadt, pending their arraignment before the Revolutionary Tribunal.

All the popular organizations are invited to cooperate in the struggle against the spoliators of food supplies.

*President of the Council of People's Commissar,*
v. ULYANOV (LENIN)

Accepted for execution,
*Military Revolutionary Committee attached to the*
*C.E.C. of the Soviets of W. and S. Deputies*
Petrograd, 23 November 1917

*

*To All Honest Citizens*
*The Military Revolutionary Committee Decrees:*

Spoliators, marauders, speculators, are declared to be enemies of the People. . . .

The Military Revolutionary Committee proposes to all public organizations, to all honest citizens: to inform the Military Revolutionary Committee immediately of all cases of spoliation, marauding, speculation, which become known to them.

The struggle against this evil is the business of all honest people. The Military Revolutionary Committee expects the support of all to whom the interests of the People are dear.

The Military Revolutionary Committee will be merciless in pursuit of speculators and marauders.

THE MILITARY REVOLUTIONARY COMMITTEE
*Petrograd, 2 December 1917*

## 59 (p. 824). PURISHKEVICH'S LETTER TO KALEDIN

The situation at Petrograd is desperate. The City is cut off from the outside world and is entirely in the power of the Bolsheviki. . . . People are arrested in the streets, thrown into the Neva, drowned and imprisoned without any charge. Even Burtzev is shut up in Peter-Paul fortress, under strict guard.

The organization, at whose head I am, is working without rest to unite all the officers and what is left of the *yunker* schools, and to arm them. The situation cannot be saved except by creating regiments of officers and *yunkers*. Attacking with these regiments, and having gained a first success, we could later gain the aid of the garrison troops but without that first success it is impossible to count on a single soldier, because thousands of them are divided and terrorized by the scum which exists in every regiment. Most of the Cossacks are tainted by Bolshevik propaganda, thanks to the strange policy of General Dutov, who allowed to pass the moment when by decisive action something could have been obtained. The policy of negotiations and concessions has borne its fruits; all that is respectable is persecuted, and it is the *plebs* and the criminals who dominate—and nothing can be done except by shooting and hanging them.

We are awaiting you here, General, and at the moment of your arrival we shall advance with all the forces at our disposal. But for that we must establish some communication with you, and before all, clear up the following points:

(1) Do you know that in your name officers who could take part in the fight are being invited to leave Petrograd on the pretext of joining you?

(2) About when can we count on your arrival at Petrograd? We should like to know in order to coordinate our actions.

In spite of the criminal inaction of the conscious people here, which allowed the yoke of Bolshevism to be laid upon us—in spite of the extraordinary pig-headedness of the majority of officers, so difficult to organize—we believe in spite of all that Truth is on our side, and that we shall conquer the vicious and criminal forces who say that they are acting for motives of love of country and in order to save it. Whatever comes, we shall not permit ourselves to be struck down, and shall remain firm until the end.

Purishkevich, being brought to trial before the Revolutionary Tribunal, was given a short term of prison. . . .

60 (p. 824). THE DECREE ON THE MONOPOLY OF ADVERTISEMENTS

1. The printing of advertisements, in newspapers, books, billboards, kiosks, in offices and other establishments is declared to be a State monopoly.

2. Advertisements may only be published in the organs of the Provisional Workers' and Peasants' Government at Petrograd, and in the organs of local Soviets.

3. The proprietors of newspapers and advertising offices, as well as all employees of such establishments, should remain at their posts until the transfer of their advertisement business to the Government . . . superintending the uninterrupted continuation of their houses,

and turning over to the Soviets all private advertising and the sums received therefor, as well as all accounts and copy.

4. All managers of publications and businesses dealing with paid advertising, as well as their employees and workers, shall agree to hold a City Congress, and to join, first the City Trade Unions and then the All-Russian Unions, to organize more thoroughly and justly the advertising business in the Soviet publications, as well as to prepare better rules for the public utility of advertising.

5. All persons found guilty of having concealed documents or money, or having sabotaged the regulations indicated in paragraphs 3 and 4, will be punished by a sentence of not more than three years' imprisonment, and all their property will be confiscated.

6. The paid insertion of advertisements . . . in private publications, or under a masqued form, will also be severely penalized.

7. Advertising offices are confiscated by the Government, the owners being entitled to compensation in cases of necessity. Small proprietors, depositors and stockholders of the confiscated establishments will be reimbursed for all moneys held by them in the concern.

8. All buildings, offices, counters, and in general every establishment doing a business in advertising, should immediately inform the Soviet of Workers' and Soldiers' Deputies of its address, and proceed to the transfer of its business, under penalty of the punishment indicated in paragraph 5.

> *President of the Council of People's Commissars,*
> V. ULYANOV (LENIN)
> *People's Commissar for Public Instruction,*
> A. V. LUNACHARSKY
> *Secretary of the Council,*
> N. GORBUNOV

## 61 (p. 825). Two Proclamations

Lenin, *To the People of Russia:*

> Comrades, workers. Soldiers, peasants—all toilers!
> The Workers' and Peasants' Revolution has won at Petrograd, at Moscow. . . . From the front and the village arrive every day, every hour, greetings to the new Government. . . . The victory of the Revolution . . . is assured, seeing that it is sustained by the majority of the people.
> It is entirely understandable that the proprietors and the capitalists, the employees and functionaries closely allied with the bourgeoi-

sie—in a word, all the rich and all those who join hands with them—regard the new Revolution with hostility, oppose its success, threaten to halt the activity of the banks, and sabotage or obstruct the work of other establishments. . . . Every conscious worker understands perfectly well that we cannot avoid this hostility, because the high officials have set themselves against the People and do not wish to abandon their posts without resistance. The majority of the people is for us. For us is the majority of the workers and the oppressed of the whole world. We have justice on our side. Our ultimate victory is certain.

The resistance of the capitalists and high officials will be broken. No one will be deprived of his property without a special law on the nationalization of banks and financial syndicates. This law is in preparation. Not a worker will lose a single kopek; on the contrary, he will be assisted. Without at this moment establishing the new taxes, the new Government considers one of its primary duties to make a severe accounting and control on the reception of taxes decreed by the former régime. . . .

Comrades, workers! Remember that you yourselves direct the Government. No one will help you unless you organize yourselves and take into your own hands the affairs of the State. Your Soviets are now the organs of governmental power. . . . Strengthen them, establish a severe revolutionary control, pitilessly crush the attempts at anarchy on the part of drunkards, brigands, counter-revolutionary *yunkers*, and Kornilovists.

Establish a strict control over production and the accounting for products. Arrest and turn over to the Revolutionary Tribunal of the People everyone who injures the property of the People, by sabotage in production, by concealment of grain reserves, reserves of other products, by retarding the shipments of grain, by bringing confusion into the railroads, the posts, and the telegraphs, or in general opposing the great work of bringing Peace and transferring the Land to the peasants. . . .

Comrades, workers, soldiers, peasants—all toilers! Take immediately all local power into your hands. . . . Little by little, with the consent of the majority of peasants, we shall march firmly and unhesitatingly toward the victory of Socialism, which will fortify the advance-guards of the working class of the most civilized countries, and give to the peoples an enduring peace, and free them from every slavery and every exploitation.

62 (p. 825).

*To All Workers of Petrograd!*
Comrades! The Revolution is winning—the revolution has won. All the power has passed to our Soviets. The first weeks are the most difficult ones. The broken reaction must be finally crushed, a full triumph must be secured to our endeavors. The working class ought to—must—show in these days THE GREATEST FIRMNESS AND ENDURANCE, in order to facilitate the execution of all the aims of the new People's Government of Soviets. In the next few days decrees on the Labor question will be issued, and among the very first will be the decree on Workers' Control over the production and regulation of industry.

STRIKES AND DEMONSTRATIONS OF THE WORKER MASSES IN PETROGRAD NOW CAN ONLY DO HARM.

We ask you to cease immediately all economic and political strikes, to take up your work, and do it in perfect order. The work in the factories and all the industries is necessary for the new Government of Soviets, because any interruption of this work will only create new difficulties for us, and we have enough as it is. All to your places.

The best way to support the new Government of Soviets in these days—is by doing your job.

LONG LIVE THE IRON FIRMNESS OF THE PROLETARIAT! LONG LIVE THE REVOLUTION!

> *Petrograd Soviet of W. and S.D.*
> *Petrograd Council of Trade Unions*
> *Petrograd Council of Factory-Shop Committees*

## 63 (p. 826). APPEALS AND COUNTER-APPEALS

*From the Employees of the State and Private Banks*
*To the Population of Petrograd*

Comrades, workers, soldiers, and citizens!
The Military Revolutionary Committee in an "extraordinary notice" is accusing the workers of the State and private banking and other institutions of impeding the work of the Government, directed toward the ensuring of the front with provisions."

Comrades and citizens, do not believe this calumny, brought against us, who are part of the general army of labor.

However difficult it is for us to work under the constant threat of interference by acts of violence in our hard-working life, however depressing it be to know that our Country and the Revolution are on the verge of ruin, we, nevertheless, all of us, from the highest to the lowest, employees, *artelshchiki*, counters, laborers, couriers, etc., are continuing to fulfill our duties which are connected with the ensuring of provisions and munitions to the front and country.

Counting upon your lack of information, comrades, workers, and soldiers, in questions of finance and banking, you are being incited against workers like yourselves, because it is desirable to divert the responsibility for the starving and dying brother-soldiers at the front from the guilty persons to the innocent workers who are accomplishing their duty under the burden of general poverty and disorganization.

REMEMBER, WORKERS AND SOLDIERS! THE EMPLOYEES HAVE ALWAYS STOOD UP FOR ALL AND WILL ALWAYS STAND UP FOR THE INTERESTS OF THE TOILING PEOPLE, PART OF WHICH THEY ARE THEMSELVES, AND NOT A SINGLE KOPEK NECESSARY FOR THE FRONT AND THE WORKERS HAS EVER BEEN DETAINED AND WILL NOT BE DETAINED BY THE EMPLOYEES.

From 6 November to 23 November, i.e., during seventeen days, 500,000,000 roubles were dispatched to the front, and 120,000,000 roubles to Moscow, besides the sums sent to other towns.

Keeping guards over the wealth of the people, the master of which can be only the Constituent Assembly, representing the whole nation, the employees refuse to give out money for purposes which are unknown to them.

DO NOT BELIEVE THE CALUMNIATORS CALLING YOU TO TAKE THE LAW INTO YOUR OWN HANDS.

> *Central Board of the All-Russian Union of Employees*
> *of the State Bank*
> *Central Board of the All-Russian Trade Union of*
> *Employees of Credit Institutions*

*

*To the Population of Petrograd*

CITIZENS: Do not believe the falsehood which irresponsible people are trying to suggest to you by spreading terrible calumnies against the employees of the Ministry of Supplies and the workers in other Supply organizations who are laboring in these dark days for the salvation of Russia. Citizens! In posted placards you are called upon to lynch us, we are accused falsely of sabotage and strikes, we are blamed for all the woes and misfortunes that the people are suffering, although we have been striving indefatigably and uninterruptedly, and are still striving, to save the Russian people from the horrors of starvation. Notwithstanding all that we are bearing as citizens of unhappy Russia, we have not for one hour abandoned our heavy and responsible work of supplying the Army and population with provisions.

The image of the Army, cold and hungry, saving our very existence by its blood and its tortures, does not leave us for a single moment.

Citizens! If we have survived the blackest days in the life and history of our people, if we have succeeded in preventing famine in Petrograd, if we have managed to procure to the suffering army bread and forage by means of enormous, almost superhuman, efforts, it is because we have honestly continued and are still continuing to do our work. . . .

To the "last warning" of the usurpers of the power we reply: It is not for you who are leading the country to ruin to threaten us who are doing all we can not to allow the country to perish. We are not afraid of threats: before us stands the sacred image of tortured Russia. We will continue our work of supplying the Army and the people with bread to our last efforts, so long as you will not prevent us from accomplishing our duty to our country. In the contrary case the Army and the people will stand before the horrors of famine, but the responsibility therefor belongs to the perpetrators of violence.

*Executive Committee of the Employees of the Ministry of Supplies*

\*

### To the Chinovniki (Government Officials)

It is notified hereby that all officials and persons who have quitted the service in Government and public institutions or have been dismissed for sabotage or for having failed to report for work on the day fixed, and who have, nevertheless, received their salary paid in advance for the time they have not served, are bound to return such salary not later than on 27 November 1917 to those institutions where they were in service.

In the event of this not being done, these persons will be rendered answerable for stealing the Treasury's property and tried by the Military Revolutionary Court.

*The Military Revolutionary Committee*

*7 December 1917*

### From the Special Board for Supplies
CITIZENS!

The conditions of our work for the supplying of Petrograd are getting more and more difficult every day.

The interference with our work—which is so ruinous to our business—of the Commissars of the Military Revolutionary Committee is still continuing.

THEIR ARBITRARY ACTS, their annulling of our orders, MAY LEAD TO A CATASTROPHE.

Seals have been affixed to one of the cold storages where the meat and butter destined for the population are kept, and we cannot regulate the temperature SO THAT THE PRODUCTS WOULD NOT BE SPOILT.

One carload of potatoes and one carload of cabbages have been seized and carried away no one knows where to.

Cargoes which are not liable to requisition (*khalva*) are requisitioned by the Commissars and, as was the case one day, five boxes of *khalva* were seized by the Commissar for his own use.

WE ARE NOT IN A POSITION TO DISPOSE OF OUR STORAGE, where the self-appointed Commissars do not allow the cargoes to be taken out, and terrorize our employees, threatening them with arrest.

ALL THAT IS GOING ON IN PETROGRAD IS KNOWN IN THE PROVINCES, AND FROM THE DON, FROM SIBERIA, FROM VORONEZH AND OTHER PLACES PEOPLE ARE REFUSING TO SEND FLOUR AND BREAD.

THIS CANNOT GO ON MUCH LONGER.

The work is simply falling out of our hands.

OUR DUTY is to let the population know of this.

To the last possibility we will remain on guard of the interests of the population.

WE WILL DO EVERYTHING TO AVOID THE ONCOMING FAMINE, BUT IF UNDER THESE DIFFICULT CONDITIONS OUR WORK IS COMPELLED TO STOP LET THE PEOPLE KNOW THAT IT IS NOT OUR FAULT. . . .

## 64 (p. 827). ELECTIONS TO THE CONSTITUENT ASSEMBLY IN PETROGRAD

There were nineteen tickets in Petrograd. The results are as follows, published 30 November:

| Party | Vote |
| --- | --- |
| Christian Democrats | 3,707 |
| Cadets | 245,006 |
| Populist Socialists | 19,109 |
| Bolsheviki | 424,027 |
| Socialist Universalists | 158 |
| S.D. and S.R. Ukrainian and Jewish Workers | 4,219 |
| League of Women's Rights | 5,310 |

| | |
|---|---|
| Left Socialist Revolutionaries | 152,230 |
| Socialist Revolutionaries *(oborontsi)* | 4,696 |
| League of People's Development | 385 |
| Radical Democrats | 413 |
| Orthodox Parishes | 24,139 |
| Feminine League for Salvation of Country | 318 |
| Independent League of Workers, Soldiers, Peasants | 4,942 |
| Christian Democrats (Catholics) | 14,382 |
| Unified Social Democrats | 11,740 |
| Mensheviki | 17,427 |
| Yedinstvo group | 1,823 |
| League of Cossack Troops | 6,712 |

## 65 (p. 829). FROM THE COMMISSION ON PUBLIC EDUCATION ATTACHED TO THE CENTRAL CITY DUMA

Comrades, Working Men and Working Women!

A few days before the holidays, a strike has been declared by the teachers of the public schools. The teachers side with the bourgeoisie against the Workers' and Peasants' Government.

Comrades, organize parents' committees and pass resolutions against the strike of the teachers. Propose to the Ward Soviets of Workers' and Soldiers' Deputies, the Trade Unions, the Factory-Shop and Party Committees, to organize protest meetings. Arrange with your own resources Christmas trees and entertainments for the children, and demand the opening of the schools, after the holidays, at the date which will be set by the Duma.

Comrades, strengthen your position in matters of public education, insist on the control of the proletarian organizations over the schools.

*Commission on Public Education attached to the Central City Duma*

## 66 (p. 830). FROM THE COUNCIL OF PEOPLE'S COMMISSARS TO THE TOILING COSSACKS

*Brother Cossacks.*

You are being deceived. You are being incited against the People. You are told that the Soviets of Workers', Soldiers', and Peasants' Deputies are your enemies, that they want to take away your Cossack land, your Cossack liberty. Don't believe it, Cossacks. . . . Your own Generals and landowners are deceiving you, in order to keep you in darkness and slavery. We, the Council of People's Commissars, address ourselves to you, Cossacks, with these words. Read them attentively and judge yourselves which is the truth and which is cruel deceit. The life and service of a Cossack were always bondage and penal servitude. At the first call of the authorities a Cossack always had to saddle his horse and ride out on campaign. All his military equipment a Cossack had to provide with his own hardly earned means. A Cossack is on service, his farm is going to rack and ruin. Is such a condition fair? No, it must be altered for ever. THE COSSACKS MUST BE FREED FROM BONDAGE. The new People's Soviet power is willing to come to the assistance of the toiling Cossacks. It is only necessary that the Cossacks themselves should resolve to abolish the old order, that they should refuse submission to their slave-driver officers, landowners, rich men, that they should throw off the cursed yoke from their necks. Arise, Cossacks! Unite! The Council of People's Commissars calls upon you to enter a new, fresh, more happy life.

In November and December in Petrograd there were All-Russian Congresses of Soviets of Soldiers', Workers', and Peasants' Deputies. Congresses conferred all the authority in the different localities into the hands of the Soviets, i.e., into the hands of men elected by the People. From now on there must be in Russia no rulers or functionaries who command the People from above and drive them. The People create the authority themselves. A General has no more rights than a soldier. All are equal. Consider, Cossacks, is this wrong or right? We are calling upon you, Cossacks, to join this new order and to create your own Soviets of Cossacks' Deputies. To such Soviets all the power must belong in the different localities. Not to *hetmans* with the rank of General, but to the elected representatives of the toiling Cossacks, to your own trustworthy reliable men.

The All-Russian Congress of Soldiers', Workers', and Peasants' Deputies have passed a resolution to transfer all landowners' land into the possession of the toiling people. Is not that fair, Cossacks? The Kornilovs, Kaledins, Dutovs, Karaulovs, Bardizhes, all defend with their whole souls the interests of the rich men, and they are ready to drown Russia in blood if only the lands remain in the hands of the landowners. But you, the toiling Cossacks, do not you suffer yourselves from poverty, oppression, and lack of land? How many Cossacks are there who have more than 4–5 *dessiatins* per head? But the landowners, who have thousands of *dessiatins* of their own land wish besides to get into their hands the lands of the Cossack Army. According to the new Soviet laws, the lands of Cossack landowners must pass without compensation into the hands of the Cossack workers, the poorer Cossacks. You are being told that the Soviets wish to take away your lands from you. Who is frightening you? The rich Cossacks, who know that the Soviet AUTHORITY WISHES to transfer the landowners' land to you. Choose then, Cossacks, for whom you will stand: for the Kornilovs and Kaledins, for the Generals and rich men or for the Soviets of Peasants', Soldiers', Workers', and Cossacks' Deputies.

THE COUNCIL OF PEOPLE'S COMMISSARS elected by the All-Russian Congress HAS PROPOSED TO ALL NATIONS AN IMMEDIATE ARMISTICE AND AN HONORABLE DEMOCRATIC PEACE WITHOUT LOSS OR DETRIMENT TO ANY NATION. All the capitalists, landowners, Generals-Kornilovists have risen against the peaceful policy of the Soviets. The war was bringing them profits, power, distinctions. And you, Cossacks, privates? You were perishing without reason, without purpose, like your brother-soldiers and sailors. It will soon be three years and a half that this accursed war has gone on, a war devised by the capitalists and landowners of all countries for their own profit, their world robberies. To the toiling Cossacks the war has only brought ruin and death. The war has drained all the resources of the Cossack farm life. The only salvation for the whole of our country and for the Cossacks in particular, is a prompt and honest peace. The Council of People's Commissars has declared to all Governments and peoples: We do not want other people's property, and we do not wish to give away our own. Peace without annexations and without indemnities. Every nation must decide its own fate. There must be no oppressing of one nation by another. Such is the honest, democratic, People's peace which the Council of People's Commissars is proposing to all Governments, to all peoples, allies, and enemies. And the results are visible: ON THE RUSSIAN FRONT AN ARMISTICE HAS BEEN CONCLUDED.

The soldiers' and the Cossacks' blood is not flowing there any more. Now, Cossacks, decide: do you wish to continue this ruinous, senseless, criminal slaughter? Then support the Cadets, the enemies of the people, support Chernov, Tseretelly, Skobeliev, who drove you into the offensive of 1 July; support Kornilov, who introduced capital punishment for soldiers and Cossacks at the front. BUT IF YOU WISH A PROMPT AND HONEST PEACE, THEN ENTER THE RANKS OF THE SOVIETS AND SUPPORT THE COUNCIL OF PEOPLE'S COMMISSARS.

Your fate, Cossacks, lies in your own hands. Our common foes, the landowners, capitalists, officers-Kornilovists, bourgeois newspapers are deceiving you and driving you along the road to ruin. In Orenburg, Dutov has arrested the Soviet and disarmed the garrison. Kaledin is threatening the Soviets in the province of the Don. He has declared the province to be in a state of war and is assembling his troops. Karaulov is shooting the local tribes in the Caucasus. The Cadet bourgeoisie is supplying them with its millions. Their common aim is to suppress the People's Soviets, to crush the workers and peasants, to introduce again the discipline of the whip in the army, and to eternalize the bondage of the toiling Cossacks.

Our revolutionary troops are moving to the Don and the Ural in order to put an end to this criminal revolt against the people. The commanders of the revolutionary troops have received orders not to enter into any negotiations with the mutinous generals, to act decisively and mercilessly.

Cossacks! On you depends now whether your brothers' blood is to flow still. We are holding out our hands to you. Join the whole people against its enemies. Declare Kaledin, Kornilov, Dutov, Karaulov, and all their aiders and abettors to be the enemies of the people, traitors and betrayers. Arrest them with your own forces and turn them over into the hands of the Soviet authority, which will judge them in open and public Revolutionary Tribunal. Cossacks! Form Soviets of Cossacks' Deputies. Take into your toil-worn hands the management of all the affairs of the Cossacks. Take away the lands of your own wealthy landowners. Take over their grain, their inventoried property and livestock for the cultivation of the lands of the toiling Cossacks, who are ruined by the war.

Forward, Cossacks, to the fight for the common cause of the people!

Long live the toiling Cossacks!

Long live the union of the Cossacks, the soldiers, peasants, and workers!

Long live the power of the Soviets of Cossacks', Soldiers', Workers', and Peasants' Deputies.

Down with the war! Down with the landowners and the Kornilovist-Generals!

Long live Peace and the Brotherhood of Peoples!

*Council of People's Commissars*

## 67 (p. 831). DIPLOMATIC CORRESPONDENCE OF THE SOVIET GOVERNMENT

The notes issued by Trotsky to the Allies and to the neutral Powers, as well as the note of the Allied military attachés to General Dukhonin, are too voluminous to give here. Moreover, they belong to another phase of the history of the Soviet Republic, with which this book has nothing to do—the foreign relations of the

Soviet Government. This I treat at length in the next volume, *Kornilov to Brest-Litovsk.*

## 68 (p. 832). APPEALS TO THE FRONT AGAINST DUKHONIN

. . . The struggle for peace has met with the resistance of the bourgeoisie and the counter-revolutionary generals. . . . From the accounts in the newspapers, at the Stavka of former Supreme Commander Dukhonin are gathering the agents and allies of the bourgeoisie, Verkhovsky, Avksentiev, Chernov, Gotz, Tseretelly, etc. It seems even that they want to form a new power against the Soviets.

Comrades, soldiers! All the persons we have mentioned have been Ministers already. They have acted in accord with Kerensky and the bourgeoisie. They are responsible for the offensive of 1 July and for the prolongation of the war. They promised the land to the peasants and then arrested the Land Committees. They reestablished capital punishment for soldiers. They obey the orders of the French, English, and American financiers. . . .

General Dukhonin, for having refused to obey orders of the Council of People's Commissars, has been dismissed from his position as Supreme Commander. . . . For answer he is circulating among the troops the note from the Military Attachés of the Allied imperialist Powers, and attempting to provoke counter-revolution. . . .

Do not obey Dukhonin! Pay no attention to his provocation! Watch him and his group of counter-revolutionary generals carefully. . . .

## 69 (p. 833). FROM KRYLENKO

*Order Number Two*

The ex-Supreme Commander, General Dukhonin, for having opposed resistance to the execution of orders, for criminal action susceptible of provoking a new civil war, is declared the enemy of People. All persons who support Dukhonin will be arrested, without respect to their social or political position or their past. Persons equipped with special authority will operate these arrests. I charge General Manikhovsky with the execution of the above-mentioned dispositions. . . .

**Chapter 12**

70 (p. 836). Instructions to Peasants

In answer to the numerous inquiries coming from peasants, it is hereby explained that the whole power in the country is from now on held by the Soviets of the Workers', Soldiers', and Peasants' Deputies. The Workers' Revolution, after having conquered in Petrograd and in Moscow, is now conquering in all other centers of Russia. The Workers' and Peasants' Government safeguards the interests of the masses and workers against the landowners and against the capitalists.

Hence the Soviets of Peasants' Deputies, and before all the District Soviets, and subsequently those of the Provinces, are from now on and until the Constituent Assembly meets, full-powered bodies of State authority in their localities. All landlords' titles to the land are canceled by the second All-Russian Congress of Soviets. A decree regarding the land has already been issued by the present Provisional Workers' and Peasants' Government. On the basis of the above decree all lands hitherto belonging to landlords now pass entirely and wholly into the hands of the Soviets of Peasants' Deputies. The Volost (a group of several villages forms a Volost) Land Committees are immediately to take over all land from the landlords, and to keep a strict account over it, watching that order be maintained, and that the whole estate be well guarded, seeing that from now on all private estates become public property and must therefore be protected by the people themselves.

All orders given by the Volost Land Committees, adopted with the assent of the District Soviets of Peasants' Deputies, in fulfillment of the decrees issued by the revolutionary power, are absolutely legal and are to be forthwith and irrefutably brought into execution.

The Workers' and Peasants' Government appointed by the second All-Russian Congress of Soviets has received the name of the Council of People's Commissars.

The Council of People's Commissars summons the Peasants to take the whole power into their hands in every locality.

The workers will in every way absolutely and entirely support the peasants, arrange for them all that is required in connection with machines and tools, and in return they request the peasants to help with the transport of grain.

*President of the Council of People's Commissars,*
V. ULYANOV (LENIN)

Petrograd, 18 November 1917

71 (p. 852).

The full-powered Congress of Peasants' Soviets met about a week later, and continued for several weeks. Its history is merely an expanded version of the history of the "Extraordinary Conference." At first the great majority of the delegates were hostile to the Soviet Government, and supported the hostile wing. Several days later the assembly was supporting the moderates with Chernov. And several days after that the vast majority of the Congress was voting for the faction of Maria Spiridonova, and sending their representatives into the Tsay-ee-kah at Smolny. . . . The Right Wing then walked out of the Congress and called a Congress of its own, which went on, dwindling from day to day, until it finally dissolved. . . .

## A Note on the Type

The principal text of this Modern Library edition
was set in a digitized version of Janson, a typeface
that dates from about 1690 and was cut by Nicholas Kis,
a Hungarian working in Amsterdam. The original matrices have
survived and are held by the Stempel foundry in Germany.
Hermann Zapf redesigned some of the weights and sizes for
Stempel, basing his revisions on the original design.